Competition Law in Latin America

Competition Law in Latin America

A Practical Guide

Second Edition

Editcd by

Julián Peña

Marcelo Calliari

Wolters Kluwer

Published by:
Kluwer Law International B.V.
PO Box 316
2400 AH Alphen aan den Rijn
The Netherlands
E-mail: lrs-sales@wolterskluwer.com
Website: www.wolterskluwer.com/en/solutions/kluwerlawinternational

Sold and distributed by:
Wolters Kluwer Legal & Regulatory U.S.
7201 McKinney Circle
Frederick, MD 21704
United States of America
E-mail: customer.service@wolterskluwer.com

ISBN 978-94-035-3695-8

e-Book: ISBN 978-94-035-3700-9
web-PDF: ISBN 978-94-035-3701-6

Editors

Julián Peña is the partner in charge of the competition law practice of Allende & Brea in Argentina, a professor at Universidad Torcuato Di Tella's Masters on Law and Economics, and the founder and moderator of ForoCompetencia. He is also Vice-Chair of the Antitrust Committee of the International Bar Association; Vice-Chair of the International Comments & Policy Committee of the Antitrust Law Section of the American Bar Association; and member of the Advisory Board of the Fordham Competition Law Institute and of the American Antitrust Institute. He has been selected twice among the 40 best under-40 competition lawyers in the world by Global Competition Review and received Lexology's Client Choice Award for antitrust in Argentina, among other recognitions. He has published many papers and given presentations on competition law around the world

Marcelo Calliari is the head of the competition law practice of TozziniFreire in São Paulo. He was a commissioner of the Brazilian antitrust agency CADE, from 1998 to 2000, and president of the Brazilian Institute of Studies on Competition, Consumer Affairs and International Trade (IBRAC), from 2010 to 2011. He is past-chair of the International Trade and Customs Law Committee of the IBA, and he has served as a non-governmental advisor to the International Competition Network (ICN) multiple times. Marcelo Calliari advises clients on all areas of competition. He holds degrees in economics and law, an LL.M. from Harvard Law School, and a PhD from the University of São Paulo (USP), and writes and speaks frequently about antitrust around the world.

Contributors

Manuel A. Abdala is a PhD in Economics from Boston University and holds a Master of Arts in Political Economy from the same school. He is currently a senior managing director with Compass Lexecon and a member of its Global Management team. He also acts as co-chair of the international arbitration practice group.

Bruno Assunção is a Bachelor of Economics from the School of Economics, Business and Accounting of the University of São Paulo (FEA-USP). Bruno has experience as a data analyst, as well as acting in the areas of competition analysis and defense.

Felix Santiago Bofferón, graduated with honors from the Faculty of Legal and Diplomatic Sciences of the Universidad Catolica "Nuestra Señora de la Asunción", partner at Peroni Sosa Tellechea Burt & Narvaja. Diploma in Competition Law from the Universidad Torcuato Di Tella, Argentina; Diploma in Competition Law and Policies from the Law School of the Universidad de Chile. Consultant of the World Bank in Competition Law for Paraguay. Co-founder and member of the Board of Directors of the Paraguayan Association of Studies on Competition Defense (APEDEC).

Alfredo Bullard González holds a Master of Laws Degree (LLM) from Yale Law School (EEUU, 1991) and Law degree from the Pontificia Universidad Católica del Perú (Lima, 1989). He is a partner at Bullard, Falla & Ezcurra Law Firm. He is president of the Technical Commission that drafted the New Peruvian Arbitration Act. He is also a member of the International Court of Arbitration (ICC) of Paris. He has participated as arbitrator in arbitration cases administrated by the International Chamber of Commerce (ICC), by CIADI, by CIAC, by Chamber of Commerce of Lima, and other arbitration centers. He has participated as arbitrator in more than 300 arbitration cases. He was a former president of INDECOPI's Tribunal for the Defense of the Competition and Protection of Intellectual Property. He is professor at Pontificia Universidad Católica del Perú. He has been visiting professor at Universidad Torcuato di Tella de Buenos Aires, Argentina, Universidad de Puerto Rico, and Escuela Superior de Economía y Negocios (ESEN), El Salvador. He is the author and co-author of several books such as "La Relación Jurídica Patrimonial. Reales vs. Obligaciones"; "Derecho y

Economía: el análisis económico de las instituciones legales". He has written various articles on issues related to his specialization.

Andrea Cadenas is a Master of Laws (LLM) from the University of Chicago, USA. She holds a Law Degree from the Pontificia Universidad Católica del Perú (PUCP). She is a senior associate at Bullard Falla Ezcurra +. Andrea has focused her practice on economic regulation, competition/antitrust, unfair competition, administrative law, civil law, and arbitration in connection with, among others, telecommunications, natural resources, and cargo transportation industries. She is professor of Competition Law at the Law School of Pontificia Universidad Católica del Perú—PUCP and professor of Regulation and Antitrust at the Law School of the Universidad de Piura.

Jonathan Clovin is an associate at Guyer & Regules, Montevideo, where his main areas of practice are antitrust, privacy, and data protection law, and international trade law. He is a member of the New York Bar and holds an LLB in English and French law from King's College London. He holds a Double Maîtrise en droits français et anglais from Université Paris 1 Panthéon-Sorbonne, a Master in International Public Management from Sciences Po Paris, and an LL.M. from Georgetown University Law Center (2012).

Ignacio de León is president of Kozolchyk National Law Center, CEO IPPBLOCK, PhD (UCL); LLM (QMC); MBA (UFM). Dr. De Leon is a specialist in innovation policy, intellectual property (IP) commercialization, entrepreneurial business finance, and private sector development. He was superintendent of the Venezuelan competition agency from 1998 to 2000.

Mateo Diego-Fernández advises clients on the legal aspects of antitrust, regulation, and international trade. He specializes in compliance proceedings for Mexican and international companies, as well as trade and industry associations, and represents clients in law enforcement matters before Mexican competition, foreign trade, and other regulatory agencies. Between 2008 and 2013, he was general director of Legal Affairs at the Federal Competition Commission. Between 1998 and 2008, he served as a counselor and then as minister in the Mexican Mission to the World Trade Organization (WTO). He has acted as legal representative of Mexico in more than thirty disputes before the WTO, in addition to serving as a panelist or chairman in eight trade disputes before the WTO, and as a facilitator in the Airbus-Boeing case. He is an appeals arbitrator at the WTO and a member of the list of arbitrators of USMCA and the World Intellectual Property Organization, as well as being on the roster of various free trade agreements. He has a law degree from the Instituto Tecnológico Autónomo de México and a Master's degree in International Relations from the Geneva School of Diplomacy and International Relations.

Alejandro Falla Jara is Master in Regulation from the London School of Economics and Political Sciences-LSE, United Kingdom. He holds a Law Degree from the Pontificia Universidad Católica del Perú. He is a partner at Bullard Falla Ezcurra +. He focuses his practice on competition law, economic regulation, telecommunications, energy and transport regulation, contracts and arbitration. He is director of the Master Program in Intellectual Property and Competition Law of Pontificia Universidad Católica del Perú. He is professor of Competition Law at the Law School of Pontificia Universidad Católica del Perú and at Universidad de Piura. He is also a professor of Regulation and Competition at the Law School of the Universidad del Pacífico. He was member of the council board of the Supervising Agency for Private Investment in Energy-OSINERGMIN. He was also president of the Supervising Commission of Advertising and Repression of Unfair Competition, member and technical secretary of the Competition Commission of the National Institute for the Defense of Competition and Intellectual Property—INDECOPI.

Fernanda Garza Magdaleno is an attorney with nineteen years of expertise on competition and international trade law. Mrs. Garza serves as counsel at the Mexican Law firm Basham, Ringe y Correa, S.C. where she focuses on competition law. She previously worked in the Competition and International Trade teams of other prominent legal firms and served as director of Proceedings at COFECE, where she led several competition proceedings. Her experience in trade law includes serving as an international official in the Legal Affairs and Rules Divisions at the WTO, where she advised dispute settlement panels on international disputes. She also worked for the Mexican Ministry of Economy, where she negotiated free trade agreements on behalf of Mexico.

Juan Cristóbal Gumucio Schönthaler is the head of the competition law practice group at Cariola Díez Pérez-Cotapos, leading several high-profile cases and transactions before the Chilean antitrust authorities and courts. He graduated from the Pontificia Universidad Católica de Chile and obtained a Magister Iuris (MJur) from the University of Oxford. He lectures in Competition Law and Intellectual Property Law at Pontificia Universidad Católica de Chile, and he has written several publications about competition law.

Juan David Gutiérrez, LLM, PhD in public policy. He is associate professor at Universidad del Rosario. Founder of the competition law and policy blog www.lalibrecompetencia.com. Co-director of the Latin American Chapter of the Academic Society for Competition Law (ASCOLA).

Felipe Irarrázabal Philippi is attorney at University of Chile (Summa Cum Laude), holds LLM degree from Yale University (1997) He was a visiting scholar (2018) at Stanford University. He is current director of CentroCompetencia (CeCo), Universidad Adolfo Ibáñez, Chile. He was former national economic prosecutor between 2010 and 2018 in the National Economic Prosecutor's Office, Chile. He was former partner at Philippi, Yrarrázaval, Pulido & Brunner between 1999 and 2010 (currently, Philippi Prietocarrizosa Ferrero DU & Uría). He was former foreign associate at Cleary Gottlieb Steen & Hamilton LLP (New York) in 1999. He is professor of competition law, Universidad Adolfo Ibáñez.

León Efrén Jiménez Domínguez serves as senior associate at Basham, Ringe y Correa, S.C. He has focused his professional experience on antitrust matters. León chairs the Youth Liaison Commission of the Mexican Association of Lawyers and has published various articles.

William E. Kovacic is professor at George Washington University. He is visiting professor at King's College in London. He was former chairman of the Federal Trade Commission.

Cristóbal Lema Abarca is a lawyer from the Universidad de Chile and is currently pursuing a Master of Science (MSc) in Economic Analysis at the Economy and Business Faculty of Universidad de Chile. He joined Cariola Díez Pérez-Cotapos in 2017, where he is part of the competition law practice group. He has written other publications about competition law, such as a critical analysis of the Chilean merger control system (part of a collaborative book, forthcoming).

Alejandro Lombardi is a vice president with Compass Lexecon based in Buenos Aires. He holds a PhD in Economics from Toulouse School of Economics. Dr. Lombardi's research and applied work specializes in the analysis of complex economic problems in the context of economic disputes and regulatory processes. He has advised public and private entities on issues of regulation, antitrust, and competition, and the quantification of damages in investment treaties and contractual disputes. Dr. Lombardi has also consulted and published on market design issues. He has worked on a wide range of industries, with special focus in the telecommunications industry. Prior to joining Compass Lexecon, he has worked in both government and consulting. Dr. Lombardi served as a member of the board of directors of Argentina's International Trade Commission and as an economic advisor at the Competition Group of UK's communications regulator (Ofcom). He also worked as an associate at LECG.

Pablo Márquez, PhD is a partner at ECIJA Colombia He was chairman of Colombia's Commission for Communications Regulation. He was also the superintendent for antitrust at the Colombian Competition Authority. Pablo Studied Law, Philosophy, and holds a master's degree in economics from the Javeriana University. He obtained a LL.M. degree from Harvard Law School and a PhD in competition law from the University of Oxford.

Marcel Medon Santos has long experience with antitrust law. He was legal coordinator and director of the Secretariat of Economic Law of the Ministry of Justice (SDE/MJ) from 2001 to 2007. He was one of the officials responsible for the implementation of the modern investigation techniques currently used by the Brazilian Competition Protection System (including dawn raids and leniency agreements). Marcel also has solid expertise in the private practice, assisting clients with risk assessment of business practices, investigation of conducts, merger review, and implementation of corporate compliance programs. He holds a postgraduate degree in Antitrust Law from FGV-SP and a graduate of the Law School of PUC-SP.

Juan Manuel Mercant is a partner at Guyer & Regules, Montevideo. His practice includes mergers and acquisitions, energy and infrastructure. He has developed his activities in the Corporate and Banking, Project Finance, and Antitrust Practice Groups. He is a professor of Project Finance and Antitrust at the Law School of the Catholic University of Uruguay. Juan Manuel holds a Doctorado en Derecho from Universidad de la República (1997). He was a foreign associate at Cleary Gottlieb.

Alfonso Miranda Londoño is a lawyer from the Javeriana University Law School in Bogotá, Colombia (1985). He has specialized in Socioeconomic Sciences in 1985 from the same University, in Banking Law from Los Andes University (also in Bogotá) in 1986 and with a Master's Degree in Law (LLM) from Cornell University in 1987. He is director of the Law and Economics Department at the Javeriana University Law School, the co-founder and director of the Centre for Studies in Competition Law—CEDEC, and a professor of Competition Law at the Javeriana University. He is also the partner that leads the Competition Law practice at Esguerra Barrera Arriaga.

Edgar Odio-Rohrmoser is a partner at Facio & Cañas, where he advises local and multinational clients on corporate matters, mergers and acquisitions, and competition matters. He has postgraduate degrees in Competition Law and Economics for Competition from King's College, London. He was a member of the competition agency in Costa Rica and consultant to UNCTAD in competition matters for Latin America. He teaches competition in La Salle University, and he is regularly invited as guest speaker in competition seminars and workshops.

Gesner Oliveira was president of CADE and Sabesp, secretary of Economic Monitoring of the Ministry of Finance, and deputy secretary of Economic Policy of the Ministry of Finance. He is professor at FGV-SP where he coordinates with the Center for Infrastructure Studies and Environmental Solutions (CEISA). He also holds a Ph.D. in economics from the University of California (Berkeley).

Juan Pablo Otero is a lawyer from the Javeriana University Law School in Bogotá, Colombia. He also holds a postgraduate degree in Regulation and Management of ICT, Telecommunications, and the Digital Ecosystem from Universidad Externado de Colombia. He is an associate of the Telecommunications and Information Technology team at ECIJA Colombia.**Andrés Palacios Lleras,** LLM, PhD. He is currently deputy superintendent of Ports.

Amílcar Peredo heads the antitrust and competition practice in the law firm Basham, Ringe y Correa, S.C. He has broad experience representing national and international clients in all areas of Competition Law. In 2004, he published one of the few books on Mexican antitrust law called (in English) "Economic Competition: Theory and Practice" which is used as a text in many Mexican universities. He obtained his law degree at the Universidad Nacional Autonoma de Mexico in 1996. He also obtained a master's degree at the Georgetown University Law Center, specializing in antitrust law. He has been a lecturer in antitrust law at two of Mexico's best-known universities.

Eduardo Perez Motta has been a partner of SAI Derecho & Economía since 2018. He has more than thirty-five years of expertise working in a wide range of subjects, including economic competition, international trade, and regulatory affairs. Since 2013, he has represented companies in the most relevant economic sectors of the Mexican economy before regulators such as COFECE and the IFT in processes related to the application of the Federal Law on Economic Competition. He has close relationships with a wide range of senior government officials and regulatory agencies. He was president of the Federal Competition Commission from 2004 to 2013. In 2012, he was elected president of the International Economic Competition Network, which brings together more than 130 competition agencies worldwide. Between 2001 and 2004, he was Mexico's ambassador to the WTO, where he chaired the council on Trade-Related Aspects of Intellectual Property Rights (TRIPS) and the Negotiating Group on Rules. Previously, he was head of the negotiation of the free trade agreement between Mexico and the European Union in Brussels. He serves on the advisory boards of the American Antitrust Institute, the Fordham Conference on International Antitrust Law and Policy in New York and Mitsui. He is currently a member of the Board of Trustees of the Colegio de México and the ABC Medical Center and participates in the Investment Committee of the CKD's of GBM.

Diego Petrecolla is a PhD in Economics from University of Illinois at Urbana-Champaign. He is a researcher at the Interdisciplinary Institute of Economic Policy of Buenos Aires (UBA-CONICET). He is professor of Microeconomics and Industrial Organization: University of Buenos Aires, Argentina. He was former President of the National Commission of Competition Defense, Argentina. He has published works on different topics, including competition policy, energy economics and inequality and income distribution.

Lucila Porto is a Master student from the Universidad de San Andrés, and a Bachelor of Economics from the University of Buenos Aires (UBA). She has published articles in the fields of tourism and regional economics.

Lucía Quesada is a professor of economics at the Universidad de San Andrés, Argentina. Between 2016 and 2020, she served as National Director of Competition Advocacy of Argentina's National Commission for Competition Defense (CNDC), in charge of market studies, competition advocacy, and international affairs. Previously, she was a senior economist at Compass Lexecon from 2012 to 2016, where she worked on advising clients on competition and regulatory issues, as well as damages assessment, an assistant professor of economics at the Torcuato Di Tella University from 2005 to 2012 and at the University of Wisconsin-Madison from 2003 to 2005. She has authored several publications related to competition and regulation. She holds a PhD in economics from the University of Toulouse, an MA in economic theory from the

University of Toulouse, an MA in economic policy from the University of Buenos Aires, and a degree in economics from the University of Buenos Aires.

Carlos Adrián Romero is a doctor in Economics (Universidad Nacional de la Plata), MSc Economics (University of Warwick, UK), and Bachelor of Economics from the University of Buenos Aires (UBA). He is a researcher at the Interdisciplinary Institute of Economic Policy of Buenos Aires (UBA-CONICET) and lecturer of Industrial Organization at the School of Economics of the UBA. He has published articles in the fields of law and economics, energy, tourism, regulation of public services, and regional economics.

Federico Rossi is a partner in the competition law practice at Allende & Brea (Argentina). He obtained a Master of Laws (LLM) in Competition Law from King's College London and a Law Degree from Universidad Austral (Argentina). He is a professor of Competition Law at the Law School of Universidad Austral (Argentina).

D. Daniel Sokol is a professor of Law at the USC Gould School of Law and Affiliate Professor of Business at the USC Marshall School of Business. He is academic director of the Center for Transnational Law and Business and co-director of the Marshall Initiative on Digital Competition. He also serves as senior advisor at White & Case LLP.

David A. Sperber Vilhelm founded the first Ecuadorian Competition Authority in Ecuador and participated in the preparation and debate in Congress of Ecuadorian Competition Act. Dr. Sperber is a partner at AntiTrust Consultores & Abogados, recognized Top # 1 by Leaders League, The Legal 500 and others, and chairs the Competition Commission of the International Chamber of Commerce—ICC Ecuador. In addition, he is a Professor at Universidad Internacional del Ecuador.

Summary of Contents

Table of Contents

Foreword

The newly revised and extended edition of *"Competition Law in Latin America: A Practical Guide"*—edited by Julián Peña and Marcelo Calliari—is a must-read for every practitioner attorney, authority, academic, and economist involved in competition law in this region. In my opinion, there is no better introduction to understand the past and current state of competition law in Latin America and the challenges that we will be facing in the years to come.

In its tireless task of keeping up-to-date, this 2022 edition has some remarkable new chapters on cutting-edge issues, actively discussed in prominent jurisdictions such as the European Union (EU) and the United States (US). Also, it incorporates two additional chapters with the competition regimes of Ecuador and Paraguay and updates the analysis in Argentina, Brazil, Chile, Colombia, Mexico, Peru, and Uruguay.

Each piece of *"Competition Law in Latin America: A Practical Guide"* covers different topics. The book can be divided into two large sections. The first on general competition issues in the region. The second are descriptions, under a standardized format which makes it easier to read, of the regulations and realities of the main Latin American countries.

The chapters of the first section explore the intricate history of competition policy in Latin America (Daniel Sokol, William E. Kovacic, Andrés Palacios Lleras, Juan David Gutiérrez, and Ignacio de León); conducts an analysis of merger control in Argentina, Brazil, Colombia, and Mexico (Diego Petrecolla, Lucila Porto, and Carlos **Adrián** Romero); provides an overview of the current situation on international cooperation among competition authorities (Eduardo Perez Motta and Mateo Diego-**Fernández**); analyzes the interaction and challenges of competition and regulation, with a deeper approach in digital markets and information and communication technologies (Manuel A. Abdala, Alejandro Lombardi, Lucía Quesada, Gesner Oliveira, Bruno Assunção, and Pablo Márquez); and lastly, describes and analyzes the state of competition policy in Central America (Edgar Odio-Rohrmoser).

In a context where progress has been uneven and there still is heterogeneity among the competition law regimes of each jurisdiction, a clear and concise understanding of the main systems promotes further developments in the region.

The book develops, through its different chapters and with a magnificent index by concepts, three general trends that work as pillars of a more general vision of the region, while addressing the most vibrant challenges that competition policy currently faces and will face in the future.

First, to a greater or lesser extent, competition policy and its institutions have had their ups and downs throughout the years. Experience has shown that prestige—and ultimately, success—of competition authorities is strongly related to the acceptance of market-oriented economies and the belief in their ability to produce better outcomes. In other words: the irruption of ideas and practices oriented towards a centralized economy—something that seduces the region from time to time—weakens the competition authorities.

Furthermore, the deeper embrace of economic analysis and deference to technical aspects strengthen competition authorities, increase their credibility, and keep them away from the political arena. Experts coincide that the strength of institutions, international cooperation, human capital, funding, independence from the government, among others, are factors that highly contribute to the success of the authorities.

Some authors describe the development of competition policy in lifecycles, others in layers of competition law regimes or waves. All things considered, this book navigates through the history of competition law in Latin America, recognizing some common factors or trends that allow understanding the differences between institutions from different jurisdictions, their strengths, and weaknesses.

Second, globalization, the digital economy, and large digital platforms have posed new challenges to competition authorities: whether competition policy is the right tool to deal with problems associated with them, how to define a relevant market in a context of multi-sided market and multihoming, what is the right tool to tackle competition problems in this context, the need to collaborate between agencies from different jurisdictions to deal with the challenges it imposes, among other relevant questions.

What path should Latin American countries follow regarding large digital platforms? An overview of the recent proposals of the EU and the US to address competition concerns in digital markets might help find the best solution for Latin America. Taking advantage of the lag that the region faces on this matter—compared to the EU, the US, and the UK—, allows us to adopt a prudent wait-and-see posture and avoid rushing into a costly and erroneous model.

Third, there is a sensitive interaction between competition and regulatory authorities in the region. Experience shows that the gradual incorporation of competition in regulated markets has helped to achieve higher levels of investment, coverage, and quality, but there is room for more. As the region still faces challenges to increase competition in regulated sectors, such as telecommunications or energy, the main challenge nowadays is to find the right equilibrium between independence and interdependence among competition and regulatory authorities.

The puzzle is completed with pieces entirely dedicated to each jurisdiction, written by practitioners with vast experience and knowledge, aiming to understand in-depth the current state of each country's competition regime. Julián Peña and

Federico Rossi for Argentina, Marcelo Calliari and Marcel Medon Santos for Brazil, Juan Cristóbal Gumucio Schönthaler and Cristóbal Lema Abarca for Chile, Alfonso Miranda Londoño for Colombia, David A. Sperber for Ecuador, Amílcar Peredo, Fernanda Garza Magdaleno, and León Efrén Jiménez Domínguez for Mexico, Felix Santiago Bofferón for Paraguay, Alfredo Bullard González, Alejandro Falla Jara, and Andrea Cadenas for Peru and Juan Manuel Mercant and Jonathan Clovin for Uruguay.

This book will help foreign lawyers and economists—from countries that do not belong to this region—, who need, for their professional practice or for the academy, to understand Latin America and its particularities.

In addition, this book is a great step to understand that we have a lot to learn among ourselves. In competition law and economics, we must be permanently looking to the north of the world, especially to the EU, the US, Germany, England, and Australia. But this "Competition Law in Latin America" reminds us that there is much wisdom, experience, and practice in our region and that translation and its consequent transplants, under continental law systems and with generally concentrated economies, shed light on present and future challenges that each of our countries must face.

Overall, this book brings together a valuable collection of essays that will enrich our vision on the functioning and challenges of competition law in Latin America. Each of its chapters, with its style and approach, allows us to delve into the past, present, and future of competition law in the region. The result is extraordinary because, like puzzle pieces, this book allows us to have a panoramic and in-depth view of the region as a whole—a picture with a lot of pixels—, with its similarities and differences.

Felipe Irarrázabal
Director of CentroCompetencia (CeCo)
Universidad Adolfo Ibáñez
Chile

Preface to the Second Edition

Competition Policy in Latin America has entered the decade of the 2020s with the same fast pace of development it had seen in the previous twenty years. So much has changed throughout the region in the last five years that, more than justifying an updated second edition of this book, it basically required it. There is still a very wide gap among different countries in the region, but the trend is that it will get smaller over time as more and more jurisdictions catch-up. Some countries started to enforce competition legislation for the first time in their history, while others updated—sometimes significantly—their legislations and institutional frameworks, and all have had to work hard at reconciling international best-practices in an interconnected antitrust world with often unavoidable local requirements, traditions, and idiosyncrasies. Some agencies have become stronger, with more investigative power, harsher penalties, and expanded jurisdiction, while others have had to withstand challenges from a variety of different sources to maintain the gains they had already made. Evolution has not been easy or necessarily linear, but overall, these efforts continually reposition Latin American authorities in the antitrust arena, granting them a growing importance both domestically and internationally.

This dynamic scenario makes this updated publication especially useful for practitioners, academics, and government officials. In order to provide a more in-depth analysis of such a complex scenario, "Competition Law in Latin America" offers two main sections. The first one includes comments and analysis on the developments sweeping the region, addressing their causes, characteristics, and impacts both domestically and internationally, as well as some of the significant challenges faced by competition authorities in the region. The variety of backgrounds of the specialists who author the different chapters in this section ensures that the reader will get a wide range of perspectives, capable of offering a more complete understanding of the current evolution of antitrust in Latin America.

The second section of the book addresses each of the main antitrust jurisdictions in the region in an in-depth and detailed manner. Written by practicing experts with considerable hands-on experience in their respective countries, each chapter in this section provides a comprehensive description and explanation of the evolution, current state and prospects for antitrust in each of the countries. The topics addressed encompass relevant institutions and legislation, cartel investigations, unilateral conducts policies and merger review, and include comments on specificities and idiosyncrasies that are so important for a correct understanding of the practical realities of competition policy and enforcement. In this sense, the chapters also include analysis on the most relevant case law, allowing the reader to gauge the positions, views, and tendencies of each competition law regime. The new edition also includes a chapter on the digital economy, a topic that is becoming increasingly more relevant across the region.

Though not uniform across all countries, the overall picture painted by this publication is undoubtedly one of a region carving a new position for itself in the antitrust world. High fines, dawn raids, leniency, criminalization, and international coordination are spreading around Latin America, and the increased enforcement has secured it a new status in the definition of a global investigation strategy. The same is true on the merger review front, as a consequence of the ever-spreading of mandatory waiting periods for mergers (with worldwide impacts) and the renewed confidence in the imposition of remedies. And the growing number of decisions regarding unilateral conduct highlights a duality that affects all competition enforcement in the region. At the same time, they look up to and try to emulate agencies from more mature antitrust jurisdictions, typically the United States and Europe, authorities in Latin America also to a large extent follow their own music, including historical and legal peculiarities or also ideological and socio-economic views and positions.

With its broad ranging and in depth-approach, this book provides a unique analysis of a challenging region that seems poised to become an increasingly important part of the international antitrust scenario. It is in this sense an essential guide for lawyers, economists, corporations, academics, and government officials interested in understanding where competition law is, and where it is going, in Latin America.

Chapter 1

The Second Wave of Latin American Competition Law and Policy

D. Daniel Sokol

Latin America has had a somewhat bumpy development in its competition law and policy evolution. Modern competition law development in Latin America began during a period of growth and economic liberalization to exit statist policies. In the contemporary period, some competition authorities have improved in their capacity. The common characteristics among them are: a deeper understanding of economic analysis resulting in a higher quality of antitrust decisions, highly trained professionals, and institutional structures that have been recalibrated (and continue to do so) to address the specific needs of the countries in question given their country level institutional backdrops. Furthermore, as the pandemic and increased digitization of the economy become a more significant part of competition agencies, the need for a re-evaluation as to the tools and processes of competition law and economic require careful consideration. Perhaps a third wave may be underway.

Latin America as a region has had a somewhat bumpy development in its competition law and policy evolution. Latin America suffered from statist economic policies into the 1990s and lagged behind United States, American, and East Asian development.[1] Modern competition law development in Latin America began during a period of growth and economic liberalization to exit statist policies. This period was known as the era of the Washington Consensus.[2] Economic liberalization worked to move towards an economic organization based on market driven policies. As a result of the

1. Sebastian Edwards, *Crisis and Reform in Latin America: From Despair to Hope* (World Bank 1995).
2. John Williamson, *What Washington Means by Policy Reform*, in *Latin American Adjustment: How Much Has Happened?* (John Williamson ed., Institute for International Economics 1990).

implementation of Washington Consensus policies, growth that had been elusive in Latin America during the 1980s (called the "Lost Decade") improved significantly in the 1990s across the region.[3] For example, whereas the 1980s had been a period of run-away inflation in many countries in the region, by the end of the 1990s, the Latin American average for inflation was less than 10% and only in two countries was the inflation rate more than 10%.[4] In the context of the Washington Consensus, competition law and policy worked among a number of other policy tools to help create economic growth strategies in Latin America including sector liberalization in utilities and finance, privatization, trade liberalization, and macro-economic reforms such as fiscal policies.

The first generation of Latin American competition reforms were significant in some sense. Antitrust authorities resulted from new competition laws and older regimes were reworked. The agencies were often filled with bright teams of lawyers and economists from other parts of government who wanted to make a name for themselves and pursue significant consumer welfare enhancing policies. The US antitrust agencies, World Bank, and others provided technical assistance and capacity building to help shape the priorities of the competition authorities, and to offer specific case assistance on conduct and merger cases, as well as assistance in competition advocacy efforts. Many competition authorities achieved tangible success in this first decade.[5]

To create better regional best practices, communication, and exchange of ideas and information across competition authorities, the Inter-American Development Bank and the Organisation for Economic Co-operation and Development (OECD) set up a yearly Latin American Competition Forum. The Forum had its initial meeting in 2003 in Paris and has moved around Latin American every year since then. The Forum was an expression of the hope of greater economic prosperity through competition law. The linkage between competition law and a broader competition policy was something that the Director General of the OECD made explicit in his opening address of the first Competition Forum. He explained:

> Competition is a policy area that has strong links to most other branches of economic policy, and virtually all sectors of the economy... We should not underestimate the importance of what we will be discussing in the coming two days. We live in a world with enormous potential for social progress—if we take the right public policy decisions. Fortunately, countries across the spectrum of development have begun to come together to forge a shared international development agenda. There appears to be broad acceptance that economic growth spearheaded by competition, investment and entrepreneurship is the best way to fight poverty and enhance public welfare. Economic reform guided by competition

---

3. Jakob de Haan, Susanna Lundström & Jan-Egbert Sturm, *Market-Oriented Institutions and Policies and Economic Growth: A Critical Survey*, 20 J. Econ. Surveys 157 (2006).
4. Anoop Singh, et al., *Stabilization and Reform in Latin America: A Macroeconomic Perspective on the Experience Since the Early 1990s*, IMF Working Paper (2005) at 3.
5. *See*, e.g., Eleanor M. Fox & D. Daniel Sokol, *Competition Law and Policy in Latin America* (Hart 2009).

> principles increases wealth, productivity, and international competitiveness. Effective competition law enforcement helps to put a stop to private, anti-competitive conduct that may eliminate or undermine the benefits of market reform and trade liberalisation.[6]

This statement expressed the prevailing sentiment at that time by those within Latin America and policy makers and academics in the US and Europe who saw in competition law and policy a set of tools to help create increased economic prosperity in a region that had gone through spurts of low economic growth and significant social inequality.

Alas, this congratulatory feeling was not to last. Corruption in Latin America, which had been endemic during the period before the Washington Consensus, remained an issue during the Washington Consensus era.[7] This presented a problem for the legitimacy of the market-based regimes of Latin America since the benefits of competition often did not reach end consumers. Further, social inequality remained significant.[8] Pushback against market reforms (perhaps because of overly broad and unrealistic promises) occurred throughout the region.

In just a few years, the tone within Latin America had changed at the macro-economic level. Populist governments had taken power in Argentina, Brazil, Venezuela, Peru, and elsewhere in a backlash against the Washington Consensus. This backlash extended to competition law and policy. More recently, a newer wave of populist backlash has occurred on both the left and the right that is distrustful of market mechanisms. Some agencies that had been very active became less so in the post Washington Consensus era as agency resources were cut or where the goals of enforcement changed from stepping in only when there was a market malfunction due to the illegal exercise of market power to one akin to a price regulator. In many of these jurisdictions, the quality of the leadership and staff in the competition authorities suffered as salaries were frozen and where the possibility to take on interesting (and economically sound) cases instead became more political and preordained in outcome.

Across both successful and less successful competition regimes, a number of critical issues limited the overall effectiveness of competition law and policy in the region. These included:

---

6. OECD, *Latin American Competition Forum* (2003), available at http://www.oecd.org/competition/latinamerica/2003%20Latin%20American%20Competition%20Forum.pdf.
7. Jean Jaques Laffont warned about the problems with importing competition regimes into developing world countries because political and economic reality differed from the theoretical prediction of "Competition is an unambiguously good thing in the first best world of economists. That would assume large number of participants in all markets, no public goods, no externalities, no information asymmetries, no natural monopolies, complete markets, fully rational economic agents, and a benevolent court system to enforce contracts, and a benevolent government providing lump sum transfers to achieve any desirable redistribution." World Bank, *Competition, Information and Development*, Annual World Bank Conference on Development Economics, 1998.
8. *See* Sebastian Edwards, Gerardo Esquivel & Graciela Márquez, *Introduction* to *The Decline of Latin American Economies: Growth, Institutions, and Crises* (Sebastian Edwards, Gerardo Esquivel & Graciela Márquez eds, University of Chicago Press 2007).

Fines that were too low. Fines were set too low to deter anti-competitive behavior in many jurisdictions. Put differently, fines served as the equivalent to a parking ticket for the behavior in question. This meant that firms had incentive to violate the law because the penalties were too low. Even where penalties were sufficient in the law, often the maximum penalty never was used in practice.

Challenges to the basis of the competition authorities powers. Often within the first ten years of agencies existence, litigants challenged the very reach of the competition authority to address certain types of conduct on either procedural or substantive grounds. In some cases, these challenges emerged not from the courts but from the legislature or executive, where entrenched interests sought to limit the discretion of the agencies, challenge their funding, or circumscribe the jurisdictional reach of the agency into certain parts of the economy through various implicit immunities via deference to sector regulation over competition law. In yet other settings, it was sector regulators (sometimes captured by the industries that they regulated) who reacted negatively to the reach of competition authorities.[9]

Agency design. The design of the agency proved ineffective given the legal, political, and economic factors in a given country.[10]

Finality of decisions. Often cases could go through many years of appeal before final disposition of a case. This led to frustration as to the effectiveness of competition law.

Agency turnover. With young agencies, the private sector or other parts of government often poached on some of the best staffers and senior leadership of the agencies through higher salaries or public sector roles that had greater power. As the competition authority improved its processes and effectiveness, the private sector experienced increased demand for expertise in the area. The natural collection of talent given the increased demand came from the agency itself. Investments in human capacity and institutional knowledge often were lost given the rapid turnover.

Digital markets. Agencies have been pushed to allocate more resources specifically towards digital issues, sometimes because of economic realities and sometimes because of political pressure. Agencies have had to address competing agencies in their own countries with some authority as to digital competition issues in overlapping and/or adjacent areas.

Even with such limitations to the effectiveness of competition regimes generally, a number of regimes in Latin America have done better in terms of effectiveness in the subsequent decades than they had in earlier decades. That is, unlike competition

9. Gesner Oliveira & Germán Orjuela, "Competition in Regulated Markets in Latin America: Overview and Challenges," in *Competition Law in Latin America: A Practical Guide* (Julián Peña & Marcelo Calliari eds, Wolters Kluwer 2016).

10. David A. Hyman & William E. Kovacic, *Institutional Design, Agency Life Cycle, and the Goals of Competition Law*, 81 Fordham L. Rev. 2163 (2013).

regimes where effectiveness declined over time, elsewhere the quality of the competition system improved both on the public and on the private sector sides of the equation. This has been the case in Chile, Mexico, Panama, Colombia, and Brazil to name just a few for a combination of factors. In some cases, the initial authority institutional design needed to be reformulated to become more effective. In some cases, this has meant combining multiple agencies (Brazil), changing the design from a commission to a singular head (Panama), changing some of the statutory powers (Mexico), creating a specialized competition tribunal (Chile) or other institutional design issues. Not surprisingly, those institutions with more stable political and economic factors (some countries such as Brazil and Chile benefitted from the commodity boom of the 2000s) also tended to have more robust competition law institutions. Recent work on the interaction of a broader competition policy and growth suggests that competition policy alone will be able to ensure highly effective competition law enforcement. Rather, effective institutions seem to affect the effectiveness of competition law.[11]

At the level of competition law and policy, those systems that have shown improved results seem to share common attributes. The first is a deeper embrace of economic analysis.[12] As agencies, courts, and law firms have become more sophisticated in their economic analysis, competition law has become more technocratic. This has improved the quality of decisions as measured by how economically sound such decisions are. This process of economic learning has created increased demand for training in law schools, business schools, and economics department. Both private practitioners and agency staff are now part of this educational pipeline. The ability of practitioners (and academics) to spend more time in the US and Europe to interact with peers allows Latin American practice to be influenced by the latest global competition law developments and develop best practices. This process of learning and multiple contact points for diffusion of international norms has resulted in a robust competition policy ecosystem in many countries, which has become self-sustaining.

A second factor that has improved competition law and policy has been a focus on end consumer related enforcement. Often this has meant prosecution decisions regarding cartels of core consumer products (food, gasoline, etc.), or issues relating to consumer finance such as pension funds or credit cards.[13] Such cases expose the general public to use and effectiveness of competition law in remedying anti-competitive behavior in a way that is tangible to them.

11. Esteban Greco, Diego Petrecolla, Carlos A. Romero & Juan P. Vila Martínez, "Competition Policy and Growth: Evidence from Latin America," in *Competition Law in Latin America: A Practical Guide* (Julián Peña & Marcelo Calliari eds, Wolters Kluwer 2016).
12. Manuel A. Abdala & Lucía Quesada, *The Use of Economic Analysis in Latin American Competition Policy* (Kluwer Law International 2016), in the first edition of this book published in 2016; D. Daniel Sokol, "The Development of Human Capital in Latin American Competition Policy," in *Competition Law and Policy in Latin America* (Eleanor M. Fox & D. Daniel Sokol eds, Hart 2009).
13. Edgar Odio-Rohrmoser, "Competition Law in Central America and the Years to Come," in *Competition Law in Latin America: A Practical Guide* (Julián Peña & Marcelo Calliari eds, Wolters Kluwer 2016).

The final factor that has changed competition law enforcement effectiveness is that institutional issues that plagued enforcement efforts in the earlier period have been somewhat resolved. As such, the institutional structures of competition enforcement have been recalibrated (and continue to do so) across the region to address the specific needs of the countries in question given their country level institutional backdrops.

This book as a collection of chapters brings together a collection of law and economics professionals who identify the latest trends in Latin American competition law, economics, and policy. They also provide analysis as to the strengths and weaknesses of policy and areas of convergence across countries in the region. Such a book fills an important gap in the English language competition policy literature for an integrated view of developments in the region and of particular countries therein. As the pandemic and increased digitization of the economy become a more significant part of focus of competition agencies, the need for a re-evaluation as to the tools and processes of competition law and economic require careful consideration. Perhaps a third wave may be underway.

CHAPTER 2

Competition Lifecycles in Latin America

*William E. Kovacic**

In light of the worldwide developments that have occurred since the late 1980s, the experience in Latin America and the remarkable expansion of regulatory competition policy raises important questions about the implementation and the success or failure of these new competition policies. This chapter analyzes how well jurisdictions have created the institutional predicates for effective policy implementation by identifying lifecycles that appear to characterize the development of new competition law systems.

A successful legal reform is very complex and challenging, and it is even more difficult in transition economies that have recently adopted competition laws. Life-cycle assessment is therefore of great relevance in determining the development of newer systems and, in this regard, there are three main vectors of implementation: (a) Early Ascent Followed by Decline, (b) The Flat Line, and (c) Gradual Upward Progression; but the road to a successful legal reform has shown to be a process of gradual improvement.

Furthermore, other factors tend to determine the rate at which new systems gain implementation proficiency, such as well-funded agencies, top rate talent in agencies and political support. In this regard, the need for this gradual approach is most pressing in countries with unfavorable initial conditions—poorly funded agencies, weak political support, and low human capital.

Lastly, when applying this gradual approach, it is vitally important that the process be monitored in a proactive manner and that regular evaluations are used as tools to improve programs and institutions. The experience suggests that the emphasis should be on institution-building as a dimension of competition law reforms.

* The author thanks Julián Peña for many useful comments and suggestions. The views expressed here are the author's only.

§2.01 INTRODUCTION

In August 1996, Indecopi, the regulatory body that houses Peru's competition agency, convened a conference in Lima to mark the fifth birthday of its creation.[1] The event attracted officials from across Latin America, as well as academics, government officials, and private practitioners from Europe and North America. More than recognition of Indecopi's formation and considerable accomplishment in institution-building, the conference provided an occasion for reflection on the development of competition law in Latin America.

In 1996 there were lots to celebrate about competition law in this part of the world. Indecopi had gained a soaring reputation, largely by virtue of the work of Beatriz Boza, the agency's first chair, and the exceptional ensemble of professionals she had recruited to fill senior management positions. No less striking were the beginnings of new competition systems in Argentina, Brazil, and Venezuela. Astute leaders headed each of these systems (Jorge Bogo in Argentina, Gesner Oliveira in Brazil, and Ana Julia Jatar in Venezuela) and attracted bright, young men and women to join them. On the whole, the early results in Latin America were encouraging and appeared to foreshadow still better days to come.

Experience over the past two decades has confounded some of the elevated expectations that flourished at the time of Indecopi's fifth birthday. Of the four jurisdictions that had ascended quickly by 1996, only Brazil's competition system today retains the full luster of its early days.[2] Yet, at the same time, the prospects of Latin American systems that seemed less promising in the mid-1990s have improved steadily. For example, the competition law regimes of Chile and Mexico started slowly, but they now stand with Brazil as cases of largely successful policy implementation. Colombia's competition regime, begun over a half-century ago, also has made notable progress in recent years.[3]

Developments in Latin America have taken place in a larger context in which, since the late 1980s, the number of jurisdictions with competition laws has grown from fewer than 20 to roughly 130.[4] Experience in Latin America and in other regions of the

1. On the formation and early years of Indecopi, see Lessons from the First Years of Indecopi: Peru's Experience in Market Regulatory Reform 1993–1998 (Beatriz Boaz ed. 1998).
2. Informative treatments of developments in Latin America since the mid-1990s include Antitrust in Emerging and Developing Countries (Eleanor M. Fox, et al. eds, 2015); Organization for Economic Cooperation and Development, Competition and Market Studies in Latin America (2015); Organization for Economic Cooperation and Development, A Follow-up to Nine Peer Reviews of Competition Law and Policy of Latin American Countries: Argentina, Brazil, Chile, Colombia, El Salvador, Honduras, Mexico, Panama, and Peru (2012); Competition Law and Policy in Latin America (Eleanor M. Fox & D. Daniel Sokol eds, 2009); Claudia Schatan, The Dynamics of Competition Policies in Small Developing Economies: The Central American countries' Experience, in New Competition Jurisdictions 91 (Richard Whish & Christopher Townley eds, 2012).
3. The modern progress of Brazil, Chile, Colombia, and Mexico is recounted in The Antitrust Review of the Americas 2016 (2015).
4. The expansion in the number of the world's competition systems and its significance for business decision making are discussed in William E. Kovacic, The United States and Its Influence on Global Competition Policy, 22 George Mason L. Rev. 1157 (2015).

world raise two basic questions about the remarkable expansion of a regulatory discipline first established in North America in the late nineteenth century. First, how successfully have the new adopters implemented their competition laws? Second, what factors account for the relative success or failure in implementation?

This chapter addresses these questions in the Latin American context by identifying lifecycles that appear to characterize the development of new competition law systems. The discussion here focuses on what it takes to build the institutions needed to apply competition law in a manner that improves economic performance.[5] The chapter does not assess how much the competition systems created since 1990 have served to reduce prices, improve product quality, or stimulate innovation. Instead, it considers how well various jurisdictions have created the institutional predicates for pursuing programs that promise to achieve these aims.

The emphasis on an institution-oriented approach reflects a growing understanding that there is a strong connection between the quality of institutional arrangements and the policy outcomes that competition law, or any other system of economic regulation, can achieve.[6] In the 1990s, as a large number of nations adopted competition laws as part of market-oriented economic reforms, there was an epidemic failure—especially among national foreign assistance programs and multinational bodies that advised nations in designing new laws—to account for the institutional arrangements that would be vital to effective implementation. To many donors, the measure of success of a technical assistance project was the adoption of a new competition statute—a readily observable, tick-the-box index of effectiveness. Here and in other contexts, implementation issues were secondary, technical details to be sorted out later on: pass the law first, and implementation inevitably will follow along in due course.[7]

Blindness to implementation afflicted the drafting of many new competition statutes. External advisors often provided off-the-rack solutions from other jurisdictions with little tailoring to account for local conditions. Glaring mismatches abounded between indigenous implementation capabilities and the demands imposed by laws best suited to well-established market economies with well-funded competition agencies and strong collateral institutions such as courts and universities.[8]

To some extent, the perceived need to imbed models tested in older competition law systems was understandable. The prevailing wisdom of technical assistance

5. Improved economic performance is not the sole aim of most competition laws, yet it is a core stated aim of most of the world's competition laws. On the diversity of objectives embodied in competition systems, *see* Symposium, The Goals of Antitrust, 81 Fordham L. Rev. 2151 (2013).
6. Annetje Ottow, Market and Competition Authorities: Good Agency Principles (2015); David A. Hyman & William E. Kovacic, Competition Agency Design: What's on the Menu?, 8 European Competition Journal 527 (2012).
7. William E. Kovacic, Lucky Trip? Perspectives from a Foreign Advisor on Competition Policy, Development and Technical Assistance, 3 European Competition Journal 319 (2007).
8. William E. Kovacic, The Institutional Foundations for Economic Law Reform in Transition Economies: The Case of Competition Policy and Antitrust Enforcement, 77 Chicago-Kent Law Rev. 265 (2001) 20.

pressed toward adopting fully-loaded competition regimes that included the complete range of policy commands that were the norm in older systems such as the European Union (EU) and the United States. This partly reflected the view that transition economies would have a single political opportunity to make basic economic reforms. Because the political will to enact reforms could evaporate, it was thought necessary to pack everything into the competition law from the outset. The possibility for future upgrades or gradual, phased implementation was seen as uncertain or unlikely.

Academic scholarship and government policymaking over the past fifteen years or so reveal increased recognition that implementation requires close attention from the first day of a law reform process.[9] Statutes with grand policy aspirations but ineffective means for implementation pointlessly consume resources, public and private, and engender cynicism about lawmaking and public administration generally. There is a healthy and growing interest in (a) how to establish and sustain the institutional foundations necessary to achieve good policy results and (b) how to measure the effectiveness of different institutional configurations.

This chapter treats the topic of agency lifecycles and policy implementation in three sections. It first considers at what point in the development of a new competition law system it makes sense to form reliable conclusions about implementation effectiveness. The chapter proposes that it takes roughly fifteen to twenty-five years from the adoption of a law to determine whether a new competition law regime is on the path to successful implementation.

The second section of the chapter describes several lifecycles that describe the development of newer systems. The 100 or so competition systems formed since the late 1980s have proceeded along different evolutionary paths. It presents four principal evolutionary paths and proposes that the path most closely associated with implementation success is a gradual upward sloping curve of progress.

The third section identifies factors that determine the rate at which new systems gain implementation proficiency. Key considerations include resources (financial outlays and human capital), agency leadership, political commitment and stability, and the quality of collateral institutions, such as courts and universities.

Several sources of information inform the paper. Three stand out. One is a benchmarking project undertaken by the George Washington University Law School's Competition Law Center. This project has collected information about ten major institutional characteristics for the world's 130 competition law systems. The process of preparing the study has provided a useful opportunity to see how individual systems have evolved. A second source of information includes reports, including "peer reviews," prepared by the International Competition Network (ICN), the Organization for Economic Cooperation and Development (OECD), and the United Nations Conference on Trade and Development (UNCTAD) on matters related to competition law

9. Eleanor M. Fox & Michael J. Trebilcock eds The Design of Competition Law Institutions: Global Norms, Local Choices (Oxford University Press, 2012).

implementation.[10] The third are interviews with current and former competition agency officials and site visits in various countries.[11]

§2.02 THE TIME FOR ASSESSMENT

When should one take stock of the progress of implementation for a new competition system? The evaluation process should be continuous and should begin from the earliest days of the new competition regime. For the new system and for supportive external observers (such as donors or foreign competition agencies that provide assistance), it is sensible to monitor progress from early days and use regular assessments as tools to improve programs or institutional arrangements.

When can we form reliable views about the quality of institutional arrangements and the capacity of an agency to perform assigned policy duties? I would suggest that it takes fifteen to twenty-five years to gauge progress in a meaningful manner. Put another way, for most jurisdictions it takes at least fifteen to twenty-five years to achieve a sound institutional footing in terms of statutory authority, judicial interpretation, internal capacity building, and improvements in collateral bodies.

For five basic reasons, the fifteen to twenty-five year milestone is a valuable point to assess implementation success. First, it provides an adequate opportunity for the competition agency to test its powers—notably, its authority to gather information (e.g., through compulsory process and searches of business premises), its mandate to challenge various forms of business behavior (e.g., abusive conduct by dominant firms, cartels, and anticompetitive mergers), and its power to impose sanctions. The agency will require time to build internal teams and processes to carry out these functions. Success in performing these tasks requires the accumulation of experience and the development of a sound institutional memory to capture knowledge gained from practice.

Second, it takes considerable time to see whether an agency has established a reputation that enables it to attract and retain good attorneys, economists, and administrative professionals.[12] Some agencies never succeed in recruiting sufficient numbers of capable staff. Others do well in the early years as enthusiasm for a new program, ambitious enforcement measures, and charismatic leadership make the agency a desirable employer. A serious test for such agencies is whether they can

10. I have participated in a number of these peer review exercises since 2011 and have co-authored UNCTAD peer reviews for Armenia, Pakistan, and Ukraine.
11. Since 2011, I have done site visits to the competition authorities of the following countries that adopted competition laws after 1990: Albania, Argentina, Armenia, Barbados, Brazil, Chile, China, Czech Republic, Ecuador, Egypt, Hong Kong, Georgia, Hungary, India, Indonesia, Ireland, Israel, Jamaica, Kazakhstan, Kenya, Latvia, Lithuania, Malaysia, Mauritius, Mexico, Mongolia, Morocco, Netherlands, Pakistan, Peru, Poland, Portugal, Russia, Singapore, South Africa, Spain, Sweden, Taiwan, Thailand, Turkey, and Ukraine.
12. On the importance of reputation and branding to an agency's performance, *see* William E. Kovacic, Creating a Respected Brand: How Regulatory Agencies Signal Quality, 22 George Mason L. Rev. 237 (2015).

become more than what amounts to an executive MBA program that identifies good talent for absorption by the private sector or by other public agencies.

Third, in nearly every jurisdiction, initial efforts to exercise these legal capabilities will elicit stout challenges by affected firms in the courts. It will require fifteen to twenty-five years to obtain judicial rulings (often from the highest court in the jurisdiction) that either sustain or forestall the agency's efforts to exercise its legal mandate. Courts in the early period also will focus closely on apparent deviations from procedural requirements established in the competition law or imposed by the jurisdiction's administrative procedure code.

Fourth, it is important to see how an agency fares following leadership changes. Some agencies have gotten off to a seemingly great start by reason of highly visible and capable leadership. Many of these agencies have descended rapidly in performance when the first-generation leader departs and a less capable successor takes office. Newer agencies, just like older agencies, can suffer from the rivalry and jealousy that can characterize relationships between current and former leaders. Several handoffs will be necessary to see if the government remains committed to appointing high quality officials, whether the agency succeeds in embedding good process and analytical capability in the institution itself (rather than relying chiefly on the skill of a given leader). After several leadership changes, it is also possible to see whether leaders have accepted a norm that defines success in terms of the agency's achievements and suppresses the impulse for individual credit-claiming and blame-casting.

Fifth, a period of fifteen to twenty-five years provides a rough idea of the depth and durability of political support for the competition law. An initial period of vigorous law enforcement can create political backlash that inspires ministers and legislators to intervene destructively in the competition agency's work; Changes in economic conditions that erode support for competition as an organizing principle of economic organization.[13] Political support also can evaporate amid political upheaval or conflict. Political upheaval can render competition law a subordinate political concern, or make the competition regime entirely irrelevant.

To a large degree, all of the considerations sketched earlier reveal the competition system's resilience. One wants to see if the agency not only has generated positive accomplishments (e.g., cartels successfully attacked and anticompetitive government policies adjusted by reason of effective advocacy), but also has shown its ability to take a punch and keep fighting well. Every competition agency gets tested by a crisis or several crises.[14] These take many forms: a major case that fails in the courts, a powerful industry lobbying campaign to induce legislators to withdraw funding or authority, an improper disclosure of confidential information that casts doubt on the

---

13. A good case can be made that the U.S. competition laws did not become mainstream elements of national economic policy until the late 1930s, following the abandonment of central planning initiatives tried in the First New Deal. This history is traced in William E. Kovacic & Carl Shapiro, Antitrust Policy: A Century in Economic and Legal Thinking, 14 Journal of Economic Perspectives 43 (2000).
14. On the struggles of the Federal Trade Commission in its early years, *see* Marc Winerman & William E. Kovacic, Outpost Years for a Start-Up Agency: The FTC from 1921 to 1925, 77 Antitrust L. Rev. 145 (2010).

agency's procedural safeguards, or, worse, an episode of corruption involving a top agency official. It is important to know if the agency can cope well with adversity and, if it has committed errors, to repair problems and do better going forward.

The factors set out here also caution against embracing unrealistic expectations about what a new competition system is likely to achieve in its first decade or so. As discussed below in section 2.04, the performance of a competition system depends crucially on matters such as funding and human capital.[15] Competition agencies that are weakly funded and situated in jurisdictions with a shallow pool of talent must proceed more gradually to implement the law than agencies blessed with substantial financial resources and first-rate talent. Even for the best-resourced agency with superb staff, it can take considerable time to become proficient in tasks such as law enforcement or competition advocacy. There is no such thing as an "easy" cartel case or "simple" dawn raid for an agency that never has done one. The essential architecture of a leniency program may seem fairly straightforward (give immunity for the first cartel member to inform), but the routine application of leniency schemes presents extraordinary complexities that can perplex even the most-experienced regimes.

The underestimation of difficulty is especially pronounced for action-forcing mechanisms that compel the competition agency to devote resources to certain types of matters. Examples include compulsory merger notification with mandatory waiting periods and administrative law requirements that force the agency to investigate all complaints brought to its attention (with little or no discretion to brush aside manifestly insignificant matters in favor of pursuing more economically meaningful priorities). There is a chronic tendency to underestimate the administrative burdens imposed by these types of requirements. This has been true for even well-resourced agencies in undertaking new programs.[16] There is a lengthy learning process by which agencies adapt to cope effectively with these and similar mandates.

§2.03 LIFECYCLES

From the accumulated experience of new systems since the late 1980s, we can observe three principle implementation vectors.

[A] Early Ascent Followed by Decline

One cohort of systems has risen early and then entered a sustained period of decline. In some cases, the first period consisted of a sharp vertical ascent followed by a descent

15. Building this crucial dimension of capacity has proven to be a difficult endeavor in Latin America. D. Daniel Sokol, The Development of Human Capital in Latin American Competition Policy, in Competition Law and Policy in Latin America 13 (Eleanor M. Fox & D. Daniel Sokol eds, 2009).
16. On the early difficulties of the Federal Trade Commission in implementing a new program of compulsory advance notification of mergers, *see* William E. Kovacic, HSR at 35: The Early US premerger Notification Experience and Its Meaning for New Systems of Competition Law, in New Competition Jurisdictions 9 (Richard Whish & Christopher Townley eds, 2012).

almost as dramatic as the initial climb. Venezuela's competition system fits this profile. In the early years, such agencies often are heralded as success stories. The ascent typically is propelled by a strong first-generation leader (e.g., Ana Julia Jatar in Venezuela) who succeeds in bringing superior talent into the agency in its first years. The decline is set in motion by various factors: departure of the charismatic leader without the development of an institutional framework to carry on the agency's work, a regime change in national leadership that results in a redirection of policy, or a legal dispute that casts doubt on the legitimacy of the framework.

In some instances, the collapse associated with this scenario is not complete, with a noticeable descent from the early period of seemingly effective implementation. Prominent examples in this category are Argentina and Peru. The agency does not crash into the ground, but descends to a level of performance that is decidedly modest by comparison to its initial accomplishments. In this case the agency stalls for some of the same reasons suggested earlier—for example, a leadership change that dramatically reorients the agency (e.g., political upheaval which led to the departure of Beatriz Boza and a curtailment of Indecopi's authority in Peru[17]) or the ascent of political philosophies that question the value of giving market-oriented reforms a decisive role in national economic policy (e.g., Argentina[18]).

Political turmoil inspired by discontent with market reforms deeply affects the competition law regime. In some instances, anti-market political movements have placed the competition policy system into a holding pattern during which the agency at best can hope to retain a critical mass of its best staff, who devote themselves during the hiatus to research and analysis tasks in anticipation of a future resumption of operations. At worst, the repudiation of market processes can convert the competition agency into a Frankenstein's monster that becomes a device for retarding, rather than promoting, competition.

[B] The Flat Line

A second vector resembles a flat line. Some new systems never get off the ground in the sense of applying advocacy or law enforcement tools effectively. A number of systems in Central America suffer from desperately weak funding that prevents the establishment of even the most rudimentary implementation programs. In other countries (e.g., Paraguay), indifferent political support has stalled the application of advocacy or enforcement powers.

In other countries, funding is more generous, but a basic infirmity in the law has prevented the application of the competition authority's enforcement tools. The

17. The narrowing of Indecopi's powers in the early 2000s is reviewed in Organization for Economic Cooperation and Development, Competition Law and Policy in Peru: A Peer Review (2004).
18. The waning of political support for the "Washington Consensus" and market-based economic policies (including competition) in Argentina and other countries in Latin American after the mid-1990s is discussed in Julián Peña, Promoting Competition Policies from the Private Sector in Latin America, in Competition Law and Policy in Latin America 469 (Eleanor M. Fox & D. Daniel Sokol eds, 2009).

competition authority of the Dominican Republic still awaits the appointment of an official who, by law, must approve the initiation of law enforcement proceedings. The new agency trains its people and engages in advocacy measures such as public education, but it is unable to apply enforcement powers that, on the surface, were a major reason to create a competition regime.

This cohort of agencies is not irretrievably failed. In some cases, the largely inactive agency has begun to build a program that has promise of putting the system on a path of upward progression. In recent years, for example, a number of agencies have overcome badly inadequate funding levels and a most unfavorable political environment to build a useful program.

[C] Gradual Upward Progression

The third vector is a path of gradual upward progression. The slope of progress can vary—some steeper (e.g., Brazil), and some more gradual (e.g., Chile and Mexico). The vector usually is not an unbroken upward arc, as the agency encounters successes and setbacks along the way. Mexico, for example, has achieved important improvements in its statutory framework and in the implementation of its law enforcement and advocacy programs. A recent change in leadership was accompanied by a wholesale change in senior management (with the departure one year ago of seventeen of the agency's top eighteen managers). Restocking the leadership team will take time and will come at some cost in performance in the short term.

In their first years, these systems usually are not identified as fast-rising stars. Over time, however, they show steady improvement and grow resilient by reason of better resourcing, staffing, program selection, and political support.

§2.04 FACTORS ACCOUNTING FOR IMPLEMENTATION SUCCESS

To study the lifecycles of various competition systems is to see factors that tend to improve the prospects for successful implementation.

[A] Funding

Well-funded agencies generally outperform poorly resourced regimes. Chile, Colombia, and Mexico are examples of agencies that have undergone gradual, steady improvements in implementation. Each received adequate outlays to begin its new competition law regime and has enjoyed strong continuing support. A condition that links many of the least successful systems is a poverty of resources from internal sources and an inability to enlist external donors to fill the gap.

[B] Human Capital

Resourcing, in turn, deeply influences a second vital condition. Well-funded agencies have greater ability to attract and return top rate talent and to spend funds for external consultants. The agency's ability to establish effective law enforcement or advocacy programs hinges largely on its human capital. As the agency's talent increases, it can undertake more ambitious programs. The level of skill should be paramount in the choice of enforcement and non-enforcement matters.

[C] Matching Commitments to Capabilities

The more effective competition systems strive to match program commitments to delivery capabilities. A weakly resourced agency must strive to select programs that it has a fighting chance to carry out successfully. This requires strong discipline in program selection to avoid making commitments to matters that the agency cannot execute successfully. A common trap in the early years is to begin a large number of highly ambitious matters that outrun the capability of staff and run serious risks of failure before the courts.

Poorly resourced systems should be wary of undertaking programs that involve large, recurring administrative tasks. Merger regimes with mandatory notification and waiting period requirements tend to impose substantial administrative burdens. A system with few resources likely will find itself overwhelmed by a merger review mechanism unless reporting thresholds are set at levels that correspond to the agency staffing.

[D] Learning

The effort to avoid mismatches requires attention to the agency's experience level. As the competition authority accumulates experience, it can reasonably seek to conduct a larger number of inquiries or undertake individual matters of greater difficulty. The more effective agencies also have made wise use of the learning of other competition law regimes—either directly from individual regimes or indirectly through the work of international bodies such as the ICN, OECD, and UNCTAD.

[E] Political Support

It is extraordinarily difficult to implement a competition policy program in a jurisdiction that is hostile to or indifferent to the aims of the law. It is still more difficult to build a program amid political entropy. Weak political support or episodes of severe political instability inevitably lengthen the period for effective implementation of the competition law.

[F] Collateral Institutions

The implementation of competition law depends heavily on the quality of collateral institutions—bodies which Allan Fels has called "co-producers." A nation with a well-functioning judicial system confers a great advantage on the development of the competition regime. A country with feeble or, worse, corrupt courts faces a lengthy process of retooling its judiciary or establishing new tribunals dedicated to competition law.

A competition system ultimately cannot thrive without the support of academic institutions that teach courses and perform research in competition law and industrial organization economics. The speed with which a jurisdiction develops a sound intellectual infrastructure will affect the pace and quality of implementation.

[G] International Cooperation

Participation in international programs—bilateral relationships, regional programs, and larger international networks—can help agencies to overcome resource limits, accelerate learning, and build political support. To an increasing degree, these mechanisms enable agencies to obtain highly valuable know-how about the substance and process of competition law, and to train agency leaders about how to deal with sensitive issues involving political pressure and relations with other public agencies.

[H] Periodic Assessment and Upgrades

The most successful implementation efforts have taken place in jurisdictions that undertake periodic reviews of the competition system. The virtuous cycle one observes in the best systems consists of a three stage process of experimentation, assessment, and refinement. Many authorities (e.g., Brazil, Mexico) have returned to the national legislature to obtain major upgrades in their systems.

§2.05 CONCLUSION

The design and successful implementation of law reform are difficult tasks in any legal system. They tend to be even more difficult in the dozens of transition economies which have adopted competition laws in the past twenty-five years.

The path to success for new competition systems generally has been a process of incremental improvement. The best experiences have taken place in jurisdictions that pursued gradual increases in the tempo and difficulty of implementation. The need for a deliberate, phased approach is the most acute in countries with unfavorable initial conditions—badly funded agencies, weak political support, and thin human capital.

Better understanding of the path of implementation to date suggests the value of greater emphasis on institution-building as a dimension of competition law reforms. It also calls for patience in setting expectations about what most regimes are likely to be able to accomplish.

CHAPTER 3

The Failed Search for the Soul of Competition Policy

Ignacio De León[*]

A recent assessment by the IDB Secretariat at the annual meeting of the Latin American Competition Forum examined the problem of "mainstreaming" antitrust policy among economic policies across the region. The background note advanced several hypotheses about why the policy does not scale to the forefront of countries economic policies. The IDB vividly stated: "*Competition Policy (...) is still a second division player waiting to be promoted to the premier league.*" (IDB, 2014: 7).[1] Antitrust policy has struggled for a long time to gain credibility among the core of economic policies, with uncertain results.

To be sure, disappointment over antitrust policy is not confined to Latin America. Assessing antitrust policy in the U.S., Crandall and Winston (2005: 4) conclude that they "find little empirical evidence that past interventions have provided much benefit to consumers." Similarly, Teece (2012: 205) indicates "the lack of compelling evidence

* The views presented here are entirely the author's and do not represent the view of the IDB.

1. The Secretariat highlighted the problem as follows:

> There is no clear picture on how competition policy principles are being used, or mainstreamed in the overall economic framework of LAC countries. The fact is that competition policy is not generally perceived by key policy makers as a fundamental pillar to boost the wealth of LAC countries. Therefore, competition policy is often inexistent in the political agenda of most governments leaving the institutional arrangements with a low-key profile and a scarce budget allocation. Moreover, competition policy issues are not generally a topic (at least directly) in most political campaigns, despite the fact that a large percentage of the population purchasing power (especially those with lower income) is affected by anti-competitive distortions in basic goods and services. In fact, in the LAC region there is a homogenized political discourse that often addresses the need to reduce consumer prices, but that seldom references competition policy as the necessary tool to that end. (IDB, 2014: 7).

indicating that antitrust is not aiding consumers is a matter of concern, and motivates inquiry here."

Two lines of thought have avoided answering the difficult question of why, unlike other regulatory policies, competition policies in Latin America (and elsewhere) have struggled to attain tangible results. The first line of analysis blames the institutional setting of developing countries for failing to enforce antitrust policy "adequately." In a recent paper, Fox and Gal (2014: 2) highlighted particular traits within developing countries such as "scarce human and financial resources, malfunctioning markets and poor infrastructure, systemic poverty, cronyism, and corruption" as responsible for their incapacity to sustain competition enforcement along international best standards.

Clearly this ethnocentric view of the policy leads to a *non sequitur*. In this circular reasoning, the lack of development displayed by these proxies undermines antitrust policy, which is intended to propel development. Upon closer inspection, it also misconstrues reality by implicitly postulating the claim that consensus exists in the implementation of antitrust policy among developed countries, which is simply not the case. Yet, this view is actually quite extended, especially among international "reviewers" who have increasingly become a source of peer pressure on what competition policy "should" and shouldn't be; these include steering mechanisms as diverse as the International Competition Network,[2] the OECD Competition Policy Committee Recommendations,[3] the OECD/IDB Latin American Competition Forum,[4] the Centre for Competition Policy,[5] and other similar mechanisms.

The second line of interpretation assumes an exculpatory position, by taking "experimentation" in the policy's wavering legal standards as a sign of virtuosity. Thus, Kovacic (2005) praises the "learning process" that allegedly accrues from tinkering with market outcomes through antitrust policy interventions, thereby resulting in changing rules developed through this process over time.[6]

By contrast, in this paper, we hold that differences do exist in policy enforcement but these should not be credited to the country's level of development; rather they stem from the contradictions of the policy's theoretical foundations. Moreover, we contend that wavering legal standards, far from encapsulating a kernel of attributed wisdom, are severe policy flaws that undermine its legitimacy. Indeed, "experimentation" in the search of optimal antitrust policy, has affected the credibility of the policy to the extent that it has rendered it impossible to define what the policy actually seeks and how it

2. http://www.internationalcompetitionnetwork.org/.
3. http://www.oecd.org/daf/competition/recommendations.htm.
4. http://www.oecd.org/competition/latinamerica/.
5. http://competitionpolicy.ac.uk/home.
6. Kovacic (2005) states: "Competition policy is a work in progress. From the adoption of the first national antitrust statute in Canada in 1889, the history of competition law has featured a continuing search for optimal statutory commands, institutional designs, and operational techniques (Gavil et. al. 2002; Chs 1, 9). Recent decades have witnessed extraordinary change as older and newer competition systems seek better practices for defining substantive commands, setting priorities, choosing cases, and selecting remedies."

measures performance results. In fact, what seems uncontestable are the erosive effects of antitrust policy over the rule of law.

Lack of credibility towards competition policy follows a deeper crisis of identity. The façade of the policy, in truth, adopts two separate, distinct operational frameworks: antitrust policy and competition advocacy, respectively. Initially, however, this was not the case. Antitrust policy historically emerged as a government attempt to curb perceived monopolistic power of industrial conglomerates and "trusts" emerged in the United States during the reconstruction after the Civil War. This endeavor, which was sustained somewhat intuitively back then, found intellectual respectability within the economics profession in the studies of the firm and competition that were conducted in the 1930s. These studies, led by Joan Robinson's model of Imperfect Competition, essentially misconstrued the competitive process as an equilibrium framework, which led scholars to support antitrust policy on flaky analytical foundations that completely disregarded the institutions where the competitive process takes place. This essay postulates that Robinson's theory produced a "cognitive dissonance" between markets and institutions that resulted in the simplistic disapproval of business agreements or unilateral practices that entrepreneurs use to develop competitive capabilities, and to seize profit opportunities through a trial-and-error learning process.

In the dominant creed that emerged since then within the economics profession market failures allegedly made it impossible to achieve Perfect Competition (PC) in product markets; thus these "imperfections" had to be corrected through government antitrust intervention so as to restore optimal equilibria lost to monopolistic behavior. Later, the policy shifted from this "rigid" analytical framework into varying degrees of more "flexible" interpretations that laid down the possible existence of "tolerable" imperfections due to their pro-competitive effects. Nonetheless, the wavering interpretation of these legal standards undermined legal certainty, which is the bedrock of market functioning.

In this essay we focus our attention on how the theoretical wellsprings of antitrust theory have rendered the policy unable to build stable legal doctrines, and to be executed consistently, which is reflected in no small part, by the lack of adequate metrics with which to measure policy performance.

The lack of precision on the policy goals has brought about a key difficulty to measure policy performance, and to make it accountable, judicially or otherwise. To be true, the literature has been very prolific in developing indicators, but these are indicators mostly related to competition agencies' performance, rather than measurements on competition dynamics itself. Moreover, as Rodriguez and DeNardis (2008) have said, they are "perceptions-based" i.e. based on the mere opinion of those who conduct the measurement; hence, they are liable to heterogeneous understanding and personal bias.

In a broader sense, the imprecision of antitrust policy goals has led enforcers into dithering policy action and subsequent loss of legitimacy. Competition agencies in the region are either excluded or simply ignored from key decision-making in economic policy matters. These agencies are sometimes not even officially acknowledged;[7] supportive competition legislation is blocked or national governments condemn them to oblivion as soon as they show a minimum degree of independence.[8]

This paper argues that the reason for this record does not rest on the lack of willingness or political clout of the competition agencies themselves, usually integrated by highly professional officials. Rather, it is found in its analytical bias, which links competition analysis to theoretical models of industrial organization without any reference to the institutions, rules or customs under which such industrial organization takes shape. In light of this neglect, antitrust policy formulates a contrived set of normative goals that have little understanding of the rationale behind firms' market conduct. Ultimately, the Achilles Heel of Competition Policy rests on its inherent disconnect with the set of institutional rules wherein business strategies take shape and can be understood.

This paper starts by highlighting how this cognitive dissonance creates a gulf of expectations between antitrust enforcement and the perceived results of such activity on the promotion of competition, as revealed in the Global Competitiveness Report survey.

Given the divergence found, we examine the historical roots of the theoretical background that gave rise to this cognitive dissonance, namely, the model of Imperfect Competition developed by Joan Robinson in the mid-1930s. We study the implications of this model into the normative analytical mindset that emerged hitherto for the assessment of competition, as well as the neglect that stirred over institutional analysis and a better understanding of the competitive implications of legal barriers.

Next, our analysis will examine how this analytical oversight made its way through antitrust policymaking. We will focus our attention on the lack of proper competition metrics with which to measure the effects of the policy; the unpredictable and unstable case law arising out of policy enforcement; the legal formalism that casts a shadow over economic substance and finally, the neglected role of competition advocacy, as opposed to the active antitrust enforcement role assumed by competition agencies.

The last section will outline some alternative metrics proposed for assessing competition.

7. The case of the Argentine Competition court illustrates the point. Created by the Competition Act of 1999 it has yet to be appointed; similarly, lagging legal reforms in Costa Rica to improve the current COPROCOM as well as the obvious resistance of countries such as Guatemala; the difficulties of Mexico's CFC state the problems of these agencies to make headway and to become relevant.
8. In 2001, the Superintendente of Colombia's SIC, tendered his resignation after his decision to block a merger in the airline industry was objected to by the Government, yielding to the pressure of vested interests in this industry; in Venezuela, the Superintendente of Pro-competencia also tendered his resignation in 2000 due to the interference of the government on Procompetencia's decisions.

§3.01 COGNITIVE DISSONANCE IN ANTITRUST THEORY

The antitrust policy agenda suffers from inherent ambiguity that is readily visible in its conflicting goals, whether economic efficiency (most often, short-term efficiency also associated to Consumer Welfare) or some distributive goal (i.e., equity).[9]

Yet, the point to be emphasized here is not about choosing between conflicting normative goals but rather to highlight that these goals emerge from the underlying inconsistencies of conventional competition theory. These theoretical inconsistencies render the ethos of the policy undefined, hence the proliferation of diverging normative policy goals.

These tensions in the agenda are traceable back to the origins of Neoclassical Industrial Organization analysis in the 1930s,[10] inaugurated by Joan Robinson's theory of Imperfect Competition (IC) (1933). Robinson's theory was purely inspired by the search of "optimal" equilibrium thinking of markets. Assuming that optimal equilibrium represented under PC was the best possible outcome of markets, Robinson displayed a picture of possible states away from PC, where businesses exploited knowledge advantages in order to seize monopoly rents.

By the same token, antitrust analysis ignored the problem of how competitive knowledge is transmitted through institutional channels; how cooperation between competitors is necessary to stabilize expectations and why contracts, customs, routines, standards, and the like emerge in order to pass valuable information on to market agents that help them overcome uncertainty that otherwise impedes investments (Richardson, 1960) or to create new knowledge through disruptive innovation, to help them overcome technological barriers impeding them access to the market (Schumpeter, 1942). None of these research themes were part of Robinson's quest, who was content with modeling market exchanges under the hypothesized departures from the "PC" situation, while postulating institutions as "givens" within which market exchanges would allegedly take place.

Under Robinson's model, equilibrium was implicit in her assumption of unchanging consumer preferences that would make part of the producer's negative slope demand curve. Each producer is a monopolist of his own production, thereby facing a negative slope demand curve; likewise, oligopolies are also protected from third party competitors. Why? Simply because Robinson postulated it so.[11]

---

9. Martin (2008) does an updated discussion along with a review of the extensive literature on this matter. In his view, how one ought to measure market performance (consumer welfare or net social welfare) remains a subject of discussion. Moreover, use of the economic welfare standard is characterized by judicial application that is inconsistent with mainstream economics.
10. This analysis has received different names: "blackboard economics"; "equilibrium analysis," or "neoclassical competition economics." For the sake of simplicity we will brand it antitrust analysis, given the implications that later would have upon the conceptualization of Industrial Organization and antitrust analysis.
11. Of course, Robinson's Imperfect Competition rested on contrived assumptions about the nature of demand. It is a demand curve conditioned by the existence of substitutes, where consumers' preferences are well defined. Unlike the previous generation of economists (notably, Alfred Marshall), who clearly foresaw changes in demand, resulting from changes in the underlying consumer preferences as the short-term evolved towards the long term, Robinson did not bother

Robinson thus postulated departures from the PC case that resulted in more complex -yet always equilibrium- models of product differentiation and advertising, thus yielding to a vantage point that favored "imperfection" over "competition." This construction, which Loasby (1989) vividly called "Joan Robinson's Wrong Turning", would be rejected by Robinson herself,[12] but by then, the intellectual support of "equilibrium" Industrial Organization postulating competition along structural models of "imperfect competition," while presenting monopolies as "exploitative" market structures was already underway.[13]

Hence, the antitrust analysis rejects, almost as a matter of principle, any analysis of the rules, contracts, laws, and standards that enable market transactions. These are simply assumed while it patronizes against the "imperfect" resource allocation within these markets, located away from PC, wherever that is. Simultaneously, it ignores the assessment of these market institutions that focuses upon transmission of competitive knowledge among market agents. Robinson's quest to formalize a competition model in terms of mathematical equilibrium analysis[14] led her to implicitly assume institutions away as exogenous "givens," rather than endogenous variables to reckon. It also bequeathed the next generation of economists (and eventually, competition scholars) a contrived "blackboard" view of static markets dominated by monopolies of varying size and "power."[15]

---

with this; nor did she clarify as to what sort of preferences would enable economic agents to reach "optimality." She simply assumed that businesses manipulated individual preferences to their benefit -i.e. monopolistic conduct, and that, in her view, explained eventual changes in the system.

12. Explicitly she said: "When I prepared *Economics of Imperfect Competition* on static assumptions, I took a wrong turning; the right road would have been to abandon static analysis and to reconcile the analysis with Marshall's theory of development."(Robinson, 1951: viii) Later, she would reaffirm this conviction: "I took the wrong turn in my analysis of imperfect competition, by concentrating on the 'imperfect' and ignoring 'competition'. Thus, instead of abandoning static analysis and trying to reconcile my analysis with Marshall's theory of development, I followed Pigou and prepared *Economics of Imperfect Competition* on static foundations."
13. By 1934 the static vision of (imperfect) competition, had been firmly established in economic thought, as well as the widespread misunderstanding on Marshall's equilibrium system. This is clearly revealed in Kaldor's impeccable logic, as follows: "long-period static equilibrium and *perfect* competition are incompatible assumptions." (Kaldor, 1969: 46) Thereafter, public policy arising from such theoretical assumption was biased against increasing returns, as potential source of monopolistic power. Evidently, such model misconstrued the creative, ongoing nature of markets. Under a dynamic perspective of markets, Kaldor's long-term equilibrium under such static bounds would have never been postulated; much less the assumption that Marshall ever founded his analysis upon the notion of perfect competition, as Kaldor naively seems to argue.
14. Interestingly, Robinson would later acknowledge her own mistake in developing her competition theory in equilibrium terms: "The neoclassical economist thinks of a position of equilibrium as a position towards which an economy is tending to move as time goes by. But it is impossible for a system to get into a position of equilibrium, for the very nature of equilibrium is that the system is already in it, and has been in it for a certain length of time. (Robinson 1953-4; quoted from Robinson, *supra* n. 11, p. 120, italics in original)."
15. The modern theory of industrial organization was born out of a number of academic projects in the United States already yielding significant results by the early 1950s. It focused on industry-wide studies, tested the hypothesis that market or industrial structures determined member firms' conduct and performance. (Corley, 1990: 88) This "finding" resulted in the core Structure-Conduct-Performance "paradigm" which still today dominates much of antitrust policy analysis. Already in 1970 a scholar said that:

This analytical paradigm, based on the "perfectibility" of markets through enlightened elimination of business "contrivances" built a naïve dent that riddled policymaking ever since. For it focused the attention into selecting whether short-run Consumer Welfare should prevail over long-run Productive Efficiency, instead of questioning whether the whole exercise was pointless, as it ignored the very object in need of analysis, namely, business institutions. Objections against the unrealism of the premises of the antitrust analysis (Chamberlin 1950, 1957; Clark, 1957: 158–156; Richardson, 1960; Kirzner, 1973)[16] were dismissed on methodological grounds by arguing in favor of predictability over realism of the models. (Friedman, 1955)[17]

Due to its analytical bias focused on market ideal outcomes, rather than on connecting institutions, antitrust analysis (and, by implication, antitrust policy) fell into a sort of "cognitive dissonance," whereby the policy has sought to attain idealistic normative goals (most often, Consumer Welfare) that have little to do with the way institutions shape business conduct; thereby rendering the policy highly ineffective in explaining the rationale behind businesses carrying out limitations to their rivalry,

---

> the public policy interest and applications are now propelling the field of industrial organization so strongly that it would be impossible to stop the momentum. Consequently, professional workers in this field have a high responsibility and an unusual opportunity. The market structure-conduct-performance approach is now a basis of analysis and for judgments in much of the work in the antitrust field in both the Department of Justice and the Federal Trade Commission. The selection and analysis of cases is being influenced to some extent by this framework of analysis as is much of the basic research and data collection." (Grether, 1970: 86).

16. Chamberlin (1957: 72) noted the incongruity of using perfect competition as a point of departure for measurement of reality:

> If all rents are included within the cost curve of the firm, equilibrium for the firm under pure competition will always involve tangency of the demand curve and the cost curve at the minimum point for the latter, and hence the equality of price and marginal cost. But it does not follow that the equilibrium of a firm under monopolistic competition may be compared with such assumed conditions *for the same firm* in order to obtain a measure of the departure from pure competition. The reason is that the definition of pure competition involves conditions beyond the individual firm. Pure competition could be realized for the firm in question only if there were a very large number of what does not and cannot exist when as in real life the demand is for a diversified product. To imagine its existence is to indulge in flights of fancy which deprive the comparisons of any useful meaning.

Chamberlin rightly notes the absurdity of this exercise when used for any other purpose different from pure mathematical conjecture.

17. Interestingly, in 1960 G.B. Richardson, focused his attention not on the "realism" of the analytical premises, but on the inner consistency of the perfect competition hypothesis as a theoretical construct, by pointing the logical contradictions implicit in the antitrust analysis, namely, that a state of competitive equilibrium can neither be maintained, achieved, or even approached unless there are entrepreneurs with differing capabilities, and the system has some level of "asymmetric information," because if they all had equal chances and knowledge of profit opportunities (i.e., the conditions that were supposed to prevail under perfect competition), no one would in fact be able to seize it or they would all race to seize it causing the market to collapse, due to overinvestments. Richardson was ignored altogether, in no small measure, due to the prevalence of the equilibrium paradigm, which simply could not assimilate the criticism into its analytical framework.

collaboration, and merging activities, with impact on the competitive processes. The following sections explore the implications of this phenomenon in more detail.

However, before we move on into exploring the implications of the "cognitive dissonance" on the assessment of antitrust policy; and its inability to fulfill its role, we should devote a few words to the nature of business practices and institutional means devised by entrepreneurs to compete in the marketplace.

Entrepreneurs compete through a trial-and-error learning process, whereby institutional arrangements are set forth and rearranged as change in the circumstances dictate. This concept is far from the "positional" character of competition that underlies in the antitrust analysis, where competition is gauged according to its distance from optimal PC.

In the trial-and-error competitiveness process, entrepreneurs profit from knowledge gaps and cracks of the market that make opportunities available only to a few. They do so through awareness that leads them into building capabilities for innovating which, by definition, entails seizing opportunities that were unseen or unreachable to others. Thus, business competition is about controlling knowledge that, if it were equally available to everyone, it would leave no business opportunity to seize. As Richardson (1960: 57) noted "a general profit opportunity, which is both known to everyone and equally capable of being exploited by everyone, is, in an important sense, a profit opportunity for no-one in particular; it will create the incentive to invest only provided some people are less able to discern it, or to respond to it, than others." Control of knowledge is therefore essential to the competitive process; exactly the opposite assumption of the antitrust analysis.

Thus, in the real world, away from idealized abstractions that assume information is available to all (but it is never explained how this is possible), constraints on some can simultaneously be resources on others. In fact, the notion of property, essential for economic development, is sustained on this very recognition. Thus, the concept of the *felix culpa* applies here in all its dimensions. Bellante (2004: 17) put it eloquently: "Society gets as much product diversity as it is willing to pay for."

In short, the "perfection" in the real world would be one where monopoly and competition coexisted. As Chamberlin (1950) had stated, in real world transactions, away from blackboard economics, "the welfare ideal itself involves a blend of monopoly and competition and is therefore correctly described as one of monopolistic competition."[18]

Yet, the antitrust analysis misconstrues the connecting role of market institutions between short-run and long-run market outcomes, the first being merely related to resource allocation of existing resources, while the long-run ones is associated to the creation of new resources through innovation. These institutions (i.e., contracts; rule of law; etc.) allow market agents to reduce their uncertainty that is enough to induce

18. Richardson (1960: 39) also said: "It does not seem to have been recognized that the fact that 'imperfections,' in some forms and degree of strength, are clearly an obstacle to adjustment, does not entitle one to conclude that it would be best if [market] 'imperfections' were absent altogether."

them to carry out investments that will enhance output in the long-run (Richardson, 1960).

In sum, business restraints are not only inevitable; they are indispensable to frame the trial-and-error competitive process. Yet, most antitrust scholars regard many of these practices "anti-competitive" due to their conceptual "imperfect competition" framework. Moreover, this framework neglects proper assessment of the institutional role played by these conducts in the market order.

Several consequences accrue from this antitrust analysis's cognitive dissonance upon the institutional role of business conducts otherwise deemed "anti-competitive." We believe this is ultimately responsible for alienating the policy from addressing the practical tasks any policymaking should accomplish: accountability, predictability and consistency. We will see them in order.

§3.02 UNFATHOMABLE COMPETITION METRICS

The first, and perhaps most significant instance of antitrust analysis' cognitive dissonance is the lack of adequate metrics to measure antitrust policy performance. Lack of accountability, thus, undermines the credibility of antitrust policy.

Competition metrics are not scarce, but abundance of alternative indicators does not yield a better understanding of the phenomenon, because these policy indicators range from those that give idiosyncratic assessment of economic competition (Rodriguez and DeNardis, 2007)[19] to those that simply elude examination of the phenomenon, and instead focus their attention on the capacity of competition agencies to deliver results.[20]

In other words, these are not metrics associated to objective ends, as one would expect out of policy intervention such as *x* number of houses built, *y* number of students graduated from high school, or *z* number of criminal cases prosecuted. In antitrust policy cases objective ends are impossible to attain because diverging views on what economic competition actually is makes policy goals a moving target. On the contrary, personal views abound on whether competition in the market has actually

19. According to these authors the extensive list of indicators of antitrust policy performance found in the literature "rely on subjective performance metrics that have undergone little direct scrutiny by users." These authors enumerate a comprehensive list of authors that include those who have relied on traditional industrial organization structural measures and variables; on qualitative assessments; on idiosyncratic surveys; and on subjective, perceptions-based surveys of performance. They additionally observe that these survey measures also figures prominently as an original source in the World Bank's composite measures of governance database (Kaufmann, Kraay and Zoido-Lobaton 1999) and the WEF Competitiveness Rankings, databases that have been richly mined by researchers and practitioners.
20. According to Kovacic (2005) there are two basic ways in which competition agencies might go about measuring the quality of their performance. The first is to evaluate the contribution of the agency's outputs (...) A second approach to evaluation is process-based. In lieu of or in addition to evaluating outcomes, an evaluation program might seek to assess the quality of the competition agency's internal operations – the mix of managerial methods and organizational choices that determine how the agency allocates and applies its resources.

increased (e.g., through improved services; better quality; enhanced access to products) or not as a result of policy interventions, simply because there is no clear indication of whether ensuing short-run price reductions compensate long-run productive efficiency losses (Tardiff, 2009).

Clearly, this is not possible in the case of antitrust analysis because it compares imperfect states of reality with the idealistic (thus impossible) conditions that would exist if PC prevailed. Such analysis cannot yield any meaningful metrics measuring tangible results, but opens the way for each analyst to include her own view of what is missing from departed "imperfect" situations away from PC, to use as proxy of what then needs to be measured. In other words, each analyst surrogates her own opinion for what is actually "competitive" and what is not. Policy interventions are seldom followed through to check whether practical results are attained due to this lack of clarity on what the goals of intervention really are.

Rodriguez and DeNardis (2007; 2008) reaffirm this view, as they put the blame not so much due to the surveyors' sensitivity to external biases, but on a deeper and fundamental "misunderstanding of the role, methodology and objectives of antitrust policy by survey respondents across countries," or the fact that those involved "hold a heterogeneous understanding of competition policy." These authors highlight how metrics of antitrust policy have focused on idiosyncratic parameters that rely on heterogeneous views of businesses on economic competition.[21] It is ironic that despite its focus on achieving optimal market outcomes, the conventional assessment actually lacks proper metrics to explain when such outcomes have been attained.

Alternatively, these measures emphasize performance indicators of *competition agencies* (Kovacic, 2006). These indirect performance standards evaluate the transparency of the executing agency; and their degree of independence (financial, operational and otherwise) from central governments. However, focusing on the expediency of the agency is a second's best metrics that does not examine the central problem of meaningful competition metrics: whether competition is actually enhanced or diminished as a result of direct policy interventions deciding on the competitive nature of businesses' strategies.

Not surprisingly "competition policy leaders have not been able to explain with hard data the benefits of competition." (IDB, 2014: 6) The very US Federal Trade Commission (FTC), which epitomizes the model of antitrust policy enforcement, noted the problem of 'direct measurement' of welfare effects following policy intervention, (and only in merger cases, because in horizontal cases, these effects are simply "assumed") indicating that "determining the optimal mix of cases to use as a benchmark for the actual mix of cases *is likely* to be somewhat subjective" (FTC, 2009:20). In fact, the subtle language used by the FTC denotes an intention to elude the

21. "Are antitrust performance indicators measuring antitrust policy performance or are they simply reflecting the heterogeneous views of businesses? There appear to be fundamental differences between businessmen's understanding of competition policy performance across countries. We speculate that this may be due to the different perception of the most immediate competitive 'threats' affecting each country's business community coupled with a misunderstanding of the role of the competition agency." (2009)

impossibility of identifying competition metrics. This language turns into overt concealment of the issue when she advocates her own "intellectual leadership" as proxy for approaching cases "when direct measurement is not feasible."[22]

This problem is directly related to the cognitive dissonance of the competition theory. The misguided approach into theoretical problems that have little connection to real market undertakings has led to a lack of objective performance indicators in antitrust policy. In short, the policy is geared towards analyzing the normative impact of blackboard, idealized markets, rather than analyzing the causal effects of policy interventions upon real business conduct.

§3.03 LEGAL UNCERTAINTY AS BY-PRODUCT OF ANTITRUST POLICY TINKERING

A second result arising from antitrust policy's lack of institutional assessment of markets is the subordinate place the policy gives to legal certainty. The literature has emphasized this problem repeatedly (Bork, 1980; Sowell, 1980; Rockefeller, 2009; De Leon, 2009) yet, the majority of competition scholars simply choose to play it down or simply ignore it altogether (Kovacic, 2005; Kovacic and Shapiro, 2000; Fox and Gal, 2014).[23] For example, Kovacic (2005: 5) indicates:

> in the sciences, an indispensable element of the process of experimentation is the systematic evaluation of the experiment's results. So it should be with experimentation in antitrust policy. The importance of uncertainty and the experimental quality of antitrust policy is apparent in several dimensions of government decision-making. Competition authorities sometimes are called upon to diagnose the competitive significance of dominant firm conduct. Claims of unlawful exclusion often require the competition agency to choose between competing explanations that posit efficiency and naked exclusion as rationales for the challenged behavior. A decision to prosecute or not to prosecute may depend upon debatable interpretations of observed behavior.

Kovacic's suggestion that antitrust experimentation is "scientific" takes for granted the static epistemological foundations of the methodology supporting such "science" which, in the light of Robinson's recant of her "wrong turning" is debatable

22. If the leadership is not obvious, the FTC recommends looking at "the outcome of enforcement actions"; "the direct impact, deterrent effect, and precedential value of these actions"; "the guidance and transparency provided by the FTC to businesses and consumers"; or "the burdens the FTC places on industry." It is really hard to fathom a more subjective proxy for performance measurement than the very opinion of the agency on its own record; not to mention the conceited reference to "intellectual leadership."
23. Speaking on the future of US antitrust, Kovacic and Shapiro (2000) indicated:

> For the future, two related challenges confront the 1990s approach to antitrust enforcement, capable as it is of generating various results. One is for economists and attorneys to devise analytical techniques that accurately identify complex business practices as being pro-competitive or anti-competitive. The second is to adapt such techniques to formulate rules that are suited to the capabilities of enforcement agencies and courts and give the business community a stable and predictable base for designing business plans.

to say the least. After all, alchemists, too, used experimentation as their main research tool but could hardly be branded as "scientists." The idea that "experimenting" (i.e., tinkering) with the market exchanges provides a kernel of the logic behind antitrust intervention. Using law as an "experimentation tool" naturally undermines the "stability" of the rule of law system, upon which economic development rests. Thus, antitrust theory euphemistically substituted the "rule of reason" for the rule of law.[24] Yet, the historical development of the rule of reason in the US antitrust policy shows that there is little "reason" behind the rule, if one considers that predictability disappears altogether from the picture. The dithering jurisprudence and subsequent changing to a succession of antitrust legal theories gives ample evidence of the changing assessment of social welfare, which is alien to a system based on the rule of law.

The broad language of the Sherman Act (1890), which chastized "every contract in restraint of trade," marked the ambiguous enforcement of the rule of reason from the very onset. Clearly, such expression could not be construed literally, and called for further casuistic revision of their welfare restrictive effects in order to distinguish between collaboration that suppressed rivalry and cooperation that promoted growth. Some of the early cases already confronted this problem, eventually leading to the "ancillary restraints" doctrine.[25] This doctrine, which at first seemed to give flexibility to the rigid word of the law, eventually was expanded to a broad array of forms of business collaboration, becoming the hallmark of antitrust policy, which would later be extended to monopolization and merger control legal doctrines in the 1930s and 1950s respectively.

In Europe, a similar phenomenon followed after the adoption of the foundational competition law provisions of the Treaty of Rome, whereby a broad prohibition was followed by a casuistic clearance procedure that eventually proved unmanageable, leading to rather uncertain categories of white, black and grey "acceptable" behavior. The Treaty of Rome of 1957, which established the European Common Market, established a broad legal prohibition encompassing "all agreements between undertakings, decision by associations of undertakings and concerted practices which may affect trade between Member States and which have as their object or effect the prevention, restriction or distortion of competition within the common market" (Article 85(1)). The drafters of the Treaty, perhaps inspired by the U.S. enforcement experience implementing the ancillary restraints doctrine, also incorporated Article

24. According to the Organization for Economic Co-operation and Development (OECD) the concept of the rule of law "first and foremost seeks to emphasize the necessity of establishing a rule-based society in the interest of legal certainty and predictability." (Maxeiner, 2008).
25. For example, the Court, in *United States v. Trans-Missouri Freight Association* (166 U.S. 290 [1897]) recognized that prohibiting all agreements which curbed commercial freedom could imperil beneficial forms of cooperation, such as partnerships. In *United States v. Addyston Pipe&Steel Co.* (85 Fed. 271 [6th Cir. 1898], aff'd, 175 U.S. 211 [1899]), the court distinguished between "naked" trade restraints, where direct rivals simply agreed to restrict output and raise price, and reasonable "ancillary" restraints, which encumbered the participants only as much as needed to expand output or to introduce a product that no single participant could offer.

85(3) which declared inapplicable Article 85(1) on those agreements otherwise violating the latter article provided such agreements meet two positive conditions and two negative conditions. The two positive conditions are that such agreements operate to help "to improve the production or distribution of goods or promote technical or economic progress" and to reserve to consumers "a fair share of the resulting profit." The two negative conditions are that no restrictions should be allowed if they are not "indispensable to the achievement of these objectives" or "afford such undertakings the possibility of eliminating competition in respect of a substantial part of the products in question." Soon it became obvious that even a system that allowed for individual authorizations based on a "statutory" rule of reason would be unmanageable, and that it needed to develop a more effective clearance procedure allowing those agreements that contributed to the economic welfare of the Common Market. The system of individual authorizations established in 1957 started being effectively implemented in 1962, but soon called for revision through a system of block exemptions that was eventually approved in 1965. The OECD (2005: 11) noted the problem arising from administering this system: "When the system was implemented in 1962, the Commission received over 35,000 notifications requesting exemption or negative clearance. Case-by-case response proved impossible; general rules were obviously needed instead. The block exemption regulation of 1965 responded to the overload." Eventually, "block exemptions" also proved too broad, thereby forcing the Commission to implement a system of "white, black and grey" lists, qualifying types of behavior within each "block." This system, however, is still perceived "too legalistic" and devoid of connection with the underlying economics of the ideal competition system (Sendra, 1992: 389)

Naturally, it is easier to assess antitrust legal uncertainty in connection with regions with broader experience. Yet, other regions that have tried to emulate the policy have run into similar problems; the case of Latin American competition agencies is quite illustrative. Here it will suffice to highlight three examples to show how the interpretation of entry barriers changes depending on the executive team in charge of the authority.[26]

The first example is Peru's changing standards regarding the analysis of monopoly power. From 1997 to 2000 Peru's Indecopi adopted a dynamic method for the analysis of the monopoly power. In the Poultry case (1997),[27] Accordingly, Indecopi brought a case against several processed chicken-meat producers for aligning prices, marketing conditions, and levels of production, thereby raising entry barriers and attempting to exclude incumbent competitors. Indecopi defined the market as consisting of those competitors who were concerned about a potential "over-supply" of live chickens. The investigated firms were afraid of an excessive supply, in Indecopi's

26. In a previous work (De Leon, 2009: 466–532) I list the following flaws displayed by case law: (i) overemphasis of price competition over other forms of competition that are not properly assessed in the standard "SSNIP" Methodology; (ii) uncertainty in the assessment of market size; (iii) uncertainty in the assessment of Barriers to Entry; and (iv) preference of short-term resource allocation over long run dynamic efficiencies. I refer the reader to this section, for an exhaustive list of cases for review.
27. Ruling 276-97-TDC/Indecopi.

opinion, since they all belonged to the same relevant market. The Tribunal for the Defence of Competition noted that: "The language used (in these communications) reveals a common concern by the attending firms (to the meeting) and a common valuation of the consequences of the announced 'over-supply'."[28] Accordingly, Indecopi's monopoly power determination not only considered structural elements such as demand substitutability, but also dynamic elements such as firms' perceptions about their competitors.

This perspective seemed to follow from Indecopi's general philosophy towards anti-competitive restrictions, which was then heavily influenced by the Chicago School of Economics and its contempt for both government restrictions and structural antitrust analysis. As the 2004 OECD Peer Review stated regarding this period:

> To some extent, Indecopi's preference for promotion over coercive action (except in striking down anti-competitive government regulations) manifested the generally accepted approach to introducing competition law and policy, but it also reflected what may sometimes have been excessive reliance on "Chicago School" theories, and some experts argued for a more proactive, law enforcement approach.

Since 2000, Indecopi's opinion towards antitrust restrictions has changed considerably. OECD and IADB (2004).

Second, Venezuela's position towards strategic barriers changed between 1998 and 2000. Prior to that time, Pro-Competencia took a tough approach towards mergers and acquisitions, as well as towards structural barriers to entry. Between 1998 and 2000, a new superintendent overhauled the structural views that guided the agency in its first years, adopting a flexible view of mergers, and emphasized a dynamic view of barriers to entry. A case in point was a merger in the agroindustrial sector. In April 2000, AgrEvo de Venezuela, S.A., requested an opinion on the potential restrictive effects of an acquisition of Rhone Poulenc's line of agrochemical products. Pro-Competencia's analysis determined that the dynamics of competition in the relevant markets, where there were companies that were larger and had a wider variety of products than the merged entity, suggested that such an acquisition would not cause or reinforce a dominant position in any of the markets in question.

Finally, the adoption of economic standards to judge market conditions often leads enforcing agencies into neglecting fundamental evidence for the sake of construing the case under accepted market structural antitrust theories.

In the Anheuser-Busch/Antartica merger review case (1997),[29] Brazil's CADE applied a potential competition doctrine that raised a clear presumption against the transaction, as it assumed increased concentration resulting from the merger to be anti-competitive. Under this theory the acquisition of a leading firm might reduce competition by eliminating the acquiring firm's impact on competition (perceived potential competition) or might reduce the prospect of future entry into the market

28. Indecopi, "Precedentes de Observancia Obligatoria en materia de Defensa de la Competencia," (Lima: Indecopi, 1999), pp 141–142.
29. CADE, File No. 0083/1996 www.cade.gov.br.

(actual potential competition). Based on this theory CADE blocked the intended joint ventures between Miller Brewing Company and Cervejaria Brahma (to produce Miller Genuine Draft in Brazil) and between Anheuser-Busch and Antartica (to increase the presence of Budweiser in the country) respectively.

In particular, CADE interpreted the association between Anheuser-Busch (a former potential competitor) and Antarctica (a leading Brazilian brewery) as raising anti-competitive concerns, because their agreement provided for discrimination of prices and market segments in which both companies were active. The structural interpretation of the competitive effects of the deal (i.e., inquiring into the market shares that would result from the deal) totally ignored the fact that market shares were notorious for shifting over time. For example, in the period from 1989 to 1995, Brahma's market share declined from 50.3% to 46.6%; similarly, Antarctica's market share had declined from 40.8% to 31.9%. Clearly there was a competitive threat to the leading firms from existing competitors. Nonetheless, CADE declined to give proper weight to this piece of evidence.

Such wavering case law clearly touches upon the fundamental problem of legal uncertainty underlying antitrust enforcement. Unlike other areas of law, antitrust case law does not provide a stable *ratio decidendi* because antitrust infractions are gauged by economic hypotheses rather than by legal precedents. These hypotheses, in turn, are contingent to the particular brand of theory supported by the authority.[30] Hence, the only "visible" reality to the antitrust agency is what she decides is "sound" according to her supported brand of theory. Thus, a cognitive dissonance emerges in the mind of whoever rests the decision-making authority.

Yet, antitrust advocates are lured into thinking that rational economic science would make policymaking scientifically rigorous and adaptable to new understandings of market reality. Kovacic and Shapiro (2000: 58) state:

> The *consciously* evolutionary quality of the U.S. antitrust statutes, with their implicit recognition of the need to adjust doctrine over time in light of experience and new learning, *gives economists considerable power to influence competition law and policy.*"(Our emphasis)

Recognition that antitrust statutes are consciously changing and that economists control policymaking display two often overlooked tenets of this policy. Preference of adaptability over predictability reveals a moral judgment that renders "rational" economic superior (kaleidoscopic?) over legal precedent. One can hear in this the overtones of the "Economic Imperialism" (Stigler, 1984) predicated by the Law and Economics school in the 1980s. The pretense of economic hypothesis applied to the understanding of business activities is part of an overarching ideology that predicated

30. Notice that these hypotheses are not related to the causal events confirming someone's liability in a wrongdoing (as in criminal law), but rather they are related to its very existence. Sowell (1980: 203) colorfully detected this flaw: "[t]here is usually nothing in antitrust cases comparable to finding someone standing over the corpse with a smoking pistol in his hand. Objective statistical data abounds, but its interpretation depends crucially on the definitions and theories used to infer the nature of the prospective process which left behind that particular residue of retrospective numbers."

economic imperialism over the analysis of non-economic markets. This trend emerged in the mid-1970s at the Department of Economics of the University of Chicago (Becker, 1976; Posner, 1973), but later extended to other academic centers (Lazear, 2000); it gained strong popularity in antitrust policy, given the inclination of antitrust scholars (Bork, 1980) to rest their assumptions on the tenets of the Imperfect Competition theory.

Interestingly, the new generation of antitrust scholars has abandoned the normative tenets of the Law and Economics school, but has maintained its epistemology of markets as enclosed structures limited by cross price elasticity; entry barriers raised by economies of scale; and market concentration as the key (if not the only) competition driver.

Likewise, this assessment perceives institutions such as contracts, rules, customs, standards, collective behavior, and the like, as "noises" extraneous to the economic models, which either ignore them as "givens" or perceive them as sources of "imperfections". The epistemology of conventional economic thinking, following Robinson's heed, emphasize "imperfections" over "competition" (Robinson, 1951: viii)

These arrangements, which under the tenets of Robinson's Imperfect Competition theory appear as suspicious attempts to divert short-run (perfect) competition into monopolistic maneuverings, acquire a totally different outlook when they are perceived under an alternative long-run institutional building assessment. In a long-run perspective, overcoming inter-temporal uncertainty is a clear reason for justifying these business arrangements. In this assessment, they enable some businesses to compete, even though if they naturally do at the expense of excluding infinite hypothetical competitors that would otherwise be under PC; exclusion that is carried out through contracts and other similar arrangements usually falling under the purview of competition statutes. In the words of Macneil (1980: 4-10) contracts are "the projection of exchange into the future." In this opposite assessment, legal precedent gives content to institutions built in (and for) the long-run.

In short, the institutional neglect of the policy deprived the enforcers of clear guidelines about what they should construe as anti-competitive; instead, it filled the policy with legal doctrines promoting ad-hoc analysis that could never satisfy the requirements of legal certainty.

§3.04 OBSESSION WITH PRE-MERGER CONTROL

Latin America offers an interesting –and often overlooked- lesson in the area of merger control on how institutions adapt legal reforms into the codified ethos of societal values. To understand how, it may be useful to trace the emergence of this scheme in the region, and compare it to other jurisdictions whose own antitrust systems served as inspiration for Latin American policymakers.

In Europe, for example, it took three full decades after the adoption of their first antitrust provisions (1957) to adopt a pre-merger control system in 1989,[31] and almost ninety years in the US after the Sherman Act (1890) before the passing of the Hart-Scott-Rodino Act in 1976.[32] By contrast, with few exceptions most Latin American countries adopted pre-merger control systems right from their start.[33] The hastiness in adopting pre-merger control was barely concealed by the recognition that some antitrust enforcement experience would be desirable before implementing a fully-fledged pre-merger control system. Even so, these laws were quickly passed, even by countries whose economy size called for less expensive means of fostering competition, such as open trade, rendering the costly implementation of pre-merger control overly excessive, even awkward, such as El Salvador, Honduras, Paraguay or Nicaragua.[34]

More importantly than wavering case law enforcement are the overarching trends that highlight even more glaringly the misplaced priorities arising from the "structural" innuendo of the imperfect competition theory. This is most visible in the growth of merger control advocated by antitrust agencies in the region.

Following heed to the predicament of competition being based upon market structure, merger control seemed the obvious choice for the highly concentrated economies of Latin American countries. After promoting generalized open trade from the mid 1980s onwards, by the early 1990s it appears obvious that certain non-tradable industries required promoting other forms of competition. Little attention was given to the modest aggregate demand of these economies as the main cause of the higher concentration rates and low specialization seen in most industrial sectors. Most advocates of expanding understaffed antitrust agencies into expensive pre-merger control were driven by the imperfect competition creed.

Almost all countries in the region established competition policies without introducing merger policies at first; later they had the policies introduced and implemented to the point of eclipsing the other areas of antitrust.

31. Council Regulation 4064/89, 1989 O.J. (L395/1), corrigendum 1990 O.J. (LL257/14), as amended by Council Regulation 1310/97, 1997 O.J. (L180/1).
32. 15 U.S.C. section 18 (1996).
33. The following countries adopted pre-merger control systems (mostly, compulsory ones), right after the adoption of their first operational antitrust statute: Mexico (1992); Venezuela (1993); Colombia (1992); Brazil (1994); Panama (1996); Nicaragua (2006); El Salvador (2004); Honduras (2007); Costa Rica (1994); Paraguay (2013), Ecuador (2011) and Uruguay (2007). Argentina passed pre-merger concentration rules nineteen yrs after its first "operational" law of 1980. Only Chile, Dominican Republic and Peru are the exceptions to the trend.
34. It is necessary to state here the heavy hand of international lending agencies like the World Bank, and of governments in countries negotiating bilateral free trade agreements with the region, such as the United States and the European Union, to introduce antitrust policies as a precondition for the disbursement of funding or trade concessions. These governments and lending agencies seldom questioned the convenience of enforcing such a costly policy in countries lacking key market institutions, much less the theoretical dissonance behind the policy.

Figure 3.1 Mexico: Pre-merger Review v. Antitrust Enforcement Review (2000–2007)

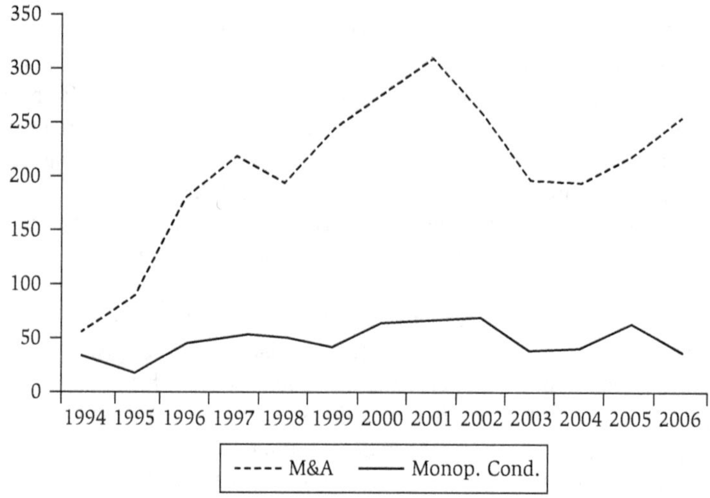

Source: CFC Annual Reports.

Figure 3.2 Brazil: Pre-merger Review v. Antitrust Enforcement Review (2000–2007)

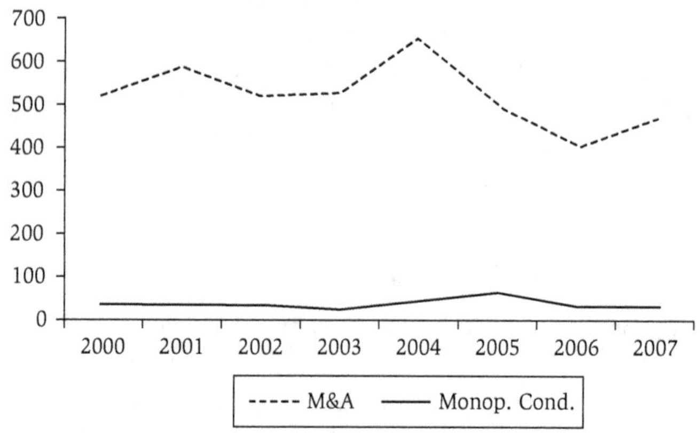

Source: CADE Annual Reports.

These two countries highlight a general trend in the region, which prioritizes pre-merger control over antitrust surveillance of monopolistic behavior, to the point of entirely eclipsing the latter.

§3.05 ANTITRUST LEGAL FORMALISM OVER ECONOMIC SUBSTANCE

The cognitive dissonance of competition theory towards institutions not only misconstrues market functioning, but also directs the analysis away from institutions that are essential to understand competition dynamics, particularly in developing countries.

Consider the case of the "shadow economy" which, according to recent estimates (Schneider, 2014), reaches a hefty 41.1% of the GDP in Latin America and the Caribbean.[35] Antitrust policy scholars adopt a peculiar bias against the "shadow economy"; this is the result of Robinson's reluctance to integrate the law and economics of her imperfect competition model into a unified analysis; instead, they opted for isolating them by idealizing the latter into the mold of PC, and simply ignoring (i.e., postulating) the former. In Robinson's approach, laws, contracts, rules, standards, customs and social conventions are just "givens" that have no other role in her analysis but to "justify" the existence of monopolistic restraints. How these institutions emerge, or whether they have universal impact or just under certain circumstances or groups, becomes completely irrelevant for the sake of her analysis. She simply adopted a legalistic assessment over market institutions that neglected those that emerged beyond the realm of formal legality.

Accordingly, antitrust advocates adopted an antagonistic view towards informal businesses, which they perceive as a source of "unfair competition" against "formal" businesses (i.e., incumbent firms). This peculiar analysis, which among antitrust advocates ranges from mistrust to outright hostility, is the by-product of the policy's cognitive dissonance towards institutions. The response of antitrust scholars, guided by a positivistic legal (i.e., formalistic) approach, is to chastise shadow economy activities as "illegal"[36] which in fact is to state the obvious, namely, that these activities

35. According to Vuletin (2008);

> the size of the informal economy in the early 2000s is found to vary considerably—from a low of around 15 percent of measured GDP for The Bahamas to a high of over 70 percent of measured GDP for Paraguay. The relative contribution of each underlying factor to the overall size of the informal economy is also estimated for each country. For some countries like Antigua and Barbuda, Barbados and Trinidad and Tobago, the key element is the tax burden. For other countries, like St. Vincent and the Grenadines, St. Lucia and Belize, the importance of the agriculture sector appears to be decisive, with around 75 percent of exports concentrated in agriculture and food products. For others like Paraguay and the Dominican Republic, labor rigidities are some of the most important factors, with minimum wages representing 170 percent and 90 percent, respectively, of the corresponding GDP per capita.

36. Actually, the condescendence of the competition literature goes further than that, by comparing the "informal economy" to the "mafia." A report from the OECD (2009:14) states:

> Nearly all the countries reported that, in principle, their competition laws applied to economic activity carried out by the informal sector. However there are significant issues in applying competition law to the informal sector. Informal firms tend to be small and highly mobile. There may be difficulty in serving legal notices. Even when prosecuted, these firms are less likely to have significant assets to pay any penalty and, in any case, may simply start up a new business elsewhere. In some countries organised

are outside of the law. Yet, formal illegality does not make them economically irrelevant, as policymakers in developing countries well know.

Furthermore, by condemning almost half of the economic activity of a standard Latin American economy onto the sidelines of competition analysis, antitrust scholars simply ignore the very significant effects that informality has upon "formal" market incumbents in terms of entry barriers in labor-intensive industries. For example, informal firms are more likely to compete effectively with established businesses in the retail and services industries, albeit in commerce of products of low added value. Similarly, they are also less likely to do so in industries dominated by higher sunk costs, i.e. construction; medical services; food distribution; and the like.

The incapacity of antitrust analysis to deal with the shadow economy cripples the antitrust assessment of industrial concentration, by overestimating the level of concentration accruing from only counting businesses in the formal economy, under the Hirschman Herfindalh methodology. But the analytical flaws of the antitrust analysis do not end here; other areas show a similar cognitive dissonance. Consider a keystone concept of antitrust policy analysis such as market definition. In the logic of the Imperfect Competition model this step is essential to establish the significance of market power, i.e. the "source" of monopolistic restrains. Market size begins on the assumption that "perfectly" homogeneous products (commodities) establish the boundaries between "markets." Yet, homogeneity is conceptually possible only if one assumes institutions entirely absent from the model: it is by doing away with them that one can possibly think of products that are exactly identical in production costs; delivery; inputs; service; and other qualities. On the other hand, any differentiating attribute resulting from institutions communicating knowledge unevenly among market agents would forcefully lead to market differentiation.

On another sphere, the cognitive dissonance of the antitrust analysis alienates antitrust policy by ruling out any consideration over the actual reality of developing countries, which is dominated by a large presence of the shadow economy. Antitrust policy, far from addressing the problem of small and medium firms who cannot overcome the transaction costs imposed by the legality prevailing in these countries chooses to ignore it.

§3.06 THE NEGLECTED ROLE OF COMPETITION ADVOCACY

The shortcomings listed in the previous sections underscore the theoretical and practical limits of antitrust policy to deliver predictable, measurable, and consistent policy results. In order to circumvent these limitations competition agencies have developed an alternative policy response aimed at promoting more competitive

crime is a component of the informal sector. Some competition authorities consider it too dangerous for their staff to prosecute anti-competitive behaviour by the mafia.

Perhaps with the exception of the smallness, one has to wonder why the description just made could not equally apply to financial scandals featured by Enron, Lehman Brothers, Barings Bank and a long list of "formal" and hitherto very respectable businesses.

markets, by focusing not on the "monopolistic" position of incumbent firms in the market, but rather on the legal impediments imposed against potential entrants to penetrate it. This solution has been branded, somewhat vaguely, as "competition advocacy."

A joint World Bank/OECD report (1998: 93) explains the meaning of competition advocacy as follows:

> [C]ompetition may be lessened significantly by various public policies and institutional arrangements as well. Indeed, private restrictive business practices are often facilitated by various government interventions in the marketplace. Thus, the mandate of the competition office extends beyond merely enforcing the competition law. (Competition agencies) must also participate more broadly in the formulation of its country's economic policies, which may adversely affect competitive market structure, business conduct, and economic performance. It must assume the role of competition advocate, acting proactively to bring about government policies that lower barriers to entry, promote deregulation and trade liberalization, and otherwise minimize unnecessary government intervention in the marketplace.

Competition advocacy is usually presented as a "complement" to antitrust enforcement, the latter being the "core" of competition policy. This is historically inexact and not based on hard evidence. In fact, compared to antitrust enforcement, which emerged through the inception of the Sherman Act in 1890, competition advocacy has a much longer tradition in the history of English Common Law, that goes back to *Darcy v. Allen* (1601), (commonly known as the Case of Monopolies), where a Common Law court reviewed a royal grant of trade privileges and struck down the grant as being void under the common law the rulings of Lord Coke (1601) (Calabresi, 2012).

Competition advocacy has evolved out of intuition as the rationale of antitrust enforcement is not driven against legal barriers that create restraints on potential competitors, but rather on the "monopolistic" condition enjoyed by incumbent firms in the market. Again, it should be remembered that the Imperfect Competition model merely postulates the existence of legal barriers forcing new entrants out of the market as explanation of why incumbent firms may impose monopolistic prices in a quest to maximize profits at the point where aggregate demand meets marginal revenues; it does not admonish against them "per se."

Resorting to advocacy has proven difficult to competition agencies for internal as well as institutional reasons. Competition authorities often lack conviction in pursuing measures against governments to which, after all, they owe their investiture or are financially dependent on; these internal constraints are usually reinforced by their lack of judicial standing to challenge government measures directly, but only through the intervention of courts. The IDB (2014: 5) indicates, "the regional consolidated trend is to grant agencies with the powers to issue opinions on a voluntary basis with no binding effects."[37] These practical constraints are added to the lack of arguments offered by the Imperfect Competition theory in favor of developing a positive agenda towards intervening upon legal restraints against potential market entrants.

Hence, it is not surprising that the allocation of resources devoted to advocacy is usually very scant. An ICN Report (2009: 12) elaborates on how many financial resources competition authorities dedicate to advocacy activities.

Table 3.1 Competition Advocacy Expenditures: Selected Years (% of Total Budget)

Country	*% of Budget*	*Country*	*% of Budget*
Brazil	20% (but it also includes merger analysis)	New Zealand	FY 2007: 2.7%
Cyprus	10%	Russia	10%
European Union	FY 2006 – 10%	Senegal	N/A
Honduras	FY 2007: 1.03% FY 2008: 2.26%	Slovak Republic	10-20%
Hungary	10%	Spain	8.5%
India	30%	Switzerland	10%
Jamaica	10%	Tanzania	33%
Japan	FY 2008: 1.5%	U.K.	6%
Korea	0.3%	U.S FTC	1-2%
Lithuania	Between 5-15%	Zambia	10-15%
Mexico	FY 2008: 3%		

Source: ICN (2009).

To be sure, several agencies noted difficulties in estimating agency resources dedicated to competition advocacy due to them often being interrelated with other agency activities. In addition, they do not specifically track competition advocacy as a separate category of expenditures. Yet, the picture displayed is very clear: the amount of resources spent on advocacy activities is only a fraction of what competition agencies devote to antitrust enforcement.

An ICN report (2002) had already noted this phenomenon:

> It is sometimes said that a successful competition advocacy effort, for example in regulatory reform, can bring about economic benefits far in excess of a single successful enforcement action, or even more than one. If that is so, then it is logical that an agency should focus most of its resources on competition advocacy, but the ICN survey showed that this is not the case. Of those countries (both developed and developing) that could identify the proportion of their resources spent on

37. "Whereas a majority of agencies are entitled to publish opinions on legislation affecting competition, only a few of these opinions are binding. Moreover, in very few instances is the legislature obliged to request agencies' opinions before approving new legislation."

advocacy, most (62%) spent less than 20% on that activity. The remainder spent between 20% and 30%.

Beyond the issue of financial sufficiency, competition agencies lack a clear estimate of the impact advocacy activities have in their working agenda. Thus, the IDB notes (2014: 2) "there is a lack of empirical data measuring the success of advocacy activities in mainstreaming competition policy principles into the overall implementation of economic policy including activities in which government institutions engage."

This assessment is not surprising. In view of the neglect of conventional competition analysis upon the institutional landscape of competitive markets, one can easily understand why measuring the impact of filtering out restrictive legal rules through competition advocacy appears unimportant in the logic of competition policy. Yet, under the institutional-based assessment advocated in this article, successful competition policymaking (i.e., advocacy) depends not so much on the (dominant) position held by the incumbent firms in the market, but on the capacity of new entrants to challenge them successfully. This capacity ultimately rests on the ubiquity and effects of legal barriers, and on the innovative capacity of the newcomers. The next section will review these.

§3.07 GAUGING INNOVATION CAPABILITIES: A NEW FOCUS FOR COMPETITION POLICY

Our previous definition of competition as a trial-and-error process underlines innovation as a cornerstone of the competitive process; therefore, a measurement of how competitive markets are, demands a prior assessment of whether barriers exist upon innovator firms to display their ingenuity and transform it into viable market products.

Entrepreneurial ingenuity confronts two types of barriers: exogenous or endogenous. Exogenous barriers are located outside the personal capacity of entrepreneurs to innovate, and usually are comprised by legal barriers (i.e., government decrees; regulations; laws; and statutes) and mores (customs; religion; and social conventions) that impose limitations upon the entrepreneurs' capacity to develop their acumen. The endogenous ones are related to the perception of entrepreneurs to discover hidden opportunities, through innovation of the production process. Problems to commercialize intellectual property in developing countries are often related to the inability or inexperience of entrepreneurs (e.g., startups) to realize the value involved on protecting their IP or even, to understand their protective dimension.

Exogenous barriers become genuine obstacles to competition because, unlike business practices, their effect is more permanent and resilient compared to the temporary monopoly positions developed by dominant firms at any point of time. In this context, legal barriers not only include general laws, but also legal concessions as well as any government permission, license or grant that, *inter alia*, creates privileges or discriminates (privileges or "above general law") among competitors, without valid technical or economic reasons that justify it so. These restrictions create an impediment for entrepreneurs to exercise their trial-and-error competitive process.

Several indicators measure different angles of the exogenous barriers on trial-and-error competition. They include the World Bank *Doing Business Report*, the World Economic Forum *Global Competitiveness Report*, the *WGI* or the *Index of Economic Freedom* published by the Heritage Foundation, as well as Gwartney, Hall and Lawson's *Economic Freedom of the World* Report (2012).[38] They all focus their attention to the transparency of the environment where the entrepreneurial activity takes place.

Endogenous barriers are harder to measure because, as Harper (2003, 119) points out, there are as yet no empirical studies that directly investigate the impact of economic freedom on people's cognition and entrepreneurial alertness. That means that finding "direct" economic indicators evidencing the lack of drive on developing economies towards dynamic competition is futile. No particular measure of economic freedom guarantees that businesses will become more "alert" or "aware" of business opportunities at hand; therefore, no quantitative measurement of this indicator can tell in advance whether firms will be more "competitive." Unlike the antitrust analysis, which links certain levels of market concentration to a probability of anti-competitive restrictions under the SCP Paradigm, this is not so in the "process" trial-and-error competition approach. Institutional transparency can only give us an indirect assessment of process competition, that is, an assessment that has to be coupled with other indicators to reach meaningful conclusions.

A safer option is to combine the previously mentioned "contextual" indicators with other proxies that can enrich the analysis with a more targeted focus on innovative processes that takes place within the firm; these are best represented by the *Global Innovation Index*. Innovation rates, measured under this index, provide proper metrics of the trial-and-error competition process.

To be sure, innovation metrics are not absent of problems in developing countries, due to the very intangible essence of innovation. According to the Oslo Manual on Innovation (2005), "innovation is the implementation of a new or significantly improved product (good or service), or process, a new marketing method, or a new organizational method in business practices, workplace organization or external relations." Though this definition covers a broad spectrum of improvements on both products and services, measuring them becomes trickier particularly in developing countries, because of the parameters used by innovation metrics, usually overstate activities such as R&D or patent registration, both seldom found in less developing

38. The report measures three factors: freedom from regulation in the credit industry; this requires that private banks supply credit to those who desire it at market-determined interest rates. A free labor market allows wages to be market determined and creates an environment with incentives to work hard such as low unemployment benefits and flexible labor laws. Finally, efficient regulation requires that business activities be free from official impediments. Prices should be market determined and barriers to entry should be low, allowing competitive practices to create efficient markets. Yet they confront a problem that the effects of many regulations cannot be measured in practice, which is why almost two-thirds of the ratings in this category are based on survey data. As regulations on business, credit, and labor markets decreases, standards of living will increase because individuals and organizations can work unhindered, eliminating the economic waste produced by bureaucracy and prohibitive standards.

countries, and underestimate innovation protected through trade secrets, or expressed in intangible knowledge.

In order to gauge innovation rates, the *Global Innovation Index* measures two essential variables: first, "Business Sophistication," which includes the speed of human capital development (knowledge workers);[39] innovation linkages (connectivity across the economic system to produce knowledge);[40] and knowledge absorption (capacity of local entrepreneurs to use foreign knowledge).[41] Second, it measures "Creative outputs," including creative intangibles;[42] creative goods and services[43] and online creativity.[44]

These innovation indicators provide a closer measure of the levels of trial-and-error competition inside firms.

Problems still remain, however, as in the case of developing countries these metrics may underscore, perhaps a little too excessively, a lack of innovation that occurs in the informal sector, which is not properly surveyed (and which accounts in some countries for more than 50% of the labor force); or overstate the relevance of indicators that are not representative of developing countries, such as the level of patenting activity, which does not fully represent the amount of real innovation that occurs within firms that decide not to use the patent system simply because it is too unreliable.

---

39. It includes: Employment in knowledge-intensive services (% of workforce); Firms offering formal training (% of firms); Percentage of gross expenditure on R&D performed by business enterprise; Percentage of gross expenditure on R&D financed by business enterprise; Weighted mean score at the Graduate Management Admission Test (GMAT) by residency and by citizenship (weighted by the total numbers of test takers); Number of test takers of the Graduate Management Admission Test (GMAT) by citizenship (scaled by million population 20–34 years old).
40. This includes: University/industry research collaboration; State of cluster development; and percentage of gross expenditure on R&D financed by abroad, i.e., with foreign financing
41. This includes: Joint ventures/strategic alliances: Number of deals, fractional counting (per trillion PPP$ GDP); Percentage of published Patent Cooperation Treaty (PCT) applications with at least one foreign inventor; Royalty and license fees, payments (per thousand GDP); High-tech net imports (% of total net imports); Computer, communications, and other services (% of commercial service imports); and foreign direct investment (FDI), net inflows (% of GDP).
42. Number of trademark registrations issued to residents by the national office (per billion PPP$ GDP); Number of international trademark registrations issued to residents through the Madrid system (per billion PPP$ GDP); ICT and business model creation (answer to the question: To what extent are information and communication technologies creating new business models, services and products in your country?); and ICT and organizational models creation (answer to the question: To what extent are information and communication technologies creating new organizational models (virtual teams, remote working, telecommuting, etc.) within businesses in your country?).
43. This measure includes: Recreation and culture (% total individual consumption); National feature films produced; Daily newspaper circulation; Creative goods exports (% of total exports); Creative services: Exports (% of total services exports).
44. This measure includes: Generic top-level domains (per thousand population); Country-code top-level domains (per thousand population); Number of video uploads on YouTube (scaled by population; and Wikipedia monthly page edits per adult).

§3.08 CONCLUSION: AN OLD POLICY, A NEW RHETORIC

The quest for the soul of Competition Policy has been disappointing. Like Janus, the Roman god of beginnings and future, the policy has two faces looking at opposite directions: One face, that of antitrust enforcement embodies a contrived view of markets that patronizes them and favors policy interventions in cases that are not theoretically warranted; this has resulted in increased competition barriers to the extent that it undermines the rule of law and increases unpredictability among entrepreneurs.

The opposite face is one of competition advocacy, which has steadily emerged to fill the gap left by antitrust enforcement's incapability to perform consistently. This understanding of competition policy, far from novel, replicates the same sort of policy intervention conducted by Common Law courts against economic privileges laid down by the Sovereign: they are aimed at emphasizing the elimination of exogenous legal barriers that create obstacles for new entrants into the market. Yet, it has another, fresh component, that is, the promotion of endogenous capabilities to do innovation. This element is more subtle and requires a policy combination of public and private support aimed at identifying potential opportunities for firms; help them commercialize their intellectual assets (i.e., intellectual property); and build an innovation ecosystem through stirring collaboration between the academia, business community, the government, and venture capital sources.

Clearly, antitrust enforcement has severe inner flaws that undermine its legitimacy; it makes no use to blame on others for their alleged "lack of understanding"; their "hidden interests"; or the "country's institutional incapacity" to enforce these provisions effectively. The IDB (2014: 6) indicates that competition agencies are unable to "educate consumers on the benefits of competition policies" thus presupposing that consumers would be better off if they were literate on Industrial Organization matters. This assumption is a derivative of a methodological error that assumes external observers to be better informed or better intentioned than market agents themselves. No explanation is given as to why we should assume that antitrust scholars actually have deciphered what competition is like better than businesses whose main daily activity –one should assume-is to compete, in order to survive.

Moreover, the claim attesting the experimentation nature of the policy as advantageous appears unconvincing particularly in the light of a sheer absence of policy metrics that could otherwise make the policy accountable. If there are no metrics capable of measuring whether policy interventions are actually successful, how can anyone say that "experimentation" or tinkering with market outcomes will do any good at all? Only indirect measures, such as counting the number of cases brought, seem to count; but then again, these metrics only seem to reinforce the self-indulgency of those who advocate antitrust enforcement at any cost.

Not surprisingly, meager results attained by antitrust enforcement in Latin America have driven competition agencies into the bandwagon of economic policy-making. They have made progress to the extent that they intuitively have stepped out of the conventional script of antitrust enforcement, and have undertaken positive steps to conduct more competition advocacy activities. Yet, there is a long way to go, if one considers the scant resources devoted to this activity by competition agencies worldwide.

Disappointment in the policy is the consequence of the failed expectations raised by the naïve normative proposal implicit in the tenets of the Imperfect Competition theory.

On the face of it, Consumer Welfare appears akin to good market functioning: in this situation, social resources are directed to those who value them the most. On closer inspection, however, such efficiency is nothing but one (extreme) case of social resource allocation that only applies to the very unlikely case of short-run allocation, within conditions of PC (infinite information; timeless exchanges; absolute product homogeneity; countless sellers and buyers). This situation, seeking mathematical elegance of equilibrium modeling, rejects long-run planning among firms; hence, entrepreneurial innovation strategies, to develop capabilities and seek market leadership.

Yet, the problem with Consumer Welfare (and other alternative short-run goals) is not only one of methodological rarity, but a less studied one: that it leads policy interventions to awkwardly play the fiddle of redistributive socialist policies, albeit in a pro-market rhetoric. Indeed, Robinson's Essay on Marxian Economics published less than a decade after her Theory of Imperfect Competition declared:

> Recent developments in academic theory have led (academic economists) to a position which in some respects resembles the position of Mark far more closely than the position of their own intellectual forebears. *The modern theory of imperfect competition, although formally quite different from Marx's theory of exploitation, has a close affinity with it.* (Robinson, 1942: 4)

Very few antitrust scholars, driven by their excitement about attacking what they perceive to be anti-competitive restraints, realize how close they align ranks to those who actually declare themselves to be enemies of the market.

In this light, antitrust scholars have entertained a superficial, idealized discussion over the normative goals that should inform competition policy, whether economic efficiency or some other social welfare value. In this subjective choice of goals, they adopt a condescending view towards developing countries, whenever these countries enforce policies that the former perceive to be away from their normative "Nirvana."

It is not surprising that competition policy goals have remained restricted to these parameters; after all, this discussion reflects the same short-term parameters of the conventional market analysis inherited from Robinson's Imperfect Competition theory that has nourished the antitrust debate. Yet, these are short-term competing goals that conceal a broader discussion between short-term goals and long-run ones.

A more meaningful discussion on the goals of competition policy should differentiate between equilibrium short-run analysis or long-run disequilibrium analysis. This discussion would differentiate between a policy that would privilege resource allocation through intervention over market dynamics, on the one hand; and a policy that would privilege long-run innovation, which directs the attention of policymakers towards eliminating legal barriers to potential entrants, even at the expense of tolerating temporal "monopoly rents."

There is no question that such a policy would fulfill the conditions one would expect of pro-market policymaking, that is, predictability, accountability and consistency. Predictability would follow because it would direct the attention of competition agencies into barriers to competition that create obstacles to potential market entrants, that are not based on their differentiated commercial risk, market facilities or technical reasons.

Accountability would follow, because unlike the imprecision of current antitrust measurement proxies, such as the Global Competitiveness Report, focusing the attention on legal barriers is easy to identify and measure, as witnessed through the emergence of numerous international indicators of institutional transparency, as seen above.

Finally, consistency would follow, because a policy focus on legal barriers would exclusively examine the impact that such rules create by discriminating businesses according to their long-run technical standards, not to their particular position in the market at one moment in time.

Twenty-five years after the inception of modern competition policy in Latin America, and in other developing countries, experience shows that the quest for economic competition demands above all unraveling the ideological confusion that pervades legal reform in developing countries, which has led them to blend government interventionism under a pro-market rhetoric.

BIBLIOGRAPHY

Bellante, Don (2004), *Journal of Business and Economics Research* 2(4), pp. 17–25.

Calabresi, Steven G. and Price, Larissa, "Monopolies and the Constitution: A History of Crony Capitalism" (2012). Faculty Working Papers. Paper 214. http://scholarlycommons.law.northwestern.edu/facultyworkingpapers/214.

Chamberlin, E.H. (1950), "Product Heterogeneity and Public Policy," *American Economic Review*, Papers and Proceedings 40(2), pp. 85–92.

Chamberlin, E.H. (1957), *Towards a More General Theory of Value*, New York and London: Oxford University Press.

Corley, T.A.B. (1990), "Emergence of the Theory of Industrial Organization, 1890–1990," *Business and Economic History*, 19 Second series, 1990 published at http://www.thebhc.org/publications/BEHprint/v019/p0083-p0092.pdf.

Crandall, R.W. and Winston, C. (2005) "Does Antitrust Policy Improve Consumer Welfare? Assessing the Evidence," *Journal of Economic Perspectives* 17(4), pp. 3–26.

De Leon, Ignacio (2009), *An Institutional Assessment of Competition Policy*, London: Kluwer Law International.

Fox, Eleanor M. and Gal, Michal S. (2014), "Drafting Competition Law for Developing Jurisdictions: Learning from Experience" New York University Law and Economics Working Papers. Paper 374. http://lsr.nellco.org/nyu_lewp/374.

Friedman, Milton (1955), "The Methodology of Positive Economics," In *Essays In Positive Economics*, Chicago: Univ. of Chicago Press, 1966, pp. 3–16, 30–43.

Gwartney, J., J. Hall and R. Lawson (2012), *Economic Freedom of the World: 2012 Annual Report*, available at: http://www.cato.org/pubs/efw/.

Grether, Ewald T. (1970), "Industrial Organization: Past History and Future Problems," *The American Economic Review* 60(2), papers and Proceedings of the Eighty-second Annual Meeting of the American Economic Association (May, 1970), pp. 83–89.

Harper, D.A. (2003), *Foundations of Entrepreneurship and Economic Development*, New York: Routledge.

IDB Secretariat (2014), *Advocacy: Mainstreaming Competition Policy into the Overall Economic Policy and Government Actions in Latin American and the Caribbean*, Latin American Competition Forum, 16–17 September 2014, Montevideo, Uruguay, OECD/IDB, DAF/COMP/LACF(2014).

ICN (2002), *Advocacy and Competition Policy*, Report prepared by the Advocacy Working Group, ICN's Conference, Naples, Italy.

ICN (2009), *Report on Assessment of ICN Members' Requirements and Recommendations on Further ICN Work on Competition Advocacy*, Presented at the 8th Annual Conference of the International Competition Network, Zurich, June 2009.

INDECOPI, (1999), "Precedentes de Observancia Obligatoria en materia de Defensa de la Competencia," Lima: Indecopi, pp. 141–142.

Kaldor, N. (1934), "The Equilibrium of the Firm," *Economic Journal*, XLIV; reprinted in N. Kaldor, Essays on Value and Distribution, London: Duckworth, 1969.

Kovacic, W. (2005), *Using Evaluation to Improve the Performance of Competition Policy Authorities*, Background Note presented by the OECD Secretariat; Roundtable on Evaluation of the Actions and Resources of Competition Authorities, OECD, Paris, 25 May 2005, DAF/COMP(2005)23.

Kovacic, W. (2006), "Using Ex Post Evaluations to Improve the Performance of Competition Policy Authorities," *The Journal of Corporation Law* 31(2) 503, Winter 2006.

Kovacic, William E. and Carl Shapiro (2000), "Antitrust Policy: A Century of Economic and Legal Thinking," *Journal of Economic Perspectives* 14(1) Winter 2000, pp. 43–60.

Lazear, Edward P. (2000), "Economic Imperialism," *Quarterly Journal of Economics* 115(1), p. 99, pp. 99–146.

Loasby, B. (1989), Joan Robinson's "Wrong Turning," In *The Mind and Method of the Economist: A Critical Appraisal of Major Economists in the 20th Century*, Hants, England: Edward Elgar.

Macneil, Ian R. (1978), "Contracts: Adjustment of Long-term Economic Relations under Classical, Neoclassical, and Relational Contract Law," *Northwestern University Law Review* 72, 854–905.

Macneil, Ian R. (1980), *The New Social Contract: An Inquiry into Modern Contractual Relations*, Yale University Press, London.

Maxeiner, James R. (Fall 2008). "Some Realism about Legal Certainty in Globalization of the Rule of Law," *Houston Journal of International law*. Retrieved 29 May 2011.

OECD (SF), *Competition Advocacy: Challenges for Developing Countries*, available at http://www.oecd.org/daf/competition/prosecutionandlawenforcement/32033710.pdf.

OECD and IADB (2004), *Competition Law and Policy in Peru: A Peer Review*, OECD/IADB, Paris: OECD.

OECD (2005), *European Commission – Peer Review of Competition Law and Policy*, OECD, Paris available at www.oecd.org/daf/competition/prosecutionandlawenforcement/35908641.pdf.

OECD (2005), *Oslo Manual Guidelines for Collecting and Interpreting Innovation Data*, 3rd edn, Paris: OECD.

OECD (2010), *Competition Policy and the Informal Economy*, DAF/COMP/GF(2009)10, Policy Roundtables, OECD, Paris.

Posner, Richard (1973), *The Economic Analysis of Law*, Boston: Little Brown.

Richardson, G.B. (1960), *Information and Investment*, Oxford University Press, Oxford.

Robinson, Joan ([1933] 1969), *The Economics of Imperfect Competition*, Palgrave Macmillan.

Robinson, Joan (1942), *An Essay on Marxian Economics*, The MacMillan Press, London.

Robinson, Joan (1951), *Collected Economic Papers* 1, Basil Blackwell, Oxford.

Rodriguez, Armando and Lesley DeNardis (2007), Examining the Performance of Competition Policy Enforcement Agencies: A Cross-Country Comparison, *Journal of Business & Economic Studies* 13(1), Spring 2007.

Rodriguez, Armando and Lesley DeNardis (2008), "Assessing Competition Policy Performance Metrics: Concerns About Cross-Country Generalisability," Government, Politics & Global Studies Faculty Publications. Paper 4. http://digitalcommons.sacredheart.edu/gov_fac/4.

Rodriguez, Armando and Ashkon Menon (2010), *The Limits of Antitrust*, London: Kluwer Law International.

Sendra, Maria (1992), "Strategic Alliances for Innovation in the Global Market of the 1990s: A Comparative Study of the Relationship between Innovation and the Patent/Antitrust Mechanisms of the United States and the European Economic Community," *Int'l Tax & Bus. Law. 382 (1992)* 9 pp. 382–407 Available at: http://scholarship.law.berkeley.edu/bjil/vol9/iss2/2.

Schneider, Friedrich, "Outside the State – the Shadow Economy and Shadow Economy Labor Force" (2014) background paper for In from the Shadow: Integrating Europe's Informal Labor, a World Bank regional report on the informal sector in Central, Southern Europe and the Baltic countries (Task number P112988 available at http://goo.gl/00q76I and http://www.econ.jku.at/schneider.

Schumpeter, Joseph (1942), *Capitalism, Socialism and Democracy*, New York: Harper and Brothers.

Sowell, Thomas (1980), *Knowledge and Decisions*, New York: Basic Books.

Stigler, George J. (1984), "Economics—The Imperial Science?," *Scandinavian Journal of Economics* 86(3), pp. 301–313.

Tardiff, Timothy (2009), "Efficiency Metrics for Competition Policy in Network Industries," *Journal of Competition Law and Economics* 6(4), 957–972.

Teece, David (2012), "Favoring Dynamic over Static Competition: Implications for Antitrust Analysis and Policy," In *Competition Policy and Patent Law under Uncertainty*, Geoffrey A. Manne, Joshua D. Wright (eds), Cambridge: Cambridge University Press.

U.S. Federal Trade Commission (2009), *The Federal Trade Commission at 100: Into Our 2nd Century. The Continuing Pursuit of Better Practices, A Report by Federal Trade Commission Chairman William E. Kovacic*, FTC, Washington, D.C.

Vuletin, Guillermo (2008), "Measuring the Informal Economy in Latin America and the Caribbean," *IMF Working Papers*, WP/08/102.

WIPO, Cornell University, Insead, (2014), *Global Innovation Index* available at https://www.globalinnovationindex.org/content.aspx?page=GII-Home.

The World Bank, OECD (1998), *A Framework for the Design and Implementation of Competition Law and Policy*, Chapter 6, Washington, D.C.

World Economic Forum (2012), *Global Competitiveness Report* available at: http://www.weforum.org/issues/global-competitiveness.

CHAPTER 4

Analysis of Merger Control Performance in Latin America: The Case of Argentina, Brazil, Colombia, and Mexico

Diego Petrecolla, Lucila Porto & Carlos Adrián Romero

This chapter analyzes the performance of a competition authority (CA) in controlling mergers and acquisitions (M&A) in Argentina, Brazil, Colombia, and Mexico. The methodology consists of a statistical analysis of M&A cases evaluated from 1999 to 2019. The chapter also compares legislation in those countries, helping to understand the implication of different M&A control designs in the authority's performance. We found a similarity in the decision scheme of all the CAs. However, some results raise suspicions about a possible lack of independence. Others, opens the discussion as to whether M&A control is really necessary or whether it represents a waste of resources.

§4.01 INTRODUCTION

Any intervention by a competition authority (CA) faces a trade-off between the costs resulting from an anti-competitive merger and acquisition (M&A) and the costs of an intervention that tries to restrict or correct them. Taking into consideration all possible interventions, we should no longer question whether the authority should intervene, but, rather, what the optimal and most efficient way to do so is. From this arises the need to measure the efficiency of the authority's performance.

The CA's objective is to defend the welfare of consumers and improve the allocation of economic resources. The control of M&A is an instrument to that end. Based on this, the authority assesses the change in the conditions of competition as a result of an M&A. The analysis it performs, the duration of the procedure, and the decisions it makes act as signals to the private sector that it is considering a concentration operation. In this regard, some investigations study the impact of an authority's decisions in relation to the composition and/or frequency of future M&A

notifications. Ideally, the decision on an operation should be such as to discourage the notification of cases that generate harmful effects on competition, but without discouraging the benign cases (Clougherty and Seldeslachts, 2013; Lee, 2015).

Other works analyze the similarity/discrepancy between the outcome that the market expects and the CA's decision. In this scenario, the response of the financial market to the announcement of an M&A would allow us to state whether the market views the operation as anti-competitive. A discrepancy between the expectations and the decision would mean that the market considers that the authority rejected an operation that it "should have approved", or vice versa (Duso, Neven, and Röller, 2007; Neven and Röller, 2002).

This chapter differs from the aforementioned and aims to evaluate the performance of the Argentine, Brazilian, Colombian, and Mexican CA by analyzing the evolution in the number of cases resolved, the result, and their duration. In addition, we include an analysis of the legislation in those countries, the changes said legislation underwent, and its impact on the performance of the authority.

The methodology enables us to obtain a holistic view of M&A control since it analyzes both "the before", that is, the design of the procedure and its theoretical implications on the efficiency of the CA, as well as "the after", that is, the actual performance.

In Latin America, Colombia was one of the first countries to introduce merger control into its legislation in 1959. In the 1990s, Mexico (1993), Brazil (1994), and Argentina (1999) did so. However, not all countries count with such experience. Some are even undergoing an early stage in the design, as is the case in Peru and Uruguay. In this context, a comparative analysis of those experiences is of interest and contributes some lessons.

The literature offers some studies that evaluate the performance of M&A control applying this type of quantitative analysis—Cardinale, Petrecolla, and Romero (2020), Del Pino (2018), Greco, Petrecolla, Romero, and Romero Gómez (2013) and Petrecolla (2007). This chapter also aims to promote learning. From this approach, we consider the works of Orbach (2000), Page (1997), and Schwindt and McDaniels (2008) that present some experiences in Peru, Brazil, and Japan, respectively.

For the construction of the database, we studied the websites of the respective CAs. The Argentine CA, the National Commission for the Defense of Competition (CNDC), publishes the opinions and resolutions referring to the M&A from 1980 to the present. In Brazil, the Administrative Council for Economic Defense (CADE) publishes statistics on resolved operations. The Colombian competition authority's website has a public document on the statistics of transactions resolved by the SIC from 1998 to the present. The current Mexican competition authority COFECE publishes statistics on its M&A control work. It also has the annual reports of the former CA. Based on this information, we built a database from 1999, the year in which Argentina introduced M&A control, to 2019.

Evaluating the performance of the CA using this type of quantitative analysis has multiple drawbacks. The performance of a CA cannot be determined only by imposing conditions or blocking a determined amount of M&A. In this regard, Kovacic (2009) proposes three criteria to evaluate whether a CA's actions are aligned with an effective

M&A control: (1) analyze whether the control resulted in lower prices and/or a higher quality of products; (2) observe whether the social costs of the exercise of defending competition (DC) have been minimized; and (3) examine whether the CA has undergone a re-evaluation process and an improvement in its performance.

As to the first, given that an analysis of the effect on prices and quality goes beyond this study, we apply a cost-error analysis. One of the great difficulties that the CA faces when evaluating an M&A is the asymmetry of the information. This situation entails a tension between two types of errors: type 1 or false positives and type 2 or false negatives. In the first, we find M&A blocks that generate pro-competitive effects, while M&A authorizations generate anti-competitive effects in the second. Based on this approach, good performance is associated with a minimization of the sum of both errors.

Regarding the second, some of the social costs of the DC exercise are the processes that exceed the optimal time and the application of conditions that require a profusion of resources for monitoring. With respect to conditionalities, those of a structural type are less costly for the CA in terms of monitoring, but since they generally require a divestment of assets, they may not minimize social costs. In addition, in cases where the notification of the transaction is *ex post,* there are disincentives to subject the parties to structural conditioning because an already consummated concentration would have to be modified.

Another aspect that influences the cost of a DC exercise is the number of cases that the authority must analyze. So, it is important not only to set a threshold at the optimum level, but also to generate the appropriate deterrent effect in such a way as to minimize the costs of the exercise (Sørgard, 2009).

Lastly, regarding evaluation, the four CAs undergo the OECD peer-reviews. This fact attests to their commitment to improve their performance. In addition, COFECE periodically conducts *ex post* evaluations of certain cases and transactions.

Lyons (2009) raises another possible approach. Following the theory of negotiation, if an agreement is beneficial both for the authority (and failing that for society) and for the companies involved, an agreement must be reached. Any prohibition and withdrawal of the parties would result in a breakdown of the negotiation. On the other hand, the M&A should be resolved in the shortest time possible since any delay implies a loss of well-being. In this context, an efficient system should be able to reach an agreement, reasonably quickly, between the authority and the parts.

Considering both approaches, the following guidelines could be outlined according to which an M&A control would be efficient:

- those operations that do not ultimately damage competition and those that present improvements should be approved;
- the procedure should take a reasonable time. However, a trade-off exists between speed and fewer type 1 and type 2 errors;
- the authority's decisions should be those that minimize the social cost of exercising DC; and
- authorities must be subjected to a continuous review process.

Considering the limitations of the chosen methodology, in what follows the chapter addresses a quantitative analysis on the evolution of the number of cases resolved, their resolution and the duration of the procedure, contextualizing it according to the criteria developed by Kovacic (2009) and Lyons (2009) (section 4.04). Before doing so, sections 4.02 and 4.03 develops and compares the competition laws in Argentina, Brazil, Colombia, and Mexico. Finally, section 4.05 concludes.

§4.02 LEGISLATION ON M&A CONTROL

[A] Argentina

At the end of 1999, Law No. 25,156 established control of M&A. In 2018, the new Law No. 27,442 was enacted. This last Law introduced several important changes in the procedure of M&A control; some of these are regarding thresholds, timing of notification, and the introduction of an accelerated procedure. However, some of the changes introduced require the conformation of the CA in order to become effective. To date, such authority has not been created. Consequently, the procedure and timing of notification of Law No. 25,156 and the thresholds of Law No. 27,442 are in force.

Law No. 25,156 establishes that the notification can be prior (ex-pre control) or up to one week after the consummation of the transaction (*ex post* control). Once notified, the CNDC must come to a decision within 45 business days. If the operation can potentially restrict or distort the competition, the term can be extended up to an additional 120 days. It may also be suspended in cases of requests for additional information. Once the deadline has passed, the operation is tacitly approved.

Although Law No. 25,156 does not explicitly distinguish between cases according to their level of risk, as of 2001, the 45 business days available to the CNDC are divided into stages according to the information forms that the parties must submit (SDCC Resolution No. 40/2001). Figure 4.1 shows the procedure once the notification has been received.

Figure 4.1 Procedure in Argentina (Law No. 25,156 and Resolution SDCC No. 40/2001)

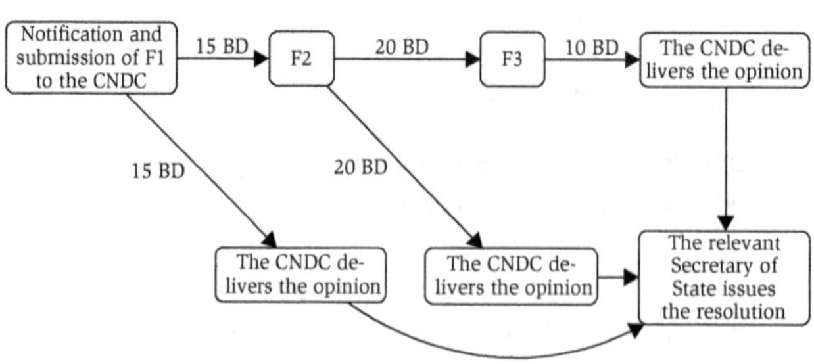

Source: Own elaboration.

When notifying, the parties must submit a first form (F1). If the information contained is not sufficient, the CNDC can request a second (F2) and third form (F3). Although there is no accelerated procedure for simple cases, the presentation of the F1 is sufficient and should resolve the case relatively faster.

Regarding CA, there is a discrepancy between what is established by law and occurs in practice. The legislation provides for the creation of an enforcement authority (tribunal),[1] which has not yet been set up. Consequently, to control M&A, the CNDC carries out the technical analysis and issues a non-binding opinion. The decision that has legal effects for the parties is the resolution of the secretariat on which the CNDC[2] depends.

Regarding the thresholds, Law No. 25,156[3] established that all M&A whose total business volume of the group of affected companies exceeded the sum of AR$ 200 million in the country had to be notified. In 2001, it added that those that do not exceed AR$ 20 million need not be notified,[4] even if the other threshold had been met. Law No. 27,442 establishes that the thresholds are to be expressed in mobile units (MU) whose value will be automatically updated using the variation of the consumer price index (CPI) published by the National Institute of Statistics and Censuses (INDEC). In addition, the threshold values become 100 million MU (approximately USD 11 million[5]), and 20 million MU (approximately USD 55,000), respectively.

Because the thresholds had been outdated by inflation, in 2017 the CNDC introduced an accelerated procedure for simple cases (OECD, 2017). In addition, Law No. 27,442 empowers the CA to submit for summary treatment low-risk operations. Finally, another of the modifications was the timing of the notification. Law No. 27,442 establishes the obligation of prior notification. However, given that the new CA has not yet been established, both the ex-pre control and the summary treatment are not in force and, therefore, the regime established in Law No. 25,156 still governs.

The M&A analysis may result in authorization, subordination to the fulfillment of conditions, or the denial of authorization. Although in practice certain variants were given to this classification, this chapter considers it conditional to any operation that is subject to some type of restriction.

The conditions are imposed by the authority and can be structural, behavioral, or modifiable in the non-competition clauses of the contracts through which the operations are carried out.

1. Law 25,156 provides for the creation of an Enforcement Court. Law 27,442 provides for the creation of a National Competition Authority (ANC), made up of the Competition Defense Tribunal (Tribunal) and two secretariats: one dedicated to the study of anti-competitive behavior and the other to control M&A.
2. It currently depends on the Ministry of Internal Trade.
3. In 2001 they were modified by Decree No. 396/2001. The threshold in force between 1999 and 2001 established that if the total worldwide invoicing of the parties were greater than AR $ 2,500 million, the operation had to be notified.
4. Except that in the previous 12 (36) months, operations have been carried out that together exceed AR $ 20 million (AR $ 60 million). The operations subject to accumulations of 12 and 36 months should have been verified in the same market.
5. We considered the price of the dollar of the BCRA for the last business day of December 2019 and the value of the MUs established in Resolution 145/2019 of 26.4.

[B] Brazil

Control of M&A[6] (Law No. 8,884) was introduced in 1994. The notification can be ex-pre or take up to 15 business days after the transaction has been consummated. It was not until 2011 that the mandatory prior control was implemented (Law No. 12,529). It took effect in 2012.

Law No. 8,884 assigned the regulatory task to the Brazilian Competition Defense System (BCDS) made up of CADE, the Secretariat of the Economic Directorate (SED), and the Secretariat of Economic Supervision (SES), dependent on the Ministry of Justice and of Economy, respectively. In this system, CADE exercises the role of administrative court, issuing final decisions. Figure 4.2 illustrates the procedure from the moment of notification.

Figure 4.2 Procedure in Brazil (Law No. 8,884)

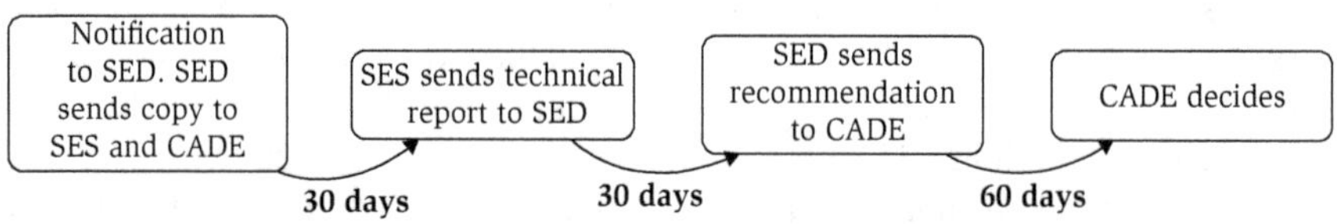

Source: Own elaboration.

SED receives the notification and delivers a copy to SES and CADE. Within 30 days, SES must send a technical report to SED, which, in turn, must send a recommendation to CADE within 30 days of receipt.[7] The decisions received by CADE from both agencies are non-binding. During the next 60 days, CADE has to pronounce on the operation; if not, it is tacitly approved. The maximum legal time is 120 days. This can be suspended if any of the agencies request further information.

Regarding thresholds, an M&A must be notified if the resulting entity controls 20% of the relevant market or if the annual sales volume exceeds BRL 400 million. In 2005, CADE modified the thresholds establishing that the market share of the resulting entity, or of at least one of the parties, should exceed 20%. In addition, the annual sales volume is restricted to that generated in the national territory.

In 2012, Law No. 12,529 established that the CA be renamed CADE. This organization condenses the tasks that were previously in the hands of the SED and the SES. In organizational terms, CADE is made up of the General Superintendency (GS),

6. The economic concentration operations achieved by law are not limited to M&A, but to all those that may limit competition in the relevant market (including agreements between competitors). However, "acts of economic concentration" and "mergers and acquisitions (M&A)" are used interchangeably.
7. In 2003, the Joint Ordinance between the SED and the SES was implemented by which both organizations could quickly analyze simple cases. In 2004, the Joint Merger Review Procedure was introduced whereby both agencies simultaneously analyze the cases and then send a joint recommendation to CADE.

the Department of Economic Investigations (DEI), and the Administrative Tribunal for Economic Defense (Tribunal). Figure 4.3 describes the new procedure.

Figure 4.3 Procedure in Brazil (Law No. 12,529)

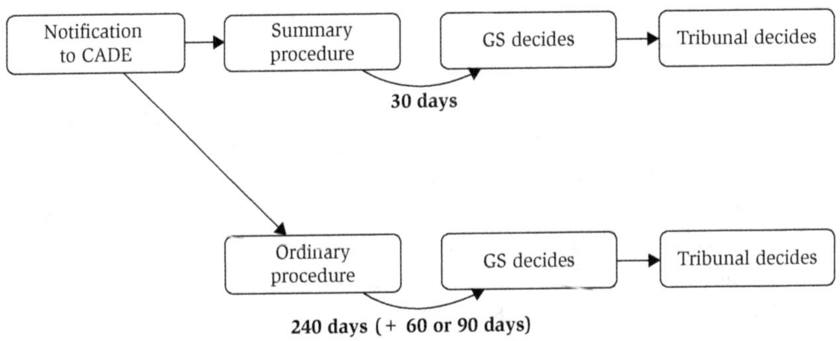

Source: Own elaboration.

The maximum time allotted to CADE depends on whether the case has been submitted to an ordinary or summary procedure.[8] In the first case, once notified, CADE has 240 days. This can be extended to an additional 90 days by decision of CADE or 60 days at the request of the lawyers of both parties. On the other hand, summary-type procedures must be completed in less than 30 days.[9] In both cases, once the deadline has passed, the operation is tacitly approved.

As of 2012, the thresholds[10] are set according to whether the annual turnover or sales during the year prior to the operation of at least one of the parties registers at least BRL 750 million (approximately USD 190 million[11]) and whether the annual turnover or sales of at least one of the other parties involved surpasses BRL 75 million (approximately USD 19 million). Unlike what Argentina stipulates, the amount of the thresholds is not adjusted automatically but can be adjusted through inter-ministerial decrees.[12]

The M&A evaluation may result in unrestricted approval, conditional approval, or rejection.[13] The final decision can be made by both the GS and the tribunal. The GS refers the cases to the tribunal when it considers that the M&A should be approved with conditions or rejected. Once received, the tribunal conducts its own investigation and issues a resolution, regardless of what was recommended by the GS.

8. Resolution No. 02/2012.
9. Resolution No. 16/2016.
10. Updated in Inter-ministerial Ordinance No. 994 of 2012.
11. The dollar price was considered for the last business day of December 2019 (BCB, 2020).
12. Law No. 12,529 (Article 88).
13. Operations may also have been closed without merit when it should not have been notified, is withdrawn by the parties or is archived.

The conditioning factors can be structural, behavioral, or both. They can even include modifications to the non-compete clause.[14] The conditions can be imposed by CADE or negotiated between the parties. In the case of negotiation, a concentration control agreement (CCA) is established, which must be approved by the tribunal to become effective.

[C] Colombia

In 1959, Law No. 155 was approved, establishing the prior control of economic concentration operations. In 1968, through Decree 2,974, the Secretariat of Industry and Commerce (SIC), currently the CA, was created (SIC, n.d.-b).

Law No. 155 established that any operation of economic concentration where the individual or joint assets of the parties involved exceed COP 20 million must be previously notified to the SIC. In 2006, through Resolution No. 22,195, the thresholds are updated and expressed in units of minimum monthly wages (MMW). Until 2010, the new threshold value was defined as 100,000 MMW (OECD, 2016). In 2010 and 2011, it is updated again reaching 150,000 MMW. From 2012 onwards, the threshold decreases, from 100,000 MMW between 2012 and 2016, and 60,000 MMW (approximately USD 14.7 million[15]) since 2017.

Regarding the scope of such thresholds, until 2015, both the thresholds corresponding to income and assets referred to those obtained worldwide. However, Resolution No. 10,930 of 2015 modifies this issue and restricts it to the national territory. With respect to the M&A reached, Law No. 155 and Law No. 1,340 only make explicit the control over operations of a vertical and horizontal nature, but not over those of the conglomerate type (OECD, 2016).

Regarding the procedure, Article 4 of Law No. 155 establishes that once the operation has been notified, and if the information referred to is submitted in full, the authority has 30 days to decide on it. This period may be suspended if the authority requests the submission of new information. If no decision is made, then the transaction is tacitly approved (OECD, 2009).

In 2009, with the enactment of Law No. 1,340, this procedure was modified, segmenting the process into two stages. Once admitted for processing, the first stage of investigation, or preliminary evaluation, begins. This lasts 30 working days, and the authority may, if the transaction does not present concerns for competition, approve it without conditions, or otherwise, initiate the next phase, or substantive study. If the latter occurs, the parties have 15 business days to provide additional information. Once provided, the authority has three calendar months to pronounce and decide on the operation. Otherwise, it is tacitly approved (Ibarra Abogados, 2019; OECD, 2009; SIC, n. d.-a). Figure 4.4 describes the new procedure from the moment of M&A is admitted.

14. Article 1,147 of the Civil Code.
15. We considered the price of the dollar of the BANREP for the last business day of December 2019 and the value of the MMW established in Decree 2,451 of 828,116.

Figure 4.4 Procedure in Colombia (Law No. 1,340)

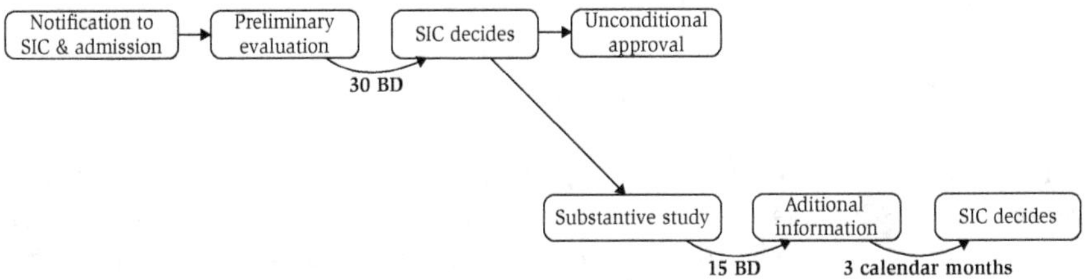

Source: Own elaboration.

There is a type of simplified analysis for transactions that, a priori, do not present competition concerns. In those cases where, despite exceeding the thresholds, the combined participation of the parties does not exceed 20% of the relevant market, the transaction is considered approved and only needs to be notified (SIC, n.d.-a). The authority has 10 business days to analyze it and confirm its reception, after which time it is tacitly approved. In the event that the authority does not have all the necessary information to verify whether or not the true joint participation is less than 20%, the parties must initiate a pre-evaluation (Ibarra Abogados, 2019).

Mergers may have the following results: approved, approved with conditions, or rejected. Any transaction that is only notified, or that ends with the authority's decision in the first phase of investigation, is approved without conditions. So, for an operation to be conditioned or rejected, it must have passed through the second stage of investigation.

The conditions may be proposed by the parties and negotiated with the authority. The parties have up to 15 working days after the second phase of investigation to propose them. They may be structural or behavioral, or both.

A difference with respect to the rest of the countries under analysis is found in Article 22 of Law No. 1,340, which establishes that in cases where conditions are imposed, the parties are obliged to pay an annual contribution to the CA. The value will be determined based on the criteria established in Resolution No. 72,896 of 2010.

Another important difference with respect to the rest of the countries is the access to information and reports made by the SIC. Prior to Law No. 1,340, the SIC did not disclose those integration analyses in which the operation was fully authorized. Thus, neither the society nor the parties had access to a version of the report, not even to a non-confidential version. In 2009, with the enactment of Law 1,340, non-confidential versions can be disclosed (OECD, 2009).

Finally, in 2019 through the approval of Law 2,010, a tax reform is carried out. Consequently, the parties must pay a filling fee for merger control procedures. The amount of the fee depends on the stage of the procedure and the threshold that has been exceeded. The value of the fee ranges between COP 2.62 and COP 37.38 million (approximately USD 799 and USD 11,406,[16] respectively). Note that, unlike the thresholds, the fee is expressed in current values. However, Law No. 2,010 contemplates an annual update (Holland and Knight LLP, 2021).

[D] Mexico

In 1992, the Federal Economic Competition Law (Ley Federal de Competencia Económica or LFCE) was enacted and became effective in 1993. With this Law, *ex ante* merger control is established, and the Federal Competition Commission (CFC) is designated as the Competition Authority. In terms of independence, the CFC was a decentralized administrative body of the Ministry of Commerce and Industrial Development, until 2012, and of the Ministry of Economy, between 2012 and 2013. The CFC had technical and administrative autonomy, but not economic independence.

In 2013, the constitution was amended and the Federal Economic Competition Commission (COFECE) was created as an autonomous constitutional body, with legal personality, budgetary autonomy, and as the Enforcement Authority of the LFCE in most of Mexico's markets.[17] In 2014, a new LFCE was enacted, which was amended in 2017 and 2021.

Initially in 1992, Article 20 of the LFCE established that if (i) the amount of the transaction was equivalent to or exceeded 12 million times the general minimum wage in effect for the Federal District (GMWDF), (ii) as a result of the transaction, the resulting firm accumulated 35% or more of the assets or shares of an economic agent whose assets or sales exceeded 12 million times the GMWDF, or (iii) if the assets or annual sales volume, jointly or individually, exceeded 48 million times the GMWDF, and such transaction implied an additional accumulation of assets or capital stock in excess of 4.8 million times the GMWDF, then the transaction had to be notified and required the commission's approval in order to be consummated.

In 2006, the values of the thresholds are restricted to those generated within the national territory. In addition, the values of the thresholds were updated to 18 million (approximately USD 98 million[18]), 18 million (approximately USD 98 million), 48 million (approximately USD 261.5 million), and 8.4 million (approximately USD 48.8 million), respectively.

Regarding the procedure, in 2014, Article 90 of the LFCE established that the parties involved in the transaction must submit the notification together with information to the commission. The commission can request additional information. After notification or receipt of additional information, the commission has 60 days to issue a

16. We considered the price of the dollar of the BANREP for the last business day of December 2019.
17. The exceptions are telecommunications and broadcasting, where the authority is the Federal Telecommunications Institute (IFT), and the financial sector, where the authority is the National Insurance and Bonding Commission (CNSF).
18. We considered the price of the dollar of the BANXICO for the last business day of December 2019 and the value of the MMW published by the National Commission on Minimum Wages.

decision (the deadline may be extended for an additional 40 days).[19] If no decision is made, then the transaction is deemed to be approved. Also, if the commission asks additional information to third parties, then they have 10 days to present the additional information. Figure 4.5 describes the new procedure from the moment of notification.

Figure 4.5 Procedure in Mexico (LFCE)

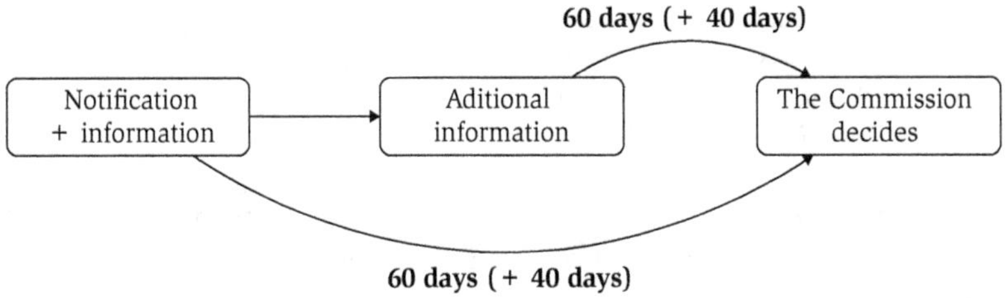

Source: Own elaboration.

Prior to notification, the parties may engage in pre-notification discussions with the CA. This represents a good opportunity to avoid errors and delays in the presentation of information once the procedure has begun. In addition, as from January 1, 2021, the parties must pay MXN 196,347[20] (approximately USD 10,419) as a filling fee (COFECE, 2021).

Although no distinction was made within the bodies of the commission, the task of investigation and analysis is in the hands of the Technical Secretariat (TS) while the resolution is issued by the plenary. This distinction is clearer in cases where it is considered necessary to impose conditions. In particular, before passing the case to the plenary, the TS must inform the parties so that they may propose remedies.

Article 21 bis of the LFCE of 2006 introduces a simplified procedure. In order to apply, the parties, at the time of notification, must demonstrate that the transaction does not have negative effects on competition.[21] Within 15 days following the notification, the commission must analyze whether the transaction should be approved or whether, on the other hand, it should not be treated in a simplified manner and should be transferred to the ordinary procedure (it starts as already notified). If the commission does not make a decision within 15 days, the transaction is deemed to be approved.

19. Between 1992 and 2006 (Article 21 of the 1992 LFCE), the Commission has 45 days from the notification or from the submission of the additional information to issue a decision. The deadline may be extended by the President of the Commission by a total of 60 additional calendar days. Between 2006 and 2014, the Commission has 35 days to issue a decision, and it can be extended by 40 days.
20. The filling fee was established in the Federal Law of Rights, and the amount was updated in Annex 19 of the Miscellaneous Tax Resolution for 2021.
21. In the 2011 amendment to the LFCE, Article 21 bis explicitly clarifies which types of transactions do not affect competition.

§4.03 COMPARISON BETWEEN LEGISLATION

Table 4.1 Summary of Some Similarities and Differences Between the Four Countries

Comparison Criteria	*Argentina*	*Brazil*	*Colombia*	*Mexico*
Does merger control exist?	Yes, since the end of 1999 (Law No. 25,156)	Yes, since 1994 (Law No. 8,884)	Yes, since 1959 (Law No. 155)	Yes, since 1993 (LFCE)
Is merger control *ex ante*?	Between 1999 and 2018 (Law No. 25,156) control could be *ex ante* or *ex post*. As of 2018 (Law No. 27,442) is ex ante[*]	Between 1994 and 2012 (Law No. 8,884) merger control could be *ex ante* or *ex post*. As of 2012 (Law No. 12.529) is *ex ante*.	Yes, since 1959 (Law No. 155)	Yes, since 1993 (LFCE)
In the case of *ex post* merger control, what is (was) the maximum time limit for notification?	Between 1999 and 2018 (Law No. 25,156), the limit was one week after the consummation of the operation.	Between 1994 and 2012 (Law No. 8,884), transactions had to be notified within 15 working days of their consummation.	-	-
Should the parties pay any fees when notifying the CA of the transaction?	No (Law No. 25,156 and Law No. 27,442).	Yes, since 1999 (Law No. 9,781).	Yes, since 2019 (Law No. 2,010) SIC is authorized to establish a notification fee (effective since 2021—Resolution No. 2,103).	Yes, since 2021 (Federal Law of Rights).

Comparison Criteria	*Argentina*	*Brazil*	*Colombia*	*Mexico*
Unit of measurement of reporting thresholds	Between 1999 and 2018 current value As of 2018 (Law No. 27,442) CPI-adjusted constant values.	Current value. The last amendment was through Interministerial Ordinance No. 994 of 2012.	Until 2006, current values (Law No. 155) Since 2006 (Resolution No. 22,195), thresholds are expressed in terms of minimum monthly wages.	Since 1992, thresholds are expressed in terms of general minimum wage.
Is the merger control procedure divided among types of operations according to their potential risk?	Yes (Law No. 25,156 and SDCC Resolution No. 40/2001), depending on the complexity of the case, there are three different resolution deadlines: 15 (F1), 35 (F2) and 45 (F3) business days after notification.	Yes (Resolution No. 02/2012), the mergers that do not pose a risk to competition undergo a less thorough analysis (summary procedure).	Yes, since 2009 (Law No. 1,340), the procedure is divided in two stages.	Yes, since 2006 there is a simplified procedure for non-risky cases. However, the requirements are very high and it is rarely used (OECD, 2020).
	In 2017, the CNDC began implementing accelerated treatment for some cases (OECD, 2017). Law No. 27,442 introduced summary treatment for low-complexity operations.		There is also a simplified procedure for not risky cases.	The ordinary procedure is not divided into stages, although if the commission does not ask for additional information, the case should be finalized earlier.

Comparison Criteria	*Argentina*	*Brazil*	*Colombia*	*Mexico*
What is the maximum resolution time?	From 1999 to the present (Law No. 25,156 and Law No. 27,442): 45 working days (with the possibility of extending 120 additional days).	Between 1994 and 2012 (Law No. 8,884): 120 days. From 2012 (Law No. 12,529): 240 days (with the possibility of extending up to 330 days).	Up to 2009 (Law No. 155): 30 days. Since 2009 (Law No. 1,340): 30 working days (first stage) or 105 working days (approx.). In the simplified analysis, SIC has 10 business days.	Up to 2006: 45 days and it can be extended by 60 calendar days. Between 2006 and 2014: 35 days and it can be extended by 40 calendar days. In the simplified analysis (effective since 2006): 15 working days. Since 2014: 60 working days (the deadline may be extended for an additional 40 days) (LFCE).
Is there tacit approval?	Yes	Yes	Yes	Yes

Source: Own Elaboration.

Notes: [*] According to Article 84 of Law No. 27,442, the *ex ante* notification will become effective one year after the National Competition Authority is formed. To date, such authority has not yet been confirmed.

Figure 4.6 presents the evolution of absolute (left) and relative (right) thresholds over time.[22]

22. The Argentinian threshold refers to the total business volume of the group of affected companies. In the case of Brazil, we considered the sum of the individual invoices of the parties as from 2012. In the case of Colombia, we considered the joint assets. Finally, for Mexico we considered the joint assets or annual sales volume. This comprises the exchange rate for the last business day of each year published in the BCRA (BCRA, 2020), BCB (BCB, 2020), BANXICO (BANXICO, 2021), and BANREP (BANREP, 2021), and indexed it by the CPI published by the United States Bureau of Labor Statistics (BLS) (US BLS, 2020).

Figure 4.6 Evolution of Thresholds

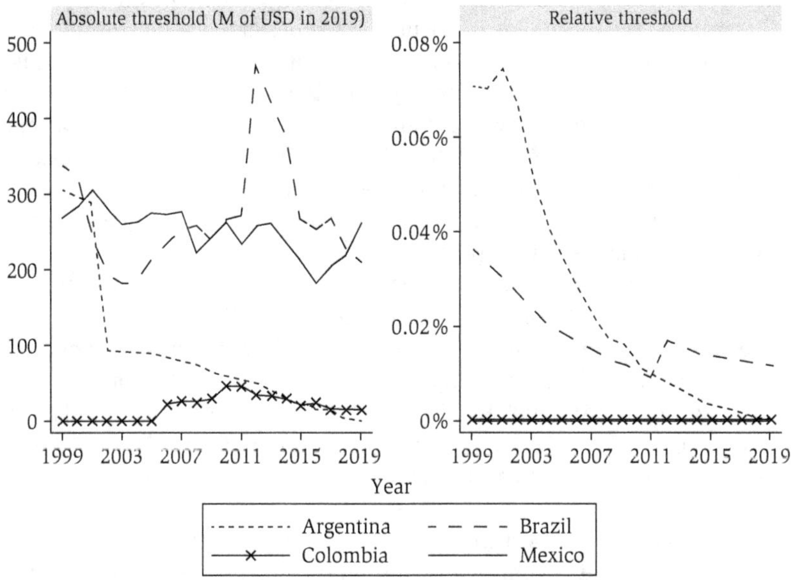

Source: Own elaboration.

Based on the evolution of the absolute threshold, the group of countries can be separated into two. On the one hand, Mexico and Brazil, who despite the variability, present an average threshold of 250.6 and 271.4 million constant dollars at 2019 prices, respectively. On the other hand, Colombia, whose average threshold is 18.3. If the aggregate average of Brazil and Mexico is compared to that of Colombia, then the former is 1,323% higher. Finally, Argentina, which moved from one group to the other, has an average threshold of 88.

Regarding the large variations in the evolution of the threshold, two large jumps can be observed. The first, in 2001 in Argentina, which can be explained by the large devaluation suffered by that country. The second, in 2012 in Brazil, is due to the major updating of the thresholds.

Since the thresholds could be related to the size of the economy, a relative comparison is necessary. Following this line of thought, the difference between the thresholds should be similar to the difference between gross domestic products (GDP) and, therefore, when comparing the relative thresholds,[23] they should not be so dissimilar. When analyzing the relative thresholds, several things can be noted. First, the relative thresholds of Colombia and Mexico are almost indistinguishable in the graph. Second, Argentina's relative threshold converges to a value similar to that of

23. We considered the value of GDP published by the World Bank (WB, 2020b), expressed in current dollars, and indexed it by the CPI published by BLS (U.S. BLS, 2020).

Colombia and Mexico. Lastly, while between 1999 and 2011, Brazil's relative threshold also shows a converging trend, in 2012 there is a jump due to the update in the thresholds. Thereafter, the trend continues to converge but at a slower rate.

Determining the thresholds is essential when designing M&A control. "A system with thresholds that are too low, where virtually all M&A must be reported, is costly and inefficient. On the other hand, if the thresholds are very high such that a large part of the operations are approved without any review, the damage to consumers can be notable" (Buccirossi, Cervone, and Riviera, 2014, p. 166). This dilemma is aligned with Kovacic's (2009) criteria. In the first case, it would not be minimizing the costs of the DC exercise or type 1 and type 2 errors. In the second, there would be adverse effects on the prices and qualities of the products.

Determining the thresholds has to do with setting their unit of measurement. In Mexico, since 1992, the thresholds have been defined in GMWDF. In Colombia, until 2006, the thresholds were defined in current currency and since 2006, they have been expressed in MMW. In the case of Argentina, it was not until 2018 that the thresholds were expressed in MU. Although Brazil does not have thresholds expressed in constant units, according to World Bank (WB, 2020a) statistics, inflation rates in 19 of the last 20 years fell below 10%. Thus, it does not represent a recurring problem for the Brazilian CA.

Another important aspect in the design of the procedure is the timing of the notification. First, an ex-pre control presents information problems both for the CA and for the parties. On the other hand, an *ex post* control would make it possible to show whether there are indeed efficiency gains. Second, any conditioning imposed on a completed operation implies higher costs than if it had been applied *ex ante*. In this line of study, the work of Cosnita-Langlais and Tropeano (2013) shows that an ex-pre control is preferable to an *ex post* one, except in those cases where the information on efficiency gains is imperfect after the operation. On the other hand, another line of study raises the relationship between the timing of the notification and the cost of deviating from the optimal duration. Along these lines, in an *ex post* control, any delay with respect to the optimum could be very costly for consumers in those cases where the operation must be subjected to conditions or even rejected. Both approaches coincide with the recommendation of the International Competition Network (ICN) to establish ex-pre control. The legislation of Colombia and Mexico established *ex ante* control from the very beginning. Brazil achieved this as of 2012. However, although Argentine legislation also provides for it, it has not yet entered into force.

Another point to compare is the accelerated procedure for non-risky cases. Argentina has still not implemented the differentiated procedure established by Law No. 27,442. On the contrary, Brazil, Colombia, and Mexico have a simplified procedure.

§4.04 ANALYSIS OF CONCENTRATION OPERATIONS

[A] Result Analysis

Table 4.2 shows the concentration cases resolved by merit by the CAs. From Argentina, we analyzed 1,310 operations. When examining the evolution of the cases, we can see that the number of opinions decreased due to the change in the thresholds in 2001. Subsequently, between 2002 and 2015, an average of 39 operations per year was recorded with the fewest cases in 2015.[24] In the 2016–2019 period, the average M&A rose to 124, with a maximum of 190 cases in 2017. The number decreased again in 2018–2019 due to the change in thresholds.

In Brazil, a total of 10,044 cases were resolved on merit. Between 2000 and 2004, there was an annual average of 534. In 2005, there was an interannual fall of 38% owing to the change in thresholds. In 2012, the absolute maximum was reached in the number of cases (712). Finally, the 2013–2019 period begins with a change in the thresholds and has the lowest average of annual resolutions (389). Furthermore, in 2017, the second lowest value was reached in the number of cases resolved in one year (363).

In Colombia, 1,316 cases were resolved, a number similar to that reported in Argentina. These cases do not include notifications (they are understood to be approved, they only have to report) or concepts (opinions on M&A cases in a sector regulated by another agency). Analyzing the total number of cases per year, two clear periods can be distinguished. The first period was between 1999 and 2006, where the annual average is 94 cases. Another period was between 2007 and 2019, where the annual average is reduced to 44 cases per year. The difference between these two stages is the thresholds. In the first stage, not only are they expressed in current units, but they are significantly lower than in the second stage.

As a point in common, note the immediate impact a change in the thresholds generates on the number of resolutions per year. This implies how important it is to determine the number and, see how the authority can influence the volume of cases for which it will have to advocate.

Finally, in Mexico, a total of 2,983 cases were resolved, equivalent to an annual average of 142 cases. Notifications that were withdrawn, closed cases and notices were excluded from the analysis. Unlike Argentina, Brazil, and Colombia, Mexico's thresholds were always expressed in constant units. The maximum number of cases resolved in a year was 242 in 2001, while the minimum was 88 in 2010.

24. The number and duration of cases in 1999 is not considered representative and, therefore, is not included in the comparisons.

Table 4.2 Resolutions by Merit According to Final Decision

Year	Argentina				Brazil				Colombia				Mexico			
	Approved without restrictions	Approved with restrictions	Dis-approved	Total	Approved without restrictions	Approved with restrictions	Dis-approved	Total	Approved without restrictions	Approved with restrictions	Dis-approved	Total	Approved without restrictions	Approved with restrictions	Dis-approved	Total
1999	6	1	0	7	215	2	0	217	117	0	0	117	153	6	3	162
2000	147	14	0	161	490	15	2	507	123	1	1	125	172	20	3	195
2001	93	5	1	99	559	12	0	571	92	2	0	94	233	8	1	242
2002	23	1	1	25	474	9	0	483	70	10	0	80	171	5	2	178
2003	34	5	1	40	484	8	0	492	47	3	0	50	127	2	1	130
2004	38	5	0	43	574	43	1	618	88	3	3	94	117	4	1	122
2005	38	5	0	43	345	37	0	382	96	3	0	99	140	8	0	148
2006	58	3	0	61	352	20	0	372	87	3	2	92	163	4	4	171
2007	32	1	1	34	490	37	0	527	58	3	1	62	162	8	1	171
2008	34	4	0	38	550	58	1	609	73	1	2	76	114	0	0	114
2009	41	5	0	46	437	19	1	457	52	0	0	52	87	2	2	91
2010	35	8	0	43	587	27	1	615	34	2	0	36	85	3	0	88
2011	31	9	0	40	649	48	0	697	39	0	0	39	105	1	0	106
2012	28	5	0	33	670	39	3	712	40	0	0	40	86	6	2	94
2013	35	6	0	41	387	47	3	437	28	3	0	31	123	5	2	130
2014	33	5	0	38	413	20	1	434	29	8	0	37	106	6	0	112
2015	17	4	0	21	376	7	1	384	42	3	1	46	141	3	1	145
2016	108	0	0	108	360	6	0	366	39	0	0	39	132	2	0	134
2017	189	1	0	190	355	5	3	363	30	3	0	33	131	8	1	140

Year	Argentina				Brazil				Colombia				Mexico			
	Approved without restrictions	*Approved with restrictions*	*Dis-approved*	*Total*	*Approved without restrictions*	*Approved with restrictions*	*Dis-approved*	*Total*	*Approved without restrictions*	*Approved with restrictions*	*Dis-approved*	*Total*	*Approved without restrictions*	*Approved with restrictions*	*Dis-approved*	*Total*
2018	145	2	0	147	384	6	1	391	28	4	0	32	172	1	3	176
2019	52	0	0	52	405	5	0	410	39	2	1	42	132	0	2	134
Total	1,217	89	4	1,310	9,556	470	18	10,044	1,251	54	11	1,316	2,852	102	29	2,983
	92.90%	6.80%	0.30%	100%	95.10%	4.70%	0.20%	100%	95.1%	4.1%	0.8%	100%	95.6%	3.4%	1.0%	100%

Source: Own elaboration with data from the CNDC, CADE, COFECE, and SIC.

When comparing the total number of solved cases, the value for Brazil is 667% higher than that of Argentina, 663% higher than Colombia, and 237% higher than Mexico. However, when comparing the decision structure, 94% of the cases were approved without restrictions (95.6% in Mexico, 95.1% in Brazil and Colombia, and 92.9% in Argentina). Five percent were approved with restrictions (6.8% in Argentina and 4.7% in Brazil, 4.1% in Colombia and 3.4% in Mexico), and 1% were rejected (1.0 % in Mexico, 0.8% in Colombia, 0.3% in Argentina, and 0.2% in Brazil). This shows that the decision structure was very similar although the number of cases differs significantly.

Analyzing year by year, Brazil is the only country in which in all the years under analysis at least one operation resolved was conditioned or rejected. In contrast, in Argentina there are two years (2016 and 2019) in which all operations were approved without conditions. The same occurred in 2008 in Mexico and in 1999, 2009, 2011, 2012, and 2016 in Colombia. In percentage terms, the year with the highest approval without conditions in Brazil was 1999 (99.0%). At the other extreme, 2013 had the lowest proportion of cases approved without conditions (88.6%). In Argentina, the lowest proportion of cases approved without restrictions is 77.5% (in 2011), in Colombia it is 78.4% (in 2014), and in Mexico 88.2% (in 2000).

We calculate the proportion of conditioned operations (rejected) and their evolution over time for which the conditioning rate (CR) and rejection rate (RR) as the quotient between the conditioned cases (rejected) and the total number of cases resolved by merit of each year. Figure 4.7 shows the value of both rates.

Figure 4.7 Conditioning and Rejection Rates

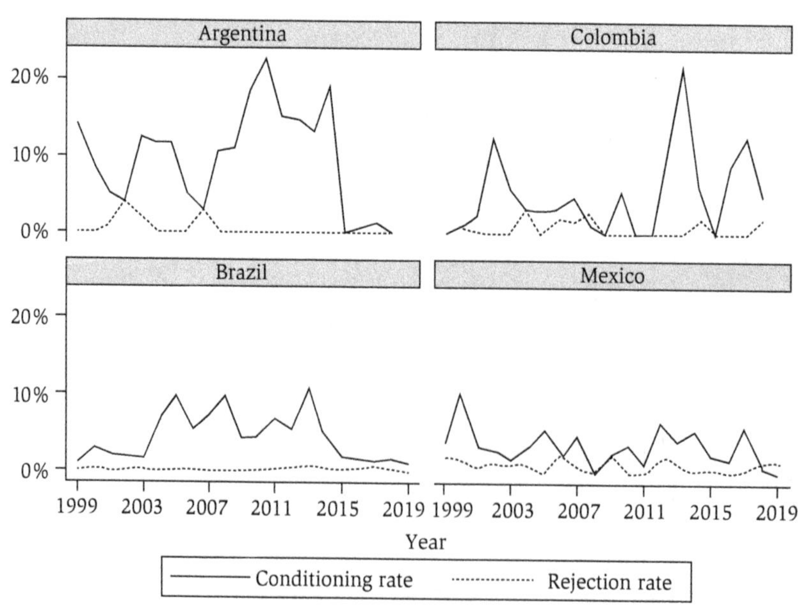

Source: Own elaboration with data from the CNDC, CADE, COFECE, and SIC.

Figure 4.7 shows a lack of stability of CRs especially for Argentina and Colombia. Against this, we can list some hypotheses. Considering the composition of cases resolved per year according to their level of risk, and the metric from which the authority judges a case as risky, we assume that only the first one varied over time, so the variability reflects different case compositions. In this way, 2011 marks the year in which the CNDC faced the highest number of risky cases, as also happened in 2014 for SIC. The opposing hypothesis assumes that only the metric varied. Using this approach, the variations in CR would respond to a relaxation or tightening of the exercise of M&A control.

The opposing role that the authority has in each of these theories is evident. In the first, it adopts a passive role and its actions do not explain variations in the CR. In contrast, the second focuses on its decisions and, since the composition of the cases remains constant, it raises suspicions about arbitrariness and a lack of independence. Faced with this dichotomy, we can propose a third hypothesis where both factors vary over time. In this scenario, the variation in CR would be the product of a conjunction between changes in the composition of cases and in the metric used.

The CA's lack of independence is no minor fact, and its consequences could compromise the effectiveness of the M&A control. The actions of a non-independent CA would not be subject to the minimization of type 1 and 2 errors but to a political issue.[25]

The literature points to the existence of a trade-off in relation to CA independence. On the one hand, a higher level of independence could generate an increase in the use of CA resources to build its reputation and improve its standing in positions of influence and political decision-making. This would lead to a redirection of resources from the performance of strictly competitive tasks to broader tasks. On the other hand, greater independence would imply that decisions would not necessarily be influenced by the political sphere. In this way, CA decisions could be guided by economic efficiency rather than political incentives (OECD and IDB, 2012).

Although an analysis of whether the four CAs are independent goes beyond this chapter, the institutional organization allows us to elucidate certain issues. Regarding Argentina, that the tribunal has not yet been instituted, that the CNDC's opinions are non-binding, and that only the resolution of the Secretary of State is legal all show a certain lack of independence. In Colombia, the independence of the SIC is a concern and there is even a call for institutional reform. Until 2015, the president of the SIC was appointed and could be removed at the discretion of the executive branch. In 2015, Decree 1,817 was issued, from which the president of Colombia ceased to have so much influence in the CA. However, in 2020, this decree is declared unconstitutional and therefore the CA's independence is set back (CPI, 2020). The literature highlights the importance of transparency of CA decisions and procedures when this body is not independent (Fels and Jennings, 2016). However, the Colombian CA until 2009 did not make public its decisions where operations were approved.

25. Furthermore, each subperiod where a different metric is applied would not be fully comparable to another subperiod, thus making an intertemporal analysis impossible. An international analysis faces a similar problem.

On the other hand, in Brazil, the exercise of DC, as of 2012, ceased to be in the hands of secretariats dependent on the Ministry of Justice and Economy and was reorganized in CADE. In this way, Brazil made progress toward greater independence. Similarly, since the 2013 constitutional reform, the Mexican CA went from being subordinated to the executive branch to having constitutional autonomy.

When analyzing the values of figure 4.7, we see that Argentina's CR and RR averaged 9.6% and 0.5%, respectively, 4.4% and 0.2% in Brazil, 3.3% and 0.9% in Mexico, and 5.1% and 0.7% in Colombia. To contextualize, the percentage of conditional cases (rejected) over the cases notified per year between 1992 and 2003 registered 2%–12% (0%–2%) for the European Union and 1%–2% (0%–1.7%) for the United States (Duso, Gugler, and Yurtoglu, 2011). On the other hand, according to OECD (2010) and OECD and IDB (2006), international experience on the percentage of M&A subject to some type of corrective action ranges between 5% and 10%.

Such low values open the discussion about whether more than optimal is approved without restrictions. A possible explanation could be that the thresholds are very low and, therefore, the percentage of complex cases is reduced. Another possible explanation rests on the deterrent effect of the previously rejected cases. This discourages the parties from conducting mergers that are likely to be rejected. In this way, the set of reported cases is biased toward non-risky cases.

Regarding the effect on performance, both theories lead to conflicting conclusions. The first of these would imply that the authority is not minimizing the costs of a DC exercise or the probability of errors. On the other hand, a composition of cases in which non-risky cases predominate might suggest that the deterrent effect was at least close to optimal since the CA managed to discourage anti-competitive cases without discouraging pro-competitive ones.

[B] Duration Analysis

Figure 4.8 shows the average duration of the resolved cases. The values of all the countries are expressed in calendar days[26] from notification to resolution.

---

26. Until 2012 CADE statistics are expressed in running days and business days from 2012. To express them in running days, we multiplied them by an annual ratio between running days over business days (Business days, 2020).

In Mexico, as of 2007, COFECE statistics are presented in business days. In order to calculate the equivalence with respect to working days, the ratio of working days over working days was calculated for each year and multiplied by the duration in working days (Working days, 2021).

Between 1999 and 2012, COFECE did not present statistics on the total average duration of procedures. Instead, the average duration is disaggregated by type of procedure. Since we do not have information on the percentage of cases resolved by procedure, this proportion was estimated. For this purpose, the years 2013–2016 were used, as they are the only ones for which we have both disaggregated information and the overall average. In this way, a system of equations can be posed in matrix form $T = D * W$ where T is a 3x1 column vector formed by the overall average duration, D is a 3x3 square matrix with the duration disaggregated by procedure and W is a 3x1 column vector of weights. By solving for $W = D^{-1} + T$. Since there are 4 years between 2013 and 2016, we estimated the first three (2013–2015) and for the second three (2014–2016). The difference in the estimated average duration according to both weights never

Figure 4.8 Average Duration (In Running Days)

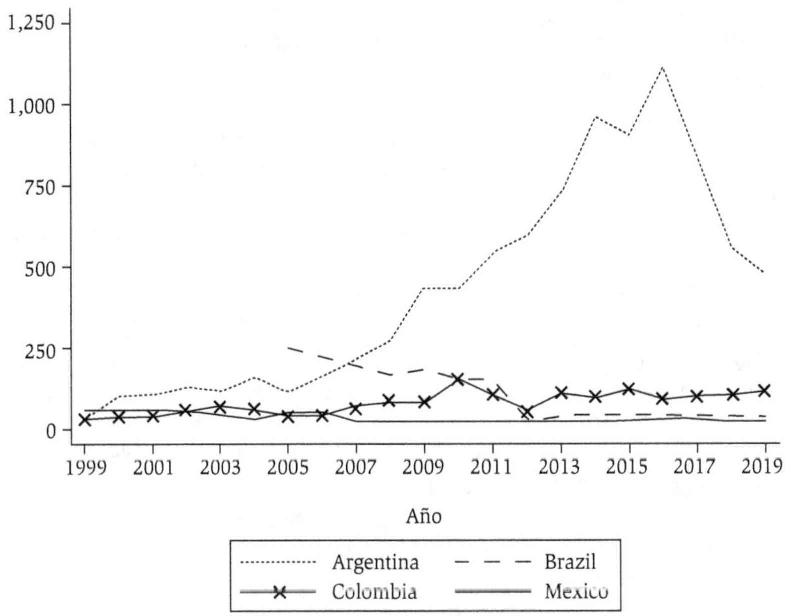

Source: Own elaboration with data from the CNDC, CADE, COFECE, and SIC.

The average duration in Argentina was 478 days[27] (approximately 16 months). When analyzing the intertemporal evolution of the duration, we find a period of growth until 2016, followed by a reversal in this trend and a reduction in the duration in the following years. The average duration went from 103 days in 2000 to 1,113 in 2016 (+ 981%), subsequently falling to 472 in 2019 (58% less than in 2016).

One hypothesis explaining the trends in duration is the composition of cases according to their level of risk. Based on this theoretical framework, and assuming that the composition is variable, a longer average annual duration could be associated with a higher proportion of risky cases in which the CA was forced to spend more time. Along this line, between 1999 and 2016, the authority would have faced an increasing number of risky cases.

Given that this approach was also used to understand the dynamics in CR, it is interesting to analyze both questions simultaneously. Assuming that the metric used by the authority remains constant, a longer average duration should be positively correlated with a higher level of intervention. However, when analyzing Figure 4.7, the relationship does not follow as expected. The relationship would seem to have been

---

differed by more than 9% nor by more than 5 days. For the estimation of the average duration, the estimation of the 2014–2016 weights was considered as it estimated a longer duration than using the 2013–2015 weights.

27. The general average is not the average between the average durations of each year because the number of cases resolved per year differs.

fulfilled in recent years where there is evidence of a lower CR than in previous years and a break in the increasing trend in duration as of 2017.

Cardinale et al. (2020) examine other possible hypotheses although all of them were discarded. These were: (i) the number of cases resolved per year, (ii) the nature of the operations (horizontal, vertical, and/or conglomerate), and (iii) the CNDC's budget for M&A analysis.

The duration in Brazil between 2005 and 2019 registered 115 days (less than 4 months). For 2005–2011, we can see a slight but constant, decreasing trend with an average annual duration of 191 days. The year 2005 recorded the maximum duration (252 days). The year 2012 showed the largest year-on-year drop (80%) and a minimum duration of 30 days. Throughout this second period (2012–2019) the values stabilized and averaged 40 days annually.

One possible cause for the decrease in the average duration is the introduction of summary treatment. The average annual duration of the cases submitted to summary treatment was 25 consecutive days, while it was 113 days under ordinary treatment. Taking that into consideration, since 2012, the proportion of cases submitted to summary treatment was approximately 85% (OECD, 2009). The accelerated procedure manages to significantly reduce the total average duration.

The differentiated procedure generates two positive effects on the authority's performance. It is possible to reduce the average analysis time and improve the allocation of resources between cases, which would imply a minimization of type 1 and 2 errors. Despite this, we can find a high percentage of cases submitted to summary treatment and their outcome in a short time. The analysis reveals the large number of cases that did not represent a risk, but that, nevertheless, were forced to notify. The Brazilian experience, then, raises the question of whether a complementary modification of the thresholds is necessary.

Colombia's average duration, without considering notifications that are already considered approved, is 67 calendar days. This average duration is 41% less than that of Brazil and 86% less than that of Argentina. Although in relative terms Colombia seems to have a more efficient system in terms of duration, there is evidence of a slight increase in duration over time. The evolution of the duration is contrary to what was expected. In 2006, the thresholds are adjusted and, in 2009 the simplified procedure was introduced. Both modifications led to believe that the average duration would decrease. However, the opposite is happening. In particular, between 1999 and 2006 the average duration recorded was 47 consecutive days. Between 2007 and 2019, this value rises to 100. Moreover, during the first period, there was never an average duration of at least 70 calendar days, while in the second period, except in 2012 (57 calendar days), the rest of the years show an average duration of more than 66 days. The maximum duration was recorded in 2015 with 124 days.

The average duration in Mexico is 39 days, 92% less than in Argentina, 66% less than in Brazil, and 42% less than in Colombia. The longest duration in Mexico was recorded in 2002 (61 days) and the shortest in 2009 (20 days). Only in 6 of the 30 years under analysis does Mexico not have the lowest average duration among the countries. In these 6 years, Mexico is surpassed once by Argentina (1999) and 5 times by

Colombia (2000, 2001, 2002, 2005, and 2006). Note that these 6 years are concentrated in the beginning of the period. In fact, the average duration between 1999 and 2006 is 52 days, while, between 2007 and 2019, it is only 26 days.

This difference in performance can be explained, in principle, by two reasons: (i) change in thresholds and (ii) introduction of a simplified procedure. Regarding the first reason, the updated thresholds could lead to a reduction in the number of cases reported and, therefore, resolved. This reduction in the total number of cases could generate a better performance in terms of time. Table 4.2 shows slight changes in the number of cases resolved. Regarding the simplified procedure, the introduction of this procedure generates a better allocation of resources and therefore a reduction in type I and type II errors.

Finally, if analyzed on a case-by-case basis, in Brazil, under Law No. 12,529, only 1% of the cases reached the maximum term of 330 days, and no operation was tacitly approved (OECD, 2019). In Argentina, although the average durations (in running days) are significantly different from what is established by law (in business days), no case was tacitly approved. This difference begs the question of how long a procedure has to be suspended so that it does not exceed the legal business day time span, but that lasts, for example, more than three years (2016) in running days. A lengthy extension in the duration implies a poor performance and a high cost for the DC exercise.

§4.05 CONCLUSIONS

The analysis of the four CAs in controlling M&A has allowed us to evaluate their performance and delineate difficulties that countries at an early stage in the design of the procedure could face.

Throughout this chapter, we studied some of the issues to be defined when designing the control: the determination of the thresholds, both in levels and their unit of measurement; the timing of the notification; the introduction of a differentiated procedure; and the maximum legal term of duration.

Regarding the thresholds, if these fall below or above the optimal level, then the efficiency in the control of M&A is diminished. Thresholds that are too low will not minimize the cost of the DC exercise or the likelihood of errors. In addition, the greater number of operations that the authority must analyze could mean a slowdown in the procedure leading to longer average durations. On the other hand, a system with thresholds that are too high would also be inefficient and consumers will experience price increases and declines in the variety and quality of the products they consume.

Colombia and Mexico were the first to set their threshold values at constant values. Mexico did so from the beginning of its merger control in 1992. Colombia, on the other hand, has done so since 2006. In countries where inflation levels are high, the unit of measurement of the thresholds is an important aspect to consider. Argentina, as of 2018, managed to solve it by setting its thresholds in MUs, which are updated according to the CPI. On the other hand, Brazil continues to express them in current values.

Regarding the timing of the notification, the four countries foresee an ex-pre control that is consistent with the recommendation of the ICN. However, in Argentina it is not yet in effect. This is no minor fact considering that an *ex post* control changes the incentives the authority faces when setting conditions. In addition, any period between the completion of the operation until the authority conditions or rejects it implies welfare losses.

The introduction of a differentiated procedure generates two positive effects on the performance of the authority. The average case analysis time is reduced and the probability of errors is minimized. However, the Brazilian experience shows how necessary it is to complement the policy with a change in the thresholds to avoid allocating resources to simple cases.

Finally, the definition of the maximum legal term available to the CA should consider not only the days of the "active" procedure, but also those days in which the procedure is suspended.

BIBLIOGRAPHY

BCB, (2020). Currency Conversion. https://www.bcb.gov.br/en/currencyconversion

BCRA, (2020). Currency rates. https://www.bcra.gob.ar/PublicacionesEstadisticas/Currency_rates.asp

BANREP (2021), Estadísticas - Tasas de cambio y sector externo - Tasa representativa del mercado (TRM - Peso por dólar). Access November 9, 2021. https://www.banrep.gov.co/es/estadisticas/trm

BANXICO (2021), Sistema de Información Económica: Tipos de cambio y resultados históricos de las subastas - Tipos de cambio diarios - (CF102). Access November 9, 2021 https://www.banxico.org.mx/SieInternet/consultarDirectorioInternetAction.do?sector=6&accion=consultarCuadro&idCuadro=CF102&locale=es

Buccirossi, P., Cervone, R., and Riviera, C. (2014). Optimal Pre-Merger Notification Thresholds: A Contribution to the Italian Debate. *Antitrust & Public Policies, 1*(3). DOI: 10.12870/iar-11061

Business days, (2020). Business Days Calculator in Brasil. https://www.dias-uteis.com/EN

Cardinale, J. Petrecolla, D. and Romero, C.A. (2020). 20 años de control de fusiones y adquisiciones en Argentina (1999–2019): Indicadores de desempeño [en línea] Ensayos de Política Económica. 2020, 3(2). Available at: https://repositorio.uca.edu.ar/handle/123456789/10730

Carletti, E., Hartmann, P., and Ongena, S. (2015). The Economic Impact of Merger Control Legislation. International Review of Law and Economics, 42, 88–104

Clougherty, J. A., and Seldeslachts, J. (2013). The Deterrence Effects of US Merger Policy Instruments. Journal of Law, Economics, & Organization, 29(5), 1114–1144

COFECE, (2021). Trámites y pagos: Pagos a través de e5cinco – Notificación de concentraciones. Access November 19, 2021: https://www.cofece.mx/tramites-y-pagos/

Cosnita-Langlais, A., and Tropeano, J. P. (2013). *Ex post or ex ante? On the optimal timing of merger control* (No. 2013-22). University of Paris Nanterre, EconomiX

CPI, (2020). The Independence of Colombia's Competition Authority: Still a Pending Task. Available at: https://www.competitionpolicyinternational.com/wp-content/uploads/2020/07/Latin-America-Column-July-2020-Full.pdf

Del Pino, M. (2018). La protección de la competencia en Argentina. Próximos desafíos de cara al futuro, En Miguel del Pino ... [*et al.*]*Comentarios a la Ley de Defensa de la Competencia* (1° ed, pp. 25–44). Ciudad Autónoma de Buenos Aires: La Ley, 2018. Available at: https://www.thomsonreuters.com.ar/content/dam/openweb/documents/pdf/arg/white-paper/Supl%20Ley%20de%20Defensa%20de%20la%20Comp_completo.pdf

Duso, T., Gugler, K., and Yurtoglu, B. B. (2011). How Effective Is European Merger Control? European Economic Review, 55(7), 980–1006

Duso, T., Neven, D. J., and Röller, L.-H. (2007). The Political Economy of European Merger Control: Evidence Using Stock Market Data. Journal of Law and Economics, 50(3), 455–489

Fels, A., Jennings, H., 2016. Competition Agencies: What If They Are Not independent? And Are There Any Disadvantages to Being Independent? Paper submitted as background material for Session III at the 15th Global Forum on Competition on December 1-2, 2016. OECD - DAF/COMP/GF(2016)11. Available at https://one.oecd.org/document/DAF/COMP/GF(2016)11/en/pdf

Greco, E. M., Petrecolla, D., Romero, C. A., and Romero Gómez, E. (2013). El control de Fusiones y Adquisiciones en Argentina (1999–2011). Indicadores de desempeño. Revista de los Contratos, los Consumidores y Derecho de la Competencia. FIDAS-LEGIS. Año 4- 2013-3

Holland & Knight LLP, (2021). JDSUPRA: SIC of Colombia Establishes Fees for Merger Control Procedures. Access November 19, 2021: https://www.jdsupra.com/legalnews/sic-of-colombia-establishes-fees-for-5971101/

Ibarra Abogados. (2019). International Comparative Legal Guides (United Kingdom). International Comparative Legal Guides International Business Reports; Global Legal Group. Access September 16, 2020: https://iclg.com/practice-areas/merger-control-laws-and-regulations/colombia

Kovacic, W. E. (2009). Assessing the Quality of Competition Policy: The Case of Horizontal Merger Enforcement. CPI Journal, 5(1), 129–150.

Lee, M. C.-K. (2015). Three Essays on the Effectiveness of Merger Control. Doctoral Thesis, Humboldt-Universität zu Berlin, Wirtschaftswissenschaftliche Fakultät. http://dx.doi.org/10.18452/17226

Lyons, B. (2009). An Economic Assessment of European Commission Merger Control: 1957–2007. Centre for Competition Policy, University of East Anglia, Working Paper 08-17

Neven, D., and Röller, L.-H. (2002). Discrepancies between Markets and Regulators: An Analysis of the First Ten Years of EU Merger Control. In Lundvall, Karl, The Pros and Cons of Merger Control: 10th Anniversary of the Swedish Competition Authority, Swedish Competition Authority, ed., Swedish Competition Authority, Stockholm, 2002, Available at SSRN: https://ssrn.com/abstract=361761 or http://dx.doi.org/10.2139/ssrn.361761

OECD. (2009). Competition Law and Policy in Colombia: A Peer Review—2009. Available at: https://www.oecd.org/daf/competition/44110853.pdf

OECD (2010), Policy Roundtables: Standard for Merger Review 2009. DAF/COMP(2009)21. Available at: https://www.oecd.org/competition/mergers/45247537.pdf

OECD. (2016). Colombia: Assessment of Competition Law and Policy. Available at: https://www.oecd.org/daf/competition/Colombia-assessment-competition-report-2016.pdf

OECD (2017). Roundtable on Safe Harbours and Legal Presumptions in Competition Law - Note by Argentina. DAF/COMP/WD(2017)68. Available at: https://www.argentina.gob.ar/sites/default/files/safe_harbours_and_legal_presumptions_in_competition_law.pdf

OECD (2019), OECD Peer Reviews of Competition Law and Policy: Brazil. Available at: https://www.oecd.org/daf/competition/oecd-peer-reviews-of-competition-law-and-policy-brazil-ENG-web.pdf

OECD and IDB (2006). Derecho y política de la competencia en América Latina: Exámenes inter-pares en Argentina, Brasil, Chile, México y Perú. Available at: https://www.oecd.org/daf/competition/40282837.pdf

OECD and IDB (2012), Follow-up to the nine peer reviews of competition law and policy of Latin American countries: Argentina, Brazil, Chile, Colombia, El Salvador, Honduras, Mexico, Panama and Peru. Available at: https://www.oecd.org/daf/competition/2012Follow-upNinePeer%20Review_en.pdf

Orbach, B. Y. (2000). Competition Policy in Transition: Lessons from Peru. In: Promperu Summer Research Fellowship, Lima: Beatriz Boza, 227.

Page, W. H. (1997). Antitrust Review of Mergers in Transition Economies: A Comment, With Some Lessons from Brazil. U. Cin. L. Rev., 66, 1113

Petrecolla, D. (2007). Mejores prácticas en materia de defensa de la competencia en Argentina y Brasil: aspectos útiles para Centroamérica. CEPAL

Schwindt, R., and McDaniels, D. (2008). Competition Policy, Capacity Building, and Selective Adaptation: Lessons from Japan's Experience. Washington University Global Studies Law Review, 7(1), 35–86

SIC. (n. d.-a). Guía de análisis de integraciones empresariales (trámites de pre-evaluación). Available at: https://www.sic.gov.co/sites/default/files/files/Proteccion_Competencia/Integraciones_Empresariales/2019/Gu%C3%ADa%20Integraciones%20Empresariales_agosto16_2019_%20(1).pdf

SIC. (n. d.-b). Historia | Superintendencia de Industria y Comercio. Access September, 16th, 2020: https://www.sic.gov.co/historia

Sørgard, L. (2009). Optimal Merger Policy: Enforcement vs. Deterrence. Journal of Industrial Economics, 57(3), 438–456

U.S. BLS, (2020). Historical Consumer Price Index for All Urban Consumers (CPI-U): U.S. City Average, All Items, Index Averages. Available at: https://www.bls.gov/cpi/tables/supplemental-files/historical-cpi-u-202006.pdf

WB, (2020a). Inflation, consumer prices (annual %) – Brazil. https://data.worldbank.org/indicator/FP.CPI.TOTL.ZG?end=2019&locations=BR&start=1999

WB, (2020b). GDP (current US$) – Argentina, Brazil, Colombia, Mexico. https://data.worldbank.org/indicator/NY.GDP.MKTP.CD?end=2019&locations=AR-BR-CO-MX&start=1999

Working days (2021), Working days in Mexico. Access November 17, 2021: https://mexico.workingdays.org/EN/

CHAPTER 5

International Cooperation Between Competition Agencies

Eduardo Perez Motta & Mateo Diego-Fernández

Competition legislations and authorities have multiplied at a relevant pace in the last decades. Today, more than 129 jurisdictions have adopted competition legislations and about 140 competition authorities have been established. Furthermore, international trade and investment has grown exponentially. As a result, several operations often involve more than one country and are subject to the scrutiny of different authorities applying similar standards. Considering this scenario, cooperation is important at least in two respects: on the one hand, it helps agencies to resolve a particular case where they do not have enough information; and on the other, it helps newer authorities to benefit from the experience of their older counterparts to refine their standards or to avoid making mistakes that are not self-evident.

For matters of this chapter, two dimensions in which cooperation takes place will be addressed. First, geographically, considering multinational cooperation through international organizations such as The United Nations Conference on Trade and Development (UNCTAD), the Organization for Economic Co-operation and Development (OECD), and the International Competition Network (ICN); regional cooperation through regional organizations such as the European Competition Network (ECN), the Nordic Alliance, the Central European Competition Initiative and the Marshfield Competition Forum, and the Centro Regional de Competencia para América Latina *(CRCAL); and bilateral cooperation. Also, topically, cooperation among authorities under the auspices of multinational or regional agreements normally refers to recommendations, guidelines, or discussions in the abstract or as part of the peer review of particular countries' legislation and policies as well as cooperation in specific cases. Also, through capacity building, better and more coherent outcomes can be obtained, and networks can be formed. While the most obvious "teachers" lay in the United States and the European Union, mid-sized authorities, such as the Mexican one, can share their experiences and disclose some of their methods to their smaller counterparts, saving them the time and resources when applying the law in particular instances.*

Twenty years ago, when Mexico's Federal Competition Commission was created, there were only a handful of competition authorities throughout the world. Back then, it would have been unthinkable to suggest that any type of cooperation between them was needed. However, competition legislations and authorities have multiplied to a point where now it is the opposite that appears unthinkable. Today, more than 120 jurisdictions have adopted competition legislations and established competition authorities.[1] Furthermore, international trade and investment has grown exponentially.[2] As a result, many operations often involve more than one country and are subject to the scrutiny of different authorities applying similar standards.

Cooperation is important at least in two respects: on the one hand, it helps agencies to resolve a particular case where they do not have enough information; and on the other, it helps newer authorities to benefit from the experience of their older counterparts in order to refine their standards or to avoid making mistakes that are not self-evident. It is therefore desirable that at least some type of coordination can be provided.[3]

The aim of this work is to provide a short overview of the current situation of international cooperation among authorities and to share some views based on our personal experience as to where the greatest benefits are. For purposes of clarity, two dimensions in which cooperation takes place will be addressed:

- Geographically
- Topically.

§5.01 GEOGRAPHICAL DIMENSION

International cooperation can take many forms. It can be either multinational or regional or bilateral.

[A] Multinational Cooperation

There are at least three organizations where cooperation is of a multilateral dimension. The UNCTAD, the OECD, and the ICN.

1. http://www.oecd.org/daf/competition/challenges-international-coop-competition-2014.htm.
2. *See* WTO World Trade Report 2014 at http://www.wto.org/english/res_e/booksp_e/world_trade_report14_e.pdf, pp 20 et seq.
3. According to the OECD/ICN 2013 survey, the top five objectives for international cooperation were (i) capacity building; (ii) facilitating investigations; (iii) avoiding conflicting outcomes; (iv) coordinating timing of procedures; and (v) effective/coherent enforcement. http://www.oecd.org/daf/competition/InternEnforcementCooperation2013.pdf.

Both UNCTAD and OECD are governmental organizations with broad agendas, where competition represents only a small portion of their work. UNCTAD's work profile is directed to help developing and least developed countries to maintain a certain level of legislative framework and to help authorities of these countries to keep minimum standards of performance. OECD, on the other hand, is focused on keeping state-of-the art standards and establishes optimal analytical frameworks. OECD members are mainly from developed countries and more advanced developing countries.

The ICN is an informal forum where authorities and non-governmental advisors (practitioners, industries representatives, and academics) work in different areas of competition. Unlike UNCTAD and OECD, ICN is basically a virtual network where members participate via either e-mail or teleconference and an annual meeting takes place. It is guided by a Steering Group of eighteen heads of agencies and carries out its day-to-day work in working groups where members of all agencies can participate. The areas in which these working groups are focused are advocacy, agency effectiveness, cartels, mergers, and unilateral conducts. Previous working groups discussed enforcement in regulated sectors and telecommunications.

[B] Regional Cooperation

Regional cooperation can take a wide variety of forms. There are regional alliances devoted solely to competition as well as competition chapters in broader regional cooperation agreements. Most regions of the world cooperate in one way or another. For example, in Europe, there is the European Competition Network (ECN), the Nordic Alliance, the Central European Competition Initiative, and the Marshfield Competition Forum. Latin America has the Centro Regional de Competencia para América Latina (CRCAL), as well as a number of competition agreements that form part of wider cooperation treaties, such as the Caribbean Community (Caricom), the Andean Pact, Mercosur, and SICA in Central America. In Africa, there is the African Competition Forum, as well as competition chapters within the Common Market for Eastern and Southern Africa (COMESA) and Southern African Development Community (SADC). Asia has the Asian Competition Forum and groups devoted to discussing competition within Asia-Pacific Economic Cooperation (APEC) and Association of Southeast Asian Nations (ASEAN).[4]

As examples, the types of work performed by ECN and the CRCAL are briefly addressed.

ECN is perhaps the most advanced regional network. Given the strength of economic integration between European Member States, cases often involve more than one member state. Therefore, ECN provides for a forum where strategies are proposed

4. *Ibid.*, pp. 84 et seq. While most of the information herein contained was taken from the OECD/ICN survey, at least two of these regional organizations were not mentioned: the CRCAL and the Asian Competition Forum. It is not clear why these fora were not mentioned, which begs the questions as to what other cooperation mechanisms were left out from the survey and their relative weight.

and where coordination between national authorities, as well as the European Commission can allocate the work in the most efficient manner in order to avoid inconsistencies. There is a sophisticated method for notifications and discussion of investigation. Member states' competition authorities are required to apply EU law if cases involve more than one of them and sometimes the European Commission can take over a particular investigation. Furthermore, a number of discussions of a systemic nature take place, such as guidance for merger application, leniency, and specific sectors of interest to them.

The CRCAL was created as a joint effort by Latin American countries to collaborate among them and to develop products tailored to their needs. Through the CRCAL, Latin American countries have issued guidelines on cartels, mergers, unilateral conducts, and horizontal issues, like exclusivities, barriers to entry and relevant markets; as well as studies in the pharmaceutical and supermarket sectors, as well as public procurement. They also organize capacity building courses and roundtables for the presentation of their guidelines or for topical discussion. For instance, two roundtables for judges of the region have been organized. It also provides for one of the most ambitious database containing resolution by regional authorities regarding cartels, unilateral conducts and mergers, allowing all authorities to have an updated vision of criteria taken by their counterparts in the region.[5]

To further promote cooperation and address common competition problems in the region, OECD and the Inter-American Development Bank hold the Latin American Competition Forum (LACF) where countries meet and exchange experiences and best practices from a regional perspective. Since 2003, the LACF has served as a venue for discussing peer reviews, working methods, and issues of common interest. At the same time as the LACF, the Ibero American Forum on Competition takes place. The Spanish National Commission for Markets and Competition and the Portuguese Competition Authority support the Ibero American Forum, which brings together competition authorities from Spanish speaking and Portuguese speaking countries in Latin America and the Caribbean.

[C] Bilateral Cooperation

Bilateral cooperation is commonly found either in a specific chapter of free trade agreements or in interinstitutional agreements between competition authorities. These documents usually contain requirements to notify investigations or merger proceedings that may affect the other party as well as procedures for the exchange of information and varying degrees of cooperation among authorities.[6]

5. http://www.crcal.org/.
6. It is possible to have more than one agreement on competition. For example, on NAFTA Chapter XV Parties (i.e., Mexico) were required to establish legislation on competition and tribunals and to keep minimum standards, while the cooperation agreement between the Comisión Federal de Competencia and the Federal Trade Commission provided for a cooperative framework with specific obligations and timetables. This can be explained by the timing of these two agreements.

§5.02 TOPICAL DIMENSION

Cooperation among authorities under the auspices of multinational or regional agreements normally refers to recommendations, guidelines, or discussions in the abstract or as part of the peer review of particular countries' legislation and policies. In addition, regional as well as bilateral cooperation agreements also establish frameworks under which parties can cooperate in specific cases and where principles for the provision of capacity building activities are set forth.

[A] Recommendations, Guidelines, or Discussions

UNCTAD's Competition and Consumer Policies Programme undertakes competition policy peer reviews, publishes the UNCTAD Model law on competition and the Handbook on competition legislation and implements sector specific and economy-wide competition and consumer policies reforms.[7]

The OECD work in competition is divided into three main areas: best practices roundtables, where experiences in certain areas are discussed; best practices recommendations, where a particular issue is analyzed and non-binding recommendations are issued; and country reviews, where the entire competition regimes of particular countries are discussed.

Roundtables on best practices have been held for almost twenty years. Both authorities and experts make submissions that are discussed at hearings and published. The topics addressed in these roundtables vary from sectorial discussions, such as pharmaceuticals, telecommunications, energy, transportation, and consumer goods; to topical discussions, such as mergers, enforcement, cartel investigation, consumer protection, public procurement, etc.

Recommendations on best practices are multi-annual works reflecting the state-of-the art policies and practices in particular issues. These are aimed at providing guidance and ultimately promoting changes in government policies. Their latest effort is an updated version of their 1967 recommendation concerning international cooperation in investigations and proceedings. This work is the response to a survey carried out in 2013 by the organization together with the ICN, which shows that international cooperation is very limited mainly due to legal and practical limitations; it analyzes the main areas where cooperation would be helpful and the advantages and disadvantages of such cooperation. It concludes with a call for enhanced cooperation in certain policy and procedural areas. Previous recommendations refer to bid rigging in public procurement (2012), structural separation in regulated industries (2011), competition

---

When NAFTA was negotiated Mexico did not have a proper competition law and when the cooperation agreement was signed, Mexico had more than a decade of experience in enforcing its domestic legislation.

7. http://unctad.org/en/Pages/DITC/CompetitionLaw/Competition-Law-and-Policy.aspx.

assessment (2009), principles for regulatory quality and performance (2005), information exchange (2005), merger review (2005), effective action against hard-core cartels (1998), and competition policy and exempted and regulated sectors (1979).[8]

Peer reviews of countries are a detailed exercise of a particular country's legislation and policy and contain recommendations that promote public debate and changes to ensure regimes that are more effective.

The ICN work has the aim of facilitating convergence and cooperation through recommendations, manuals for case handling and enforcement, reports, templates on legislation and rules of different countries, databases, toolkits, and workshops. The ICN claims that most agencies use and distribute their materials and products, and that they actively work towards applying their recommendations. Steering Group projects refer to advocacy, outreach, international coordination, enforcement cooperation, investigative process, and work with courts and judges.[9]

Furthermore, at a regional level the establishment of common standards, guidelines, or efforts for the convergence of national regimes and coherence in the enforcement of the laws can be helpful in that it eliminates the need for developing similar documents in each jurisdiction and interpreting the differences among them. This work can save time and other resources and allows for greater convergence in the application of regimes based on similar cultural bases and legal systems.

Recommendations, guidelines, best practices and other documents may refer to the same or similar principles, procedures, or investigative tools. While these initiatives enrich the knowledge of authorities, practitioners, and academics alike it might be possible that some of this work might become irrelevant or a repetition of other efforts being made elsewhere. Therefore, it might be useful reflecting as to whether some coordination between agencies would be desirable.

[B] Cooperation in Specific Cases

This type of cooperation is particularly useful to ensure effective enforcement of different legal regimes where cross-border practices or transactions take place. When authorities agree to seek waivers for exchanging confidential information among them or to alert each other when investigations that may affect them take place or that a merger has been notified helps them to be better prepared to fulfill their legal obligations. The benefits of this type of cooperation are immediately tangible, since it allows agencies to obtain information that companies may not be willing to share with them. It is also useful in order to ensure that merger analyzes on transnational transactions do not result in contradictory rulings, where one jurisdiction may authorize the merger, others may impose remedies and/or others may deny authorization where similar market conditions prevail.[10]

8. http://www.oecd.org/daf/competition/recommendations.htm.
9. http://www.internationalcompetitionnetwork.org/.
10. One would have to recognize cases where completely different market conditions prevail in different countries. For example, the deal involving Anheuser Busch InBev and Cerveceria

Given the nature of international cartel investigations or merger proceedings, close cooperation among authorities is essential to ensure effective application of competition regimes. Otherwise, companies would be inclined to cooperate only with the most efficient agencies or the authorities based on the jurisdictions where their main economic interests are and would try to block efforts by authorities with less investigative resources or where they have small subsidiaries. For instance, lack of cooperation with the Mexican CFC by two merging companies in an international transaction required such authority to seek information with its counterparts and to obtain the types of remedies being offered in other countries and share this information with other Latin American agencies. As the companies did not offer such level of commitment, the result was a negative resolution on the part of the Mexican authority leading to a cascade of negative resolutions in the entire region. At the end, these companies ultimately offered the same level of remedies they had submitted in more advanced jurisdictions and obtained positive resolutions, but only after months of discussions that have kept the entire international obligation pending.

[C] Capacity Building

Given the size of their economies, the experience of their enforcers, the many trial-and-error processes among authorities, or the particular formation of their staff members, some agencies are better equipped to look at the right places to seek tools to help them find solutions in applying the law. Through capacity building, better and more coherent outcomes can be obtained and networks can be formed. While the most obvious "teachers" lay in the US and the EU, mid-sized authorities, such as the Mexican one, can share their experiences and disclose some of their methods to their smaller counterparts, saving them the time and resources when applying the law in particular instances.

This is especially useful for agencies that, given their small economy, do not have that many cases, as well for others that do not exclusively deal with competition, but also with consumer protection, telecommunications, or other issues preventing them from specializing in merger proceedings, studies of relevant market, coordinated effects, or other very specific tools required to apply competition law and regulations.

However, unless public servants who benefit from this capacity building are offered some stability, this type of cooperation may only provide for short-term benefits that will be lost as they leave their agencies.

§5.03 CONCLUSIONS

As globalization becomes more intense, greater cooperation among antitrust authorities increases in importance. Multinational, regional, and bilateral arrangements often

---

Modelo required structural remedies in order to be approved in the United States, where in Mexico it was a relatively straightforward case of a company changing hands with no further competition concern.

share similar features, and authorities can choose from different models and decide what type of cooperation they prefer.

Multinational, regional, and bilateral cooperation have some complementarities. Whereas the wider-ranging fora might be helpful in providing state-of-the art recommendations on particular topics, regional cooperation might be helpful in translating these principles into guidelines that are most suited for particular realities, and bilateral cooperation is most useful in solving particular cases. Having said that, the establishment of recommendations, guidelines, and best practices might result in forum shopping. One may question whether this is the optimal outcome or whether coordination in some areas (e.g., recommendations or guidelines) might be more useful.

Bilateral and regional cooperation is, in our view, the most immediately relevant tool that agencies have and the one where results are more readily visible.

Technical cooperation through capacity building is useful for smaller agencies, but only provides for short-term relief.

CHAPTER 6

Histories of Competition Law in Latin America

Andrés Palacios Lleras & Juan David Gutiérrez

In this chapter we present a characterization of three types of competition law regimes in Latin America that have followed each other since the second half of the twentieth century. Each type, or "layer," corresponds not only to a particular historical period, but also to a particular group of ideas about competition and of regulation. First, we conclude that there are important differences among the different competition law regimes of the region. Such heterogeneity may be determined by a range of factors, such as the enforcers' technical capacity, their independence, or the overall ideology of each regime; in any case, there is little empirical evidence that accounts for these divergences. Second, the reforms introduced during the 1990s were not as sweeping as the conventional narrative suggests. The second generation regimes resemble their forebearers in important aspects, such as relying on public enforcement through competition agencies. Third, there are important aspects of Latin American competition law where there is preciously little research, for example, about the early adoption and implementation of competition laws, and the evaluation of the impact of antitrust enforcement.

§6.01 INTRODUCTION

The history of Latin American Competition Law (hereinafter LACL) is usually described as a process of improvement through continuous legal reform.[1] The typical

1. Twenty-three countries in Latin America and the Caribbean have enacted national competition laws: Argentina, Barbados, Bolivia, Brazil, Chile, Colombia, Costa Rica, Curaçao, Ecuador, El Salvador, Guyana, Honduras, Jamaica, Mexico, Nicaragua, Panama, Paraguay, Peru, Dominican Republic, The Bahamas, Uruguay, Trinidad & Tobago and Venezuela. The scope of The

history can be summarized as follows: between the 1950s and the 1990s, few Latin American States had competition law regimes (hereinafter CLRs). The few CLRs in place were misguided, too general and seldom enforced.[2] This resulted from the adherence to economic policies that favored protectionism over competition. However, the crises of the 1980s led to a reexamination of the importance of competition for Latin America's development. As a result, during the 1990s, new CLRs were adopted and previously existing regimes were amended by drawing from the institutions and the ideas that characterized competition law and policy in the United States (US), the European Union (EU), and European national states such as Spain. Also, the negotiation of trade agreements of Latin American countries with the US and the EU between the 2000s and the mid-2010s contributed to the amendment of the regimes in place.[3] While this process has been more successful in some states than in others, the trend suggests that Latin America now embraces competition in ways that are congenial with how it is implemented in other states.[4]

In this chapter we rely partially on this narrative and present a characterization of the three types of CLRs that have followed each other since the second half of the

Bahamas's competition law is limited exclusively to telecommunications. Supranational competition laws have been enacted in the framework of the Andean Community of Nations (CAN), the Caribbean Community (CARICOM), and the *Mercado Común del Sur* (Mercosur). For an overview of the competition law systems in Latin America and the Caribbean, *see*, *Derecho de la competencia en América Latina y el Caribe: Evolución y principales retos*, in "Anuario de Derecho de la Competencia" 123–152 (La Ley, Paraguay, 2021).

2. For example, according to G. Coloma from 1923 to 1980 only four cases were decided by the Argentinian competition authority. German Coloma, *The Argentine Competition Law and Its Enforcement*, in *Competition Law and Policy* 94 (Fox & Sokol eds, Latin America, Hart Publishing, UK 2009).
3. For example, this is the case of Peru, El Salvador, and Dominican Republic. Due to the Association Agreement between the EU and the Central American region, Guatemala agreed to enact a national competition law by 2016. Several bills have been studied by the National Congress of Guatemala but none of them have been approved up to date.
4. The best example of this narrative is, Julián Peña, *The Consolidation of Competition Law in Latin America* 2 CPI Antitrust Chron. 2 (2011). More critical views can be found in Julián Peña, *The Limits of Competition Law in Latin America*, in *The Global Limits of Competition Law* (D. Sokol, & Ioannis Lianos eds, Stanford U. Press 2012), and especially De León, Ignacio, *An Institutional Assessment of Antitrust Policy: The Latin American Experience* (Kluwer Law International 2009) (providing a historical approach to the roots of the problems of CLRs). Overall criticisms of how the CLRs interact with larger legal issues can be found in Ana Maria Alvarez & Pierre Horna, *Implementing Competition Law and Policy in Latin America: The Role of Technical Assistance*. 83 Chi.-Kent L. Rev. 91 (2008). Analysis of recent developments can be found in Alfonso Miranda Londoño *Competition Law in Latin America Main Trends and Features*. CEDEC Working Paper (2012), Carlos Pablo Marquez, *Competition Law in Latin America and the Caribbean: Statutory Harmonization and Convergence* (January 10, 2010). Luis Fernando Álvarez-Londoño. *Últimas Tendencias En Derecho De La Competencia En América Latina*. 116 Vniversitas 247 (2008) and Juan D. Gutiérrez, *Competition Laws in Latin America and Caribbean: History, Enforcement and Amendments*. Pontificia Universidad Javeriana, Competition Law & Economics Working Paper 07-05 (2007). Critical appraisals from a policy perspective can be found in Moisés Naím & Joseph S. Tulchin (eds) *Competition Policy, Deregulation, and Modernization in Latin America* (Lynne Rienner Publishers 1999). Coate, Malcolm B., et.al. *Antitrust In Latin America: Regulating Government and Business*. 24 U. of Miami Inter-Am. L. Rev. 37 (1992). Rafael German, *Latin American Antitrust*. Law. Am. 1 (1982).

twentieth century.[5] Each type, or "layer," corresponds not only to a particular historical period, but also to a particular group of ideas about competition and regulation. As a metaphor, the "layers" are useful for describing legal changes and, in particular, changes involving the development of new legal materials.[6] By endorsing this "layered" view, we highlight particular elements that have shaped the evolution of LACL, leaving the endorsement of normative judgments to our readers.

§6.02 THE PIECES AND THE WHOLE

Our research of the history of LACL suggests that there are at least three distinctive layers of legal materials, involving both abrupt and smooth changes.[7] Each layer has a set of distinctive features that are worth comparing in order to appreciate their own characteristic elements. We consider that it is important to consider (i) the principles and purposes that inspire the CLRs (or "rationales"), (ii) the scope of the laws and their application, (iii) the degree of independence of the enforcement institutions, and (iv) relative size and operation. In what follows, we briefly describe the different layers, characterize each of these features, and offer some brief examples. Table 6.1 offers a summary.

Table 6.1 "Layers" of Competition Law Regimes by Traits[8]

	Developmental (1910s–1990)	*Neoliberal (1990–2000)*	*Institutionalist (2000–Present Day)*
Rationales	Social justice, promote national development.	Promote economic welfare, beneficial for consumers.	Promote economic welfare and national competitiveness.
Scope	General prohibitions and discretionary exemptions.	General and specific prohibitions, limited fines, merger review provisions.	General and specific prohibitions, increased fines, leniency regimes, new investigative powers for agencies, incentivize private enforcement,

5. We rely on this periodization and some of the traits identified in Peña, *supra*. (2011), but nonetheless we are skeptical of the sense of improvement this narrative conveys, and in general with concept of "progress" in social science.
6. Palacios Lleras, Andres. PhD dissertation (In file with authors).
7. Besides consulting secondary sources and reflecting on our own experience as competition law practitioners, in September 2014 we conducted ten structured (written) interviews with colleagues from five different countries (El Salvador, Dominican Republic, Colombia, Ecuador, and Guatemala). The names of the interviewees are not disclosed, but all of them have first-hand knowledge of the legislative and enforcement history in their respective countries. They draw their insights from their active role as government officials, legal advisors, or scholars.
8. Peña *supra* (2011), Palacios Lleras (*supra*).

	Developmental (1910s–1990)	*Neoliberal (1990–2000)*	*Institutionalist (2000–Present Day)*
			inclusion of new agents and markets subject to law, cooperation with other competition agencies, and prosecution of international cartels.
Independence	Dependent enforcement agencies	Semi-autonomous agencies, timid separation of functions.	Autonomous agencies, clear(er) separation of functions.
Composition, size and operation	Limited resources, lawyerly staff.	Limited resources, staff of lawyers and few economists.	More resources, staff increase, lawyers and economists.
Sources of resistance[9]	Business associations	Business associations, sector-specific firms (particularly agroindustry).	Business associations, sector-specific firms (particularly agroindustry and "national champions"). Exceptionally sectors with executive government.
Country specific cases (examples)	Mexico (1917, 1934), Argentina (1923, 1946), Chile (1959), Colombia (1955, 1959), Brazil (1962)	Chile (1973, 1999), Colombia (1991, 1992), Mexico (1992), Venezuela (1992), Brazil (1994), Costa Rica (1994), Argentina (1999).	Chile (2002, 2003, 2009, 2015), El Salvador (2004, 2007), Mexico (2006, 2011, 2013, 2014, 2017), Colombia (2009, 2014), Peru (2008), Panama (2007), Dominican Republic (2008), Brazil (2011, 2012), Peru (2015), Chile (2016), Argentina (2018), Costa Rica (2019).

[A] Developmental (1910s–1990s)

The first CLRs appeared after a series of constitutional changes that, by the mid-twentieth century, paved the way for the regulatory developmental state.[10] These

9. The information regarding the resistance to LACLs enactment and enforcement is drawn from both local press accounts and personal interviews conducted by the authors.
10. In doing so, the first CLRs coincide with the State-led development that dominated economic planning in Latin America between 1930s and 1960s. E. Cárdenas, J. A. Ocampo, & R. Thorp,

regimes had three central characteristics. First, they mixed developmental concerns with issues about fairness and equity. As a result, they contained provisions that condemned certain anticompetitive practices depending on how they affected key economic sectors and whether they amounted to a form of abuse to the detriment of local producers or citizens at large. Second, the provisions of these regimes gave considerable discretion to the enforcement bodies by creating strong prohibitions and ample exemptions. These allowed enforcers to determine whether a particular practice should be punished, exempted, or addressed via other mechanisms (such as imposing price controls). Enforcers could issue rulings imposing fines and orders to cease and desist. Finally, the enforcement bodies had little political and budgetary autonomy; more often than not, they were administrative agencies that were attached to a ministry, the appointment of its leading official was done by the president or the ministries, and their staff was minimal. Overall, these first CLRs gave LACL an administrative ethos that continues to define it today. Moreover, some of the provisions enacted during this period continue to be in force today, such as Article 1 of Colombia's law 155 of 1959.[11]

An interesting example of this type of regime can be appreciated in Colombia's law 155 of 1959. As its predecessor (Decree 2061 of 1955), this law establishes a general prohibition addressing anticompetitive agreements and unilateral practices taking place in different economic sectors that establish "inequitable prices at the expense of consumers." Notably, the law also provides to the government the discretion to exempt firms or sectors from the application of this prohibition if such application affects their stability.[12] Both the prohibition and the exemption remain in force.[13]

We contend that the development and salience of the initial CLRs was determined by the capacity of different social actors to oppose, delay, or limit their application. There is some evidence from Colombia, for example, pointing to resistance from business associations to the enactment of law 155 of 1959.[14] However, given the ethos of the regulation of this period, we consider that firms affected by the first CLRs were most likely able to secure an exemption depending on their political leverage. Also, the little research on this particular period makes it difficult to understand the interrelation between competition and other policies.

Introduction, in *An Economic History of Twentieth-Century Latin America*, vol. 3 (Cárdenas, Ocampo, and Thorp eds, New York, Palgrave 2000).

11. Palacios Lleras, *supra*.
12. For a description of the evolution and implementation of the so-called block exemption in Colombia, *see* J. D. Gutiérrez, "Protección de la competencia en las cadenas de valor agropecuarias en Colombia, 1994–2015" in "El desarrollo equitativo, competitivo y sostenible del sector agropecuario en Colombia" (C. G. Cano, A. M. Iregui, M. T. Ramírez, y A, M. Tribín eds., 603–657, Bogotá: Banco de la República y CAF - Banco de Desarrollo de América Latina, 2016).
13. Colombia. Ley 155 de 1959. Article 1.
14. J. Cortazar, *Colombian Competition Law Regime*, In: *Concurrences* N° 2-2012.

[B] Neoliberal (1990s–2000)

The fiscal crisis of the 1980s contributed to the demise of developmental ideas and policies that characterized Latin America until then.[15] In that decade many of the region's economic problems were attributed to the execution of the developmental model in the 1950s and 1960s.[16] Conversely, the ideology that promoted open trade and market-oriented policies became dominant in the region by mid-1980s and during the 1990s.[17] In doing so, it also opened the door for new reflections about the importance of protecting competition.

The second generation of CLRs had three central characteristics. First, these regimes drew considerably from law and economics perspectives originating in the US and the EU. These regimes eschew considerations about development in favor of focusing on efficiency and consumer welfare. As such, they can no longer be considered part of or complimentary to development policies. Second, most of these regimes focus on anticompetitive agreements, unilateral conducts, and mergers. Just as the regimes of the previous generation, they have general provisions condemning anticompetitive behaviors, but they have specific provisions forbidding anticompetitive agreements (such as cartels) and unilateral conducts (such as predatory prices), and in some instances, a merger review regime. Third, the enforcement bodies were also modified with the purpose of fostering some political independence and technical prowess.[18] These second generation of CLRs gave to LACL the distinctive technocratic ethos it currently enjoys.

A good example of the approach to competition of this period can be evidenced in México's 1992 *Ley Federal de Competencia Económica*. Several aspects of this law are notorious, of which we briefly mention three. First, the law is straightforward in stating an economic welfare approach toward competition and, therefore, at odds with the more social justice rationale of Article 28 of the Mexican constitution.[19] Second, the law incorporates foreign theories about economic analyses that are consistent with this approach, like the distinction between absolute and relative monopolistic practices based on the welfare effects that certain practices may have despite their effects on

15. The State-led development policies applied in Latin America were characterized by an increase of the Government's economic intervention in the markets through foreign trade (tariff and non-tariff) and exchange restrictions, a direct entrepreneurial role, and a closer relationship with businesses. E. Cardoso & A. Helwege *Latin America's Economy: Diversity, Trends and Conflict* (Cambridge, MA: MIT Press 1992).
16. Cfr. R. Thorp, *Progress, Poverty and Exclusion: An Economic History of Latin America in the 20th century* 181(Washington, DC: IDB 1998). J. L. Love, *The Rise and Fall of Structuralism*, in *Economic Doctrines in Latin America* 101 (Valpy FitzGerald and Rosemary Thorp eds, New York, Palgrave MacMillan 2005). However, contemporary economists such as D. Rodrik, E. Cárdenas, J. A. Ocampo, and R. Thorp have argued that the problems caused by macroeconomic or financial mismanagement ("macro-mess") should be distinguished from the direct effects implementation of the "structuralist" model.
17. R. Thorp (1998), *supra*. E. Cárdenas, J. A. Ocampo, and R. Thorp (2000), *supra*, p. 4.
18. With the exceptions of Chile, Jamaica, and Panama that established judicial antitrust enforcement systems in which the powers to prosecute and adjudicate are separated and allocated to different state authorities.
19. Ley Mexico, Federal de Competencia Económica (1992). Article 2.

rivalry.[20] Third, the law created a specialized enforcement agency that was deemed to be semi-autonomous from other administrative institutions.[21]

The fates of the neoliberal CLRs adopted during this "layer" were quite varied. All the new CLRs faced considerable difficulties; we contend that the political support they received within and outside the government determined their capacity to overcome them. As in the past, business associations and large firms resisted the enforcement of the CLRs; however, some government sectors also contested the development of these regimes. Mexico and Chile provides interesting examples of the challenges competition law enforcement faced during the 1990s. In the former, the *Comisión Federal de Competencia* struggled with the recurrent use of *amparo* actions by investigated parties before the judiciary that prevented it from continuing with its investigations and collecting fines.[22] In the latter, the return to democracy in 1990 led to a profound challenge to the legitimacy of the *Fiscalía Nacional Económica*.[23] In other jurisdictions, the initial support for neoliberal CLRs waned during the years following their enactment, such as in Argentina, Peru, and Venezuela. Especially in Argentina and Venezuela, their governments withdrew the initial support given to their CLRs, and by the late 1990s they relied considerably more on price controls. Finally, during this period strong interest groups curtailed the birth of a new breed of CLRs, mainly in Central America, the Caribbean, and the smallest economics of South America.

[C] Institutionalist (2000: Present Day)

The CLRs adopted or amended during the 1990s aimed to establish competition as a guiding principle of all economic activity. However, the activities of the enforcement bodies faced important problems that prevented them from accomplishing their tasks effectively. Among those problems are (i) their political dependency, (ii) the absence of a deterrent effect, and (iii) the lack of adequate staff (especially economists) and overall political support.[24] Hence, we refer to this "layer" as "institutionalist" because the new rules focus on strengthening the institutional foundations of enforcement to improve its effectiveness. In doing so, this new layer involves a continuation of previous trends.

This third "layer" has its own characteristics. First, the new rules adopted involved both local and regional processes; while the rules were adopted by the

20. *Ibid.*, Articles 8 & 9, 10–13.
21. *Ibid.*, Articles 23–29.
22. Fernando Sánchez Ugarte, *Diez Años De Política De Competencia*. In *La Primera Década De La Comisión Federal De Competencia*. Comisión Federal de Competencia (2004).
23. Palacios Lleras, *supra*. Also, Bernedo, *supra*, pp. 135–149 (referring the critics charged against the *Fiscalía Nacional Económica* for its enforcement activities and the responses by the government).
24. For example, the current competition law in Argentina, enacted in the year 1999 through the Act No. 25,156, created a new antitrust authority, the *National Court for the Defense of Competition*, which has not yet been installed and so the National Commission for the Defense of Competition has been maintained in its place.

relevant authorities of each state, they were often conceived and discussed in specialized regional forums comprised of enforcement bodies, global and regional experts, and global institutions. In particular, the Organization for Economic Cooperation and Development (OECD) and the Inter-American Development Bank (IDB) became a major source for devising and recommending particular amendment to specific CLRs via activities such as peer reviews and summits. Just as well, since the 2010s there have been many cooperation activities between Latin American States and other states in the Americas, Europe, and Asia. This has contributed to the development of joint, cross border prosecution of cartels. For example, the competition authorities of Brazil, Colombia, and Chile have recently prosecuted international cartels cases involving products and services as varied as refrigeration compressors (Brazil, 2012), diapers (Colombia 2014), and shipping services (Chile 2015).[25] Second, the amendments of the 2000s and after focus mostly on two issues, namely improving the technical capacity and political independence of the enforcement bodies and prosecuting cartels. In particular, the changes observed grant more resources to enforcement bodies and modify their structure to grant them more independence and to separate decision making from prosecution. They also adopt harsher fines (in some instances, criminal punishments), more intrusive investigatory faculties (e.g., to conduct dawn raids) and leniency regimes, in order to better fight cartels. (Leniency regimes were crucial in the prosecution of the cartel cases mentioned earlier.) However, not all the changes are in the same direction, for in some cases the applicable rules grant new exceptions.[26] Third, local competition authorities have embarked in making their efforts very well-known among their populations mostly through the use of mass media. For example, the competition authority of El Salvador launched in 2013 a mobile application that allows citizens to obtain information about antitrust cases and share the information through social media. Other competition authorities of Latin America, particularly Mexico, Ecuador, and Colombia also use social media like Twitter to divulge their activities and engage with citizens.

A good example of these reforms is Chile's law 19.911 of 2003. This law reflects the discussions that were taking place regarding the overall legitimacy of the competition law regime in place during the 1990s. It created a specialized judicial tribunal that replaced the previous commissions, which were in charge of reviewing anticompetitive practices and imposing fines. In doing so, it further contributed to the separation of investigative and decision-making functions, and the tribunal itself asserted its independence when discussing competition law issues. The law also raised the applicable fines substantially.[27]

25. It is worth highlighting a case presented by the *Fiscalía Nacional Económica* on Jan. 27, 2015, to the Competition Tribunal of Chile against six vehicle-shipping companies from Chile, Korea, and Japan. It probably represents the highest international profile case of the Chilean authority. The authority requested the tribunal fines that amount to USD 75 million (the second highest in history) and its grounds rely on the evidence facilitated by two leniency applicants. Global Competition Review, "Chile condemns international shipping cartel," Jan. 30, 2015.
26. For example, in the Andean Community, Panama, and Colombia.
27. Chile, law 19.911 of 2003.

As in the previous two "layers," business associations, agroindustry sectors, and recurring defendants are major sources of resistance toward the CLRs, and both political lobbying and strategic litigation are part of their strategies. In some countries, however, a lack of political support for competition continued to place competition well behind other policies and concerns. Moreover, in a few countries, another strategy has consisted in introducing new or further exceptions to the enforcement of competition law that benefits certain sectors, particularly agricultural.[28] Finally, in several new jurisdictions, the vocal opposition to the enactment of CLRs has transformed into a silent resistance to the establishment and improvement of new competition authorities.

Dominican Republic, El Salvador, and Guatemala exemplify the last point. The case of the Dominican Republic is quite striking: despite the fact that the law was enacted in 2008, the law only came into full effect in early 2017. In the case of El Salvador, Article 136 of the 1950 Constitution established that economic freedom would be guaranteed by the state, and Article 110 of the 1983 Constitution prohibited monopolistic practices. Moreover, one of the few economic points that the government and guerrillas included in the 1992 peace agreements was that the government must prevent monopolistic practices.[29] In spite of all these antecedents, successive bills failed to be approved in Congress, and only until 2004, the competition law was enacted and its enforcement started approximately three years later. Finally, in Guatemala, despite the fact that Article 130 of the 1985 Constitution mandates the development of laws that prohibit monopolistic practices, none of the bills presented before the Congress have been openly and thoroughly debated; Guatemala remains as one of the few countries of Central America, with Belize, that lacks a CLR. It seems that part of the strategy of the opponents consists on preventing competition law and policy to become a priority in the national economic agenda.

There are two cases that we consider merit special consideration to illustrate the heterogeneity of LACLs in this period—México and Venezuela. As we mentioned earlier, the Mexican CLR adopted in the 1990s faced considerable difficulties in terms of effective enforcement. The CLR was amended first in 2006 and then in 2011 precisely to address these issues by reinforcing the institutional capabilities of the *Comisión Federal de Competencia Económica*. However, before these reforms "settled in" they were superseded by a new set of reforms in 2013 and 2014. The latter reforms included an amendment to Article 28 of the 1917 Mexican constitution and a new competition statute (albeit quite similar to the previous one). Notably, they elevate to constitutional level the competition enforcement agency, create an enforcement agency exclusive for the telecom sector, and enable the enforcers to remove "barriers to competition." As a result of these amendments, the Mexican CLR acquired a regulatory outlook. The case

28. Juan D. Gutiérrez, *Competition Law Goals in Agricultural Markets: A Latin American Perspective*, in *The Goals of Competition Law* 450–475 (D. Zimmerman ed., Edward Elgar, UK 2012). Juan D. Gutiérrez, *Agricultural Exceptions to Competition Law*, in *Revista de Derecho de la Competencia* 173–287 (CEDEC X, Bogotá: Universidad Javeriana, Facultad de Ciencias Jurídicas, 2010).
29. Daniel Olmedo, *Pasado y presente de la defensa de la competencia*, May 3, 2012, available at: http://www.elsalvador.com/mwedh/nota/nota_opinion.asp?idCat=50839&idArt=6865356.

of Venezuela is quite different. During the 1990s, the Venezuelan enforcement agency became well regarded among the Latin American competition law community. However, Hugo Chavez's government did not share such regard, and withdrew its support to this agency. In 2014, a new competition law was enacted, and like its predecessors, it grants the government considerable discretion regarding its enforcement. There is very little information about the enforcement activities undergone by the *Superintendencia Antimonopolio*; in any case, the contrast between the enforcement activities taking place in these two countries evidences the diversity regarding CLRs in this region.

The advent of the "Neo Brandeis" movement in the US may bring about important changes to LACL.[30] The current regimes are starting to exhibit symptoms of fatigue, among other things, because they have not been as successful as expected in safeguarding consumers from anticompetitive behaviors. Consider for example leniency regimes; just as in other regions, leniency filings are declining in the Americas. According to the US Justice Department, the number of cases filed and of corporations and individuals charged has diminished since 2015.[31] In México, leniency applications dropped from the levels of previous years to levels undisclosed by the competition authority; arguably, this has been because said authority removed the benefits to applicants that did not cooperate fully.[32] A debate about a related issue took place in Chile during 2020. In that year, the Supreme Court of Justice overruled a decision by the competition tribunal that relied on the prosecutor's decision to extend the benefits of leniency to the organizer of a cartel.[33] While Chilean law allows this outcome, it was received negatively by practitioners, who claim that it creates unnecessary uncertainty. After all, leniency has not been central to the prosecution of cartels and is not necessarily well understood and accepted, as acknowledged by the cartel prosecutor.[34] Finally, the markets and political systems of Latin America and the Caribbean are still characterized by economic and political concentration. In this vein, reports published by international organizations such as the United Nations Development Programme and The World Bank, have recently pointed out that antitrust enforcement should be strengthened in order to curb anticompetitive practices in the region.[35]

30. See Lina Khan, *The New Brandeis Movement: America's Antimonopoly Debate*. 9 Journal of European Competition Law and Practice (2018).
31. Department of Justice. Criminal Enforcement Trend Charts Criminal Enforcement Trends Charts through Fiscal Year 2020. Available at https://www.justice.gov/atr/criminal-enforcement-fine-and-jail-charts. Accessed on October 31.
32. Garcia Santos, et al., *Mexico*, in *The Public Competition Enforcement Review* (Aidan Synnott ed., 13th edition, UK, 2021).
33. Corte Suprema, causa 1531-2018 of January 6, 2020. Available at: https://www.fne.gob.cl/wp-content/uploads/2020/01/sent_cs_01_2019.pdf (Accessed on October 31, 2021).
34. Ricardo Riesco "*Dia de la Competencia 2020*" Fiscalía Nacional Económica (2020). Available at https://www.fne.gob.cl/wp-content/uploads/2020/12/Discurso-DDLC-2020.pdf (Accessed on October 30, 2021)
35. See, UNDP. "Regional Human Development Report 2021 | Trapped: High Inequality and Low Growth in Latin America and the Caribbean." United Nations Development Programme (UNDP), 2021. Martínez, Martha, Tanja Goodwin, Dennis Sanchez, y Noella Carreras. "Fixing Markets, Not Prices: Policy Options to Tackle Economic Cartels in Latin America and the Caribbean", The World Bank, 2021.

§6.03 CONCLUSIONS

Our review of the history of LACL is suggestive and prevents us from making definitive conclusions about the effectiveness of the different legal institutions involved. Our analysis is (mostly) descriptive, but we offer three considerations that might be useful for the further historical understanding of competition law in this region.

First, the overall institutional make-up of LACL suggests that there are important differences among the different CLRs of the region.[36] While certainly there are similarities, the institutions and their enforcement are not uniform across the region. Such heterogeneity may be determined by a range of factors, such as the enforcers' technical capacity, their independence, or the overall ideology of each regime; in any case, there is little empirical evidence that accounts for these divergences.

Second, the changes introduced during the 1990s were not as sweeping as the typical narrative suggests. This is not to say that they were not important; consider, for example, the change in rationales (from "developmental" to "neoliberal") of the CLRs. However, the second generation regimes resemble their forebearers in important aspects. For example, they continue to rely on administrative agencies and their procedures, instead of establishing different enforcement systems that could be based on general or specialized courts. Such reliance highlights the importance that executive branches have in Latin American regulation, despite their many problematic issues. It also furthers the idea that competition law enforcement requires highly specialized institutions manned by well-trained legal and economic consultants.[37]

Third, there are important aspects of LACL where there is preciously little research. In general, thorough research on the history of LACL is rather scarce.[38] Moreover, an evident "research vacuum" concerns the first "layer" presented here. It has become common place to say that the first CLRs were seldom enforced, although a few thorough investigations suggest that they were actually enforced on a regular basis.[39] A second "research vacuum" involves measuring the effects of the decisions taken by the enforcement agencies. Indeed, there is information about the resources

36. An informal history of LACL is accounted by the Latin American law and policy blog www.lalibrecompetencia.com. Since 2007, nineteen scholars and practitioners of different nationalities write blog posts about the trends in their respective country.
37. Palacios Lleras, *supra*.
38. Notable exceptions are Ignacio De León, *An Institutional Assessment of Antitrust Policy: The Latin American Experience* (Kluwer Law International, The Netherlands 2009) and *Latin American Competition Law and Policy: A Policy in Search of Identity* (Kluwer Law International 2001). Palacios Lleras, Andrés, *Competition Law in Latin America: Markets, Politics, Expertise.* Ph.D. dissertation available at https://discovery.ucl.ac.uk/id/eprint/1529869/ (Accessed October 31, 2021). There are other case studies for individual countries. Regarding Chile, *see* e.g., Patricio Bernedo, *Historia de la libre competencia en Chile, 1959* (Fiscalía Nacional Económica, Santiago de Chile 2013). Other case studies that are worth noting include Brazil, El Salvador and Colombia: Francisco Ribiero & Marcelo Maciel Torres, *History of the Competition Policy in Brazil: 1930–2010*, 57 Antitrust Bull., no. 2/ Summer 207–257 (2012). Arrieta de Carsana, Liliam, *Evolución histórica de la legislación histórica de competencia en El Salvador*, in "Revista Cuadernos," Universidad Dr. José Matías Delgado, El Salvador, 2013, pp. 56–89. Miranda Londoño, Alfonso, *Origen y evolución del derecho de la competencia en Colombia. La Ley 155 de 1959 y su legado*, in Rev. Derecho Competencia. Bogotá (Colombia), vol. 6, n° 6, 65–148, 2011.
39. *See* e.g., Dale B. Furnish, *Chilean Antitrust Law*, 19 Am. J. Comp. L. 464 (1971).

and staff of the competition authorities, but little analysis about their impact. The only competition agency of the region that periodically evaluates the impact of its enforcement activities is Mexico's Federal Economic Competition Agency (COFECE). Hence, we simply do not know if the fines and orders imposed by the enforcement activities contributed in positive ways to making markets more competitive and efficient or, on the contrary, they stifled competition and failed to address crucial issues. Hence, we remain cautious in stating that the legal reforms have had a positive effect on different sectors and markets.

The history of LACL is a field that has sparked little interest among the legal community. There are many aspects that deserve further attention, and the established histories could be improved and amended. More importantly, further research could provide more comprehensive understandings of how this field of law works, and how it can be improved. If anything, we are certain that a lack of awareness about the history of this field opens the door to facile presumptions and erroneous policy recommendations.

CHAPTER 7

Latin America's Digital Markets: Competition or Regulation?

Manuel A. Abdala, Alejandro Lombardi & Lucía Quesada[*]

In the last decade, digital markets have become the center of the debate among competition experts and practitioners. There is an increasing number of antitrust investigations against large digital platforms. However, there is a debate as to whether competition policy is the right tool to deal with the competition problems associated with large digital platforms. The United States and the European Union are currently discussing new legislative proposals to impose ex ante *regulation on key digital platforms. Latin America is not a stranger to this debate, although, countries in the region are taking a cautious, case-by-case approach to this problem. In this chapter, we argue that Latin American countries have good reasons to adopt a conservative approach, at least until there is further clarity as to what is the right regulatory model to follow. While the costs of early adoption of an unproven regulatory model can be substantial, the benefits of rushing to adopt a position in this debate can be limited for Latin American countries. Until there is a clearer picture, there are opportunities to mitigate potential consumer harm.*

§7.01 INTRODUCTION

Over the past decades, the increasing relevance of digital trade and services has created numerous new challenges to competition policy and antitrust authorities.

---

* The authors' views are their own and do not represent the views of other experts at Compass Lexecon or its clients.

Currently, there is worldwide debate on whether the competition regime needs to be adapted or complemented to deal with these challenges. Some jurisdictions, notably Europe and the US, have taken initial steps to address this issue and established initial proposals to regulate digital markets.

Latin American countries are starting to think about what path they should follow. While much of the competition concerns are similar to those faced in developed countries, some issues are specific to Latin America. Global digital platforms such as Google and Facebook pose similar challenges across the world. The relevance of digital platforms with less global reach, however, differs across countries, making it necessary to analyze some competition issues at a local level from scratch. Latin American countries often have limited resources to perform complex analyses. Moreover, Latin American countries tend to have weaker institutions than developed countries, and political economy issues interfere with regulatory effectiveness and credibility.

In this context, what should Latin American countries do to address the challenges of digital markets? Should they embrace the regulatory wave or should they keep relying on competition enforcement tools? A sensible answer to these questions requires an analysis of the pros and cons of the different alternatives that consider the specificities of the region.

In this chapter, we first analyze the current status of the debate around competition in digital markets to identify the challenges faced by Latin American countries. In doing so, we revisit the competition concerns surrounding digital platforms and the challenges in dealing with such issues with the existing tools from the antitrust legislation and standard practices. Next, we provide an overview of the recent proposals in Europe and the US to address those issues. Finally, we discuss whether Latin American countries should start thinking about their own proposals. We offer some remarks about the challenges Latin American countries face in this debate and conclude by explaining why Latin America may benefit from following a conservative, case-by-case approach until there is further clarity about the proper regulatory model to adopt.

§7.02 THE COMPETITION VERSUS REGULATION DEBATE IN DIGITAL MARKETS

[A] Competition Risks in the Digital World

The digital world comprises a heterogeneous set of platforms that enable economic and social interactions. There are different economic elements about the way these platforms operate that may pose competition concerns.

In a report prepared for the European Commission (EC), Crémer et al. (2019) identified three key characteristics of the digital economy that could create strong competitive advantages to incumbent platforms. These are (a) extremely-high economies of scale, (b) network externalities, and (c) the ability to gather large amounts of personal data.[1] To this list, Furman et al. (2019), in a report prepared for the UK government, add another characteristic: (d) demand limits to switching.[2]

Each of these features, and more so all of them collectively, can create strong disadvantages for entrants and prevent market contestability. The concern is that a more efficient or innovative player might not successfully enter the market if it cannot attract a sufficiently large number of users, which, in turn, becomes difficult when high switching costs are involved.

These factors also imply that digital markets will end up showing high levels of concentration and a trend toward having a few, very large, global players. While such a trend is driven by economic efficiency considerations, much like in the case of natural monopolies, concerns arise regarding the potential anticompetitive behavior of dominant firms seeking to either (1) maintain their dominant position or (2) extend their market power to related or adjacent markets (leverage or self-preferencing).

As to large platforms' potential pre-emptive behavior, there have been several remarkable acquisitions of new entrants by dominant market players over the past decade.[3] In most cases, those new entrants were not providing precisely the same services as the acquirer, arguably not operating in the same relevant market, and even not generating revenues. On the other hand, in some cases, the target firm could become a direct competitor to the acquirer in the future after achieving a sufficiently large scale. The literature nowadays calls this kind of acquisition a "killer acquisition,"[4] a term coined by Cunningham, Ederer, and Ma (2021) in the context of the pharmaceutical industry.[5]

Regarding the risk of leverage of market power, the digital industry has a long history of cases of cross-market abuses. Starting from the Microsoft-Netscape browser case, competition authorities worldwide have raised several concerns about the possibility of vertical abuses and favoritism. Such concerns are flourishing and encompass all relevant platforms, including digital marketplaces, search engines, and social networks, among others.[6]

---

1. Crémer, J, Y-A de Montjoye, and H. Schweitzer. 2019. "Competition Policy for the digital era: Final Report."
2. Furman, J., Coyle D., Fletcher, A., McAuley, D., and P. Mardsen. "Unlocking digital competition. Report of the Digital Competition Expert Panel".
3. Some examples are the acquisition of Instagram and WhatsApp by Facebook or the acquisition of Waze by Google.
4. Motta, M and M. Peitz. 2020. "Intervention triggers and underlying theories of harm: Expert Advice for the Impacy Assessment of a New Competition Tool."
5. Cunningham, C., F. Ederer, and S. Ma. 2021. "Killer Acquisitions." *Journal of Political Economy*. Vol. 129(3), pp. 649–702.
6. The extent of potential concerns in the digital world is extremely wide and constantly evolving. There are other potentially concerning aspects, such as algorithmic collusion that do not fit in the scheme described above. For the purpose of simplicity, we limit our description to the issues related to market power.

[B] Challenges in Dealing with Competition Concerns with the Traditional Tools

In evaluating competitive conditions in digital markets, competition authorities face multiple challenges associated with the economic complexity of the digital environment.

Evaluating competitive conditions in rapidly evolving markets of highly differentiated products and services has always been challenging, and digital markets are not an exception. Digital market boundaries are often unclear and can change rapidly, making market definition a complex exercise. In the words of Professor Salop, "platforms no doubt would argue that competition is 'just a click away.'"[7] In this dynamic environment, there is a concern that the rigorous competition policy standards might not be fast enough to prevent harm in an effective way.

Digital platforms operate in several interconnected markets at the same time (multi-sided markets). In these markets, platforms often internalize network externalities by adopting complex pricing and commercial strategies. For example, platforms usually charge only one side of the market for services while subsidizing the other side. In this context, identifying exclusionary behavior can be highly challenging. Efficient pricing policies in multi-sided markets might appear anticompetitive when we analyze each side of the market in isolation. In addition, competing platforms often have very different business models, making competition analysis even more challenging.[8]

There is also a growing concern that competition agencies are not appropriately questioning killer acquisitions simply because they do not meet their scrutiny thresholds, such as minimum turnover limits for notification. While agencies have shown flexibility to evaluate some of these mergers,[9] a debate remains whether better thresholds are required.

[C] The Debate in Europe, the UK, and the US: Are New Tools Required?

In response to these challenges, developed countries nowadays debate new proposals to tackle the issues discussed earlier. In all cases, these proposals introduce some form of specific *ex ante* regulation applicable to critical platforms in the digital arena.

In the US, a bipartisan initiative has issued a new proposed legislative agenda comprising five different bills.[10] Under the 2021 American Innovation and Choice

7. Salop, S. 2021. "Dominant Digital Platforms: Is Antitrust Up to the Task?" *The Yale Law Journal Forum*. Vol. 130, pp. 563-587.
8. This is the case, for example, of Google and Apple when competing on mobile phone operating systems.
9. For example, in the EU, the European Commission was able to review the Facebook/WhatsApp merger despite WhatsApp having a low turnover, by means of the case referral mechanism. *See* OECD. 2020. "Start-ups, Killer Acquisitions, and Merger Control – Background Note."
10. *See*, e.g., Congressman David Cicilline. "House Lawmakers Release Anti-Monopoly Agenda for "A Stronger Online Economy: Opportunity, Innovation, Choice." June 21, 2021, available at https://cicilline.house.gov/press-release/house-lawmakers-release-anti-monopoly-agenda-stronger-online-economy-opportunity; and Ghaffari, S. and S. Morrison. "What you need to know

Online Act,[11] there would be "designated platforms," which regulators would define. The act would target self-preferencing by platforms. The 2021 Platform Competition and Opportunity Act[12] would deal with killer acquisitions. It would prevent "dominant firms from acquiring competitors, potential competitors, and firms or assets that would reinforce their monopoly power." The 2021 Ending Platform Monopolies Act[13] would target conflicts of interest by cross-ownership of platforms and thereby incentives for self-preferencing. Finally, the 2021 Augmenting Compatibility and Competition by Enabling Service Switching Act[14] would target data-gathering advantages by requiring platforms to make user data interoperable and portable with other platforms.

In Europe, the 2020 Digital Markets Act (DMA) proposes a new set of rules for online platforms qualifying as "gatekeepers."[15] These are platforms with (a) a strong economic position, (b) a strong intermediation position, and (c) an entrenched durable position in the market. The DMA would impose interoperability and data sharing obligations and would prevent self-favoring by the platforms. Regarding killer acquisitions, the EC is currently assessing whether its merger regime is sufficient to force notifications of such transactions or if it needs to be adjusted. There are, however, no proposals on the table yet.[16]

In the UK, the so-called new pro-competitive regime for digital markets, launched in 2021, proposed the creation of a new "Digital Markets Unit" within the CMA.[17] The Digital Markets Unit would have the power to designate firms with "Strategic Market Status" after conducting an evidence-based assessment showing that they have substantial and entrenched market power. Firms with a Strategic Market Status would have to follow a code of conduct. The code would seek to promote (a) fair trade to prevent exploitative conduct, (b) open choices to prevent extension of market power and exclusionary conduct, and (c) trust and transparency to promote informed decisions. The Digital Markets Unit would also have the power to intervene to tackle the root causes of entrenched market power. Finally, the British government is

about the House's opening bid to rein in Big Tech." *Recode*. June 11, 2021, available at https://www.vox.com/recode/22529779/antitrust-bills-house-big-tech.

11. H.R.3816 - American Choice and Innovation Online Act, available at https://www.congress.gov/bill/117th-congress/house-bill/3816/text.
12. H.R.3826 - Platform Competition and Opportunity Act of 2021, available at https://www.congress.gov/bill/117th-congress/house-bill/3826/text?r=5&s=1.
13. H.R.3825 - Ending Platform Monopolies Act, available at https://www.congress.gov/bill/117th-congress/house-bill/3825/text.
14. All Information (Except Text) for S.2658 - ACCESS Act of 2019, available at https://www.congress.gov/bill/116th-congress/senate-bill/2658/all-info.
15. European Commission. 2020. Proposal for a REGULATION OF THE EUROPEAN PARLIAMENT AND OF THE COUNCIL on contestable and fair markets in the digital sector (Digital Markets Act), available at https://eur-lex.europa.eu/legal-content/en/TXT/?uri=COM%3A2020%3A842%3AFIN.
16. Note by the European Union to the OECD Roundtable. "Start-ups, killer acquisitions and merger control." June 2020, available at https://one.oecd.org/document/DAF/COMP/WD(2020)24/en/pdf.
17. *See* "A new pro-competitive regime for digital markets." *Gov.UK*. July 2021, available at https://www.gov.uk/government/consultations/a-new-pro-competition-regime-for-digital-markets.

currently considering a new merger regime for firms with "Strategic Market Status" in dealing with killer acquisitions.

There are evident similarities in the proposals in Europe, the US, and the UK. Notably, the three of them consider having designated entities subject to new special regulatory rules, which target self-preferencing and access to data. These, however, are still just proposals and there are likely to be amendments before they become final.[18] Many issues are still to be defined, such as exactly which platforms will fall in the category of designated entities in each jurisdiction. For example, while it is clear that the most prominent platforms such as Google and Facebook will become designated entities, it is yet unclear whether smaller platforms such as Booking.com will fall in this category. It is also unclear how new rules would be policed and enforced.

Finally, detractors of the proposals highlight the risks that they pose. The introduction of blanket conduct rules to tackle competition problems without analyzing whether a competition concern exists in each case can have obvious negative consequences, particularly in terms of incentives to innovate.

§7.03 CHALLENGES IN LATIN AMERICA: WHAT CAN WE LEARN FROM THE DIGITAL DEBATE?

Latin America is no stranger to the digital platforms debate. In the last few years, there has been a myriad of papers, blogs, conferences, and webinars in which Latin American competition experts, both practitioners, and academics, discuss how to address the challenges that digital markets pose. The lack of international consensus regarding how to adjust rules implies that there is no proven model to introduce. Despite that, competition authorities in Latin America have already faced some cases related to digital markets, and the frequency of such cases will likely increase as digital markets develop further.[19] In this context, how should Latin American competition agencies and policymakers handle digital markets?

We argue in the remainder of this chapter that, at the moment, it appears reasonable for Latin America to adopt a wait-and-see posture until there is further consensus in the developed world. Rushing to adopt one of the schemes proposed can have substantial drawbacks. At the same time, it appears that there will be opportunities for Latin American countries to mitigate the adverse effects of not having digital markets regulation early on. These include the possibility of free-riding on developed countries' legislation and relying on the protection offered by competition policy.

---

18. On March 25, 2022, the Council of the European Union and the European Parliament reached a provisional agreement on DMA. *See* "Digital Markets Act (DMA): agreement between the Council and the European Parliament." European Council. March 2022, available at https://www.consilium.europa.eu/en/press/press-releases/2022/03/25/council-and-european-parliament-reach-agreement-on-the-digital-markets-act/.
19. Brazil is the country with the largest number of cases involving digital markets according to Gutiérrez, J.D. and M. Abarca. 2020. "Challenges to competition and innovation in digital platform markets: Insights from Latin American cases." Available at https://lalibrecompetencia.com/2020/11/15/plataformas-digitales-y-derecho-de-la-competencia-en-america-latina-y-el-caribe/.

[A] Rushing to Adopt a Regulatory Model Might Be a Mistake

In principle, developed countries seem to be aiming in the same direction. The US, Europe, and the UK are all considering imposing *ex ante* regulation schemes to limit the ability of large digital platforms to behave in an anticompetitive fashion. Yet, there might be considerable differences in how each of the proposed regulatory models plays out. Proposals are far from being ready and already display essential differences. For example, Europe's DMA seems to be mostly rules-based: Gatekeepers would be screened based on a series of absolute criteria (such as the number of users), and they would be subject to a pre-defined set of "dos and don'ts" rules. In contrast, the UK proposals lean toward a principles-based approach, where platforms should adhere to certain principles.[20]

Differences in regulatory models may have a material effect on policy outcomes. In this sense, the early adoption of a wrong regulatory approach can carry high costs.

Adopting a regulatory model that is different from those in the developed countries would be a high-risk choice. If global platforms must follow a hard-to-comply code of conduct in a single small country, then they might decide not to provide services in such a country. Adopting one of the regulatory models in developed countries can avoid this risk, making it easy for global platforms to comply with local regulations.

As discussed, however, it is not yet clear which of the regulatory models proposed in developed countries will be better. There is little benefit of committing early to one of those models, but the costs can be high. Regulation has an effect on investment and innovation. A comparative analysis of the history of broadband regulation illustrates how regulatory choices affect the dynamics of the markets.

In the late 1990s, both the US and Europe took decisive regulatory actions to encourage competition in telecommunications markets by introducing mandatory wholesale access regulations.[21] The initial approach to promote competition in these markets was to unbundle the local loop[22] and mandate network access conditions to facilitate the entry of new players in the competitive segments of the network. As in the case of digital regulations, the focus of regulation was to ensure that third parties could access the essential bottleneck by preventing self-preferencing and foreclosure of new entrants in competitive segments.

Soon after the US and Europe took their initial steps in that direction, technological changes allowed cable networks to compete with telecommunication companies by

20. Van der Brande, T. "Rules-based versus principles-based regulation - is there a clear front-runner?" *Ofcom Economic Insights*. August 2021.
21. In the US, regulation was put in place in 1996, through the Telecommunications Act. In Europe, after an initial interim regulatory regime that started in 1998, the European countries adopted a common framework in 2003 that subsists to the present date. *See* Cave, M., C. Genakos, and T. Valetti. 2019, "The European Framework for Regulating Telecommunications: A 25-year Appraisal." *Review of Industrial Organization*. Vol 55, pp. 47–62.
22. The local loop comprises the infrastructure between a local exchange and the final premises in a fixed telecommunications network. This infrastructure was understood to be very costly to replicate, and thus had the characteristics of a natural monopoly.

providing similar services. In addition, there was a strong demand for innovation and investments in the regulated segments of telecommunication networks to transform traditional copper network local loops into fiber loops to keep up with the need for internet services. The access rules in place posed a critical challenge to achieving that goal.

In tackling these challenges, the paths of the EU and the US diverged. The US quickly rewound from access regulation, particularly on fiber-based broadband networks.[23] In contrast, Europe maintained a strong regulatory footprint, with rules that needed to handle the complexity of dealing with rapidly changing market conditions, the periodic redefinition of access conditions that changed with technologies, and the differences in competitive conditions within each country. Some authors link the divergence between the US and EU approaches with the differences in investment outcomes and innovation levels in both regions.[24] As a result, the US achieved high levels of fiber penetration significantly earlier than Europe.[25] For example, by 2012, 82% of US households had access to fiber-based networks, whereas that proportion was only 54% in Europe.[26]

The history of broadband regulation reminds us that there can be a tension between regulation and incentives to invest and innovate. The choice of a regulatory model has an impact on outcomes regarding the type and pace of innovation. Such tension is even more evident in digital markets, essentially driven by fast-paced innovation. Moreover, the risk of adversely affecting investments and innovation through tight regulation might be more extensive in Latin America than in developed countries. The reason is that Latin American countries have weak institutional frameworks where the risk of opportunistic behavior or regulatory failure is perceived as high by investors.

In all, Latin American countries can benefit from postponing the adoption of a regulatory model until there is greater clarity on how each proposal works out and how digital markets continue to evolve.

23. For example, in 2003 the FCC (regulatory authority in the US) stated the following: "...we have come to recognize more clearly the difficulties and limitations inherent in competition based on the shared use of infrastructure through network unbundling. While unbundling can serve to bring competition to markets faster than it might otherwise develop, we are very aware that excessive network unbundling requirements tend to undermine the incentives of both incumbent LECs and new entrants to invest in new facilities and deploy new technology." *See* Federal Communications Commission. 2003. FCC 03-36. "Review of the Section 251 Unbundling Obligations of Incumbent Local Exchange Carriers (CC Docket No. 01-338); Implementation of the Local Competition Provisions of the Telecommunications Act of 1996 (CC Docket No. 96-98); Deployment of Wireline Services Offering Advanced Telecommunications Capability (CC Docket No. 98-147)" p. 7.
24. *See* Yoo, C. 2014. "US vs European broadband deployment: What do the data say?" *University of Penn.* Institute for Law & Economics Research Paper No. 14-35.
25. *See* Cave, M., C. Genakos, and T. Valetti. 2019, "The European Framework for Regulating Telecommunications: A 25-year Appraisal." *Review of Industrial Organization*. Vol 55, pp. 47–62.
26. *See* Yoo, C. 2014. "US vs European broadband deployment: What do the data say?" *University of Penn.* Institute for Law & Economics Research Paper No. 14-35.

[B] Opportunities to Mitigate Delays in the Choice of a Regulatory Model

Delaying the adoption of a regulatory model, however, might be detrimental to consumers if there is a risk that unregulated digital platforms could cause consumer harm. There are at least two factors that make us think that mitigation of such risks is possible.

First, unlike other regulated entities, most digital platforms are global companies operating worldwide. These companies might not be able to adopt different commercial policies across the globe or even have economic incentives to do so. Hence, rules in the developed world may have spillover effects that indirectly affect how digital companies operate in other markets. In other words, to some extent, Latin American countries will be able to free-ride on the regulatory efforts of developed countries.

Free-riding will not always be effective, in any case. Key platforms in specific markets (such as Amazon in the US) only have a limited presence in some Latin American countries. In turn, some large local platforms such as Mercadolibre might fall outside the radar of developed countries' regulations.

Nevertheless, Latin American countries still have competition policy tools to deal with problems that are specific to the region. There are recent examples in the region that show that this is not a mere theoretical possibility. For instance, both Brazil's Administrative Council for Economic Defense (CADE) and Argentina's National Commission for the Defense of Competition (CNDC) recently have taken measures to prevent Whatsapp from sharing information obtained from users with its parent company, Facebook.[27] As another example, in 2018, CADE's tribunal achieved a settlement with travel aggregators Decolar, Expedia, and Booking, to limit the scope of price-parity clauses such that hotel chains could publish best offers in competing platforms or offline sales.[28]

All in all, Latin American countries have more to gain by postponing the potential implementation of a regulatory scheme for digital markets. In the meantime, it seems reasonable that they keep relying on *ex post* competition enforcement, based on a case-by-case approach. Such a policy would allow flexibility to adapt to changing conditions and minimize potential adverse effects on innovation.

---

27. CADE. "WhatsApp is committed to complying with Cade, ANPD, MPF and Senacon recommendations regarding the privacy policy." August 20, 2021, available at https://www.gov.br/cade/pt-br/assuntos/noticias/whatsapp-se-compromete-a-atender-recomendacoes-do-cade-anpd-mpf-e-senacon-em-relacao-a-politica-de-privacidade. *See also* CNDC. "Nuevas Condiciones del Servicio y Políticas de Privacidad de WhatsApp." May 17, 2021, available at https://www.argentina.gob.ar/noticias/nuevas-condiciones-del-servicio-y-politicas-de-privacidad-de-whatsapp-0.
28. CADE, Administrative Inquiry No. 08700.005679/2016-13, TECHNICAL NOTE No. 10/2018/CGAA2/SGA1/SG/CADE.

CHAPTER 8

Competition in Regulated Markets in Latin America: Overview and Challenges

Gesner Oliveira & Bruno Assunção

This chapter analyses the legal competition framework on infrastructure in Latin America, reviewing recent developments and trends in the water, sanitation, electricity, gas, telecommunications, and transportation sectors. Since 2014, when the last assessment was conducted, the antitrust agencies in Latin America were empowered with a broader range of powers to fight anticompetitive practices in the region, notably regarding merger controls, and analysis of abuse of dominant position. Moreover, countries such as Brazil, Chile, and Mexico have protocols of understanding in force between the anticompetitive agencies and the regulatory authorities in the infrastructure sectors, as well as agreements with international organizations and agencies. On the other hand, there are shortcomings that still need to be addressed regarding the competition and regulatory framework in the region, especially in respect of mandatory opinions on draft legislation by the competition agencies. The chapter also briefly reviews the regulatory framework on infrastructure in the region. Finally, theoretical institutional models for the legal competences and relationships between the regulatory and competition agencies are presented.

§8.01 INTRODUCTION

This chapter reviews the main improvements and trends observed in the competition and regulatory framework of infrastructure sectors in Latin America, particularly, the water, sanitation, electricity, gas, telecommunications, and transportation sectors.[1]

1. This chapter aims at updating the original article prepared in 2014.

The proven limitations of the centralized and public scheme for the provision of infrastructure services in the region encouraged the adoption of a new models based on the principles of decentralization, private participation, and promotion of competition since the 1990s. Three decades after the progressive adoption of the new configuration, important advances were made in terms of coverage, quality, and cost efficiency in all the sector mentioned. Moreover, improvements have been made since 2014, when the last assessment was conducted. Nonetheless, important objectives remain unaddressed.

This chapter is organized in five sections. Besides this Introduction, §8.02 gives a brief overview of the situation of competition promotion in infrastructure regulated sectors in Latin America. Section §8.03 contains a review of the current market, institutional and regulatory challenges in the region. Section §8.04 presents an array of possible institutional frameworks for competition and regulatory agencies, as a required step to achieve the sectors goals. Section §8.05 sets forth the major conclusions of this analysis.

§8.02 OVERVIEW OF THE COMPETITION FRAMEWORK IN LATIN AMERICA

Over the last thirty years, most Latin American countries have implemented a competition framework that includes a competition act and an antitrust agency. Moreover, significant improvements have been made, with most countries strengthening their antitrust agencies and legal framework with a broader range of responsibilities and actions aimed at bringing competition policy to the forefront of the region's economic policies.

Nonetheless, there are still shortcomings in the institutional design identified in the region, which partially obstructs further competition promotion policies: (i) scarce level of research regarding the consequences of institutional arrangements in competition policy outcomes; (ii) a limited degree of independence in relation to the executive branch, such as the existing procedures to designate the directors of the agencies (Umaña, 4). Aware of these issues, in 2015, the 13th IDB-OECD Latin American Competition Forum discussed the measuring of competition advocacy's impact in Latin America and the Caribbean, which recognized the fundamental importance of such assessments.

Recent enhancements in the strength of antitrust agencies in the region can be evidenced by the broader array of powers endowed in relation to law enforcement, advocacy, and rulemaking activities. Table 8.1 shows the portfolio instruments of some selected antitrust agencies in Latin America.

Table 8.1 Portfolio Instruments of Antitrust Agencies in Latin America

	Portfolio Instruments[2]			
Countries	*Law Enforcement*	*Advocacy*	*Rulemaking: Issue of Guidelines or Secondary Legislation*	
	Power to Investigate Cartels	*Mandatory Opinions of Draft Legislation*	*Merger Control*	*Analysis of Abuse of Dominant Position Cases*
Argentina	Yes	No	Yes	Yes
Brazil	Yes	No	Yes	Yes
Chile	Yes	No	Yes	Yes
Colombia	Yes	Yes	Yes	No
Costa Rica	Yes	Yes	Yes	Yes
Ecuador	Yes	No	Yes	Yes
Honduras	Yes	No[3]	Yes	Yes
Mexico	Yes	No	Yes	Yes
Nicaragua	Yes	No	Yes	Yes
Panama	Yes	Yes	Yes	Yes
Peru	Yes	No	Yes	Yes
Uruguay	Yes	No	Yes	Yes
Venezuela	Yes	No	No	No

Source: CNDC (Argentina); Cade (Brasil); FNC (Chile);[4] Coprocom (Costa Rica);[5] SCPM (Ecuador); CDPC (Honduras);[6] Cofece (Mexico); Procompetencianic (Nicaragua);[7] Acodeco (Panama);[8] Indecopi (Peru);[9] Comisión de Promoción y Defensa de la Competencia (Uruguay);[10] The George Washington Competition Law Center.

2. Updated by the author. Information regarding Colombia and Venezuela were not updated in this version due to the lack of data.
3. The agency has the power to issue an opinion on draft legislations, but it is up to the agency to do so, it is not mandatory.
4. Available at: https://www.fne.gob.cl/en//about-us/fiscalia-nacional-economica/.
5. Available at: https://www.coprocom.go.cr/acerca_coprocom/quienes%20somos.html; http://www.pgrweb.go.cr/scij/Busqueda/Normativa/Normas/nrm_texto_completo.aspx?param1 = NRTC&nValor1 = 1&nValor2 = 90054.
6. Available at: https://www.cdpc.hn/?q = www.funciones; ttps://www.cdpc.hn/sites/default/files/Privado/marco_legal/LeydeCompetencia_Honduras.pdf.
7. Available at: http://procompetencia.gob.ni/?p = 510; http://procompetencia.gob.ni/wp-content/uploads/2015/03/Ley-No.601-y-Reglamento-Refundida-20161.pdf.
8. Available at: https://acodeco.gob.pa/inicio/ley-45-de-31-de-octubre-de-2007/.
9. Available at: https://www.gob.pe/4193-instituto-nacional-de-defensa-de-la-competencia-y-de-la-proteccion-de-la-propiedad-intelectual-que-hacemos; https://www.indecopi.gob.pe/en/clc-que-hacemos; https://www.indecopi.gob.pe/documents/1902049/3918907/DL + 1034.pdf/9fbfc613-bf1b-e1bf-4930-9c6dcdf3dd09
10. Available at: https://www.gub.uy/ministerio-economia-finanzas/defensa-de-la-competencia; https://www.impo.com.uy/bases/leyes/18159-2007.

All the competition agencies analysed here have the power to investigate cartels; to exert merger controls, to analyse potential abuse of dominant position as well as to issue guidelines and make recommendations regarding competition law, or other type of competition advocacy powers.

However, regarding the advocacy power of competition institutions, measured here as the requirement for the agencies to issue mandatory opinions on draft legislation that might affect competition, only three (23.1%) of the thirteen countries of the representative sample (Colombia, Costa Rica, and Panama) have this provision, while in the remaining 10 (76.9%) countries, the opinion of the agency is optional.

The observed landscape in the region regarding advocacy power can be explained by different factors, which are not fully developed:

- Population's lack of awareness regarding the benefits of competition for consumer welfare which can be described as lack of competition culture.
- Recent anti-market trends by national governments.
- Conflict between competition objectives and other areas of public policies.
- Ambiguity in defining what constitutes anticompetitive behaviour in the judicial system.
- Executive/legislative application of competition policies disregarding consumer welfare as their primary goal.

Coordination and cooperation between competition and regulatory agencies are relevant aspects to improve results from competition authorities. Agreements or protocol definitions between competition and regulatory agencies are important to avoid overlapping responsibilities and to strengthen pro-competitive activities and public understanding. Table 8.2 shows whether the competition agencies have agreements with authorities from regulated infrastructure sectors.

Table 8.2 Agreements Between Competition and Regulatory Agencies

Countries	*Protocols or Memoranda of Understanding*				
	Telecommunication	*Energy*	*Transport*	*Other*	*International Organizations and Agencies*
Argentina	No	No	No	No	Yes
Brazil[11]	Yes	Yes	No	Yes	Yes
Chile	No	Yes	Yes	Yes[12]	Yes
Colombia	No	No	No	Yes	Yes

11. There is an agreement between Cade and the National Agency of Petroleum, Natural Gas and Biofuels ('ANP'); also, there is a recent Memoranda of Understanding between Cade and the National Agency for the Waterway Transportation ('ANTAQ').
12. Other agreements available at: https://www.fne.gob.cl/advocacy/acuerdos-nacionales-de-cooperacion-2/.

Countries	*Protocols or Memoranda of Understanding*				
	Telecommunication	*Energy*	*Transport*	*Other*	*International Organizations and Agencies*
Costa Rica	Yes	No	No	No	Yes
Ecuador	No	No	No	No	Yes
Honduras	Yes	No	No	Yes	Yes
Mexico	Yes	Yes	No	Yes	Yes
Nicaragua	No	No	No	No	Yes
Panama	No	No	No	Yes	Yes
Peru	Yes	Yes	Yes	Yes	Yes
Uruguay	No	No	No	Yes	Yes
Venezuela	No	No	No	No	Yes

Source: CNDC (Argentina); Cade (Brasil); FNC (Chile); Coprocom (Costa Rica);[13] SCPM (Ecuador); CDPC (Honduras); Cofece (Mexico);[14] Procompetencia (Nicaragua);[15] Acodeco (Panama);[16] Indecopi (Peru); Comisión de Promoción y Defensa de la Competencia (Uruguay); The George Washington Competition Law Center.

Based on data from thirteen Latin American countries, it is possible to observe some improvement in the recent years regarding the interaction between regulatory and competition promotion agencies. All countries are members of the International Competition Network (ICN). Nine competition agencies have at least one cooperation agreement with a regulatory agency, but only five of them have an agreement with telecom regulatory agencies. This shows that there is plenty of room for the increase of such agreements. Nonetheless, the effectiveness of these agreements should be subject to constant review.

§8.03 OVERVIEW OF REGULATED MARKETS IN LATIN AMERICA

Latin America still experiences a deficit in terms of quantity and quality of network services, evidenced by the increasing gap between their supply and demand. Besides the challenges concerning the current levels of access/consumption, quantified by local governments and multilateral organizations, the expanding difference between

13. Available at: ttps://www.coprocom.go.cr/publicaciones/convenios_acuerdos.html.
14. Available at: https://www.cofece.mx/publicaciones/marco-juridico-y-normativo/#normateca-4; https://www.cofece.mx/wp-content/uploads/2017/12/ift-cfce-convenio_24_10_2013.pdf.
15. Available at: ttps://www.sc.gob.sv/index.php/sala_multimedia/acuerdo-cooperacion-instituto-nacional-promocion-la-competencia-procompetencia-nicaragua/.
16. Available at: https://acodeco.gob.pa/inicio/convenios-nacionales/.

the volume of trade in the region and its infrastructure stock[17] illustrates the deficiencies on the supply side, as shown in Figure 8.1.

Figure 8.1 Evolution of Infrastructure and Trade Volume Index (1990 = 100)[18]

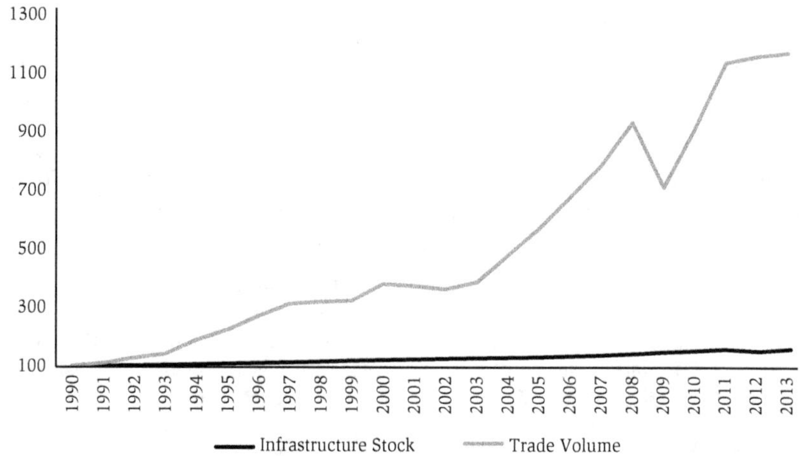

Source: Authors (with IDB and IMF data).

In that respect, insufficient investment is one of the main causes identified for the lack of infrastructure in the region. The aforementioned scenario occurs, in part, as a result of a downward trend in infrastructure investment since the mid-1980s, attenuated by the 1990s wave of privatization of network services which, nonetheless, has steeped downwards again in recent years. Particularly, Brazil has seen a sharp decline in infrastructure investment from more than 5% of GDP in the 1970s to a level slightly more than 2% in the recent past.

17. The infrastructure index is used as a proxy for supply, while the trade index is a proxy for demand. Due to the nature of the mentioned variables, the comparison should be observed only as a general trend.
18. Figure 8.1 is based on a representative sample of Latin American countries. Specifically: Argentina, Brazil, Colombia, Costa Rica, Ecuador, Honduras, Mexico, Panama, Peru, Uruguay, and Venezuela. The infrastructure stock index is constructed based on the IMF database, and the trade volume index is constructed based on the IDB datasets.

Figure 8.2 Investment on Infrastructure in Latin America[19] *($ Billion)*

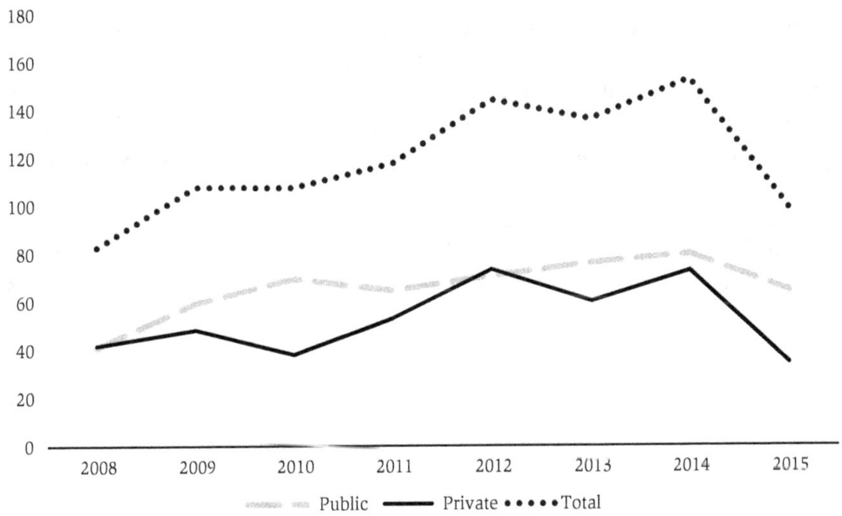

Source: Authors (with IDB data).

Despite the progressive reduction of investment in infrastructure, the sector has undergone significant transformations. During the 1980s, network services provision followed a centralized model for planning, decision making, and investment. Public monopolist firms were responsible for production and tariffs determined by national or federal agencies.

Although important advances in terms of overall coverage were gained through public investment, the model collapsed due to the high inefficiency of firms, considerable deficits generated by unsustainable levels of public subsidies, slow technological advance, management decisions heavily influenced by political interests, and macroeconomic pressures (reduction of commodity prices, elevated international interest rates, and a critical level of debts).

As a response, since the 1990s, the region began a series of structural changes to the model of provision of network services, partially influenced by ideological principles promoted by the World Bank and the International Monetary Fund. Specifically, private participation and capital were introduced to the sector, based on a new institutional framework, where the planning, regulation, production, and supervision responsibilities were decentralized and reassigned.

19. The chart was constructed by the arithmetic sum of the public and private investments of a representative sample: Argentina; Brazil; Colombia; Costa Rica; Dominican Republic; Honduras; Mexico; Nicaragua; Panama; Peru; Paraguay and El Salvador. Argentina and Paraguay have no private investment data for 2015 and the Dominican Republic has no public investment data for 2008.

As summarized in Figure 8.2, the role of general policy definition was assigned to a ministry, and coverage/production decisions were redirected to local/regional authorities or a network administrator. The investment was open to the private sector, and supervision authority was given to an independent regulatory agency.

At the same time, in the electricity, gas, and telecommunications industries, competition was introduced through vertical disintegration, responsibility for service provision designated to local governments or firms in the market (public, private, or mixed), and price definition was delegated to regulatory agencies (network access) or the market.

While in the water, sanitation, and transportation industries, only competition for the market was allowed, the price determination role was given to the regulatory agency and service provision responsibility was designated to local governments or firms of the sector.

Table 8.3 Infrastructure Services: Institutional and Competition Framework

	Water and Sanitation	*Electricity*	*Gas*	*Telecommunications*	*Transportation*
Policy/Planning	Ministry (policy) and Local/Regional Government (directly responsible)	Ministry (policy) – Network Administrator/ Regulator	Ministry (policy) – Network Administrator/ Regulator	Ministry (policy) – Network Administrator/ Regulator	Ministry (policy) and Local/ Regional Government
Service Provision	Local Autonomous Agencies, Local Government or Private	Local Government or Private	Public or Private Firms (Predominantly private)	Public or Private Firms (Predominantly private)	Local Government or Private
Investment	Private-Public (predominantly public)	Private-Public (predominantly private)	Private-Public (Predominantly private)	Private-Public (Predominantly private)	Private-Public (predominantly public)
Competition	Competition for the market	Vertical Disintegration: Generation (Competition), Transmission (Monopoly or Competition) – Distribution (Monopoly or Competition).	Vertical Disintegration – Downstream (Competition for exploitation) – Upstream (Monopoly or	Fixed Network (Monopoly or Competition), Mobile Services (Competition), Internet (Competition)	Competition for the market

	Water and Sanitation	*Electricity*	*Gas*	*Telecommunications*	*Transportation*
Price Definition	Regulator	Generation (Market) – Transmission (Market or Regulator), Distribution (Market and Regulator).	Downstream (Market) – Upstream (Market for Wholesale and Regulator for Retail)	Market. Network access prices are Regulator.	Regulator
Supervision	Independent Regulator	Independent Regulator	Independent Regulator	Independent Regulator	Independent Regulator

Source: Julián Peña & Marcelo Calliari, Competition Law in Latin America: A Practical Guide, First Edition (2016).

It is important to consider that the presented structural changes in network services provision constitutes only a general pattern in the region, with some exceptions or variations in relation to the adopted model. Similarly, the moment of adoption initiated in the 1990s for most countries and industries, yet there are a few cases where the mentioned process is still on-going.

The main institutional, regulatory and sector challenges for the infrastructure services under analysis are presented in the following sub-sections.[20]

[A] Water and Sanitation

Investment in water and sanitation in Latin America is long overdue. According to IDB data, Latin American countries invested on average 0.3 % GDP in water and sanitation between 2008 and 2015. It is necessary to attain universal coverage and increase the quality of services in urban areas. At the same time, it is required to expand coverage in rural areas and in wastewater treatment.

Although there has been significant improvement in the water and sanitation coverage in the region, this progress fell short of the rest of the world. As of 2017, the percentage of people without access to an improved water source[21] diminished 5.8 percentage points (p.p.) in Latin America, against a reduction of 7.4 p.p. in the rest of the world. Similarly, the share of people without access to an improved sanitary installation fell by 14.1 p.p. in Latin America against 16.3 p.p. in the world.

As an example, the deficit in a large country such as Brazil is enormous, with almost half of the population without access to sanitation services. On the other hand, in this respect, Brazilian government has signed a new regulatory framework in 2020 which is expected to increase private participation and investments in the sector and to improve water and sanitation conditions in the country.

Regarding regulation, it is important to set tariffs that guarantee financial sustainability, achieve effective implementation of existing regulatory methodologies, reduce fragmentation to exploit economies of scale, improve consumer protection policies, diminish the probability of capture by increasing the regulator's degree of independence and technical expertise, adequate regulation to public firms (still predominant in the market), stimulate private investment and promote cost efficiency by inducing competition (open network access).

20. The following overview of the sector challenges is based on the document by Santiago, Priscila Braga. Infraestrutura: experiência na América Latina. Comissão Econômica para a América Latina e o Caribe - CEPAL. Brasília, DF: CEPAL. Escritório no Brasil/IPEA, 2011, and on the paper by Ricardo J. Sánchez et al.: Inversiones en infraestructura en América Latina Tendencias, brechas y oportunidades. Comissão Econômica para a América Latina e o Caribe - CEPAL. Santiago, CL, 2017.
21. An improved water source (or improved drinking-water source or improved water supply) is a term used to categorize certain types or levels of water supply for monitoring purposes. It is defined as a type of water source that, by nature of its construction or through active intervention, is likely to be protected from outside contamination, in particular with fecal matter.

[B] Electricity

Current levels of coverage are more than 95% in Latin America. Nonetheless, in terms of population, there are still more than 20 million persons still waiting to be connected to the electricity grid in the region.

In relation to production of electricity, the main challenges are to increase cost efficiency that can be effectively transferred to 'retail' consumers, to promote the adoption of green energy sources (Brazil is in the avant-garde on this matter) while diversifying the options for the generation of electricity and to implement more efficient technologies.

Regarding the institutional and regulatory aspects, the central issues are to move towards the implementation of complete vertical and horizontal disintegration to effectively promote competition,[22] reduce the degree of concentration in the industry in open network markets,[23] open network access in some regions (to allow market contestability), coordinate regulatory frameworks to promote network integration between countries, increase the regulator independence to reduce the probability of capture by the regulated and redefine the areas of service to enable subsidy schemes for small scale markets and low-income population.

[C] Gas

Although important gas reserves in Latin America are concentrated in but a few countries (Venezuela, Argentina, and Brazil), apart from Uruguay and Paraguay, all South American countries possess proved deposits of natural gas, which in total sum up to 7.5 trillion m^3 and correspond to 4% of the world's reserves. Currently, 26% of the primary energetic resources used in Latin America correspond to natural gas.[24] In 2016, the total production in the region was 178.8 trillion m^3, 5% of the world's output. This leaves the reserves production ratio (R/P) in 42.1 years, against 52.4 years for the world average. On the other hand, regional integration of networks still constitutes a challenge, especially regarding the implementation of stable supply agreements in the long run.

Although for the Latin America as a whole supply and demand for natural gas are at an equilibrium, Brazil, Argentina, Chile, Uruguay, and in a lesser degree Colombia and Venezuela do not produce enough to meet their respective demands and need to resort to importing natural gas. On the other hand, Bolivia, Peru, and Trinidad and Tobago are net exporters of the commodity.

---

22. The industry presents three different models according to the degree of the existence of competition: (i) open-access networks: Nicaragua, Bolivia, Salvador, Panama, Guatemala, Peru, Ecuador, Dominican Republic, Chile, Colombia, Argentina, Venezuela, and Brazil) (ii) Unique buyer: Suriname, Guyana, Honduras, Jamaica, Costa Rica, Uruguay, and Mexico (iii) State Monopoly: Cuba, Paraguay, Haiti, Barbados, and Grenada (Santiago, 18).
23. Herfindal-Hirshman index of 2006–2007 for open network countries: Argentina (1.1190), Colombia (1.305), Brazil (2.044), Peru (2.319), Chile (3.541), Salvador (5.090) (Santiago, 19).
24. Available at: https://repositorio.cepal.org/bitstream/handle/11362/44596/1/S1801057_es.pdf.

Institutionally, there is not a unique model adopted for provision in the region. Upstream, the public sector still plays an important role, while in Mexico and Venezuela the exploitation is a state monopoly. Downstream, the trend is open access networks with regulated prices (if there is excess capacity); at the same time, distribution is open to competition, but 'retail' consumers pay regulated prices.

The industry operates smoothly in Brazil, Colombia, and Peru, where there is vertical disintegration, open access to networks, and an adequate level of return (Santiago, 30). In Brazil, the federal government and competition agency are on-going on a series of institutional reforms focused on promoting increased competition and development in the gas sector.[25]

[D] Telecom

Landline, mobile, and Internet services have not reached international levels of coverage in the region yet. However, the expansion of landlines has dramatically decreased, while mobile and Internet services are rapidly expanding above the scale of landlines penetration. Nevertheless, coverage and quality, in an industry in continuous adjustment due to rapid technological changes, are still objectives to pursue in Latin America (Santiago, 31–33).

It is worth noting that improvements in the landlines service were highly influenced by the reduction of technology costs (digitalization and automation) and competition promotion (elimination of exclusive periods of exploitation), rather than by privatization alone.[26]

A new challenge the region shall face in the short term is the implantation and of the 5G technology, ensuring the desired quality and impact upon the IoT. For example, in Brazil, it is expected that all the twenty-six states' capitals plus the federal district are covered by the technology by 2022. On the other hand, only by 2028 the entire country should have full access to 5G connections. In Argentina, the technology should be made available only after 2022 or 2023. In Colombia, according to the regulatory authorities, 80% of the country's rural areas shall be covered by 2025. Nevertheless, the importance of a speedy implementation of the 5G technology cannot be overstated, especially when it is considered that both the United States and China are already competing for the leadership of the 6G, which should be commercially available in the early 2030s. That is, Brazil and probably Argentina should only complete their 5G coverage on the brink of a new technological breakthrough.

Concerning regulatory aspects, the challenges on a highly concentrated sector like telecommunications consist of achieving the transfer of efficiency gains to consumers through prices, stimulating network convergence to continue a gradual transition from market regulation to competition promotion, and strengthening consumer

25. Available at: https://www.gov.br/mme/pt-br/assuntos/secretarias/petroleo-gas-natural-e-biocombustiveis/novo-mercado-de-gas.
26. Venezuela and Panama are examples where, even though privatization was introduced, competition was restrained for a period to promote infrastructure expansion. However, firms strategically refrained from complete coverage in order to gain higher returns.

protection policies. In most markets, barriers to entry continue to be high and regulatory efforts have not been sufficient to facilitate entry.

[E] Transportation

Similar to other infrastructure services, transportation capacity is below the required levels to promote trade and economic growth, which constitutes one of the main challenges of the industry. In Brazil, the largest country in Latin America, only 12.4% of its roads were paved as of 2018. For the analysed countries, six countries were lower than the 20% threshold and only Panama has more than 40% of paved roads in 2015.

On the other hand, between 2007 and 2015, the growth rate of paved roads has exceeded the increase in the total road network in the region. Nonetheless, in some countries such as Peru, this increase has been the result of the incorporation of the officially registered network.

Regarding the region's railroads, not only its current density (measured by the railroad extension per 100 km^2 of territory) is significantly below that of developed countries, but also the development of new lines has been stagnated for most Latin American countries. Moreover, an important share of the region's railroads is out of service: in Colombia, as of 2015, 48 % of its railroads were not operational.

Auction for the market (Concessions) constitutes the primary form of competition. As of 2004, there were 243 road concessions in the region, equivalent to 35,112 Km, indicating that this is still a predominantly public activity (Santiago, 39).

At the institutional level, the objective is to define and implement coherent and unified transportation policies, encourage private investment (public and private partnerships), and continue promoting competition.

§8.04 INSTITUTIONAL MODELS FOR THE RELATION BETWEEN REGULATORY AND COMPETITION AGENCIES

The situation of the infrastructure sector in Latin America in the recent years, among other factors, evidence the necessity of stimulating investment in order to reach coverage goals and stimulate economic prosperity. At the institutional level, as discussed earlier, it is still required to strengthen the independence of regulatory agencies and increase the coordination of activities between competition and regulation authorities, as a first step to effectively promote competition in the industry.

A key factor to achieve coverage goals is to generate an adequate institutional framework, with a clear distribution of responsibilities and continuous coordination between regulatory and competition agencies. In this regard, a revision of the different existent institutional functions for competition promotion and regulatory activities, evidence the following three basic functions:

(i) Technical Regulation (TR): definition of standards, goals, and rules for agents in regulated industries.

(ii) Economic Regulation (ER): establishing the price, tariffs, and quantities conditions in regulated industries.
(iii) Competition Legislation (CL): implementation of the competition law repressing and preventing anticompetitive practices.

In addition, as indicated in Table 8.4, the limits between the promotion of competition and regulation present variations according to the different market structures. There are several possibilities in terms of market structure. For simplicity, we consider general stylized models which serve to point out how the relative importance of competition and regulatory agencies vary according to the extent to which market imperfection is present. The greater the market imperfection (the extreme case being the natural monopoly) is, the greater is the role of the regulatory agency. However, in most markets of modern economies, both agencies do have a role, and they must coordinate their activities to be effective. The agreements reached between competition agencies and regulatory agencies in the recent years play an important role in this sense.

Table 8.4 Limits Between Competition Promotion and Regulation

	Perfect Competition	*Competitive*	*Imperfect Competition*	*Natural Monopoly*
Competition Promotion	–	X	XX	X
Regulation	–	–	X	XX

Source: Authors.

In an ideal market with perfect competition, the intervention of regulatory or competition promotion agencies is not essential. Market mechanisms would be sufficient to obtain optimal equilibrium and efficiency. In the remaining three market structures, the role of regulation and competition promotion varies according to their characteristics. While regulation plays a more important role in a natural monopoly market, the promotion of competition tends to be relatively more relevant in markets characterized by imperfect competition.

Institutional frameworks should distribute the three mentioned institutional functions to be undertaken by regulation and competition agencies, towards which four models can be suggested:

- Model 1 – Antitrust Exemption: the regulatory agency is empowered to perform the three basic functions (TR, ER, and CL) and the competition agency does not have any involvement.
- Model 2 – Competing Responsibilities: regulatory and competition agencies define antitrust penalties and economic regulation rules together, while technical regulation is conducted solely by the regulatory agency.

- Model 3 – Complementary responsibilities: the regulatory agency is responsible for economic and technical regulation and the competition promotion agency is in charge of implementing the existing competition legislation (there is no overlap of duties).
- Model 4 – Antitrust Regulation: the competition agency is responsible to perform the three basic functions (TR, ER, and CL), without the intervention of the regulatory agency.

Figure 8.3 Possible Institutional Frameworks Between Competition and Regulation Agencies

Model 1. Antitrust Exemption

	CL	TR	ER
CPA	–	–	–
RA	X	X	X

Model 2. Competing Responsibilities

	CL	TR	ER
CPA	X	–	X
RA	X	X	X

Model 3. Complementary Responsibilities

	CL	TR	ER
CPA	X	–	–
RA	–	X	X

Model 4. Antitrust Regulation

	CL	TR	ER
CPA	X	X	X
RA	–	–	–

Source: Julián Peña & Marcelo Calliari, Competition Law in Latin America: A Practical Guide, First Edition (2016).

The implementation and effectiveness of each presented institutional model vary among industries and countries, depending on the market dynamics, institutional history, technological level, among other factors.

For example, in the United States, the antitrust exemption (Model 1) would be a fair description of the agricultural sector, while the banking industry is under the competing responsibilities framework (Model 2); at the same time, the telecommunication sectors of most Latin American countries apply the Complementary responsibilities approach (Model 3) and, in Australia, the Antitrust Regulation prevails (Model 4).

§8.05 CONCLUSIONS

Despite the significant institutional advances of the infrastructure sector in Latin America in the last thirty years, there are still important challenges in terms of investments, coverage, and quality that are relevant for the economic and social development of the region.

In this respect, the gradual introduction of competition in regulated sectors has been identified as a factor that plays a key role in achieving these goals. The rapid growth of coverage of the telecommunication and energy industries of Latin America evidence the improvements that competition can bring about.

Despite the challenges, the promotion of competition and its agencies are beginning to play a more forefront role in the public policies formulation and implementation. Albeit some competition agencies lack the required institutional attributions, resources, and advocacy capacity to successfully pursue their objectives, countries such as Brazil, Mexico, Chile, Colombia, Costa Rica, and Peru have shown significant progress at the institutional level.

Latin American countries have made great improvements in the merger control and abuse of dominant position competencies in the most recent years, with the majority of them enabling their respective agencies to discourage these practices. Moreover, although the competition agencies still play for the most part a secondary role in the competition advocacy activities, and there are but a few cooperation agreements between competition and sectoral regulation agencies, these have also shown improvement recently. Brazil's Cade is one of the exceptions in the region, having many protocols of understanding with other regulatory agencies in the country, as well as other international agencies. Moreover, in the last two years, it has played a significant role in the promotion of competition in the petroleum and natural gas sectors.

At the same time, important institutional and regulatory challenges were identified in the water, sanitation, electricity, gas, telecommunications, and transportation sectors in the region. The most relevant can be encapsulated in the following points:

(i) generate incentives to increase public and private investments;
(ii) improve the degree of independence of regulatory and competition agencies;
(iii) advance in the introduction of competition in regulated markets (vertical disintegration, open-access networks, etc.); and
(iv) increase the degree of interaction between competition and regulatory agencies.

An independent regulator reduces the political pressures on the agency, increasing regulatory stability and predictability, which in turn is a determinant factor to stimulate private investment.

Technological convergence and interdependence among sectors are a current trend in regulated industries. Thus, to effectively introduce competition in a vertically disintegrated chain of production, it is necessary to establish a coherent and clear distribution of responsibilities between the regulatory and competition promotion agencies, as well as continuous coordination among regulatory authorities.

In the last section, we presented different possible arrangements to distribute basic roles between the competition and regulation agencies, according to the market characteristics and objectives being pursued. Nonetheless, the discussion is focused on presenting existing alternatives, rather than suggesting specific institutional frameworks. The structure of the regulatory and competition agency should be established according to a diversity of factors, such as institutional flexibility, efficiency, bureaucratic transaction costs, the existence of economies of scale or scope, institutional history, responsibilities overlap, among others. There is not a single model that could be recommended to all countries.

As a general and final point, the overview of the Latin American experience of competition in regulated markets suggests that the elimination of the enormous infrastructure gap in emerging countries depends on pro-competitive regulation and not on the elimination of competition under the pretext of the existence of a natural monopoly.

BIBLIOGRAPHY

Calderón, C.; Servén, L. Tendencias en Infraestructura en América Latina 1980-2001. Grupo Regional de Trabajo Tarifas y subsidios. Washington D.C.: PPIAF y Banco Mundial, 2004.

Carciofi Gaya. Una Nota Acerca de la Expansión del Comercio y las Necesidades de Infraestructura en América Latina. Carta Mensual Octubre 2007, Instituto para la Integración de América Latina, 2007.

George Washington Competition Law Center. Worldwide Competition Database. George Washington University, 2014. Web. Sep. 20, 2014. http://www.gwclc.com/World-competition-database.html.

Kovacic & Lopez-Galdos, Benchmarking Competition Systems: A Global Survey of Major Institutional Characteristics, UNCTAD 2012.

Sánchez, R., Lardé, J., Chauvet, P. and Jaimurzina, A., 2017. Inversiones en infraestructura en América Latina: tendencias, brechas y oportunidades. Web https://repositorio.cepal.org/bitstream/handle/11362/43134/1/S1700926_es.pdf.

Santiago, Priscila Braga. Infraestrutura: experiência na América Latina. Comissão Econômica para a América Latina e o Caribe - CEPAL. Brasília, DF: CEPAL. Escritório no Brasil/IPEA, 2011. Web http://www.cepal.org/cgi-bin/getProd.asp?xml=/publicaciones/sinsigla/xml/9/43439/P43439.xml&xsl=/tpl/p9f.xsl&base=/publicaciones/top_publicaciones.xsl.

Di Sbroiavacca, N., Dubrovsky, H., Nadal, G. and Contreras Lisperguer, R., 2019. Rol y perspectivas del gas natural en la transformación energética de América Latina: aportes a la implementación del Observatorio Regional sobre Energías Sostenibles. Web https://repositorio.cepal.org/bitstream/handle/11362/44596/1/S1801057_es.pdf.

Umaña Mario. Session III – Advocacy: Mainstreaming Competition Policy into the Overall Economic Policy and Government Actions in Latin American and the Caribbean. Latin America Competition Forum, Montevideo, Uruguay: September 2014. Web http://www.oecd.org/officialdocuments/publicdisplaydocumentpdf/?cote=DAF/COMP/LACF%282014%298&docLanguage=es.

CHAPTER 9

Competition Law in the ICT Industry in Latin America

Pablo Márquez & Juan Pablo Otero

This chapter aims at introducing the trends and analysis that competition law and regulators in Latin America have undertaken in the Information and Communication Technology (ICT) sector with an emphasis in decisions and cases in the telecommunications infrastructure. The text seeks to provide a critical analysis of the cases regarding competition law in the ICT industry, exploring the developments that certain regional authorities have provided and present a critical framework for the analysis of competition law under the new market circumstances. This chapter starts with the analysis of competition law in ICTs showing the new characteristics of ICT Ecosystem and the role of platform economics, shortly explaining what the telecom sector was, its decline to incept into the ICT sector, and how the new ICT industry works. The next section includes a brief analysis of dominance regulation and abuse of dominance, highlighting dominance in competition law and regulation, and the ICT and telecommunications case law in Latin America. After that, the chapter reviews procompetitive and anticompetitive agreements between competitors and the enforcement of anticompetitive agreements in Latin America, covering the recent trend to consolidation in the different layers of the ICT ecosystem, including the analysis and explanation of the latest mergers in the sector in Latin America. The chapter concludes stressing the importance that competition authorities in the region develop a framework of the analysis and enforcement of competition law in the ICT sector.

§9.01 INTRODUCTION

Contemporary discussion regarding the role of antitrust law as a tool to enhance markets dynamics has focused on a wide variety of deep and complex issues. The most avant-garde side of the literature is preoccupied discussing issues including the role of antitrust law in fintech, the role of antitrust regulations in satellite constellations, the standard of analysis of killer acquisitions, or the role of antitrust in data-driven business models.[1] Latin American authorities are far from such discussions yet, but still in the path to discuss technological convergence. This chapter addresses such discussions in the Latin American ICT ecosystem.

During the last years, the ICT industry has witnessed and discussed the effect in the dynamics of competition technological convergence – this is the use of a single infrastructure to serve all the services provided. Convergence has already been implemented and deployed, and the telecommunications antitrust literature is still undergoing the analysis of the procompetitive and anticompetitive hurdles that this phenomenon brings to the dynamics of competitive interaction.[2] In addition, despite all the discussion and analysis undertaken, competition authorities around the world are still pending to fully approach to the implications of technological convergence, platforms economics, and the cross relation between data-driven business models in the dynamics of competition in telecommunications markets and their impact in the assessment of market power.[3] Latin American competition law authorities are taking short and prudent steps towards the analysis of the ICT industry as shown in this review.[4]

In this short piece we aim at introducing the trends and analysis that competition law and regulators in the region have undertaken in the ICT sector with an emphasis in decisions and cases in the telecommunications infrastructure. Our aim is to provide a critical analysis of the cases regarding competition law in the ICT industry, exploring the developments that certain Latin American authorities have provided and provide a critical framework for the analysis of competition law under the new market circumstances.

1. *See* Economides, Nicholas and Lianos, Ioannis, 'Restrictions on Privacy and Exploitation in the Digital Economy: A Market Failure Perspective' (27 January 2021). Journal of Competition Law and Economics, Forthcoming, NET Institute Working Paper No. #20-05, NYU Stern School of Business Forthcoming, Available at SSRN: https://ssrn.com/abstract = 3686785 or http://dx.doi.org/10.2139/ssrn.3686785; Bryan, Kevin A., and Erik Hovenkamp. 'Antitrust Limits on Startup Acquisitions.' Review of Industrial Organization, vol. 56, no. 4, March 2020, pp. 615–636.
2. A few recent papers on the topic: First, Harry, Digital Platforms and Competition Policy in Developing Countries (12 May 2021). Harry First, Digital platforms and competition policy in developing countries, Concurrences N° 2-2021, Art. N° 100661, https://www.concurrences.com/fr/revue/issues/no-2-2021/articles/digital-platforms-and-competition-policy-in-developing-countries, Available at SSRN: https://ssrn.com/abstract = 3864953.
3. See: Larsson, Stefan. 'Putting Trust into Antitrust? Competition Policy and Data-Driven Platforms.' European Journal of Communication, vol. 36, no. 4, August 2021, pp. 391–403; Sheppard, Susanna. The EU's Traditional Analysis of the Facebook, WhatsApp Deal – Do We Like it? Society for Computers and Law, 2014. En: http://www.scl.org/site.aspx?i = ed38934.
4. *See*, for example, G. Núñez y F. Da Silva, 'La libre competencia en la era digital y la pospandemia: el impacto sobre las pequeñas y medianas empresas', Documentos de Proyectos (LC/TS.2021/15), Santiago, Comisión Económica para América Latina y el Caribe (CEPAL), 2021; Pereira, Verónica et al. 'The Impact of Legislation on the Development of IPTV in Latin America'. Revista Ibérica de Sistemas e Tecnologias de Informação; Lousada N.° E26 (Feb 2020), pp. 296–308.

This chapter starts with the analysis of competition law in ICTs showing the new characteristics of ICT ecosystem and the role of platform economics. In this section, a short explanation of what was the telecom sector, its decline to incept into the ICT sector, and how the new ICT industry works, in terms of its layered ecosystem, its competitive dynamics and the challenges for competition authorities, also keeping an eye on the consequences of COVID-19, which gave a boost to the sector and made ICT services even more important.

After this general approach, a brief analysis of dominance regulation and abuse of dominance is discussed, highlighting dominance in competition law and regulation and the ICT and telecommunications case law in Latin America. After the review of procompetitive and anticompetitive agreements between competitors and the enforcement of anticompetitive agreements in Latin America, a section covers the recent trend to consolidation in the different layers of the ICT ecosystem. In this section, a theory in ICT mergers is explained based on international case law, and the current analysis in the latest mergers in the ICT sector in Latin America is discussed. We conclude stressing the importance that competition authorities in Latin America develop a framework of the analysis and enforcement of competition law in the ICT sector and the case for the specialization of competition enforcers in ICTs.

Before starting, a few notes regarding the current state of development of the telecommunications industry and the ICT sector in Latin America. Broadly defined, the telecommunications sector is the addition of two very large markets: the mobile and the fixed industry. The ecosystem that surrounds both, however, includes several other markets and industries linked but never interconnected as they currently are,[5] such as the Over-the-Top (content services industry).[6]

Regarding the telecommunications industry, during the last thirty years, Latin American telecoms sector has transformed substantially. The mixture between government privatisations, public-private-partnerships, and several other strategies have led to a fast pace growing sector, attracting investments and new competition from local companies and from abroad, and a continuously dynamic sector,[7] fostering the emergence of several platforms, apps, super apps, and other sharing economy entrepreneurs.[8]

5. *See* Beatriz Kira, Vikram Sinha, and Sharmadha Srinivasan, Regulating Digital Ecosystems: Bridging the Gap between Competition Policy and Data Protection, *Industrial and Corporate Change*, vol. 30, no. 5, Oct. 2021, pp. 1337–1360, https://doi.org/10.1093/icc/dtab053 (Claiming that the antitrust literature has not yet explored the interface between data protection and antitrust systematically); Fransman, Martín. *The New ICT Ecosystem*. CUP, 2010, pp. 21–34.
6. Ganuza, Juan José and Viecens, Maria Fernanda. Over-the-Top (OTT) Content: Implications and Best Response Strategies of Traditional Telecom Operators. Evidence from Latin America, 4 July 2014, pp. 7–9.
7. Brereton, Collin. Rapid Growth Heralds a Great Future, in: Communications Review: Exploring the Telecom Markets in Latin America. A journal for telecom, cable, satellite and Internet executives, Vol. 16, no. 2. PricewatershouseCoopers, 2011, pp. 8–9 Available at: https://www.pwc.com/ve/es/publicaciones/assets/communications-review-latin-america-vol16-no2.pdf.
8. *See* International Telecommunications Union. *Measuring the Information Society Report 2018*. ITU Publications, 2018. Volume 1 and 2. Available at: https://www.itu.int/en/ITU-D/Statistics/Pages/publications/misr2018.aspx.

The mobile voice market in Latin America has grown at a very good pace during its two decades of development, however, it still lacks effective competition; concentration rates are above Europe and the United States – measured by the HHI[9] based in users.[10] Latin America, Africa, and Asia are the regions with the largest growth rates, but only the Latin American countries have reached penetration levels above 100%.[11] Regarding Internet access, according to the International Telecommunications Union (hereinafter ITU), the Americas has the lowest growth in fixed broadband penetration. Regarding fixed and mobile broadband Internet access, the development of Latin American indicators has been remarkable, only comparable with sets of other developing jurisdictions.

There are, however, several restrictions to the healthy growth of the industry. First, and most importantly, most consider that competition is weak and insufficient, leading to high prices and slow connections in the broadband market.[12] In addition, infrastructure growth has not reached all areas in most jurisdiction (with the notable exception of Colombia that has connected all municipalities with fibre optics during the last five years and that has programs that promote the elimination of barriers and the effective deployment of infrastructure in all municipalities[13]) and cellular mobile dependency, making a slow transition to an internet based and converged market. Competition policy is here to change most of this pervasive market structures, and the purpose of this chapter is to analyse the work done in Latin America, during the last twenty years and based on such work provide a framework of analysis for the future of competition law and policy in the ICT ecosystem.

We must also mention, of course, the COVID-19 pandemic and its effects on competition, particularly in the ICT sector. The proliferation in the use of the Internet, the consumption of goods and the provision of Over-The-Top services due to isolation generated those markets with different dynamics to the traditional ones, became relevant. This is currently, and will continue to be in the coming years, a challenge for competition authorities, which face conditions that do not allow them to take regulatory measures in the way they usually do. These are complex markets, making it difficult to analyse relevant markets, horizontal and vertical integrations, market power situations and even monopolies.[14]

9. The Herfindahl-Hirschman Index (HHI) measures market concentration to determine market competitiveness, and it is calculated by adding the results of the squared market share of the companies in a given sector or market.
10. Campbell, Glen, *The Year Ahead: Global Wireless Matrix*, Bank of America, 2014.
11. ITU Telecommunication Development Bureau. International Telecommunications Union, ICT facts and figures. ITU, Geneva, 2014, pp. 2–3.
12. OECD, ICCP Committee. *Review of Telecommunication Policy in Colombia*. 2014, pp. 15–38.
13. *See* República de Colombia, Comisión de Regulación de Comunicaciones. *Código de buenas prácticas al despliegue de infraestructura*. Versión 2020. Available at: https://crcom.gov.co/uploads/images/files/Buenas_Practicas_Despliegue_2020.pdf.
14. G. Núñez y F. Da Silva. *La libre competencia en la era digital y la pospandemia: el impacto sobre las pequeñas y medianas empresas*. Documentos de Proyectos (LC/TS.2021/15). Santiago, Comisión Económica para América Latina y el Caribe (CEPAL), 2021, pp. 7–9 Retrieved from: https://www.cepal.org/sites/default/files/publication/files/46663/S2100020_es.pdf.

§9.02 COMPETITION LAW IN ICT: FROM THE TELECOMMUNICATIONS SECTOR TO THE ICT ECOSYSTEM

In this section, a brief analysis of competition law in ICTs will be provided. First, a short explanation of what the telecom sector was, its decline to incept into the ICT sector, and how the new ICT industry works, in terms of its layered ecosystem, its competitive dynamics, and the challenges for competition authorities.

[A] The Telecommunications Sector

The telecommunications sector is composed of a set of markets interlinked to provide communications services, that is, any form of remote communications mediated by technological instruments.[15] Regularly, communications technologies are arranged in networks, on which participants can transmit, receive, or transport information through dedicated or shared channels.[16] This 'network' of elements that can be aimed to receive or transmit (e.g., handhelds) or to transport or code (e.g., backbone of fiber optics) and seen from distance constitutes a large machine devoted to interconnect machines to people, people to people, people to machines, or machines to machines.

In this process multiple economic and market relations arise.[17] End users have an economic relation with network providers and network providers with other larger, or farther-reaching network providers, and network providers. All these economic relations happen in a retail channel as well as in a wholesale channel.[18] Until very recently, from this grid of economic relations, but still the case of many developing countries and in most Latin American countries, voice communications have dominated the industry as the largest and most important market and the largest revenue generator.[19]

This brief description of the telecommunications market shows that having regard to these two layers of participants in the market, end users and networks, the transport layer became the most important undertaking in the industry, above terminal manufacturers, and end users. Moreover, giving the network and the termination and in some cases transport monopolies, most regulatory interventions in the industry were aimed at controlling the abuse of market power and other forms of illicit exploitation of a market advantage.

15. *See* Chiang, Mung and Brinton, Christopher. *Networks Illustrated,* EdWiser Scholastic Press, 2013; Dodd, Annabel Z. *The Essential Guide to Telecommunications*, 5th Edition, Prentice Hall Professional, 2012.
16. Chiang, Mung and Brinton, Christopher. *Networks Illustrated*. EdWiser Scholastic Press, 2013, sect. 7.1.
17. Dodd, Annabel Z. *The Essential Guide to Telecommunications,* 5th Edition, Prentice Hall Professional, 2012.
18. *Ibid.*, Chapter 3.
19. *Ibid*

[B] From Telecommunications to ICT

During the last decade, networks have changed and migrated to data networks where voice is reducing its importance, giving room to IP communications based on text, images, and video.[20] Service providers such as OTTs, – this is communications services providers over an internet connection – have, despite long started, used the transport layer to deliver their services to end users. This, to a large extent, will continue to be the case because it represents benefits for market players and consumers. The provision of OTT services eliminates barriers and reduces information asymmetries, enables access to new products, and allows small companies to have a global reach. All this fosters competition.[21]

All this relationships between end users and service providers have generated new economic realities by increasing or shrinking the scope of different markets (such as television and audio-visual services) and different forms to exercise market power.[22] OTT service providers, in most cases, are competing head to head with the traditional telecom operators with services that over the Internet can replace voice, television, or other value-added services that long before were exclusively provided by operators through means different from the Internet. In most cases, OTT do not have to comply with all the legacy regulations[23] that are regularly enforced and applied to network providers, creating, different regulatory environments that might create substantial competitive advantages.[24] However, several other collaborative OTT-Operator models have aroused,[25] giving rise to other antitrust concerns regarding the 'addition' of market power[26] and the use of service bundles and sponsored data to provide packages to users that were before sold separately.[27] The Colombian communications regulator

20. *See* República de Colombia, Comisión de Regulación de Comunicaciones. *Redes móviles en Colombia. Análisis y hoja de ruta regulatoria para su modernización.* 2019. Available at: https://www.crcom.gov.co/uploads/images/files/Documento-Modernizacion-redes-moviles.pdf.

    In this document, the Colombian regulator reviews and makes a comparative analysis of the technical evolution of mobile networks and regulatory modernization measures. It shows the progress made in this area in Colombia and in some countries in the region.
21. Lancieri, Filippo and Sakowski, Patricia, Competition in Digital Markets: A Review of Expert Reports (30 January 2021). 26 Stan. J.L. Bus. and Fin. 65 (2021), pp. 92–93 Available at SSRN: https://ssrn.com/abstract=3681322 or http://dx.doi.org/10.2139/ssrn.3681322.
22. *See* Thépot, 'Florence, Market Power in Online Search and Social-Networking: A Matter of Two-Sided Markets.' World Competition, Kluwer Law International, vol. 36, no. 2, 1 June 2013.
23. Australian Communications and Media Authority (ACMA). *Broken Concepts: The Australian Communications Legislative Landscape.* Published by the Australian Communications and Media Authority (2011).
24. *See* GSMA, *White Paper: The OTT Opportunity for Operators.* In: http://www.gsma.com/membership/wp-content/uploads/2013/10/White-paper-Aug2013.pdf.
25. *See* Kineto, The Telco-OTT opportunity. 2013. In: http://kineto.com/pdf/The-Telco-OTT-Opportunity.pdf.
26. John M. Newman, 'Antitrust in Digital Markets.' *Vanderbilt Law Review*, vol. 72, 1497 (2019) Available at: https://scholarship.law.vanderbilt.edu/vlr/vol72/iss5/2.
27. AsiaInfo. Quantity & Quality: The business case for a profitable operator/OTT partnership model. 2014.

recently conducted a study on the role of OTT services in the communications sector in Colombia, which may shed light on what we have been saying.[28]

All these 'new' economic relationships have just started to be a concern for competition regulators and antitrust authorities around the globe. In Latin America, just during 2014 some jurisdictions have started to find that there might be some antitrust concerns from exclusionary conduct of network operators that may disrupt the net neutrality principle,[29] or by OTTs that have competitive advantages due to niche entry and other market inefficiencies. Little attention has competition authorities and regulators given to the bundling of services by dominant operators of different platforms, such as the network operators and some service providers, the reverse payment agreements by service providers to network operators that might bypass the competitive neutrality principle and could lead to restrict the access of competitors to final consumers.

[C] The New ICT Industry/Ecosystem: Dynamics and Challenges for Competition Authorities

The disruption in the telecom market of service providers gave rise to several other economic relations that were not linked before which have made the telecommunications sector transform into a larger sector with a wider set of actors and participants interlinked, interconnected, and mutually coexistent in symbiotic relations that have produced an 'ecosystem'.[30] This ecosystem pushes market participants to compete and cooperate, to survive.

Recent ITU studies indicate that mobile network operators and OTT service providers need each other. Each has an effect on the demand and revenues of the other, as one offers the connectivity needed to provide services and the other offers the content for which consumers demand internet connectivity.[31]

Under this model, several other undertakings, before only adjacent in a telecom operator industry, are now even more important than networks in the creation of value for consumers.[32] Then, manufacturers are now a fundamental part of the ecosystem providing online services and operative systems. Telecom operators are now widening the scope of their value chain by providing content to end users or value-added services to content providers. Network equipment manufacturers are entering the device and handset markets. Content providers are entering the operative systems markets and

28. Reública de Colombia, Comisión de Regulación de Comunicaciones. *El rol de los servicios OTT en el sector de las comunicaciones en Colombia.* 2019. Available at: https://www.crcom.gov.co/uploads/images/files/ESTUDIO-OTT-COLOMBIA.pdf.
29. FCC, CRC, Subtel Chile.
30. *See* Taylor, Richard D., Metaphor as Policy: The Case of the 'Broadband Ecosystem' (31 March 2014). 2014 TPRC Conference Paper. Available at SSRN: http://ssrn.com/abstract=2418258 or http://dx.doi.org/10.2139/ssrn.2418258.
31. International Telecommunications Union. *Repercusiones económicas de los servicios OTT en los mercados nacionales de telecomunicaciones/TIC.* UIT-D Comisiones de Estudio. Producto anual 2019-2020. Retrieved from: https://www.itu.int/en/ITU-D/Study-Groups/2018-2021/Documents/2020/470102_Question3-1and4-1S.pdf.
32. *See* OECD, ICCP. Internet Economy Outlook, 2013, pp. 101–128.

have produced marketplaces for applications. Handset manufacturers as well as telecom operators are now entering the apps market through the development of applications or introducing their own platforms for the distribution of applications.[33] In addition, most participants of the market are also gathering user's information to boost their advertising business and their revenues coming from publicity.

These interconnected businesses have created new cost functions and structures, new network externalities and have changed the basic market analysis that was prevalent in the world of telecommunications. Regulation and competition law analysis must change to this new reality and include, not segments of the chain, as the regular market definition techniques prescribe, but the complete set of interconnected economic relations, having much more regard to the prospects of the market than its past. The role of regulators and competition authorities must have regard to the need to provide a level playing field and ensure the competitive process.

[D] The Characteristics of the ICT Ecosystem: Challenges for Competition Authorities

This whole process is regularly described with three different characters that easily explain why the 'ecosystem' requires different regulatory and academic approaches than the one applying regularly to markets.[34]

The first is the existence of dynamic efficiencies or fast dynamism. This characteristic of the ICT sector not extensively present in the former telecom sector is the large reliance on short-term innovation and product differentiation to drive industry growth and the industry's profitability.[35]

The second character is the increasing reliance on platforms competition to grow and differentiate, as explained earlier. The existence of these two-sided markets and platforms to meet both market sides is what makes the economics of complementary goods and services much more important to understand the links among the different participants in the ecosystem.[36] Antitrust issues may be seen in a traditional fashion when those platforms also create compatibility issues or vertical integration restraints that nowadays are necessary to participate in the ICTs markets.[37]

---

33. Koslowski, Thomas G., Patricia H. Longstaff, Miguel Vidal, and Thomas Grob. 'Resilience Analysis of the ICT Ecosystem.' In *23rd European Regional ITS Conference, Vienna 2012*, no. 60390. International Telecommunications Society (ITS), 2012.
34. *See* Oz Shi, *The Economics of Network Industries*, Cambridge University Press, 2001; Patrick Tucker, *The Naked Future: What Happens in a World That Anticipates Your Every Move?* Penguin, 2014; Jeffrey A. Eisenach and Ilene Knable Gotts. *In Search of a Competition Doctrine for Information Technology Markets: Recent Antitrust Developments in the Online Sector*. In: Communications and Competition Law Key Issues in the Telecoms, Media and Technology Sectors. Wolters Kluwer, Aspen, 2015; Jeffrey A. Eisenach. *Broadband Competition in the Internet Ecosystem*. America Enterprise Institute, 2012.
35. See Eisenach and Gotts. *In Search...*, p. 71.
36. *Ibid.*, p. 71. See also Evans, David S. and Mariscal, Elisa V., *Market Definition Analysis in Latin America with Applications to Internet-Based Industries* (26 June 2013). Available at SSRN: http://dx.doi.org/10.2139/ssrn.2285400.
37. *Ibid.*, p. 72.

The third characteristic of these markets is the existence of network externalities on almost every chain of the value chain. Consumers are more likely to buy a product when faced with products with large numbers of users.[38] It is not just a matter of the scale of users, but also, as explained by Eisenach, of the scope of users. Most platforms grant more value to users and advertisers when they have a large set of different users.[39]

This framework of analysis facilitates the conclusions regarding the need of a different approach in ICT sectors antitrust and regulatory analysis. Competition authorities and regulators have piecemeal doctrines and theoretical frameworks that allow them to study sectors that possess the latter characteristics. However, there are no regulatory or antitrust enforcement developments that may lead to standards or rules regarding conduct or structures in the presence of network externalities, platforms, and dynamic efficiencies,[40] which traditionally may be deemed as anticompetitive.

§9.03 DOMINANCE, ABUSE OF DOMINANCE, AND ITS ENFORCEMENT IN ICT

Having regard to the latter section, dominance regulation and abuse of dominance cases in the ICT sector should follow different perspective than the one that followed until now, having regard to the wide spectrum in the ICT's ecosystem. From market definition to the analysis of the exercise of market power, it is necessary that antitrust authorities reframe the use of regulatory instruments to impose remedies in markets where an abuse exists.

Dominance is a legal as much as an economic concept, but larger than mere market power.[41] Dominance goes beyond independency of pricing and goes as far as the possibility to exclude.[42] This, as in the case of market power, is also a matter of

38. See Oz Shi. *The Economics of Network Industries*, Cambridge University Press, 2001.
39. *See* Sarit Markovich and Johannes Moenius. 'Winning while losing: Competition dynamics in the presence of indirect network effects.' International Journal of industrial Organization, vol. 27, 2009, pp. 346–357.
40. 'IT markets have characteristics that limit the usefulness of these traditional approaches, often in ways that are not yet well understood. We begin by describing the characteristics that distinguish IT markets from more traditional ones and then discuss some of the challenges these characteristics pose for traditional antitrust doctrine.' Jeffrey A. Eisenach and Ilene Knable Gotts. *In Search of a Competition Doctrine for Information Technology Markets: Recent Antitrust Developments in the Online Sector.* In: Communications and Competition Law Key Issues in the Telecoms, Media and Technology Sectors. Wolters Kluwer, Aspen, 2015.
41. *See* O'Donoghue and Padilla, *The Law and Economics of Article 82 EC*, p. 108 (stating that in EU competition law, there is an economic concept of dominance; however, this does not correspond with the legal definition); Hovenkamp, *Federal Antitrust Policy: The Law of Competition and Its Practice.* West Academic Publishing, p. 271a–b, (showing that in US antitrust law, dominance is a concept larger than mere market power).
42. *See* Areeda and Hovenkamp, *Antitrust Law*, §3A-651a. According to Areeda and Hovenkamp, exclusionary acts are actions by a dominant undertaking that 'are capable of creating, enlarging or prolonging monopoly power by impairing the opportunities of rivals' and that either 'do not benefit consumers at all'; 'are unnecessary for the particular consumer benefits that the acts produce' or 'produce harms disproportionate to the resulting benefits.'

degree; And of course, the scope of the conduct regarding the market where the conduct takes place and the impact of such in the value chain and the 'ecosystem'. This is particularly important in the ICT sector as most conducts that may seem very likely to constitute an abuse are mere matching the competition actions and other conducts that may seem inoffensive in other markets - such as a conglomerate merger - may affect the whole ecosystem.

The economic perspective of dominance in telecommunications and ICTs is regularly associated with the exercise of market power in the network or the platforms where there might be monopoly power.[43] Under this perspective, most Latin American economies have developed regulations or ex post and antitrust interventions to cope with the challenges that dominance imposes. Most of the cases pertain to the telecom sector where network operators are considered dominant over their network use and therefore are proved to have the ability to 'raise price above the competitive level'[44] or introduce margin squeezes on competitors, refusals to deal or exploitative prices among other conducts.

All these definitions show that there have been different approaches to dominance, and the effect of such approaches has a different outcome in the Latin American jurisdictions. Regulatory approaches to dominance in the telecommunication industry tend to be much more intrusive than the approaches taken by competition authorities. This does not mean that both the different authorities follow different rules but that the remedies considered are definitively much more precise when defined by a regulator of competition.[45]

Enforcement of dominance in ICTs in Latin American economies has been wide, and most dominance cases in the region refer to dominance in telecommunications markets. Few cases have been opened regarding the IT industry, this although most emerging economies have highly concentrated industries, and the IT industry is regularly based on IP network interfaces.[46]

Some cases are very interesting as they go against the common wisdom. For example, Mexico's Competition Commission found that not even a market share of 98% is enough to define dominance or 'substantial market power' in the telecommunications market. In the *Teléfonos de Mexico*[47] case, the commission found that Telmex had 98% of fixed (land) lines in the telephony services market.[48] However, such a fact was not enough, and the commission went further to determine the barriers to entry in

43. Elhauge, Einer R., 'Defining Better Monopolization Standards'. Harvard Law and Economics Discussion Paper No. 434 p. 257. Available at SSRN: https://ssrn.com/abstract=437863
44. Landes, William M. and Posner, Richard A., 'Market Power in Antitrust Cases', 94 Harvard Law Review 937 (1980) p. 937.
45. See for example the remedies imposed by the Colombian Communications' Regulator regarding the dominance in the mobile voice market taken in 2012 and its impact (Riascos et al., Measuring Welfare effects of dominance regulation in the mobile voice industry in Colombia, 2012, On File with the Author, 2015) and the remedies imposed by the competition authority in a case involving an abuse in the mobile voice industry in Colombia taken by SIC.
46. *See* Gal MS. *Competition Policy for Small Market Economies*, Harvard University Press, 2003.
47. *Comisión Federal de Competencia v Teléfonos de México* Expediente No. DE-45-2000 Comisión Federal de Competencia, México.
48. *Ibid.*, p. 11.

to the subservices in which Telmex had pricing power in order to find the company dominant.[49] The only problem with this case is that all the arguments were based on static efficiencies and the singular markets defined and not on the impact such decision has on the ecosystem. On the other hand, in *Will v. Claro Chile*,[50] the Chilean Tribunal considered that the market share by the defendant, Claro, was 16.1% in the market for fixed telephony, which was large compared to the 0.3% market share by the defendant. However, the tribunal disregarded Claro's dominant position by comparing Claro's shares with those of Movistar and Entel, which for the year in question were respectively 44% and 32%.[51]

Excessive pricing and margin squeeze cases were very common. In Colombia, in the case *Orbitel v. Comcel, Telefónica and Tigo*[52] the superintendent for competition, accused the largest mobile telephony undertakings in the country of charging high and excessive prices to fixed telephony companies for the termination of calls in their mobile network. According to the superintendent, without any significant difference in cost structures, mobile telecommunication companies charged fixed telephony firms a rate per minute that was substantially higher (66% and 69% depending on the cost assessment methodology)[53] than the rates charged for calls terminated in the fixed network. The deputy concluded that, given the market structure and considering a reasonable profit and the probable effects of macroeconomic shocks on rates, there were no reasonable explanation for the rates charged to fixed telecommunications companies, and therefore such charges constituted an 'exacerbated' and 'inequitable' price.[54] However, the competition authority held in a brief paragraph that the mere difference between a theoretical price and the actual prices charged are not a per se violation of Article 1 of Law 155 of 1959, since high prices were a consequence of dominance, not an abuse itself.[55]

Also in *CMET v. Compañía de Telecomunicaciones de Chile S.A.*,[56] CMET accused the Chilean Telecommunications Company (CTC) of price predating in the market of fixed telephony.[57] According to the Chilean National prosecutor, price predation could not occur, since the duration of the discount regarded as predatory was only for a month; therefore it did not have the likelihood of excluding or disciplining a well-established company from the market.[58] In *Avantel, Alestra and Marcatel v. Telmex*, the Federal Competition Commission of Mexico investigated whether Telmex has

49. *Ibid.*
50. *Will S.A. v. Claro Chile S.A.* Sentencia 110 de 2011 Tribunal de Defensa de la Libre Competencia, Chile.
51. *Ibid.*, §§17-18.
52. *See Orbitel v. Comcel, Telefónica y Colombia Movil* Informe Motivado Superintendencia de Industria y Comercio, Colombia.
53. *Ibid.*, p. 22.
54. *Ibid.*, p. 28.
55. *See Orbitel v. Comcel, Telefónica y Colombia Móvil* Resolución 18954 de 2009, Superintendencia de Industria y Comercio, Colombia.
56. *CMET v. Compañía de Telecomunicaciones de Chile S.A.* Rol N° 977-07 FNE, Fiscalía Nacional Económica, Chile.
57. *Ibid.*, §4.
58. *Ibid.*

abused its dominant position in the resale of telecommunication services, in particular in the resale of 'long distance transmission capacity' and 'interconnection services' in the national market.[59] The Mexican Competition Authority found several signals of abuse such as the fact that Telmex charged its competitors twice for certain services, or that wholesale long distance calls prices were higher than retail prices, or denial and reluctance to provide services to competitors, and therefore the authority sanctioned Telmex for impeding the provision of interconnection and resale services to its competitors and reducing competition in such telecommunications markets and imposed several remedies in order to restore competition in the market.[60]

In other margin squeeze case, the Federal Competition Commission of Mexico[61] fined Telcel – a mobile operator – for abusing its dominance in the Mexican mobile telecommunications markets. The Mexican authority found that Telcel engaged in a non-transitory pricing scheme in which the undertaking charged its competitors fees for wholesale termination in its own network larger than the retail prices offered by Telcel to its own customers in the retail market, making its competitors impossible to match Telcel prices without incurring a loss. Telcel appealed the commission's ruling, and in 2012, the commission accepted to reduce the fines imposed subject to the condition that Telcel reduces its fees to competitive prices.[62]

Regarding tying, in *CFC v Telmex*,[63] the Mexican competition authority found that the Mexican telecommunications company was abusing its dominant position by obstructing other agents' access to internet services by tying their service of local telephony to the internet access service, a market where the Telmex was dominant, thus impeding entry and consequently reducing consumer welfare.[64] Similarly, in 2014, the superintendent for Market Power Control, of Ecuador, imposed a fine against Conecel–Claro – a subsidiary of the Telmex group, for abusing its dominant position in the passive infrastructure lending market, where the company was considered to be dominant in Ecuador. According to the Ecuadorian Competition Authority, Claro abused its dominant position by imposing unjustified exclusivity clauses to land lenders that limited the possibility of other market participants to deploy infrastructure

59. DE-033-99; this account is based on OECD Policy Round table, Margin Squeeze, DAF/COMP(2009)36, 2010, pp. 164–165; D. Sokol, Fourth Annual Latin American Round Table On Competition & Trade. Brooklyn Journal of International Law, vol. 27, no. 1, 2001.
60. Cited by: Cave, Martin, A. Andreas Avgousti, and Adrian Foster. Strengthening Competition Policy in Latin American Countries. Centro Regional de Competencia en America Latina, México, July, 2013. In: http://crcal.org/guias-y-estudios/estudios/estudios-de-sector/doc_download/12-strengthening-competition-policy-in-latin-american-countries-the-application-of-competition-law-in-the-telecommunications-sector, p. 54.
61. Federal Competition Commission of Mexico, Communiqué 04-2011 Interconnection Related Monopolistic Practices. DE-037-2006. The decision can be found at http://resoluciones.cfc.gob.mx/DOCS/Asuntos%20Juridicos/V45/6/1518064.pdf.
62. Federal Competition Commission of Mexico, Communiqué 04-2011 Interconnection Related Monopolistic Practices. The decision can be found at http://resoluciones.cfc.gob.mx/DOCS/Asuntos%20Juridicos/V45/6/1518064.pdf.
63. *Comisión Federal de Competencia v. Grupo de Telecomunicaciones Mexicanas S.A. de C.V.*
64. *Ibid.*, §IV.a; §IV.b.

in such sites or deal with other undertakings to reduce the costs of infrastructure deploying.[65]

In *GMT v. Telmex*,[66] also Telmex was accused of tying and bundling the fixed telephony service with the fixed Internet service, not giving the chance to consumers to unbundle and acquire such services separated. In addition, GMT alleged that the tying made by the dominant undertaking was leveraging its dominant position in the broadband market to the fixed market making uneconomical the participation of GMT in the fixed telephony market. The Mexican Competition Authority defined the relevant market as the market for the fixed broadband access with a regional scope. The authority considered that there was no nationwide market as 5% of municipalities had more than one participant in both markets. In addition, having evidence that there was competition in 5% of municipalities, there was no evidence that they could not compete on the merits - they could easily invest - and, therefore, the tying was not anticompetitive offer. The Mexican Authority definitively made a mistake interpreting the behaviour of the dominant undertaking. First, the relevant market was poorly defined; from a very poor understanding of bundling in telecommunication services to the definition of entry barriers (last mile). Second, there was evidence in the case that the dominant's offer was designed as a system to limit access to the fixed telephony market by leveraging its broadband market power to the fixed telephony market making fixed telephony companies' offer uneconomical.

Also, in *SIC v. Colombia Telecomunicaciones S.A.*,[67] the Colombian Authority found that Colombia Telecomunicaciones - Coltel - was the dominant undertaking in the market for data and cross-connection through submarine cable. The authority found Coltel's dominant position just by looking at the market structure and considered the fact that there was a single operator with, therefore, a 100% market share, giving such an undertaking the ability to independently and unilaterally determine prices and other market conditions.[68] The competition authority closed the investigation by signing a consent decree, despite there was evidence that Coltel was price discriminating tying its interconnection service with the international capacity service and had the capacity to squeeze its competitors markets.[69]

As margin squeeze cases, refusals to deal have been a common set of cases for the antitrust decisions in the communications industry. In the case *Tele Cable Centro Occidente S.A. v. Grupo Televisa*,[70] Grupo Televisa was accused and found abusing its

65. SCPM v Conecel. Superintendencia de poder de mercado. Exp.: 0009-SCPM-CRPI-2013. In: http://base.crcal.org/documentos/bd60386f-40d3-4d08-a7ed-6558fd83d479/Ecuador-CNT-2014-CONECEL_SA.pdf.
66. *Grupo de Telecomunicaciones Mexicanas S.A. de C.V. v. Telmex*, Recurso de reconsideración. Expediente No. RA-014-2011 y Expediente 07-2011.
67. *Superintendencia de Industria y Comercio v. Colombia Telecomunicaciones COLTEL S. A. E.S.P.* Resolución 60145 de 2009 Superintendencia de Industria y Comercio, Colombia.
68. *Ibid.*, §§7.1-7.8.
69. *See*: *SIC v Coltel*. Resolución 43253 de 2010. Superintendencia de Industria y Comercio. In: http://www.sic.gov.co/drupal/sites/default/files/estados/RESOLUCION_43253_DE_20_DE_AGOSTO_DE_2010_GARANTIAS_COLTEL.pdf.
70. *Tele Cable Centro Occidente S.A. v. Grupo Televisa*, Comisión Federal de Competencia Económica, México. Expediente RA-26-2007.

dominant position in the market of wholesale television content in different categories of content due to its denial of access to sixteen television signals (content produced by Televisa). The Mexican authority considered that only the wholesale market of public television was open for antitrust scrutiny, as only such content was a necessary input in the market of cable television as not having those signals made it impossible for the company to compete in the market.[71]

Similarly, in *Axtel v. Teléfonos de Mexico and Teléfonos del Norte*,[72] Axtel, a fixed telephony operator in Mexico complained to the CFC that the Telmex Group, through both of its companies, abused its dominant position in the market of wholesale telephony termination, transport, and lending of dedicated links for local and long distance calls.[73] The companies, according to the CFC, delayed and obstructed Axtel's participation in the market by refusing to deal with Axtel the lending of its dedicated accesses and interconnection required to provide services of long distance and local calls, broadband Internet, and other communications in the Mexican fixed communications markets, services where the compliant competed with the defendant.[74] The Mexican CFC also proved that Telmex Group, in order to provide interconnection services, asked Axtel specific information about the needs of Axtel's clients, and then denied the service to Axtel in order to provide the service directly to Axtel's clients.[75]

In Chile the entrance of new operators in the mobile industry was pushed by the Chilean competition watchdog, the National Economic Prosecutor, which, by a complaint presented by the Ministry of Communications - SUBTEL, investigated whether the mobile network operators refused to deal with Mobile Virtual Operators - MVNOS - and obstructed their entrance to the market. The Chilean Tribunal for Competition found, based on the evidence presented by National Economic Prosecutor, considered that the three mobile companies (Telefonica, Entel PCS, and Claro) did not refused to deal or denied access to essential facilities required to participate in the mobile market, mostly due to the fact that there was no regulation. The prosecutor, appealed before the Supreme Court which held that the mobile network operators did restrict competition in the market, and, with the purpose to reduce the intensity of competition, artificially restricted entry and refused to deal with MVNOs.[76] A similar

71. *Tele Cable Centro Occidente S.A. v. Grupo Televisa,* Comisión Federal de Competencia Económica, México. Expediente RA-26-2007. *In:* http://www.cfc.gob.mx:8080/cfcresoluciones/Docs/Asuntos%20Juridicos/V35/21/1331194.pdf.
72. *Axtel v Telefonos de Mexico and Telefonos del Norte,* Comisión Federal de Competencia Económica, Mèxico, Expediente DE-008-2010.
73. *Axtel v Telefonos de Mexico and Telefonos del Norte,* Comisión Federal de Competencia Económica, México, Expediente DE-008-2010, OPR.
74. *Ibid.*, pp. 330-341.
75. *Ibid.*, pp. 430-431.
76. Supreme Court Decision 104_2011. Cited by: Cave, Martin; A. Andreas Avgousti, and Adrian Foster. Strengthening Competition Policy in Latin American Countries. Centro Regional de Competencia en America Latina, México, July, 2013. In: http://crcal.org/guias-y-estudios/estudios/estudios-de-sector/doc_download/12-strengthening-competition-policy-in-latin-american-countries-the-application-of-competition-law-in-the-telecommunications-sector, p. 56.

case happened in the Colombian mobile industry where the Colombian Communications Regulator – CCR – imposed obligations on Coltel, in order to allow interconnection and deal with MVNOs that wanted to enter the Colombian market but were imposed impossible conditions by incumbent operators and were therefore restricted to enter the market.[77] During the proceedings of an interconnection case, the CCR defined that such practice may violate competition law and current access and interconnection regulations and ordered incumbent operators to allow access to MVNOs and facilitated this operator's entry into the market.

Despite the above, we should also mention that the Chilean National Economic Prosecutor's Office dismissed a complaint filed by *WOM S.A.* against *Entel PCS, Telefónica Móviles Chile S.A.* and *Claro Chile S.A.* (incumbent operators) for abuse of dominant position, which was allegedly exercised through anticompetitive practices aimed at excluding *WOM* from the mobile telephone market. The head of the antitrust division of the Chilean competition watchdog stated that there was no evidence of anticompetitive behaviour, and therefore recommended that the complaint be dismissed.[78]

On the other hand, price predation and price discrimination cases have not been very common but in *Impsat S.A. v. Advance Comunicaciones S.A., Telecom Soluciones S.A., Startel S.A., Telefónica de Argentina S.A. y Telecom Argentina STET France Telecom S.A..*,[79] Impsat accused several companies in the market of data transmission in Argentina to be price predating. The Argentinean Commission, using the average variable costs standard (hereinafter AVC), stated that in these markets variable costs are so low that it will be very difficult to demonstrate that prices are lower than such.[80] In *Impsat*,[81] the Argentinean authority decided that not only the restrictions to competition must be proven, but also the restriction to the 'general economic interest', because 'there are anticompetitive conducts that may not engender an actual or potential damage to the general economic interest'.[82] In addition, during 2010 the Chilean Competition watchdog, the National Economic Prosecutor, filed a complaint before the Competition Tribunal due to the on-net/off-net price discrimination made by mobile operators in the mobile communications retail market. According to the prosecutor, such price discrimination was imposing barriers to entrants discouraging consumers as tariffs to the largest networks were much more expensive than those paid by costumers of the incumbents. The tribunal held that such practice created an artificial – not cost-related – and endogenous barrier to entry, in a market already characterized by high exogenous barriers to entry. The tribunal held also that the on-net/off-net price discrimination was not per se anticompetitive, and therefore,

77. *Ibid.*
78. *See* República de Chile, Fiscalía Nacional Económica. Denuncia por eventuales prácticas anticompetitivas en el mercado de la telefonía e internet móvil. Rol N° 2407-16 FNE, 2017. Available at: https://www.fne.gob.cl/wp-content/uploads/2017/05/inpu_05_2017.pdf.
79. *See Impsat v. Telefónica de Argentina S.A et. al.* Dictamen No. 442. Ministerio de Economía y Producción. Comisión Nacional de Defensa de la Competencia, Argentina.
80. *Ibid.*, p. 121.
81. *Impsat v. Telefónica de Argentina S.A et. al.*
82. *Ibid.*, §66, §161; *See A. Gas y otros v. AGIP Argentina S.A.*

imposing restriction to such discrimination may hinder consumers by limiting operators' possibilities to offer new and innovative plans.[83]

Also, in *Telefónica v. América Móvil Peru*, the Peruvian Tribunal for the Defense of Competition and Unfair Competition decided that there was no act of unfair competition by América Movil which offered its customers the possibility to download a famous ringtone for free knowing that it was mandatory to pay for Internet access, making the content not necessarily free for consumers. On the other hand, in the same case the tribunal ordered América Móvil to stop certain advertising campaign where subjective factors made consumers prone to be mistaken regarding the quality of service granted by América Móvil.[84]

There is also a recent case in which dominance was declared but the authority did not take ex ante measures. In January 2021, the Colombian Communications Regulatory Commission found *Claro Colombia's* effective dominant position in the mobile services market.[85] The regulator found that (i) there is no effective competition; (ii) economies of scale and scope are a significant advantage for *Claro Colombia*; (iii) barriers to market entry persist; and (iv) other operators have not been able to compete for large market shares. This was reaffirmed on appeal.[86] Despite the above, the Regulatory Commission did not take special regulatory measures against *Claro Colombia*.

Finally, we must refer to the search engines market. It is well known that the European competition authorities have analysed Google's dominant position in this market and different jurisdictions have, on different occasions, sanctioned the company for abusing its market power. Well, in Latin America, the Conselho Administrativo de Defesa Econômica (CADE), Brazil's competition authority, has not lagged and has investigated Google for alleged conduct that could potentially affect free economic competition.[87] CADE investigated whether Google did indeed manipulate its search engine algorithms to favour its service to the detriment of neutrality and to the detriment of its competitors. Finally, in 2019 the authority concluded that it could not prove manipulation of Google's organic search algorithms in the Brazilian market and,

83. República de Chile, Tribunal De Defensa De La Libre Competencia, Instrucciones de carácter general N° 2/2012. Santiago, dieciocho de diciembre de dos mil doce. ROL: NC N° 386-10. Instrucción General Sobre los Efectos en la Libre Competencia de la Diferenciación de Precios en los Servicios Públicos de Telefonía 'Tarifas On-Net / Off-Net' y de las Ofertas Conjuntas de Servicios de Telecomunicaciones. http://www.fne.gob.cl/wp-content/uploads/2012/12/inst_02_2012.pdf.
84. Tribunal de Defensa de la Competencia y de la Propiedad Intelectual, Sala de Defensa de la Competencia. RESOLUCIÓN 2758-2010/SC1-INDECOPI. Expediente 099-2009/CCD. 20 de Octubre de 2010.
85. República de Colombia, Comisión de Regulación de Comunicaciones. Resolución CRC 6146 de 2021.
86. República de Colombia, Comisión de Regulación de Comunicaciones. Resolución CRC 6380 de 2021.
87. *See* Conselho Administrativo de Defesa Econômica. Processo Administrativo 08012.010843/2011-94. Available at: https://sei.cade.gov.br/sei/modulos/pesquisa/md_pesq_processo_exibir.php?2pXoYgv29q86Rn-fAe4ZUaXIR3v7-gVxEWL1JeB-RtUgqOwvr6Zlwydl0IhRNSr2Q22lByVKByYDYwsa13_JxqldakEIsAfM40O_nlair2nlnoNzF4h6tAzo-cc8tTVt.

on the contrary, proved efficiencies for both consumers and advertisers. As a result, the investigation was closed.[88]

The case law for abuse of dominance, which as we have seen is abundant in Latin America for telecommunications markets, shows two particular facts: first, either in recent as in pre-convergence stages, the notion of dominance is based on market definition and not in the ecosystem, making the reach and depth of the analysis of communications and IT markets, subsidiary in the best case scenario; and second, most antitrust agencies and regulators had not yet developed a framework to face difficult cases where there are interlinked services involved, and therefore many Type 1 and Type 2 errors may have aroused.

§9.04 AGREEMENTS BETWEEN COMPETITORS: FROM ILLICIT COLLABORATION TO COMPETITION

The existence of provisions prohibiting anticompetitive agreements in Latin American markets is usual among different jurisdictions, at both the regional and the national level. It is not necessary to explain here why enforcement of competition law in Latin America is regularly more preoccupied with anticompetitive agreements and more specifically cartels, as it is not necessary to analyse the provisions prohibiting cartels as common understanding and certain harmonization between regimes have been held by the different authorities. However, cartels and anticompetitive agreements have been one of the areas of enforcement with the most cases and that have had the largest attention by competition authorities.

The traditional cannon of competition law regularly deems as illegal many acts, contracts, or agreements where competitors either downstream or upstream to reduce rivalry or attempt to reduce rivalry and increase prices, reduce quality, or share the market. Regularly, as well the competition and antitrust *cannon* considers that most agreements between competitors reduce rivalry and only a very few of them may have procompetitive outcomes that may increase consumers' welfare.

It is also a fact that in the ICT sector, there are multiple interrelations between competitors that collaborate in different areas to compete in the multiple services provided. In fact, it is becoming a common trend in the market that most agreements and collaborations between competitors are regularly aimed at providing much more value to consumers and not to reduce rivalry between market participants. However, traditional analysis of horizontal effects – such as the effect on prices – must be looked from a different perspective. Antitrust doctrine based on the simple observation that after certain transaction or agreement, there are stable or even lower prices for consumers is not necessarily a guarantee that an operation is free from antitrust risk or scrutiny. It is now the case that the effects from one operation in a particular market may be seen in other related or interlinked markets or even in distant services with just

88. See Conselho Administrativo de Defesa Econômica. Processo contra Google no mercado de busca na internet é arquivado. Retrieved from: https://www.gov.br/cade/pt-br/assuntos/noticias/processo-contra-google-no-mercado-de-busca-na-internet-e-arquivado.

far interlinked by behavioural considerations. This consideration is applicable not only to agreements between competitors but also to mergers.

Case law in Latin America in this area is scarce. There are only few cases where competition authorities have found a cartel in telecommunications, IT, or other communications' services as this is a 'winner takes all' industry and rivalry is a common place. Cartels are therefore almost inexistent; illicit collaboration between competitors is not a common area of antitrust scrutiny and analysis. A few cases are worth analysing.

In 2010,[89] the Colombian Competition Authority, opened an investigation against the largest broadcasters of public television in Colombia - Caracol and RCN - for an agreement in which the parties bought and limited the access to television rating measures made by IBOPE and limited the scope of measuring excluding from it international networks and other local broadcasters. The authority found that, both companies received the largest amount of revenues for television advertising in the country and examined whether such kind of collaboration agreement between the parties was procompetitive as the parties considered it to be, finding that it looked much more like a purchasing cartel than a collaboration agreement and disregarded the Défense according to which the agreement was procompetitive as it guaranteed the advertising market with a rating tool.[90]

In 2004, the Venezuelan SVS,-yes, there is competition law in Venezuela, initiated an investigation in order to determine whether RCTV and Venevision - the media in opposition to the government had an agreement to define advertising spots prices, quality conditions, and market shares in the advertising in public television market. According to the report, RCTV and Venevision were found to be acting to 'offer advertisers preferential prices for advertising space' restricting the access of other television networks to the market of advertising in TV programmes. The SVS considered that both companies were creating an artificial barrier to competition granting RCTV and Venevision advantages that led to an increase in market concentration.[91]

Similarly, in *CNC v. Multicanal and CableVision S.A.*[92] the Argentinean Competition Commission found that Multicanal and Cablevision were accused and later on fined for having an agreement to share the cable television market in the city of Santa. The commission found that, based on a complaint presented in the year 1998 by the

89. SIC v Ibope, Caracol y RCN. Resolución 20065 de 2010. Superintendencia de Industria y Comercio. See: http://www.sic.gov.co/drupal/sites/default/files/estados/Resolucion_200065_de_2010_Apertura_de_Investigacion_Ibope.pdf
90. *SIC v Ibope, Caracol y RCN*. Resolución 23890 de 2011. Superintendencia de Industria y Comercio. En: http://www.sic.gov.co/drupal/recursos_user/documentos/normatividad/Publicaciones_Despacho_3/sicdecisiones2/RESOLUCIONES_COMPETENCIA_ANOS/2011/RESOLUCION_23890_DE_29_DE_ABRIL_DE_2011_SANCION_IBOPE.pdf. Also Cited by: Competition Committee. Competition Issues in Television and Broadcasting. DAF/COMP/GF(2013)13.
91. Cited by: OECD, Competition Committee. Competition Issues in Television and Broadcasting. DAF/COMP/GF(2013)13.
92. Ministerio de Economía y Finanzas Públicas. Resolución 219 de 2010. Comisión de Defensa de la Libre Competencia. Expediente No. 234-14/98. See: http://www.mecon.gov.ar/cndc/dictamenes/c.460.pdf.

Consumer's Association ADELCO, the parties CableVision and Multicanal acquired the companies VCC and CableVideo and instead of competing for such customers simply divided the market in zones and agreed to share the total number of users that the acquired companies had in such areas.[93]

In all these cases, the competition authorities considered that the parties agreed to exclude or harm competitors in the market where these companies participated, but never found that the parties investigated, may harm other markets or may have an impact in other markets where there was direct or indirect participation of the companies.

A similar story has been seen with certain collaboration agreements, where the parties collaborate to compete, a phenomenon known in the literature as co-ompetition.[94] For example, in 2013, the Colombian Competition Authority examined a joint venture to share active and passive network elements to provide 4G services between Telefonica and Tigo, the second and third largest mobile telecommunications operators in Colombia. The parties notified the transaction as a merger as there is no legal provision that defines a different procedure for collaboration agreements between competitors in Colombia. The authority concluded that the parties should not notify such transaction as being a cooperation agreement that did not suffice the criteria of control under the law as it was not a merger for Colombian law.[95] Despite the analysis of the authority is based on the lack of procedural rules to exempt or clear certain agreements between competitors, the transactions was indeed a merger using Colombian criteria of control. The reason behind such an interpretation is that the authority did not check whether the agreement included active network elements that may allow the parties involved to coordinate on service terms, quality, and other very important variables that definitively affect their differentiation in the 4G data market.

On the other hand, in 2008 the Colombian Competition Authority found that the largest participants in the mobile telecommunications markets, COMCEL and TELEFONICA, infringed the competition provisions by coordinating and abusing their dominant position in the wholesale mobile communications call termination market. The authority found evidence that both undertakings abused their monopoly position in their networks by charging high rates to call termination when such calls came from fixed operators. This strategy was found as a mechanism to reduce calls originating from fixed operators and therefore reduce the access to the mobile termination market.[96] In 2010, the competition authority, chaired by Gustavo Valbuena, reviewed

93. Ministerio de Economía y Finanzas Públicas. Resolución 219 de 2010. Comisión de Defensa de la Libre Competencia. Expediente No. 234-14/98. See: http://www.mecon.gov.ar/cndc/dictamenes/c.460.pdf, pp. 23-31.
94. Brzica, Danes, and Koloman Ivanicka. 'Innovation-Oriented Regions and Co-Ompetitive Business Behavior as Source of Business Dynamics.' *Innovation As A Source Of The Competitiveness*: 56. En: http://www.staniewski.vizja.pl/pdf/INNOVATION_AS_A_SOURCE_OF_THE_COMPETITIVENESS.pdf#page=55.
95. Resolución 93346 de 2013 http://www.sic.gov.co/drupal/recursos_user/documentos/Competencia/Integraciones/Resoluciones/Integraciones/2013/Diciembre/13-269270-16.pdf.
96. Minister of Commerce, Industry and Tourism, Superintendent of Industry and Commerce, Resolution Number 29631, 20 August 2008. File Number 04126607.

its decision and dropped all charges and considered there was no infringement of competition laws. Due to such a sudden and unanticipated change of perspective regarding the case by the same officer, the competition authority has been sued for 4.8 billion Colombian pesos, the largest amount a governmental organization has been sued, due to carelessness and negligence in the exercise of its supervision powers.

§9.05 MERGERS: THE PATH TO CONSOLIDATION IN THE DIFFERENT LAYERS OF THE ECOSYSTEM

Mergers reviews have always been a very interesting and common feature in the development of competition law in Latin America. Except for Peru, all Latin American countries have a post- or pre-merger notification and review regime. This has made most authorities to consider mergers in most communications and information technologies sectors.

The number of acquisitions and other forms of partnership that led to control under antitrust laws in the ICT industry has grown exponentially in the previous decade. This phenomenon is a consequence of the changes and challenges introduced by OTTs and the industry convergence, that has imposed new marketing and competition standards to the industry participants. These acquisitions, as was said earlier, regularly do not seem to have an impact on the markets where the companies participate, but most acquisitions have an impact on other markets that may be out of the regular standard of antitrust scrutiny.

Several transactions and cases have happened in Latin America. In the triple play and mobile market, several concentrations have taken place but there are a few worth to highlight. In the mobile market, the *UNE/Tigo* merger in Colombia led to the consolidation of a mobile communications operator – participating in the mobile voice and data markets – with a mobile and fixed communications operator – participating in the triple play fixed communications market and the mobile data market – making the sector in the country much more dynamic in the whole communications ecosystem. The competition authority on the one hand considered that despite there was dominance in certain area of the country by UNE, such dominance was not enough to impose a condition to the merger as the dominance was previous to the transaction. On the other hand, the authority considered that the transaction should be conditioned due to accumulation of spectrum in the high bands resulting from the merger which surpassed the regulatory limits.[97]

A similar remedy was imposed in *BellSouth Chile Inc./Telefonica Moviles S.A.* The Chilean authority examined the acquisition of the Chilean subsidiaries of BellSouth Corporation by Telefonica, the Spanish operator of telecommunication services. Both companies participated in the mobile telecommunication services and consolidated the operation of two competitors in the mobile market. The resulting market structure,

97. Resolución 32199 de 2014. Superintendencia de Industria y Comercio. 2 En: http://www.sic.gov.co/drupal/recursos_user/documentos/normatividad/Resoluciones/2014/Resolucion_32199_2014.pdf.

despite being very relevant in the analysis, did not led the tribunal to further study the particulars of the mobile market but the concentration of spectrum allocations to the parties involved. The tribunal imposed structural condition to the operation imposing the parties to transfer of 25 MHz of spectrum to a third party in a strategic band such as 850 MHz.[98]

But the same approach on concentration of spectrum exploitation rights was not taken by the Argentinean authority in *Telefónica Móviles S.A./Bellsouth* where the former acquired the assets of Bellsouth in Latin America. The Argentinian Competition Commission decided not to block the transaction despite the evident overlap of both participants in mobile market and its likely leveraging effect in other communications markets. According to the competition authority, both companies participated in the mobile and fixed local and long-distance telephony, as well as in the carrier and the data access markets. In most markets concentration was low, and the commission was satisfied that the transaction did not raise many concerns as market concentration was small. However, in the mobile markets concentration was high, and the commission knew that the company will become the dominant operator not only in the mobile market but also in the wholesale mobile termination market, and, in addition, the new company would be the largest holder of spectrum, surpassing the 85 MHz limit defined by the regulations.[99]

A very good decision understanding the importance of convergence and the importance that advertising and other markets have in the communications markets was the Argentinean Commission, CNDC, in *Grupo Clarin, Fintech, Multicanal, CableVision et. al.*[100] The merger entities participated in the cable television market, the internet access market, the content production market, the data transport market, and advertising markets. This structure was due to the structure of the operation where several of the companies participating in the market had interest in one or two markets and the whole transaction could lead to a single operator that could provide duo and triple play services in most regions of the country. The CNDC made a traditional horizontal, vertical, barriers to entry and efficiencies analysis, concluding that there are no barriers to competition to telecom companies that could prevent them to compete against this new company in the triple play market.[101] However, the transaction was

98. Resolution No. 02/2005, Acquisition of BellSouth Chile Inc. and BellSouth Chile Holdings Inc. (together BellSouth) by Telefonica Moviles S.A. Cited by: Cave, Martin; A. Andreas Avgousti, and Adrian Foster. Strengthening Competition Policy in Latin American Countries. Centro Regional de Competencia en America Latina, México, July, 2013. In: http://crcal.org/guias-y-estudios/estudios/estudios-de-sector/doc_download/12-strengthening-competition-policy-in-latin-american-countries-the-application-of-competition-law-in-the-telecommunications-sector.
99. Cave, Martin; A. Andreas Avgousti, and Adrian Foster. Strengthening Competition Policy in Latin American Countries. Centro Regional de Competencia en America Latina, México, July, 2013. In: http://crcal.org/guias-y-estudios/estudios/estudios-de-sector/doc_download/12-strengthening-competition-policy-in-latin-american-countries-the-application-of-competition-law-in-the-telecommunications-sector. Notificación Art. 8 De La Ley N. 25.156 (Conc. 0448).
100. Dictamen No. 637 de 2007. Comisión Nacional de Defensa de la Competencia (CNDC). *CableVisión Multicanal et. al.*, 7 December 2007.
101. *Ibid.*, pp. 95-96.

conditioned[102] but widely criticized,[103] since it was not clear that telecom operators could enter the TV market to offer triple play bundles. The transaction was later stopped by a decision ordering a divestiture[104] based on an alleged infraction competition law ordering a divestiture;[105] such decision that was annulled by the Supreme Court considering it illegal as the judge had no jurisdiction over the case.[106]

However, in the Chilean Cable Television Market Liberty Comunicaciones De Chile Uno Ltda. and Cristal Chile Comunicaciones S.A.[107] merged in 2004. The tribunal found that the companies participated in the national triple play market but considered the three services, that is, the cable TV, the broadband Internet access, and the fixed telephony, as three different markets. While studying the transaction, the tribunal considered that despite there were several risks associated with the merger, the market provided several procompetitive outcomes by reducing the costs to provide such services to consumers facilitating penetration and other efficiencies that made the creation of a dominant undertaking less problematic, but anyway subject to conditions. The conditions were in some cases behavioural, including restrictions regarding imposing the obligation to sell to consumers every service independently, and some structural remedies such as the prohibition to deal with exclusive content in cable television as well as the prohibition to provide satellite television services, among many other including pricing.[108]

Also, regarding the content market, some acquisitions scrutinized by Latin American authorities, for example in *America Online/Time Warner* merger,[109] Argentina's CNDC studied the merger of these two companies in the markets of the

102. *See* Arballo, Gustavo. Fusión Cablevisión - Multicanal: análisis del dictamen de la CNDC. 17 December 2007. In: http://www.saberderecho.com/2007/12/fusin-cablevisin-multicanal-anlisis-del.html.
103. Galperin, Hernán; Cabello, Sebastián M., *see Convergencia tecnológica y armonización regulatoria: el caso argentino*. CEPAL – Colección Documentos de proyectos. pp. 24-25 (2008) Available at: https://repositorio.cepal.org/bitstream/handle/11362/45995/1/LCW183_es.pdf; Bizberge, Ana. *Audiovisual Media Regulation in the 21st Century in Argentina and Brazil*, Revista Mexicana de Opinión Pública. Vol. 19, July-December 2015, pp. 13-39.
104. In a decision a judge form the Mendoza Province considered that the parties should, among other, split networks and head ends 'that corresponded to the absorbed multi-channel of remaining were according to Cablevision prior to the concentration between the two companies', divide subscribers, accounts for the collection of revenues, accounting, and legal, administrative, and computer and management systems, as well as, stop the conjunct commercial use of Cablevision and multichannel brands. *See*: El Pergaminense, 22 December 2011. http://www.elpergaminense.com/index.php?articulo_id=4634.
105. *Ibid.*
106. Supreme Court of Justice of Argentina. 25 February 2014. *See*: http://www.sij.gov.ar/sentencias.
107. TDLC. Resolución N° 01 /2004. Liberty Comunicaciones De Chile Uno Ltda. and Cristalchile Comunicaciones S.A. Cited by: Cave, Martin; A. Andreas Avgousti, and Adrian Foster. Strengthening Competition Policy in Latin American Countries. Centro Regional de Competencia en America Latina, México, July 2013.
108. *Ibid.* In: http://crcal.org/guias-y-estudios/estudios/estudios-de-sector/doc_download/12-strengthening-competition-policy-in-latin-american-countries-the-application-of-competition-law-in-the-telecommunications-sector.
109. Dictamen 144. Comisión Nacional de Defensa de la Competencia (CNDC). America Online Inc. and Time Warner Inc. October 24, 2000. *America Online/Time Warner*, CNDC, Argentina. Cited by: Evans, David S. and Mariscal, Elisa V., Market Definition Analysis in Latin America

production and commercialization of contents for TV and Internet and the advertising market. It was, of course, the year 2000, and therefore, both markets were defined as non-complementary and there was no analysis of two-sided markets or two-sided market effects. In both the cases, there were no competition concerns raised by the authority; however, the analysis made in the last two cases did not consider the fact that there are strong network externalities coming from this merger and its possible outcome in competition, mostly in the advertising market.[110] The latter was the main argument in the CableVisión/Multicanal Merger, in which the analysis made by the CNDC remarkably based its arguments in the issue of convergence and the impact of convergence in competition in the triple play market and the advertising markets impact on the industry's value chain.[111]

A similar approach has been taken in the online advertising market. In Microsoft/aQuantive the Brazilian SDE studied the merger between Microsoft, a developer and seller of computer software, and aQuantive a company participating in the digital advertising sector. At first sight, the two companies seemed not to have any market overlap that may raise antitrust concerns, and therefore, the decision was to clear the transaction with no objections.[112] It is clear that the SDE considered that there was no horizontal overlap between the different companies and approved the transaction.[113] It is important to see, however, that Microsoft indeed regularly purchases online advertising services and the acquired company received approximately 90% of its revenues from Microsoft, making sense to a vertical integration between both firms.[114]

Also, in *Yahoo/Starmedia*[115] the Brazilian SDE and CADE studied the transaction, as both Starmedia and Yahoo participated in the internet search market, and the companies had revenues coming from different sources including advertising revenues. As explained by Evans and Mariscal, the Brazilian authority considered that the

with Applications to Internet-Based Industries (26 June 2013). Available at SSRN: http://dx.doi.org/10.2139/ssrn.2285400, p. 39.

110. *Ibid.*
111. Dictamen No. 637 de 2007. Comisión Nacional de Defensa de la Competencia (CNDC). *CableVisión Multicanal et. al.*, 7 December 2007, §283 y ss.
112. Ato de Concentraçao No 08012.008554/2007-11. Ministério Da Justiça. Secretaria de Direito Econômico. Microsoft Corporation and aQuantive Inc. June 12, 2007. Cited by: Evans, David S. and Mariscal, Elisa V., Market Definition Analysis in Latin America with Applications to Internet-Based Industries (26 June 2013). Available at SSRN: http://dx.doi.org/10.2139/ssrn.2285400, pp. 39-44.
113. *Ibid.*, pp. 41-44.
114. *Ibid.*, pp. 39-44.
115. Ato de Concentraçao No. 08012.000182/2002-61. Ministerio da Justiça. Conselho Administrativo de Defesa Econômica. Yahoo! Do Brasil Internet y Starmedia do Brasil Ltda. Cited by: Evans, David S. and Mariscal, Elisa V., Market Definition Analysis in Latin America with Applications to Internet-Based Industries (26 June 2013). Available at SSRN: http://dx.doi.org/10.2139/ssrn.2285400, pp. 39-44 and Ato de Concentraçao n° 08012.000212/2003-11. Ministério Da Justiça. Secretaria de Direito Economico. Yahoo! Inc. y Inktomi Corporation. January 14 2003. Cited by: Evans, David S. and Mariscal, Elisa V., Market Definition Analysis in Latin America with Applications to Internet-Based Industries (26 June 2013). Available at SSRN: http://dx.doi.org/10.2139/ssrn.2285400, pp. 39-44.

market of advertising should be narrowed down to the internet advertising market due to the lack of substitutability of the different advertising channels.[116]

Meanwhile, in the internet sales market, Mexico's competition authority (COFECE) objected in 2019 to the merger transaction between *Wal-Mart International Holdings, Inc, Cornershop (Holdco), Cornershop Technologies LLC* and *Shareholder Representative Services LLC.*[117] The commission made its decision due to a high potential to affect the market of online stores and platforms that offer the logistic service of immediate purchase and delivery of products offered by self-service stores, through the internet and apps. COFECE points out that there could be risks related to the slowdown in the growth of competitors of both Walmart and Cornershop, mainly due to two situations: (i) free access could be violated and discrimination could occur and (ii) the information gathered by the intervening parties could be used strategically to strengthen Walmart's dominant position.[118]

The acquisition of a participant in the apps and OS market and one participant in the manufacturing market, in the previous years, may not have been studied by competition authorities but the new bundling techniques may lead to such approach. That is why in *Google/Motorola,*[119] Google's main line of business is search, on one side, and online advertising on the other side. In addition, Google has engaged in several other ventures, including providing and manufacturing an open architecture operating system for mobile devices, Android. Motorola marketed hardware for cell phones and tablets, and home appliances including broadband access solutions. The Argentinian Commission for Competition found that there was no horizontal but a vertical overlap and concluded that despite the existence of such overlap there was no evidence of a potential refusal to distribute the software between google and other manufacturers.[120]

Brazil's SEAE reviewed the acquisition of Akwan by Google Brasil in 2005. Both companies were regarded as having a similar line of business: search for final consumers with revenues generated mainly through the sale of Internet advertising space. But the line of business was not translated into one two-sided market, but instead SEAE defined the relevant markets under review as (1) Internet search technology, (2) Internet advertising space, and (3) corporate search, which was an additional service offered by Akwan and not by Google. As was the case of Argentina before, two-sided markets were defined as two one-sided markets, and even within those services, there were further narrow classifications: in Internet search technology, the authority distinguished between search firms that offered their own searching

116. See Ato de Concentraçao n° 08012.000182/2002-61.
117. Estados Unidos Mexicanos, Comisión Federal de Competencia Económica. *Versión pública de la resolución del expediente CNT-161-2018.* Dirección General de Concentraciones. 27 de mayo de 2019. Available at: https://www.cofece.mx/CFCResoluciones/docs/Concentraciones/V6008/9/4845885.pdf.
118. *Ibid.* pp. 79-86.
119. Google/Motorola was also reviewed and approved by CADE. It is currently under review in Argentina by the CNDC. Cited by: Evans, David S. and Mariscal, Elisa V., *Market Definition Analysis in Latin America with Applications to Internet-Based Industries* (26 June 2013). Available at SSRN: http://dx.doi.org/10.2139/ssrn.2285400, pp. 39-44.
120. *Ibid.*

capabilities and those that searched linking to other search engines. SEAE ultimately approved the transaction.[121] In the fixed Internet market, Colombia's competition authority is studying the feasibility of the merger between *UFINET Colombia* and *Empresa de Telecomunicaciones de Bogotá (ETB)*. The two companies announced a merger operation[122] through which they seek to offer wholesale fiber optic service in Bogotá and its surroundings. The SIC objected to the operation representing a high risk to competition, as it could potentially restrict access to their infrastructure unilaterally. Both parties filed an appeal for reconsideration of the SIC's decision, which has not been ruled upon at the time of writing this chapter.

§9.06 CONCLUSION: THE NEED OF A FRAMEWORK OF COMPETITION LAW ANALYSIS FOR CONVERGED TELECOMMUNICATIONS MARKETS IN LATIN AMERICA

The legislation and competition case laws analysed show that there is a lot of room for improving the current framework of antitrust analysis in the communications and information technologies ecosystem. As was shown, in most Latin American cases the ICT ecosystem is shown as a set of different markets, partially related markets, or non-interlinked markets. In most cases, the reviews were done as if they were mere conglomerates. This perspective lacks the analysis of the dynamic efficiencies created by innovation and the business circle that multi-sided and multi-platform economies present and ignore the different dimensions of technological convergence in the dynamics of competition.

As was said earlier, the ICT 'ecosystem' requires different regulatory and academic approaches than the one applying regularly to static markets.[123] The existence of dynamic efficiencies makes the ICT sector rely on *short term* innovation and product differentiation to drive industry growth and the industry's profitability.[124] Also, the increasing reliance on platforms, platforms competition and two-sided

121. Ato de Concentraçao n° 08012.006162/2005-47. Ministério Da Fazenda. Secretaria de Acompanhamento Econômico. Google Brasil Internet Ltda. y Akwan S.A. August 26, 2005.
122. See República de Colombia, Superintendencia de Industria y Comercio. Inicia el procedimiento administrativo de la operación de integración empresarial entre UFINET COLOMBIA PARTICIPACIONES S.A.S. y EMPRESA DE TELECOMUNICACIONES DE BOGOTÁ S.A. E.S.P. Available at: https://www.sic.gov.co/sites/default/files/files/2021/21-69461%20orden%20de%20publicaci%C3%B3n%20UFINET%20LATAM%20S_L_U_%20-%20ETB.pdf.
123. See Oz Shi, *The Economics of Network Industries*, Cambridge University Press, 2001; Patrick Tucker, *The Naked Future: What Happens in a World That Anticipates Your Every Move?* Penguin, 2014; Jeffrey A. Eisenach and Ilene Knable Gotts. *In Search of a Competition Doctrine for Information Technology Markets: Recent Antitrust Developments in the Online Sector*. In: Communications and Competition Law Key Issues in the Telecoms, Media and Technology Sectors. Wolters Kluwer, Aspen, 2015; Jeffrey A. Eisenach. *Broadband Competition in the Internet Ecosystem*. America Enterprise Institute, 2012; Paul Heidhues, et al, *More Competitive Search through Regulation*. Yale Tobin Center for Economic Policy. Policy Discussion Paper No. 2, 20 May 2021. Available at: https://tobin.yale.edu/sites/default/files/Digital%20Regulation%20Project%20Papers/Digital%20Regulation%20Project%20-%20Search%20-%20Discussion%20Paper%20No%202%20(1).pdf.
124. See Eisenach and Gotts. *In Search...*, p. 71.

markets as means to grow and differentiate, make the economics of the ICT ecosystem focus on complementary goods and services. This theory, poorly developed from the antitrust perspective until now, is relevant to understand the links between the different participants in the ecosystem[125] and to dismiss antitrust issues when those platforms also create compatibility issues or vertical integration restraints that nowadays are necessary to participate in the ICTs markets.[126] Finally, the ICT ecosystem is based on the existence of network externalities on almost every part of the value chain where consumer grant more value to users and advertisers when they have a large set of different users.[127]

This framework of analysis facilitates the conclusions regarding the need of a different approach in ICT sectors antitrust and regulatory analysis. Competition authorities and regulators have piecemeal doctrines and theoretical frameworks that allow them to study sectors that possess the latter characteristics. However, there are no regulatory or antitrust enforcement developments that may lead to standards or rules regarding conduct or structures in the presence of network externalities, platforms, and dynamic efficiencies[128] which traditionally may be deemed as anticompetitive. Thus, it is important for academics and regulators to broaden the framework for action and interpretation, considering the conditions of these new markets, proposing new alternatives that will help to make them more dynamic and foster competition in them.[129]

Having the latter in mind, it is necessary to determine new approaches to market definition and market power analysis in the ICT ecosystem as these concepts are still based on economic theory created to tackle static industries with insignificant innovation and a low pace of transformations.

In highly innovative markets, it must be considered that in most cases differentiated goods or services place us in monopolistic competition or must be considered that the products with high technological content are initially offered at a very high

125. *Ibid.*, p. 71. See also Evans, David S. and Mariscal, Elisa V., *Market Definition Analysis in Latin America with Applications to Internet-Based Industries* (26 June 2013). Available at SSRN: http://dx.doi.org/10.2139/ssrn.2285400.
126. *Ibid.*, p. 72.
127. *See*: Sarit Markovich and Johannes Moenius *Winning while Losing: Competition Dynamics in the Presence of Indirect Network Effects*. International Journal of industrial Organization, vol. 27, 2009, pp. 346-357.
128. 'IT markets have characteristics that limit the usefulness of these traditional approaches, often in ways that are not yet well understood. We begin by describing the characteristics that distinguish IT markets from more traditional ones and then discuss some of the challenges these characteristics pose for traditional antitrust doctrine.' Jeffrey A. Eisenach and Ilene Knable Gotts. *In Search of a Competition Doctrine for Information Technology Markets: Recent Antitrust Developments in the Online Sector.* In: Communications and Competition Law Key Issues in the Telecoms, Media and Technology Sectors. Wolters Kluwer, Aspen, 2015.
129. See Fiona M. Scott Morton, et al. *Equitable Interoperability: The 'Super Tool' of Digital Platform Governance.* Yale Tobin Center for Economic Policy. Policy Discussion Paper No. 4, 13 July 2021. Available at: https://tobin.yale.edu/sites/default/files/Digital%20Regulation%20Project%20Papers/Digital%20Regulation%20Project%20-%20Equitable%20Interoperability%20-%20Discussion%20Paper%20No%204.pdf.

price and this price will drop when the costs of its creation are recovered, without having to consider that the price is excessive.[130]

Regarding networks and network externalities, it must be considered that operators to own a service network that generates positive externalities must have acquired a large market share. Some operators can hold a dominant position which does not necessarily means that there is a failure in the market. This may occur when a network's connections are incompatible with other networks,[131] or when, in multiple-sided markets, the platform imposes a price – that is, not a market price or a cost-based price – on the most inelastic side, that may, subsequently finance the most elastic side, which does not necessarily imply a crossed subsidy.[132] Concerning the issue of technological convergence, it must be considered that it leads to new substitutability relationships hence to new market definitions and operator's dominant positions, since products and services that were not considered part of the same product market, are now part of it.[133]

The latter shows that new methods to determine markets reach and interconnections may bring other old fashion concepts to life and limit the use of other notions rooted in the common wisdom.[134] The latter includes not only reshaping the notion of relevant markets as they are today installed in decision and policy makers,[135] rethinking the mechanisms to assess market power and focus on entry and long-term competitive constraints in dynamic and highly innovative markets, including remedies to better impose regulatory and ex post antitrust remedies. This job, however, is yet incomplete and there is need of much more analysis and theoretical proposals that lead competition authorities' work.[136] Today the best rule is to prefer a false negative than a false positive, as the latter may impair innovation and damage consumers permanently, the former can be corrected with time once information provides better facts for decision making.

130. Pleatsikas, C., and Teece, D. 'The Analysis of Market Definition and Market Power in the Context of Rapid Innovation.' International Journal of Industrial Organization, vol. 19, no. 5, 2001, pp. 665-693.
131. Economides, N. *Public Policy in Network Industries in Handbook of Antitrust Economics (Vol. 1)*, The MIT Press, 2008.
132. Evans, D. S., and Noel, M. 'Defining Antitrust Markets When Firms Operate Two-Sided Platforms.' Colum. Bus. L. Rev., 667, 2005.
133. OECD. Competition Committee. Defining the Relevant Market in Telecommunications, 2014. Available in http://www.oecd.org/daf/competition/Defining_Relevant_Market_in_Telecommunications_web.pdf.
134. See Evans, David S. and Mariscal, Elisa V., *Market Definition Analysis in Latin America with Applications to Internet -Based Industries* (June 26, 2013). Available at SSRN: https://ssrn.com/abstract=2285400 or http://dx.doi.org/10.2139/ssrn.2285400
135. See: Kaplow, Louis, 'Market Definition: Impossible and Counterproductive (February 2014).' Antitrust Law Journal, vol. 79, no. 1, 2013. Available at SSRN: http://ssrn.com/abstract=2402953.
136. Jeffrey A. Eisenach and Ilene Knable Gotts. *In Search of a Competition Doctrine for Information Technology Markets: Recent Antitrust Developments in the Online Sector.* In: Communications and Competition Law Key Issues in the Telecoms, Media and Technology Sectors. Wolters Kluwer, Aspen, 2015, pp. 70, 90. '… enforcers continue to struggle to devise a coherent alternative framework… the tensions regulators will continue to face in the years ahead, as well as the challenges facing academics and practitioners in terms of developing more useful frameworks and analytical tools.'

CHAPTER 10

Competition Law in Central America and the Years to Come

*Edgar Odio-Rohrmoser**

This chapter describes and analyzes the competition legal framework in the Central American countries, and the possible developments in the region in the next few years. The countries covered in the discussion are Costa Rica, El Salvador, Guatemala, Honduras, Nicaragua, and Panamá. The chapter compares the general aspects of the competition law, including foreign aid, the institutional arrangements, investigative powers of the authorities; the regulation of cartels and unilateral conduct, merger review; and the existing regulations at the regional level. The chapter also explores the possibilities offered by the current legal framework of the region to prevent, investigate, and punish cross-border anticompetitive conducts at the regional level.

§10.01 INTRODUCTION

Many people, especially from other parts of the world see Central America as a region where countries are very similar and are already, or should already be integrated. Similarities are based on historical reasons since Guatemala, Honduras, El Salvador, Nicaragua, and Costa Rica, were once a province of the Spanish Empire. Spanish is the official language in all countries, and Catholicism is still the prevalent religion. Countries are also very small, compared to most countries of the world. From a legal perspective, all countries follow the civil law system, they all have presidential systems, and there are similarities in their main pieces of legislation: civil, commercial, criminal, labor, and administrative.

* The author wishes to thank Juan Pablo Lara associate at Facio & Cañas, for his support in the research and discussions we had. Any error in the content of this chapter is the sole responsibility of the author.

However, despite all such similarities, the countries remain as separate sovereign states since their independence in the nineteenth century. Integrationist efforts from a political perspective failed in the nineteenth century, but economic integration in the second half of the twentieth century has been more successful, albeit a long period of stagnation and regression due to the political and military conflicts that affected most countries during the 1980s. More progress has been made in the recent past towards a customs union. But political and cultural differences remain. Political integration is still a no go for some countries. And yet, this has not been an obstacle for people and governments from other countries in the world to continue focusing on the similarities among the countries of the region. For multinational corporations, it is common to have offices or headquarters in one country to oversee the rest of the countries, sometimes even the Caribbean. For countries of different parts of the world, it is not rare to have an ambassador based in one country of Central America, with duties in other countries of the region.

In 2004 the United States entered into a Free Trade Agreement with Guatemala, Honduras, El Salvador, Nicaragua, Costa Rica, and Dominican Republic (CAFTA).In June 2012, the European Union (EU) negotiated and entered into an Association Agreement with the region, including Panama (EU-CA Association Agreement). Both agreements are evidence that the Central American countries are seen by many as a region where similarities outbalance diversity.

In the light of increasing economic integration, the countries had already contemplated the need for a regional regulation on competition, when they entered into the "Protocol to the General Treaty on Central American Economic Integration (Protocolo al Tratado General de Integración Económica Centroamericana. Guatemala 1993).[1] This commitment was later reinstated in the Framework Agreement for the Establishment of Central American Customs Union (Convenio Marco para el Establecimiento de la Unión Aduanera Centroamericana, signed by Guatemala, Honduras, El Salvador, Nicaragua, and Costa Rica. Guatemala 2007).[2]

Pursuant to the EU-CA Association Agreement, a Central American competition regulation and a competition authority shall be established according to Article 25 of the "Protocol to the General Treaty on Central American Economic Integration" and Article 21 of the Framework Agreement for the Establishment of Central American Customs Union, within a period of seven years from the moment the agreement comes into force. Before that, all countries must have a competition law and a designated competition authority no later than three years from the moment the agreement comes into force. This is applicable to Guatemala, which is the only country in Central America that does not have a competition law and a competition authority yet.

Thus, in a sense, the EU-CA Association Agreement urges the countries of the region to implement what they had already agreed to do on two previous occasions.

1. "Article 25: In the trade sector, the Parties agree to adopt common regulations to prevent monopolistic activities and to promote free competition in the countries of the region." (free translation)
2. "Article 21: The States shall develop a regional regulation on competition policy." (free translation)

But now the commitment is much more specific. Title VII of the EU-CA Association Agreement contains a general provision according to which the parties shall adopt or maintain in force comprehensive competition laws which effectively address the anticompetitive practices:

> a.) agreements between undertakings, decisions by associations of undertakings and concerted practices between undertakings, which have as their object or effect the prevention, restriction or distortion of competition; b.) any abuse by one or more undertakings of a dominant position or a substantial market power or notable market participation; and c.) concentrations between undertakings, which significantly impede effective competition; are incompatible with the Association Agreement.

The Parties shall also establish or maintain competition authorities designated and appropriately equipped for the transparent and effective implementation of the competition laws.[3]

The EU-CA Association Agreement does not force the parties to remove public enterprises or enterprises entrusted with exclusive rights or monopolies. Such entities shall be subject to competition laws insofar as it does not obstruct the performance of the particular tasks assigned to them. No discrimination should be exercised by these entities regarding the conditions under which goods or services are purchased or sold by natural or legal entities of either of the parties. Competition authorities may exchange non-confidential information, and they can request cooperation from each other relating to enforcement activities.

On December 20, 2020 the Council of Ministers for Economic Integration (COMIECO) issued the Reglamento Centroamericano de Competencia, resolution No.441-2020. The purpose of this regulation is to promote cooperation and competition advocacy at a regional level. This is clearly a good step to ensure cooperation among the competition authorities of the region and towards building mechanisms to investigate cross-border anticompetitive conducts in the regions, which should be a priority at a regional level.

§10.02 GENERAL CONDITIONS OF COMPETITION IN THE REGION

There are structural reasons in these countries that tend to limit competition even in the presence of international trade liberalization, particularly: (a) competition culture is very limited, (b) economic power concentration, (c) limited financial and human resources, (d) small local markets, (e) entry barriers, (f) sectors exempted from competition law, and (g) prices set in regulated markets based on cost—plus instead of using competition criteria. Besides, state intervention in key sectors of the economy and the heavy protectionist barriers levied during the Import Substitution Model were still very much in place when the competition laws were enacted.

At the institutional level, the authorities of each country make significant efforts to build their technical capacities and investigate anticompetitive conducts. But in most

3. *See* Articles 278 and 279.

cases, the authorities are not provided with the resources they need. Except for the El Salvador and Panama, the authorities of the rest of the countries have very limited resources compared to the region and compared with the regulatory agencies in their respective country.

Competition law in these countries came in place as part of the liberalization and privatization process that started in the late 1980s and early 1990s. Rivera and Schatan characterize three types of scenarios:

(1) Countries with vast economic reforms, including a competition law: Panama, El Salvador and Honduras.
(2) Countries with privatization and trade liberalization, but with weak regulatory framework and late competition law: Nicaragua and Guatemala (still with no competition law).
(3) Countries with more limited privatizations and economic reforms but with a competition law: Costa Rica. The State is still present in many key sectors of the economy, including telecommunications, energy, banking and oil.[4]

Taking into consideration the characteristics noted above, the limited resources and the level of expertise, some have argued that competition policy in these countries should focus on promoting competition to develop an entire new business culture, and removing the barriers to entry. They argue that the focus should be on the investigation of hard core cartels. Investigation of unilateral conduct should come next given the difficulties of measuring efficiencies in this type of conduct, and finally the investigation of concentrations.[5]

These countries also need to improve the coordination between competition policy and other related areas such as consumer protection, unfair competition, intellectual property, deregulation, industrial and agricultural policy, international trade; and regulated sectors of the economy. The mandate of the competition law in most of these countries does not give enough power to the competition authority to ensure competition a key role in the policy and decision making in these areas.

At the regional level, as economic and customs integration continues to grow, the risk that economic agents engage in anticompetitive practices, particularly horizontal agreements, also increases.[6] Therefore the need for effective cooperation in the investigation of cross-border anticompetitive conducts should be addressed, as it was very well argued by Sittenfeld and Valbuena:

> This necessity for cooperation is even greater in the case of Nicaragua and all Central American countries, as they are small commercially integrated economies and therefore practices committed in one country can quite likely have effects in

4. Rivera and Schatan, p. 38. Although in Costa Rica telecommunications and banking were open to competition several years ago.
5. De León, p. 45.
6. *See* UNCTAD: " Recomendaciones para mejorar la cooperación regional en Centroamérica."

another (or others) and the strategies of the companies operating in the region may not vary greatly between countries.[7]

Therefore, even though each country (except Guatemala) has a competition law and policy, and a local competition authority to enforce the law, enforcement is still weak at the national level in most countries, and almost non-existent at the regional level. However, given the commitment assumed by the countries in international regional agreements, including the newly issued Reglamento Centroamericano de Competencia, and the growing economic integration, we should expect more cooperation among the authorities.

§10.03 INTERNATIONAL COOPERATION

Competition policy development in the region has been fostered by international cooperation. All countries have benefited from assistance and cooperation from international agencies such as the United Nations Conference on Trade and Development (UNCTAD), the Organisation for Economic Co-operation and Development (OECD), the Inter-American Development Bank (IDB), and the World Bank, notably Costa Rica with its recent incorporation as member of the OECD. Cooperation has also come from countries with more developed agencies like Canada, US, Spain, Portugal, México, Brazil, and Chile.

The following countries have undertaken a peer review from the OECD. El Salvador was the first one, when the report was written by John Clark in 2008; and again on 2020, when Diego Petrecolla wrote the report. Panama did it in 2010, the report was written by Daniel Sokol with the contribution of John Clark and Diego Povolo, William Kovacic and Caldwell Harrop as examiners. The Honduras' OECD Peer Review was written by Enrique Vergara in 2011. Meanwhile Costa Rica went through the peer review process with UNCTAD, which was presented in the International Group of Experts in 2008, the report was written by Diego Petrecolla. Nicaragua did the same in 2012. The Nicaraguan Peer Review was also made by UNCTAD, and the report was written by Pamela Sittenfeld and Gustavo Valbuena. Costa Rica also undertook the OECD Peer Review in 2014, and the report was written by Paolo Benedetti. As part of the process to join the OECD, a second and more detailed review was made on 2016 and the recommendations of this report were the basis of a major reform of the competition law in the country.[8]

The authorities of the region formed the Central American Competition Group in 2006 which has helped them to keep in contact with each other and share information about the type of cases they are handling. They have even progressed to developing specific projects on a regional basis, including market studies and a study to explore ways to integrate the systems. But there is still a long way to go before the authorities are able to investigate cross-border anticompetitive conduct in the region, under a full cooperation scheme. A necessary condition and possibly the first major step towards

7. UNCTAD, Peer Review, Nicaragua, p. 55.
8. Law for the Strengthening of Competition Authorities, Law. 9736, Sep. 9, 2019.

that end seems to be the exchange of confidential information, but very little progress has been made to agree on such sort of cooperation. Different concepts of confidential information both within each country and between countries; and how confidentiality information has to be handled vis-à-vis the right of defense of the parties within the proceeding (*see* the discussion in El Salvador),[9] the need to determine mechanisms to request the information, the need to ensure information will remain confidential, and the resistance from the private sector, are among the reasons that explain why progress in this specific aspect has been so difficult.

§10.04 THE COMPETITION LAW IN EACH COUNTRY

The influence of the original Federal Competition Law of Mexico on the structure and content of the competition laws of the Central American countries is very clear.

Costa Rican Law was enacted in 1994 and amended in 2012 and again in 2019, Panama's in 1996 and amended in 2007, El Salvador's in 2004 but the law took effect until 2006, and it was very soon amended in 2007, Honduras' in 2006 and amended in 2015, and Nicaragua's in 2006. Guatemala has not passed a competition law even though the congress has reviewed several bids during the last two decades. A new bid is now being discussed. It is still a question whether Guatemala will pass a competition law.

In some cases, exogenous elements had an influence in passing the competition law. In Costa Rica, the law was a condition to the approval of a package of loans granted by multinational organizations such as the World Bank. In Panama, it was necessary as part of the institutional arrangement developed to become a member of the World Trade Organization. In El Salvador, a number of external factors were important, the economic reforms that followed the Chapultepec accords in 1992 that put an end to the twelve year Civil War, included a commitment to competition and consumer protection,[10] but at the end, a local negotiation with local interests groups from the local business community and from both political parties was the key element to finally pass the law in 2004. In Honduras, the law was part of a new institutional arrangement development following CAFTA. In Nicaragua, entering into CAFTA and the support from international agencies like United Nations, GTZ, and the UK was necessary to pass the law.[11]

The following is a summary of the general information about the competition law of each country.

9. *See* articles written by Díaz Rodríguez Francisco, as Superintendente of El Salvador and Olmedo Daniel.
10. OECD, Peer Review, El Salvador, p. 10.
11. UNCTAD, Peer Review, Nicaragua, p. 6.

	Costa Rica	*El Salvador*	*Guatemala*	*Honduras*	*Nicaragua*	*Panama*
Year of the Law	*1994–2019*	*2004*	*N/A*	*2005*	*2006*	*1996*
Law	Ley para la Promoción de la Competencia y Defensa Efectiva del Consumidor. Ley General de Telecomunicaciones.[12] Ley de Fortalecimiento de las Autoridades de Competencia	Ley de Competencia	N/A	Ley para la Defensa y Promoción de la Competencia	Ley de Promoción de la Competencia No.601	Ley que dicta normas sobre protección al consumidor y defensa de la competencia y otra disposición
Authority	Comisión para Promover la Competencia (COPROCOM) Superintendencia de Telecomunicaciones (SUTEL)	Superintendencia de Competencia (SC)	N/A	Comisión para la Defensa y Promoción de la Competencia (CDPC)	Instituto de Promoción de la Competencia (Procompetencia)	Autoridad de Protección al Consumidor y Defensa de la Competencia ACODECO

12. Due to space constraints the content of this law is not discussed in this chapter, although the competition provisions contained in this law are very similar to the competition provisions discussed herein.

	Costa Rica	*El Salvador*	*Guatemala*	*Honduras*	*Nicaragua*	*Panama*
Year of the Law	*1994–2019*	*2004*	*N/A*	*2005*	*2006*	*1996*
Horizontal Conduct	Section 11 Absolute monopolistic practices Per se rule	Section 25 Agreement Among Competitors. Per se rule	N/A	Section 5 Restrictive practices forbidden by their nature Per se	Section 18 Agreements among Competitors. Per se rule	Section 13. Absolute monopolistic practices Not per se rule
Vertical Agreements	Section 12 Relative monopolistic practices Rule of reason	Sections 26 and 27 Conduct among non-competitors and abuse of dominance. Rule of reason	N/A	Section 7 Restrictive practices forbidden according to their effect Rule of reason	Section 19 Practices among economic agents non-competitors Rule of reason	Section 16 Relative monopolistic illicit practices Rule of reason
Merger control	*Ex ante* first phase Thirty days and second phase ninety days	*Ex ante* ninety days	N/A	*Ex ante* forty-five days	*Ex ante* thirty plus ninety days	Voluntary sixty days
Investigation starts	Ex officio or by complaint	Ex officio or by complaint	N/A	Ex officio or by complaint	Ex officio or by complaint	Ex officio or by complaint

Since Costa Rica was the first country to enact the law, the authority and the local community have gained more experience than the rest of the agencies in the region, but over the years El Salvador and Panama have devoted more resources to their authorities and have caught up in expertise and sophistication of cases investigated and resolved, with Honduras and Nicaragua catching up in their experiences but still with limited resources. However, ACODECO (Panama) has jurisdiction on both competition and consumer protection, and it is said that the majority of resources are devoted to the latter.[13]

The objective of the competition laws of these countries is to promote competition, improve economic efficiency, and increase consumer welfare. The law's intent is to limit anticompetitive conducts from undertakings. Although with somewhat different names, the concepts of horizontal conducts, vertical restraints, abuse of dominance, and merger control are present in the law of all countries, with the differences and particularities that are noted below. According to Sittenfeld, these differences become more accentuated in the way each authority interprets and applies the law.[14]

In Costa Rica, Nicaragua, and Panamá, anticompetitive conducts are divided between absolute monopolistic practices, relative monopolistic practices, concentrations, and unfair competition. In El Salvador, the distinction is between agreements among competitors, agreements among non-competitors, abuse of dominance, and concentrations. The distinction in Honduras is between restrictive practices forbidden by its nature and practices forbidden by the effects. Meanwhile in Nicaragua, the law divides the conducts in monopolistic practices, abuse of dominance, and unfair competition.[15] However, there are important differences in some respects such as the nature and degree of independence of the competition authority, the procedures, exemptions from the law, the application of the per se rule to horizontal conducts, merger notification, intellectual property, nature and severity of the sanctions, leniency programs, etc. Thus, similarities are important, but the differences may be more significant. In his comparative study, Bendaña identifies the main similarities and divergences among the laws and concludes that one difficulty for the implementation of a regional set of rules is the differences that exist among countries. He also points out to the benefits that a harmonization process would bring.[16]

The following sub-sections explore the main similarities and differences of the competition law of the countries and their application, particularly with regard to the anticompetitive practices that must be addressed by the law, based on comparative law, literature on the field and according to the EU-CA Association Agreement. If significant differences exist, then it can be expected that moving towards a regional competition law will be very difficult. If, on the contrary, these conducts are addressed in a similar way, the question would be whether this could facilitate moving on towards a regional set of rules and enforcement at a regional level.

13. OECD, Peer Review, Panamá, p. 61.
14. Sittenfeld, Pamela. Interview.
15. Rivera and Schatan, p. 45.
16. Bendaña, "Análisis crítico de la legislación de competencia en Centro América, Panamá y República Dominicana," p. 18.

However, the real question is how to prevent, detect, investigate, and sanction cross-border anticompetitive conducts at a regional level. It seems that having a regional set of rules and a regional agency is one way to deal with this. But another way may be to strengthen the rules of cooperation among the agencies and make cooperation binding. With the enactment of the Reglamento Centroamericano de Competencia, the countries might be moving towards the latter.

[A] Cartels

In El Salvador, section 25 of the law forbids the following agreements among competitors: to fix sale or purchase prices or other conditions, to limit output, public and private bid rigging, and market sharing in any form. Although not expressly indicated, the applicable standard is the per se rule. The list however, does not seem to be exhaustive.

In Honduras, sections 5 and 6 also contemplate the typical hard core cartels: price fixing, output reduction, market sharing and bid rigging, which are subject to the per se rule.

In Nicaragua, section 18 contemplates the anticompetitive practices between competitors to fix price, market sharing, horizontal boycott, output restriction, and bid rigging, which are subject to the per se rule.

In Panamá, section 13 of the law also lists price fixing and information exchange to fix prices, output reduction, market sharing, and bid rigging as illegal agreements among competitors. However, the law does not contemplate the per se rule for these agreements. Moreover, according to section 5 of the law, an agreement that increases efficiency and does not affect consumer welfare does not harm competition. And section 6 of the law exempts agreements to improve production or distribution of goods, promote technological or economic progress, and improve consumer welfare; provided the agreements are to exchange technological information, to develop or use infrastructure, equipment, or production facilities, to use storage, distribution, or distribution facilities, or to export goods.

In Costa Rica, section 11 of the law lists the absolute monopolistic conducts including price fixing, output reduction, market sharing, public bid rigging, horizontal boycott (joint refusal to deal), and information exchange with the purpose or effect of any of the other horizontal conducts. All these conducts are per se illegal. According to the law, the authority shall put especial attention to those markets with fewer players. However, there is no definition of such type of markets. However, the law for the Strengthening of the Competition Authorities introduced a "de minimis" provision according to which conducts, either horizontal or vertical are excepted if the undertakings involved have a total market share less than 5%.

[B] Unilateral Conduct

In El Salvador, sections 26 and 27 contemplate agreements among non-competitors and abuse of dominance. Section 26 includes a non-exclusive list of agreements like tie ins, vertical boycott, and exclusive dealing. These conducts are subject to the rule of reason. Section 28 articulates the concept of the relevant market based on substitutability. Section 29 contemplates the factors to determine if a dominant position exists. Efficiency defense is admissible in this type of conduct. Article 30 of the law prohibits abuse of dominance. The non-exclusive list includes preventing entry or expansion of competitors, predatory pricing, and price discrimination. Section 17 of the Regulations of the law contemplates some indicators of the abuse of dominance, some of which might be considered an abuse on its own: increasing cost of entry, limit access to input, cross subsidies, and price discrimination.

In Honduras, section 7 lists the conducts forbidden by their effects if they restrict, limit, reduce, or harm competition. These conducts include the imposition of territory, market or client restrictions, tie ins, resale price fixing, vertical boycott, imposition of ancillary restraints, exclusive dealing, predatory pricing, output or distribution restriction, exclusivity discounts; but the list is not exclusive. These conducts are subject to the rule of reason. Market definition also refers to substitutability, according to section 2 of the law; and more detailed parameters are set in the regulations. However, the Peer Review noted that they are rarely incorporated into the analysis. The review also calls for more spread use of tools like the hypothetical monopolist and cross elasticity to make the analysis more technically consistent.[17]

In Nicaragua, section 19 of the law contemplated conducts among non-competitors, as follows: (a) exclusive distribution, (b) resale price maintenance, (c) tie ins, (d) exclusive dealing, (e) unjustified refusal to deal, (f) discriminatory treatment, (g) vertical boycott, and (h) predatory conduct. The list should be considered exhaustive.[18] This type of conducts is subject to the rule of reason, as per section 20 of the law. Definition of the relevant market is based on product substitutability. And the description of a dominant position also refers to the traditional definition, but there is no reference to joint dominance.

In Panama, section 16 of the law lists the relative monopolistic illicit practices, which can be unilateral or concerted conducts, as follows: (1) exclusive distribution, (2) resale price maintenance, (3) tie ins, (4) exclusive dealing, (5) refusal to deal, (6) vertical boycott, and (7) predatory conduct. Paragraph (8) seems to include an attempt to monopolize and paragraph 9 any other act that may limit access to the market or harm competition. The relevant market is called pertinent market, but it is also described in terms of substitutability (section 18) and market power is called substantial power, which is described also following common understanding of the concept, as the capacity to act and price unilaterally in the market.

In Costa Rica, section 12 of the law lists the relative monopolistic practices and includes: (a) exclusivity agreements and vertical market segmentation, (b) resale price maintenance and the imposition of other conditions to reseller, (c) tying and reciprocity, (d) exclusive dealing, (e) vertical boycott, (f) predatory pricing when the incumbent sells below average cost for long periods and there are indicators that losses may

17. OECD, Peer Review, Honduras, p. 30.
18. UNCTAD, Peer Review, Nicaragua, p. 11.

be recovered by future price increases, except for sales promotions and product introduction to the market, (g) refusal to deal, (h) price discrimination/discriminatory treatment, (i) increasing the cost of a competitor with no justification, (j) the request to, or the obligation of the supplier to change, modify or substitute its trademark as a condition to sell its goods or services; or to request the supplier for the production of similar goods or services for a private trademark, (k) any other conduct intentionally implemented to drive competitors out of the markets or prevent their entrance, (l) additional obligations that according to the business traditions are not part of the object of the transaction, (m) the threat of termination in order to obtain payment or other business conditions different from the generally accepted business conditions, (n) cross subsidies, and (o) margin squeeze. All these conducts are subject to the rule of reason. So, they shall be presumed valid and legal unless COPROCOM determines in an investigation that the following three elements are present: (i) the economic agent has substantial power in the relevant market, (ii) the conduct is listed in article 12, and (iii) the object or effect is the improper displacement of other undertakings from the market, a substantial limit to access the market or the granting of exclusive benefits to one or more people. The relevant market is defined as usual in terms of substitutability and substantial power in terms of the ability of an economic agent to act in the market independently of the competitors.

[C] Merger Review

El Salvador has an *ex ante* merger control system, as mandated in section 33 of the law, for all concentrations where the combination of total assets exceeds 50,000 minimum salaries, or total income exceeds 60,000 minimum salaries. Although the law does not specify whether assets or revenue must be located in El Salvador, the authority considers a "local nexus" is required, and therefore assets or revenues must be local.[19] The superintendency has ninety days to issue a decision, and if there is no decision the merger may take place.

In Honduras, the CDPC is authorized by law and the regulations to establish specific notification thresholds, which it did based on indexed (to minimum wages) values of assets, volume of sales, and market shares (more than 20% market share). The 20% market share threshold is low compared to international standards, and the OECD has recommended the elimination of this criteria from the notification thresholds.[20] The CDPC established thresholds to move the analysis to a second face. The CDPC also reviews mergers in the regulated markets. So, many resources are devoted to merger control. All cases have been approved, but in thirteen cases conditions have been imposed. The analysis has to be completed in forty-five days.

In Nicaragua, section 24 defines the type of transactions that are considered concentrations, all of which entail some sort of change of control; and that subject to the threshold established in section 25 shall be subject to *ex ante* notification.

19. OECD, Peer Review, El Salvador, p. 20.
20. OECD, Peer Review, Honduras, p. 72.

Thresholds are more than 25% market share and combined gross income of entities involved above 642.847 minimum salaries. Joint Ventures (established for a limited period) and mergers involving a firm in insolvency condition are permitted. The standard for the analysis is whether the merger reduces or harms competition. The efficiency defense is acceptable. A filing fee must also be paid as follows: (a) USD 50,000 for concentrations affecting more than 25% of the relevant market, and for up to USD 5 million; (b) USD 75,000 for concentrations affecting more than 25% of the relevant market, and for USD 5 to USD 10 million; and (c) USD 100,000 for concentrations affecting more than 25% of the market, and for more than USD 10 million. Procompetencia has thirty business days to complete a preliminary analysis, but a second phase may be necessary in more complex cases.

In Panama, mergers are also defined in terms of change in control. But in this country notification is voluntary. This is why ACODECO has reviewed very few cases. But ACODECO may challenge a merger within three years after closing. Most notified mergers have been approved. Only in two cases conditions have been imposed, and in only one case the merger was not approved. The standard for the analysis is unreasonable harm to competition. ACODECO shall consider the efficiencies created by the merger. There is no mention of consumer welfare as part of the analysis. Joint Ventures for a limited period of time and concentrations involving a firm operating with losses and a declining market share are not prohibited. ACODECO must issue the opinion in sixty days; otherwise the merger is automatically approved. The notification does not prevent the parties from completing the merger, unless ACODECO gets a court order.

The Costa Rican competition law contemplated a merger control system since it was enacted in 1994. But there was no pre-merger notification obligation, thus control was *ex post*. It was in this context that COPROCOM started the investigation of a merger that ended up with the USD 2.0 million in fines. For some time COPROCOM allowed voluntary notifications, until the 2012 amendment of the law came into effect and implemented a compulsory notice starting April 2013. The system however was not technically *ex ante*, because notice could be filed before closing or no later than five days after closing. However, the Law for the Strengthening of the Competition Authorities established a whole new *ex ante* merger control regime that applies also to mergers in the telecommunications markets that have to be notified before SUTEL. Under these rules COPROCOM and SUTEL only rejected one case each. Now there is a two-phase procedure. The first phase is thirty days long, and the second phase is ninety days. If the concentration does not pose risks to competition, then it must be approved in the first phase. The analysis standard is harm to competition instead of the focus on market structure usually applied by COPROCOM.

[D] Cases

The following is just a sample of cases in each country that indicates all authorities are familiar with anticompetitive conducts, the way to investigate them, and that they have been able to sustain most of the sanctions imposed despite numerous reviews by courts.

In El Salvador, the most relevant case has been the sanctioning of a hard core cartel in the wheat flour (USD 4 million in fines) which the authority ruled after finding evidence in the first ever dawn raid conducted by the superintendency and continues to be the iconic case; and one case involving the most important gas stations.[21]

In Honduras, experience shows that it has been difficult for the CDPC to prove the amount of the benefit obtained by the economic agents with implementation of the anticompetitive conduct. So, the highest fines have been based on 10% of the sales of the economic agents. Cartels have been detected and sanctioned in the drugstore, cement, and sugar markets.[22]

In Nicaragua, the Constitutional Court granted an appeal ("amparo") to several banks that claimed Procompetencia did not have jurisdiction to resolve cases on the financial sector (confirming regulated sectors are excluded from the superintendency's authority), following a ruling on an interest rate fixing case in the credit card market. The superintendency of Banks, however, did not open an investigation on the credit card market after this Constitutional Court ruling, leaving the case unchecked.[23] In a refusal to deal the case, Tropigás de Nicaragua was fined with USD 22,000. The decision was confirmed in the appeal by the Board of Procompetencia. Procompetencia have also reviewed mergers in several markets. All cases reviewed have been approved, some subject to conditions, like the merger in the hydrocarbons market and the merger in the poultry market (conditions imposed were criticized by the Peer Review Report).[24]

In Panamá, cartels have been detected in the transport of goods between the Free Trade Zone of Colon and Panama City, laundries, gasoline stations, flour, medical oxygen (bid rigging), airlines, car and fire insurance, and rice, sugar, and milk markets.[25] There have been fewer cases of vertical conduct. The case filed by ACODECO against the Panama Refinery in the gasoline and diesel market is one of them. In this case, the refinery was charged with favouring an affiliate and the best client in detriment of the other clients, when determining the order in which gasoline and diesel would be served to the tank trucks of its clients (the refinery had eliminated the first come first served rule). In 2018, ACODECO prevailed in a case against the largest brewery of Panama, for blocking entrance using exclusive dealing agreements.

In Costa Rica, COPROCOM investigated and sanctioned a price fixing cartel in the pension funds market. The total amount of fines to the parties involved was approximately USD 4 million, but the court preemptively suspended the obligation to pay the penalty and subsequently annulled the opinion. The largest fine imposed to a single economic agent was USD 2 million (approximately this amount based on exchange rate of the moment). The case is also special because it was on a merger review case that

21. OECD, Peer Review, p. 18.
22. Ayes, Rubin. Interview.
23. UNCTAD, Peer Review, Nicaragua, p. 41.
24. *Ibid.*, p. 51.
25. OECD, Peer Review, Panamá, p. 19.

COPROCOM started ex officio. This happened before the amendment of the law introducing the compulsory notice was passed. COPROCOM also detected and sanctioned a vertical boycott. In this case, local car dealers of foreign manufacturers got together to press the local insurance company, to modify a system for the purchase of repair parts. The modification limited the opportunities of other players to participate in the system. The most recent relevant cases are one of vertical restraints in the drugstore market where a vertically integrated laboratory and drugstore chain was heavily fined for imposing discriminatory conditions to its competitors at the retail level. The other case is the rejection of the largest retail company attempt to buy its third largest competitor. In this case COPROCOM posed greater concerns on the possible effects on the upstream level alleged by supplier, than the potential efficiencies that the concentration might have brought to consumers.

[E] Authorities

The superintendency of El Salvador is part of the executive branch but has technical and financial independence. There are three members of the board, the superintendent is a full time employee appointed by the president of the country and is a member of the board. Following the 2007 amendment of the law, the powers of the authority include dawn raids and leniency program. Leniency can be granted only to the first applicant, but exemption of fines is only partial. Of all agencies the superintendency of El Salvador is by large the one with better resources in terms of budget and staff, with more than thirty employees.

In Honduras, the CDPC has three members, all appointed by congress for a seven-year term, and their term expires at the same time. The commission has technical and financial independence.

Procompetencia in Nicaragua has a board of three members, appointed by the president of the country and ratified by absolute majority in congress. They serve for five years on a full time and exclusive basis, but their appointment is not coterminous.

In Panama, ACODECO is a fully independent entity led by only one administrator appointed by the executive and ratified by congress, for a seven-year term (which may be renewed one time).

In Costa Rica, COPROCOM has three commissioners and two alternates. They are full time employees. They are appointed by the executive but can be vetoed by congress. They serve for six years, and their appointment cannot be renewed. Their terms are not coterminous. COPROCOM is still part of the Ministry of Economy and Industry, but it is independent on budgetary and technical matters. The Law for the Strengthening of the Competition Authorities granted COPROCOM and SUTEL larger advocacy and investigative powers. Advocacy powers now include the possibility to issue opinions and recommendations on regulations issued by other authorities. These recommendations are not binding, but the authority that does not adopt them must issue a written explanation of its reasons. The agencies also have the capacity to challenge before court any regulation or law that limits competition.

[F] Investigation and Procedures

In all countries the investigation may start by a complaint or ex officio. The authority may order preemptive measures and the decisions may be reviewed by court.

In El Salvador, a final decision must be issued within twelve months, but this period can be extended for another twelve months. According to Escolán, this is happening too often.[26] The superintendency was given regular investigation powers normally given in other jurisdictions, including the capacity to do dawn raids. The fining power includes fines up to 6% of a firm's total annual sales in El Salvador; 6% of firm's total assets in El Salvador; and between two times and ten times the estimated gain resulting from the anticompetitive conduct, in cases of particularly serious offenses.

In Honduras, investigations must be completed in six months, which is considered too short to complete an investigation.[27] The CDPC can make dawn raids, the 2015 amendment introduced a leniency program, but there are no early termination or settlement provisions. The highest penalty is three times the amount of the benefit obtained by the undertaking with the anticompetitive conduct, or up to 10% of gross profit of the last fiscal year; if the benefit cannot be determined. But if the undertaking accepts the charges, then a 30% reduction of the penalty may apply, as per section 51 of the law.

In Nicaragua, section 48 of the law contemplates a complete exemption under the leniency program, but there has not been any case yet. The executive regulations to implement the leniency program were published in March 5, 2021 in La Gaceta No.45, No.31, establishing the procedural rules of the program, so there are no registered cases yet. Early termination or settlements are not expressly contemplated in the law. Interim measures may be ordered at the request of a party. Maximum penalties for horizontal agreements are up to 10% of sales of the last fiscal year, and up to 6% in the case of vertical conduct and unfair competition. Decisions are issued by the President of Procompetencia. In case of non-compliance with final decision, Procompetencia may order the shutdown of the business activities until the decision is fully complied with. Article 273 of the Criminal Code contemplates anticompetitive practices as a:

> criminal offense by way of imposing resale prices or sharing information for the same purpose or with the same effects, limiting production, sharing market and excluding competitors from the market. The crime would be committed when an agreement exists which restricts competition and puts the country's economic stability at risk or affects basic goods. To date no such case has been tried in criminal courts.[28]

In Panamá, section 104 of the law contemplates a reward to the person who filed the complaint equal to 25% of the penalty imposed. Panama contemplates leniency provisions for horizontal conducts. But given the small size of the country and the vast

26. Escolán, Celina. Interview.
27. OECD, Peer Review, Honduras, p. 10.
28. UNCTAD, Peer Review, Nicaragua, p. 14.

net of family and social connections between persons in key positions in the local business community, the success of this program may be limited.[29] Maximum penalty is USD 1,000,000 for hard core cartels; and the criminal code contemplates penalties for price fixing in public bids. The authority can perform dawn raids, which has been used two or three times per year, and they can perform competition audits to specific players to monitor the market and ensure anticompetitive conducts do not reappear. Once the investigation phase is completed with evidence of the existence of anticompetitive conduct, ACODECO has to file a complaint before court. Private parties may also file complaints and join complaints filed by ACODECO. Thus, only courts can determine the existence of an anticompetitive conduct. Once a court has issued a decision confirming the existence of an anticompetitive conduct, ACODECO has to determine the penalty and the remedies (behavioural or structural). But if there is a private claim, the court would rule on it. Judges may triple the amount of damages. Mergers that are voluntarily notified to ACODECO are reviewed by ACODECO, but the decision may be appealed before court. The law contemplates the possibility to settle the case during the judicial phase, which requires consents from the Procuraduría General, the council of ministers and the judge. Informal agreements before the filing of the complaint are also permitted.

In Costa Rica, the Law for the Strengthening of the Competition Authorities created a whole new procedure, applicable only for the investigation of horizontal and vertical anticompetitive conducts, and other offenses contemplated in the competition law. The main purpose of the reform was to separate the investigation and the decision-making phase, and to move the hearing to the second phase, so that the parties can directly argue before the commissioners. The law also introduced a preliminary phase to allow the staff to determine whether the case has merits to open a formal investigation. Even though the law contemplates specific terms of 12 to 18 months for the preliminary phase, 10 to 16 months for the investigation phase, and 7 to 8 months for the final decision, unfortunately the law does not contemplate any consequences if these terms elapse. The 2012 amendment of the law granted COPROCOM the capacity to make dawn raids, with a court order. This capacity has not been exercised yet. The amendment also granted COPROCOM the ability to reach agreements for early termination of cases, but for cartel cases the applicant must admit the participation in the conduct and the benefit is only a 10% reduction of the fine. Cartels and vertical restraints are considered very serious offenses and are punished with a fine between 5% and 10% of annual sales of the economic agent.

§10.05 POSSIBLE DEVELOPMENTS

Given the state of development of the competition law and policy in the region, an obvious question arises as to whether the Central American countries will be able to establish and implement effective mechanisms to prevent, detect, investigate, and punish cross-border anticompetitive conducts in the region.

29. OECD, Peer Review, Panamá, p. 23.

The more recent step toward that end is the Reglamento Centroamericano de Competencia. This regulation creates a regional competition committee that is already integrated by representatives of the competition authorities of each country and started meeting immediately. This committee is not a tribunal and does not have investigative powers, which means investigation of cross-border conducts is still difficult in the region. However, the committee has to promote competition in the region and create cooperation mechanism among the authorities. This includes the creation of mechanisms for information exchange among the authorities and the capacity to make market studies in key sectors of common interest and at a regional level, which the committee is already planning. So, although there is still a long way to having effective mechanisms to investigate cross-border conducts, this committee may be one more step in that direction. The mission of this committee should be to expose the need to keep moving toward that end.

At a country level, the first issue to note is that Guatemala, despite a long lasting discussion of several initiatives in congress, does not have a competition law yet. The EU-CA Association Agreement establishes an individual commitment of each country first to have its own law and its own authority, within three years from the time the agreement comes into effect. This raises a lot of questions about the competition conditions on the market, the entity, the infrastructure, human, financial and other basic resources need for the existence of a competition authority; and the building of adequate expertise in competition in the country.

Second, the 2020 OECD-BID peer review on El Salvador issued several recommendations to the country, that include changes in the law, changes in the Superintendencia, and changes in the technical analysis of the cases. Implementation of these recommendations is not easy and it takes time, especially those that require changing the law. So, new developments in El Salvador in the next few years should be related to the recommendations from the OECD.

Third, following the enactment of the Law for the Strengthening of Competition Authorities, in Costa Rica, COPROCOM and SUTEL have to issue the regulation of the law and guidelines on several topics. These regulations and guidelines were due by the end of 2020, but they have not been issued yet. The delay is caused by the pandemic but also by lack of coordination between the two agencies and the Ministry of Economy. So, a new development in the country should be the publication and implementation of these regulations. Another development that should be expected in Costa Rica should be brought by a corruption scandal that recently erupted, regarding braveries to public officials paid by the two largest companies in the public infrastructure market. This is being pursued by the public prosecutor, but the President requested COPROCOM to launch an investigation for possible bid rigging. Hopefully this will make the authority in Costa Rica and in the other countries to dedicate more efforts and resources to the investigation of bid rigging in key markets.

In sum, Central American countries have made good progress since the competition laws were enacted, and the agencies make continuous efforts to build adequate technical capacities to investigate anticompetitive conducts and review mergers, despite the limited resources in most cases. Their voluntary submissions to peer reviews are evidence of their commitment to keep up with best practices. However, as the result of these reviews evidence, there are still many things to improve at a national level in each country. At a regional level, there are not yet proper mechanisms to investigate and punish cross-border anticompetitive conducts in the region. The way to accomplish this may be by the implementation of the EU-CA Association Agreement, or the efforts from the newly created regional competition committee. How long this would take is still an open question.

BIBLIOGRAPHY

Treaties, Laws, and Regulations

Agreement Establishing an Association between Central America, on the one hand and the European Union and Its Member Estates, on the other. 2012

Convenio Marco para el Establecimiento de la Unión Aduanera Centroamericana. 2007

Costa Rica: Ley de Promoción de la Competencia y Defensa Efectiva del Consumidor. No. 7472 Dec. 20, 1994

El Salvador: Ley de Competencia Executive Decree N° 586 Dec. 22, 2004

Honduras: Ley para la Defensa y Promoción de la Competencia Executive Decree N° 357-2005. Dec. 29, 2005

Nicaragua: Ley de Promoción de la Competencia. Law No. 601 Sep. 28, 2006

Panamá: Ley que dicta normas sobre protección al consumidor y defensa de la competencia y otra disposición. Law No. 45. Oct. 31, 2007

Protocolo al Tratado General de Integración Económica Centroamericana. 1993

Reglamento Centroamericano sobre Competencia. COMIECO Resolución No.441-2020

Books and Articles

Bendaña, Julio C. "Análisis Crítico de la Legislación de Competencia en Centroamérica, Panamá y República Dominicana." COMPAL, Programa Regional, 2010

Conferencia de las Naciones Unidas para el Comercio y el Desarrollo. "Recomendaciones para mejorar la cooperación regional en Centroamérica." Ginebra, Suiza, 2011

De León, Ignacio. "Condiciones y políticas de competencia. Economías pequeñas de Centroamérica y el Caribe." Fondo de Cultura Económica, 2006. La Promoción de la Competencia en Centroamérica. Dificultades y Posibilidades

Díaz Rodríguez Francisco, "Sobre confidencialidad y derecho de defensa." Artículo publicado por el Diario de Hoy, El Salvador, 1 de setiembre de 2014

Hernández, René and Schatan, Claudia. "Condiciones y políticas de competencia. Economías pequeñas de Centroamérica y el Caribe." Fondo de Cultura Económica, 2006. Políticas de Competencia y de Regulación en el Istmo Centroamericano

Horna, Pierre. "Can Accountability and Effectiveness Go Hand in Hand? Lessons from Two Latin American Competition Networks." In *Informal International Lawmaking*. Torkel Opsahl Academic E Publisher. The Hague, 2012

Odio, Edgar. Costa Rica Chapter, in "The Dominance and Monopolies Review" Second Edition Edited by Dolmans, Maurits, Law Business Research, 2014

Odio, Edgar. Costa Rica Chapter, in "The Merger Control Review" Fifth Edition Edited by Knable Gotts, Ilene, Law Business Research, 2014

Olmedo, Daniel. "Superintendencia de Competencia e información confidencial." Artículo publicado por el Diario de Hoy, El Salvador, 22 de agosto de 2014

Rivera, Eugenio y Schatan, Claudia. "Centroamérica y México: políticas de competencia a principios del siglo XXI." 2008. Naciones Unidas, CEPAL. Introducción

Rivera, Eugenio y Schatan, Claudia. "Centroamérica y México: políticas de competencia a principios del siglo XXI." 2008. Naciones Unidas, CEPAL. Los mercados en el Istmo Centroamericano y México: qué ha pasado con la competencia?

Sittenfeld, Pamela. "Centroamérica y México: políticas de competencia a principios del siglo XXI." 2008. Naciones Unidas, CEPAL. Ventajas y limitaciones de la experiencia de Costa Rica en materia de políticas de competencia: un punto de referencia para los demás países de la región centroamericana

Ministerio de Economía Industria y Comercio. Memoria Institucional. 2013

United Nations Conference for Trade and Development. "Cross-Border Anticompetitive Practices: The Challenges for Developing Countries and Economies in Transition." Intergovernmental Group of Experts on Competition Law and Policy, Twelfth session. Geneva, July 9–11, 2012

Peer Reviews

OECD. "El Salvador- Peer Review of Competition Law and Policy." Country Studies, 2008. Clark, John

OECD. "Derecho y Política de la Competencia en Honduras." Country Studies, 2011. Vergara, Enrique

OECD. "Derecho y Política de la Competencia en Panamá." Country Studies, 2010. Sokol, Daniel

OECD. "Competition Law and Policy in Costa Rica" Country Studies, 2014. Benedetti, Paolo.

OECD – BID "Exámenes Inter-Pares de la OECD y el BID sobre el Derecho y Política de Competencia. El Salvador. 2020"

UNCTAD. "Voluntary Peer Review of Competition Law and Policy: Nicaragua." 2013. Sittenfeld, Pamela and Valbuena, Gustavo

UNCTAD. "Voluntary Peer Review on Competition Policy: Costa Rica." 2008. Diego Petrecolla

Interviews

Ayes, Rubin. Former Member of the "Comision para la Defensa y Promoción de la Competencia" of Honduras

Escolán, Celina. Former Superintendent of the "Superintendencia de Competencia" of El Salvador

Sittenfeld, Pamela. Former Director of the Technical Staff of the "Comisión para Promover la Competencia" of Costa Rica

CHAPTER 11

Competition Law in Argentina

Julián Peña & Federico Rossi

§11.01 INTRODUCTION

Argentina's first comprehensive and modern antitrust regulation was Law No. 22,262 of 1980.[1] During the initial twenty years (1980–1999), antitrust enforcement was focused on anticompetitive conducts, whereas since year 2000 antitrust enforcement has moved to predominantly focus on merger control.

Law No. 22,262 of 1980 introduced many new features, such as the creation of the *Comisión Nacional de Defensa de la Competencia* (CNDC), the rule of reason approach to anticompetitive conducts, and the concept of abuse of dominant position, all of which are reflected in the following Antitrust Law (No. 25,156) that was enacted in September 1999, but for the first time created a merger notification procedure.[2]

Antitrust policy acquired constitutional status through the 1994 amendment to the Argentine Constitution, which in its section 42 states that the federal authorities shall provide for 'the defense of competition against any kind of market distortions'.

Today, Law No. 27,442[3] (the 'Antitrust Law'), which was enacted on May 15, 2018, and came into force on May 24, 2018, substantially amended Argentina's antitrust regime, with the underlying rationale of modernizing Argentinian antitrust law and bring it in line with international best practices. The Antitrust Law governs all competition matters (i.e., cartels, unilateral conducts, and merger control), and its enforcement is vested in the Secretariat of Trade of the Ministry of Production (the

1. Law No. 22,262 enacted on 1 August 1980. There were some previous antitrust laws (No. 11,210 of 1923 and No. 12,906 of 1946) that dealt with certain anticompetitive conducts but received little to no enforcement at all.
2. Law No. 25,156, 20 September 1999, B.O. 29233 (Arg.).
3. Law No. 27,442, 15 May 2018, B.O. 33870 (Arg.) (*Ley de Defensa de la Competencia*).

'Domestic Trade Secretariat'), which is assisted by the CNDC (together with the Domestic Trade Secretariat, shall be hereafter referred to as the 'Antitrust Authority').

§11.02 CARTELS

[A] Relevant Legislation

Cartels are regulated by Chapter I of the Antitrust Law, notably, by sections 1 and 2. In addition, in December 2018, the CNDC issued a Guideline for Business Associations and Chambers and Professional Associations and Colleges aimed at preventing the creation of cartels in the framework of trade associations[4] and laying out certain rules and best practices to avoid the exchange of commercially sensitive information among competitors.

Section 1 of the Antitrust Law sets forth the guiding principle to analyse any anticompetitive conduct, which provides that:

> Agreements between competitors, economic concentrations, acts or conducts, in any form manifested, related to the production and exchange of goods or services, which have the object or effect of limiting, restricting, falsifying, or distorting competition or access to any market or that constitute an abuse of a dominant position in a market, in a manner that may be harmful to the general economic interest, are prohibited.

More specifically, section 2 of the Antitrust Law covers cartel behaviour and establishes that:

> Agreements between two or more competitors, consisting of contracts, agreements or arrangements constitute practices that are absolutely restrictive of the competition and are presumed to be harmful to the general economic interest, whose object or effect is to:
>
> a) Arrange, directly or indirectly, the sale or purchase price of goods or services at which they are offered or demanded in the market;
> b) Set obligations to (i) produce, process, distribute, purchase or commercialize only a limited or restricted quantity of goods, and/or (ii) provide a restricted or limited number, volume or frequency of services;
> c) Horizontally allocate, divide, distribute, assign or impose zones, portions or sectors of markets, consumers or sources of supply;
> d) Establish, arrange or coordinate bids or abstention in bids, contests or auctions.

Strictly related to section 2 of the Antitrust Law, section 29 of the Antitrust Law (also a provision introduced in 2018) provides that the Defense of Competition Tribunal, in accordance with what is established in the regulation, may issue permits to enter into contracts, agreements, or arrangements that relate to conducts included in section 2 of the Antitrust Law, that according to the reasonable discretion of the

4. CNDC, GUIDELINE FOR BUSINESS ASSOCIATIONS AND CHAMBERS AND PROFESSIONAL ASSOCIATIONS AND COLLEGES (2018) (Arg.).

tribunal are not harmful to the general economic interest. In turn, the regulation (i.e., section 29 of Decree 480/2018 – the 'Regulatory Decree') established that the Defense of Competition Tribunal shall verify the fulfilment of the following conditions to grant a permit to an agreement that relates to section 2 conduct:

(a) Contribute to improve the production or allocation of goods and/or services;
(b) Promote technical or economic progress;
(c) Generate specific benefits for consumers;
(d) Not impose on the companies in question any restriction that is not indispensable to the fulfillment of the purposes set forth in the preceding paragraphs (a), (b) and (c);
(e) Not afford such companies the possibility to eliminate competition in a significant portion of the affected market.

The presumption of illegality of cartels set forth in section 2 and the permits system of section 29 are both new features introduced by the Antitrust Law.

Pursuant to section 2, certain types of agreements between competitors are presumed to be anticompetitive and harmful to the general economic interest, which would exempt the Antitrust Authority from the heavy burden of proving that certain types of agreements between competitors (i.e., those relating to price-fixing, output-fixing, market allocation, and bid-rigging) in practice had anticompetitive effects.

Conversely, under the previous legal framework, the Antitrust Authority had the burden of proving (1) the existence of an agreement or coordinated practice; (2) the capacity (i.e., market power) of the investigated parties to be able to potentially cause a damage to the general economic interest in a properly defined relevant product and geographic market; (3) that the agreement or coordinated practice distorted competition in the relevant market; and (4) an actual or potential damage to the general economic interest. With the former antitrust legislation, all types of anticompetitive conduct (including hard-core cartels) had to be analyzed under the rule of reason or an effects-based approach. Consequently, even if the Antitrust Authority obtained direct evidence of a cartel, it had to prove the anticompetitive effects of such conduct and how such conduct affected (or could have affected) the general economic interest.

Since the legal presumption of section 2 is a novel feature recently introduced by the Antitrust, there is no certainty as to how the Antitrust Authority will interpret and apply such presumption in practice, and, subsequently, whether the courts will confirm the Antitrust Authority's approach. There are many cogent reasons to argue that congress has created a rebuttable presumption of illegality for a closed number of agreements between competitors (i.e., the four types of agreements between competitors comprised in section 2 of the Antitrust Law). Such presumption would relieve the Antitrust Authority from demonstrating that the agreements included in section 2 of the Antitrust Law actually had anticompetitive effects (since these are presumed by law), and the burden to prove that the investigated agreement had no net anticompetitive effects would shift to the investigated parties.

First, nothing in the wording of section 2 of the Antitrust Law indicates that the presumption therein established is irrebuttable. Second, the legislative debates that led to the enactment of the Antitrust Law, specifically refer to the fact that the presumption of section 2 is rebuttable, and that the source of such presumption is the competition law of the European Union (EU). On a different, yet related note, the influence of EU legislation in relation to merger control and the abuse of dominance is patent and indisputable in the Antitrust Law. Therefore, a reasonable and consistent approach would favour an interpretation whereby the analysis of anticompetitive conducts also follows the legislation of the EU. Third, the permit system (regulated in section 29 of the Antitrust Law and section 29 of the Regulatory Decree) is a verbatim copy of article 101 (3) of the Treaty on the Functioning of the EU. Fourth, a per se approach to cartels (i.e., one of automatic condemnation or irrebuttable presumption in relation to the anticompetitive effects of certain types of agreements) would hardly be compatible with the constitutional safeguards of due process of law and right to fair trial. On the other hand, the EU's analytical system of 'by object restrictions' and 'by effects restrictions' of competition, whereby the alleged infringers can always submit an efficiencies defense would certainly seem more consistent with the Argentinean constitutional regime.

In addition, it is worth mentioning that the Antitrust Authority in *CARBAP*[5] has held that agreements between competitors are not illegal when fostered by state action.

Since the general economic interest concept is not defined in the Antitrust Law, its conceptual broadness has led to different interpretations in the case law since it was first introduced by Law No. 22,262 of 1980. This broad concept grants the Antitrust Authority ample discretionary powers to determine its content; however, it also raises the burden of proof that the Antitrust Authority has in order to be able to consider an anticompetitive conduct as unlawful.

The interpretation of the general economic interest concept has changed over time. In the first two decades since its introduction in 1980, the general economic interest concept was assimilated to the 'correct market functioning' (e.g., *Agip*,[6] among others). However, since the late 1990s, the case law moved towards interpreting such concept as referring to economic efficiency (e.g., *YPF*,[7] among others), thus, assimilating the general economic interest to the economic concept of 'total surplus', that is, the sum of both the consumers' surplus and the producers' surplus in a given market.

Regarding the standard of proof of the damage to the general economic interest, the case law has held different criteria: in some cases, the courts held that the damage

5. CNDC, 9 August 2007, Conduct Decision No. 556.
6. National Supreme Court of Justice, 23 November 1993, 'Lara Gas y otros c/ Agip y otros.'
7. National Supreme Court of Justice, 2 July 2002, 'Yacimientos Petrolíferos Fiscales S.A. s/ ley 22.262 – Comisión Nacional de Defensa de la Competencia – Secretaría de Comercio e Industria.'

should be proven (e.g., *Shell*[8]), while in other rulings the courts allowed the Antitrust Authority to presume the existence of such damage (e.g., *Loma Negra*[9]).

The National Supreme Court of Justice has held that cartels have enough capacity to affect the general economic interest since they deprive consumers of the benefits that should be obtained if prices and quantities were determined through competition. Thus, in case there is overt collusion, the courts tend to presume the existence of damage to the general economic interest. Contrarily, in cases relating to covert collusions, the National Supreme Court of Justice has held that the existence of parallel pricing is not enough to prove the existence of a cartel.

The case law has always found price-fixing, quantity-fixing, bid-rigging, and horizontal market allocations to be illegal when these practices have been properly ascertained by the Antitrust Authority.

[B] Extraterritoriality

An anticompetitive conduct that took place outside the territory of Argentina is covered by the Antitrust Law as long as it had effects in the domestic market. Section 4 of the Antitrust Law adopts the so-called Effects Doctrine and introduces the principle of extraterritorial application of the Antitrust Law. However, there has not been any known case relating to the extraterritorial application of the Antitrust Law that derived in the sanction of cartels adopted abroad.

[C] Investigations

[1] Authorities

[a] Policy, Politics, and Institutions

The Antitrust Law is enforced by the Antitrust Authority, which at present is vested in the Domestic Trade Secretariat, which is appointed and removed by the president of Argentina. However, the Antitrust Law envisions the removal of all decision-making powers from the Domestic Trade Secretariat and provides for the creation of a new, more independent antitrust authority.

The Domestic Trade Secretariat, which has decision-making powers, is assisted by the CNDC, which is a technical agency with investigatory and advisory powers. The Domestic Trade Secretariat generally follows the recommendations issued by the CNDC and very rarely takes a different position.

The CNDC is composed of five members. The President of the CNDC is appointed by the President of Argentina who can remove him or her without cause. The

8. Court of Appeals of Posadas, 30 May 2008, 'Shell Gas S.A. y Total Gaz Argentina S.A. s/ ley 25.156 Ministerio de Economía y Producción Sec. de Comercio Interior Comisión Nacional de Defensa de la Competencia.'
9. Court of Appeals in Criminal Economic Matters, 26 August 2008, 'Loma Negra Compañía Industrial S.A. y otros.'

remaining four commissioners, two of which must be lawyers and two of which must be economists, are also designated by the President of Argentina but their term in office is four years, which can be renewed indefinitely.

Cartel investigations are carried out by the CNDC, which issues a non-binding report with recommendations to the Domestic Trade Secretariat, which adopts the final decision.

An important goal of the Antitrust Law is to provide more independence to the antitrust enforcement authority. To that end, the Antitrust Law foresees the removal of the decision-making powers from the Domestic Trade Secretariat and provides for the creation of a new, more independent antitrust authority, the National Competition Authority (*Autoridad Nacional de la Competencia*). The National Competition Authority shall be composed of three bodies:

1. The Defense of Competition Tribunal: shall be composed of five members and decide all matters relating to the Antitrust Law.
2. The Anticompetitive Conduct Secretariat: shall investigate and prosecute all matters related to anticompetitive conduct before the Defense of Competition Tribunal, and
3. The Economic Concentrations Secretariat: shall be responsible for the preliminary assessment of economic concentrations within the framework of the merger control regime and for issuing legal opinions for the Defense of Competition Tribunal to rule on these cases.

The Defense of Competition Tribunal shall be composed of five members and decide all matters relating to the Antitrust Law.[10] The Anticompetitive Conduct Secretariat shall investigate and prosecute all matters related to anticompetitive conduct before the Defense of Competition Tribunal, and the Economic Concentrations Secretariat will be in charge with conducting the preliminary assessment of economic concentrations under the merger control regime and issuing opinions for the Defense of Competition Tribunal to adjudicate in such cases.[11] Although all three bodies will make up the National Competition Authority, each shall possess technical autonomy.[12]

Pursuant to a temporal clause embedded in section 80 of the Antitrust Law, pending establishment of a National Competition Authority, the Domestic Trade Secretariat and CNDC will continue in their antitrust enforcement roles.[13] In the interim, the Domestic Trade Secretariat serves as the adjudicating authority; whereas the CNDC acts as an advisory and investigatory technical agency.[14]

10. Article 28, Law No. 27,442, 15 May 2018, B.O. 33870 (Arg.).
11. Articles 30–31, Law No. 27,442, 15 May 2018, B.O. 33870 (Arg.).
12. Articles 28, 30–31, Law No. 27,442, 15 May 2018, B.O. 33870 (Arg.).
13. Article 80, Law No. 27,442, 15 May 2018, B.O. 33870 (Arg.).
14. The CNDC is composed of five members. The President of the CNDC is appointed by the President of Argentina. The remaining four commissioners, two of which must be lawyers and two which must be economists are also designated by the President of Argentina but their term in office is four years, which can be renewed indefinitely. Articles 7–8, Law No. 22,262, 6 August 1980, B.O. 24474 (Arg.).

Therefore, since as of December 2021 the National Competition Authority has not been established, the Antitrust Law remains to be enforced by the Domestic Trade Secretariat with the technical assistance of the CNDC.

[b] *Resources and Priorities*

The enforcement of the Antitrust Law, despite its obvious technical content and policy aims, has always been to a very large extent politically driven, due to the following two main reasons: (i) the CNDC depends on the Domestic Trade Secretariat, which is appointed and removed by the President of Argentina, thus the enforcement agenda of the CNDC follows the guidelines ordered by the Domestic Trade Secretariat, which in turn follows the economic policy of the executive branch; and (ii) pursuant to the Antitrust Law, the Antitrust Authority has the absolute discretion to advance those claims it desires, while claimants – despite being entitled to file claims – do not have legal instruments to force the CNDC to investigate a given conduct.

Although the Antitrust Authority has expressly stated that cartels are hard-core offenses and the 'supreme antitrust evil', its efforts to detect and sanction cartels have been historically low. Recurrent economic and financial crisis, price controls and business cooperation formally or informally fostered by the different governments, and a dirigisme approach to economic policy, are some of the causes that have contributed to a low track record in tackling cartels.

The introduction of the first-ever antitrust leniency program as part of the enactment of the Antitrust Law in 2018, foresaw an uptick in the investigation of cartels. However, more than three years have elapsed since the launch of the leniency program and as of December 2021, there are neither leniency applications nor cartel investigations that have derived from a leniency application.

[c] *Inter-agency Cooperation*

Argentina has signed agreements both within Mercosur (*Mercado Común del Sur*) and bilaterally with other competition agencies.

In December 1996, Mercosur's founding members (i.e., Argentina, Brazil, Paraguay, and Uruguay) signed the Fortaleza Protocol of Defense of Competition to be applied to anticompetitive conducts affecting trade among its members that had a local effect in one of them. The Fortaleza Protocol was ratified by the Brazilian and Paraguayan congresses but was never approved by Argentina or Uruguay.

Even though the Fortaleza Protocol was never ratified, the Mercosur working group for competition matters (Working Group No. 5) kept meeting at least twice annually. In 2002, Mercosur adopted the Agreement on the Implementation of the Fortaleza Protocol. In 2004, through Common Market Council (CMC) Decision No. 4/2004, Mercosur approved the Consensus on the cooperation among competition agencies. In 2006, it approved CMC Decision 15/2006 establishing a system of exchange of information and consultation in the field of merger control. In 2010, Mercosur approved the CMC Decision No. 43/2010 an Agreement for the Defense of

Competition in Mercosur which replaced the Fortaleza Protocol. This agreement was ratified so far only by Argentina (in April 2011) and Uruguay (in January 2014).

Due to the new agreement so-called Agreement of Competition Defense of the MERCOSUR signed in 1996 with the objective of cooperation and exchange of information among the competition authorities of its members, the Cooperation Agreement was executed by Argentina and Brazil in September 2007.

In relation to the bilateral cooperation agreements, Argentina and Brazil were among the first countries to sign bilateral cooperation agreements in 2003. Although there has been very limited formal cooperation, there is some sporadic, informal communication regarding specific matters either through the postal system or by telephone.[15] In June 2011, the CNDC requested some information from its Brazilian counterparts using the mechanism established in the bilateral cooperation agreement, and the Brazilian agencies responded in August of the same year, though no information has been given on the content of the request.[16] In October 2011, the CNDC and Ecuador's competition agency signed a bilateral cooperation agreement, and in September 2017, the CNDC signed a similar agreement with Peru's INDECOPI.

Despite the above, in practice the inter-agency cooperation displayed by the Antitrust Authority has ranged from low to almost inexistent in both cartel and merger cases.

[2] Procedure

Pursuant to section 34 to 54 of the Antitrust Law, a cartel investigation may be initiated by the filing of a claim by any individual or company, ex officio by the Antitrust Authority or through a leniency application. Once a claim is filed, it is at the Antitrust Authority's sole discretion whether to conduct an investigation or not since there are no legal instruments to force the Antitrust Authority to do so.

Once an investigation is initiated, the Antitrust Law grants the investigated parties a fifteen-business day period to submit their explanations regarding the alleged anticompetitive conduct. If the Antitrust Authority, after reviewing the explanations and evidence filed by the investigated parties, concludes that there are grounds to file formal charges, it issues a resolution opening a formal investigation and grants the accused parties a twenty-business day period to file their defenses and offer evidence. On the contrary, should the explanations filed by the investigated parties rule out the existence of an anticompetitive conduct, then the Antitrust Authority issues a resolution closing the investigation.

Pursuant to the Antitrust Law, the evidence-production period shall last a maximum period of ninety business days (which may be extended to further ninety business days, if necessary). After the evidence-production period is finalized, the accused parties have six business days to file their arguments in connection with the

15. OECD, International Enforcement Cooperation, Paris 2003, Secretariat Report on the OECD/ICN Survey on International Enforcement Cooperation, p. 90.
16. See CNDC New Section (2013), available at www.cndc.gov.ar.

evidence produced throughout the investigation. Pursuant to section 42 of the Antitrust Law, the decisions adopted by the Antitrust Authority regarding the evidence produced during the investigation cannot be appealed to the Court of Appeals, but can be the object of an administrative appeal with the same Antitrust Authority. Once the parties file their arguments on the evidence, the Antitrust Authority has sixty business days to issue its final resolution.

Despite the above-explained timeline set forth in the Antitrust Law, in practice, cartel investigations that finished with the imposition of a fine by the Antitrust Authority took approximately between four and eight years.

Other significant powers that the Antitrust Authority has during the investigation according to section 30 of the Antitrust Law are to hold hearings with the presumably responsible individuals, claimant, affected parties, witnesses or experts, take their declarations and order confrontations, review of the books, documents, and other elements of the investigation, control stocks, and confirm origins and cost of raw materials or other goods, access the places subject to inspection with the consent of their inhabitants or by means of a court order, among others.

The limitations to the Antitrust Authority's investigatory powers to safeguard the rights of defense of companies and/or individuals are the ones established by the Argentine Constitution, such as the due process of law and property rights.

Furthermore, during the proceedings, pursuant to section 44 of the Antitrust Law, the Antitrust Authority may issue injunctions (i.e., preliminary cease and desist orders) ordering the accused parties to suspend the conduct under analysis until a final resolution is issued.

In addition, section 45 of the Antitrust Law provides the possibility for the investigated parties to propose a voluntary suspension of a conduct subject to approval of the Antitrust Authority. However, the approval by the Antitrust Authority of a commitment offered by the accused parties in a cartel investigation seems highly unlikely. Despite the fact that compromises would not appear to be available in cartel cases, the Antitrust Authority has recently accepted a compromise in the Prisma case, even when the theory of harm put forward by the CNDC in its investigation included collusive conduct.[17]

As explained in further detail below, once the final decision is issued by the Domestic Trade Secretariat, it can be appealed within fifteen business days with the Federal Civil and Commercial Court of Appeals (or the corresponding Federal Court of Appeals in the provinces).

At present, most of the investigatory powers described above are entrusted to the CNDC.[18] However, once the National Competition Authority is established, the Anti-competitive Conduct Secretariat shall investigate and prosecute all matters related to anticompetitive conduct before the Defense of Competition Tribunal.

17. Secretaría de Comercio [SeCom] [Secretariat of Trade], 31/10/2018, 'Investigación de oficio contra Prisma Medio de Pago S.A. y sus accionistas en los términos del art. 1 y 2, inc. A), F), G), H), J), K) y L), de la Ley 25.156 (C.1613)', (Arg.).

18. Resolution 359/2018 of the Secretariat of Trade details the investigatory and prosecutorial powers vested on the CNDC until the National Competition Authority is established.

[D] Sanctions and Remedies

[1] Administrative Sanctions

Pursuant to section 55 of the Antitrust Law, the sanctions that may be imposed on the individual or companies found to be involved in a cartel are the following:

A. The cessation of the acts or conducts prohibited by the Antitrust Law and, if relevant, the removal of their effects;
B. Fines of (i) up to 30 percent of the turnover of the product to which the infringement relates during the last fiscal year multiplied by the number of years of infringement. This amount cannot exceed 30 percent of the consolidated turnover archived by the offender's economic group in Argentina during the last fiscal year; or (ii) up to double the economic benefit derived from the infringement. In the event that fines cannot be calculated using either method (i) or (ii), fines for each offender cannot exceed 200 million Administrative Units (as of April 2022, approx. US$ 141 million). If the fine can be calculated according to the two criteria established in points (i) and (ii), the higher fine will be applied. In case of recidivism, the amount of the fine shall be doubled for those companies that have been sanctioned in the previous ten years for anticompetitive infringements.
C. In case of breach of injunctions issued pursuant to section 44 of the Antitrust Law or compromises reached with the Antitrust Authority according to section 44 of the Antitrust Law, a daily fine of up to 0.1% of the Argentinean turnover of the infringing economic group during the previous year. If a fine cannot be determined using this methodology, the amount of the daily fine cannot exceed 750,000 Administrative Units (as of April 2022, ARS 62.6 million, approximately US$530,000).
D. Order measures aiming at eliminating the distorting effects over competition or the request to a competent judge to order that the offending companies be dissolved, liquidated, spun off or divided.
E. Suspension from the National Registry of State Suppliers for up to five (5) years. The exclusion may be for up to eight (8) years in case of the bid-rigging conducts established in section 2, paragraph (d) of the Antitrust Law.

Section 57 of the Antitrust Law makes companies liable for the conduct of individuals who acted on their behalf, with the help or for the benefit of the company, even if the company's representation is rendered ineffective.

Similarly, section 58 of the Antitrust Law provides the joint and several liability of directors, managers, administrators, trustees, or members of the Statutory Auditors Office, agents or legal representatives of the infringing legal entity who by means of their action or omission of their duties of control, supervision, or security, had contributed, encouraged, or allowed the infringement to the Antitrust Law.

Lastly, as a new feature introduced by the Antitrust Law in 2018, section 58, third paragraph, establishes that controlling companies may be joint and severally liable for the illegal conduct of their subsidiaries and controlled legal entities. Put differently, the Antitrust Authority has the power to and may seek to collect the full amount of the fine from the controlling entities (even if these are foreign companies) as a consequence of the illegal activities of their subsidiaries.

[2] Criminal Sanctions

Unlike Law No. 22,262 of 1980, the current Antitrust Law does not foresee criminal sanctions for individuals involved in anticompetitive conducts.

However, section 300 of the Argentine Criminal Code provides that:

> any individual that may contribute to an increase or decrease in the price of a product by means of false news, fake negotiations or through the negotiations with the main holders of said product, in order to sell or to refrain from selling it a certain price, shall be sanctioned with imprisonment from six months to two years.

More specifically, section 309 of the Argentinian Criminal Code contemplates imprisonment for a period of one to four years for individuals who engage in the same conduct established in section 300, but in relation to any financial instrument.

It is not clear that any of these provisions has ever resulted in the effective imprisonment of any individual. Despite their existence, public criminal prosecutors do not appear to have applied them in practice, and it would be reasonable to argue that cartels are *de facto* not criminally sanctioned in Argentina.

Despite the fact that sections 300 and 309 have not been applied in practice, the Antitrust Law enacted in 2018, expressly indicates that successful leniency applicants 'shall be exempted from the sanctions provided in sections 300 and 309 of the Criminal Code and any prison sanctions that may in any form be applicable for engaging in anticompetitive conducts'.[19] This provision was certainly included for the sake of conveying certainty and thus inducing leniency applications, but also introduced certain uncertainty as to whether sections 300 and 309 of the Criminal Code could be applicable to cartels.

However, as explained, there are no known cases in which either criminal prosecutors or Criminal Courts have sanctioned an individual based on section 300 of the Argentine Criminal Code. Furthermore, the most renowned cartel cases sanctioned in Argentina (notably, the cement cartel, the medical oxygen cartel, and the medical gelatine cartel) did not entail any criminal prosecution.

[3] Private Actions and Follow-On Actions

Pursuant to section 62 of the Antitrust Law, any person damaged by an anticompetitive practice may seek damages under civil and commercial law before a competent judge. The Antitrust Law states that follow-on damages actions will be subject to an expedited (rather than ordinary) procedure set forth in the Code of Civil and Commercial Procedure. The Antitrust Law appears not to limit which parties have standing to seek

19. Article 61, para. 2, Law No. 27,442, 15 May 2018, B.O. 33870 (Arg.).

damages. Accordingly, it is reasonable to conclude that both direct and indirect purchasers have standing to sue for damages, this conclusion is supported by the wording of section 65 of the Antitrust Law, which refers to both 'indirect' and 'direct' purchasers.

The private antitrust litigation system embedded in the Antitrust Law (originally established in Law 22,262 of 1980) has received scarce application.

For the first time, in 2009 a first instance judge granted compensation for the damages caused by the infringement of the Antitrust Law in *Autogas*. The judge ordered YPF – Argentina's largest producer and distributor of Liquefied Petroleum Gas (LPG) to pay Autogas – a LPG distributor a compensation of roughly ARS 13 million, plus interest, for the damages caused by YPF's abuse of its dominant position.

The decision was successfully appealed by the parties, and in 2017 the Attorney General's Office issued its legal opinion declaring the previous ruling arbitrary to the extent that it establishes the quantification of the damage on aspects distorted by the conduct whose reparation is pursued, as well as on the elements that are not sufficiently related to the conclusion it reaches.

This disqualified the decision as a valid judgment because it placed the parties in a state of defenselessness due to the impossibility of knowing the basis of the decision and evaluating its relevance. In addition, it concluded that the appealed decision did not constitute a reasonable application of the current law to the circumstances of the case.

As to the background of the *Autogas* private antitrust litigation case, YPF was sanctioned by the Antitrust Authority in 1999 for abuse of its dominant position in the LPG market, in which it had a 53% share. The fine was later confirmed by the National Supreme Court of Justice in 2002. YPF was fined with approximately ARS 109 million. According to the Antitrust Authority, YPF sold LPG in the local market at a higher price than it did in foreign markets, and banned its foreign LPG purchasers from re-exporting the product into Argentina. YPF's behaviour artificially raised the local price of LPG through creating a supply shortage in the local market. At the same time, since YPF was active at both the production and distribution levels, it increased its market share in the latter from 10% to 40%, by driving many distributors such as Autogas out of business.

Before filing an action with the first instance judge, Autogas filed a complaint with the Antitrust Authority, which was dismissed arguing that the rise in LPG prices was passed on by distributors to end-consumers, which were the only ones harmed by YPF's behaviour. Subsequently, based on the 1999 precedent and on the facts proved in the case by the Antitrust Authority, Autogas sued YPF seeking compensation for the damages caused by its anticompetitive conduct and grounded its claim on civil law principles.

In addition, in another case private litigation case stemming from YPF's abuse of a dominant position of 1999, damages were awarded to a consumers' association by the Court of Appeals of La Plata in 2017.[20]

20. 'Unión de Usuarios y Consumidores c/REPSOL –YPF s/Repetición', (Arg.). Cámara Federal de La Plata [CNLP].

[E] Leniency

The current Antitrust Law created Argentina's first antitrust leniency program. The main features of the program are set forth in sections 60 and 61 of the Antitrust Law. The leniency program became effective upon the entry into force of the Antitrust Law.

The features of the leniency program established by the Antitrust Law are the following:

- Leniency will be available only in relation to agreements between competitors that are deemed as practices 'absolutely restrictive of competition' pursuant to section 2 of the Antitrust Law. Therefore, it does not cover vertical agreements and/or unilateral behaviour.
- Leniency will be available to both companies and individuals involved in a cartel.
- The first applicant to provide evidence that allows the Antitrust Authority to determine the existence of the conduct will obtain civil and criminal immunity.
- Provided that additional evidence of the cartel is furnished, subsequent applicants will obtain criminal immunity as well as reductions in the fines that would have otherwise be applicable ranging between 50% and 20%, depending on the chronological order in which applications were lodged.

The common requirements to benefit from leniency, regardless of being the first applicant or not, are (i) to immediately cease participation in the cartel, unless otherwise ordered by the antitrust authority to avoid tip-offs; (ii) to cooperate fully, continuously, and diligently with the Antitrust Authority throughout the whole proceeding; (iii) not to destroy or conceal evidence related to the cartel; and (iv) not to have made public the decision to apply for leniency (except for other antitrust authorities). The identity of all leniency applicants will be kept confidential by the Antitrust Authority.

[F] Appeal

Once a cartel infringement decision is issued by the Domestic Trade Secretariat, it can be appealed by the infringing companies and individuals to the Civil and Commercial Federal Court of Appeals. In its turn, the Federal Court of Appeals' decision may be appealed, as a last resort, before the National Supreme Court of Justice. In fact, the most important cartel cases decided by the Antitrust Authority have been appealed and confirmed by the National Supreme Court of Justice (i.e., the cement cartel and the medical oxygen cartel).

Pursuant to section 66 of the Antitrust Law, the following Antitrust Authority's decisions can be appealed:

(a) imposition of fines;
(b) cease and desist orders;

(c) the prohibition of an economic concentration transaction or the imposition of conditions;
(d) dismissal of a claim filed before the Antitrust Authority;
(e) rejection of a leniency application; and
(f) injunctions adopted pursuant to section 44 of the Antitrust Law.

However, the courts have consistently construed that the above list is only illustrative and that any other decision adopted by the Antitrust Authority that causes sufficient and irreparable harm can be appealed by the addresses of such decision.

Pursuant to section 67 of the Antitrust Law, an appeal does not suspend the effects of the decision issued by the Antitrust Authority (except for fines imposed under item (a) above in which case the parties may not pay the fine amount provided they submit a surety bond).

Section 67 of the Antitrust Law provides that appeals should be filed within fifteen business days as of the notification of the Antitrust Authority's decision. The Antitrust Authority then has ten business days to send the administrative file to the Federal Civil and Commercial Court of Appeals (or the corresponding Court of Appeals in the provinces).

In addition, a court fee of 1.5% of the amount of the fine must be judicially deposited by the appellant once the appeal arrives to the Court of Appeals or shortly thereafter.

[G] Precedent Cases

[1] Cement Cartel

In July 2005, after a seven year long investigation that included the first dawn raid ever performed by the Antitrust Authority in Argentina, the Antitrust Authority imposed fines to several cement companies totaling ARS 309 million due to their involvement in a nationwide price-fixing and territorial market allocation scheme, implemented by means of an information exchange system that last 18 years and which detailed the sales of each producer to each customer in Argentina allowing the parties to collude. The cement market being a very concentrated market, these practices not only allowed the above-mentioned companies to fix prices, exchange information, and distribute the sales territory, but also prevented other companies from entering the market.

The following cement companies were fined by the Antitrust Authority: Loma Negra C.I.A.S.A. (ARS 138.7 million), Juan Minetti S.A. (ARS 100.1 million), Cementos Avellaneda S.A. (ARS 34.6 million), Petroquímica Comodoro Rivadavia S.A. (ARS 6 million), and Cemento San Martín S.A. (ARS 28.5 million).

The Antitrust Authority's infringement decision was subsequently confirmed by the Court of Appeals and the National Supreme Court of Justice in May 2013.

[2] *Medical Oxygen Cartel*

In July 2005, the Antitrust Authority sanctioned four medical oxygen suppliers for their participation in a bid-rigging cartel with fines totaling ARS 70.3 million.

During its investigation, which included dawn raids to the premises of the alleged offenders, the CNDC proved that the oxygen medical companies colluded their participation in tenders for the supply of medical oxygen to private and public hospitals. By means of these practices, the companies fixed their prices, allocated customers, and prevented competitors from entering the market. The cartel was implemented at a national level and lasted, at least, five years (between 1997 and 2002).

The Antitrust Authority fined the following companies for their involvement in the cartel: Air Liquide Argentina S.A. (ARS 24.9 million), Praxair Argentina S.A. (ARS 26 million), AGA Argentina S.A. (ARS 14.2 million), and Indura Argentina S.A. (ARS 5.1 million).

The Antitrust Authority's decision in the oxygen cartel was confirmed by the National Supreme Court of Justice in June 2015.

[3] *Automobile Cartel*

The highest fine ever imposed in Argentine antitrust history was on December 12, 2014, when the Domestic Trade Secretariat closed the case against several car companies imposing a fine amounting a total of ARS 1,060 million, to the following automotive companies: Toyota Argentina S.A: ARS 104.2 million, Volkswagen Argentina S.A.: ARS 150 million, General Motors Argentina S.R.L: ARS 150 million, Renault Argentina S.A.: ARS 150 million, Ford Argentina S.C.A: ARS 150 million, Fiat Auto Argentina S.A: ARS 150 million, Peugeot – Citroën Argentina S.A: ARS 150 million, and Honda Motor de Argentina S.A: ARS 56.1 million.

The Antitrust Authority's decision considered that the automobile companies had engaged in illegal price-fixing by means of selling automobiles in the Province of Tierra del Fuego at the same price (or even higher price) than those charged for the same automobiles in the continental territory of Argentina. Pursuant to a 1972 federal law, products and services sold in the Province of Tierra del Fuego are exempted from certain national taxes (such as VAT, income tax, and export or import taxes), which means that prices should be lower in the Province of Tierra del Fuego due to the tax exemptions. The fact that cars were sold in Province of Tierra del Fuego at a price that was similar to the price charged by car manufacturers in the rest of the territory of Argentina led the Antitrust Authority to understand that the companies were fixing the price of cars sold in Tierra del Fuego.

On August 14, 2015, the Federal Court of Appeals of Comodoro Rivadavia annulled and thus reversed the Antitrust Authority's infringement decision arguing that (i) there was no evidence of cartel behaviour, and (ii) there were several plausible justifications for the prices charged by the car manufacturers other than the cartel hypothesis entertained by the Antitrust Authority. Thereafter, the Supreme Court of

Justice confirmed the Court of Appeals decision setting aside the Antitrust Authority's decision. This was the first important cartel decision adopted by the Antitrust Authority that was not confirmed by the courts.[21]

§11.03 UNILATERAL CONDUCT

[A] Relevant Legislation

Anticompetitive unilateral conducts are governed by sections 1, 3, 5, and 6 of the Antitrust Law.

As explained earlier in the Relevant Legislation section for Cartels, section 1 of the Antitrust Law contains the general guiding principle establishing that anticompetitive conducts shall be prohibited only if they affect the general economic interest, whereas section 3 of the Antitrust Law provides a non-exhaustive list of anticompetitive unilateral conducts (including, but not limited to, resale price maintenance, tying, price discrimination, predatory pricing, exclusive dealing, and refusal to deal), which will be considered an infringement to the Antitrust Law insofar as they are deemed to harm the general economic interest. Therefore, unilateral conducts are assessed under an effects-based approach pursuant to which the Antitrust Authority shall balance the anti-competitive effects and the pro-competitive effects (if any) of the conduct and determine whether it has a net negative effect on consumer welfare. In turn, sections 5 and 6 of the Antitrust Law address the definition of dominant position.

[B] Assessment of Dominance

Pursuant to section 5 of the Antitrust Law, a company has a dominant position when, for a certain product or service, it is the only supplier or buyer either within the national market or in one or several parts of the world; or when despite not being the only supplier or buyer, it is not exposed to substantial competition; or when, due to the level of vertical or horizontal integration, it can determine the economic viability of a competitor.

Pursuant to section 6 of the Antitrust Law, to establish the existence of a dominant position, the Antitrust Authority shall consider the following circumstances:

(a) the degree of substitutability of the product or service involved, whether of national or foreign origin, and the conditions and timing of such substitutability.

21. Another important cartel decision not confirmed by the Court of Appeals was the medical gelatine decision adopted by the Antitrust Authority on 10 December 2015. On 16 April 2019, the Federal Civil and Commercial Court of Appeals reversed the Antitrust Authority's infringement decision since the five-year statute of limitations period had expired, arguing that more than five years had elapsed between the time the infringement ended and the time the Antitrust Authority issued its decision. The Supreme Court of Justice dismissed the Antitrust Authority's extraordinary appeal on 10 March 2020, thus confirming the Court of Appeals' ruling.

(b) the level of entry barriers in the relevant market; and
(c) the degree in which the alleged offender can unilaterally determine prices or restrict supply as well as the extent to which competitors can counteract such power.

Despite the limited guidance provided in the Antitrust Law to determine with precision when a company would be deemed to hold a dominant position, the Antitrust Authority through its case law has laid down certain parameters to that end. The Antitrust Authority's case law on exclusionary abuses of a dominant position has been condensed in the 'Guides for the Analysis of Exclusory Abuse of Dominance cases' (the 'Dominance Guides') issued by the CNDC in May 2019.

To establish the existence of dominance, the Antitrust Authority must first define the relevant market, both at a product and at geographic dimension. To that end, the Antitrust analyses the characteristics of the product, its price, and the purposes of consumption to determine the demand-side substitutability of the product. In relation to the price of the product, the Antitrust Authority uses SSNIP test to determine the relevant market, by assessing how consumers' demand will respond to a small but significant and non-transitory price increase.

Once the relevant market affected by the alleged abusive conduct is defined, to determine whether the company has a dominant position, the Antitrust Authority measures the market power of the company, chiefly, by reference to its share in the relevant market. The Dominance Guides establish that if a company has a market share less than 40%, it is highly unlikely that it will be deemed to hold a dominant position (even being the market leader). This is confirmed by the Antitrust Authority's case law, since only companies holding 50% or more of the market have been held liable for an abuse of a dominant position. For instance, in the *YPF* case of 1999, the CNDC considered that YPF – Argentina's state-owned gas and oil company – had a dominant position in the LPG market holding a 50% share, and in the most recent dominance case of 2015, the CNDC considered that Clorox Argentina held a dominant position in the domestic bleach market with a 50% share.

Having a high market share for a long period of time is a necessary, but not a sufficient condition to be considered to hold a dominant position, therefore, the Antitrust Authority will look at other market factors, such as the market share held by competitors and barriers to entry.

[C] Abuse of Dominant Position

The three cumulative conditions that the Antitrust Authority shall ascertain to sanction an abuse of dominance are as follows:

(a) *Existence of a dominant position*: please refer to section B above relating to 'Assessment of Dominance'.
(b) *Existence of an abusive conduct*: As to its effects, an abuse of a dominant position can be either exclusionary (when the main effect of the practice is the

exclusion of competitors from the market or to prevent the entrance of potential ones) or exploitative (when the main effect of the conduct is that the dominant firm illegally appropriates the consumer's surplus). The Antitrust Law forbids those conducts that seek to displace other competitors from the market, to block their access to a market, and to illegally obtain an exclusive competitive advantage. Examples of abuse of a dominant position include:

(i) *Resale Price Maintenance*: unilateral conduct whereby a dominant manufacturer fixes the retail price at which the distributors must resell its products. Minimum resale prices are prohibited, whereas, in certain cases, maximum resale prices may not be banned insofar as they prevent distributors from exploiting certain consumers. Pursuant to the case law, recommended or suggested resale prices by a dominant company are permitted (provided these are truly suggested and no negative consequence for the distributor derives from deviating from the suggested resale price).

(ii) *Refusals to deal*: The refusal to deal has to be unjustified in order to be considered illegal. It has been considered illegal when the refusal to deal is based on discriminatory reasons.

(iii) *Discriminatory pricing*: Price discrimination is considered illegal when a product is sold to different buyers at different prices without a valid business justification.

(iv) *Tying and bundling*: This type of conduct is considered illegal when in order to purchase a product in which the seller has a dominant position (i.e., the tying product), the buyer is also required to purchase another good not related to the main product (i.e., the tied product) in order to increase its market share of the tied product's market.

(c) *Potential damage to the general economic interest*: The Antitrust Authority shall analyze whether the conduct has the potential to damage the general economic interest. In doing so, it shall balance the pro-competitive effects of the conduct (i.e., efficiencies) *vis-à-vis* the anticompetitive effects of the conduct.

[D] Investigation (Authorities, Procedure, Powers, Burden of Proof, Appeal)

Please refer to the description provided in the Cartel section regarding the applicable authority, its powers, the burden of proof, and the appeal process.

[E] Sanctions and Remedies

Please refer to the description provided in the cartel section regarding sanctions.

[F] Precedent Cases

The Antitrust Authority has historically applied a more flexible approach when analyzing unilateral conducts vis-à-vis agreements between competitors. This clearly demonstrates that the Antitrust Authority is more interested in pursuing practices related to collusive practices than unilateral practices.

[1] YPF

In 1999, YPF – the main local Liquified Petroleum Gas (LPG) producer in Argentina – was fined ARS 109 million for abusing its dominant position in the LPG bulk market in Argentina by engaging in price discrimination. YPF was found liable of charging artificially higher prices in Argentina by reducing LPG supply through exporting part of its production and forbidding the import of such product into the country. YPF had a share of 50% in the LPG market, while it also controlled two of the three ports that allowed imports and exports of LPG. The infringement decision issued by the Antitrust Authority was ratified by the National Supreme Court of Justice.

[2] Trisa

In 2002, in *TRISA*,[22] the Antitrust Authority imposed sanctions on three cable TV operators and two TV content producers, co-owners of the exclusive rights to broadcast live first division soccer matches in Argentina for fixing minimum prices in connection with said exclusive rights. The TV content producers had signed identical vertical agreements with the three cable TV operators, setting a minimum price for the pay-per-view of live football matches. The Antitrust Authority concluded that the agreements were a consequence of a collusive behavior between the cable TV operators and the TV content producers.

The Court of Appeals revoked the Antitrust Authority's decision, holding that the TV content producers were the ones that imposed the minimum prices and redefined the relevant product market. It broadened the definition of the relevant product market from live first division soccer matches (which was the definition originally adopted by the Antitrust Authority to analyze the case) to all soccer matches, which in fact was a very competitive market. Hence, the Court of Appeals held that there was no dominant position in the relevant market since the accused parties did not have enough market power and, thus, no possible damage to the general economic interest could follow. Therefore, it considered the minimum price maintenance practice as lawful.

22. Court of Appeals in Criminal Economic Matters, 29 August 2003, 'VCC S.A.; Multicanal S.A., Cablevisión TCI S.A. y otros s/Inf. Ley 22.262.'

[3] Clorox

On April 17, 2015, the Domestic Trade Secretariat, after a nine-year-long investigation conducted by the CNDC, imposed a fine on Clorox Argentina S.A. ('*Clorox*') worth ARS 50 million for abusing its dominant position in the domestic water bleach market by means of inducing wholesalers to implement a 'price gap' scheme between Clorox's premium water bleach *Ayudín* and lower-quality water bleaches offered by competitors, which resulted in a significant increase in the price of the bleach offered by Clorox's competitors.

The *Clorox* case was initiated in 2006, following a claim filed with the CNDC by Clorox's competitor Queruclor S.R.L. manufacturer of water bleach *Querubín-*, which alleged that it was unable to effectively compete in the water bleach market due to Clorox's anticompetitive practices. Claimant argued that Clorox provided wholesalers with economic incentives to increase the price at which they sold competing water bleaches, and thus reduce the price differential between Clorox's premium water bleach and those of the competing brands, from almost 63% (in place prior to Clorox's alleged anticompetitive scheme) to 30% (in place during Clorox's alleged anticompetitive scheme).

According to the CNDC, through the scheme, Clorox forced wholesalers - under the pain of reducing or eliminating discounts and bonuses on its products - to set higher prices for competing lower-quality bleaches so that customers would choose (or have strong incentives) to purchase Clorox's premium-quality water bleach in view of the artificially reduced price differential. As a result of Clorox's conduct, when water bleach consumers had to decide whether to buy Clorox's water bleach *Ayudín* (the better known and positioned brand in the Argentine market) or a water bleach from another brand, customers were inclined to purchase Clorox's water bleach given the absence of significant differences in price.

After analyzing the information submitted by the claimant as well as the evidence gathered in testimonial hearings (in which most of the wholesalers confirmed Clorox's alleged anticompetitive practices), the CNDC concluded that Clorox, which held a 50% share in the water bleach market, abused its dominant position to the detriment of the general economic interest: (i) by limiting competition since non-premium products could not compete with Clorox's *Ayudín* if they were offered at the same price; (ii) by artificially increasing the entry barriers in the water bleach market for new competitors; and (iii) for the damage that Clorox's practices brought about to customers since the prices of Clorox's competitors increased by approximately 50%.

On March 18, 2016, the Antitrust Authority's decision was revoked by the Court of Appeals since the five-year statute of limitations period had expired.[23]

23. Cámara Nacional de Apelaciones en los Penal Económico Sala B [National Court of Appeals in Criminal Economic matters], 16/03/2016, 'Clorox Argentina S.A. sobre Apelación Resolución Comisión Nacional de Defensa de la Competencia Ley 25.156', (Arg.).

[4] SADAIC

In 2018, the Domestic Trade Secretariat, following the recommendations of the CNDC, imposed a fine worth ARS 42.7 million to the Argentinean Society of Music Authors and Composers (SADAIC), a music collective society, for abusing its dominant position (it held a legal monopoly) in violation of the Antitrust Law by charging excessive and discriminatory fees to certain hotels for the secondary reproduction of music.[24] This decision was subsequently overturned by the Court of Appeals in Civil and Commercial matters on the grounds that there was insufficient evidence to assert that excessive prices had been charged.[25] The Court of Appeals confirmed nonetheless the Antitrust Authority's decision as to the need for executive branch to regulate SADAIC's tariffs to hotels, although it set aside the finding of infringement as well as the fine.

[5] Quilmes

In August 2021, the Antitrust Authority sanctioned Quilmes[26] – an AB Inbev subsidiary –, for an abuse of its dominant position in the national beer market. The investigation began in 2016 as a result of the claims filed by two competitors. The Antitrust Authority's investigation indicated that Quilmes implemented a set of loyalty strategies (i.e., exclusivities and mixed discounts, among others) in the On-Premise and Off-Premise beer channels, which resulted in a vertical foreclosure of the market for current and potential competitors. The Antitrust Authority imposed a fine worth ARS 150 million (since the case was analyzed under the former antitrust law) and ordered Quilmes to adjust its commercial strategy to be compliant with the Antitrust Law. The Antitrust Authority's decision is currently under appeal.

§11.04 MERGER REVIEW

[A] Relevant Legislation

The merger control regime was a novel introduction of the Antitrust Law passed in 1999 and was adopted following the merger control regulations in force in the EU.[27]

24. Secretaría de Comercio [SeCom] [Secretariat of Trade], 26/06/2018, 'Federación Empresaria Hotelera Gastronómica de la República Argentina s/solicitud de intervención de la CNDC (C. 1302)', (Arg.).
25. Cámara Civil y Comercial Federal Sala III [Court of Appeals in Civil and Commercial matters], 20/08/2019, 'Federación Empresaria Hotelera Gastronómica de la República Argentina c/SADAIC y otros/apel. Resol. Comisión Nacional de Defensa de la Competencia', (Arg.).
26. Secretaría de Comercio [SeCom] [Secretariat of Trade], 24/08/2021, Compañia Industrial Cervecera S.A. y Compañía Cervecerias Unidas de Argentina S.A. contra Anheuser Busch Inbev N.C. / S.A. y Cervecería y Maltería Quilmes S.A.I.C.A.A. y G.S. / Infracción Ley 25.156 (c.1589)
27. Consequently, the Antitrust Authority has closely followed the European Commission's notion of control (i.e., European Commission's notice on the concept of concentration) on a series of Advisory Opinions overtime. This position was enshrined on Advisory Opinion No. 124 of 6 July 2001, in which the Antitrust Authority stated that 'it has considered as valuable and applicable by analogy to our national legislation said foreign doctrine.'

Before that, mergers were analyzed by the Antitrust Authority only if they were considered to be anticompetitive and were assessed under the general legal framework for anticompetitive conducts.[28]

Chapter III of the Antitrust Law (sections 7 through 17) sets forth the legal framework applicable to merger control. In furtherance of provisions of the Antitrust Law, the following regulations have been issued to complement the merger control regime:

(i) Resolution No. 40 of 2001 of the former Secretariat of Competition and Consumer Defense, which details the information that shall be furnished by the notifying parties to the Antitrust Authority as part of the notification of an Economic Concentration,
(ii) Resolution No. 208 of 2018 of the Secretariat of Trade, which sets forth the criteria and methodology to be used by the Antitrust Authority to analyze whether an Economic Concentration restricts competition (the 'Merger Guidelines'), and
(iii) Resolution No. 26 of 2006 of former Secretariat of Technical Coordination, which regulates the procedure for Advisory Opinion requests, a process designed for the parties to a transaction to request the Antitrust Authority to issue a formal decision on whether the transaction is subject to a mandatory merger control filing.

[B] Authorities

As explained earlier, like in cartel and dominance cases, the authority that enforces merger control in Argentina is the Domestic Trade Secretariat, which is assisted by the CNDC.

In the specific case of merger control, the CNDC analyzed the notified transactions and issues a non-binding report for the Secretariat of Domestic Trade to adopt a decision.

According to section 14 of the Antitrust Law, the Antitrust Authority has the power to either approve, reject or to subject the approval of a Concentration Transaction to the fulfilment of certain undertakings (e.g., divestiture of certain assets or business lines).

28. There is only one known case in which the Antitrust Authority analyzed an acquisition of control prior to the implementation of the merger control regime. In *Castro c/ Standard Electric y otros* (1985), a claim was filed with the Antitrust Authority alleging that Siemens' acquisition of Standard Electric Argentina S.A. was anticompetitive, however, the Antitrust Authority, which analyzed the merger under the general rules applicable to anticompetitive conducts, dismissed the claim and closed the investigation arguing that the target fell under the scope of the failing firm defense.

[C] Triggering Events and Thresholds

[1] Qualitative Threshold: Acquisition of Control or Substantial Influence

The Antitrust Law requires the parties to notify and obtain the approval of the Antitrust Authority for certain economic concentrations (the 'Economic Concentration'), which are those meeting the qualitative criteria set forth in section 7 and quantitative thresholds provided in sections 9 and 11 the Antitrust Law.

Economic Concentrations affected by the Antitrust Law are those resulting in the direct or indirect acquisition of control or substantial/decisive influence of one or more companies, businesses, or assets. The Antitrust Law provides in section 7 a non-exhaustive list of Economic Concentrations that must be notified to the Antitrust Authority, including mergers, transfers of on-going concerns, stock acquisitions, assets acquisitions, shareholders agreements, joint venture agreements, and any other agreement granting legal or *de facto,* control or substantial influence over the management decisions of a company, business, or asset.

In the highly political transaction *Multicanal-Cablevisión*, the Antitrust Authority through Advisory Opinion No. 219 dated March 21, 2006, acknowledged that the acquisition of a 20% interest in a competitor, even with the right to appoint two out of ten directors, did not grant either control or substantial influence over the target. The acquisition did not grant veto rights over key decisions such as budget or business plans. Consequently, the Antitrust Authority understood that 'the rights granted by the agreement refer exclusively to those issues regarding the protection of a financial investment and does not grant by itself the possibility to exercise control or substantial influence over the target' (...) 'since these do not relate to the competitive activities of the company', thereby concluding that it did not qualify as an Economic Concentration pursuant the Regulations.

However, in another highly political transaction, the Antitrust Authority took a detour from its traditional interpretation on the concept of control, broadening the scope of cases that fall under such concept. In this regard, in its 2009 decision in the *Telefónica-Telecom* case ('Telefónica-Telecom') the Antitrust Authority understood, regardless of the fact that the European Commission had previously decided that there was no acquisition of control, that Telefónica de España had acquired a controlling interest over its competitor Telecom Italia because it obtained a substantial influence over key administration decisions by the fact that it had the right to appoint two directors in the board of its main competitor. For context purposes, it is worth mentioning that, at that time, Telefonica de España controlled Telefonica Argentina and Telecom Italia controlled Telecom Argentina, which were the two main telephone, mobile phone, and Internet service providers in Argentina.

In this sense, the Antitrust Authority held in In *Telefónica-Telecom* that

> [i]f through an agreement a person acquires, by means of the exercise of its rights in a corporate structure, the possibility to determine its own competitive behaviour

(although not that of the target being acquired), it must be understood that said person has been part to an Economic Concentration.

In a nutshell, the Antitrust Authority held that a minority shareholding acquisition could be an Economic Concentration under the Regulations if by means of the transaction the acquirer gains access to confidential information of a competing company and can, as a consequence, modify its competitive behaviour in the market. Furthermore, the Antitrust Authority pointed out that 'the concept of control has to be analyzed together with other factual and legal considerations'.

With *Telefónica-Telecom*, the Antitrust Authority departed from its well-established case law according to which minority stake acquisitions only amounted to an Economic Concentration insofar that they granted veto rights over the competitive strategy of the target company (i.e., decisions relating to matters such as budget, business plan, investments, and appointment of senior management).

[2] Quantitative Thresholds

Pursuant to section 9 of the Antitrust Law, an Economic Concentration must be notified to the Antitrust Authority if the combined Argentine annual net sales of the acquiring group and the acquired group exceed 100 million administrative units (approx. USD 77.4 million considering the exchange rate of December 31, 2021) and either the amount of the Argentine portion of the transaction or the value of the assets to be transferred in Argentina exceeds 20 million administrative units (approx. USD 14.2 million, as of April 2022).[29]

[D] Exemptions

Section 11 of the Antitrust Law exempts the following Economic Concentrations from an otherwise mandatory merger control notification:

1. Acquisitions of companies in which the buyer already owns more than 50% of the shares and of the voting rights, as long as it does not entail a change in the nature of control of the company (i.e., from sole to joint control or from joint to sole control);
2. Acquisitions of bonds, debentures, notes and non-voting shares;
3. Acquisitions of a single Argentine company by a foreign company which owns no assets in Argentina (excluding those held for residential purposes) or shares in other Argentine companies, and had no significant, regular and periodic exports to Argentina during the preceding 36 months (the so-called 'New Comer' or 'First Landing' exemption); and

29. Without prejudice to the above rule, those transactions for less than 20 million administrative units must be notified where the acquiring group was involved in a concentration transaction in Argentina valued in 20 million administrative units, during the preceding twelve-month period, or 60 million administrative units, during the preceding thirty-six months period.

4. Acquisitions of companies in liquidation that did not transact business in Argentina in the preceding year, except if the main activity of the target company is the same than that of the acquirer.

The above being exemptions to the mandatory notification principle must be construed in a restrictive manner.

[E] Pre-merger Control Regime or Post-merger Control Regime

Pursuant to a transitory clause embedded in the Antitrust Law, until one year after the creation of the new National Antitrust Authority, the notification of a reportable Economic Concentration may take place anytime (as from the moment the parties execute some sort of binding legal document) up to one week after the closing or the acquisition of control, whichever happens first. Therefore, at present, there is no stand-still obligation, and the notifying companies may consummate a reportable Economic Concentration without first having antitrust approval, and to notify up to one week thereafter. Even if closing without prior antitrust clearance is allowed under the current regime, the Antitrust Authority always retains the power to – partially or totally – undo Economic Concentrations that are considered to be anticompetitive and harmful to the general economic interest. This situation has led that in most cases, the purchaser assumes both the legal and financial risks of a negative decision from the Antitrust Authority rejecting the proposed transaction or ordering divestments. Besides assuming the risk of a negative decision by the Antitrust Authority, neither there are consequences derived from closing prior to antitrust clearance nor can there be fines for doing so.

Once one year elapses from the creation of the new National Antitrust Authority (although its creation is uncertain at the present time) and thus the above-mentioned transitory clause in the Antitrust Law expires, the ex-ante merger control regime shall become operative. At that time, the consummation of a reportable Economic Concentrations or the acquisition of control without the prior authorization from the Antitrust Authority will be prohibited and sanctioned accordingly. The Antitrust Law does not stipulate a specific deadline for the notification once the ex-ante regime becomes effective. However, it would be in the parties' interest to file as early as possible to obtain a clearance decision from the Antitrust Authority and thus be legally allowed to close the Economic Concentration.

[F] Intra-group Transactions

Based on the economic reality principle (also known as the 'substance over legal form' principle) set forth in section 4 the Antitrust Law and on the notification exemption for those Economic Concentrations in which the purchaser already owns more than 50% of the shares and votes of the target company, the Antitrust Authority has built a well-established case law under which intra-group corporate reorganizations are not subject to merger control notification.[30] The Antitrust Authority has consistently construed that internal group reorganizations (i.e., the acquisition of or merger between legal entities within the same economic group) are exempt from mandatory notification because they do not entail a change of control of one or more companies or assets, since the companies or assets being transferred remain under the control of the same economic group. Technically speaking, there is in fact an acquisition of control, but there is no obligation to notify because, pursuant to the economic reality principle, the control of the acquired entity remains within the same economic group.

[G] Substantive Test for Assessing Mergers

The substantive test for the analysis of Economic Concentrations is provided in section 8 of the Antitrust Law, which establishes that those transactions that have the object or effect of restricting or distorting competition in a manner that may harm the general economic interest are prohibited. Hence, the same substantive test is applicable to assess mergers and anticompetitive conducts, such as cartels and abuses of dominant position. The general economic interest concept has been interpreted by the Antitrust Authority and the courts as comparable to the concept of economic efficiency, although more inclined to consumer surplus rather than to total surplus. In short, as a general rule all Economic Concentrations are permitted except those whose object or effect is to eliminate a competitor or to substantially reduce competition in a manner that harms the general economic interest.

The Antitrust Law does not conclusively establish when an Economic Concentration substantially reduces competition or when it has enough entity to harm the general economic interest; notwithstanding, the Merger Guidelines provide certain parameters and criteria for the Antitrust Authority and companies to assess the legality of a prospective Economic Concentration.

In its review of an Economic Concentration Transaction, the Antitrust Authority first defines the relevant product market (i.e., those products that are offered by both parties) and the geographic market (i.e., the territory where the merging entities offer the relevant products). Afterwards, it considers the effect of the Economic Concentration Transaction on the market structure, considering not only the merging parties' resulting combined market shares but also entry barriers, competition derived from imported products, efficiency gains, and potential competitors within a determined relevant market.

Pursuant to the Merger Guidelines, the existence of a high level of concentration in the relevant market, or a substantial increase in its level of concentration as a consequence of an Economic Concentration Transaction, is a necessary but not a sufficient condition for the transaction to be objected. In that regard, an Economic Concentration Transaction resulting in a high combined market share may be approved if it generates efficiencies that can be translated to customers (e.g., through lower

30. Antitrust Authority's Advisory Opinions Nos 6, 15, 19, 25, 29, 35, 36, 37, 38, 48, 49, 53, 106, 114, 145, 146, 148, 150, 152, and 154, among several others.

prices or innovative products). For the purposes of analyzing market shares, the Antitrust Authority gives priority to the turnover data over volume data.

For the purposes of analyzing the quantitative effects of a given Economic Concentration Transaction in the relevant market, the Antitrust Authority bases its analysis on the 2001 Merger Guidelines, which are, in turn, based on the 1992 Horizontal Merger Guidelines issued by the US Government. Pursuant to the 2001 Merger Guidelines, the Antitrust Authority shall use the Herfindahl-Hirschmann Index (HHI) as the instrument to measure the level of market concentration. An HHI level of 10,000 points represents a monopoly whereas an HHI level of 0 points represents the ideal of a perfect competition market.

Generally, most of the Economic Concentration Transactions (approximately 95%) reviewed by the Antitrust Authority since the introduction of the merger control regime in 1999 obtain the appropriate antitrust clearance, reducing to a minimal number the cases in which the Antitrust Authority subordinates the approval to certain conditions (mainly divestments). It is not possible to determine a specific market share that the Antitrust Authority would consider questionable, since as stated earlier, the analysis is made on a case-by-case basis considering several factors such as the structure of the market, entry barriers, imports, and efficiencies achieved by the transaction under review.

Thus far, the Antitrust Authority has only rejected four Economic Concentration Transactions, in all of which the merging parties achieved through the transaction a market share close to 100%, thus creating a monopoly (i.e., *OCA/Correos Argentinos* in 2001, *LAPA/Aeropuertos 2000* in 2002, *Esmeralda Televisión/Venado Tuerto TV* in 2003, and *YPF/Dapsa* in 2006).

In the recent merger between Mirgor and Brightstar, the CNDC has issued an objection report in June 2021 including an injunction based on section 44 of Law 27,442, under which the parties and all their controlled and/or controlling companies were required to keep their respective businesses separate in the same manner as they were before the closing of the merger, until the merits of the present case are resolved and the case is final. The transaction was later approved subject to certain conditions in December 2021.

There are two highly political cases (i.e., *Cablevision/Multicanal* in 2007 and *Telecom/Telefonica* in 2009), which have both been at the same point approved and disapproved by the Antitrust Authority and the courts, however, these cases should not be taken into consideration due to their particularities. In the case of a rejection, the Antitrust Authority has the power to order the parties to revert the deal and to return to each other the price paid in exchange of the purchased assets.

However, since most rejections are issued well after the parties had already closed the deal and merged their commercial operations, in practice the Antitrust Authority requests the purchaser to find a suitable new purchaser for the acquired assets or business in order to restore competition.

The new purchaser of the business has to be approved by the Antitrust Authority, which generally grants the term of one year (which could be extended in time if it is shown that serious efforts were made to sell the requested assets) to do so. The price to be paid by the new purchaser of the assets is freely negotiated between the parties, notwithstanding, it is important to mention that the new purchaser may use as leverage to obtain a lower price the fact that one of the parties is legally obliged to sell the assets in a given period of time.

Although there have been cases in which the Antitrust Authority has imposed conditions when the parties had combined market share of less than 50%, generally divestments have been imposed to Economic Concentration Transactions creating a combined market share larger than 60%.

However, in November 2009, the Antitrust Authority ordered a divestment in a transaction in which the parties attained a combined market share of 34% because none of the other competitors had a market share higher than 5%[31] that could represent an effective competition to the merged entity. In the case of divestments, the process has the same characteristics as those applicable to rejections that were described in the preceding paragraph.

Lastly, it is worth mentioning that since there are no clear rules as to the procedure and timing of divestments, the Antitrust Authority proceeds on a case-by-case basis, tailoring divestments according to the special features of the Economic Concentration Transaction under analysis.

Therefore, the Antitrust Authority is open to negotiate the extent and implementation of the divestments with the merging parties, as long as they ensure to the Antitrust Authority that the divestments will restore the anticompetitive effects caused by the Economic Concentration Transaction. For example, the purchaser can negotiate with the Antitrust Authority to divest pre-owned assets instead of assets acquired through the notified Economic Concentration Transaction.

[H] Notification Procedure and Timetable

Pursuant to the Antitrust Law, Economic Concentrations must be notified by the direct acquirer (or its immediate controlling entity or the parent entity of the economic group). In the case of mergers, notification shall be made by the 'merging' and the 'merged' entity. In all cases, notification by the seller is voluntary; however, the Antitrust Authority may expressly require the notification to be also performed by the seller, depending on the circumstances of the economic concentration under review.

Filing can be made up to one week after closing of the Economic Concentration. However, a pre-merger control regime will enter into force one year after the time the new National Competition Authority is effectively established.

As to the timing of clearance, section 14 of the Antitrust Law provides that the Antitrust Authority has a maximum of forty-five business days after the filing date to issue a decision. The time period for the resolution may be extended for up to 120 additional days for the issuance of the resolution, by means of a well-founded opinion. Said term may be suspended until the parties respond to the objections presented by

31. CNDC Merger Decision No. 759, *Schering Plough Corporation/Organon Biosciences N.V.*, dated 19 October 2009.

the Antitrust Authority. If no decision is issued within this period, then the Economic Concentration Transaction is to be considered tacitly approved with the same legal effects than an express approval (section 15).

However, in practice, the forty-five business day period is repeatedly suspended by the Antitrust Authority through the issuance of several additional information requests, which takes approximately twenty months on average to get clearance in non-complex concentration transactions. In complex cases, a decision by the Antitrust Authority may take considerably longer (up to three or four years).

It is important to highlight that since the Antitrust Law allows the parties to proceed with the closing of the Economic Concentration Transaction prior to the Antitrust Authority's decision (and thus normally the purchaser assumes the risk of a negative antitrust decision), the negotiation and submissions with the Antitrust Authority are generally substantially prepared with the input of the purchaser. However, the Antitrust Authority has the power to undo the Argentine portion of an Economic Concentration Transaction that is considered to be anticompetitive.

[I] Consequences of a Failure to File

Pursuant to section 55 of the Antitrust Law, failure to or a delay in filing may be fined by up to 0.1% of the consolidated turnover at national level recorded by the economic group to which the offenders belong, during the last fiscal year. The fine imposed can be up to a sum equivalent to 750,000 administrative units per day (i.e., approximately USD 400,000 in December 2021).

Directors, managers, controllers, officers, and corporate attorneys who by their action or omission contributed to the failure to file or late notification are jointly liable for the fine. However, as of today, the Antitrust Authority has never sanctioned individuals due to failure to file or late filing and fines had always been imposed on legal entities.

[J] Third Party Involvement in Notification Process

Only the parties that notified the Economic Concentration Transaction to the Antitrust Authority are part of the notification process and can access the file. Third parties, such as competitors or clients of the parties, may be requested to file documents or may be invited to testify as witnesses, but are not allowed to access the file. This has been the interpretation given by the CNDC, which has been ratified by the Court of Appeals in *Isenbeck*. However, there have been some merger cases interrupted by judicial claims initiated by third parties, such as *Belmonte* and *CCU*. Pursuant to section 13 of the Antitrust Law, third parties can object to the merger in writing, and any such opposition or objection must be notified to the merging parties; however, the competition authority is not bound by representations and objections submitted by third parties when making a merger decision.

[K] Remedies

The Antitrust Law does not establish a mechanism for remedy negotiation or a standard approach to the terms and conditions to be applied to the divestment. Before reaching a decision, the Antitrust Authority will inform the parties of its objections by means of a reasoned report and will convene them to a special hearing to consider possible measures to mitigate the negative effect on competition.

However, since 2004 the CNDC has started to negotiate the acceptable remedies with the parties and has been more flexible on negotiating the remedies with the parties. Moreover, since the Antitrust Law does not establish a mechanism for remedy negotiation, the process may begin as soon as the parties or the CNDC consider that there will be a need for a remedy in order to approve the Economic Concentration Transaction.

The Domestic Trade Secretariat within this framework issued the corresponding resolution by which the operation was approved subject to a commitment consisting of a series of structural and behavioral measures.

The structural measures included the divestiture of forty operating cash trucks corresponding to the greater Buenos Aires area fleet and one corresponding to the Mar del Plata fleet to an existing or potential local competitor other than PROSEGUR, as well as the relocation of twenty operating cash trucks corresponding to the greater Buenos Aires area fleet to other geographic areas of Argentina where PROSEGUR provides cash transportation and processing services.

[L] Penalties

Since, under the current regime, filing of an Economic Concentration Transaction can be made up to one week after closing, no gun jumping penalties (derived from the implementation of a transaction prior to its approval) are applicable in Argentina.

However, the delay in submitting a notification with the Antitrust Authority within the one week after closing deadline, has been consistently fined by the Antitrust Authority.

[M] Appeal

Please refer to the appeal heading developed earlier in the cartels section.

[N] Specific Industries

The Antitrust Law does not contain any particular provision regarding Economic Concentration Transactions taking place in specific industries of the economy.

Pursuant to section 4 of the Antitrust Law, all individuals and legal entities, either private or public, are subject to the provisions of the Antitrust Law. Therefore, Economic Concentration Transaction between regulated companies also falls under the scope of the Antitrust Law. In addition, section 17 of the Antitrust Law establishes that in the event of an economic concentration involving companies whose activity is regulated by the state, the Antitrust Authority is obliged to request the regulatory agency to issue a report whereby the latter expresses its opinion as to the effects of the economic concentration in the competitive landscape of the regulated market or its compliance with the specific regulatory framework.

The regulatory agency has fifteen business days to issue its report as from the Antitrust Authority's request and during such term the merger review period is not suspended.

The results of the report issued by the regulatory agency are not binding for the Antitrust Authority's analysis of the Economic Concentration transaction at hand.

Notwithstanding the above explained, it is important to point out that certain regulatory frameworks have their own specific provisions regarding changes of control of regulated companies. For example, a change of control of an insurance company could be subject to the approval of both the Superintendence of Insurance (should such change of control be notifiable pursuant to the insurance regulations) and the Antitrust Authority (if such change of control meets the thresholds set forth in the Antitrust Law).

CHAPTER 12

Competition Law in Brazil

*Marcelo Calliari & Marcel Medon Santos**

§12.01 INTRODUCTION

At its tenth anniversary, Brazil's current antitrust regime (instituted by Law No. 12,529/2011, the antitrust law, which came into force in May 2012) finds itself in a fairly consolidated position both domestically and internationally, with the country being generally considered among the most active, respected, and relevant antitrust jurisdictions. Though the agency CADE (the Administrative Counsel for Economic Defense) was founded in 1962, it has undergone significant statutory and structural reforms since then, with Law No. 12,529/2011—along with much ensuing regulation—bringing a significant step forward in what has been a broadly stable (even if not totally linear) progression toward greater independence and effectiveness.

Major changes that were implemented in 2011/2012 have indeed proven in the decade since to have been valuable improvements to the system, from the profound institutional revamping to the adoption of a pre-merger notification regime, besides ensuring independence and longer fixed terms to more officials within the authority, clarification of the leniency and settlement programs, consolidation of investigative powers, adjustment to fine criteria, and other streamlining measures.

CADE has since been composed of three autonomous distinct bodies: the General Superintendence, the Administrative Tribunal (Tribunal), and the Department of Economic Studies.

The General Superintendence is the division in charge of merger analysis and antitrust investigations.

* The authors would like to acknowledge the assistance provided by TozziniFreire associates João Paulo Salviano da Costa, Luiz Eduardo Jahic, and Nicholas Cozman in the preparation of this chapter.

The Tribunal is a decision-making body with a plenary composed by six commissioners and one president responsible for issuing final decisions on anticompetitive conducts and on mergers challenged by General Superintendence. Though part of the same agency, the Tribunal and the General Superintendence are independent from each other so as to ensure decisions are taken with a fresh full review vis-à-vis the investigation that preceded it.

The Department of Economic Studies in its turn is a division headed by a chief economist, which is responsible for the preparation of economic studies and opinions, ex officio or at the request of: (i) the Tribunal's Plenary and its President, (ii) the Reporting Commissioner, or (iii) the General Superintendent, updating and ensuring the technical and scientific accuracy of the decisions made by the agency.

Apart from the changes implemented in the institutional system, the new antitrust law also promoted substantial changes to the merger review regime as well as improvements to the tools for cartel investigation.

The pre-merger control regime, including a bar on closing prior to clearance, had caused some uncertainty prior to its adoption, has not only functioned fairly well but also been improved upon in the last ten years. More than 90% of the notifications are now handled under the fast-track Summary Proceeding and have been consistently decided under the limit of thirty days of the regulation, while a double turnover threshold increased the nexus of notifiable transactions to Brazil. The antitrust law also reduced the number of transactions to be notified to CADE by increasing the thresholds for notifications related to the companies' annual turnover.

On the conduct front, CADE consolidated its position among the leading cartel enforcement agencies, with domestic and international investigations leading to very significant fines, while the leniency and settlement programs saw a marked improvement over the last ten years. Unilateral conduct became an explicit focus of the agency, and several investigations are ongoing, though that effort still needs to be fully realized.

However, if the improvement of the system in the last ten years is impressive and indisputable, then significant challenges remain and will need to be addressed for CADE to maintain its position and evolve. Reducing the length of investigations, resolving procedural bottlenecks, re-balancing incentives to increase the attractiveness of leniency, improving consistency and predictability in decisions, minimizing the effects caused by changes in staff, under-funding, improving unilateral conduct investigations are just some of the issues the Brazilian antitrust regime will have to face to write the next chapter in what has so far been—rare in Brazilian institutional history—a sixty-year-long success story.

[A] The Brazilian Antitrust Legislation

The antitrust law in Brazil (above mentioned Law No. 12,529/2011) is directly derived from the Federal Constitution of 1988, which defines "free competition" as one of the principles of the economic order (Article 170).

More specifically, Article 173, paragraph 4, of the Federal Constitution of 1988 provides that "[t]he law shall repress the abuse of economic power that aims at the dominance of markets, the elimination of competition, and the arbitrary increase of profits."

Besides the Constitution and the antitrust law itself (Law No. 12,529/2011), resolutions developing the framework of the Brazilian Antitrust Law are constantly being enacted and updated by CADE in order to improve the current system.

Other important related legislation that also affects the enforcement of antitrust law in Brazil include statutes such as the Civil Procedure Code (Law No. 13,105 of 2013), Public Civil Action Law (Law 7,347 of 1985), Consumers Defense Code (Law 8,078 of 1990), Economic Crimes Law (No. 8,137 of 1990), Public Procurement Law (Law No. 8,666 of 1993), Law of Intellectual Property and Unfair Competition (Law No. 9,279 of 1996), Administrative Procedural Law (Law No. 9,784 of 1999), Brazilian Civil Code (Law No. 10,406 of 2002), Anti-Bribery Law (Law No. 12,846 of 2013), and Economic Freedom Law (Law 13,874 of 2019).

§12.02 CARTELS

[A] Relevant Legislation

Cartel enforcement in Brazil is a combination of administrative and criminal regimes. Law 12,529/2011 regulates the administrative enforcement, while Law 8,137/1990 sets forth cartels as a crime against the economic order.

According to Article 36 of Law 12,529/2011, acts which have as an objective or may have the following effects shall be considered violations, regardless of fault and even if the effects are not achieved:

(i) to limit, restrain, or in any way injure free competition or free initiative;
(ii) to control the relevant market of goods or services;
(iii) to arbitrarily increase profits; and
(iv) to abusively exercise a dominant position.

The law considers "dominant" any company or group of companies that are capable of unilaterally or jointly changing market conditions or that control 20% or more of a relevant market. This provides a rebuttable presumption of dominance for companies with more than a 20% share in a relevant market. CADE seldom resorts to this presumption, but that has happened and companies in that position should be aware of such possibility.

Paragraph 3 of Article 36 lists examples of conducts that may constitute violations in case the effects mentioned above are produced or may be produced. Agreements, manipulation, and adjustments among competitors to fix prices of goods or services, to control production, to divide regions, clients, distributors, or suppliers, to rig bids, besides other types of collusive behavior, are among such conducts.

Chapter III of Law 12,529/2011 presents in Article 37 the applicable fines in case of a violation. The fines for corporations that take part in cartels range from 0.1% to 20% of companies' turnover in Brazil in the branch of business activity in which the violation occurred, in the year preceding the launching of the administrative proceeding. Penalties for individuals in managerial positions range from 1% to 20% of the penalty imposed on the company. As for individuals in non-managerial positions, fines can range from BRL 50,000 to BRL 2 billion.

Several other penalties can also be imposed by CADE, from debarment regarding public bids to the divestment of assets.

Besides administrative fines and other administrative penalties, individuals (not companies) are also subject to criminal charges in cartel cases. The current criminal sanctions for cartels according to Law 8,137/1990 are imprisonment from two to five years and a criminal fine (for which there is no defined range and is left to the discretion of the judge according to general criminal law principles).

[B] Extraterritoriality

The Brazilian Antitrust Law is applicable to any conduct capable of producing effects in the Brazilian territory regardless of where it is practiced. Conducts fully or partially practiced abroad are under the Brazilian jurisdiction if they produce or are capable of producing effects in Brazil. CADE has already understood that exports of a cartelized product to Brazil are sufficient to establish its jurisdiction. Furthermore, indirect sales of a cartelized product (such as when it constitutes an input to a product that is exported to Brazil) would also affect the Brazilian marketplace thus violating the law.

In accordance with such rationale, a collusive practice carried out exclusively abroad might be under the jurisdiction of the national antitrust authorities if any Brazilian market is affected.

[C] Investigations

[1] Authorities

[a] CADE's General Superintendence (General Superintendence)

Pursuant to Article 12 of Law 12,529/2011, the General Superintendence is charged with launching and carrying out investigations, both regarding mergers and anticompetitive practices, and issuing non-binding opinions with its findings that may serve as a basis for the decisions to be taken by the Tribunal. The General Superintendence is also empowered to execute search and seizure warrants (with court authorization), as well as to negotiate and execute leniency agreements and settlements, both conditioned on confirmation by the Tribunal.

[b] CADE's Department of Economic Studies (Department of Economic Studies)

The Department of Economic Studies, headed by a Chief Economist, is responsible for the preparation of economic studies and opinions, ex officio or at the request of the CADE Plenary, President, Reporting Commissioner, or General Superintendent.

[c] CADE's Tribunal

The Tribunal is an adjudicatory body comprised of a President and six Commissioners, all appointed by the President of the Republic, subject to hearings and approval by the Federal Senate.

The term of office of the Tribunal's members requires exclusive dedication[1] and is of four years. Consecutive terms for reappointment are prohibited.

As a decision-making body, decisions issued by the Tribunal's members are taken by majority voting. The Tribunal's decisions cannot be reviewed within the Federal administration and can only be challenged in the courts.

Pursuant to Article 9 of Law 12,529/2011, the Tribunal's Plenary duties include the following tasks, among others:

- Decide on the existence of violations to the economic order and apply the penalties set forth by the Brazilian Antitrust Law.
- Take the necessary steps to cease violations of the economic order, within the deadlines it may determine.
- Approve the terms of settlements in cartels and in unilateral conduct investigations.
- Confirm the immunity of leniency applicants, verifying if its conditions were fulfilled.
- Respond to consultations.
- Decide on merger reviews challenged by the General Superintendence, blocking a transaction, approving it fully or determining remedies for approval and executing settlements with the relevant parties.

[2] Policy, Politics, and Institutions

CADE, as noted earlier, is today the central player in the enforcement of the Brazilian Antitrust Law.

CADE's General Superintendence holds the investigative role and is the body in charge of all investigations, of both merger reviews and anticompetitive conducts. Its head is appointed by the President of the Republic, ratified by the Federal Senate, and has a fixed term of two years.

1. Except for those constitutionally permitted as the teaching profession, for instance.

This means that the launching of new investigations is decided by an independent, not politically subordinate authority.

Besides the General Superintendence and the Department of Economic Studies, other two entities participate in the antitrust investigations and merger review procedures: the internal CADE Attorney General's Office and the Federal Prosecution Office.

The CADE Attorney General's Office is, in general, responsible for providing legal assistance to the agency, defending CADE's decisions in the courts and issuing, whenever required by a Commissioner or by the General Superintendent, a legal opinion related to the proceedings under CADE's jurisdiction.

As with the General Superintendent and the members of the CADE Tribunal, the CADE Attorney General is appointed by the President of the Republic, with confirmation by the Federal Senate, and has a fixed term of two years. The Attorney General participates, without right to vote, in meetings held by the Tribunal, providing assistance and clarification as required.

The Federal Prosecution Office is an independent institution in the Brazilian legal system, which holds as its constitutional mission, among many attributions, to defend the public interest and overall monitor compliance with the federal legislation. It is represented at CADE by a Federal Prosecutor who is responsible for issuing opinions on investigations of anticompetitive practices, ex officio or upon request of the Reporting Commissioner.

[3] Resources and Priorities

Besides streamlining the institutional model that existed pre-2011, the current Brazilian Antitrust Law also brought the improvement of expanding CADE's workforce staff.

Over the past five years, CADE's budget has remained steadily more than BRL 35 million reais.[2] In terms of finance, the administrative activities of CADE are headed by the President of the Tribunal, who coordinates and supervises the duties of the officers within the agency.

The General Superintendence is a managing unit for administrative and financial purposes, and its General Superintendent shall order the expenses related to the respective budgetary actions. Annually, the President of the Tribunal, after consultation with the General Superintendent, submits CADE's proposal for budget and staffing placements to the federal government.

2. CADE's budget is similar to the competition authorities' of Latin American countries which only have a fraction of Brazil's population, such as Chile and Colombia. Transparency Portal: http://www.portaltransparencia.gov.br/orcamento/despesas?paginacaoSimples=true&tamanhoPagina=&offset=&direcaoOrdenacao=asc&de=2017&ate=2021&orgaos=OR30211&colunasSelecionadas=ano%2CorgaoSuperior%2CorgaoVinculado%2Cfuncao%2CsubFuncao%2Cprograma%2Cacao%2CcategoriaEconomica%2CgrupoDespesa%2CelementoDespesa%2CorcamentoInicial%2CorcamentoAtualizado%2CorcamentoRealizado%2CvalorEmpenhado%2CpercentualRealizado. CADE's budget is similar to the competition authorities of smaller Latin American countries, such as Chile and Colombia.

Though CADE's budget has increased significantly since the enactment of the current law, it continues to be seriously underfunded, especially taking into consideration the number of cases for which it is responsible.

[4] Inter-agency Cooperation (International)

In relation to inter-agency cooperation, CADE has become increasingly more active and is recognized as an important player among competition agencies in the international scene.

Cooperation with other enforcement agencies has been significantly developed in recent years, with several cooperation agreements in force with many antitrust agencies worldwide: Canada, Colombia, Costa Rica, Chile, China, the European Union, Ecuador, India, France, Japan, Mercosur Countries, Peru, Portugal, Russia, Spain, South Africa, South Korea, and the United States.[3]

Formal and informal contacts, discussions, and memoranda of understandings between the Brazilian authorities and those of other jurisdictions are steadily increasing, especially relating to the investigation of international cartels and are stimulated by repeated contacts in international organizations, including especially the ICN (International Competition Network), the BRICS (Brazil, Russia, India, China, and South Africa) initiative, and the OECD (Organization for Economic Cooperation and Development). Coordination regarding review of mergers with multi-jurisdictional implications is also constantly taking place, with discussions regarding both the analytical framework and the design of remedies.

CADE's agreements with foreign competition authorities do not establish any obligation of providing confidential information, but usually include provisions on coordination of parallel investigations, exchange of information, consultations, or staff exchanges between the authorities. Much of the actual coordination in merger and cartel investigations currently takes place outside of formal agreements, through direct and informal contacts and by way of waivers provided by relevant parties.

[D] Procedure

The administrative proceeding for the imposition of sanctions to violations to the competition law ("administrative proceeding") is the formal procedure followed by General Superintendence and the Tribunal to promote a cartel investigation. It can be initiated through a leniency agreement, a third-party complaint, a whistle-blower, or by CADE itself ex officio.

The Brazilian Antitrust Law allows the General Superintendence not only to make inspections at companies' offices but also to request to carry out dawn raids upon a court's authorization, seizing any documents, business books, computers, or equipment relevant to the investigation.

3. As of December 2021.

The search warrant provided by a court might also comprise the companies' employees' private objects, and it may allow for the search of private homes, in case such measure is necessary to uncover specific evidence. The original documents and equipment collected during the inspections and dawn raids must be returned to the companies and to the individuals. For that reason, CADE usually certifies the origin of electronic data and obtains copies of the seized materials. There is no timetable stipulated by law for returning the material to the owners. It varies from case to case, depending mainly on the quantity of documents CADE will need to keep for the investigation.

In accordance with Article 53 and the subsequent ones of Law 12,529/2011, the administrative proceeding must follow the phases and steps described below.

[1] Initial Phase of the Proceeding, Service of Process, and Presentation of Defense

The General Superintendent launches the administrative proceeding based upon a Technical Note, which reports the investigated facts and presents the grounds for the accusation of companies, entities, or individuals. The General Superintendent's decision to launch an investigation is published in the Federal Official Gazette. After issuing the Technical Note, the General Superintendence must issue formal notifications by mail to serve each defendant.

Serving defendants has been one of the main hurdles for efficient investigations in Brazil, especially when dealing with international cartels, since every single company and natural person must be individually served before the case can move. This means that not locating a defendant in a foreign country can stall the investigation for months. The agency has been trying to find ways to deal with this procedural problem, either by service through a public notice (which in any case is only allowed after the agency can show that it has tried several ways to locate the defendant) or by severing the investigation so that un-served defendants are moved to a separate proceeding with separate files, and the main case against the others can move ahead. It remains, however, one of the challenges in terms of speeding up investigations in Brazil.

The deadline for all the defendants to present their defense starts to run after the last notice of service is filed into the case records. The deadline is thirty calendar days. The law also gives the possibility for the defendants to request an extension for ten additional days. Therefore, the typical deadline for defense is forty days after the receipt of service of the final defendant is placed into the files.

In the defense, each of the defendants presents its procedural and substantive arguments regarding the charges and specifies the evidence it intends to produce, including the identification of up to three witnesses.

[2] *Evidentiary Phase*

...gally, there are no pre-determined terms for the evidentiary phase, which includes app...arings of defendants, cooperating parties (such as leniency and settlement and the ... and witnesses, the latter being under oath, and presentation of evidence any additiona...sing of all the information by the General Superintendence, as well as phase can take fro...estigation the authorities may want to carry out. In practice, this do voluntarily present a...few months to a few years. Defendants and third parties can and ...tional materials and meet with case officials throughout this phase.

Regardless of how long the evidentiary phase takes, once the General Superintendence concludes the investigation, it notifies the defendants to present their final arguments within five business days.

[3] *General Superintendence's Issuance of Legal Opinion*

Within fifteen business days after the presentation of the final arguments, the General Superintendence will send the proceeding files to the Tribunal, with a new Technical Note describing the whole investigation, detailing and assessing the evidence, and providing its final opinion suggesting either the dismissal of the charges or the conviction of each of the defendants. This opinion does not bind the Tribunal.

[4] *Remittance of the Proceeding to the Tribunal*

When the Tribunal receives the files, the case is assigned, randomly, to a Reporting Commissioner. The Reporting Commissioner may also carry out additional investigation. The defendants and the leniency applicant (when applicable) can and typically do access the Reporting Commissioner and other members of the Tribunal at this stage to present their arguments, usually both in person and in writing.

There is no deadline for the Reporting Commissioner to bring the case to the ...lenary.

...unal's Trial

... can bring the case for trial whenever he/she believes it is ... the public, transmitted live on the Internet, and ...fter the decision, the result is published in the ...ble.

...unal may be challenged by a request ...ommissioner within five days, suspend...

...es within the
...ation upon the
...commissioners
...be the advantage
...or of the advantage
...a newly formed slim
...position will continue

original decision. The final decision rendered by CADE will only become enforceable after its publication in the Federal Official Gazette. This appeal is not meant to question the merits, but rather to resolve omissions, contradictions, or obscurities the decision may contain.

[7] Judicial Appeal

All CADE decisions can be challenged in civil court. Such challenges can climb up the judicial appeals ladder and often take many years to be resolved. In order to appeal, parties must either deposit the amount of the fine with the court.

The Brazilian Courts may also accept bonds or bank guarantees to suspend the enforceability of the fine imposed by CADE. However, the courts usually require that they follow certain parameters: the value of the bond should represent the updated amount of the fine according to the Special System for Settlement and Custody (SELIC) interest rate plus 30%, while also being valid for at least two years. Brazilian courts have required that the guarantee is purchased in Brazil.

[E] Sanctions and Remedies

[1] Sanctions

[a] Administrative Sanctions

Chapter III of Law 12,529/2011 provides in Article 37 the amount of fines to be imposed in case of cartels. The law applies both to companies, companies' administrators, public or private legal entities, and individuals involved in cartel activities. Besides the administrative fines and other administrative penalties, the individuals are also subject to criminal charges in cartel cases.

In accordance with Article 37, points I, II, and III, the practice of cartel subjects offenders to the following penalties:

I. In the case of a company, a fine of 0.1% to 20% of the gross sales of the company, group or conglomerate, in Brazil, in the last fiscal year before the launching of the administrative proceeding, in the branch of business activity in which the violation occurred, which must never be less than the advantage obtained, when such estimation is possible.[4]

The term "branch of business activity" raised much discussion since it was a new and unclear expression introduced by the Law 12,529/2011. To resp

4. Estimating the advantage obtained from the violation has prompted years of deb[ate] [...] CADE Tribunal, as the majority position has always been to base the fines calc[ulation] [...] gross revenues obtained in the year prior to the investigation. However, seve[ral] [...] over time have defended a dissenting view that the main criteria shoul[d] [...] obtained when such estimation by CADE is at all possible. This position in [...] obtained has gained traction in 2021 particularly in bid-rigging cases, wh[...] [ma]jority believes such exercises are [...] Whether this ne[...] [...] [thou]gh future changes to the tribunal's [...] remains uncertai[n]

to that uncertainty, CADE's Resolution No. 3 of 2012 defined the scope of that concept by establishing 144 fields of activity based on an industrial classification used by other government authorities and on additional work carried out by the Department of Economic Studies. Resolution No. 18 of 2016 added a provision to said Resolution giving CADE power to adjust the definition of field of activity according to the characteristics of the conduct when the definition given by the list provided leads to a disproportionate and unreasonable fine. This is still subject to debates in many concrete cases.

In cases in which a company's turnover in the branch of business activity is not possible to be defined, the authority can use the total company or conglomerate turnover approach.

II. in the case of individuals without a managerial position as well as any association of persons or other legal entities that do not have a turnover (such as trade associations), the fine will be fixed between BRL 50,000 and BRL 2 billion.

III. in the case of an individual with a managerial position (an "administrator," typically considered to be a director named in the by-laws), when negligence or willful misconduct is proven, the fine will be of 1% to 20% of the fine applied to company, in the case set forth in point I above, or to the relevant legal entities, in the cases set forth in point II above.

CADE has historically seen cartels as the most harmful violation and therefore deserving of a more severe treatment, reason why the agency usually imposes the penalties for cartels in the upper band of the legal range. For hard-core cartels, the authority usually considers 15% of the company's revenue in year prior to the investigation as the reference rate for the calculation of the fine, with the rate varying from 12% to 20% depending on aggravating and mitigating circumstances. On the other hand, for other concerted practices, such as soft-core cartels, the authority usually favors a reference rate at 12% of the company's revenue in the year prior to the launching of the investigation, varying from 5% to 12% based on the circumstances of the case.

CADE has also been placing the amount of fines to be imposed to associations and other legal entities without a turnover at a higher level than it used to be before the enactment of the Law 12,529/2011, though still much lower than those for companies. In relation to the application of penalties to administrators and other individuals involved in the practice of cartels, CADE often considers fines close to the lower levels provided by the law to be sufficient penalty for natural persons.

In case of recurrence in the cartel practice, the fines to be applied to all the three groups of offenders described in the points I, II and III of Article 37 above are doubled. It is also important to note that the fines applied by CADE are subject to monetary adjustment over time, which can have very significant impacts to the values in question. Brazilian law does not establish the index to be used or the period in which the correction is applied. However, according to recent decisions issued by the Brazilian courts,[5] the most conservative view is to consider the SELIC index calculated

5. "CADE's fines must be monetarily adjusted in accordance with the same adjustment criteria applied to the federal taxes paid with delay." (Vote issued by Justice Souza Prudente. Writ of Mandamus No. 2009.34.00.028359-0. Federal First Regional Court).

from the Financial Statement's base-date of the last fiscal year before the launching of the investigation until the time of the full fine's payment by the defendant.

From a monetary adjustment's perspective, SELIC has monthly and yearly values, published by the Brazilian Central Bank.[6] This is especially important for investigations that take several years, since the SELIC correction will be applied to the base fine of the year before the investigation was launched up until the decision is taken, sometimes increasing the fine by extremely significant amounts.

Besides administrative fines, the current law also provides for other possible penalties, such as prohibiting companies from taking part in public bids for at least five years—which can in many cases have a more significant impact for defendants than a fine—, publication of the CADE's decision in local newspapers, among other sanctions in accordance with Article 38 of Law 12,529/2011.

[b] Criminal Sanctions

The State and Federal Police and the Public Prosecution Offices (both at federal and state levels) are the authorities in charge of criminal enforcement, investigating cases, and bringing them before criminal courts either by their own initiative or when informed by CADE. Criminal cases run separately and independently from the administrative investigations carried out by CADE and may reach different outcomes.

[c] Private Actions and Follow-On Actions

Private damages actions are allowed not only by the Brazilian Civil Code (Law No. 10,406 of 2002) and the Consumers Defense Code (Law No. 8,078 of 1990), but also explicitly by the antitrust law itself, and they can be presented to civil courts either as a follow-on to a CADE investigation or decision, or completely independently as stand-alone claims. Public damages actions can also be brought by public prosecutors acting on behalf of the public harmed by a cartel, based on the Public Civil Action Law (Law No. 7,347 of 1985).

[2] Remedies

Besides fines, CADE might also determine structural and/or behavioral remedies in order to discourage the cartel's continuation and/or to repair market structures affected by the conduct, aiming to restore the competition environment.

Fines and cease and desist orders are much more common than structural remedies in cases of anticompetitive conducts. In a 28 May 2014 decision, CADE for the first time imposed structural remedies in addition to fines and other administrative sanctions in the case of the cement cartel convicted by the Tribunal. In this case,

6. Historical SELIC data available at: https://www.bcb.gov.br/controleinflacao/historicotaxasjuros.

besides the fines applied to six companies, six individuals, and three associations totalizing BRL 3.1 billion, CADE also determined structural and behavioral remedies. As structural remedy, CADE imposed the divestment of cement and concrete plants, and also prohibited the cartelized companies from carrying transactions among themselves in the cement and concrete sector for a period of five years.

Although explicitly provided in the Brazilian Antitrust Law, this use of structural remedies by CADE in the cement cartel's decision raised several debates and judicial challenges, which are still ongoing.

[3] The Cease and Desist Agreements (Settlements)

According to CADE's Internal Rules[7] and Guidelines for Settlements,[8] the agency may execute with a defendant a cease and desist commitment (formally called "Termo de Compromisso de Cessação" or TCC in Portuguese) related to the practice under investigation, at the discretion of the authority if it understands that it is convenient and advances the interests protected by law.

A settlement with CADE must contain the following elements:

(i) specification of the defendant's obligations not to practice the investigated activity, as well as other obligations deemed applicable;
(ii) the setting of fines to be paid in case of failure to comply, in full or in part, with the undertaken obligations; and
(iii) the setting of pecuniary contributions (as the fines in the context of a settlement are known) to be paid, when applicable.

[4] Settlement's Benefits

There are four predefined bands of percentage discounts for pecuniary contributions that vary according to the degree of collaboration and the chronological order of signature of the settlement agreement.

The first bands with the largest discount apply when the settlement takes place while the case is still being investigated, so the settlement must be proposed while the case is still with General Superintendence. In this case, the negotiation takes place with the General Superintendence (pending final confirmation by the Tribunal) and the bands of discounts are the following: the first one will have a discount from 30% to 50% of the applicable fine; the second one from 25% to 40%; from the third onwards, the discount cannot be higher than 25%.

If the settlement is proposed after the General Superintendence has already issued its legal opinion on the case and forwarded it to CADE's Tribunal, then the

7. Approved by Resolution No. 22 of 2019 and updated by Regimental Amendment No. 1 of 2020.
8. The authority's guidelines for Settlement Agreements were published in December 2016 to consolidate the best practices adopted by CADE and provide a framework for the authority and parties interested in negotiating Settlement Agreements.

negotiation takes place directly with the Tribunal and the maximum penalty reduction is of 15%.

[a] *Timing of a Request for Settlement*

As noted earlier, the request for settlement might be presented by the defendant at any time from the launching of the investigation by the General Superintendence up to the beginning of the CADE Tribunal's judgment session. The sooner the agreement is requested, the greater the fine reduction for the defendant is expected, as per the bands described above. In any case, if the company is not satisfied with the direction of the settlement negotiations, the option remains for it to stop the process at any point. However, a settlement proposal can only be presented once, and a negotiation that is unsuccessful for whatever reason prevents a defendant from trying to settle again in the same proceeding.

[b] *Procedure*

Procedurally speaking, once a settlement proposal has been submitted, negotiations will commence between CADE (by means of a Settlement Negotiation Committee) and the defendant.

After presenting the proposal for settlement, the negotiation period will be opened through a decision issued by the General Superintendent or the Reporting Commissioner (depending on when the proposal was made and to whom, as described earlier), who will determine the negotiation period and appoint three or more CADE's servants to compose the Settlement Negotiation Committee.

During the negotiation period, several meetings with the Settlement Negotiation Committee may occur for the defendant to negotiate the amount of the pecuniary contribution to be paid as well as the extent and wording of the settlement's statement (which includes an admission of participation) to be presented by the proponents.

Once the negotiation with the Settlement Negotiation Committee is over, the General Superintendent or Reporting Commissioner provides a deadline for the proponents to submit the settlement's final proposal, which is then submitted to CADE's Tribunal for approval during a plenary session.

The plenary of CADE's Tribunal is entitled to wholly accept or reject the proposed settlement, but it is not able to propose any changes to its terms. The settlement proposal itself does not suspend the administrative proceeding, which only happens after the parties duly sign the settlement with CADE. The administrative proceeding then remains suspended until CADE verifies that the parties have complied with all the settlement's terms, conditions, and obligations imposed by CADE within the established deadline in the settlement.

There have been cases at CADE of unsuccessful proposals for settlement, due to one or both parties—CADE and the proponent of the settlement—not agreeing with the outcome of the negotiation. The rule is that a failed proposal cannot be used to harm the party or affect the final outcome of the administrative proceeding, and the presentation of a proposal for settlement to CADE does not imply an admission of the illegal practice. In case of a failed proposal, CADE's officials must return to the party all documents received during the negotiation and cannot use the information received against the proponents. The General Superintendence, however, may launch investigations to examine facts connected to a failed proposal provided that evidence comes from an independent source by any other means.

The execution of the settlement suspends the administrative proceeding only regarding the defendant who has signed the commitment, and the investigation will follow its regular course in relation to the other defendants. After execution, the settlement agreement (though not the evidence or statements provided) becomes public at CADE's website.

[c] *Requirements for Settlements in Hardcore Cartel Cases*

[i] Admission of Participation

In cartel cases, CADE's internal regulations impose the admission of "participation in the conduct under investigation" as a mandatory requirement for settlement. Even though the settlement proponent is not obliged to admit the "violation of the law," by admitting the "participation in a conduct," proponents are admitting to the facts described therein which may create exposure for civil damages claims by third parties injured by the admitted practices. Such an admission to the facts may also expose the individuals to criminal prosecution.

However, the same results may occur if defendants decide not to settle and are convicted at the end of the administrative proceeding. The difference is the moment when the defendants will be exposed to such risks: the moment they settle or the moment they are convicted. It is important to mention, however, that civil and criminal actions can be filed anytime, even if there is no conviction from CADE. Obviously, their legal strength will vary if filed before or after a CADE decision. Nevertheless, courts can consider that defendants practiced a cartel violation when deciding damage claims, regardless of a CADE decision.

From an individuals' perspective, an admission of participation in a conduct under investigation may harm their defenses in the criminal sphere. Even though they do not admit to a violation of the law, they must admit facts of the cartel investigation. On the other hand, individuals can and often do have their cooperation considered by the criminal prosecutors and courts when determining their sentences.

There are other factors that must be taken into account. One of them is purely economic, in the sense that, depending on the discounts obtained, the amount to be paid due to the settlement may be significantly lower than the fine expected in case of condemnation by CADE.

Another factor relates to the company's image and reputation, considering how it wants to be seen when facing accusations of wrongdoings: denying the charges and litigating for five to ten years or more, or admitting the practice and settling with the authorities and engaging itself in implementing and enforcing a compliance program.

[ii] Settlement Amount: Payment Contribution

As seen earlier, the settlement proposal must contain a pecuniary contribution to be paid in cases of hard-core cartels.

The pecuniary contributions are formally legally different than fines. The first ones are an amount voluntarily paid by the settlement's applicant. Fines are the amount imposed by CADE to the defendants in case of condemnation.

It should be noted that the settlement amount can never be less than the minimum fine for anticompetitive conduct provided in the Brazilian Antitrust Law foreseen in Article 37 of Law 12,529/2011, as explained above.

Many of the latest cease and desist commitments signed in accordance with the Antitrust Law by individuals and to administrators have stayed at or close to the minimum levels of pecuniary contributions (respectively BRL 50,000 and 1% of the fine imposed on the company).

Just as the fines applicable by CADE in case of conviction, settlement contributions are also subject to monetary adjustment by the SELIC rate mentioned earlier. This must be considered when deciding to accept a certain amount, since what is agreed with CADE is the base contribution based on the turnover of the year prior to the beginning of the investigation. If the investigation began several years before the settlement takes place, the monetary correction by SELIC (as described above) could increase the amount of the contribution by a significant percentage, often more than 50%.

[F] Leniency

[1] Enforcement

The Brazilian leniency program is set forth at Articles 86 and 87 of the Brazilian Antitrust Law and from Articles 197–211 of CADE's Internal Rules. In March 2016, CADE issued guidelines to set a framework for the authority and parties interested in negotiating leniency agreements, which were updated in June 2020. The General Superintendence is in charge of negotiating and executing leniency agreements. Although leniency agreements are not subject to review and/or approval by the CADE Tribunal, the latter has to verify, at the end of the case, whether the beneficiary of the leniency application complied with its terms and conditions, and to confirm the leniency agreement executed by the General Superintendence.

Normally, the applicants receive full administrative and criminal immunity. The benefits derived from leniency applications are extended to the individuals involved in the infringement provided that they also agree to join as co-applicants and sign the leniency agreement together with the company. Different from some other jurisdictions, it is important to highlight that leniency is only available for the first party to report a violation.

[2] *Benefits and Types of Leniency*

According to the Brazilian antitrust legislation, the execution of the leniency agreement prevents criminal enforcement upon the individuals[9] who have signed the agreement, in addition to the extinction (in cases of full immunity) or reduction (in cases of partial immunity) of the administrative applicable sanction, as further detailed below.

It is important to stress that the leniency program does not bar damages claims. The existence of a leniency agreement may technically allow or even facilitate such litigation.[10]

[3] *Full Immunity*

Provided that General Superintendence is unaware of the existence of the violation up to the moment the application for leniency is made, the applicant for leniency will benefit from full immunity from both (i) the administrative fines and other penalties; and (ii) the criminal penalties which include both prison terms and monetary fines for individuals.

Immunity (both administrative and criminal) will only be extended to individuals involved in the practice provided that they individually confess to the practice and sign the agreement along with the company.

[4] *Partial Immunity*

In cases in which the General Superintendence is already aware or suspicious of the existence of the antitrust violation, and has already launched an investigation on it, full immunity will no longer be available. However, partial leniency will entitle the applicant to have whichever penalty is imposed by the authorities reduced by one to two thirds, depending on the effectiveness of the cooperation provided, and on the good faith of the applicant when complying with the terms and conditions of the leniency agreement. Full criminal immunity still applies to the individuals that sign this type of agreement.

[5] *Leniency Plus*

The Brazilian leniency regime provides a "leniency plus" option, whereby any co-participant in a cartel under investigation who comes forward with evidence regarding another concerted practice still unknown to the authorities will be granted a

9. There is no corporate criminal liability for antitrust violations in Brazil.
10. The Brazilian Congress is currently discussing Legislative Bill No. 11275/2018, which aims to regulate damages claims and strike a balance between incentives for such claims and the leniency program. Under the current proposal of the bill, as of December 2021, participants in competition wrongdoings would remain jointly liable, also being subject to double damages claims, whereas leniency signatories would be removed from the joint liability and would only be subject to single damages.

reduction of one third in the penalties applicable to the first investigation. Said co-participant also enjoys full immunity for the second practice, for which it was the first one in.

CADE granted its first "leniency plus" benefit in 2015, in the context of the settlement agreement between CADE and Construções e Comércio Camargo Corrêa S/A - CCCC,[11] regarding the investigations of a cartel formed by construction firms to rig bids promoted by government-owned oil company Petrobras. Because another participant of the supposed cartel had previously signed a leniency agreement in the same case, CCCC was not allowed to do so as well. However, because the company provided information regarding another case previously unknown to CADE (the cartel formed between construction firms to fix prices in tenders conducted by Eletrobrás Termonuclear S/A – Eletronuclear regarding the Angra 3 nuclear power plant[12]), the authority granted CCCC a "leniency plus" discount in the Petrobras cartel investigation, reducing the applicable penalties by one third.

This was added to the 40% reduction granted due to the settlement agreement itself. Even so, the fine amount agreed to by the company after all the reductions was BRL 104,006,119.70. Several other leniency plus agreements have followed since.

[6] Requirements

The basic principle of the Brazilian leniency program is full cooperation with the authorities. To qualify for full immunity, the applicant must be the first one in, confess the violation and bring information to the authorities before they have any knowledge about the anticompetitive practice. In addition, it must continue to collaborate and bring additional information throughout the investigation and to abide by confidentiality rules.

The legislation formally requires documentary evidence. The Brazilian authorities understand the burden that the delivery of written statements may represent to the applicant, and have adopted, inasmuch as possible, oral procedures in the leniency application. However, the formal acceptance of the application always results in a written agreement executed between the applicant and the General Superintendence, besides the delivery of documentary evidence and a detailed statement describing the practice.

In short, basic requirements for a successful application are the following:

- the applicant must be the first to qualify with respect to the alleged or investigated infringement;
- the applicant must cease its involvement in the cartel as of the date of the leniency application;
- the General Superintendence shall not have sufficient evidence to ensure the conviction of the applicant at the time the leniency is proposed;

11. Requirement for Settlement No. 08700.007402/2015-44, related to Administrative Proceeding No. 08700.002086/2015-14.
12. Leniency Agreement No. 6/2015, in Administrative Proceeding No. 08700.007351/2015-51.

- the applicant must confess its participation in the cartel and fully cooperate with the investigation; and
- the cooperation must result in the identification of other participants of the practice, and in evidence of their participation in the practice.

[7] Procedure

To benefit from the leniency program, the interested party must submit a proposal either through a confidential written or oral statement before the General Superintendence containing the following information:

(i) The applicant's identification.
(ii) Brief description of the facts related to the violation, explaining the applicant's involvement.
(iii) List of the names of the co-participants, and
(iv) Date by when the applicant is able to submit evidentiary material, documents, or oral hearing of witnesses (typically the authority grants thirty days, extendable upon justification by the applicant).

The General Superintendence has adopted a marker system that has proven effective and facilitates asking for leniency, even with a telephone call. Given that leniency in Brazil is only available to the "first one in," the best time to approach the General Superintendence is as soon as practicable and involves a risk-assessment by the potential applicant. There is no requirement to have evidence at the time of requesting the marker, and some applicants choose to carry out their fact-finding internal investigation already under the protection of a marker, while others prefer to have a complete picture of the possible violation prior to approaching the authority. There is no downside to letting a marker elapse if the applicant later decides not to pursue the leniency course.

Depending on the quality of the evidence presented to CADE when starting the negotiations, the company may need to carry out further internal investigation to determine whether it has sufficient evidence of the infringement that could be submitted to the authorities, but as mentioned it can do so under the protection of the marker.

In the event the leniency proposal is not accepted, the authority issues a letter of rejection establishing that the application should not be disclosed to the public and the documents submitted by the applicant should be returned. The letter also sets forth that the authority will not use the information and documents to which it had access for any purpose. It is nevertheless possible for CADE to launch an investigation grounded in independent evidence collected by other means.

There is no guarantee of leniency during the marker phase, and the authority will require a certain threshold of evidence of the practice and of effects in Brazil in order to agree to sign an agreement. Once the agreement is executed, the applicant will not lose its expected immunity unless due to a serious breach of the cooperation obligations.

As mentioned above, after the signature of the agreement the beneficiary has to comply with obligations of cooperation and confidentiality, which will ultimately be examined and confirmed by CADE's Tribunal at the end of the case.

[8] Appeal

CADE's final decisions are not subject to review in the administrative sphere. However, the parties have the constitutional right to appeal to the Judiciary.

Actions challenging decisions by CADE are filed before Federal Courts, beginning with a Court of First Instance and may ascend successively to higher courts even up to the Federal Supreme Tribunal, the Brazilian Supreme Court.

A final judicial ruling on an administrative decision may take several years. However, it is possible for the parties to try to obtain from the judiciary, in a few weeks, an injunction suspending the effects of CADE's decision, provided that they deposit the amount of the fine with the court or present a bond or guarantee.

In case the appealing parties do not get an injunction suspending a CADE order, they will have to first comply with CADE's decision until a final judicial decision is issued.

[G] Precedent Cases

The highest fine ever imposed in a cartel case in Brazil refers to the investigation carried out in the cement cartel.[13] In August 2013, CADE's Tribunal applied to six companies, six individuals, and three associations fines totalizing BLR 3.1 billion. The Tribunal also determined the divestment of plants by the companies, and restriction on carrying transactions in the cement and concrete sector for five years.

Other relevant case was the subway cartel decided by CADE in 2020. Fines imposed amounted to roughly BRL 445 million.

It is also noteworthy to mention the condemnation of the cartel in the national salt market in 2018. CADE imposed fines that amounted to BRL 289 million. This case is currently pending a judicial appeal.[14]

The examples above are an indication of CADE's willingness to impose heavy fines on cartel cases.

Some examples of cartel cases analyzed and condemned by CADE since 2018 include:

- The international cartel in the market of underground and submarine cables, with effects in Brazil: fines applied totalized BRL 20,9 million;[15]

13. Administrative Proceeding 08012.011142/2006-79.
14. Administrative Proceeding 08012.005882/2008-38.
15. Administrative Proceeding 08012.003970/2010-10.

- The bid-rigging cartel in the national health sector: fines applied totalized BRL 55,4 million;[16]
- The cartel in the market of automotive filters for supply to spare parts sectors: fines applied totalized BRL 235 million.[17]
- The national cartel in the market of flexible packaging: fines applied totalized BRL 306 million.[18]
- In the context of settlement agreements in the Carwash investigations,[19] in 2018 alone, 16 agreements were executed, leading to the payment of BRL 897.9 million by the settling parties.[20]

§12.03 UNILATERAL CONDUCT

[A] Relevant Legislation

Law 12,529/2011 provides in its Article 36 a long list of examples of conducts that can be undertaken by firms, either jointly or individually, which may be deemed as antitrust violations. Among them are the more common unilateral practices of exclusive dealing, tie-ins, price discrimination, resale price maintenance, predatory pricing and refusal to deal, as well as more arcane ones, such as excessive pricing or halting, or significantly reducing production without cause. However, according to the statute, the practices included in this list, and any others, will only be considered a violation of competition law if they also fall under another provision, which lists effects such as to limit or in any way restrict competition, or constitute an abuse of a dominant position. This construction is widely considered as meaning that the listed conducts are not illegal "per se."

Since the list is not exhaustive, the Brazilian antitrust authority may consider other practices as unlawful ones, depending on their potential to cause deleterious effects to competition. In all cases, the assessment on the anticompetitive nature of a certain conduct will always be made by the authorities by means of an evaluation of whether such practice is capable of causing a substantial and unjustified restraint to competition, based on and following the rule of reason. Perhaps a peculiar aspect of the

16. Administrative Proceeding 08012.009732/2008-01.
17. Administrative Proceeding 08700.003340/2017-63.
18. Administrative Proceeding 08012.004674/2006-50.
19. "Carwash investigations" refer in a broad sense to both criminal and administrative probes carried out by Brazilian authorities, such as the Federal Public Prosecution Office, the Federal Judiciary, CADE, and the Federal Court of Accounts, in connection with accusations of bid-riggings, corruption, and other violations involving Brazil's Government-run oil company Petrobras, several of its private suppliers, and politicians. The CADE investigations targeted mainly companies and related individuals accused of having rigged Petrobras's bids.
20. Settlement Requirements 08700.001880/2016-21, 08700.002014/2016-58, 08700.003677/2016-90, 08700.003679/2016-89, 08700.004337/2016-86, 08700.004341/2016-44, 08700.005045/2016-61, 08700.005078/2016-19, 08700.007077/2016-09, 08700.007078/2016-45, 08700.008066/2016-38, 08700.008074/2016-84, 08700.008158/2016-18, 08700.008159/2016-62, 08700.008223/2016-13 and 08700.008245/2016-75.

Brazilian legislation is that there is no need for an anticompetitive practice to effectively achieve its purposes or effects for it to be deemed unlawful. The current legislation explicitly allows for the punishment of the intent to violate the law, regardless of the practice having been effectively carried out or not. Penalizing attempts however is more easily done regarding cartels than unilateral conducts, as in the latter case the effects of the practice are in general part of the finding of illegality.

In practical terms, regarding unilateral practices, the focus is on the potential harm of the conduct under investigation. As per Article 36 of Law 12,529/2011, the potentially harmful effects punishable by the Brazilian legislation are: I. limiting, restraining or in any other way harming the competition environment or free enterprise; II. dominating a relevant market; III. increasing profits on a discretionary basis; or IV. abusively exercising a dominant position. As mentioned, points I and IV are the ones most commonly resorted to by the authorities.

[B] Assessment of Dominance

The Brazilian statute adopted both the lessening of competition (Article 36, I) and abuse of a dominant position (Article 36, IV) as approaches to identify antitrust violations, including the unilateral ones, though in practice there is not much elaboration on the distinction between them. According to the Brazilian antitrust legislation, the existence of a dominant position is presumed whenever an individual firm or a group of companies has a share of 20% of a relevant market. This is a rebuttable presumption, and the authorities rarely rely upon it, usually finding it necessary to justify their own findings of market power or of dominance even for market shares much higher than 20%, on a market-by-market and case-by-case basis. The law in any case provides the option of resorting to the rebuttable presumption of dominance at a 20% market share, and the authority can take (and in fact has on occasion taken) advantage of it, meaning that companies with market shares above that threshold should be aware of that possibility.

In order to assess the existence of a dominant position, the authority starts by defining both the product and geographic dimensions of the relevant market affected by the practice, taking into consideration actual or potential substitutability among relevant products and/or services, and then examines the market shares of the main players of such market. Though not explicitly mentioned, in practice, there is almost a safe haven presumption of absence of market power whenever the market share does not reach 20%. Significant market shares lead to further investigation of market conditions, such as rivalry, barriers to entry, and countervailing bargaining power by customers, for example, so as to verify the existence of market power.

[C] Abuse of Dominant Position

If a showing of dominance is not necessary, for a determined unilateral conduct to be deemed unlawful there is almost a requirement that at least market power be identified (even if in practice, the concepts of dominance and market power are often used interchangeably in Brazil). Since the applicable legislation recognizes that unilateral practices can generate benefits (by way of increased economic efficiency, for instance), the anticompetitive character of such conducts is always examined individually and following reasonability criteria (rule of reason), searching to identify the net effect of the conduct vis-à-vis a consumer welfare standard.

Any unilateral practices capable of affecting a certain relevant market and if resulting in any of the deleterious effects (regardless of whether these effects are actually produced in practice) may be deemed as unlawful on antitrust grounds, especially in cases in which there is no reasonable economic justification to support it.

[D] Investigation

The first step taken by the authority during an investigation when assessing the illegality of a certain unilateral conduct is to identify the existence of the conduct itself—such as does the exclusivity claimed to be harmful actually exist or not, and what is the evidence available in this regard. The second stage of the analysis is then to determine whether there is any market power attributable to the agent and whether the practice produces effects in a substantial share of the market that is the target of such conduct. If market power is identified, the third stage in an investigation is to analyze the actual practice in the context of its market. This phase involves a rule of reason assessment of the logic and intent of the practice, on one hand, and of its concrete or potential impacts on the other hand. Finally, if negative effects are identified, then the authorities will verify whether there are any positive effects generated by the practice that may offset the harm caused, in a balancing exercise that takes into account the net result in terms of consumer welfare.

These three phases of the investigation can be further detailed as follows. The first step is the identification of the alleged illicit conduct, including the entities and individuals involved, as well as the products and markets. It also includes an assessment of the rationale of the practice from the point of view of the companies involved. In the second step of the investigative phase, the authorities will define and analyze the relevant markets affected by the conduct. The 'hypothetical monopolist' test is used for the definition of the relevant market. The conditions of competition in the market are examined, including rivalry, barriers to entry, the degree of concentration, and the contestability of the relevant market by means of imports or new entries.

The third and final step of the analysis deals with the assessment of the conduct under investigation. First, the authority will determine whether the companies have market power or not, and then they will verify the anticompetitive effects of the restraint in the relevant markets. For this analysis, several different aspects are taken into consideration, including portion of the relevant market affected by the unilateral restraint, the duration of the restrictive practice, the assessment of the barriers to entry in the markets affected by the unilateral restraint, the past behavior of the companies in the relevant market related to concerted practices, among others. Subsequently, following the rule of reason, the authority will analyze the possible benefits and efficiencies generated by the restraint under investigation, in a balancing exercise that takes into account the net result in terms of consumer welfare. Unilateral restraints are unlikely to be deemed unlawful whenever the agent does not have any market power.

[1] Authorities, Procedure, and Investigative Powers

The investigation of anticompetitive unilateral practices is performed by CADE's General Superintendence and the ultimate decision is taken by CADE's Tribunal.

Investigations on unilateral practices derive mainly from complaints filed by third parties (anonymously or not) or ex officio. The Brazilian leniency program is not applicable to unilateral practices given the nature of the violation not being collusive, so that there are no investigations on unilateral practice being launched as a result of leniency applications.

The investigation of unilateral conduct is structured based on a three-phase procedure, which is also applicable to collusive conducts, and starts and evolves according to the strength of the evidence of the violation under investigation as assessed by CADE's General Superintendence on a case-by-case basis: (i) preparatory proceeding for an administrative inquiry; (ii) administrative inquiry; and (iii) administrative proceeding. It is possible that a case does not go through by all three phases, depending on the strength and level of evidence available to the authority, and a complaint can lead directly to the launching of an administrative proceeding if the evidence is strong enough.

Preparatory proceedings and administrative inquiries can be closed and dismissed at CADE's General Superintendence's own discretion. Any interested party can nevertheless challenge such dismissal to the General Superintendent, and any Commissioner of CADE's Tribunal can request the case files for a further examination in order to confirm dismissal or order the continuity of the investigation, whether by means of the same type of procedure or conversion into a further one. The decision to close and dismiss an administrative proceeding must necessarily be validated by CADE's Tribunal. Preparatory proceedings and administrative inquiries can be kept confidential by the authority, depending on the interest of the investigation. The investigative phase in all three stages includes presentation of additional clarifications/information/documents by involved parties (voluntarily or upon request by the authority), consultation with third parties, meetings with parties, and hearing of depositions of defendants and witnesses, the latter being under oath, according to Brazil's Civil Procedure Code (Law No. 13,105 of 2015).

Dawn raids can be used in unilateral conduct cases but in practice, they are usually only resorted to in case of cartel investigations.

CADE's General Superintendence and the Commissioners of CADE's Tribunal are empowered to impose preventive measures (similar to injunctions) in administrative inquiries or administrative proceedings, whenever there is evidence or reasonable concern that the defendant's actions, directly or indirectly, cause, or might cause, harm to the market that is irreparable, difficult to repair, or that may render the final result of the proceeding ineffective. Violations of such injunctions are usually subjected to daily fines which may vary between BRL 5,000 and BRL 250,000. Defendants can appeal the imposition of preventive measures to the plenary of CADE's Tribunal, and also to civil courts.

[2] *Burden of Proof*

Under the Brazilian due process of law, CADE bears the burden of proof, although parties normally try to demonstrate the lawfulness of the conduct under investigation. CADE has tried to create an exception in cases involving resale price maintenance, attempting to treat them as "hard core" restraints whose lawfulness would only be recognized if investigated parties succeed in demonstrating the efficiency gain derived from the practice, showing that the positive effects generated in the market derived from the practice ended up being transferred to the end consumer. The case is currently being challenged in the Judiciary and so far a Court of First Instance has refused this new CADE understanding of presumptive illegality.[21]

[3] *Appeal*

At the administrative level, CADE's decision is final and binding. From CADE's final decision it is possible to file a motion for clarification, which aims to clarify omissions, contradictions, or obscurities in the decision. A dissatisfied party can always take CADE's decision to court, but court procedures usually take a long time and, when related to sanctions imposed by CADE, may require that an injunction is obtained to suspend the enforceability of CADE's decision. In cases of pecuniary fines, as noted above, a judicial deposit or a bank guarantee is required as a condition for the appeal to be processed.

[E] Sanctions and Remedies

Companies and individuals found guilty for taking part in unilateral anticompetitive practices are subject to the same sanctions already described above for collusive practices. Companies are subject to fines that range from 0.1% to 20% of the gross turnover achieved by the entity or its group in the field of activity affected by the practice. Individual administrators who are part of the company's management are subject to fines that range from 1% to 20% of the fine applied to the company, while the remaining individual employees are subject to fines that range from BRL 50,000 to BRL 2 billion. Other penalties may include obligation to publish CADE's decision in a major newspaper at its own expenses, cease and desist orders, and restrictions from contracting with the government. Recidivism causes fines imposed to be doubled.

Despite the fact that the legal provision applied to collusive and unilateral restraints is the same, in practice the average percentage of the fines effectively applied

21. CADE's final decision in the Administrative Proceeding 08012.001271/2001-44 as of January 2013, which is currently being challenged before Brazilian Courts and pending a final decision on its merits. See further details in item section §12.03 [E] [3].

by the authority to unilateral violations tends to be much lower than the one applied to collusive behavior, typically ranging around the lower end of the legal band.

Finally, with the enactment of Law 12,529/2011, provisions considering unilateral conducts as criminal offenses were revoked and cartels remained as the only anticompetitive conduct with criminal liability.

[1] Remedies in Unilateral Conducts

Remedies imposed by the authority on unilateral restraints vary on a case-by-case basis depending on the nature of the violation, as further detailed in section §12.03 [E] [3] below. Contracts containing unlawful unilateral restraints can either be subjected to an amendment to eliminate the problematic provision or be considered void if the unilateral restraint is the core object of the agreement. Often remedies in unilateral cases involve behavioral obligations to act or not to act in a certain way, such as granting access or not discriminating other players.

[2] Settlements in Unilateral Conducts

Companies or individuals involved in unilateral practices investigations can enter into cease and desist commitments with the authority any time before the final decision is issued. Applicable rules are the same as the ones already detailed above for collusive violations. Proposals to settle will be examined by the authority at its own discretion depending on whether it deems convenient and appropriate to settle.

Settlement agreements are always conditional on the settling defendant agreeing to cease the practice under investigation among other obligations that may be required by the authority on a case-by-case basis. Similarly to collusive practices, proposing to settle in unilateral conduct investigations is also a one-shot deal, meaning that defendants can only propose to settle once. If negotiations do not move in an acceptable way, defendants can give up on their proposal to settle anytime with no major consequences other than wasting their one-time opportunity to settle.

Settlement agreements typically do not include a conclusion on the merits of the case and do not result in a confession or admission of unlawfulness of the practices under investigation.

Although settlement negotiations can take place with CADE's General Superintendence, they need to be later validated by CADE's Tribunal necessarily before a final decision on the main investigation is rendered. The investigation against the settling defendant will be suspended after the execution of the agreement, and it will remain so depending on the period of duration provided therein the settling defendants will be granted to comply with the terms and conditions negotiated with the authority. Unlike investigations on hard-core cartels, payment of a monetary contribution is not mandatory in unilateral conduct cases. According to a CADE report on settlement agreements between 2012 and 2019, the average payment in settlement negotiations involving unilateral conduct investigations was of 1.56% of the company's turnover in the year prior to the launch of the proceeding.[22]

[3] Precedent Cases

Case law shows that the vast majority of investigations carried out by the Brazilian antitrust authority on unilateral conducts involved some type of practice whose objective was to exclude competitor firms from the market or prevent other companies from competing with the dominant firm. Among the decisions rendered by CADE on unilateral restraints, maybe the two most famous and relevant ones are the convictions of bearings manufacturer SKF for resale price maintenance[23] and of beer manufacturer AMBEV for an anticompetitive rebates program.[24]

The investigation against SKF was launched in 2001 following a complaint presented by the Brazilian Consumer Protection Office (PROCON) but a decision was only rendered in January 2013, as a result of a convoluted investigative phase full of backs-and-forth. Throughout the investigation the authority reached the conclusion that SKF had indeed imposed commercial conditions on its distributors for a brief period. However, in 2008 the then investigative arm of the antitrust authority issued an opinion for the dismissal of the case, as the practice had no identifiable effects and had generated efficiencies to SKF's distribution network by expanding intra-brand competition on the quality service dimension when it eliminated the free-riding effect. The matter was then subject to intense controversy in 2009 at CADE's Tribunal, with a final decision being rendered only in January 2013 by majority voting (4x2 decision).

The commissioners that accepted the opinion of CADE's investigative body voting to dismiss the case grounded their decision following the rule of reason. Among arguments brought in favor of dismissing the case were the facts that there was no evidence in the case records that led to the conclusion that SKF's distributors had actually followed the commercial impositions made by the manufacturer; the absence of market power on the side of SKF; and the significant intra-brand rivalry that made it impossible for the practice to have had negative effects (of which there was in any case no evidence in the file). On the other hand, among the votes for the conviction of SKF was the leading one rendered by the then President of CADE, followed by other three Commissioners. Although these votes differed in terms of arguments, they all followed the leading one which expressly stated when making his vote public that he was changing the analysis methodology for vertical restraints, in particular for resale price maintenance.

22. Report released in March 2021. Available at https://cdn.cade.gov.br/Portal/centrais-de-conteudo/publicacoes/TCC%20na%20Lei%20n%C2%BA%2012.52911/TCC%20na%20Lei%20n%C2%BA%2012.529-11.pdf.
23. Administrative Proceeding 08012.001271/2001-44. TozziniFreire was counsel for SKF in this case defending the company against the charges brought by CADE and in the on-going appeals process against the decision in the courts.
24. Administrative Proceeding No. 08012.003805/2004-10.

The leading vote that resulted in the conviction of SKF relied on the 20% rebuttable presumption of dominance (SKF's market share was in between 25% and 30% depending on the relevant market definition adopted), and discarded the need for CADE to demonstrate the actual existence of market power. It also highlighted the oligopolistic nature of the industry that made the practice even more dangerous. The vote also discarded the relevance of the facts that the practice only lasted seven months and that there was no evidence of whether distributors actually followed the impositions and considered it basically "per se" illegal. It argued that the mere existence of a possible punishment, even if never adopted, would be sufficient to result in a "moral coercion" of distributors and in a reduction of intra-brand competition.

Finally, based on this new almost 'per se illegality" presumption, the decision stated that the burden of the proof shifted to SKF, concluding that the company had failed to demonstrate sufficient countervailing efficiencies deriving from the practice being transferred to end consumers, and imposed a fine equivalent to 1% of SKF's gross turnover in Brazil. As noted above, this decision of CADE is currently being challenged on its merits by SKF before Brazilian courts and still pending a final decision, though CADE has lost in the Court of First Instance.

Since then, CADE has decided other cases touching on RPM but seeming to adopt a different approach, more based on the rule of reason, and to move away from SKF. As this remains the leading case on the subject however, the situation continues to be uncertain. In 2016, CADE reviewed a minimum price policy announced by Continental Tires. While this decision[25] did not expressly reverse the one in SKF, CADE acknowledged that such practice could be deemed legal when the undertaking lacks market power, the policy is unilateral and does not serve as an instrument for collusion, and distributors who do not follow the policy are not punished.

More recently (2021), CADE reviewed a proposed maximum suggested retail pricing policy by fuel distributor Ipiranga.[26] The agency once again noted that, given that the prices were a suggestion, the policy was unilateral and no penalty mechanisms were in place, the practice was legal. Nevertheless, it noted that prices suggested should always be lower than those already in place and needed to be custom-made for each reseller, and not a general suggestion.

CADE has launched several investigations on unilateral restraints concerning the beer manufacturer AMBEV, leader in the Brazilian marker for beers. The most important of these investigations is the one dealing with a rebates program called "Tô Contigo," whose goal was to benefit retail stores willing to join the program with loyalty rebates and discount bonuses. During the investigation into the lawfulness of this rebate program, CADE ended up concluding that, even if not formally, in practice it implied exclusive dealing elements preventing/discouraging participant retailers from selling products of competitors and limiting end consumers' choice. In 2009, the practice was deemed unlawful by CADE, and AMBEV was convicted to pay a fine that amounted at that time to BRL 352 million. This decision was challenged by AMBEV

25. Consultation 08700.004594/2018-80.
26. Consultation 08700.002055/2021-10.

before Brazilian courts, and parties have recently reached a settlement that led to the payment of the fine by AMBEV with a discount of 20% on the total amount.

CADE has also been active in investigating unilateral practices in digital platforms. In 2018, it executed a settlement agreement with online travel agencies ("OTAs") Booking.com, Despegar.com, and Expedia, by means of which the undertakings agreed to no longer require price parity from hotels on the platform in comparison with their offers on competing platforms, on the grounds that this requirement prevented competition between platforms. CADE, nevertheless, allowed the OTAs to request parity in relation to the hotels' own websites. No payment was required from the investigated parties and there was no finding of illegality.

Over the past few years, a relevant portion of CADE's case law on unilateral practices has revolved around terminal handling charges imposed on warehousing operators by port operators, which have been considered abusive for being charged in duplicity. CADE has reiterated its case law originally established in 2006[27] and most recently in 2020 on numerous occasions stating that these charges were illegal, even in face of new regulation from the relevant regulatory agency stating that they were not illegal from their perspective. CADE has been deciding that even if a charge is allowable from a regulatory perspective, an abuse of dominant position within the antitrust sphere is still possible and should be reviewed.

Another major sector which was the focus of CADE's practice was financial services. In 2017,[28] CADE executed a settlement agreement with Banco Itaú (Brazil's largest private bank) to ensure that Hipercard-issued cards were available to merchant networks other than Itaú's own. In 2018, CADE once again executed a settlement agreement with Itaú and payment card acquirer Rede in an investigation into a refusal from Itaú of accepting to offer credit based on payments receivable that were due by Rede's competitors; this time, CADE required a payment of BRL 21 million. In 2019, CADE imposed a preventive measure on Itaú when investigating a campaign by Rede where it provided advance payments for credit card transactions, provided that the customer chose to receive such amounts via Itaú's banking services. In 2020, another bank (Bradesco) agreed to BRL 24 million as a result of an administrative proceeding[29] which investigated its refusal to provide information to the GuiaBolso financial application at the request of customers—making it more difficult for GuiaBolso to compete with Bradesco to some extent.

Besides those major cases, a significant part of all investigations on unilateral conducts that resulted in penalties in Brazil involved exclusivity arrangements, many of them related to a practice by local medical cooperatives called Unimed (a type of health-care-plan-like arrangement). Several dozens of investigations have been launched in Brazil (each focusing on a geographically specific entity) since the implementation of former Law 8,884/94 aiming at verifying whether the exclusivity

27. Administrative Proceedings 08012.007443/1999-17, 08012.003824/2002-84, 08012.005422/2003-03, 08012.001518/2006-37, 08700.005499/2015-51, among others.
28. Administrative Inquiry 08700.000018/2015-11.
29. Administrative Proceeding 08700.004201/2018-38.

requirement imposed by such medical cooperatives on their member doctors constituted an illegal unilateral practice.

In these cases, the authority typically found that the medical cooperative investigated counted as its members a significant proportion (sometimes up to 90%) of the doctors in the respective town or city. In these circumstances, CADE understood that such exclusivity arrangement prevented new health care providers from entering the market and created difficulties for competing players, as it blocked access to the specialized professionals, the most important input in this market.

Another important and highly publicized case on exclusive dealing involved one of the most famous luxury shopping malls in the city of São Paulo, Shopping Iguatemi. In a controversial split decision, CADE imposed a pecuniary penalty of 1% of the mall gross revenues for anticompetitive unilateral conduct. Iguatemi included in its rental agreements with many of its stores a clause that barred them from opening outlets in other luxury shopping malls in the city of São Paulo. During the investigation, the authority found that Iguatemi's market share in its relevant market (of approximately 30.9% of the rental revenues of luxury shopping malls in such area, and 29.0% of revenues of such shopping mall sales) gave it a position that these stores could not afford to do without. CADE further considered that, given the importance of the set of stores subjected to the exclusivity obligation in the market for luxury shopping malls, the practice would have the effect of barring entry or making it more difficult for other players to compete against Iguatemi in that market.

Anticompetitive conduct on intellectual property has also been pursued. In 2015, Eli Lilly was fined BRL 36 million for sham litigation.[30] The company was accused of obtaining exclusive rights over a drug by omitting relevant information in a court proceeding where it requested such right. CADE understood that Eli Lilly was aware that its previously granted patent request was related to the production process, and not the rights for exclusive sales, when it used such an argument in court to obtain exclusivity and subsequently increase prices for the drug. Eli Lilly is currently challenging CADE's decision in court. On another occasion, CADE dismissed an investigation of car manufacturers for enforcing exclusive intellectual property rights over the parts used in their cars also in the aftermarket segment by suing manufacturers who were producing unlicensed parts.[31]

Predatory pricing has an interesting history in Brazil. Although several investigations have been launched and carried out, so far no case of this nature has resulted in a conviction by CADE. The most recent cases on predatory pricing were all dismissed, since the Brazilian antitrust authority found there were not enough elements that would justify a conviction. CADE case law indicates that prices that are higher or at least equivalent to the products' average variable costs will not be considered as predatory. Further, these decisions show that predatory pricing characterization requires evidence that the investigated company will somehow benefit from the conduct. Generally speaking, this would imply high barriers to new entrants, and

30. Administrative Proceeding 08012.011508/2007-91.
31. Administrative Proceeding 08012.002673/2007-51.

a dominant position that would allow the company to practice monopolist prices after the exclusion of competitors and recoupment of losses. In practice, CADE set a very high bar and has made it consistently clear that it will be very difficult for a complainant to make a successful predatory pricing case.

Finally, excessive pricing has never been convicted by CADE, although an investigation into unjustified price increases by medical supplies companies was launched early in the COVID-19 pandemic and is still ongoing.

§12.04 MERGER REVIEW

[A] Relevant Legislation

Brazil adopted in 2012 a pre-merger review system with a mandatory bar on closing until the agency clears a transaction. The main legislation applicable to merger cases is Law 12,529/2011 plus a series of resolutions issued by CADE. Guidelines on gun jumping, antitrust remedies, and horizontal mergers were also made available by the authority in recent years. Relevant regulations on merger control include Resolution No. 2/2012 that clarifies the concept of economic group for purposes of merger control, exemplifies cases that are eligible to the Fast-Track Proceeding, and clarifies what types of minority interest acquisitions are subject to mandatory notification; and Resolution No. 17/2016 that further details the concept of associative agreements.

[B] Authorities

Merger cases are initially submitted to CADE's General Superintendence, the investigative body of the Brazilian antitrust authority and, if challenged, are ultimately decided by CADE's Tribunal. CADE's General Superintendence has the power to clear transactions that are harmless to competition, and does so in the vast majority of cases. The Department of Economic Studies also plays an important role in more complex merger review cases by supporting the authority with market and economic studies.

[C] Triggering Events and Thresholds

Merger control rules are applicable to deals that have effect in Brazil, but those include even ones with limited nexus with the country. The existence of a legal entity or of assets located in Brazil, and any sales, even if only through exports, and in very small amounts, (there is no *de minimis* exemption provided by Brazilian merger control legislation or established in regulation or case law) are sufficient to satisfy the effects test. There is no specific treatment for foreign investment in Brazil or foreign-to-foreign transactions, and merger review provisions apply similarly across the board.

According to the statute, all deals that fall under the provision for Acts of Concentration[32] (Article 88 of Brazilian Antitrust Law) are subject to mandatory pre-merger approval of CADE, provided they produce effects in Brazil and parties meet the double gross turnover threshold.

The double gross turnover threshold is of a gross turnover in Brazil in the year prior to the one that the deal occurs in excess of BRL 750 million by one party to the deal (either buyer or seller) and of BRL 75 million by the other party—parties considered as the consolidated economic group to which they belong.

For purposes of analysis of the thresholds criteria, one should consider the composition of the economic groups of the buyer and seller on the date of transaction. In practice, this will be the date of execution of the contract to be potentially notified to CADE's merger review.

Thus, for the calculation of the economic group's gross revenue for CADE's purposes, the gross revenue of companies that were part of that group in the year prior to the transaction, but which were sold before the date of execution of the contract, must be disregarded. On the other hand, the sales, in the last fiscal year, of companies that were not part of the group in the year prior to the transaction but were acquired by the group before the date of execution of the contract must be considered.

The economic group comprises all companies subject to common control and all companies in which the ultimate controller directly or indirectly holds an interest of 20% or higher. In cases of private investment funds being directly involved in the transaction, the economic group comprises the economic group of each investor holding an interest of at least 50% in the investment fund and all the companies in which the investment fund holds directly or indirectly an interest of at least 20%.

In March 2021, however, CADE's General Superintendence decided to include the manager's economic group as part of an investment fund's economic group. In the Merger Review related to the purchase of participation in Kepler Weber S.A. by the Multimercado Investment Fund Profit 1552, managed by Tarpon,[33] CADE understood that the manager controlled the fund's activities. Therefore, the gross revenues of both manager's and fund's investors' groups should be added up for the purpose of verifying the thresholds for mandatory submission.

Regarding acquisitions of minority interests, although Brazilian competition legislation does not provide for any definition of control, CADE states broadly that control involves the ability to interfere with the activities of a company or undertaking. Generally speaking, in order to provide greater clarity to the obligation to notify than just the broad notion of control, CADE adopted some objective criteria regarding the dimension of the minority stake being acquired, and Resolution No. 2/2012 provides what types of acquisitions of less than 50% or control will be subject to notification: (i) when the acquisition grants to the buyer the status of main individual investor of the

32. When (i) two or more companies that were previously independent merge; (ii) one or more companies acquire the control or parts of other company(nies); (iii) one or more companies acquire another company(nies); two or more companies enter into an associative agreement, consortium or joint venture.
33. Act of Concentration 08700.000180/2020-04.

target; (ii) when the buyer is not horizontally or vertically related to the target, if the acquisition amounts to an interest equal to or higher than 20%, considering the buyer is a new investor—if it is not, the buyer must already have an interest of 20% and one of the sellers must be individually divesting an interest of at least 20%; (iii) when the buyer is horizontally or vertically related to the target, if the acquisition amounts to an interest equal to or higher than 5%, considering the buyer is a new investor—if it is not, the buyer must already have a 5% interest and the increment to the previous participation must be of at least 5%. The assessment of the existence of horizontal or vertical relations must be made considering all the companies belonging to the economic groups of involved parties. Consolidation of control by means of acquisition of minority interests by an already sole controller is not subject to notification.

Resolution No. 2/2012 also provides for circumstances in which subscription of securities and public takeover bids will be of mandatory submission. Provided that the effects and turnover tests are met, the subscription of securities convertible into stock interest must be notified if the future conversion into stock interest would constitute a notifiable act or if such securities already grant to the owner the right to interfere in the management of the target (rights to appoint officers or board members, vote or veto rights on competitive sensitive matters), except for those already provided by law. Deals carried out by means of public takeover bids are not exempted from merger control in Brazil but may be closed before clearance by CADE, though parties are prohibited from exercising any political powers until final clearance. Upon request, CADE may exceptionally grant authorization for the exercise of political rights associated with securities if necessary to protect the value of the investment.

Brazilian law has a peculiar requirement of notification for associative agreements. In order to clarify this obligation, CADE issued Resolution No. 17/2016, which provides the criteria on associative agreements that constitute an Act of Concentration and therefore are of mandatory submission if the effects and turnover tests are satisfied. These include all types of agreements that (i) last two years or longer, (ii) establish a common enterprise between at least two economic groups with competing activities in the relevant market object of the contract for the exploration of economic activity, and (iii) result in profit/loss sharing in such activity. Continuity of existing agreements beyond a 2-year duration or undetermined period depends upon CADE's clearance.

Deals that do not meet mandatory notification thresholds can still be subject to merger review upon request of CADE within a period of one year as of its closing. CADE has used this prerogative at least four times already,[34] asking parties to file deals that had not been subject to the regular statutory pre-merger notification obligation.

34. APAC 08700.005079/2019-06 (Prosegur and Acel) 08700.006355/2017-83 (SM Empreendimentos Farmacêuticos and All Chemistry), 08700.009828/2015-32 (Guerbet and Mallinckrodt), 08700.006497/2014-06 (Greca Distribuidora de Asfaltos Ltda., Betunel and Centro Oeste Asfaltos).

[D] Exemptions and Intra-group Transactions

A few scattered decisions rendered under the former statute had suggested that in deals in which the amount of sales in Brazil is minimal and irregular, there could be no obligation of submission. However, this has never coalesced into a consistent position, there has not been any precise definition by CADE as to what level of sales in Brazil could be considered irrelevant for the purpose of defining effects, and the agency has consistently stayed away from adopting any sort of *de minimis* exemption for filings in Brazil. In fact, the agency has also reviewed (thereby recognizing the obligation to file) transactions involving minute sales in Brazil.

The only clear exemptions concern fully intra-group transactions, and joint ventures, consortiums, or associative agreements formed with the specific purpose of participating in public bids and the agreements derived from these public bids.

[E] Pre-merger Control Regime

There is no deadline for filing in Brazil but transactions of mandatory notification cannot be closed or implemented before clearance. Infringing parties are subject to payment of fines ranging from BRL 60,000 to BRL 60 million, besides possibly having the deal declared null and void and facing a behavioral investigation in case the deal is considered harmful on its merits.

CADE may upon request allow parties to adopt measures toward the implementation of the deal prior to final clearance. However, this process normally requires a lengthy and uncertain negotiation with the authority, remaining as a rare and exceptional measure. In order to benefit from said previous authorization from CADE, parties must demonstrate that the measures intended to be implemented will cause no irreparable harm to competition, can be completely reverted if CADE later deems the deal harmful on the merits, and the financial losses the target company would face if said measures are not pursued are significant and irreversible. CADE requires such requests to be accompanied by documents, financial reports, certificates, and so forth. In the absence of this previous authorization, any failure to comply with the bar on closing provision can be interpreted by the authority as gun jumping and subject parties to the sanctions already mentioned above. In May 2015, the authority published its guidelines providing additional clarity on what can and cannot be done by parties while clearance is still pending.

Since the enactment of the pre-merger regime in 2011, several fines have been imposed on parties for measures considered as gun jumping, including: generation of effects prior to the formal agreement itself,[35] decision-making/controlling powers from one party on the other;[36] absence of antitrust suspensive clause in the agreement;[37]

35. Acts of Concentration 08700.005775/20013-19, 08700.007899/2013-39, 08700.008292/2013-76, 08700.002285/2014-41, 08700.000631/2017-08, 08700.001886/2019-41, 08700.000422/2020-51 and 08700.002914/2020-81.
36. Act of Concentration 08700.005775/2013-19 and 08700.004924/2015-94.

exchange of commercially sensitive information;[38] operational merger between parties;[39] and payment of the price of the agreement (in total or partially).[40]

In 2015, in the Goiás Verde Alimentos Ltda./Brasfrigo Alimentos Ltda. Merger Review,[41] CADE imposed penalties for gun jumping which went beyond monetary fines: even though the transaction itself was fully approved, the buying party was prohibited from using the purchased brand for a period of two years, besides having to pay a fine of BRL 3 million—the same value as the gun jumping fine in the OGX Petróleo e Gás/Petrobras merger review case, which related to a much larger transaction with larger parties involved in it.[42]

This penalty was imposed due to the fact that, in this case, the parties did not voluntarily submit the transaction to CADE's approval, which was taken by the authority as a severe breach of good faith. In 2016, the authority for the first time applied the sanction of nullity due to gun jumping, suspending the effects of the contract concluded between Shimano and Blue Cycle for the exclusive distribution of products in Brazil.[43]

As for carve-outs, in 2016, CADE for the first time stated explicitly that they are not permitted. In the Cisco/Technicolor Merger Review,[44] parties closed the deal prior to CADE's clearance, though carving out Brazil, as the operation was essentially abroad, involving only minor assets in Brazil. The authority, though, deemed the arrangement unlawful and fined parties BRL 30 million.

A notable change in CADE's procedure regarding gun jumping took place in July 2019, with the release of CADE's Resolution No. 24/2019. Before said Resolution, CADE would first decide the gun jumping matter, and then would rule on the merger. This undermined the calculation of the gun jumping fine, as CADE should consider competition concerns derived from the transaction as one of the legal factors for such calculation. The Resolution set guidelines that provide more objective and less discretionary criteria for the calculation of gun jumping fines. Since then, the application of aggravating and mitigating factors, as well as the values or ranges of values, are pre-established, turning the calculation clearer and more predictable.

[F] Substantive Test for Assessing Mergers

As noted before, the Brazilian Antitrust Law contains both a dominant position test and a lessening or restriction of competition test. Although not much elaboration has been

37. Acts of Concentration 08700.005775/2013-19, 08700.007899/2013-39 and 08700.008292/2013-76 and 08700.000137/2015-73.
38. Acts of Concentration 08700.005775/2013-19, 08700.007899/2013-39 and 08700.008292/2013-76.
39. Act of Concentration 08700.007899/2013-39, 08700.007553/2016-83 and 08700.003660/2019-85.
40. Acts of Concentration 08700.008289/2013-52, 08700.008292/2013-76 and 08700.005455/2019-54.
41. Act of Concentration 08700.010394/2014-32.
42. Act of Concentration 08700.005775/2013-19.
43. Administrative Proceeding 08700.002655/2016-11.
44. Act of Concentration 08700.009018/2015-86.

done regarding either one, or the distinction between them, in practice most decisions tend (usually implicitly) to focus more on the dominant position test, meaning that a deal will normally be cleared if not deemed to create or strengthen a dominant position, even without a deeper analysis of possible broader lessening of competition effects. Coordinated effects used to be rarely assessed, but are progressively becoming more of a concern. The economic efficiency defense is expressly accepted by the Brazilian Competition Law within certain conditions, which include evidence that the gains will also benefit consumers. Although they are regularly analyzed and taken into account in substantially complex transactions, it is fairly uncommon for CADE to authorize a deal that is considered harmful based solely on compensatory efficiencies.

[G] Notification Procedure and Timetable

[1] Filing Preparation and Notification

Notifications should preferably be submitted jointly by the parties and after formalizing the transaction. The law does not exclude however that filings are made based on initial non-binding agreements, such as letters of intent or memoranda of understanding. There is no statutory distinction between different parties to a deal, so that all parties (including the seller) are responsible for filing (one filing is made per deal only), and all can be punished for non-compliance. As of January 1, 2016, according to Law No. 13,196, of December 1, 2015, the flat filing fee per filing to be paid to CADE is set to BRL 85,000.

Filing requires the preparation of a notification form (either a simpler form for transactions that are eligible for the Summary Proceeding, or a complete form for deals subject to the Ordinary Proceeding). Both forms require corporate information on the parties and their economic groups, and on the transaction itself, and a relevant market definition up front. Estimates of market shares for the parties and their main competitors and data on clients and suppliers are also required, as well as some elaboration on barriers to entry and other market conditions. The information is requested in a substantially more detailed way in the complete form.

There is significant room for pre-notification discussions with the authority in cases that cannot benefit from the Summary Proceeding. During these confidential discussions, parties present a draft of the notification form and meet with representatives of CADE's General Superintendence, advancing the most challenging aspects of the upcoming analysis prior to the formal filing. These pre-notification discussions are not a statutory requirement but have become basically mandatory for Ordinary cases. As the countdown of the authority's deadline for review is only triggered after the authority deems the filing complete after submission, pre-notification discussions can avoid unnecessary delays in the merger review analysis after notification. Also, remedies can start being negotiated at this preliminary phase, so that a proposal of remedies can be presented simultaneously with the filing, significantly shortening the period of review. The authority can ask for waivers during the pre-notification discussions stage to be able to consult with third parties but those are granted by parties at their own criteria.

Different from many other jurisdictions, antitrust filings are given almost full publicity after submission (excluding confidential information), including to third parties. After notification and once satisfied with the completeness of the filing, CADE publishes in the Federal Official Gazette a summary of the notification and name of the parties and inviting comments from anyone. The notification form, submissions by the parties and by third parties, responses to requests for information, all became publicly available (including online), and redactions are granted by the agency upon request and on a very restricted basis. Proposals of remedies and related negotiations are treated confidentially, with the exception of the market testing sometimes carried out by the authority. A clearance decision is also published in the Federal Official Gazette and the reasoning made available to anyone. In challenged cases that reach CADE's Tribunal, the decision will be taken in a public session. The entire content of merger review cases, except for confidential information, is made publicly available after clearance.

[2] Review Phase

Horizontal deals that do not result in a combined market share in excess of 20%, or up to 50% provided that the Herfindahl-Hirschmann Index (HHI) variation is below 200, or vertical deals in which the parties do not have a share of at least 30% in any of the vertically related markets are among simpler cases that can benefit from the Summary Proceeding. Other hypotheses of Summary Proceedings include joint ventures involving two independent companies for the formation of a new company under common control aiming to operate in a market whose products or services will not be horizontally or vertically related, and situations of mere substitution of economic agents in the market, with no new horizontal, vertical, or conglomerate relations due to the transaction.

Within the General Superintendence, all cases are first analyzed by a specific unit in charge of a preliminary triage in order to verify if the agency agrees with the parties' characterization of the deal as a Summary or Ordinary Proceeding and the information provided. The latter ones are to be sent to one of CADE's specialized units (according to the market area involved) for further analysis. The final decision comes from the General Superintendent, who can approve the merger outright as normally done for summary proceeding cases or ordinary cases that are not considered as harmful to competition. More complex cases normally take longer, and they are analyzed by CADE's Tribunal if they are challenged on its merits (i) by CADE's General Superintendence—normally backed up by studies produced by the Department of Economic Studies—, (ii) by third interested parties admitted in the merger review, and (iii) by CADE's Tribunal when any commissioner requests the case files for a further review after clearance by CADE's General Superintendence.

If the merger review is to be analyzed by the Tribunal, a commissioner will be assigned to the case by draw. Remedies can be negotiated either with CADE's General

Superintendence or CADE's Tribunal, though the latter always gives the final word. A report and a decision vote will be prepared by the Reporting Commissioner and then submitted to the full Tribunal during a public session. The final decision at the tribunal is taken by a majority vote.

[3] Timetable

Under the Brazilian Antitrust Law, the maximum period of analysis is of 240 days, which can be extended for up to an additional 60 days at the applicants' request, or 90 days at CADE's own initiative if necessary to conclude the analysis.

By means of Resolution No. 16/2016, CADE established a 30-day deadline for CADE's General Superintendence to clear Summary Proceedings. CADE's General Superintendence has been consistently clearing this type of proceeding within this deadline.

Applicants must respect an additional fifteen-day waiting period after clearance from CADE's General Superintendence (refraining from consummating the deal), during which the decision can be challenged at CADE's Tribunal. The additional waiting period when CADE's Tribunal clears the deal is of five days for possible requests for clarification. The time frame for Ordinary cases may substantially vary depending on the complexity of the case.

[H] Consequences of a Failure to Notify

Failure to notify (gun jumping) potentially renders the transaction null and void. In addition, and more frequently, CADE may impose a pecuniary penalty ranging from BRL 60,000 to BRL 60 million, and also launch an administrative proceeding if the deal is considered harmful to competition.

Pecuniary sanctions can be collected from any of the parties of the transaction, whichever is easier for CADE. Failure to pay the fine will lead CADE to start proceedings for collection in a Federal Court.

[I] Third-Party Involvement in Notification Process

Clients, suppliers, and competitors are often involved in high-profile cases, voluntarily or upon request by the authorities. Third parties aiming to actively participate in the merger review may request admission to CADE's General Superintendence within fifteen days as of the publication of the Act of Concentration in the Federal Official Gazette. Once admitted, they can present submissions, request meetings with officials, or even appeal against a clearance made by the General Superintendence. Often, the authority also brings clients and competitors into the process by sending them official requests for opinions and additional information, and their input is traditionally taken into consideration. Third parties that act in bad faith with a goal to stall or delay a review may receive penalties that vary from BRL 5,000 to BRL 5 million.

[J] Remedies and Ancillary Restraints

CADE has very broad enforcement powers, with the law expressly allowing it to take whatever measures are deemed necessary to remedy damages caused by an anticompetitive transaction, including up to dissolution or break-up of a company. As an administrative authority, CADE can request judicial backing to carry out in force its decisions as well as the collection of fines or the performance of a specific obligation.

The remedies have to be specific, in that they must address the competition problems raised by the deal, and they have to be adequate to the market. CADE explicitly favors structural remedies over behavioral ones, especially in horizontal deals, though behavioral remedies are often adopted in vertical transactions, if deemed sufficient and more proportionate. In most cases, the agency is more concerned with the effects of the remedies on consumers rather than on competitors.

In 2018, CADE launched its Guidelines for Antitrust Remedies on best practices and procedures for determining, applying, and monitoring antitrust remedies. One type of practice that has been increasingly used to speed up resolution of complex mergers and ensure the effectiveness of the remedies is the adoption of a fix-it-first or upfront-buyer approach. In Hypera/Boehringer Ingelheim,[45] the parties received the CADE approval subject to the sale of a line of medicines from the buyer to another pharmaceutical company, and União Química was then presented by the purchaser as the upfront buyer, which CADE also approved.

Timing will depend on the specific remedy being adopted by the authorities. Vertical issues are becoming more important in the review and several remedies have already been imposed based on foreclosure or essential facility-like theories. As noted above, in more complex cases CADE tends to pay growing attention to coordinated effects of the transaction.

CADE decisions routinely address non-compete provisions. In 2009, CADE released two internal rulings based on its case law and consolidating the understanding about such ancillary restraints. By means of said internal rulings, CADE consolidated the understanding that it will accept non-compete agreements in joint ventures, provided that they have a close relationship with their corporate purposes and their relevant markets, and they last as long as the joint venture itself. In the case of acquisitions, CADE has also consolidated its understanding that an acceptable period for non-compete agreements is five years as of the transaction, provided that it is limited only to the relevant product and geographic markets involved in the transaction. CADE has frequently ordered the parties, even in foreign-to-foreign mergers, to change the original agreement if a non-compete clause provides for a longer period or comprises a broader territory or wider product scope. Exclusivity arrangements can also be covered by the decision, and CADE has in the past ordered the elimination or modification of exclusivity clauses it did not deem reasonably justified.

45. Act of Concentration 08700.001255/2020-66.

[K] Penalties

Besides the above explained fines that may be imposed by CADE in cases of failure to notify or gun jumping, the approval of Act of Concentrations may be revised and even unwound by the Tribunal, ex officio or upon request of the General Superintendence, if the decision is based on false or misleading information provided by the parties or in case of non-compliance with any of its obligations imposed as a condition for the approval of the deal. Companies found guilty of providing false or misleading information are subject to the payment of fines that range from BRL 60,000 up to BRL 6 million, besides the adoption of any other appropriate measures. Failure to pay the fine will lead CADE to start proceedings for collection in a Federal Court.

[L] Appeal and Judicial Review

Administrative appeals against CADE's decisions on merger cases are very limited and submitted to the same CADE Tribunal that issued the decision in the first place. This means that decisions are rarely changed in the administrative sphere, unless there is evidence of a new fact or document that could result in a more favorable decision. However, the parties always have the right to go to court to challenge a CADE decision.

With the pre-merger notification system, parties have less incentive than in the previous post-closing system to take the discussion on the merits of the case to courts due to the bar on closing. Before, they would have closed the transaction by the time the CADE decision was awarded, so that typically the years of judicial appeal would run with the transaction already implemented. Today, since closing cannot take place prior to clearance, a transaction that is blocked by the agency may have to wait several years until its attempt to reverse the agency decision comes to a result in the courts—a timeline that obviously discourages most such appeals, as is the case in several other jurisdictions with similar systems.

In any case, as mentioned earlier, the Brazilian Constitution provides for the judicial review of administrative acts. If the capacity of the courts to go over procedural aspects is unlimited, then there is some deference awarded to CADE regarding substantive issues, though exactly how much remains unclear and will only be decided by the judiciary itself as more appeals reach the higher courts.

[M] Specific Industries

The Antitrust Law provides no sector exemptions, and CADE exercises its jurisdiction across all industries. The one grey area used to be the banking sector, the object of a long jurisdictional dispute between CADE and the Central Bank. In 2012, the Central Bank issued a new regulation on merger control, and now it is clearer that the Central Bank will perform its regulatory role also with respect to antitrust aspects. Financial institutions are therefore obliged to submit antitrust filings not only with CADE, but also with the Central Bank. As of February 2018, the two agencies entered into an agreement to close a judicial dispute that lasted years in the higher courts. By means of a Memorandum of Understanding, CADE and the Central Bank set the procedures for analyzing mergers and anticompetitive conducts in the Brazilian financial system. Parties need to get clearance from both agencies in order to implement a notifiable transaction in this sector. An important exception is the recognition, by CADE, that the position of the Central Bank will prevail when a transaction is deemed necessary to prevent systemic risk. In such cases, CADE shall accept the position issued by the Central Bank and will immediately approve the Act of Concentration. This is expected to be a very rare situation, if it ever comes to pass.

Transactions in certain other regulated sectors may also require not only the standard merger review clearance by CADE, but also special clearance by their respective sector regulators or agencies. Depending on the nature of the transaction, this may be the case, for example, in the telecommunications industry, insurance, oil and gas, electricity, aviation, health insurance, securities, and hydro transportation. Other than the Central Bank systemic-risk exception mentioned above, no other regulated-sector clearance requirement affects the regular merger review process and independent decision-making power by CADE.

CHAPTER 13

Competition Law in Chile

*Juan Cristóbal Gumucio Schönthaler & Cristóbal Lema Abarca**

§13.01 INTRODUCTION

The present chapter contains a brief overview of the Chilean competition system, its main current issues, the competition legal framework, and the treatment that has been given to different potential anticompetitive conducts.

The current Chilean competition system is relatively recent, the existing Competition Court (*Tribunal de Defensa de la Libre Competencia*, hereinafter "*TDLC*") was created seventeen years ago, and other very important institutions (e.g., mandatory merger control, criminal liability for cartels) were introduced just a few years ago.

Consequently, the case precedents of the TDLC and the Supreme Court, as well as the guidelines issued by the National Economic Prosecutor Office (*Fiscalía Nacional Económica*, hereinafter "*FNE*") are under constant evolution in different aspects, following in many ways the criteria established by more consolidated legislations and especially considering the case law of the European Commission and the US Courts.

[A] Competition Legal Framework

The Chilean competition system is mainly contained in:

- *The Political Constitution:*[1] Article 19 N. 21 of the Political Constitution sets forth the general grounds of the Chilean competition system. It guarantees to

* The original version of this chapter was written by Juan Cristóbal Gumucio Schönthaler & Guillermo Frene Candia with the collaboration of Elías Astudillo. The revision of cases, bills, and documents ended in October 2021, so any matter occurred after such date is not explained in detail in this chapter.

1. Note that the current Political Constitution of Chile might be replaced during 2022 or 2023 given the Constitutional Convention that was implemented to discuss a new magna carta.

everyone the right to develop any economic activity that it is not contrary to morale, public order or national security, pursuant to the relevant legislation.

- *The Decree Law N. 211*: The DFL N. 1 of 2005 reinstated and redrafted the text of the Decree Law N. 211 of 1973, which contains the Antitrust Law in Chile (hereinafter the "*DL 211*" or "*Competition Law*"). Pursuant to the Law the main bodies in charge of promoting and protecting free competition in Chile are the TDLC and the FNE.
- *Other statutes*: Other relevant statutes are the Unfair Competition Act (Law No. 20,169); the Consumer Protection Act (Law No. 19,496); the Freedom of Opinion and Information Act (Law No. 19,733); the General Banking Act (DFL No. 3 of 1997 that reinstated and redrafted the General Banking Act (DFL No. 252 of 1960) and other laws); Water Supply and Sewerage Services Act (DFL 382); the Public Ports Act (Law No. 19,452); the Casinos Act (Law No. 19,995); the Criminal Process Code; and the Civil Procedure Code, which governs some procedural aspects of the antitrust proceedings before TDLC.
- *Internal regulations established by the TDLC*: The TDLC has issued twenty-one internal instructions (*Auto Acordados*), fourteen of which are currently in force, relating to procedural matters. The main instructions are *Auto Acordados* No. 5, No. 16, and No. 19. The former sets forth procedural rules regarding contentious and non-contentious cases. *Auto Acordado* No. 16 sets the standards with respect to confidentiality and reservation of the information submitted to the TDLC during proceedings, while the latter describes the digital procedure for cases starting from 2020.
- *Case law*: Chile does not follow the common law system, based on binding precedents. However, the provisions of the DL 211 have been shaped and defined through several rulings issued by the Supreme Court, the TDLC and, in relation to the recently implemented merger control system, the FNE.

[B] The Evolution of the Chilean Competition System

The origin of the competition system in Chile can be placed in 1959, when the first statute related to competition matters, Law No. 13.305, was enacted. This statute, which reproduced some ideas and concepts from the American Sherman Act, created a commission to review claims of anticompetitive conducts and prohibited the offense of monopoly, defined, in summary, as any conduct undermining the freedom of competition.

Notwithstanding the above, it is in 1973, with the enactment of DL 211, that the current Chilean competition system was established. DL 211 has been amended several times. According to the original wording of the DL 211, there were three different authorities involved in competition law:

- *The Resolutive Commission*: this commission worked as a court reviewing and ruling on acts or transactions that allegedly violated the law and acted as an appeal board reviewing the decisions of the Preventive Commissions. The

decisions of the Resolutive Commission could be appealed before the Supreme Court in certain cases.
- *The Preventive Commissions*: There were thirteen commissions, each located in the different regions of Chile, with broad attributions to review acts and transactions, but they could not impose fines or order remedial actions.
- *The FNE*: The FNE was an independent entity from the abovementioned commissions. The FNE could conduct investigations for potential violations of the Competition Law and prosecute such violations before the Resolutive Commission.

In 2004, important amendments were introduced by Law No. 19,911, whose main purpose was to strengthen the independence, specialization, and dedication of the competition authorities; hence, the following amendments were enacted:

- The Resolutive and Preventive Commissions were abolished.
- The TDLC was created to replace such Commissions.
- The criminal penalties were abolished.

In 2009, a new amendment to DL 211 was introduced by Law No. 20,361, aiming to improve the independence of the TDLC's members, and to grant the FNE with additional attributions to investigate collusion. Among other relevant changes introduced by this law, we can list the following:

- The introduction of new attributions to the FNE to investigate cartels allowing dawn raids, intercept telephonic communications, etc.
- The creation of a leniency program.
- The increase of the fines in cartel cases, from up to UTA 20,000 (*Unidad Tributaria* Annual or yearly tax unit) to up to UTA 30,000.[2]
- The extension of the statute of limitations.

Finally, in 2016, the last amendment to DL 211 was introduced by Law No. 20,945. Among the main modifications are:

- The criminalization of hardcore cartels.
- The elimination of the "market power" requirement for hardcore cartels.
- The prohibition of interlocking between competitors.
- The creation of an obligation to report, ex-post, acquisitions of minority shareholdings in competitors.
- A substantial increase in the amount of fines and inclusion of other potential sanctions.
- The creation of a mandatory merger control system.
- Attribution of TDLC to know follow-on damage actions arising from competition infringements.

2. The UTA is an index that varies in time. Based on the average value of UTA and dollar for 2021 (626,487 Chilean pesos and 750 Chilean pesos, respectively) 1 UTA is equivalent to approximately USD 835.

[C] The Current Organic Structure

Since the enactment of Law No. 19,911 in 2004, the authorities in charge of defending and promoting free competition are the TDLC and the FNE. In addition, the Supreme Court has played a significant role in our competition system because most of the relevant cases have been decided by the court (including some relevant reversals of TDLC's decisions in recent cases), due to its broad attributions to review the decisions of the TDLC in antitrust and merger control[3] cases when a special revision recourse (*recurso de reclamación*) is filed by a party or the FNE.

[D] Future Developments

In March 2020, the government submitted a bill to the parliament, which introduces several amendments to the DL 211, although the bill has not advanced in the legislative process since April 2020. The main amendments of the bill are the following:

- *Powers of the FNE relating to collusion*: the bill proposes to give additional investigative powers to the FNE for collusion cases, such as requesting the lifting of the banking secrecy and photographing, filming and recording individuals.
- *Increase of imprisonment for Collusion*: the bill proposes to punish collusions regarding essential goods or services (*bienes o servicios de primera necesidad*) with up to five to ten years of imprisonment (instead of three to ten years of imprisonment, as it is currently for collusion regarding such goods and services and others).
- *Anonymous whistleblower*: the bill proposes to create the figure of individual anonymous whistleblowers on top of leniency regulation and the possibility of making a claim (*denuncia*) before the FNE asking the confidentiality of the identification of the claimant.

Also on the legislative side, there is a bill mainly aimed to systematize economic criminality (in broad terms), which for the competition system contained in the DL 211 includes the following main changes:

- *Criminal prosecution in case of essential goods*: the bill proposes to make mandatory the submission of a criminal complaint (*querella*) by the FNE when the collusion affects essential goods.
- *Parallel proceedings*: the bill proposes that FNE must submit the criminal complaint within ninety days counted since the submission of the competition

3. Under current merger control system, FNE's prohibition can be appealed before the TDLC (*recurso de revision especial*) and, if the TDLC approves the transaction subject to mitigations different to the last ones offered to the FNE, the parties and the FNE can file a special appeal (*recurso de reclamación*), but so far, no case under this system has been decided by the Supreme Court.

lawsuit (*requerimiento*). This would make the criminal and competition procedures to advance in parallel.
- *Confidentiality of the information*: the bill proposes to allow the criminal prosecutor (*Ministerio Público*) to request the lifting of the confidentiality of determined pieces of competition case file for its use in the criminal procedure.

In the context of the pandemic outbreak and the extraordinary measures most authorities have adopted, both the FNE and the TDLC have issued specific guidelines and/or regulations to try to adjust their functions to the current times. On the one side, the FNE issued a public statement indicating that DL 211 does neither have any applicable exemption nor mandatory ex-ante review system for collaboration agreements, although these, unlike cartels, can be legal, particularly if due to the current situation some degree of collaboration among competitors is necessary for an efficient production and distribution of goods and services.[4] On the other side, the TDLC issued internal regulations (*Auto Acordados*) adopting its functioning to home office and extraordinarily allowing, while the state of catastrophe decreed due to the pandemic, the execution of acts or agreements subject to a non-contentious consultation procedure before the TDLC renders a decision,[5] especially if these refer to goods or services indispensable to maintain the supply chain, the continuity of transport services, and the delivery of remedies or medical supplies.[6] The TDLC's plenary session also suspended the evidentiary terms of the procedures in similar terms to the rule applicable to general tribunals pursuant to Law No. 21,226,[7] but evidentiary stages are currently ongoing.

Finally, like in other jurisdictions, digital markets have been a rising topic. For example, the FNE approved two transactions concerning Cornershop, a groceries delivery app,[8] and drafted a specific section about digital platforms and markets on its new guideline for the Analysis of Horizontal Concentrations.[9] TDLC also addressed the

4. FNE, "Declaración Pública", April 3, 2020, available in: https://www.fne.gob.cl/wp-content/uploads/2020/04/Declaraci%C3%B3n-P%C3%BAblica-FNE-030420.pdf.
5. Normally, facts, acts or contracts subject to a non-contentious procedure are suspended, so in the terms of the TDLC itself, this would be the equivalent to a "provisional authorization."
6. Auto Acordados Nos. 20 and 21, respectively, both available at: https://www.tdlc.cl/auto-acordados/. Note that, as far as we are concerned, no fact, act or agreement has been consulted before the TDLC pursuant to the extraordinary permit of internal regulation No. 21.
7. "Acuerdo del Tribunal de Defensa de la Libre Competencia con Ocasión de la Publicación de la Ley N° 21.226 y de Estado de Catástrofe", April 2, 2020, available in: https://www.tdlc.cl/wp-content/uploads/2021/07/ACUERDO-DEL-TRIBUNAL-DE-DEFENSA-DE-LA-LIBRE-COMPETENCIA-abril-2020-marzo-2021-julio-2021.pdf. The applicable rules were continuously updated by the TDLC according to the advance of the pandemic in Chile and the new legislation governing judicial procedures.
8. Cases Nos. F161-2018 (acquisition by Walmart) and F217-2019 (acquisition by Uber). The acquisition by Walmart was not carried out because it was forbidden by the Mexican authority *Comisión Federal de Competencia Económica*, COFECE (*see* https://www.cofece.mx/wp-content/uploads/2019/08/AnCAs-CornerShop-12agsoto2019.pdf).
9. Published for comments until June 11, 2021 available in: https://www.fne.gob.cl/wp-content/uploads/2021/05/Guia-para-el-Analisis-de-Operaciones-de-Concentracion-Horizontales-mayo-VF.pdf. Final version has not been published yet.

digital economy on its 2021 annual public account[10] and was part of its recent judgment rejecting the lawsuits of taxi drivers against Uber, Cabify, and Easy Taxi (all transportation apps) for alleged abuse of dominance, predatory pricing, and unfair competition.[11]

§13.02 CARTELS

[A] Relevant Legislation

The legal regime applicable to competition in Chile is contained in DL 211. Article 3 sets forth, as a rule, that any act or agreement that prevents, restricts, or hinders competition, or tends to produce said effects, shall be sanctioned.

In addition to providing a broad definition of anticompetitive conducts, the law subsequently sets forth that:

> the following will be considered as, among others, facts, acts or conventions that impede, restrict or hinder competition or tend to produce said effects:
>
> a) Agreements or concerted practices that involve competitors among them, consisting of fixing purchase or sale prices, limiting production, allocating territories or quotas, or affecting the result of bidding processes, as well as the agreements or concerted practices that, conferring them market power, consist of determining commercialization conditions or excluding current or potential competitors.[12]

Given the modification introduced by Law No. 20,945, now DL 211 considers two types of collusions: those that require market power and those that do not require such power, i.e., hardcore cartels. In recent cases, the Supreme Court and the TDLC held that the per se rule applies to the so called hardcore cartels (i.e., those referred to fixing purchase or sale prices, limiting production, allocating territories or quotas, or affecting

10. Public account of TDLC's President Enrique Vergara Vial, pp. 10–12, available in: https://www.tdlc.cl/wp-content/uploads/2021/05/Cuenta-P%C3%BAblica-2021-TDLC.pdf.
11. TDLC's Ruling No. 176 (2021), "Sindicato de Trabajadores Independientes Chile Taxi v Maxi Mobility Chile II SpA. and others" (pending appeal before the Supreme Court). Digital markets were also a relevant element of TDLC's decision lifting remedies to a radio owner, because the TDLC concluded that traditional radios and digital radios and online music platforms are part of the same relevant product market (both from the advertisers' and the consumers' perspectives). TDLC's Resolution No. 64/2021, "Consultation of Grupo Latino de Radiodifusión SpA to lift mitigation measures", para. 52.
12. Free translation of:

> "Se considerarán, entre otros, como hechos, actos o convenciones que impiden, restringen o entorpecen la libre competencia o que tienden a producir dichos efectos, los siguientes:
>
> a) Los acuerdos o prácticas concertadas que involucren a competidores entre sí, y que consistan en fijar precios de venta o de compra, limitar la producción, asignarse zonas o cuotas de mercado o afectar el resultado de procesos de licitación, así como los acuerdos o prácticas concertadas que, confiriéndoles poder de mercado a los competidores, consistan en determinar condiciones de comercialización o excluir a actuales o potenciales competidores."

the result of bidding processes), under which it would not be necessary to prove anticompetitive effects.[13]

Our case law has consistently held that collusion is the most serious and harmful conduct against competition.[14] As the Supreme Court explains: "of all behaviors which undermine competition, collusion constitutes the most reprehensible, the most serious, inasmuch as it involves the coordination of anticompetitive behavior of firms."[5]

According to the TDLC's most recent case law,[15] the following requirements must be proved to determine there is a collusion:

- *The existence of an agreement*: This agreement may be express or tacit, written or oral, of instant or delayed execution, formal or informal, including contracts, conventions, dealings, promises, understanding protocols, "gentlemen agreements", behavior guidelines, among others.[16]

  About this element, the Supreme Court has stated that hub & spoke schemes, collusive agreements, or concerted practices have the same essential core, that is, the adoption of a common rule that influences a competitive variable (in the case decided by the court, fixing prices).[17]
- *Involving competitors*: The agreement or concerted practice must include two or more competitors, but under current wording of Article 3 letter a) of DL 211 intervening parties that are not competitors might also be sanctioned. Although hub & spoke schemes have been condemned in Chile, so far noncompeting companies that are part of the collusion have not been sanctioned.[18]
- *The object of the agreement must be one or more competitive variables:* One or more of the following competitive variables might be the object of the agreement: fixing sale or purchase prices, limiting production, allocating territories or quotas, bid rigging, determining other commercialization conditions, or excluding current or potential competitors.

13. Supreme Court (2020), File No. 15005-2019, "FNE v CCNI S.A. and others", c. 27; and TDLC's Ruling No. 175 (2020), "FNE v. Sociedad de Transportes Avda. Alemania-P. Nuevo S.A. and others", c. 66. In TDLC's ruling there is an interesting minority vote by the two economist judges who argued that there is no per se rule in DL 211 and that even for hard-core cartels an effects analysis, albeit succinct, should be made, like a quick look rule (citing NCAA *v.* Board of Regents in the USA). TDLC's Ruling No. 175 (2020), minority vote.
14. TDLC's Ruling No. 148 (2015), "FNE v. Asfaltos Chilenos S.A. and others", c. 132; and TDLC's Ruling No. 175 (2020), "FNE v. Sociedad de Transportes Av.da Alemania-P. Nuevo S.A. and others", c. 135.
15. TDLC's Ruling No. 175 (2020), "FNE v. Sociedad de Transportes Avda. Alemania-P. Nuevo S.A. and others", c. 24.
16. *Ibid.*, c. 25.
17. Supreme Court (2015), Case No. 9361-2019 "FNE v Cencosud S.A. and others", c. 8. However, this case was brought by the FNE, and the *Supermarkets* were sanctioned by the TDLC and the Supreme Court, under the previous version of DL 211.
18. For example, in *Supermarkets*, colluded supermarkets were sanctioned, but the relevant providers (hubs) were not (in fact, they were not accused of collusion).

- *That conferred market power*: For agreements with the object of determining "other commercialization conditions" or excluding current or potential competitors,[19] the infringers must also have obtained market power.

The Supreme Court also recognized these elements, adding that there must also exist a "common will and decision to carry out the agreement," although such common will does not imply that the agreement must cause effects to be sanctioned, because the adoption of the agreement and the capability of producing anticompetitive effects is enough.[20]

The statute of limitations is generally three years from the execution of the anticompetitive conduct. In case of cartels, the statute of limitations will be five years from the extinction of the effects attributed to the conduct.

[B] Extraterritoriality

The TDLC has asserted jurisdiction over conducts executed abroad that produce effects in Chile. In this regard, the TDLC stated that:

> a position contrary to the one described above would generate the perverse incentive to leave unpunished those who, wanting to undermine competition in the Chilean markets, expressly adopt anti-competitive decisions or execute actions to implement them outside of Chile, traveling for such purpose to another country, or using media or intermediaries which are not located in Chile, in such regard, although the effects of these decisions and actions would affect our markets, there would be no submission to this Tribunal.[21]

That position was upheld by the Supreme Court, which in the same case affirmed that:

> taking into account that the purpose of the regulations contained in Legal Decree No. 211 is to protect free competition in Chile, it is clear that our courts do indeed have jurisdiction to judge those attacks which had an effect in Chile, or had the ability to have it, wherever the place they were executed or concluded. (...) Accepting this allegation of the appellant would imply that said infringement, which would have also affected Chile, could not be controlled, or punished by the country's courts. Thus, to the extent that the alleged collusive agreement denounced by the FNE reached the local market—through the implementation of concerted prices on the Chilean clients—and affected it, it is clear that the Chilean courts have the necessary authority to judge and punish said infringement.[22]

---

19. And also, for any agreement covered by previous versions of DL 211, before the amendment of Law No. 20,945.
20. Supreme Court (2020), Case No. 16986-2020 "FNE v Laboratorios Baxter and Sanderson", c. 4. In the same sense, Supreme Court (2020), Case No. 278-2019, "FNE vs Fresenius and others", c. 7 and, emphasizing the subjective element, Supreme Court (2016), Case No. 5128-2016, "FNE v. Asfaltos Chilenos S.A. and others", c. 7–8.
21. TDLC's Ruling N° 122 (2012), "FNE v. Tecumseh Do Brasil Ltda. and other", c. 6.
22. Supreme Court (2013), Case N° 5308-2012, "FNE v. Tecumseh Do Brasil Ltda. and other", c. 2.

Furthermore, Law No. 20.945 also modified Article 6 number 11 of the Organic Code of Courts, exceptionally subjecting to the Chilean jurisdiction, crimes and felonies committed abroad that constitute hardcore cartels and therefore, constitute criminal offenses according to Article 62 of DL 211.

[C] Investigations[23]

[1] Authorities

[a] Policy, Politics, and Institutions

The authority in charge of the investigation of competition infringements is the FNE, while the TDLC is the court that has the power to impose sanctions and measures.

According to Article 5 of DL 211, the TDLC is an independent jurisdictional body, subjected to Supreme Court's oversight which function is to prevent, correct and punish offenses to competition.[24]

The TDLC is currently comprised of five members: three lawyers and two economists. It is chaired by a lawyer appointed by the President of the Republic from a list of five candidates chosen by the Supreme Court. With respect to the other members, one of the lawyers and one of the economists are appointed by the Central Bank of Chile, and the others are appointed by the President of the Republic from a list of three candidates nominated by the Central Bank.

According to Article 18 of the DL 211, the TDLC has the following attributions and duties to protect and promote competition:

- To review, upon request of private parties (lawsuits) or the FNE (*requerimientos*), the acts that might constitute infringements to DL 211.
- To review, upon request by the FNE, the parties or a third-party with legitimate interest, facts, acts or contracts in force or to be executed, other than concentration transactions, as non-contentious matters that may infringe Competition Law. The TDLC may set forth the conditions that the relevant fact, act or contract must fulfill in order to be compliant with Competition Law.
- To issue general instructions in accordance with the law, which must be considered by private parties on their acts or contracts.[25]

23. Note that §13.02[C][1]; §13.02[C][2]; §13.02[D]; and §13.02[F] also apply to unilateral conducts unless expressly indicated otherwise.
24. Article 5 of DL 211.
25. The TDLC has issued four general instructions. There are two related to the instructions that municipalities must follow on solid waste market's bidding processes (General Instructions No. 1 of 2006 and No. 3 of 2013). The other two refer to telephony and telecommunications market, and the imposition of limits to differentiate between the price of on-net and off-net calls (General Instructions No. 2 of 2012 No. 4 of 2015). In addition, there are several instructions issued by the Resolutive Commission. Among others, some of the most relevant are: Decision No. 445, related to the air transportation market; Decision No. 488 related to the electricity market; Decisions Nos. 634, 638 and 729 related to the laboratories/pharmaceuticals market; and Decision No. 666 relating to credit interest rates, some of which are currently abrogated.

- To propose to the President of the Republic the amendment or abrogation of legal and regulatory provisions which may be contrary to Competition Law, and to propose the enactment of legal or regulatory provisions to encourage competition or to regulate certain activities which take place under non-competitive conditions.
- To know the special appeal (*recurso de revisión especial*) that the parties to a concentration transaction might submit against FNE's decision prohibiting such transaction.

In addition, there are special laws, e.g., the Public Ports Act,[26] which grant further powers to the TDLC.

According to Article 33 of DL 211, the FNE is a decentralized independent public service subject to the surveillance of the President of the Republic through the Ministry of Economy, Development, and Tourism. This agency has broad legal attributions to investigate potential anticompetitive conducts, to start legal procedures, and to represent the general interests of society in such matters.

The FNE is chaired by the national economic prosecutor, a lawyer designated by the President of the Republic. The national economic prosecutor can only be removed from his duties by the following causes: (i) the end of its legal period; (ii) voluntary resignation accepted by the President of the Republic; (iii) manifest negligence in the performance of his/her duties; or (iv) incapacity. The removal must be determined by the President of the Republic, with a favorable opinion by the Supreme Court, at the request of the Minister of Economy. The opinion of the Supreme Court must be issued by the court's plenary.

The FNE is currently organized in eight different divisions (i) Mergers, (ii) Litigation, (iii) Unilateral Abuses, (iv) Studies, (v) Administration and Finance, (vi) Cartels, (vii) Monitoring, and (viii) Institutional Relations and Leniency.

Among its powers and duties, the FNE can investigate potential infringements to DL 211, prosecute anticompetitive conducts before the TDLC and the Supreme Court, act as an amicus curiae in procedures in which it is not a party, and supervise the compliance with TDLC's, Supreme Court's and its own decisions. In addition, the FNE can reach out-of-court settlements with the companies subject to its investigations, conduct market studies and, similarly to TDLC's powers, propose to the President of the Republic the amendment, abrogation, or the enactment of legal or regulatory provisions.

Since the national economic prosecutor has independence from all authorities in the exercise of its duties, he/she may consequently defend the interests entrusted to him/her the manner deemed lawful, according to his/her own assessment. As a result, the FNE can determine its internal organization, its policies and priorities, and carry out different actions aimed to promote competition.

26. Article 14 of the Law No. 19452 (Public Ports Act) states that the Chilean State may grant concessions to private companies to operate the ports, if there is another port with similar characteristic in the same region. Otherwise, it will be necessary for a prior clearance from TDLC, which will regulate the concessions' conditions.

The FNE has issued guidelines to provide certain guidance in some relevant matters. The guidelines are not binding, but they constitute a significant reference for economic agents to develop their commercial activities. These guidelines are:

- Internal guidelines for the development of investigations ("*Internal Instructions*").[27]
- Internal guideline about leniency in collusion cases ("*Leniency Guideline*").[28]
- Guideline for the analysis of vertical restrains ("*Vertical Restraints Guideline*").[29]
- Internal guideline for the development of market studies.[30]
- Internal guideline for the exercise of criminal actions for collusion crime.[31]
- Internal guideline for the request of fines.[32]
- Guideline for the Analysis of Horizontal Concentrations ("*Horizontal Mergers Guidelines*").[33]

In addition to these guidelines, the FNE has issued some advocacy documents ("*Materiales de promoción*") which address several matters with the purpose of promoting competition. Some of these documents are:

- Public procurement and competition.[34]
- Trade associations and competition.[35]
- Forestry activities and free competition.[36]

27. "Instructivo interno para el desarrollo de investigaciones de la Fiscalía Nacional Económica", May 2013, available in https://www.fne.gob.cl/wp-content/uploads/2017/05/Instr._investi gaciones_2013.pdf.
28. "Guía Interna sobre Delación Compensada en Casos de Colusión", March 2017, available in: https://www.fne.gob.cl/wp-content/uploads/2017/03/Guia_Delacion_Compensada.pdf.
29. "Guía para el análisis de restricciones verticales" June 2014, available in https://www.fne.gob .cl/wp-content/uploads/2017/10/Gu%C3%ADa-Restricciones-Verticales.pdf.
30. "Guía Interna para el Desarrollo de Estudios de Mercado", October 2017, available in: https:// www.fne.gob.cl/wp-content/uploads/2017/10/Guia_Estudios_Mercado_Final_oct2017.pdf.
31. "Guía Interna para la Interposición de Querellas por el Delito de Colusión", June 2018, available in: https://www.fne.gob.cl/wp-content/uploads/2018/06/Gu%C3%ADa-de-Querellas-final-definitiva.pdf.
32. "Guía Interna para Solicitudes de Multa de la Fiscalía Nacional Económica", August 2019, available in: https://www.fne.gob.cl/wp-content/uploads/2019/08/Gu%C3%ADa-de-multas. pdf.
33. "Guía para el Análisis de Operaciones de Concentración Horizontales", May 2021, published for comments, available in: https://www.fne.gob.cl/wp-content/uploads/2021/05/Guia-para-el-Analisis-de-Operaciones-de-Concentracion-Horizontales-mayo-VF.pdf. This Guideline was prepared to replace the old 2012 Horizontal Mergers Guideline.
34. "Compras Públicas y Libre Competencia" (Material de Promoción No. 1), April 2011, available in: https://www.fne.gob.cl/wp-content/uploads/2017/10/Material-de-Promoci%C3%B3n-1-Compras-p%C3%BAblicas-Abr2011-1.pdf.
35. "Asociaciones Gremiales y Libre Competencia" (Material de Promoción No. 2), August 2011, available in: https://www.fne.gob.cl/wp-content/uploads/2011/08/guia_-asociaciones_-gremiales.pdf.
36. "Las Actividades Silvoagropecuarias y la Libre Competencia", December 2011, available in: https://www.fne.gob.cl/wp-content/uploads/2011/12/dip.uagricola.pdf.

- Competition compliance programs.[37]
- Public sector and competition.[38]
- Report on minority shareholdings and interlocking between competitors.[39]
- Compilation of old investigations regarding school uniforms, supplies and textbook markets,[40] and health industry.[41]

Finally, in exercise of the power to conduct market studies introduced by Law 20,945, the FNE is currently carrying out studies about some markets[42] and has issued several studies related to diverse industries.[43] All these market studies have ended in legal or regulatory recommendations to the President of the Republic.

[b] Resources and Priorities

The FNE's resources are determined by law. In order to allocate them efficiently, the FNE has discretionary power to prioritize tasks, and it has mentioned that its focus is mainly on cases that may produce relevant effects on the market. In this regard, the FNE has sometimes announced its priorities on specifics markets, e.g., energy, private health, etc. In any case, cartel cases are on top of the list, and there is a specialized division dealing with cartels.

[c] Inter-agency Cooperation (International)

The cooperation between the FNE and other agencies is not limited to cartel cases. The FNE is continuously participating in international *forae* and activities related to competition legislation and policy aiming to develop reciprocal collaboration with other agencies of the world and adopting the best international practices.

In exercise of Article 39 letter l) of DL 211, the FNE has signed several International Cooperation Agreements with the competition agencies of Colombia,

37. "Programas de Cumplimiento de la Normativa de Libre Competencia" (Material de Promoción No. 2), June 2012, available in: https://www.fne.gob.cl/wp-content/uploads/2012/06/Programas-de-Cumplimiento.pdf.
38. "Sector Público y Libre Competencia, Evaluando sus Actuaciones desde la Perspectiva de la Competencia", June 2012, available in: https://www.fne.gob.cl/wp-content/uploads/2012/06/Guia-final-sector-publico.pdf.
39. "Participaciones Minoritarias y Directores Comunes entre Empresas Competidoras", November 2013, available in: https://www.fne.gob.cl/wp-content/uploads/2013/11/Participaciones-minoritarias.pdf.
40. "Criterios de Libre Competencia en el Mercado de Uniformes, Útiles y Textos Escolares", January 2015, available in: https://www.fne.gob.cl/wp-content/uploads/2015/02/prom_01_2015.pdf.
41. "Recopilación de las Investigaciones de la Fiscalía Nacional Económica: Una Mirada de Libre Competencia a Ciertos Aspectos de la Industria de la Salud", February 2016, available in: https://www.fne.gob.cl/wp-content/uploads/2016/02/Informe-de-Salud.pdf.
42. For example, a study about the funeral market started on December 21, 2021.
43. Such as pension annuities, notaries, school textbooks, remedies, public procurement and gas market. All available in: https://www.fne.gob.cl/estudios-de-mercado/estudios/estudios-de-mercados-actuales/.

Peru, Brazil, Canada, Costa Rica, Ecuador, El Salvador, United States, Mexico, and Spain.[44] In addition, even though they are not strictly limited to the FNE, the Free Trade Agreements and Economic Complementation Agreements (FTA) currently in force between Chile and many countries,[45] contain competition law provisions which impose upon Chile a number of obligations in competition matters. Finally, in terms of international *forae*, the FNE has contributed with the Organization for Economic Cooperation and Development (OECD) and has been part of different workgroups of the International Competition Network (ICN).[46]

The cooperation with other agencies has been relevant in past cartel cases,[47] providing the FNE with relevant information on its investigations.

[2] Procedure

In this topic it is relevant to differentiate between the procedural issues related to the FNE's investigations and the lawsuits filed before the TDLC.

[a] Procedure Before the FNE

The FNE has the powers set up in Article 39 of DL 211 to carry on its investigations and follows its Internal Instructions. The Internal Instructions regulate the process, timeframe, and other aspects of FNE's investigations.

According to the Internal Instructions, an investigation may be initiated ex officio or by a complaint. If a complaint is submitted to the FNE, an admissibility test[48] must be performed which, in principle, cannot exceed four months.[49] The Internal Instructions do not establish a deadline to conclude the investigations, but according to its paragraph 38, they should be conducted within a reasonable period.[50]

44. For further information, *see* https://www.fne.gob.cl/internacional/acuerdos-de-cooperacion/.
45. For example, FTA Chile-Canada, FTA Chile-Central America, FTA Chile-USA, FTA Chile-Mexico, FTA Chile- Peru, ECA Chile-MERCOSUR, FTA Chile-Republic of Korea, Economic Association Agreement Chile-Japan, Transpacific Strategic Economic Partnership Agreement Chile-New Zealand, Brunei Darussalam and Singapore, FTA Chile-Australia, Economic Association Agreement Chile-European Union, and the FTA Chile-EFTA. Some of these agreements (e.g., Transpacific Strategic Economic Partnership Agreement between Chile, New Zealand, Brunei Darussalam and Singapore, and Economic Association Agreement between Chile and the European Union) establish the obligation to inform to the other parties of an application of the law that could affect its interest.
46. For further information, *see*: https://www.fne.gob.cl/internacional/foros-internacionales/oecd/. In the past the FNE made some contributions to activities of the Asia Pacific Economic Cooperation (APEC).
47. For example, in the *Car Carriers* case, already decided by the Supreme Court.
48. The FNE may not initiate an investigation, when (i) the complaint relates to acts or conventions that are not or may not appear as constituting breaches of DL 211; (ii) the conduct should be known by other government agencies; (iii) the action is time-barred; (iv) there is not enough evidence; or (v) it seems unjustified to initiate an investigation. Internal Instructions, para. 28.
49. This term may be extended by valid justification, for a period that could not exceed two months. Guidelines, paras. 25–27.
50. Considering (i) its nature; (ii) the merits of the proceeding; (iii) the scope or complexity of the specific case; (iv) the lack of collaboration by the affected parties or third parties; and in general

Article 39 of DL 211 establishes that the FNE has, among others, the following attributions during its investigations: (i) subject to TDLC's authorization, not to inform the start of an investigation to an affected (investigated) party; (ii) to determine that an investigation is under reserve, subject to communicating such decision to TDLC's president; (iii) to request collaboration and information by public entities; (iv) to request information from any individual or private entity (investigated parties and third-parties); (v) to summon or request a written declaration by the representatives, managers, consultants, employees, and executives of the entities or persons that could have knowledge of facts, acts, or conventions relevant to the investigations (investigated parties and third-parties); (vi) to declare as confidential pieces of the investigation's case file;[51] and (vii) to request support from the Police.

In addition, since 2009,[52] the FNE has special intrusive powers in the investigations relating to collusion, which has used in several cases with and without leniency applications, which include:

- Entering public or private premises, if necessary, aided by public force.
- Registering and seizing all types of objects and documents that may prove the existence of an infringement.
- Authorizing the wiretapping of all types of communications.
- Ordering to any company that offers communication services to provide copies and records of communications transmitted or received.

DL 211 sets forth that these attributions may be used by the FNE only in serious and qualified cases, after an authorization granted by a Judge of the Court of Appeals of Santiago with prior approval by the TDLC. The authorization must precisely specify the measures, its duration, and the persons who will be affected by it.[53]

(v) all the circumstances that may determine the exercise of its powers and the accomplishment of the FNE's duties in the case. Internal Instructions, para. 38.

51. If (i) it is necessary to protect the identity of the persons that have declared or submitted information before the FNE according to leniency procedure, (ii) the file has formulas, strategies, trade secrets or any other element which revealed could significantly affect the competitive development of their owner, or (iii) if it is necessary to safeguard the efficiency of the investigation. Article 39, letter a) paragraph three of DL 211.
52. As mentioned earlier, the bill submitted by the government in 2020 proposes to give additional investigative powers to the FNE for collusion cases, such as requesting the lifting of the banking secrecy and photographing, filming, and recording individuals.
53. The exercise of these attributions by the FNE has led to some procedural issues, which have been dealt with by the courts. For instance, in *Poultry Meat*, one of the defendants requested the Court of Appeals to obtain the restitution of the documents seized by the FNE during the investigation, arguing that its possession by the FNE, once the latter filed a lawsuit before the TDLC, affected its right to defense, since it could not know the content of the seized documents. The court ruled in favor of the defendant. Ruling of the Court of Appeals of Santiago, Case No. 2440-2012 "Asociacion de productores avicolas de Chile A.G v. FNE." Current practice allows the investigated parties (as well as third-parties) to request, during the relevant investigation, copy of the documents and information seized by the FNE, and the parties to a judicial procedure should also have access to it (although the FNE does not normally submits its investigation case file together with its lawsuit). There are some complications with such access, given the need to safeguard confidential information and, hence, of producing public versions that have sensitive information redacted.

According to the Internal Instructions, an FNE's investigation may conclude by:

- The submission of a lawsuit before the TDLC.
- The submission of a consultation in a non-contentious procedure before the TDLC.
- An out-of-court settlement pursuant to Article 39 ñ) of DL 211 that must be approved by TDLC.
- The submission to the TDLC of a request to issue general instructions or a report according to a sector-specific law.[54]
- A decision closing the investigation.[55]

[b] *Procedures Before the TDLC*

Articles 18–30 of DL 211 regulate the contentious procedure designed to deal with offenses against competition, such as collusion, abuse of dominant position, predatory practices, and failure to comply with certain of the merger control rules.

According to Articles 18 and 20, the contentious procedure may be initiated by a lawsuit filed by the FNE (*requerimiento*) or any person with a legitimate interest (*demanda*). The TDLC cannot act ex officio in relation to contentious procedures about potential infringements to DL 211.

When a lawsuit has been filed, the defendant has between fifteen and thirty business days to respond. Once the defendant has submitted its response, or if the deadline for responding has elapsed, Article 22 of DL 211 sets forth that the TDLC may open a settlement stage between the parties (normally, summoning them to a hearing). Settlements are fairly common in non-collusion cases but are rare in collusion cases.

If the settlement fails, or the TDLC does not consider pertinent to open the settlement stage, it will start an evidentiary term of twenty days. After such period, public hearings shall be held. Finally, the TDLC will have forty-five days to render its decision.[56]

54. The Internal Instructions, that has not been updated since the enactment of Law 20,945, also consider the possibility of the FNE requesting the TDLC to propose to the President of the Republic enactments, amendments or the abrogation of legal or regulatory provisions, but this alternative seems unlikely now that the FNE has the power to make such proposals directly.
55. In particular, in the following cases: (i) when the existence of facts, acts or conventions that constitute violations of DL 211 (or the participation in the same of one or more natural or legal persons), cannot be proven; (ii) when there are no sufficient facts in the investigation that allow for bringing an action before the TDLC or courts of justice; (iii) when the matter has been object of a prior decision of the TDLC or courts of justice; (iv) when there has been a change in circumstances, so that effects against Competition are no longer observed; (v) when there are reasons of efficiency and efficacy to conclude the investigation considering the nature of the investigation, the persons affected, and the effects on the markets; and (vi) when the investigation does not appear proportional or justifiable to protect the general interest of the society or competition in the market. Internal Instructions, para. 88.
56. On average, the TDLC takes 97 days to issue its judgments, so the legal deadline is normally not met by the TDLC ("¿Cuánto tarda el Tribunal de Defensa de la Libre Competencia y la Corte Suprema en Resolver Asuntos de Libre Competencia? CeCO UAI, p.8), but there are no sanctions associated to its breach.

The average duration of this procedure is approximately twenty months before the TDLC, and for collusion cases, this may go up to approximately thirty months.[57]

[D] Sanctions and Remedies

[1] Administrative Sanctions

Article 26 of DL 211 allows the TDLC to impose different administrative sanctions, i.e., the modification or termination of acts, contracts, covenants, systems, or agreements and the dissolution of partnerships, corporations, and other private entities that intervened in the aforementioned acts,[58] on top of the application of other type of preventive, corrective, or prohibitive measures pursuant to Article 3 of DL 211.[59]

Article 26 letter of DL 211 also allows the TDLC to impose fines[60] of up to 30% of the sales of the offender corresponding to the product or service line related to the infraction during the period in which the offense was perpetrated, or up to double the economic benefit gained from the infraction; and when it is not possible to determine the amount of the sales or the economic benefit, the fines can go up to UTA 60,000 (approximately USD 50.1 million). There have been only a few rulings applying the new provisions on the applicable fines introduced by the Law No. 20,945,[61] and only one about collusion: *Temuco Transport* in which the total fines imposed to the 11 companies was approximately UTA 1,200 (approximately USD 1 million). In this case, albeit the TDLC did not have detailed information about the sales or the economic benefit, it calculated the fines starting from the base amount requested by the FNE (but prorated it according to each infringer's market share), recognizing as mitigating factors the intervention of public authorities, the absence of previous convictions, the

---

57. "¿Cuánto tarda el Tribunal de Defensa de la Libre Competencia y la Corte Suprema en Resolver Asuntos de Libre Competencia?, CeCO UAI, pp. 6–7 and 10–11.
58. Article 26 states that:

    (…) In the final ruling, the Tribunal can adopt the following measures:

    a) Modify or terminate acts, contracts, covenants, systems or agreements contrary to the provisions of this law;
    b) Order the modification or dissolution of partnerships, corporations and other legal persons of private law that could have intervened in the acts, contracts, covenants, systems or agreements referred to in the previous letter (…).

59. TDLC standard and consistent current practice is to impose the obligation to adopt a competition law compliance program to the colluded companies. *See*, e.g., *Temuco Transport*.
60. To determine the fines, DL 211 considers, among others, the following circumstances: (i) the economic benefit obtained as a result of the violation; (ii) the severity of the conduct; (iii) the deterrence effect; (iv) recidivism, having been sanctioned for competition infringements in the last 10 years; (v) the economic situation of the infringer; and (vi) the collaboration the infringer provided to FNE before or during the investigation.
61. *See*, for example, TDLC's Ruling No. 173 (2020), "FNE v. Asociación Nacional de Fútbol Profesional (ANFP)". Although the Supreme Court criticized TDLC's methodology to calculate the fine, it upheld the ruling. Supreme Court (2021), Case No. 94.189-2020.

early withdrawal from the collusion (before FNE filed its lawsuit), and the collaboration with the FNE.[62] This approach is generally aligned with FNE's methodology and parameters contained in its Internal Guideline for the request of fines.

The fines can be imposed to the corresponding legal entity,[63] its directors, managers, and to every individual that intervened in the relevant infringement.[64] Fines to individuals have been imposed in several cases.[65]

In addition, Law No. 20,945 introduced an additional sanction for collusion cases: prohibition to celebrate contracts with state organisms, companies in which the state makes contributions, National Congress and the judiciary, as well as being awarded with any state concession, for up to five years. So far, this sanction has not been applied.

[2] Criminal Sanctions

Since the last reform, DL 211 establishes criminal liability for some hardcore cartels, specifically to the individuals "who execute or order the execution, carry out or organize an agreement involving two or more competitors among them, for fixing sale or purchase price of goods and services in one or more markets; restricting its output or supply; divide, allocate or distribute territories or market shares; or affect the result of biddings organized by public companies, private providers of public services or public organisms."[66] The applicable sanctions are from three years and one day of imprisonment up to ten years of imprisonment (including effective imprisonment of at least one year) and the disqualification to hold the position of director or manager of a listed corporation (or corporations subject to the rules of listed corporations), of state-owned companies or those in which the state has an interest; or of a professional association or union. Until now no criminal prosecution has started because, based on

62. TDLC's Ruling No. 175 (2020), "FNE v. Sociedad de Transportes Avda. Alemania-P. Nuevo S.A. and others", c. 128–143.
63. In case of fines imposed to legal entities, their directors, managers and the individuals who benefited from the relevant act are severally and jointly liable, as long as they intervened in the corresponding infringement.
64. The fines imposed to individuals cannot be paid by the legal entity or company employing them or by its shareholders or partners. In addition, the fine cannot be paid by any other entity of the same business group, its shareholders or partners.
65. *See*, e.g., TDLC's Rulings Nos. 145 (2015), "FNE v. Asociación Gremial de Ginecólogos Obstetras de la Provincia de Ñuble and others"; 133 (2014) "FNE v. Pullman Bus Costa Central and others"; and 128 (2013), "FNE v. ACHAP A.G. and others"; 74 (2008), "FNE v. AM Patagonia S.A. and others".
66. Free translation of:

> "El que celebre u ordene celebrar, ejecute u organice un acuerdo que involucre a dos o más competidores entre sí, para fijar precios de venta o de compra de bienes o servicios en uno o más mercados; limitar su producción o provisión; dividir, asignar o repartir zonas o cuotas de mercado; o afectar el resultado de licitaciones realizadas por empresas públicas, privadas prestadoras de servicios públicos, u órganos públicos...".

Before such reform, no express criminal liability existed for anticompetitive behaviors, but there were a couple of unsuccessful attempts to apply provisions of the Criminal Code (articles 285 and 286) to cartels, particularly to executives involved in *Pharmacies*, which were acquitted.

the current Competition Law, the criminal case can only start after the TDLC and/or the Supreme Court have condemned a cartel. Since the law 20,945 was enacted in August 2016, there is still some time before the first cartel cases are criminally prosecuted, but some cases of a collusion that occurred after the entry into force of such law have been submitted by the FNE, e.g., *Valuables Transport*.

[3] Private Actions and Follow-On Actions

According to DL 211, the FNE and any other interested party (individuals and private or public entities) may file a lawsuit before the TDLC, for alleged collusion or other anticompetitive conducts.

The TDLC and the Supreme Court have stated that in order to have *locus standi* the plaintiff must be affected by the anticompetitive conduct:

> To consider an economic agent a direct victim of an offence against free competition, it must have current or potential participation in the market directly affected by the anticompetitive activity of other economic agents or have current or potential participation in other related markets that would be reasonably affected in an indirect manner by the alleged unlawful activity.[67]

Applying such standard, the TDLC has recently affirmed that a company that did not participated in a particular tender process but is active in the market related to it, has standing to file a lawsuit for practices that allegedly affected such tender and market.[68] Also, the Supreme Court, revoking a TDLC's decision, has stated that consumer associations are allowed to file actions for alleged exclusionary abuses.[69]

Concerning damage actions, the current version of Article 30 of DL 211 allows any economic agent affected by an anticompetitive conduct to seek compensation for damages before the TDLC, in a summary procedure, based on the ruling issued by the TDLC itself.[70] Damages actions have a four-year statute of limitations counted from the

---

67. Free translation of:

> (...) para que un agente económico pueda ser considerado victima directa de un atentado en contra de la libre competencia, ha de participar actual o potencialmente en el mercado que es directamente afectado por la presente actividad anticompetitiva de otro agente económico, o bien en otros mercados conexos que puedan razonablemente verse afectados en forma indirecta por esa actividad supuestamente antijurídica.

TDLC's Ruling No. 98 (2010), "Fundación Chile Ciudadano and other v. VTR B.A. Chile S.A.", c. 18. This criterion was confirmed by the Supreme Court when it upheld TDLC's Ruling (Supreme Court (2016), Case No. 2680-2010, "Fundación Chile Ciudadano and other v. VTR B.A. Chile S.A. ", c. 4) and, more recently, by the TDLC (TDLC's Ruling, "Constructora Denco Limitada v. Servicio de Salud de Osorno", c. 3).

68. TDLC's Ruling No. 168 (2019), "Constructora Denco Limitada v. Servicio de Salud de Osorno", c. 4–6.
69. Supreme Court (2016), "Conadecus v. Telefónica Móviles Chile S.A. and others", Case No. 11.363-2015, c. 8–10.
70. Despite the wording of Article 30 of DL 211, the Supreme Court has distinguished whether a damages lawsuit is filed (i) based on TDLC's ruling or (ii) if such ruling is only referenced as background information, only concluding that in the first situation the TDLC is the exclusive

date that the ruling becomes final, and the compensation must cover all the damages caused during the period of the infringement.

Regarding class actions for damage, Law 20,945 modified Article 51 No. 10 of Law 19,946, expressly allowing class actions to be filed before the TDLC when the consumers' collective or diffuse interest is affected.[71] Such actions can be filed by the National Consumer Service (hereinafter, "Sernac") or consumer associations.

Based on the newly granted power to know follow-on actions, nine damages procedures have been started before the TDLC, but so far none of these have ended through a definitive ruling. Of these, two were filed by a competitor affected by the collusion,[72] and the rest were lodged due to collusions that affected consumers.[73] Furthermore, Sernac started, in virtue of one of its new attributions, collective voluntary procedures to reach a settlement with two of the companies involved in the *Supermarkets* collusion, but settlements were not agreed so that Sernac opted to file a lawsuit before the TDLC.[74]

---

competent court, leaving the matter of the competent court for the second scenario open. Supreme Court, Case No. 11667-2019 "ODECU vs Empresa de Transportes Rurales Tur Bus SpA", c. 9. In fact, the possibility of a general Civil Court knowing damage actions that reference a TDLC's ruling as background was expressly accepted by a minority vote of the Appeal Court in this same procedure. Ruling of the Court of Appeals of Santiago, Case No. 2419-2019 (Civil) "ODECU v. Empresa de Transportes Rurales Tur Bus SpA.", minority vote (1-2).

Furthermore, on procedures started before the last amendment to DL 211, (i) Supreme Court even admitted the submission to a local Civil Court (in charge of follow-on actions at the time) of a lawsuit for an infringement to Consumer Law due to the same facts of Poultry Meat collusion before the TDLC had declared the existence of such collusion (Supreme Court, Case No. 62144-2016 "Sernac v. S.C.A Chile S.A."); and (ii) the Supreme Court ordered the compensation for pecuniary and moral damage based on general torts despite the same behaviors that gave rise to torts were not considered an abuse of dominance (Supreme Court (2011), Case 3516-2009, "Sociedad Agrícola Río Sur Ltda. y Otro con Amín Merino Carlos Fernando y Otro"), thus recognizing some kind of standalone action when these are not based on Competition Law infringements, but on breaches to other laws such as Civil Code or Consumer Protection Act, even if the underlying conduct is the same.

71. Before the amendment to DL 211, there was no clear provision on this matter, although regarding *Pharmacies* collusion, follow-on actions submitted by Sernac on behalf of consumers' interests were admitted to procedure. Ruling of the Court of Appeals of Santiago, Case No. 3908-2013 "SERNAC v. Farmacias Ahumada and others."
72. "Sandra Fuentes Salazar and others v. Empresa de Transporte Rurales Limitada and others", Case No. CIP-1-2017 (lawsuit withdrawn, *Buses*); and "Papelera Cerrillos S.A. v CMPC Tissue and other", Case No. CIP-3-2020 (ongoing, *Tissue*).
73. Five by consumers' associations: "CONADECUS v Agrosuper S.A. and others", Case No. CIP-2-2010 (ongoing, *Poultry Meat*); "Agrecu v. Cencosud S.A. and others", Case No. CIP-5-2020 (ongoing, *Supermarkets*); "Arcam v NYK and others", Case No. CIP-6-2020 (ongoing, *Car Carriers*); "Conadecus v. Walmart Chile S.A.", Case No. CIP-8-2021 (ongoing, Supermarkets); and "Conadecus v. SMU S.A.", Case No. CIP-10-2021; and two by Sernac: "Sernac v. Cencosud S.A.", Case No. CIP-7-2020 (ongoing, *Supermarkets*); and "Sernac v. SMU S.A. and Walmart Chile S.A.", Case No. CIP-9-2021 (ongoing, *Supermarkets*).
74. Procedures started through exempted Resolution Nos. 875 (2019) and 496 (2020) (https://www.sernac.cl/portal/609/w3-propertyvalue-64485.html#recuadros_articulo_1768_group_pvid_66422), ended on August 2021 (https://www.sernac.cl/portal/604/w3-article-63111.html), and then Sernac filed a lawsuit that derived in Case No. CIP-9-2021 (*see supra* n. 73).

Under the old system in which damage actions derived from antitrust offenses were decided by general civil courts, only a handful of cases associated to collusions existed:[75]

- *Tissue*: Sernac, two consumers' associations and one of the involved companies reached a settlement,[76] while there is still a pending appeal regarding the rejection of the lawsuit against the other company. This is the first collective compensation settlement and was agreed even before the condemnatory ruling for infringement to Competition Law was issued.
- *Poultry Meat*: Sernac and a consumers' association filed lawsuits based on the condemnatory ruling for infringement to Competition Law before general Civil Courts, but both actions were rejected.[77]
- *Pharmacies*: After a judgment ordering the payment of a compensation by the colluded companies, two of them settled with Sernac and three consumer

75. Also, few damage actions were brought for infringements other than collusion, such as (i) predatory pricing: Court of Appeals of Santiago (2004), Case No. 5954-1999 (Civil), "Pivcevic Rajcevis Andrés Nicolás v. LAN Chile S.A." (ordering the payment of consequential damages and loss of profits but not moral damage, although the case is mixed with collusion allegations); Santiago Civil Court No. 26 (2009), Cases Nos. C-13727-2007 "Cementa S.A. v. James Hardie Fibrocementos Ltda" and C-191-2007 (one judgment in favor of the defendant and one against it, but both settled while the appeals were pending); and Court of Appeals of Santiago (2010), Case No. 6721-2009 (Civil) "TV Cable Loncomilla S.A. v. Ricardo Barra Yates and others" (ordering the payment of consequential damages and loss of profits); and (ii) abuse of dominance: Santiago Civil Court No. 10 (2005), Case No C-782-2004, "Sound Color v. United International Pictures Chile" (rejected because TDLC acquitted the defendant from the alleged abuse); Court of Appeals of Santiago (2011); Case No. 1520-2010, "Philip Morris Chile Comercializadora Limitada v. Compañía Chilena de Tabacos S.A." (ordering the payment of loss of profits only); Court of Appeals of Santiago (2014), Case No. 2957-2013 (Civil), "Rivas Morel, María Luz con Sociedad Educacional American British School" (ordering the payment of consequential damages and loss of profits but not moral damages); Santiago Civil Court No. 20 (2015), Case No. C-24288-2012 "ETCOM S.A. v. Telefónica Moviles de Chile S.A.", Santiago Civil Court No. 22 (2015), Case No. C-20891-2013, "OPS Ingeniería Limitada v. Telefónica Móviles Chile S.A.", and Court of Appeals of Santiago, Case No 661-2015, "Interlink Global Chile Ltda. v. Telefónica Móviles de Chile S.A", (one judgment in favor of the defendant and two against it); and Court of Appeals of Santiago (2018), Case No. 1110-2016 (Civil) "Voissnet S.A. v. Telefónica Chile S.A." (ordering the payment of loss profits, pending appeal before Supreme Court).
76. *See* resolution dated April 1, 2017 and settlement document of January 27, 2017 (submitted at Court on February 20, 2017) of Santiago Civil Court No. 10, Case No. 29214-2015, "Conadecus v. CMPC Tissue and other"; and, given the appeals submitted by other parties, the resolutions of Court of Appeals of Santiago dated September 1, 2017 (Case No. 5731-2017 (Civil)) and of Supreme Court of May 17, 2018 (Case No. 44484-2017).
77. Santiago Civil Court No. 29, Case No. C-28470-2015, "Sernac v. Agrícola Agrosuper and others" (rejected due to absence of contractual relationship between the companies and the consumers and inappropriateness of collective procedure of Consumer Law to seek compensation for infringements to Competition Law); and Santiago Civil Court No. 17, Case no. C-27058-2015, "Conadecus v. Agrícola Agrosuper and others" (rejected due the incompetence of the Court to know the action). One of the follow-on damage procedures currently in progress before the TDLC based on the new version of article 30 of DL 211 is related to *Poultry Meat* collusion ("CONADECUS vs Agrosuper S.A. and others", Case No. CIP-2-2010, *see supra* n. 73 and accompanying text).

associations,[78] while there are appeals pending regarding the third pharmacy. These are the first collective compensation judgment and settlement based on a previous condemnatory ruling for infringement to Competition Law. The settlement is the first instance in which the "Cy-près distribution" or "fluid recovery" mechanism is used to compensate the diffuse damage suffered by the unidentifiable consumers that were not able to purchase the products.

[E] Leniency

In 2009, Law No. 20,361 created Article 39 bis of DL 211 introducing a leniency program to combat collusions. This was subsequently modified by Law 20,945. The current version grants (i) to the first applicant an exemption to the fine and to the dissolution of the involved legal entity, and an exemption from criminal liability based on Article 62 of DL 211 to individuals,[79] and (ii) to the second applicant, it reduces the fine up to 50% and the criminal penalty up to one grade.[80]

To obtain these benefits, the applicant must fulfill the following requirements:

- provide precise, truthful, and verifiable background information representing an effective contribution to produce enough evidence to sustain a lawsuit before the TDLC;[81]
- maintain the application confidential until the FNE has filed the lawsuit or has ordered to close the investigation, unless the FNE expressly authorizes its disclosure; and
- terminate its participation in the cartel immediately after submitting its application.

The TDLC may not grant the leniency if it determines that the applicant organized the cartel and forced the other parties to participate. Applying this rule, the Supreme Court revoked the benefit granted to one of the two companies involved in the *Tissue* case, because such company "not only organized the collusive agreement under examination, but also exercised economic coercion over its competitor PISA in order to lead it to become part of it and, later on, to ensure its permanence in it."[82]

---

78. *See* resolutions dated November 13 and 25, 2020 of Santiago Civil Court No. 10, Case No. 1940-2013, "Sernac v. Farmacias Cruz Verde S.A. and others".
79. Individuals awarded with this benefit might be executives, employees, workers, consultants, or representatives of a legal entity applicant; executives, employees, workers, consultants, or representatives of such entities making an independent application (in which case no benefit is received by the legal entities); or individuals that are economic undertakings in the market (in which case its executives, workers, consultants, or representatives may also be benefited). Leniency Guideline, paras. 15–17.
80. Individuals can be the same as the ones awarded with criminal liability exemption (*see supra* n. 79).
81. According to the FNE, this is the case, in general when the evidence or indicia is capable of proving the collusion or enables the FNE to justify the exercise of any of the powers established in Article 39 letter n) of the DL 211 (intrusive powers). Leniency Guideline, para. 53 (6).
82. Free translation of:

In the criminal procedure, Article 63 of DL 211 sets forth that the involved parties are obliged to provide to the criminal prosecutor and court the same background information submitted to the FNE, and the individual must declare as witness.

Complementing the Competition Law, the FNE issued a Leniency Guideline setting out the following statements that, on top of those related to the legal requirements, must be made by the applicant to obtain the leniency benefit:[83]

- That it understands it must fulfill all the requirements to which the granting of the benefits is subject to and accept the terms and conditions of this guideline.
- That it will collaborate with the FNE during its investigation and before the TDLC, as well as in the subsequent criminal investigation and procedure (if any).
- That it neither organized the collusive conduct nor coerced others into entering it.

Up to October 2021, eight leniency cases have been disclosed: (i) *Refrigerators Compressors*, whereby the TDLC acknowledged full immunity to Tecumseh do Brasil Ltda.; (ii) Ruling N. 133-2014,[59] whereby the TDLC acknowledged the full immunity to Atevil Mecánica Diesel S.A.; (iii) *Asphalt*, whereby the TDLC acknowledged the full immunity to Enex; (iv) *Tissue*,[84] whereby the TDLC acknowledged the full immunity to CMPC Tissue (then revoked by Supreme Court) and a reduction in the applicable fine to SCA Chile (formerly PISA, now called Essity); (v) *Medicine Vials*, whereby the TDLC acknowledged the full immunity to Biosano S.A.; (vi) *Car Carriers*, whereby the TDLC acknowledged the full immunity to Compañía Sudamericana de Vapores and a reduction in the applicable fine to Nippon Yusen Kabushiki Kaisha; (vii) on December 2019, in *Salmon Feed*, the FNE filed a leniency-based lawsuit against a group of four salmon feed producers, requesting full immunity for one of the defendants;[85] and (viii) on October 2021, in *Valuables Transport*, the FNE filed a leniency-based lawsuit against three companies of transport of cash and other valuables and six executives of such companies, requesting full immunity for one of the executives.[86]

> no sólo organizó el acuerdo colusorio en examen, sino que, además, ejerció coacción de carácter económico sobre su competidor PISA a fin de conducirlo a formar parte de él y, más adelante, a asegurar su permanencia en el mismo.

Supreme Court, Case No. 63600-2019, "FNE v. CMPC and SCA Chile", c. 35. Supreme Court did not grant the first applicant leniency benefit to the coerced competitor (which was the second leniency applicant).

83. Leniency Guidelines, para. 53.
84. In the context of the *Tissue* leniency and investigation, the FNE found out an alleged collusion in the diapers market, but the action to pursue such conduct was time-barred. FNE's Closing Report (2016), Case No. 2362-15, "Reserved Investigation".
85. "FNE v. Biomar Chile S.A. and others", Case No. C-386-2019. FNE also conducted dawn raids.
86. "FNE v. Brinks S.A. and others", Case No. C-430-2021. FNE also conducted dawn raids.

[F] Appeal

Article 27 of DL 211 sets forth that any of the parties, including the FNE, may file a special appeal (*recurso de reclamación*) against the TDLC's ruling, which shall be decided by the Supreme Court. The appeal must be filed within ten business days from the ruling's notification, and the procedure before the Supreme Court has a duration of approximately fourteen months, regardless of the nature of the alleged infringement.[87]

[G] Precedent Cases

Some of the most relevant collusion rulings are the following:

- *Temuco Transport*: The TDLC condemned several passenger public transport companies for having jointly determined the maximum number of buses in their fleets (i.e., limit production in the market) and imposed fines between 20.6 UTA and 160.5 UTA (approximately between USD 17,000 and USD 134,000).[88] This is the first collusion case in which the new rules to determine fines are applied, but there are appeals pending before the Supreme Court.
- *Car Carriers*: The TDLC declared that three companies agreed to respect accounts/clients for the deep sea transportation of vehicles in the Europe and/or American routes (but not for all the routes/companies accused by the FNE), acknowledged the fine exemption for the first leniency applicant and the reduction in the applicable fine for the second applicant, imposing to the latter a fine of 7,615 UTA (approximately USD 6.4 million), and imposed a fine of 2,894 UTA (approximately USD 2.4 million) to the third company.[89] The Supreme Court partially overturned TDLC's ruling, deciding there was also a collusion between five companies (four of which were not sanctioned by the TDLC) for one specific account/client in the Asia route (but not for all the accounts/clients of this route accused by the FNE) and imposing fines between 3,818 UTA (for the second leniency applicant, on top of the one imposed by the TDLC, approximately 3.2 million) and 10,517 UTA (approximately USD 8.8 million).[90]
- *Supermarkets*: The TDLC condemned three supermarket chains for being part of an agreement or concerted practice to fix, through their providers, poultry meat supermarkets' retail price equal or above its wholesale price and imposed fines between 3,438 UTA (approximately USD 2.9 million) and 5,766 UTA (approximately USD 4.8 million) to the three companies.[91] The Supreme Court generally doubled the fines imposed and, particularly for Walmart, it decided

87. "¿Cuánto tarda el Tribunal de Defensa de la Libre Competencia y la Corte Suprema en Resolver Asuntos de Libre Competencia?, CeCO UAI, pp. 6–7 and 10–11.
88. TDLC's Ruling No. 175 (2020), "FNE v. Sociedad de Transportes Avda. Alemania-P. Nuevo S.A. and others".
89. TDLC's Ruling No. 171 (2019), "FNE v. CCNI S.A. and others".
90. Supreme Court (2020), Case No. 15005-2019, "FNE v. CCNI and others".
91. TDLC's Ruling No. 167 (2019), "FNE v. Cencosud S.A. and others".

that having a competition compliance program was not a mitigation factor to reduce the applicable fine (unlike TDLC's position on this point).[92] This is the only hub & spoke collusion that has been treated as such, although the providers were neither condemned nor accused as the hubs of this scheme.

- *Medicine Vials:* The TDLC declared that three companies executed and implemented an agreement to affect public tenders for the acquisition of generic medicine contained in small size vials (medicine vials), acknowledged the fine exemption for the leniency applicant and imposed a fine of 30,000 UTA (approximately USD 25 million) to one company and of 2,463 UTA to the other (approximately USD 2.2 million).[93] The Supreme Court reduced the fines to 18,000 UTA (approximately 15 million) and 2,000 UTA (approximately 1.7 million), respectively.[94]
- *Tissue*: The TDLC declared that two companies executed and implemented an agreement with the objective of assigning market shares and fixing the sale price of tissue products, acknowledged the fine exemption for the first leniency applicant and a reduction in the applicable fine for the second applicant, imposing to the latter a fine of 20,000 UTA (approximately USD 16.7 million).[95] The Supreme Court revoked the leniency benefit for the first applicant for having organized the collusion and coerced the other company, imposing a fine of 20,000 UTA to it.[96]
- *Asphalt*: The TDLC declared that four asphalt companies colluded to assign clients and their construction works in relation to three categories of clients/works (but not for all the ones accused by the FNE), acknowledged the fine exemption for the leniency applicant and imposed fines between 718 UTA (approximately USD 600,000) and 1,790 UTA (approximately 1.5 million) to the other three companies.[97] The Supreme Court partially overturned TDLC's ruling, deciding there was a collusion in only one of the three categories of clients/works and reducing the fines to 429.1 UTA (approximately USD 360,000) for one company and to 257.4 UTA (approximately USD 215,000) for each of the other two.[98]
- *Poultry Meat*: The TDLC declared that the three main Chilean poultry companies and their trade association colluded to agree to limit the production and to allocate market quotas; and imposed fines of 30.000 UTA (approximately USD 25 million) to two of the companies and a fine of 12,000 UTA (approximately

92. Supreme Court (2020), Case No. 9361-2019, "FNE v. Cencosud S.A. and others". Furthermore, the Supreme Court ruled that the existence of a compliance program cannot be applied as an exemption from liability, because it is not legally established as such. Supreme Court (2020), Case No. 9361-2019, "FNE v. Cencosud S.A. and others", c. 51.
93. TDLC's Ruling No. 165 (2018), "FNE v. Fresenius and others".
94. Supreme Court (2020), "FNE v. Fresenius and others", Case No. 278-2019.
95. TDLC's Ruling No. 160 (2017), "FNE v. CMPC Tissue and other".
96. Supreme Court, Case No. 63600-2019, "FNE v. CMPC and SCA Chile".
97. TDLC's Ruling No. 148 (2015), "FNE v. Asfaltos Chilenos S.A. and others".
98. Supreme Court (2016), Case no. 5128-2016, "FNE v. Asfaltos Chilenos S.A. and others".

USD 10 million) to the third company.[99] In addition, the TDLC ordered the dissolution of the trade association, and the Supreme Court imposed it a fine of 2,000 UTA (approximately USD 1.7 million) to it.[100]

- *Buses*: After a partial settlement with the FNE, the TDLC found collusion between several buses' companies to block the access of competitors to some land terminals, imposing fines between 52 UTA and 1,800 UTA (approximately between USD 43,000 and USD 1.5 million).[101]
- *Refrigerators Compressors*: The TDLC found collusion between two producers of low power hermetic compressors, to artificially increase the price of this input that was essential for refrigeration equipment, acknowledging the fine exemption for the leniency applicant and imposing a fine of 10,500 UTA (approximately USD 8.8 million) to the other defendant,[102] which was reduced by the Supreme Court to 5,000 UTA (approximately USD 4.2 million).[103] This was the first leniency case.
- *Pharmacies*: After a settlement by the FNE with one of the defendants that acknowledged its participation in the infringement, the submission of background information and a payment of 1,350 UTA (approximately USD 1.1 million) in lieu of a fine, the TDLC declared the existence of a collusion between the three most important pharmacies to increase the price of 206 drugs and imposed a fine of 20,000 UTA (approximately USD 16.7 million) to each of the other two companies that did not settle.[104] That amount was the highest applicable fine in the old version of DL 211.

Since the amendments introduced by Law 20,361 in 2009 are applicable,[105] the FNE has not lost a single collusion case, although in some of them its theory of the case has not been fully accepted, for example, discarding the existence of some of the

99. TDLC's Ruling No. 139 (2014), "FNE v. Agrícola Agrosuper S.A. and others". TDLC also imposed the obligation to ask authorization for ex-ante concentration transactions in the poultry market, but Supreme Court left this measure without effect.
100. Supreme Court (2015), Case No. 27181-2014, "FNE v. Agrícola Agrosuper S.A. and others".
101. TDLC's Ruling No. 134 (2014), "FNE v. Empresa de Transportes Rurales Ltda. and others". There are several collusion cases in public transportation markets, i.e., Temuco Transport and Buses, TDLC's Rulings Nos. 141 (2014), "FNE v. Sociedad de Transportes Linea Uno Collico S.A. and others"; 137 (2014), "FNE v. Casther and others"; 136 (2014), "FNE v. Servicios Pullman Bus Costa Central S.A. and others"; 133 (2014) "FNE v. Pullman Bus Costa Central and others"; 102 (2010), "FNE v. Asociación Gremial de Dueños de Buses Agmital"; 94 (2010), "FNE v. Transportes Central Ltda. and others"; and 82 (2009), "FNE v. Asociación Gremial de Buses Interbus and others".
102. TDLC's Ruling No. 122(2012) "FNE v. Tecumseh Do Brasil Ltda. and other".
103. Supreme Court (2013), Case no. 5308-2012, "FNE v. Tecumseh Do Brasil Ltda. and other".
104. TDLC's Ruling No. 119 (2012), "FNE v. Farmacias Ahumada S.A. and others". This kind of ad-hoc during-trial leniency was also used in other cases, such as Buses, other related to public transportation and TDLC's Ruling No. 112 (2011), "FNE v. Radio Valparaíso Ltda. and others".
105. Before such amendments, there were fewer collusion cases and mixed results, existing some condemnations (*see*, e.g., Supreme Court (2012), Case No. 10954-2011, "FNE v. Abercrombie & Kent S.A. and others"; and TDLC's Ruling No. 63, "FNE vs Almacenes Paris and Falabella") and acquittals (v.gr. TDLC's Ruling No. 57, "FNE v. Isapre ING S.A. and others"; and Supreme Court (2007), Case No. 5057-2006, "FNE v. Air Liquide Chile S.A. and others").

anticompetitive agreements accused by the FNE and/or declaring some of these to be time barred in *Car Carriers* and *Asphalt*.

§13.03 UNILATERAL CONDUCT

[A] Relevant Legislation

As mentioned earlier, the legal regime applicable to competition in Chile is contained in Article No. 3 of DL 211, which sets forth, as a general rule, that any act or agreement that prevents, restricts, or hinders competition, or tends to produce said effects shall be sanctioned.

In addition, DL 211 provides some examples to illustrate said general rule. Article 3 letter a) refers to cartels, whereas letters b) and c) relate to unilateral conducts, dealing with abuse of dominance and predatory practices and unfair competition, respectively:

> the following will be considered as, among others, facts, acts or conventions that impede, restrict or hinder competition or tend to produce said effects: (...)
>
> b) The abusive exploitation by an undertaking, or a group thereof, of a dominant position in the market, imposing sale or purchase prices, tying sales to another product, allocating territories or quotas or imposing other similar abuses.
> c) Predatory practices or unfair competition conducts, carried out with the purpose of reaching, maintaining, or increasing a dominant position.

In addition, the FNE issued Vertical Restraint Guidelines that, even though they do not bind courts or private undertakings, they are an important element of analysis to avoid the risk of prosecution by the FNE before the TDLC.

According to the Guidelines, vertical restraints may be pro-competitive or anti-competitive and the FNE will focus its assessment on the effects rather than form. To assess whether vertical restraints shall be deemed competitive or anticompetitive, the FNE will evaluate: (i) the market shares of the parties; (ii) the risks of anticompetitive effects; and (iii) its efficiencies.

The FNE sets out a *de minimis* rule if the parties involved in a vertical restraint have 35% or less market share in their respective markets;[106] below such threshold the FNE will deem, in principle, that the relevant restraint is legal, and no further investigation is necessary. If the market share of one of the parties is higher than the referred threshold, then the FNE will evaluate its effects.

106. Vertical Restraints Guidelines, pp. 7–8. This threshold is not an absolute "safe harbor" because it will not apply if there is an accumulative effect of similar vertical restraints or in some other extraordinary cases qualified by the FNE (such as RPM).

The Guidelines set forth that the main potential risks are the facilitation of coordinated conducts[107] and blocking or delaying competitors' entry or expansion in the markets (foreclosure).[108]

In the assessment of potential risks, the FNE will consider, among other factors, competition conditions (related to the market), such as the market concentration, the market position of the parties and competitors, the existence of entry barriers, cumulative effects of similar restraints in the market, the presence of economies of scale and scope, the maturity of the market and the consumer search costs; and characteristics of the vertical restraints themselves, like the scope, type, and duration of the restraints, percentage of the sales (or purchases) covered by the restraints, other restraints agreed between the same parties, and the number of clients affected.[109]

Regarding the efficiencies derived from a vertical restraint, the FNE listed, among others, the elimination of double marginalization (referred to the vertical coordination problem in the determination of prices), the avoidance of "*free riding*" (related mainly with the provision of services to final consumers), and the prevention of "*hold-up problems*" (related to sub optimal specific investments). The parties must prove that the efficiencies are truthful (apt to solve a coordination issue among the parties), that they constitute an effective counterweight to the potential risks, and that there are not less restrictive means to reach the same goals.[110]

[B] Assessment of Dominance

The TDLC has ruled that a dominant position implies:

> an undertaking with significant market power that can act independently from its competitors, clients and providers, because there is no effective competitive pressure that can be exerted against it—this is, disciplining power of actual or potential competitors or an eventual counterweight power—so that it is capable of setting conditions that it would not have been able to obtain without such high market power.[111]

107. Guidelines refer to (i) "Sham vertical agreements" (downstream firms may use vertical restraints to maintain a cartel); (ii) "Hub and spoke cartels" (downstream firms may use a common supplier to exchange information and coordinate); and (iii) the use of vertical restraints to facilitate the coordination of a cartel in the upstream market, through more transparency, which allows to find the eventual deviation of the parties more easily. In addition, the Guidelines state that even in the absence of collusion, certain vertical restraints may soften inter-brand competition by weakening intra-band competition. The Guidelines give three examples: "common agency," "interlocking relationships," and "strategic delegation." Vertical Restraints Guidelines, pp. 6–10.
108. For example, RPM (which might prevent the entry of hard-discount retailers), exclusivities or conditional discounts (which may raise rivals' costs); and tying and bundling (which may be capable of leveraging the dominant position from one market to another). Vertical Restraints Guidelines, pp. 11–12.
109. Vertical Restraints Guidelines, pp. 13–16.
110. *Ibid.*, pp. 16–20.
111. Free translation of:

> "agente económico que tiene un poder de mercado sustantivo y que puede actuar con independencia de otros competidores, clientes y proveedores, porque no existe una

Complementing such definition, and given that DL 211 neither define "dominant position" nor provide any further guidelines for its assessment, different rulings have established some criteria that may indicate its existence,[112] for instance:

- the number of companies and the concentration in the relevant market;
- the market share of a company;
- the presence of barriers to entry and to expansion;
- the relationship between a company and its suppliers and distributors (including if there are exclusivities involved);
- the existence of countervailing power, such as buying power;
- the size of the competitors;
- whether a product has substitutes;
- a company's cost structure;
- the importance of innovation;
- the products' differentiation;
- the market contestability;
- the presence of an essential input; etc.

In terms of the undertakings that can have a dominant position, Article 3 of DL 211 considers both individual and collective dominance. The FNE, the TDLC, and the Supreme Court have considered the latter type of dominance in relation to different types of behaviors.[113]

> presión competitiva eficaz que pueda ser ejercida contra él – esto es, un poder disciplinador por parte de los competidores actuales o potenciales o bien, de un eventual poder de contrapeso-, de modo que está en posición de fijar condiciones que no habrían podido ser obtenidas de no mediar la existencia de ese alto poder de mercado"

TDLC's Ruling 174 (2020), "Banco BICE v. Banco Estado" (pending appeal before the Supreme Court), c. 88 and, in the same sense, TDLC's Ruling No. 176 (2021), "Sindicato de Trabajadores Independientes Chile Taxi v. Maxi Mobility Chile II SpA. and others", c. 76.

112. E.g., TDLC's Rulings Nos. 26 (2005) "Philip Morris v. Chiletabacos"; 31 (2005) "FNE v. Rendic Hnos. S.A."; 39 (2006) "Producción Química y Electrónica Quimel S.A. v. James Hardie Fibrocementos Ltda."; 55 (2007) "FNE v. Lan Airlines S.A. and Lan Chile Cargo S.A."; 78 (2008), "GPS Chile S.A. v. Entel PCS S.A."; 80 (2009) "GPS Chile S.A. v. Entel PCS S.A."; N. 97-2010 "Voissnet S.A. v. Compañía de Telecomunicaciones de Chile S.A."; 124 (2012) "FNE v. Cámara de Comercio de Santiago A.G."; 153 (2016), "Demanda de Constetel Ltda. en contra de Telefónica Móviles Chile S.A."; 154 (2016), "Conadecus v. Telefónica Móviles Chile S.A. and others"; and 176 (2021), "Sindicato de Trabajadores Independientes Chile Taxi v. Maxi Mobility Chile II SpA. and others".

    Similar elements are mentioned by the FNE as "competition conditions" that are relevant to analyze the risks of vertical restraints (*see supra* n. 109 and accompanying text).

113. FNE's Closing Report (2018), Case No. 1966-11 (2415-16), "Ex officio investigation of potential anticompetitive conducts of Soprole Inversiones S.A. and Nestlé Chile S.A."; TDLC's Ruling Nos. 7 (2004), "FNE and appeals of Soprole and Loncoleche against Decision No. 1/96 of Regional Preventive Commission IX" c. 46, and 176 (2021), "Sindicato de Trabajadores Independientes Chile Taxi v. Maxi Mobility Chile II SpA. and others", c. 73 and 76; and Supreme Court (2018), "Conadecus v. Telefónica Móviles Chile S.A. and others", Case No. 73923-2016, c. 13.

[C] Abuse of Dominant Position

DL 211 does not sanction the mere existence of a dominant position but sanctions the abuse of such a position.

The TDLC have established, and the FNE has prosecuted, some conducts that can qualify, under certain circumstances, as abuses of dominant position pursuant to Article 3 of DL 211, some of which will be summarized below.

Besides abusive conducts, the last subsection deals with interlocking, which was introduced as a specific competition infringement by Law No. 20,945 which added the letter d) to Article 3 of DL 211.

[1] Exploitative Practices

Exploitative excessive prices: In the past, the TDLC had been reluctant to define a price as excessive in absence of a conduct which was deemed abusive.[114]

Consistently, in previous cases, the TDLC sanctioned for abusive exploitation some companies which arbitrarily discriminated, made unjustified charges and/or breached the applicable legal or contractual rules, but such discrimination, charge and/or breach was necessary in order to find an exploitative conduct.[115]

In 2014, the TDLC changed its prior criterion in a divided decision whereby it decided that, although the defendants had not breached DL 211, the TDLC would be able to sanction excessive pricing following a two-stage test. First, defendant has a dominant position that is not the result of past investments or innovation, and there are high and non-transitory entry barriers. Second, the prices charged are extremely high when compared with several benchmarks and standards.[116]

In more recent cases, the TDLC has maintained this position, but it has not condemned companies for excessive pricing.[117]

---

114. TDLC's Ruling No. 93 (2010), "FNE v. Empresa Eléctrica Atacama S.A."
115. E.g., TDLC's Ruling Nos. 55 (2007) "FNE en contra de Lan Airlines S.A. y Lan Chile Cargo S.A."; 73 (2008), "Requerimiento de la FNE contra Empresa Eléctrica de Magallanes S.A."; 75 (2008) "Atrex and others v. SCL"; 76 (2008), "GTD Teleductos S.A. v. EFE"; 85 (2009); "Constructora e Inmobiliaria Independencia Ltda. v. Aguas Nuevo Sur Maule S.A."; and 100 (2010), "Nutripro S.A. v. Puerto Terrestre Los Andes Sociedad Concesionaria S.A. and Fisco" (revoked by the Supreme Court).
116. TDLC's Ruling No. 140 (2014), "Condominio Campomar v. Inmobiliaria Santa Rosa de Tunquén Ltda.", c. 16-18. This was a 3-2 decision whereby the minority judges rejected the possibility of sanctioning excessive prices.
117. TDLC's Ruling No. 163 (2018), "Alimentos Bio Bio Ltda. y Otros. Contra Alimentos y Frutos S.A. y Otros." (involving also allegations of abuse of economic dependence). Minority vote of judge Domper repeated its position against sanctioning this practice. FNE has adopted a similar approach when closing its investigations. FNE's Closing Report (2018), Case No.2548-19, "Issuance of international driving permit".

Arbitrary discrimination: Giving a different treatment to similar transactions without an objective justification may be a breach of DL 211 under certain circumstances.[118] Referencing international doctrine, TDLC has said that "price discrimination is the sale of different units of the same product at price differentials that do not correspond to cost differences, [so that] the provided services must be comparable in term of costs to determine if there was an arbitrary discrimination on prices or commercial conditions."[119]

A price difference or different commercial conditions may, however, be justified under objective criteria, such as the distinct characteristics or nature of the services or products, or the cost differences to render the services to diverse clients.[120]

Also, both TDLC and Supreme Court have recognized that arbitrary discrimination can be a source of exclusionary concerns ordering to apply objective, general, and non-arbitrary criteria to make differences.[121]

[2] Exclusionary Practices

Tying (and bundling): If a provider imposes the commercialization of one product or service tied to the purchasing of another product or service, its conduct may constitute an abusive practice.

The TDLC has established that there is an anticompetitive tying if: (i) the tied products or services are different, and it is not possible to acquire them separately; (ii) the defendant has market power on the tying product or service; (iii) the practice must

118. E.g., Ruling No. 76-2008 "GTD Teleductos S.A. v. EFE,", in which the TDLC determined that the defendant abused its dominant position discriminating prices charged for the "*atravieso*" service, without a valid economic justification, establishing that the differences were not based on costs reasons, but on elements as the clients' willingness to pay.

119. Free translation (quotations omitted):

> "la discriminación de precios es "la venta de diferentes unidades del mismo producto a diferenciales de precios que no corresponden a diferencias de costo" (G. Niels, H. Jenkins y J. Kavanagh, Economics for Competition Lawyers, Oxford University Press, 1ª ed., 2011, p. 181); en tanto que la jurisprudencia de este Tribunal ha establecido que los servicios prestados deben ser comparables en términos de costos para poder determinar si existió una discriminación arbitraria de precios o de condiciones comerciales".

TDLC's Ruling No. 158 (2017), "Telestar Móvil S.A. v. Entel PCS Telecomunicaciones S.A. and others", c. 72. In the same sense, TDLC's Ruling No. 156 (2017), "Netline Mobile S.A. contra Entel PCS Telecomunicaciones S.A. y otros", c. 128.

120. E.g., TDLC's Rulings No. 110 (2011) "Will S.A. v. Claro Chile S.A." (elements of an arbitrary discrimination were not proved because the defendant charged different prices for non-identical services) and 107 (2010) "Comercial y Agrícola Verde Sur Ltda. v. Petróleos Transandinos S.A." (the difference between the prices charged to different clients was not arbitrary, having a reasonable explanation on the different costs to provide the products to different clients).

121. Supreme Court (2011), Case No. 6100-2010, "Nutripro S.A. v. Puerto Terrestre Los Andes Sociedad Concesionaria S.A. and Fisco", c. 13; TDLC's Ruling No. 107, "Comercial y Agrícola Verde Sur Ltda. v. Petróleos Transandinos S.A.", c. 107; and TDLC's Resolution No. 47 (2015), "Servicios Equifax Chile Ltda. Consultation on Servicio de Información Comercial Exchange ", para. 79.

exclude competitors or impede the entry to the market of competitive products to the tied product; (iv) the practice does not have an alternative explanation other than the abuse of market power.[122]

For some telecommunications services, the TDLC has also addressed tying on its General Instructions, prohibiting telecom companies to condition, explicitly or implicitly, the acquisition of one service to other.[123] In the same General Instructions, the TDLC dealt with bundling determining that bundles of telecom services must have a price higher than (i) the price of the most expensive single service, in bundles of two services, or (ii) the sum of all the services' price except for the cheapest one, in case of bundles of three or more services.[124]

FNE's position on these practices can be summarized as "tying seems, in principle, more harmful to competition than bundling".[125]

Refusal to deal: The TDLC has ruled that a refusal to deal must be understood, in a broad sense, as an "unjustifiably refusal to enter into contracts abusing a dominant position."[126]

The TDLC has found an anticompetitive refusal to sell if: (i) the conduct substantially affects the ability of an undertaking to act in the market, due to the impossibility to obtain the necessary inputs to develop its activity; (ii) such situation was a consequence of a lack of competition among the providers of the goods or services subject to the refusal to deal; and (iii) the affected undertaking must be willing to accept the generally applied commercial terms.[127] Furthermore, the Supreme Court has sanctioned this behavior (revoking TDLC's acquittal) obliging the companies to

---

122. *See* TDLC's Ruling No. 97 (2010), "Voissnet S.A. v. Compañía de Telecomunicaciones de Chile S.A.", imposing a fine of 5,000 UTA for tying internet services to telephone services. Also, FNE's Closing Report (2015). Case No. 2316-14, "Claim of a private party against S.A.C.I. Falabella y CMR Falabella", para. 17 and, similarly, but rephrasing some conditions (replacing (iii) by coercion and referencing also exploitative effects), FNE's Closing Report (2016), Case No. 2338-15, "Ex officio investigation in the elevators market", para. 30.
123. TDLC's General Instruction No. 2 (2012), "Procedure for the issuance of General Instructions on the effects on competition of price differentiation of telephony public services "on-net/off-net tariffs" and joint offers of telecom services", section B.4, as modified by TDLC's General Instruction No. 4 (2015). Prohibition of tying was later introduced by Chilean Telecom Undersecretary through Telecommunication Services Regulation, article 15 letter e) (between services) and 16 (between services and equipment).
124. TDLC's General Instruction No. 2 (2012), "Procedure for the issuance of General Instructions on the effects on competition of price differentiation of telephony public services "on-net/off-net tariffs" and joint offers of telecom services", section B.3, as modified by TDLC's General Instruction No. 4 (2015).
125. Vertical Restraints Guidelines, p. 22.
126. TDLC's Ruling No. 16 (2005), "UIP Chile Ltda. and Andes Films S.A. against Decision No.1.277 of the Central Preventive Commission,", c. 24, in which the TDLC stated that refusal to deal is anticompetitive when it prevents an agent from having free access on equal terms (compared to its competitors) to the goods and services that are essential to carry-out its activities, further affirming that a refusal to deal is in accordance with Competition Law if the provider establishes general, objective, and reasonable conditions and its client does not accept them.
127. TDLC's Resolution No. 19-2006 "Consultation of PACX South America S.A.", c. 7; and Rulings Nos. 64-2008 "Micom S.A. v. Enap", c. 11; and 107-2010 "Comercial y Agrícola Verde Sur Ltda. contra Petróleos Transandinos S.A.", c. 26.

make offers of the relevant services based on general, uniform, objective, and non-discriminatory criteria.[128]

FNE has identified these same elements adding that the inputs must be indispensable to compete, such that the refusal to deal eliminates or significantly reduces competition, and that the refusal must lack an objective reason or justification.[129]

Refusal to give access to essential facilities or inputs has been approached similarly to traditional refusal to sell adding, based on the essential facilities doctrine (*doctrina de las facilidades esenciales*), that the facility or input need to be non-replicable, indispensable to compete in the market and provided by only one company.[130] In relation to pre-existing merger remedies, Supreme Court has also imposed measures for a refusal to purchase that amounted to a breach of such remedies.[131]

Another conduct related to refusal to sell (and to arbitrary discrimination) is margin squeeze, which happens "when a vertically integrated firm uses its upstream market power to squeeze its competitors' margins in the downstream market, with an exclusionary object or effect".[132] Following such definition, the TDLC identified the following elements of this anticompetitive behavior: (i) a vertically integrated company with market power upstream due to the provision of an essential input for the downstream market; (ii) squeeze, for a long period, its downstream competitors' margin (i.e. reducing or simply eliminating such margins); and (iii) such squeeze is produced because the sale price of the product does not give enough margin to competitors to remain competitive downstream.[133] In more recent cases, TDLC has complemented the two latter elements by stating, based on compared doctrine, that: (a) the dominant vertically integrated firm must make an efficient rival's activities

128. Supreme Court (2011), Case No. 7781-2020, "FNE v. Telefónica Móviles de Chile S.A. and others", in which the Supreme Court sanctioned three companies for exclusionary refusal to sell due to the absence of digital and analogical phone services offers to mobile virtual operators.
129. FNE's Closing Reports (2016) in Cases Nos. 2338-15, "Ex officio investigation in the elevators market", para. 43 and 2338-15, "Claim of a private party against LG Electronics Chile Ltda.", para. 11; and 2355-15, "Claim of a private party for potential infractions to competition in the money exchange offices market", c. 13.
130. TDLC's Ruling No. 124, "FNE v. Cámara de Comercio de Santiago A.G.", c. 11 (regarding provision of digital detailed credit information)
131. Supreme Court (2019), Case No. 8313-2018, "TVI v. VTR Comunicaciones SpA" (regarding purchase of pay-TV channels).
132. Free translation of:

> "se produce cuando una empresa integrada verticalmente utiliza el poder de mercado que posee en el mercado "aguas arriba" para estrangular los márgenes de sus competidores en el mercado "aguas abajo", con el objeto o efecto de excluirlos".

TDLC's Ruling No. 89 (2009), "OPS Ingeniería Ltda. and others v. Telefónica Móviles de Chile S.A.", c. 95.

133. TDLC's Ruling No. 89 (2009), "OPS Ingeniería Ltda. and others v. Telefónica Móviles de Chile S.A.", c. 96, in which the TDLC condemned a telecom company for discriminating against its downstream competitors in the sale price of its mobile phone services, thereby squeezing their margins.

non-profitable; (b) the pricing strategy must lack an objective justification; and (c) anticompetitive effects of the conduct must be proved.[134]

Exclusivities (and conditional discounts): The authorities have considered that exclusivities, as well as other vertical restraints, should be analyzed based on the rule of reason, that is, analyzing the current or potential effects in the markets.[135] Particularly, these vertical restraints could be anticompetitive if they foreclosure the market, excluding current or potential competitors.[136]

TDLC has indicated that exclusive distribution agreements, in which a provider designates only one undertaking to distribute its products in a given territory, can prevent or hinder competitors' entry in two situations (i) when there is not enough inter-brand competition; and (ii) when, existing several producers of the same good or of substitute goods, all or most of them have appointed one exclusive distributor.[137]

The FNE and private parties have filed many lawsuits against undertakings with a high market share, challenging exclusive dealings whereby suppliers prevent its clients from distributing competing products, such as cigarettes, matches, detergents, ice creams, beverages, and beers. In some of these, the TDLC issued a condemnatory ruling, stating that the defendant abused its dominant position through exclusivities, among other practices, to raise entry barriers and/or exclude competitors.[138] In many cases, the plaintiffs settled with the defendants with a commitment to change all or part of the accused behavior.[139]

Many exclusive dealing cases included claims against conditional discounts. Although discounts are a common commercial practice, TDLC have ruled that these may infringe competition rules, for example, in cases where there were exclusivity

134. TDLC's Rulings Nos. 156 (2017), "Netline Mobile S.A. contra Entel PCS Telecomunicaciones S.A. y otros", c. 93; and 158 (2017), "Telestar Móvil S.A. v. Entel PCS Telecomunicacions S.A. and others", c. 59 (rejecting margin squeeze, discrimination, and refusal to sell allegations that would amount to breaches of Supreme Court's previous ruling—*see supra* n. 128 and accompanying text).

135. TDLC's Ruling Nos. 126 (2012) "Mundo Petit v. Infanti,", c. 78; TDLC's resolution approving a settlement (2014), "FNE v. Unilever Chile S.A.", c. 5 and 7; and Vertical Restraint Guidelines, p. 6.

136. TDLC's Ruling Nos. 26 (2005), "Philip Morris v. Chiletabacos", c. 22; 90 (2009), "FNE v. Cía. Chilena de Fósforos S.A.", c. 89; 115 (2011), "FNE v. Cía. Chilena de Tabacos S.A", c. 22; 126 (2012) "Mundo Petit v. Infanti,", c. 80-81; and TDLC's resolution approving a settlement (2014), "FNE v. Unilever Chile S.A.", c. 8.

137. Ruling No. 126 (2012) "Mundo Petit v. Infanti," in which TDLC acquitted an exclusive distributor for lack of market power and because the exclusivity did not foreclose the market, given that among other considerations, the plaintiff had the possibility to access to a wide supply of substitute products.

138. TDLC's Ruling Nos. 26 (2005), "Philip Morris v. Chiletabacos", in which the dominant cigarettes firm was sanctioned for exclusionary behavior to raise strategic entry barriers consisting in exclusivities, refusals to sell and provision of economic benefits to prevent the sale of competing products; and 90 (2009), "FNE v. Cía. Chilena de Fósforos S.A.", in which the dominant firm was sanctioned for exclusivity clauses and for granting exclusivity discounts and conditional discounts for reaching sale goals with the object and purpose of creating artificial entry barriers to the match market.

139. Case Files Nos. Case File N. 153-2008, "FNE v. Cervecera CCU Chile Ltda." (beers); 221-2011, "FNE v. Embotelladora Andina and Coca Cola Embonor" (soft drinks); 230-2011, "Industria de Alimentos Trendy S.A. v. Nestlé Chile S.A." (ice creams); and Case File N. 249-2013, "FNE v. Unilever Chile S.A." (detergents).

discounts or discounts devised to cover all the purchases of the distributor.[140] In one of these cases, the TDLC ordered the condemned undertaking that its discounts and contractual terms must be based on general, uniform, and objective circumstances, or in costs justifications, applicable to any client that is in the same position.[141]

FNE has mentioned that exclusive dealing seems, in principle, more harmful to competition than incremental discounts based on sales goals.[142] Furthermore, recently the FNE closed without further action an investigation for retroactive conditional discounts, despite the investigated undertaking had a dominant position in some markets.[143]

Resale Price Maintenance (RPM) and Recommended Retail Price (RRP): RPM consists of a practice whereby a supplier imposes a retail price to its client, who must distribute the product at the price set by the supplier, while through RRP a supplier suggests a recommended price, which is not binding for the distributor.[144]

RPM and RRP have received different treatment by the authorities. TDLC has indicated that for RPM or RRP to be offenses to competition two conditions are necessary: (i) a producer must impose the price as a vertical restraint, preventing its retailers from competing based on this factor (intra-brand competition); and (ii) there must be a severe limitation to competition between different brands of the product or services, i.e., absence of effective inter-brand competition.[145] The FNE has stated that elimination of intra-brand competition should not produce direct competition risks if there is high inter-brand competition and RPM relating to minimum resale prices, is the most dangerous vertical restraint,[146] while RPP and RPM related to maximum resale prices pose less risks.[147]

[3] Predatory Practices

Article 3 letter c) of DL 211 forbids predatory practices and unfair competition not only if carried out by a dominant undertaking with the purpose of *maintaining* or *increasing* its market power, but also if they are executed by a non-dominant firm to *reach* a dominant position. TDLC has referenced this element as a "potential dominance,"

140. TDLC's Ruling Nos. 26 (2005), "Philip Morris v. Chiletabacos"; and 90 (2009), "FNE v. Cía. Chilena de Fósforos S.A.".
141. TDLC's Ruling No. 90 (2009), "FNE v. Cía. Chilena de Fósforos S.A.".
142. Vertical Restraints Guidelines, p. 22.
143. FNE's Closing Report (2020), "Ex officio investigation in the appliance markets".
144. Vertical Restraint Guidelines, p. 5 (chart 1).
145. TDLC's Ruling 131 (2013), "Electrocenter Ltda. v. Nokia Chile S.A.", c., rejected a "three-way" RPM allegation because the mandatory nature of the price instruction was not proved, and the market had a reasonable degree of competition.
146. Vertical Restraint Guidelines, p. 5 (chart 1).
147. *Ibid.* and FNE's Closing Report (2020), Case No. 2400-16, "Investigation about the competition conditions in the market for maintenance of vehicles with valid warranty", paras. 67–68.

which means that the defendant must have a real possibility of achieving such position.[148]

Predatory pricing: A predatory pricing conduct may occur when an undertaking sells below cost during a set time in order to eliminate or discipline a competitor and, afterwards, raise its price above competitive level to recoup its losses.[149]

According to the TDLC, three elements are necessary to configure predatory pricing: (i) the defendant must have a reasonable expectation to recover its short-term losses by virtue of its market power in the relevant market; (ii) the defendant must offer its goods or services below a relevant measure of costs,[150] for a period of time enabling him or her to displace its competitors; and (iii) the defendant must act with the intention of excluding its competitors.[151] An old ruling of the Supreme Court interpreting Article 3 letter c) of DL 211, did not request a dominant position to condemn.[152]

Sham Litigation:[153] The TDLC has punished companies for sham litigation when they have abusively filed judicial and administrative actions to impede the entry of a competitor.

The TDLC has mentioned certain elements, among others, to identify when the exercise of judicial and administrative actions may become a sham litigation: (i) defendant must have filed the actions; (ii) with the unequivocal object to restrict or hinder the entry of competitors to the market; (iii) in case the defendant has exercised

148. TDLC's Ruling Nos. 151 (2016), "Metalúrgia Silcosil Ltda. v. Masisa S.A. and other", c. 19; and 176 (2021), "Sindicato de Trabajadores Independientes Chile Taxi v Maxi Mobility Chile II SpA. and others", c. 68.
149. FNE's Closing Report (2016), "Claim of a private party for potential abuse of dominance in the buses market for the Salamanca-Santiago route", para. 21.
150. TDLC has used the "avoidable costs", i.e., costs directly affected by changes in the volume of supply, or in the quality of the goods or services, including variable costs and some fixed costs, but not sunk costs. Ruling No. 78 (2008), "GPS Chile S.A. v. Entel PCS S.A.", c. 3 and 19 et seq. FNE has identified the same elements, but has considered average variable costs, given the difficulty in determining the marginal costs that would be the most appropriate type of cost. FNE's Closing Report (2018), "Claim against Buses Orellana for potential abuses in the Santiago-Bollenar route", para. 26 (and footnote 23).
151. *See*, e.g., TDLC's Rulings Nos. 78 (2008), "GPS Chile S.A. v. Entel PCS S.A.," c. 3, in which the TDLC rejected a lawsuit for predatory pricing because the defendant did not have market power; 103 (2010), "Comercial Arauco Ltda. v. D&S and other," in which the TDLC rejected the predatory pricing claim and declared that short-term promotions, including loss leading strategies, is not a practice that must be considered per se against competition; and 110 (2011), "Will S.A. v. Claro Chile S.A.", c. 26, in which the TDLC did not accept the hypothesis of predatory pricing because the applicant neither prove that the defendant provided its services below relevant costs nor that defendant had market power.
152. Supreme Court (2006), Case No. 3449-2006, "Producción Química and Electrónica Quimel S.A. v. James Hardie Fibrocementos Ltda.", c. 6, the Supreme Court condemned a firm that was not the leader of its market for selling its products below the production cost to eliminate the competition, gain market power and, in the long term, obtain supra-competitive gains.
153. This conduct, at least in relation to judicial actions, is also punished by article 4 letter g) of the Unfair Competition Act but can be categorized as a subtype of predatory practice (not based in price) instead as a kind of unfair competition conduct.

two or more actions, these are contradictory; and (iv) the actions have impeded or delayed the entry of competitors or have tended to produce such effects.[154]

Such criteria have been applied by the TDLC to acquit and condemn defendants accused of sham litigation.[155]

[4] Unfair Competition

Article 3 of the Unfair Competition Act sets forth that an unfair competition act consists of "any behavior contrary to good faith or morality that, by unlawful means, aims to divert clientele of an undertaking."[156]

In Chile an unfair competition conduct may be punished by the Unfair Competition Act and judged by civil courts; or, under certain conditions, by the DL 211. The element that determines if a conduct of unfair competition may be prohibited by DL 211 is market power: if the conduct was carried out "with the purpose of reaching, maintaining or increasing a dominant position," such conduct would be in breach of DL 211.

Some of the unfair competition acts which have been prosecuted before the TDLC are the following:[157]

- *Misappropriating another's reputation*: The imitation of distinctive signs, such as trademarks, could constitute an anticompetitive practice when it might generate confusion to the consumer, either directly (confusion about the

154. TDLC's Ruling No. 125 (2012), "Laboratorio Recalcine S.A. v. Roche Chile Ltda.", c. 22. FNE has identified the same elements when closing its investigations. FNE's Closing Report (2014), "Claim of trade association against Colbún for potential anticompetitive conducts", paras. 28–30.
155. *See*, e.g., TDLC's Rulings Nos. 46 (2006), "Recalcine S.A. v. Novartis S.A.," in which the TDLC rejected the claim because, although the legal actions were dismissed, the defendant could have legitimately thought that its rights were violated; and 47 (2006), "FNE v. Sociedad Punta de Lobos S.A.", in which the TDLC imposed a fine to the defendant because it concluded that its different legal actions were contradictory and its real object was to impede the entry of a competitor to the market.
156. Free translation of "(...) es acto de competencia desleal toda conducta contraria a la buena fe o a las buenas costumbres que, por medios ilegítimos, persiga desviar clientela de un agente del mercado."
157. Article 4 of the Unfair Competition Act gives several examples of unfair competition practices such as: (a) improperly taking advantage of the reputation of others; (b) misleading about the source or quality of the nature, components, characteristics, price, production mode, brand, quality or quantity and, in general, of the real benefits of the offered goods or services; (c) undermining third-party's reputation; (d) aggravating statements regarding nationality, beliefs, ideology, private life or any personal circumstance of the third-party that has not direct relation with the quality of the provided goods or services(v) any comparison of goods, services, activities or premises with those of a third party, when these are based on background information that is not truthful and provable or that in any other way infringes Unfair Competition Act; the use of expressions aimed to ridicule another trader without any objective reference; (vi) the abusive exercise of legal actions with the purpose of hindering the operation of another trader, among other practices.

products) or by association (confusion about the source), becoming an unfair utilization of the reputation or the efforts of others.[158]

- *Disparaging acts*: Based on TDLC's previous case law, sending letters or making verbal communications aimed at discrediting a competitor product or service may breach the DL 211 if: (i) these contain false or incorrect statements about the services or products offered by the affected competitor; and (ii) have been executed with the purpose of discrediting such competitor to divert its clientele.[159] Based on such case law, TDLC condemned a company for sending letters to its competitor's potential clients claiming non-proven breaches to its intellectual property rights and announcing legal actions,[160] but the Supreme Court revoked TDLC's decision stating that to be unfair competition the relevant conduct must be executed through illegitimate means. According to the Supreme Court, the relevant letters were a legitimate and auto-compositive mean to address the situation, non-judicial mean that can only be subject to the restrictions of legal actions, which only exceptionally can constitute unfair competition.[161]
- *Comparative and Misleading Advertising*: Regarding misleading advertising, whether it is comparative or not, the TDLC has identified the following elements to become an anticompetitive behavior: (i) the information contained in the advertisement must be false or misleading; (ii) relate to one of the characteristic features of the product or service;, and (iii) generate, or tend to generate, a significant effect in the purchase of goods or services, causing to mistakenly purchase a product that, in the absence of such advertising would not have been purchased.[162]

[5] Interlocking

Although interlocking is neither a collusion nor an abuse of dominance, Law 20,945 introduced this figure as an infringement to competition law by adding the letter d) to

158. TDLC's Ruling No. 24(2005), "Laboratorio Knop Ltda., en contra de Farmacias Ahumanda S.A. y otros.", c. 9, in which TDLC condemned a dominant company for unfair competition imitating a product of the plaintiff.
159. Ruling No. 130 (2013), "Beatriz Zuberman Comercializadora E.I.R.L. v. One Smart Star Number Chile S.A.", c. 9, the TDLC sanctioned a company for sending cease and desist letters to its competitor's current and potential clients based on patent infringement containing false statements, instead of exercising the legal actions that the industrial property law contemplates.
160. TDLC's Ruling No. 164 (2018), "Oscar Morales L. v. Trefimet".
161. Supreme Court (2020), Case No. 26525-2018, "Oscar Morales L. v. Trefimet", c. 11-17.
162. TDLC's Rulings No. 58 (2007), "Ricardo Rodríguez y Cía Ltda. v. Epson Chile S.A.", c. 21, the TDLC did not find a causal relationship between the advertising campaign and the plaintiff's market share reduction, but ordered the defendant to abstain advertising suggesting that its products are the only original ones available in the market; and, following this same approach, 103 (2010), "Comercial Arauco Ltda. v. D&S and other," the TDLC condemned a company because its comparative pricing advertising contained false information and was not objective, thus having the potential to affect purchase decisions and divert clientele.

Article 3 of DL 211. Such provision forbids interlocking between competitors, that is, the "simultaneous participation of a person in relevant executive positions or as a director in two or more competing companies",[163] provided that (i) each competitors' businesses have annual revenues for sales, services, and other operational activities of more than 100,000 *Unidades de Fomento* (Chilean adjustable units, "*UF*") (approximately USD 4 million);[164] and (ii) the simultaneous participation in the abovementioned positions lasted for 90 calendar days since the end of the year in which the relevant companies exceeded the sales threshold.

We are aware of two investigations about interlocking that were closed and have been made public,[165] and of two recent actions filed before the TDLC in which the FNE is claiming indirect interlocking is against Article 3 letter d) of DL 211 without the need to prove effects on competition or market power.[166]

[D] Investigation

[1] Authorities

The authorities involved in the investigation of unilateral abuses are those referred in case of cartels,[167] namely the TDLC and the FNE.

163. Free translation of the first part of article 3 letter d) of DL 211:

> "d) La participación simultánea de una persona en cargos ejecutivos relevantes o de director en dos o más empresas competidoras entre sí, siempre que el grupo empresarial al que pertenezca cada una de las referidas empresas tenga ingresos anuales por ventas, servicios y otras actividades del giro que excedan las cien mil unidades de fomento en el último año calendario. Con todo, sólo se materializará esta infracción si transcurridos noventa días corridos, contados desde el término del año calendario en que fue superado el referido umbral, se mantuviere la participación simultánea en tales cargos."

164. UF is the Chilean adjustable unit and its the average value for 2021 was 29,802 Chilean pesos, so 1 UF is equivalent to approximately 40 USD. Unlike the merger control regime thresholds, there are no specific guidelines on how to convert this amount to foreign currency, so that the USD amount might vary depending on whether current or last year UF is used and whether current or last year average USD is utilized.
165. FNE's Closing Report (2021), Case No. 2638-20, "Claim against Jack Mosa for purchase of shares in Parque Arauco" (closing the investigation because involved companies were not competitors, so interlocking prohibited by article 3 letter d) of DL 211 did not occur); and Closing Report (2021) Case No. 2578-19, "Ex officio investigation regarding the participation of Glencore and Anglo American in the ownership and management of Compañía Minera Doña Iñés de Collahuasi" (closing the investigation because the entity in which there was common ownership and management was not a competitor of the shareholders, so that the interlocking prohibited by article 3 letter d) of DL 211 did not occur).
166. "Requerimiento de la FNE en contra de Hernán A. Büchi Buc y otros," Case No. C-436-2021; and "Requerimiento FNE contra Juan José Hurtado Vicuña y otros," Case No. C-437-2021.
167. Section 13.02[C][1].

[2] Procedure

The procedural rules that govern the investigations of the FNE and the cases carried out before the TDLC are the same that were referred in case of cartels.[168]

[3] Powers

In cases of unilateral abuses, the FNE has the same attributions that were mentioned earlier regarding cartels,[169] except for intrusive measures (Article 39 n) and leniency (Article 39 bis) which only apply for collusion.

[4] Burden of proof

Plaintiffs must prove the infringements. Defendants must prove their defenses. Article 1,698 of the Civil Code, which applies to all civil procedures in Chile as well as to competition matters before the TDLC, including abuses of dominance and collusion procedures, states that the burden of proof is on those that argue the existence or the extinction of an obligation.[170]

To assess the evidence, Article 22 of DL 211 sets forth that TDLC must follow the rules of sound critical approach (*reglas de la sana crítica*) in the contentious procedures regarding competition infringements (both collusion and abuse of dominance).[171]

Chilean authorities have generally adopted a "rule of reason" approach which is not limited to unilateral abuses.[172] Accordingly, a conduct may constitute a violation of the Law if it impedes, restricts, or hinders competition (actual effects) or tends to cause such effects (potential effects).

Finally, in relation to the standard of proof, the TDLC and the Supreme Court have repeatedly and consistently stated that for collusion, as well as for other infringements to DL 211, it is necessary to provide "clear and conclusive evidence" (*prueba clara y concluyente*),[173] as an intermediate standard between beyond all reasonable doubt (normally used in criminal contexts) and preponderance of evidence

168. Section 13.02[C][2].
169. *Ibid.*
170. TDLC's Ruling No. 176 (2021), "Sindicato de Trabajadores Independientes Chile Taxi v Maxi Mobility Chile II SpA. and others", c. 64-66 and Supreme Court (2010), Case No. 5443-2009, "Constructora e Inmobiliaria Independencia Ltda. v. Aguas Nuevo Sur Maule S.A.", c. 6.
171. Article 30 of DL 30 replicate this approach for damage procedures before TDLC.
172. The exceptions would be hard-core cartels (*see* §13.02[A]), interlocking, some breaches to merger control rules and to the obligation to report minority shareholdings in competitors that the FNE has argued to be "formal" infringements that do not require actual or potential effects to be sanctioned (*see* §13.03[C][5]; §13.04[E]; and §13.04[I], respectively).
173. Supreme Court (2012), Case No. 2578-2020, "FNE v. Farmacias Ahumada and others", c. 11, TDLC's Ruling No. 160 (2017), "FNE v. CMPC Tissue and other", C. 7; and Supreme Court (2020), Case No. 278-2019, "FNE vs Fresenius and others", c. 8. In *Tissue*, there is an interesting minority vote of two (now former) judges arguing that the applicable standard should be balance of probabilities. Ruling No. 160 (2017), "FNE v. CMPC Tissue and other", minority vote (1-27).

or balance of probabilities (*preponderancia de prueba* or *balance de probabilidades*, normally used in civil contexts).

[5] Appeal

The rules that govern the appeal against TDLC's rulings are the same that were referred for collusion cases.[174]

[E] Sanctions and Remedies

The sanctions and remedies that were mentioned earlier regarding cartels are applicable in unilateral conduct cases,[175] except for the prohibition to celebrate contracts with the state and other public institutions, which is only available for collusion, and criminal penalties, which can only be imposed in relation to individuals involved in hardcore cartels.

[F] Precedent Cases

Most of the cases decided by the TDLC refer to unilateral conducts and abuse of dominant position; the most relevant of these cases were explained earlier in this chapter.[176]

§13.04 MERGER REVIEW

[A] Relevant Legislation

Law No. 20,945 created a "new" merger control system in Chile, which entered into force in June 2017, by introducing a new section IV to DL 211.[177] The legal regulation has been complemented by several materials issued by the FNE or other authorities, such as Exempt Resolution Nos. 667 (2016) and 157 (2019), setting the merger sales thresholds; the Regulation on the Notification of a Merger Operation issued by the Economy, Development and Tourism Ministry on March 1, 2017, replaced by a new Regulation that entered into force on November 2, 2021 ("*Merger Regulation*"), listing the information and documentation that must be submitting in a filing; FNE's Jurisdiction Guide of June 2017 ("*Jurisdiction Guideline*"), explaining concentration transactions subject to FNE's review; FNE's Remedies Guide ("*Remedies Guideline*"),

174. Section 13.02[C][2].
175. Sections 13.02[D][1] and 13.02[D][3].
176. Section 13.03[C].
177. Before that, due to the lack of specific merger control provisions in DL 211, an ad-hoc system was utilized, based, on the substantive side, in the general prohibition of Article 3 para. 1 of DL 211 and, on the procedural side, in the investigations conducted by the FNE according to its old Horizontal Mergers Guidelines (version of 2012) and in TDLC's non-contentious procedure and, to a minor extent, contentious procedure.

outlining FNE's preferences in terms of remedies; FNE's Practical Guide to the Application of Notification Thresholds for Concentration Operations in Chile, describing how to calculate sales for the thresholds Furthermore, the FNE issued the Pre-Filing Instructive, addressing the contacts between the parties and the FNE before the filing (known as "pre-notification"), and launched for public comments a new Horizontal Mergers Guideline.[178]

Only concentration transactions are subject to this ex-ante control system, which are defined by Article 47 of DL 211 as:

> any fact, act or convention, or combination thereof, which results in two or more undertakings that are not part of the same business group and that are previously independent from each other, ceasing to be independent in any scope of its activities by one or more of the following ways:
>
> a. By merging, regardless of the legal structure of the merging entities or of the merged entity.
> b. By the acquisition by one or more undertakings of rights that allow, directly or indirectly, individually or jointly, to decisively influence in other undertaking's management.
> c. By their association, under any structure, to create an independent and different economic agent, that conducts its business in a permanent manner.
> d. By the acquisition by one or more undertakings of the control over the assets of other undertaking by any title.

Based on such definition, FNE has recognized that collaboration agreements between competitors are not subject to concentration transactions control.[179] This kind of collaboration agreements are subject to the general rules of DL 211, particularly its Article 3, and should be analyzed comparing its effects, efficiencies, and risks to determine if they are legal or not.[180] However, it is important to bear in mind that the TDLC has affirmed that these agreements are seen with suspicion, existing a strong presumption against them, and that the risks and benefits measurement should be carried out with particular care.[181]

[B] Authorities

The authority in charge of the merger control system is the FNE, which receives the filings by the parties, carries out the investigations, and must approve or reject the

178. Both available in: https://www.fne.gob.cl/fne-actualiza-y-fortalece-regimen-de-control-de-operaciones-de-concentracion-con-nueva-guia-e-instructivo/.
179. Jurisdiction Guideline, p. 4. The exception, as also identified by the FNE, would be the creation of an independent, permanent, and new undertaking among competitors (Jurisdiction Guideline, p. 4), in other words, what is commonly known as a full-function joint venture that is covered by the definition of article 47 letter c) of DL 211.
180. FNE, "Declaración Pública", April 03, 2020, available in: https://www.fne.gob.cl/wp-content/uploads/2020/04/Declaraci%C3%B3n-P%C3%BAblica-FNE-030420.pdf.
181. TDLC's Resolution No. 54 (2018), "Consultation of Asociación Chilena de Empresas de Turismo A.G. about concentration transaction between LATAM Airlines Group, American Airlines Inc. and others", paras. 13 and 16.

notified concentration transactions. TDLC and Supreme Court have a limited intervention in case a special appeal (*recurso de revisión especial*) is submitted against FNE's prohibition decision.[182]

[C] Triggering Events and Thresholds

According to Article 48 of DL 211, ex-ante mandatory filing applies for concentration transactions that have an impact in Chile and surpass both sales thresholds set forth by the FNE through a resolution. The copulative sales thresholds in force for 2021 are:[183]

i. Collective Threshold: That the sum of the sales in Chile of the undertakings that pretend to concentrate have reached, during the year previous to the filing, amounts equal to or greater than 2,500,000 UF (approximately USD 102 million); and
ii. Individual Threshold: That in Chile, at least two of the undertakings that contemplate to concentrate, have separately generated sales, during the year previous to the filing, for amounts equal to or greater than 450,000 UF (approximately USD 18.3 million).

If one or both thresholds are not met, the parties are allowed to make a voluntary notification. In terms of information to be submitted, procedure, and FNE's attributions, voluntary and mandatory filings are subject to the same rules.

[D] Exemptions

There are no exemptions other than the transaction not qualifying as a concentration transaction (e.g., in the case of intra-group reorganizations)[184] or not meeting the sales thresholds.

[E] Pre-merger Control Regime or Post-merger Control Regime

Pre-merger notification regime: Chile now has a pre-concentration transaction control regime. If sales thresholds are met, then parties are obliged to make a filling and, if these are not surpassed, then parties may choose to make such filing. In both scenarios,

182. More details in §13.04[L].
183. Set by FNE's Exempted Resolution No. 157 of March 25, 2019, which are applicable since August 9, 2019. The previous and lower thresholds were set by FNE's Exempted Resolution No. 667 of November 24, 2016.
Note that, for the sales calculation, it is relevant to distinguish between merger and joint ventures (Article 47 letters a) and c) of DL 211), on one side, and acquisition and assets' acquisitions (Article 47 letters b) and d) of DL 211), on the other. In case of merger and joint ventures or other similar commercial partnerships the sales of the parties and those of their business groups must be considered. For acquisitions and assets' acquisitions sales of the acquirer, of the acquirer's business group and of the acquired entity (and its subsidiaries) or generated with the acquired assets must be considered.
184. More details in §13.04[F].

according to Article 49 of DL 211, a standstill obligation applies to the concentration transaction since the filing is made and until a final and unappealable resolution or ruling ends the procedure.

According to Article 32 of DL 211, there is a sort of antitrust immunity in favor of the concentration transactions approved by the FNE.[185] In virtue of this provision, these transactions cannot be subsequently challenged and shall not carry further antitrust liability for the intervening parties, unless afterward, and based upon new background information, the concentration transaction is qualified as contrary to competition. However, the effects of such new qualification only apply for the future and not retroactively.

In addition, the FNE has the discretionary power to start investigations regarding concentration transactions that, without having surpassed the sales thresholds, are not voluntarily notified by the parties.[186] The FNE shall have a term of one year from the execution of the concentration transaction to open an investigation regarding it.

Finally, there are special rules for certain industries or business areas that also require filings before the FNE or other authorities, in which case there might be parallel pre-transaction procedures.[187]

Post-closing report of minority shareholdings in competitors: On a separate but somehow related regulation, law 20,945 also added an Article 4bis to DL 211, creating an obligation to inform to the FNE the acquisition, by a company or an entity of its business group, a direct or indirect interest of more than 10% of a competitor's equity, considering both stakes held in its own name and those held by third parties in their benefit. This must be done within sixty days after the closing of the transaction.

The obligation to inform shall be triggered only where the acquiring company (and its business group) and the target had, separately, annual revenues for sales, services, and other ordinary course of business activities of more than 100,000 UF (approximately USD 4 million) in the previous year.[188]

FNE may decide to start investigations regarding such minority shareholdings acquisitions to determine if there are any breaches to Article 3 of DL 211. So far, very few cases have occurred relating to this new minority shareholdings' regulation, and

185. This provision also applies for the acts or contracts reviewed and approved by the TDLC in virtue of a non-contentious procedure.
186. Regarding non-notified concentration transactions that did surpass the thresholds, *see* §13.04[I].
187. More details in §13.04[N].
188. Unlike the merger control regime thresholds, and just as it occurs with interlocking provision (*see supra* n. 164), there are no specific guidelines on how to convert this amount to foreign currency.

most of these refer to unreported acquisitions of minority shareholdings[189] or reports filed after the relevant deadline.[190]

[F] Intra-group Transactions

Intra-group reorganizations or transactions are not subject to ex-ante control, given that Article 47 of DL 211 requires the undertakings involved to be independent and to belong to different business groups.

In general terms, the FNE confirmed this perspective on its Jurisdictional Guideline, stating that "internal restructuring or transactions within a business group will not be considered as a concentration transaction".[191]

[G] Substantive Test for Assessing Mergers

Following the example of other jurisdictions, the substantive standard to review concentration transactions is the substantial lessening of competition (*reducción sustancial de la competencia*). Particularly, Articles 54 and 57 of DL 211, which apply to the end of phases I and II, respectively, set forth that FNE must: (i) approve a concentration transaction without remedies if it concludes it is not apt to substantially lessening competition; (ii) approve a concentration transaction with remedies if it concludes that, subject to these, it is not apt to substantially lessening competition; or (iii) prohibit a concentration transaction if it concludes that it is apt to substantially lessen competition (but decisions forbidding a concentration transaction can only be issued in phase II).

According to the new Horizontal Mergers Guidelines, the FNE considers that normally transactions below a certain concentration threshold have a negligible potential to substantially reduce competition. Consequently, the FNE will rule out further analysis if after the concentration transaction:

i. the Herfindahl Hirschman Index (HHI) is less than 1500;
ii. the HHI is higher than 1500 but below 2500 (this index value reflects a moderately concentrated market) with a delta HHI below 200;

189. *See*, e.g., FNE's Closing Report (2021), Case No. 2638-20, "Claim against Jack Mosa for purchase of shares in Parque Arauco" (closing the investigation because claimed purchase of shares was not in a competitor of the acquiring party); and TDLC's resolutions approving settlements (2020) in cases C No. 388-20, "FNE v. Banmédica S.A." and C No. 389-20, "FNE v. Sociedad de Inversiones Los Orientales Limitada" (settlements after the FNE filed lawsuits for not having reported a minority shareholding in an alleged competitor).

190. TDLC's resolution approving an out-of-court settlement (2018) in case AE No. 15-18, "Out-of-court settlement between FNE and International Mainstream Renewable Power Limited" (out-of-court settlement with FNE after a minority shareholding in a competitor was reported sixty-seven days past the applicable deadline).

191. Jurisdiction Guideline, para. 21. However, this analysis must be done case by case given that the concept, definition, and scope of business group may vary among jurisdictions and, more importantly, FNE interprets control and decisive influence in a rather broad and extensive manner not necessarily aligned with Chilean Securities Law (Law No. 18,045) which legally defines what a business group is, so that changes in the nature of control may trigger filings.

iii. the HHI is higher than 2500 (this index value reflects a highly concentrated market) with a delta HHI below 100.[192]

FNE will analyze with more detail the concentration transactions exceeding these thresholds or, even if these are not surpassed, if certain special circumstances exist, such as: (i) one of the involved entities is a potential competitor or a recent entrant with a small share not reflective of the share it might obtain in the near future; (ii) one of the involved entities is a maverick; (iii) the parties are close competitors; (iv) market structure is prone to coordination or there are indicia of recent coordination; and (v) existence of consumer association's claims regarding the effects of the transaction.[193]

Further elaboration on this standard, FNE has stated that a transaction can be expected to produce a substantial lessening of competition when its materialization "may grant, reinforce or increase the capacity of the entity resulting from the Transaction to by itself (unilateral risk) or together with others (coordinated risk), significantly deteriorate the competitive conditions of the respective market compared to the counterfactual."[194] After explaining the types of risks that might flow from concentration transactions and their characteristics for some specific markets and transactions, the Horizontal Mergers Guidelines recognizes two counterweights to such risks: clients bargaining power and efficiencies.

FNE distinguishes between two general categories of efficiencies: productive and dynamic efficiencies. Regardless of the type of efficiency, for these to be considered by FNE on its analysis these must meet the following conditions: (i) be verifiable (i.e., be proved by the parties); (ii) inherent to the concentration transaction (i.e., not achievable through less restrictive means); and (iii) apt to compensate the increased market power obtained by the merged entity (i.e., sufficient, timely and transferable to consumers).[195]

Although there has not been much judicial review or case law, in the only concentration transaction subject to this regime in which the TDLC has issued a judgment ("*Ideal-Nutrabien*"), the two judges of the minority vote stated that "the substantial lessening of competition is only established in DL 211 as a parameter that binds the FNE".[196]

[H] Notification Procedure and Timetable

Procedure before the FNE is separated in two main stages: phase I and phase II.

192. Horizontal Mergers Guideline, para. 35.
193. *Ibid.*, para. 36.
194. *Ibid.*, para. 39.
195. *Ibid.*, para. 152 et seq. Equivalent elements were recognized by the TDLC under the old "merger control" system, e.g., in TDLC's Resolution No. 43, "SMU Consultation on the effects in competition of the merger of the entities SMU S.A. and Supermercados del Sur S.A.", par. 13.6.
196. TDLC's Resolution No. 166 (2018), "Special revision appeal of Ideal S.A and other against FNE's resolution of May 10, 2018", minority vote (9).

The Merger Regulation includes regular, simplified and simplified (without overlaps) notification mechanisms. Thus, before submitting a notification, parties must assess the horizontal or vertical overlaps that might exist between their activities and their market shares on the involved markets. If there are overlaps, depending on their market shares the simplified or regular mechanism will apply. The regular notification requests more information. However, for all the mechanisms the procedure is the same.

The parties can also approach the FNE with informal pre-filing consultations ("pre-notification"). According to the Pre-Filing Instructive, pre-notification can be used to analyze or discuss matters such as: (i) if the transaction qualifies as a concentration transaction; (ii) the type of concentration transaction according to Article 47 of DL 211; (iii) calculating the thresholds; (iv) existence or inexistence of product or geographic overlaps; (v) difficulties in defining the relevant markets; (vi) information to be submitted; (vii) applicability of the simplified notification mechanism; and (viii) possibility of being exempted to submit certain background information.[197]

[1] Phase I

Once the parties have notified the concentration transaction, the FNE has ten business days to declare whether the filing is complete or not. If the FNE declares the filing incomplete, the parties would have ten additional business days to submit the missing information. Then, the FNE has once again ten business days to declare whether the filing is complete or not. Neither the DL 211 nor the infra-legal regulation establishes a maximum number of occasions in which the FNE might declare the filing incomplete.

When the FNE decides to declare the filing complete, it shall start an investigation (the thirty business days of phase I), communicating its decision to the parties and to the public. During phase I, the case file is confidential, so that neither the parties nor third parties can access it.

Over the course of the investigation, the FNE may exercise any of the attributions applicable to potential infringement investigations, except for the ones reserved for collusion cases.[198]

Within thirty business days following the start of phase I of the investigation, the FNE shall approve the transaction, subject or not to mitigation measures, or extend the investigation for a maximum of ninety additional business days (phase II) if it deems that the concentration transaction may substantially lessen competition if it is closed without mitigation measures or subject to the measures offered by the parties. In such case, proceeding moves to phase II.

Phase I may be suspended once for up to thirty business days if the FNE and the parties agree to do so, and it is automatically suspended for up to ten business days

197. Pre-Filing Instructive, para. 16.
198. *See* §13.02[C][2].

each time the parties submit a mitigation proposal.[199] There is no limit on how many mitigation proposals can be submitted.

According to FNE's statistics, the average duration of the procedures ended in phase I with an unconditional approval is twenty-three business days, while procedures ended in this same phase subject to remedies last in average seventy-six business days.[200] Note that such periods do not consider the time between the filing is made and the moment in which the FNE declares it complete, which according to third-parties studies last in average thirty calendar days.[201]

[2] Phase II

If the FNE decides to move the investigation to Phase II, it shall inform the parties, agencies, and authorities directly concerned and the undertakings that likely have an interest in the concentration transaction, as well as publish the relevant resolution (confidential information redacted) on its website. Recipients of this communication, as well as any third party interested in the concentration transaction, including suppliers, competitors, clients or consumers, may submit information to the investigation within twenty business days following the publication of the resolution extending the investigation to FNE's website.

During phase II, the case file is public, but parties and third parties can request confidential treatment of their submissions, responses, and documents. Hence, the case file that is available for public access has the confidential information redacted.

Within the ninety-business days of phase II, the FNE shall approve the transaction, subject or not to mitigation measures, or prohibit the transaction, if it concludes that the transaction has the ability of substantially lessening competition.

Phase II may be suspended once for up to sixty business days if the FNE and the parties agree to do so, and it is automatically suspended for up to fifteen business days each time the parties submit a mitigation proposal.

According to FNE's statistics, the average duration of phase II of investigations ended in phase II is 123 business days.[202] Considering the time between the filing is made and the moment in which the FNE declares it complete, phase I and phase II,

199. But the FNE may react sooner than the 10 business days.
200. Considering the concentration transactions notified between June 1, 2017 and September 27, 2021. Statistics available in: https://www.fne.gob.cl/wp-content/uploads/2021/11/Estadisticas_Division_Fusiones_Septiembre_2021.pdf.
201. Considering the concentration transactions notified between June 1, 2017 and January 15, 2020. "¿Cuánto tardan las investigaciones de la Fiscalía Nacional Económica en materia de fusiones?, CeCO UAI, p. 7.
202. Considering only the duration of phase II (not of phase I) of the investigations about the concentration transactions notified between June 1, 2017 and September 30, 2021. Statistics available in: https://www.fne.gob.cl/wp-content/uploads/2021/11/Estadisticas_Division_Fusiones_Septiembre_2021.pdf.

third parties' studies have indicated that the entire procedure for cases ended in phase II last in average 274 calendar days.[203]

Until September 2021, there have been twelve investigations that have advanced to phase II. Of the investigations already terminated, four ended with an unconditional approval,[204] three with approvals subject to mitigation measures,[205] and three were prohibited by the FNE,[206] although one (*Ideal-Nutrabien*) was approved by the TDLC.[207]

[I] Consequences of a Failure to File

In case a transaction qualifies as a concentration transaction pursuant to Article 47 of DL 211 and surpasses both the collective and the individual thresholds, pursuant to Article 48 of DL 211 it is mandatory for the parties to file a notification before the FNE. If not, gun jumping is sanctioned in Article 3 bis letter a) of DL 211.

Article 3 bis letters b) to e) also considers other specific infringements in the context of merger control that are subject to these same sanctions: (i) violation of the standstill obligation (i.e., closing a concentration transaction notified voluntarily or mandatorily before the relevant decision is issued); (ii) breach of the approved remedies; (iii) close a concentration transaction forbidden by the FNE, the TDLC, or the Supreme Court; and (iv) notify a concentration transaction submitting false information.

In relation to such infringements, TDLC may impose the general measures and sanctions contemplated in Articles 3 and 26 of DL 211 that are applicable to other anticompetitive behaviors (with the exception of the prohibition of entering into contracts with the state and other public institutions, which is only available for collusion) that were explained above.[208] Regarding failure to notify, the TDLC may impose a fine of up to 20 UTA (approximately USD 16,700) for each day of delay

---

203. Considering the concentration transactions notified between June 1, 2017 and January 15, 2020, for 6 of which the procedure ended in phase II. "¿Cuánto tardan las investigaciones de la Fiscalía Nacional Económica en materia de fusiones?", CeCO UAI, p. 8.
204. Cases Nos. F85-2017, "Concentration transaction between Essilor International and Luxottica Group"; F135-2018, "Acquisition of the shares of Grupo Empresas Navieras SAAM Puertos and Ransa Comercial in Terminal Puerto Arica by Inversiones Neltume and Inversiones y Construcciones Belfi"; F217-2019, "Acquisition of Cornershop by Uber Technologies, Inc.; and No. F216-2019, "Acquisition of assests of Inmobiliaria y Administradora CGL Limitada by Compañía de Petróleos de Chile COPEC S.A."
205. Cases Nos. F116-2018, "Acquisition by Turner International Latin America, Inc. of Canal del Fútbol"; F233-2020, "Merger between Fiat Chrysler Automobiles N.V. and Peugeot S.A."; and F220-2019, "Acquisition of control in GrandVision N.V. (Rotter & Krauss) by EssilorLuxottica S.A."
206. Cases Nos. F90-2017, "Concentration transaction between Ideal S.A. and Nutrabien S.A."; F101-2017, "Concentration transaction between Banco Santander – Chile and Sociedad de Recaudación y Pagos de Servicios Limitada"; and F178-2019, "Acquisition of Clinica Iquique S.A. by Red Interclínica S.A."
207. TDLC's Resolution No. 166 (2018), "Special revision appeal of Ideal S.A. and other against FNE's resolution of May 10, 2018". Details about the appeal available against FNE's prohibitions and against certain TDLC's rulings can be found in §13.04[M.
208. *See* §13.02[D][1].

counted from the closing of the concentration transaction pursuant to Article 26 letter e) of DL 211.

Until now there have been only two judicial cases. In one the FNE claimed that the parties closed a concentration transaction subject to a standstill obligation (notified to the FNE but approval pending) in breach of Article 3bis letter b), despite the carve-out implemented for Chile. The parties finally settled.[209]

In the other, the FNE accused a breach of a specific remedy subject to which a concentration transaction was approved and the submission of false information during the procedure, which did not affect FNE's decision.[210] The parties partially settled regarding the first infringement, while the case is still ongoing in relation to the second conduct.[211]

FNE did not invoke current or potential effects as part of its allegations in these cases and, furthermore, it strongly argued in the second one that a specific result or anticompetitive consequences for consumers, competitors, distributors or, in general, the market are not needed for these infringements to be sanctioned.

[J] Third Party Involvement in Notification Process

The FNE can (and normally do) require information to third parties, including suppliers, clients, and competitors. In phase II, the FNE must inform such decision to these third parties, as well as to the relevant authorities. In this sense, all these third parties are allowed to intervene both in phase I and phase II, but have a more formal stance in the latter, which even allow them to appear in the appeal procedure's public hearing before the TDLC if they submitted background information within 20 days from the publication in FNE's website of the resolution advancing to phase II.

Third parties are not allowed to "offer" remedies, but they might suggest specific remedies as part of their responses to FNE's requests for information or their voluntary submissions in the procedure. Also, the FNE has the attribution to market test the remedies asking third parties to determine if these mitigate the potential risks derived from the concentration transaction.

Also, based on Articles 31 bis and 57, third parties are not allowed to appeal against FNE's decisions.

[K] Remedies

According to Article 53 of DL 211, the parties are the only ones allowed to offer mitigation measures to the FNE (i.e., FNE cannot unilaterally impose these)[212] to

209. TDLC's resolution approving a settlement (2018), "FNE v. Minerva S.A. and other".
210. Article 3bis letters c) and e) of DL 211, respectively.
211. TDLC's resolution approving a partial settlement (2021), "FNE v. The Walt Disney Company and other".
212. In practice, FNE does suggest the type of remedies it would find suitable and would accept to approve the concentration transaction. Also, note that TDLC and Supreme Court could impose remedies other than the ones offered by the parties (*see* §13.04[M]).

address the potential risks that the concentration transaction might generate. As indicated above, each time the parties make a remedies proposal, the phase I or the phase II are suspended for up to ten and fifteen business days, respectively.

On its Remedies Guideline, FNE states that these must be (i) effective to prevent the substantial lessening of competition; (ii) feasible to be implemented, carried out, and monitored; and (iii) proportionate to the competition risk detected.[213] FNE makes a broad differentiation between structural remedies (i.e., divestments) and other mitigation measures (including quasi-structural and behavioral remedies), stating that, at least for horizontal concentration transactions, it will prefer structural remedies.[214] FNE also considers the possibility of having a monitoring trustee, either for the divestment procedure or to monitor compliance with behavioral remedies.[215]

Until September 2021, FNE has approved fourteen concentration transactions subject to mitigation measures. Of these, four were subject to structural/divestment remedies (in some cases combined with ancillary measures),[216] and ten to other remedies (such as firewalls, behavioral measures, etc.).[217] In addition, in *Ideal-Nutrabien*, TDLC approved the horizontal concentration transaction subject to the behavioral remedies offered by the parties, revoking FNE's prohibition decision.[218]

[L] Penalties

Please *see* §13.04[I] Consequences of a Failure to File.

213. Remedies Guideline, paras. 8–13. Similar requirements have been identified by the TDLC, *see*, e.g., Resolution No. 166 (2018), "Special revision appeal of Ideal S.A and other against FNE's resolution of May 10, 2018", c. 134.
214. Remedies Guideline, paras. 30–38.
215. *Ibid.*, paras. 87–92.
216. Cases Nos. F80-2017 "Concentration transaction between Dow Chemical Co. and DuPont Co."; F97-2017, "Concentration transaction between Bayer AG and Monsanto Company"; F108-2017, "Merger between Linde Aktiengesellschaft and Praxair, Inc."; and F220-2019, "Acquisition of control in GrandVision N.V. (Rotter & Krauss) by EssilorLuxottica S.A."
217. Cases Nos. F81-2017, "Concentration transaction between Time Warner Inc. and AT&T Inc."; F83-2017, "Concentration transaction between Maersk Line and Hamburg Sud."; F87-2017, "Concentration transaction between Atlantia SpA and Abertis Infraestructuras S.A."; F109-2017, "Concentration transaction between AZA Participaciones SpA, Matco Cables SpA and others"; F116-2018, "Acquisition by Turner International Latin America, Inc. of Canal del Fútbol"; F137-2018, "Concentration transaction between Atlantia SpA, ACS, Actividades de Construcción y Servicios S.A. and Hochtief A.G. and Abertis Infraestructuras S.A."; F155-2018, "Acquisition of 21CF by Disney"; F159-2018, "Acquisition of control by Producción e Inversiones Aleste Limitada and Sociedd de Inversiones AH Limitada in Fidelitas Entertainment SpA"; F222-2019, "Acquisition of control in HBO Ole Partners by HBO Latin America Holdings, L.L.C."; and F233-2020, "Merger between Fiat Chrysler Automobiles N.V. and Peugeot S.A.".
218. TDLC's Resolution No. 166 (2018), "Special revision appeal of Ideal S.A and other against FNE's resolution of May 10, 2018".

[M] Appeal

The parties have ten days to file a special appeal (*recurso de revisión especial*) against FNE's prohibition decision. Third parties are not allowed to file such appeal and approval decisions are not appealable.[219]

After the appeal is submitted, TDLC will order the FNE to share the case file and will summon to a public hearing that takes place within sixty days of the receipt of the case file, in which can participate the FNE, the appealing party, and certain third parties.

TDLC must issue its ruling based on the background information contained in the case file, the expositions in the public hearing, and other information gathered ex officio or after request of any party to the procedure, within sixty days from the public hearing.

TDLC can approve or prohibit the concentration transaction and, as a general rule, no appeal can be filed against such decision. Only if the TDLC approves the concentration transaction subject to remedies other than the last proposal made by the parties before the FNE, both the parties and the FNE can file a special appeal (*recurso de reclamación*) to be decided by Supreme Court.[220]

[N] Specific Industries

There are some laws relating to special sectors that contemplate mandatory pre-closing filing before the FNE or sectorial authorities that might overlap with concentration transaction control. We briefly describe some examples below; please note that in some of the listed cases, the analysis that the corresponding authority will conduct, is not related to the competitive effects of the transaction:

- Article 38 of the Freedom of Opinion and Information Act sets forth that any relevant change in the property or control of a media company (e.g., newspapers, magazines, etc.) must be notified to the FNE, within thirty days of its completion. However, in case of a media company which holds a concession granted by the state (e.g., free-to-air television, radio), the operation needs prior authorization by the FNE. The FNE must issue a favorable report within thirty days from the filing. If the decision is unfavorable, TDLC will resolve the matter in a non-contentious proceeding, according to Article 31 of DL 211.

219. Note, e.g., that a third-party tried to file a reconsideration motion against an approval decision of the FNE, which was rejected by the authority. FNE's Closing Resolution (2021), Case F-255-2020.

220. Same appeal applicable to TDLC's rulings on collusion and unilateral abuses, for which there is further detail in §13.02[F]. So far, there are no special appeals (*recursos de reclamación*) submitted in merger control cases.

- Articles 17 and 18 of the Casino Act state that the transfer of shares of a company that operates a casino needs the authorization of the superintendence of Casinos. Every new shareholder shall be subject to the legal requirements and the background check by the superintendence as if it were the original shareholder.
- Article 35 bis of the General Banking Act establishes that certain transactions regarding banks can only occur with prior authorization by the Securities Market Commission ("*CMF*"). The CMF can approve or deny the transaction within sixty days of the notification.
- Articles 64 and 65 of the Water Supply and Sewerage Services Act, state that a merger between two or more companies requires prior approval of the Superintendence of Sanitary Service, which has sixty days to issue a decision. Moreover, it sets forth that the person or the group of persons with a joint action agreement, which have the control or decisive influence in the administration of a utility company (qualified by the TDLC as a natural monopoly on distribution of electricity or local telecoms), which has more than 50% market share in a given area, cannot own or control a water supply company in the same area.
- Article 14 of the Public Ports Act states that the Chilean State may grant concessions to private companies to operate ports, as long as there is another port with similar characteristics in the same region. Otherwise, a prior clearance by the TDLC is necessary, which will regulate the applicable conditions. Furthermore, the TDLC has established restrictions to horizontal and vertical integration with competitors and clients operating within the same port or region.

CHAPTER 14
Competition Law in Colombia

Alfonso Miranda Londoño

§14.01 INTRODUCTION

Colombia is organized as a centralized republic under a presidential system of government based on the rule of law and the exercise of checks and balances by the different branches of power. The country has sound democratic institutions and a constitutional history for almost 300 years.

State intervention in the economy was introduced into the constitutional doctrine of the country since the constitutional reform of 1936. Such intervention has permitted the exercise of economic freedom within the *"Social Market Economy"* established by the 1991 Political Constitution.[1]

Colombia, like other countries in Latin America, issued its first antitrust legislation at the end of the fifties, following the example of the United States (US) and the European Union (EU). However, the laws were not applied in this first era, mainly due to the economic protectionism of the Latin American governments before the nineties, which was at odds with a truly competitive environment.[2]

Evolution of Colombia's Antitrust Laws can be divided into two main periods. The first period began with the expedition of Law 155 of 1959 (Law 155), which

1. The Constitutional Court has issued rulings such as decisions C-074/1993 and C-040/1993 reinforcing economic freedom within the "Social Market Economy".
2. Throughout most of the twentieth century, Colombia just as other nations in Latin America implemented a development policy called "Protectionism" as per the recommendations of the Economic Commission for Latin America and the Caribbean—ECLAC (CEPAL in Spanish). This institution was created under the name of ECLA by means of a resolution adopted by the Economic and Social Council 106 (VI) on February 25, 1948, and it has been operating ever since. Subsequently the range of functions was extended so that the Caribbean countries could be included, and it began to operate under the name Economic Commission for Latin America and the Caribbean—ECLAC (the Spanish acronym CEPAL was not replaced) by virtue of Resolution 1984/67 of July 27, 1984.

contained the first comprehensive regulation of Antitrust Law in Colombia and ended with Special Decree 2153 of 1992 (Decree 2153). The 1991 Political Constitution was issued during this first phase. This event had an enormous significance for Competition Law in Colombia, because the new constitution established Free Economic Competition as a key political principle.

The second period began when Decree 2153 was issued and continues to this day. This second phase is marked by a consistent progress in the enforcement of the law, and in the development of the case law, the doctrine, and the technical capability of the authority, which is now more experienced and mature, with a prominent position among its peers in Latin America.

Decree 2153 reorganized the Competition Authority and structured competition infringements into several categories including (i) the general prohibition, (ii) anti-competitive agreements, (iii) anti-competitive acts, (iv) abuse of a dominant position, and (v) violation of the merger control regulations.

In 2009, Congress enacted Law 1340 (Law 1340) which introduced major modifications to Colombian Competition Law, some of which are:

- Appointment of the Superintendence of Industry and Commerce (SIC) as the National Competition Authority, with almost exclusive jurisdiction for the application of Colombia's competition laws.
- Clarification of the rules for the application of special competition regimes in coordination with the general competition regime.
- Stronger application of competition advocacy and coordination between public authorities for the purpose of applying competition laws.
- Modification of the thresholds and procedures for merger review.
- Introduction of a requirement that, if a party under investigation decides to offer the SIC a settlement, it can do so only during the initial stages of the procedure, so that the SIC does not progress through the entire investigation only to have to consider a settlement proposal at the end.
- Introduction of a leniency program aimed at fostering collaboration between the companies and administrators involved in anti-competitive conduct. Effective and timely cooperation could lead to partial or total immunity from the sanctions that the SIC can impose.
- More active participation of third parties in the investigation of anti-competitive practices and in merger review procedures.
- An important increase in the fines as explained later.
- Extension of the statute of limitations for imposing fines in antitrust investigations from three to five years.
- Special mechanisms for state intervention in the agricultural sector. Eventually, these mechanisms may be used to exclude conduct and situations from the scope of application of competition laws.

Anti-competitive practices are analysed under the general prohibition contained in Article 1 of Law 155, read together with Article 46 of Decree 2153, and the prohibitions against specific actions are contained in Decree 2153: Articles 47 (horizontal and vertical agreements), 48 (unilateral conducts) and 50 (Abuse of Dominant Position). The National Competition Authority, the Superintendence of Industry and Commerce (SIC) oversees enforcing these provisions.

Most recently Law 2195 of 2022 reformed two mayor aspects of Colombia's antitrust legislation; the first being its leniency program (Article 66), and the second one being the fines that the competition authority can impose (Articles 67 and 68).

The structure of the Colombian competition laws allows for the application of two different systems of analysis to the investigation of anti-competitive conducts, that resemble the per se *rule* and the *rule of reason*.[3]

While the legislation specifically lists certain types of prohibited conducts, anti-competitive conducts that do not fall under these specific categories may be investigated by the SIC as an infringement of the general prohibition against anti-competitive behaviour using a system that resembles the *rule of reason*. Accordingly, the SIC will take into consideration the relevant market, the nature, purpose, and effect of the conduct and then balance the pro-competitive versus the anti-competitive effects of the conduct to establish if it results in a violation of the general prohibition.

On the other hand, the conducts described in the legislation are investigated according to the specific characteristics and elements of each conduct in a sort of per se *rule* of analysis. This means that when the authority studies a specifically prohibited conduct, it will focus on the demonstration of the elements of such conduct that are considered by law as anti-competitive; and in most of the cases it will not accept explanations of legal or economic nature trying to demonstrate that the investigated conduct is not illegal. For example, Article 47 (6) of Decree 2153 prohibits agreements that limit technical development or intend to do so. The authority will not accept evidence or arguments trying to demonstrate that the conduct caused no harm or that it was done with a beneficial intent or effect, because the law has defined such conduct as anti-competitive.

Even though this is the general situation regarding the interpretation of the specifically defined conducts, it must be recognized that in the past decade the SIC has

3. The per se rule of analysis has been the focus of academic debate, but the Competition Authority in Colombia as well as the Colombian Council of State seem to have solved it already. In fact, in 2000, ANDEVIP (Case 29302/00—ANDEVIP) was sanctioned by the SIC. This case involved a group of security companies that agreed on a price. They based their defence by arguing that the Superintendence of Surveillance and Private Security had issued a regulation stipulating that charging less than ten minimum monthly legal wages was equivalent to breaching tax and labour laws. Regardless of this circumstance, the SIC proceeded to sanction the company as it considered that there had been a price fixing agreement. During the reconsideration plea before the authority and the judicial proceedings that followed, the companies involved disputed the position of the SIC and claimed that having entered into an agreement was not tantamount to acting against the law as their purpose was not to restrict free competition. The first instance judicial sentence revoked the decision of the SIC as it considered that entering into a price fixing agreement was not enough to impose a sanction and that the SIC had to prove that the objectives of the law were in fact breached (in particular, consumer welfare, efficiency, and market access). Such stance actually posed a threat to the per se rule of analysis in Colombian Antitrust Law. Subsequently, the ruling was reversed by the Council of State, which ruled that demonstrating the conduct of the prohibited behaviour was enough to impose sanctions.

considered in a handful of cases that vertical price fixing agreements may be considered legal, notwithstanding the fact that Article 47 (1) of Decree 2153 defines as anti-competitive all price fixing agreements, without distinction on whether they are horizontal or vertical. In these cases, the authority has shifted the burden of proof, which means that by default the vertical price fixing agreement is considered illegal unless the investigated companies are able to demonstrate the pro-competitive advantages of the conduct.

The focus of the authority has been the fight against cartels. There are, however, cases on unilateral conduct, abuse of dominance, and the enforcement of the merger review regulations.

These functions are the core of what Law 1340 calls *"Competition Protection,"* but the SIC is an authority with many other functions: It has been granted administrative and judicial capacity to decide unfair competition and consumer protection cases; it is also the data protection, intellectual property, and metrology (measurements and standards) authority.

In the area of competition protection, some of the most significant cases especially during the nineties were related to the agricultural sector (sugar, rice, chocolate, onions, milk), and to other key economic activities, such as cement, fuel, and telecommunications. During the last decade, the authority will focus on the application of the so called *Anti-Corruption Statute,* Law 1474 of 2011 (Law 1474), which makes bid rigging in public contracting both an anti-competitive agreement and a criminal offense. It seems possible that in the immediate future, the SIC will analyse the digital markets, taking into consideration also that it has been granted functions related to the application of the competition, consumer protection, and data protection regulations.

§14.02 CARTELS

[A] Relevant Legislation

Article 1 of Law 155 and Article 46 of Decree 2153 prohibit, in general, all conducts that limit free competition. Nevertheless, Article 47 of Decree 2153 specifically prohibits horizontal and vertical agreements either "by its object or by its effect". Among other agreements, Article 47 prohibits; price fixing (horizontal and vertical), discrimination, horizontal territory and customer allocation, quota arrangements, technology or raw materials limitations, obstruction or blocking access to market distribution, tying, and bid rigging.

Article 45 (1) of Decree 2153, defines the term "agreement" for purposes of antitrust laws: An agreement is defined as a contract, convention, concerted practice of conscious parallelism. This means that the SIC will investigate both express and tacit agreements. The tacit collusion cases are considered as concerted practices and conscious parallelism. In both cases the authority will endeavour to demonstrate the so called plus factors to assert that tacit conduct amounts to an anti-competitive agreement.

[1] Horizontal Price fixing

Colombia is no exception as to what entails the most basic violations of competition legal rules and in that sense, horizontal price fixing is one example. Agreements entered with the object or effect of directly or indirectly fix prices are deemed per se unlawful according to Article 47 (1) of Decree 2153. As said before, there is no distinction in the law between horizontal and vertical price fixing, both types being clearly prohibited and deemed per se illegal by the law. As mentioned, there is a handful of cases during the past decade, in which the SIC has considered that vertical price fixing agreements may be considered legal. In those cases, the authority has shifted the burden of proof and required that the accused companies demonstrate the pro-competitive effects of the vertical price fixing agreements that will otherwise be considered illegal.

Directly or indirectly fixing prices is considered by the SIC as equally harmful just as doing it in terms of maximum or minimum prices. Back in 2004, a transportation association was sanctioned by the SIC because the companies that belonged to the association entered into an agreement which sought to protect customers from excessive pricing (Case 21821/2004—Transportation Companies).

In the case of other types of defences submitted relating to the per se illegality rule of horizontal price fixing, a 2000 case is worth noting: Back in that year, the SIC issued a decision against real estate agents that subscribed an agreement which set out a commission by which they charged their customers 3% (Case 27759/1999 and 7508/2000 Realtors). The defendants stated that there was a commercial custom that under the terms of the Code of Commerce was mandatory. The SIC did not agree and considered that no commercial custom could go against the law and imposed fines on all companies that took part in the price fixing agreement. In the end, the decision was upheld by the judiciary.

[2] Horizontal Agreements to Allocate Costumers or Territories

Article 47 (3) of Decree 2153 expressly prohibits agreements with the purpose or effect of allocating markets among producers or distributors. Hence, horizontal market allocation agreements, which include customer, supplier, or geographic market allocation are per se illegal.

Back in 1999, the SIC initiated an investigation against the cement manufacturers and their association (Colombian Cement Institute—ICPC (17464/1999—Cement—ICPC) due to an alleged horizontal market distribution agreement which violated Article 47 (3) of Decree 2153 and an agreement to share confidential and commercially sensitive information thereby violating Article 1 of Law 155. The SIC sought to prove that the cement companies had portioned the country among themselves and that they also monitored the compliance of the agreement by submitting to ICPC a weekly report about locations and customers where sales took place and by receiving a report from the institute informing each company about the same pieces of information.

The companies based their rationale on the features of the product and the cost of transportation which caused their selling the product, above all, in areas close to the plant. They offered a guarantee (settlement) to the authority, comprising among other elements, an information protocol that did not enable them to monitor sales made by their competitors. The SIC accepted the guarantee (settlement) proposal, investigation was closed, and no sanctions were imposed.

Agreements having the purpose or effect of assigning, distributing, or limiting the sources of supply of raw materials are prohibited by Article 47 (5) of Decree 2153. The Sugar Cane Manufacturers Case is a good example (Case 6839/2007—Sugar Cane Mills): the SIC considered that the sugar cane manufacturers had portioned the sugar cane growers in a way that they could only sell the crops to the mills that had been assigned. Within the same investigation, the sugar cane manufacturers were also accused and finally sanctioned for an alleged agreement that established a price formula. However, regarding the horizontal agreement to allocate the growers and their farms, the manufacturers were able to prove that no agreement had been entered and that it was due to the technical features of the process and the potential degradation of the raw material that each mill preferred to purchase the crops from closest possible farms. The SIC accepted the argument and the manufacturers were not sanctioned for this conduct.

There is no express prohibition against vertical market distribution (e.g., vertical territorial exclusivity granted by a manufacturer to its distributors) which does not mean that such agreements are permitted from the legal standpoint. They are just not illegal per se, but they can always be investigated pursuant to the general prohibition set forth in Article 1 of Law 155 along with Article 46 of Decree 2153 (Rule of Reason analysis).

Postobon, Panamco (Coca-Cola), and Bavaria (Case 19644/2000—Soft Drinks), three soft drinks manufacturers, were investigated in 1999 by the SIC. It was argued that the producers and the distributors had entered into vertical and horizontal price fixing agreements and into horizontal and vertical market allocation, thereby violating Article 47 (1) and (3) of Decree 2153 respectively. As to the first allegation, the companies that were investigated submitted that the manufacturers had imposed the price of sale to retailers on the distributors. As to market allocation, they submitted that no horizontal agreement had been entered but that they merely granted territories to their distributors for cost reduction purposes and efficiency (in their distribution channels) and inter-brand competition increases. Their submissions were successful, and the authority accepted their arguments in the sense that there had been no per se violation and that pursuant to the Rule of Reason, unilaterally imposing prices on their distributors and awarding territories for logistics purposes in fact represented pro-competitive effects and promoted inter-brand competition. The SIC accepted the settlement (guarantees) proposal and terminated the investigation with no sanctions. It also accepted the price imposed on the distributors and the logistics related vertical market allocation.

There is a general prohibition under Article 1 of Law 155 and Article 46 of Decree 2153 (Rule of Reason analysis) by which non-competition agreements can be investigated. There has not been a broad development of this concept on the part of the SIC, but it is accepted that non-competition clauses can be included on certain occasions if they are reasonable, limited in time, and have a meritorious object (e.g., in a merger deal to avoid confusion or unfair trade practices).

Apart from these two main forms of restrictive agreements, there are other restrictive agreements that are specifically prohibited and are considered as per se illegal:

- Agreements entered with the purpose or effect of assigning production or supply quotas are considered per se illegal under Article 47 (4) of Decree 2153.
- Agreements entered with the purpose or effects of limiting technical developments are considered per se illegal under Article 47 (6) of Decree 2153.
- Agreements entered with the purpose or effects of conditioning the supply of a product to the acceptance of additional obligations that by their nature did not belong to the objective of the transaction, are considered per se illegal under Article 47 (7) of Decree 2153.
- Agreements entered with the purpose or effect of abstaining of manufacturing a product or providing a service, or to affect the levels of production, are considered per se illegal under Article 47 (8) of Decree 2153.
- Bid rigging agreements aimed at tampering with public bids distribute contracts or fixing the terms of the proposals are considered per se illegal under Article 47 (9) of Decree 2153.
- Agreements entered with the purpose or effect of obstructing access of other economic agents to the market or the distribution channels, are considered per se illegal under Article 47 (10) of Decree 2153.

[B] Extraterritoriality

As a matter of principle, Colombian authorities including the SIC will exercise jurisdiction within the boundaries of the territory of the country and very rarely will they try to exercise jurisdiction abroad.

About the application of Competition Laws, Colombia, as many other jurisdictions applies the "effects theory", which means that any conduct that produces anti-competitive effects in Colombia can be investigated by the SIC. According to Article 2 of Law 1340:

> The set of rules and regulations governing competition protection shall apply to whoever performs any economic activity or to anyone who affects or may affect such performance, regardless of its form or legal nature and in relation with those conducts that have or may have a total or partial effect upon the national markets, whatever the activity or economic sector may be. (Underlined)

This means that the SIC can investigate the conduct of persons who are acting abroad if their actions affect free competition in the Colombian markets. In these multijurisdictional cases, the SIC may face several challenges including among others: (i) procedural problems related to service of process, (ii) collection of fines, (iii) the exchange of information due to confidentiality laws, (iv) gathering of evidence, and (v) incentivise leniency program cooperation.

Regardless of the challenges that the effects theory may present, it is imperative to recognize that the SIC along with other jurisdictions and Competition Authorities in Latin America, have implemented an important number of Cooperation Agreements in diverse areas of antitrust enforcement, the most representative being the leniency programs.

[C] Investigations

Violation of competition law in Colombia is subject to administrative investigations aimed to protect the constitutional principle of free competition in favour of the people. It is a general protection and therefore the authority can initiate the investigations officiously or following an accusation.

[1] Authorities

The principal feature of law 1340 is the appointment of the SIC as the National Competition Authority. Law 1340 grants the SIC the sole power to apply competition laws in all areas, including specialized sectors such as public utilities, banks and insurance, health, transportation, and ports, etc.

The law gives the SIC antitrust enforcement faculties previously granted to other Agencies like the Superintendence of Public Utilities, the Superintendence of Banks, the Superintendence of Ports and Transportation, the National Television Commission, and the Aeronautic Authority.

Pursuant of Chapter III of Law 1340, modified by Law 2195 of 2022 and Decree 4886 of 2011, modified by Decree 092 of 2022, the SIC has been given, among other functions, the following powers, and responsibilities:

- The SIC has the power to investigate and sanction anti-competitive practices in all sectors of the economy.
- In 1998, the SIC was given administrative and judicial powers to decide unfair trade and consumer protection cases.
- The SIC is the merger control authority in all cases and sectors except for the merger transactions in the financial and aeronautic sectors. In the first case, as described later in this chapter, the superintendence of banks is in charge of studying the transactions, whereas in the second case, the aeronautic authority—"Aerocivil", is in charge.
- The SIC is the trademark and patent authority. It also maintains the industrial property registry.

- The SIC is in charge of the application of the data protection statute.

Pursuant to the issuance of Law 2195 of 2022 which made some modifications to the leniency program and the system of fines, on January 24, 2022, the government issued Decree 092, which represents the most recent reform in the structure and functions of the Competition Authority. In addition, the decree seeks to strengthen the application of the rules related to the competition, consumer, and data protection rules; and creates a new set of functions related to competition compliance.

Another important modification is that since January 1, 2022, the SIC will not be the superior of the chambers of commerce and therefore will not decide the appeals presented against their decisions. This modification is consistent with the provisions contained in Law 2068 of 2020, which awarded those functions to the superintendence of corporations.

In order to strengthen data protection, the decree created the *Office of Habeas Data* within the office of the superintendent delegate for data protection and modified the functions of the superintendent delegate in order to enhance the protection of personal data.

Some of the most significant functions of the *Office of Habeas Data* are, among others, the following:

- Ensure the processing of personal data.
- Manage the National Registry of Databases.
- Advance the inquiries, investigations, procedures, and administrative actions related to the violations of the data protection Laws.

The decree also reinforced competition protection and enforcement; but most importantly it made a big step in the implementation of the Competition Compliance Policy, by creating a *Compliance Office* as part of the office of the superintendent delegate for competition protection. Some of the most significant functions of the *Compliance Office* are, among others, the following:

- Follow-up on the obligations created to the investigated parties, of the guarantees (settlements) accepted by the superintendent of industry and commerce, for the anticipated termination of the administrative investigations initiated for the breach of the antitrust and unfair competition regulation.
- Monitoring of the conditions established by the superintendent of industry and commerce in the face of requests for consolidation, integration, merger, and obtaining control of supervised companies.
- Instruct the procedures on the breach of the obligations; (i) arising from the anticipated termination of investigations pursuant to the acceptance of guarantees (settlements), (ii) from reporting a business integration, and (iii) arising from the acceptance of a business integration under conditioning.
- Monitor the effective adoption of compliance programs.

[a] Policy, Politics, and Institutions

Like in most Latin American countries, in Colombia public enforcement of the Competition Laws is the general rule, which means that the main weight in the application of the law depends on the activity of the SIC, as said before, an administrative authority in charge of the application of competition laws in all sectors of the economy.

The SIC conducts investigations that are administrative in nature (not judicial) aimed to find out if there has been a violation of the competition laws, case in which the violation is prohibited, and a fine is respectively imposed.

The SIC has no capacity to order indemnification of damages to third persons affected by the anti-competitive behaviour. It is also important to convey that except for bid rigging in state contracts, the infringements of competition laws such as price fixing and quota arrangements are not considered criminal offenses, and that as an administrative authority the SIC has no jurisdiction over these crimes, which are investigated by the attorney general's office and decided by the criminal judges.

[b] Resources and Priorities

Nowadays the SIC is perceived as an effective authority with increased strength for the application of competition laws. This is due to the legislative changes introduced by Law 1340, Decree 019 of 2012 (Decree 019) and Law 1474, which *inter alia* have allowed the authority to marshal important resources for the application of Competition Laws. Since then, the SIC has been strengthened in aspects such as (i) bigger budget, (ii) more prepared personnel, (iii) increase in the capacity to impose bigger fines, (iv) internal structure, and others

While in 2009 the SIC had a budget of 16 million USD (4.5 of which were destined to investment), for the year 2014, the authority was assigned a budget of USD 59 million (28 of which were destined to investment), which means that the budget has been multiplied by three. Currently the budget assigned for the year 2021 is approximately 64 million USD (with 35 million destined to investment), which reflects the progressive increase in the economic capacity of the competition authority.

In 2006, the SIC had 390 public officials and by 2013 the entity was already 673 strong and remains to this date approximately in that range, but the difference is that apart from the almost 700 public officials the SIC hires nearly 2.000 independent contractors that help in the different areas of work. But even more significant is the increase in the fines: In 2010 the SIC imposed 13 million USD in fines and in 2013 the fines amounted to 108 million USD, while between 2018 and July 2021 the SIC has collected approximately 69 million USD. There is no doubt that thanks to its increased capacity and strength the SIC can face new challenges and protect competition in a more technical and effective way.

As said before, in the area of competition protection some of the most significant cases in the nineties were related to the agricultural sector (sugar, rice, chocolate, onions, and milk) and to other key economic activities, such as cement, fuel and telecommunications.

Even though bid rigging agreements are forbidden since 1992 with the issuance of Decree 2153, and the SIC carried on investigations such as the one in Case 21822/2004, this conduct acquired its real importance with the introduction of the so called *Anti-Corruption Statute* (Law 1474), which makes bid rigging in public contracting both an anti-competitive agreement and a criminal offense.

As a result of the criminalization of bid rigging, the SIC was authorized to create the so called *Elite Anti-Collusion Group* with additional personnel and budget, that allowed it to investigate 358 cases in 2015 and 149 cases in 2016, which shows the importance that the SIC has given to the fight against collusion in public contracting.

The first time in which bid rigging was investigated and sanctioned both as an anti-competitive agreement and a criminal offense was in Case 12992/2019 related to the public contracts of the National Learning Service (SENA) in which the SIC conducted the administrative investigation and imposed sanctions of approximately 1.1 million USD; whereas the office of the attorney general conducted the criminal investigation as a result of which the instigator of the conduct was sentenced to forty-eight months in jail, and the other persons involved in the criminal conduct were sentenced to thirty-six months.

The SIC and the attorney general's office also conducted competition and criminal investigations related to the *Lava Jato* case in Colombia (Ruta del Sol II). It can be expected that in the following years the SIC will focus on bid rigging and in the competition cases related to the digital markets and digital platforms, especially since the SIC is the competition, consumer protection, and data protection authority.

[c] Inter-agency Cooperation (International)

As National Competition Authority, the SIC develops important interaction and cooperation with other competition authorities. A selection of those interactions is described here:

- Pursuant to Article 14 of Decision 608 of the Andean Community of Nations (CAN by its Spanish initials), the General Secretariat of the CAN will request the cooperation of the national authorities of the countries affected by the anti-competitive conducts investigated by the Commission. For the Commission to start an investigation, it is necessary that the conduct has community dimension, that is, that the conduct affects the markets of more than one member country.
- On July 4, 2007, Congress approved Law 1143 that contains the Free Trade Agreement between Colombia and the US. Pursuant to the FTA, each party agreed to maintain a competition law and as well as an authority to apply it, with the obligation to grant the accused persons due process, right of defence and the possibility to impeach the decisions of the competition authority before an independent tribunal. Pursuant to Article 13.3 of the Treaty, the

parties agreed to cooperate with each other in the area of competition policy to achieve an effective application of the competition laws.

- In September 2014, the FTC and the DOJ signed a cooperation agreement with the SIC. According to the statement released by the agencies, the new agreement contains provisions for antitrust enforcement cooperation and coordination, conflict avoidance and consultations with respect to enforcement actions, and technical cooperation. The agreement also contains confidentiality protections. The Colombian Authority has been able to forge a strong enforcement relationship with the U.S. Antitrust Agencies over the years; both bilaterally and under the terms of the U.S.-Colombia Trade Promotion Agreement.
- Similar provisions are contained in other Free Trade Agreements like the one signed between Colombia, Perú and the EU.
- Colombia participates as an observer in the Competition Committee of the OCDE since 2011 and attends Competition Forums on a regular basis. It also hosted the ninth meeting of the OECD-IDB Latin American Competition Forum in 2011 and was accepted in 2020 as member number 37 at the OECD, where the superintendent has a seat at the Competition Commission.
- The SIC also participates in the International Consumer Network—ICPEN, where Colombia has already occupied the presidency.
- Finally, Colombia is an active participant in the International Competition Network—ICN, with an active participation in several groups: currently as chair of the Competition Advocacy Group.

During the past decade, the SIC has celebrated an important number of cooperation agreements with other jurisdictions and competition authorities to strengthen the antitrust enforcement and free competition in the Colombian markets.

[2] Procedure

The SIC can initiate a preliminary investigation officiously or following accusations from any citizen. There is no time limit for the preliminary investigation; it can last for some months and, in some cases, even years. During this period the file of the preliminary investigation is kept confidential. It is also important to keep in mind that during this stage neither there are investigated parties, nor are there any charges brought forward for the allegedly commission of any presumptive anti-competitive conduct or action.

If during the preliminary investigation, the Competition Authority finds compelling evidence that an anti-competitive infraction was committed, it will then initiate a formal investigation by means of a public resolution, directed towards specific persons and/or corporations. The formal investigation can last between twelve and twenty-four months (approximately), but there is no limit to the time it can last, other than the statute of limitations for imposing a fine, which is of five years from the date of the conduct or the last event of the conduct if it is continued in time.

In those cases, in which the investigation is initiated following an accusation (and not officiously), the SIC will call for a settlement hearing between the investigated parties and the accusers to promote an agreement regarding the settlement of their private interests. If such settlement is achieved, then it will not affect the continuation of the investigation, for the SIC is protecting the public interest. In practice, these hearings have not been very effective, because the continuation of the investigation disincentivize the investigated parties to reach a settlement. It is important to note that in this type of administrative investigation the SIC has no judicial powers to adjudicate damages to the victims of the anti-competitive conducts. The damages will have to be pursued using judicial or class actions before the judiciary.

The resolution that opens the formal investigation is notified to the accused persons who will have a term of twenty working days to present and request evidence and if they decide so, to offer "*garantías*" (settlement), a procedural benefit that allows the investigated parties to request the anticipated termination of the investigation, without sanctions, by offering to the authority that they will behave in a form consistent with competition laws and the compliance with a set of obligations including a collateral in the form of a bond. The benefit of this *settlement* is that the investigation is terminated immediately without sanctions and without a definition regarding the legality or illegality of the investigated conducts.

The superintendent can accept or not the *settlement* at his/her sole discretion, depending on their sufficiency to convince the superintendent of the compliance of the investigated companies with competition law. Since the introduction of the leniency program in Colombia, the SIC has accepted this kind of settlement in very few occasions.

If a *settlement* is not offered or accepted, the SIC will gather the evidence in the form of administrative visits, depositions, expert opinions, interrogations, documents, and the like. Once the evidence is gathered the attorneys for the investigated parties will be invited to present their case orally and following the superintendent delegate for competition will file a "*Motivated Report*" with the superintendent, assessing the evidence and recommending imposing fines or to acquit the investigated parties. The motivated report will be communicated to the companies under investigation, and they will be able to present their final allegations to the superintendent.

The superintendent will evaluate the motivated report presented by the delegate and the final allegations presented by the companies and after listening to his/her council, he/she will issue a final decision in the form of a resolution in which he/she will sanction or acquit the investigated persons.

Against this decision the parties can present a reconsideration plea, which should be decided in two months, unless new evidence is requested by the accused and ordered by the SIC. Once the superintendent decides this plea, the case is over before the administration. The decision is final and can be enforced by the authority including the collection of the fine.

The final resolution issued by the SIC can be challenged before the administrative judges to obtain its annulment and the indemnification of the damages produced by the decision to the accused. Therefore, the final authority of any antitrust case is the council of state. The judicial review of the SIC's decision can last between five and twelve years (meanwhile the decision is effective).

[D] Sanctions and Remedies

[1] Administrative Sanctions

As said before, the SIC can declare the violation of competition laws, order the investigated companies to stop their illegal conduct, and impose fines both to the companies and to the natural persons involved.

One of the changes of Law 2195 of 2022 is the notorious increase in the capacity of the SIC to impose fines as we explain in this section. It is important to consider that previously, under Decree 2153, Article 4 (15) and Article (16) stipulated that the maximum fine could go up to 2,000 minimum monthly wages at the moment of the sanction (in 2022 approximately USD 507.356) to the companies and 300 minimum monthly wages (in 2022 approximately USD 76.103) for the natural persons involved; whereas, under law 1340 Articles 25 and 26, the SIC could impose to the companies up to 100,000 minimum monthly wages (in 2022 approximately 25.3 million USD) or up to 150% of the profits obtained with the anti-competitive conduct; and up to 2,000 minimum monthly wages (in 2022 approximately USD 507.356) to the natural persons involved. There is an important addition about the paragraph of article 26—Law 1340 which contained an express prohibition to the investigated companies to pay or ensure the fines imposed to the natural persons. This rule is maintained in the new law.

The original Article 25 of Law 1340 gave the SIC some criteria for the application of the fines to companies: (i) the impact that the conduct has on the market; (ii) the size of the affected market; (iii) the benefit obtained by the offender with the conduct; (iv) the degree of participation of the accused; (v) the procedural conduct of the investigated parties; (vi) the market share of the infringing undertaking, as well as the part of its assets and/or sales involved in the infringement; and (vii) the patrimony of the infringer.

With these criteria, in several cases the fine has been aggravated without exceeding the maximum legal limit.

The original Article 26 of Law 1340 gave the SIC some criteria for the application of the fines to natural persons: (i) persistence in the conduct, (ii) the impact that the conduct has on the market, (iii) reiteration of the prohibited conduct, (iv) the procedural conduct of the investigated parties, and (v) the degree of participation of the accused.

As explained before, recently Law 2195 of 2022 reformed the sanctions previously established first in Decree 2153 and then in Law 1340 of 2009, and specifically modified Articles 25 and 26 of Law 1340. In that regard, Article 67 of Law 2195 allows the SIC to apply to both natural and legal persons one of the following systems of fines, whichever yields the higher cap for the calculation of the sanction, pursuant to the applicable criteria specified in the law. So, for the violation of the competition laws, the SIC may impose the fine to the investigated parties, based on the following criteria:

- The operating income of the offender in the fiscal year immediately preceding that of the imposition of the fine. In this event, the fine may not exceed 20% of such income.
- The patrimony of the offender in the fiscal year immediately preceding the year in which the sanction is imposed. In this event, the penalty may not exceed 20% of the value of the patrimony of the offender.
- In those cases, in which the anti-competitive practice is related to a contract, the fine will be calculated in minimum legal monthly wages. In this event, the fine may not exceed 30% of the value of the contract.
- In those cases in which it is possible to quantify the profits that the offender derived from the conduct, the Superintendence of Industry and Commerce may impose as a penalty, up to 300% of the value of those profits, provided that this percentage is higher than the greater of the limits established in the criteria previously explained.

The graduation of the fine must always be made based on the following criteria as long as it is applicable: (i) The suitability of the conduct to affect the market or the affectation to it; (ii) The nature of the goods or services involved. (iii) The degree of participation of the person involved. (iv) The duration of the conduct. (v) The market participation of the infringer in the market in which he/she participates.

Once the criteria for the calculation of the fine has been chosen according to the previously established rules, and taking into account that the superintendence has to use the rules that allows for the highest penalty cap, the authority will apply the criteria for aggravation and mitigation of the fine in order to graduate the sanction to be applied to the instant case. Article 67 provides as grounds for aggravation of the sanctions the following hypotheses: (i) The infringer acted as leader, instigator or in any way promoter of the conduct. (ii) The continuation of the infringing conduct after the investigation has been initiated. (iii) The recidivism or existence of precedents in relation to infractions of the competition laws, or to the breach of commitments acquired with or of the orders issued by the Competition Authority. (iv) The procedural conduct of the infringer tending to obstruct or delay the procedure, including the presentation of applications that are obviously inappropriate.

For each of the aggravating circumstances previously described, the superintendent may increase the fine to be imposed up to 10%, without exceeding, in any case, the sanctioning limits provided for in the law and described above.

The superintendent may also reduce the applicable fine in case that the infringer accepts the charges presented to him/her in the opening resolution, provided however that the investigated person has not been recognized as a collaborator (or leniency applicant) within the leniency program, because in those cases the conditions and reductions of the leniency program are the ones that apply.

In addition to the sanctions applicable to the economic agents (whether they are legal entities or natural persons), Article 68 of Law 2195 modifies the sanctions applicable to the facilitators of the conduct. For that purpose, the law defines the "facilitators" as natural or legal persons that collaborate, authorize, promote, foster, execute, or tolerate anti-competitive conducts.

The superintendence may impose to the facilitators that incur in the above mentioned conducts in regard to anti-competitive practices, a fine of up to 2,000 minimum monthly wages (in 2022 approximately USD 507.356).

To determine the actual fine, the SIC must take into consideration the following criteria for its graduation: (i) the degree of involvement of the facilitator in the conduct of the market agent, (ii) the recidivism or existence of a precedent in regard to the violation of the competition laws or to the breach of commitments acquired with or orders issued by the Competition Authority, and (iii) the patrimony of the facilitator.

Without prejudice to the criteria for the application of the sanctions to be imposed to the facilitators and the criteria considered to graduate the fine, the law also provides aggravating circumstances. (i) Continue to facilitate the infringing conduct once the investigation has begun. (ii) The recidivism or existence of a precedent in regard to the violation of the competition laws or to the breach of commitments acquired with or orders issued by the Competition Authority. (iii) The procedural conduct of the facilitator tending to obstruct or delay the processing of the process, including the presentation of applications that are obviously inappropriate.

The impact on the fine for incurring in any of the grounds for aggravation will be up to 10% of the amount of the fine to be imposed, without exceeding in any case the sanctioning limits provided for in the law for each cause. The fine will be aggravated in this way for each cause of aggravation in which it is incurred.

As said before, there is an important addition in paragraph two of Article 68 of the new law, which contains an express prohibition to the investigated companies, their parent companies, their subsidiaries, or any corporation belonging to the same business group, to pay for or insure the fines imposed to the facilitators. Infringement of that prohibition in itself constitutes an anti-competitive practice.

It must be noted that the SIC can impose fines not only for anti-competitive conduct, but also for the obstruction of investigations; infringement of the merger control regulations; failure to comply with orders; failure to comply with obligations acquired pursuant to guarantees (settlement) accepted for the anticipated termination of investigations or the conditions accepted for the approval of a merger transaction.

[2] Criminal Sanctions

Colombian Antitrust Law has no criminal liability tradition. Nevertheless, in 2011, Law 1474 (*Anticorruption Statute*) determined that bid rigging in governmental contracts carried criminal liability. This means that the conduct prohibited in Article 47 (9) of Decree 2153 of 1992 has administrative, civil, and criminal liability.

Article 47 (9) of Decree 2153, 1992, that introduces Article 410A of the criminal code, expressly defines as a criminal offence anti-competitive agreement in the following terms: "9. Those whose purpose is to collude in bids or contests or those whose effect is to allocate contracts' awards, distribute contests or fix the terms of proposals."

This prohibition refers to collusion in bids issued by private and public entities. Only bid rigging in state contracts will produce criminal liability, being one of the challenges for antitrust legislation in this jurisdiction.

In addition, it also introduces a new incentive for the prosecution of bid rigging. The paragraph of Article 410A provides for leniency program collaborators a penalty adjustment that reduces their sentence in one third, exonerate them of a 40% fine product of the criminal investigation, and reduces their inability to subscribe state contracts from eight to five years. It is important to note that the introduction of the criminal sanctions, even with the mentioned reductions for the leniency applicant, act as a deterrent for the use of the leniency program, because it is not possible for the SIC to grant immunity to the first leniency applicant and the partial reductions that the *Anticorruption Statute* offer must be approved by the criminal authorities and not by the SIC.

In this regard it must also be mentioned that there are some other criminal offences in the criminal code that can indirectly protect Free Competition like: Article 304—Damage to raw materials, agricultural, or industrial products; Article 301—*"Agiotaje"*; and Article 298—Speculation.

[3] Private Actions and Follow-On Actions

Private Antitrust Litigation has not properly developed yet in Colombia. This is because there are no punitive damages in the Colombian system; thus, people can only sue for actual damages.

Antitrust cases are generally dealt with in administrative proceedings initiated officiously by the authority. In most antitrust investigations, there is no accusation from a victim or third-party in general.

The damages caused by anti-competitive conducts cannot be claimed within the administrative proceedings carried out by the SIC, and as a matter of fact the authority has no power to award such damages because that can only be done by the judge. This does not mean that parties affected by the conduct cannot claim for damages, it only means that there is less incentive to do so. The parties affected can either file a civil action to obtain the damages caused by the conduct, or if there is a specific group affected, a class action can be filed. The General Procedure Code of Colombia lowered the requirements that must be fulfilled to present class actions.

As said before, the SIC cannot refer to damages arising of the antitrust conducts it investigates. Nevertheless, a fine imposed by the SIC serves as a very solid evidentiary support on which to base a civil or class action.

Currently, as a direct consequence of the prosecution of different cartels (cement, sugar, diapers, soft tissue, and notebooks, among others), some class and group actions that look to obtain damages caused by the conduct have been brought forward. Nevertheless, there has been no significant precedent that properly develops Private Antitrust Litigation.

[E] Leniency

The leniency program was introduced in Colombia by Article 14 of Law 1340,[4] which states that the SIC can grant benefits to the participants of a conduct that breached antitrust laws when they collaborate with the competition authority by facilitating information and evidence regarding the existence of an anti-competitive conduct and the identification of the other participants. The law provides the following rules for the operation of the leniency program: 1) neither the instigators nor the promoters of the conduct are eligible to apply for the benefits of the program, 2) The degree of the benefits may be the total or partial exoneration of the sanctions, depending on the usefulness and quality of the information and evidence provided by the collaborator, and 3) The collaboration with the authority is also rated by the efficiency of the information and evidence adduced to reach a decision and the stage of the process in which the information is provided to the authority.

Decree 253 of 2022[5] further regulates the leniency program as follows:

- The procedure for application to the benefits, including the order of precedence for the applications (*marker*); the maximum number of applications allowed; the opportunity to present the application referring to the stages of the investigation procedure in which an application can be validly presented; and the requirements of the application, among other things.
- The rules for signing a collaboration agreement with the authority.
- The rules for reduction of the fines, including the parameters for total and partial exoneration of the fine.
- The rules for the additional benefit that the collaborators may obtain.
- The rules of confidentiality of the program including the secrecy of the applicant's identity, and the term for the confidential treatment of the information and evidence that the applicant brings to the authority.

The objective of the program is to create mechanisms of collaboration with the authority that can facilitate the prosecution of antitrust conducts. In Latin America, there is a growing tendency to implement this kind of programs as an additional tool for the competition agencies. In many countries, these programs have proved to be effective in the fight against *"hard core"* cartels. In Colombia, there have been some initial successful cases, but the leniency program also faces challenges as explained below. The Colombian leniency program does not offer monetary rewards to the leniency applicants like in other jurisdictions.

According to the reports published by the SIC, between 2009 and 2018, thirty-one applications for the program were received from which five investigations were initiated, and in three of these five investigations sanctions were imposed. Some of the most representative cases where leniency was crucial for the investigation are:

4. Article 14 of Law 1340 of 2009 was modified by Article 66 of Law 2195 of 2022.
5. Decree 253 of 2022 modified Decree 1523 of 2015 which previously modified Decree 1074 of 2015, which in turn derogated Decree 2896 of 2010.

Case 43218/2016. Diapers Cartel: In case 43218/2016 the SIC investigated and sanctioned the corporations; Kimberly, Tecnoquímicas, Productos Familia, Tecnosur, Drypers Andina, and the natural persons involved in the facts of the case, for the violation of the general prohibition, and for celebrating an anti-competitive agreement to fix prices.

During the preliminary investigation, Kimberly successfully collaborated with the antitrust agency and obtained total exoneration of the sanction, of approximately 23 million USD then for the corporation and approximately 80 thousand USD then for each Natural Person, for being the first application and successfully collaborating during the investigation. Productos Familia also collaborated with the SIC and obtained a reduction of 50% in the applicable fine.

For the other corporations and natural persons involved, the SIC imposed the maximum possible legal sanction.

The leniency application of Kimberly in the Diapers Cartel allowed the SIC to open another two investigations related to the same facts: the Soft Paper and Notebooks Cartel Investigations explained below.

Case 31739/2017. Soft Tissue Cartel: In case 31739 the SIC investigated Kimberly, Productos Familia, Papeles Nacionales, Cartones y Papeles del Risaralda, and Drypers Andina, for price fixing. Kimberly was the first collaborator, Productos Familia S.A. was the second, and Cartones y Papeles del Risaralda was the third collaborator. The SIC determined that the first and third collaborators met all requirements needed to obtain the leniency program benefits, nevertheless the second collaborator breached the leniency agreement and therefore did not receive its respective benefit.

Notebook Cartel Case 54403/2016: In case 54403 the SIC investigated Kimberly, Scribe, and Carvajal for price fixing. Kimberly and Scribe presented an application to the leniency program. Since Kimberly had sold its Notebook business to Scribe in 2011, they were both successfully admitted by the SIC as first collaborators due to the "predecessor—successor" doctrine, and therefore received the total exoneration of the fine.

Lava Jato Case—"Ruta del Sol II": In Case 82510 the SIC imposed sanctions of approximately 76 million USD to Odebrecht and its partners in the Ruta del Sol II project. During the course of the investigation Gabriel Ignacio García Morales, Vice Secretary of Transportation and Acting Director of INCO and INVIAS, collaborated with the authority, admitted to having received a USD 6.5 million dollars fine from Odebrecht and received the total exoneration of the fine, but had to face a prison sentence.

Some of the main challenges regarding leniency program incentive and applications are: (i) the confidentiality both of the identity of the leniency applicant and of the information contained in the leniency file, a problem that has been recently addressed by article 66 of law 2195 of 2022, which introduced two new paragraphs to Article 14 of law 1340 of 2009, strengthening the confidentiality rules of the leniency program and partially solving this challenge, although it is yet to be seen how it is implemented; (ii) the reputational costs that companies face even when they have cooperated with the SIC; (iii) the transfer of evidence presented during the administrative investigation in private or class action lawsuits seeking to recover damages and the right of defence of the leniency applicant; (iv) the possibility of being labelled as the promoter or instigator of the anti-competitive agreements that would lead to losing the benefits; (v) the criminalization of competition law; and (vi) the supranational application of Andean Decision 608 of 2005, among others.

Finally, there are some anti-competitive conducts that may have consequences other than administrative fines. As mentioned earlier, since 2011, bid rigging has been considered a crime in Colombia. A hypothetical leniency applicant wishing to admit a bid rigging conduct may still face criminal charges as the program was not conceived to cover criminal liability, a circumstance that disincentivises applicants of collaborating with the competition authority due to the criminal liability that they might face.[6]

Recently, Article 14 of Law 1340 of 2009 underwent a major modification. Article 66 of Law 2195 of 2022 incorporated three paragraphs, two of them related to confidentiality rules in the leniency program, one of them related to the responsibility of the collaborator of a leniency program.

Regarding the rules of confidentiality, the first paragraph of Article 66 of the new Law 2195 of 2022 protects with confidentiality the identity of the collaborators or leniency applicants within a leniency program, as well as the evidence that they provide in the context of the investigation. In addition, the second paragraph of Article 66 protects with confidentiality the negotiations that may lead to the leniency agreement between the SIC and the leniency applicant.

Without prejudice to this new rule of confidentiality, law 1340 of 2009 and decree 1523 of 2015 (modified by decree 253 of 2022) already had rules related to the confidentiality of the identity of the whistleblower and confidentiality of the information provided by the whistleblower, as per Article 2.2.2.29.4.3. of Decree 1523 of 2015 the identity of the whistleblower is considered confidential. Likewise, Article 2.2.2.29.4.4. of Decree 1523 of 2015 provides that the leniency program application, negotiation, and files are separate from that of the investigation, and consequently all the evidence and information contained therein is reserved, a rule that agrees with the provision of the recent reform.

In addition to these two provisions on confidentiality, the third paragraph of Article 66 of the new law incorporates an exception to the regime of joint liability for damages caused by an anti-competitive agreement. Consistent with the measures that have been adopted in the EU to protect the leniency program and at the same time foster the indemnification of damages to the victims, the new Law 2195 of 2022 provides that the leniency applicant will only respond in proportion to its participation in the causation of damages to third parties by virtue of anti-competitive agreement.

Recently, the leniency program underwent a major modification: decree 253 of 2022 modified decree 1523 of 2015 which regulated the leniency program in Colombia. Its two main innovations where (i) modification of the leniency program criteria to

6. In addition, the Colombian Criminal Code includes other conducts such as "agiotaje", which makes it a criminal offense to alter prices of "first-necessity" products, raw materials, or services subject to public procurement. If a leniency applicant is hypothetically prosecuted for "agiotaje," then the leniency agreement would not give him or her protection against criminal liability.

graduate the benefits, which from now on will depend on the moment when the application is presented, and (ii) It limits the number of applications to three. Other reforms are:

- It specifies the definition of the instigator or promotor of the conduct, which is the person that forces others to participate in an anti-competitive conduct where two or more agents of the market participate in a joint way.
- It expands the definition of the facilitator of anti-competitive conducts to include those persons that promote or impulse the anti-competitive conduct.
- It eliminates the presumption that the applicant to the program is not the promotor or instigator of the anti-competitive conduct.
- It establishes to new conditions to grant the leniency program benefits: (i) it expressly forbids the authority to grant the benefits to the promoter or instigator of the anti-competitive conduct, and (ii) it forbids the authority to grant the benefits of the leniency program to more than three applicants.
- It modifies the application of the leniency benefits depending on whether the application was presented before or after a formal investigation was initiated: (i) If the application is presented before the authority has initiated a formal investigation the first applicant could be totally exonerated of the fine to be imposed, the second applicant can receive a partial exoneration between thirty and fifty percent of the fine to be imposed, and the third and last applicant may receive a partial exoneration of up to 25 percent of the fine to be imposed; (ii) If the application is presented after the authority has initiated a formal investigation, the first applicant could receive a partial exoneration of up to 30 percent of the fine to be imposed, the second applicant can receive a partial exoneration of up to 25 percent of the fine to be imposed, and the third and last applicant may receive a partial exoneration of up to 15 percent of the fine to be imposed.
- It also modifies the application of the additional benefits to the leniency program (*Leniency plus*) depending on whether the application was presented before or after a formal investigation was initiated: (i) If the application for the additional benefits is presented before the authority has initiated a formal investigation, the applicant can obtain an additional reduction of 20% of the fine to be imposed; (ii) If the application for the additional benefits is presented after the authority has initiated a formal investigation, the applicant can obtain an additional reduction of 10% of the fine to be imposed.
- It eliminates the presumption that that leniency program application meets all the legal requirements when the authority keeps silent within the next five days from the filing of the application.
- It modifies the treatment that the law gives to the evidence that the applicant provides to the authority as a result of its collaboration in case he/she desists of the leniency application or rejects the application. In this case once the decision to reject the application is notified, the authority can only incorporate into the investigation proceedings the evidence provided by the applicant with his/her irrevocable consent.

[F] Appeal

As said before, against the final decision of the SIC there is no appeal before a superior authority. The parties can present a reconsideration plea before the superintendent, which should be decided within two months unless new evidence is requested by the investigated parties and ordered by the SIC. Once the superintendent decides this plea, the case is over before the administration. The decision is final and must therefore be enforced by the authority, including the collection of the fine.

As also described before, the final resolution issued by the SIC can be challenged before the administrative judges to obtain its annulment and the indemnification of the damages produced by the decision to the accused. The judicial proceedings may last between 5 and 12 years. Meanwhile the decision from the SIC stands effective including the collection of the fine.

[G] Precedent Cases

It must be said, that to this date, horizontal price fixing agreements remain as the main cause for antitrust investigations in Colombia. There have been price fixing investigations in many economic sectors, but it seems important to highlight the investigations related to the agricultural sector, where the SIC has developed cases against the industries that acquire the crops from the producers:

- Investigation against the rice mills for an agreement to fix the price of the green paddy rice (Case 22065/2005: Rice Mills).
- Investigation against the Chocolate companies for an agreement to fix the price of the cocoa beans (Case 52202/2009: Chocolate Manufacturers).
- Investigation against the sugar manufacturers for an agreement to fix the price of the sugar cane (Case 6839/2007 and 42411/2010: Sugar Cane Mills).

There have been important cases related to horizontal agreements in other sectors of the economy. Some of these cases are summarized below.

[1] Case 6839/2010: Sugar Cane Mills

In Case 6839/2010 Sugar Cane Mills, the SIC claimed that some sugar manufacturers set the price of sugar cane through a formula that used the sugar sale final price. The SIC questioned the application of different formulas and why they never resulted in the sugar cane producers sharing more than 50% of the revenues from the sale of sugar. In the end, the authority deemed such as an indirect agreement entered to fix the prices of sugar cane.

[2] Case 51694/2008: Cement

The SIC imposed fines on four cement manufacturers: Cementos Argos, Holcim Colombia, Cemex Colombia and Cementos Andino (Case 51694/2008: Cement) for having entered a price fixing agreement. In the opinion of the SIC, no economic rationale existed that could justify such pricing, being therefore a very high probability that such companies had subscribed an agreement to fix prices.

[3] Case 27762/1999: Milk

Derilac and Colanta (Case 27762/1999: Milk), two dairy products manufacturers were the subjects of an investigation initiated by the SIC on the grounds of price fixing. This investigation was decided back in 1999. The SIC concluded that an agreement existed from the fact that the same retail price was shown in the milk bags throughout 1997, 1998, and 1999 and that the price increases were also the same. In this case, the SIC stated that no explicit oral or written agreement had to be executed for a parallel practice to exist: the conduct itself proved the price fixing agreement. In the end, the SIC sanctioned the companies and the Council of State upheld its decision.

[4] Case 08732/2002: Gas Stations

Case 08732/2002: Gas Stations comprised an investigation that was decided based on a price fixing agreement that resulted in prices increases of four—star gasoil. One of the gas stations, called "La Pedregosa," owned by Rafael Ortiz Mantilla was included in the investigation. This case highlighted that price increases were introduced at the same time. In the end, the Council of State upheld the decision.

§14.03 UNILATERAL CONDUCT

[A] Relevant Legislation

In Colombia, the legal framework underlying unilateral action is contained in the following legal rules: (i) Article 1 of Law 155 along with Article 46 of Decree 2153 that set forth the general prohibition; (ii) Article 48 of Decree 2153 that governs unilateral conducts or anti-competitive acts; and (iii) Article 50 which prohibits dominant position abuse.

The dominant position of any investigated company must be duly demonstrated and as per Article 45 (4) of Decree 2153, it is considered that a company enjoys a dominant position when it has the power to directly or indirectly affecting the market conditions.

The three types of anti-competitive acts set out in Article 48 of Decree 2153 of 1992 are the following ones: (i) consumer protection laws advertisement regulations violations, (ii) influencing companies into increasing prices or refraining from reducing prices, and (iii) unilateral refusal to deal or discrimination against a company as a form of retaliation resulting from its pricing policies.

There are six types of behaviours that amount to dominance abuse set out in Article 50 of Decree 2153: (i) predatory pricing, (ii) vertical discrimination or exploitative abuses, (iii) tying, (iv) horizontal discrimination or anti-competitive abuses, (v) regional predatory pricing or leveraging, and (vi) obstruction or blocking access to markets or distribution channels.

The authority has focused its efforts rather than on unilateral conduct, on repressing cartels and horizontal agreements in general. Nonetheless, there have been several investigations regarding predatory pricing and undue influences for purposes of price increases.

[B] Assessment of Dominance

As per Article 45 (5) of Decree 2153, the dominant position of a company is established when it has the chance of directly or indirectly affecting market conditions. The SIC determines whether there is dominant position by defining a relevant market based on the product, geography, and temporal standpoint and utilizing tools such as the SSNIP test. Upon defining the relevant market, the SIC proceeds to examine the market concentration assisted by concentration indexes such as HHI, NEE, CR4 as well as others, and finally, entry barriers and market contestability, in case that the company in fact has a dominant position.

The Legal Framework for Competition in Colombia has no law, regulation, jurisprudence, or theory enabling the presumption of dominance when there is a certain percentage of market concentration. Nonetheless, Article 14(13) of Law 142 of 1994 (Public Utilities Law), a public utility company with a market share equal to or more than 25% in the corresponding market is deemed a dominant company. This rule is only applicable to public utilities.

[C] Abuse of a Dominant Position

[1] Predatory Pricing

Article 50 (1) of Decree 2153 prohibits predatory pricing, a conduct aimed at setting prices below costs and eliminating competitors or deterring other companies from accessing markets or expanding their operations. However only dominant undertakings are considered when assessing whether there is a violation of the legal rule contained in Article 50 (1) or not. As mentioned above, pursuant to Article 45 (5) of Decree 2153, a company has a dominant position when it can effectively affect directly or indirectly the conditions in a market.

An assessment of pricing versus total average costs (not variable costs) is made at the time of investigation (Case 30835/2004: Mushrooms[7]) but there is no legal requirement to do so. As to the "*intenti*" requirement to eliminate a market competitor or preventing market access or business expansion, the SIC has considered that the behaviour of the agent and the economic rationale shall be taken into consideration to deduce the intention. In the Mushroom case, the SIC determined that the company's behaviour was a reasonable one as the price reduction did not take place for a long period of time or was unreasonable considering the context of the market.

This type of conduct could also be analysed under the general prohibition of the unfair trade law, contained in Article 7 of Law 256, 1996 (Law 256). In this case, the authorities that can have jurisdiction over this type of cases, meaning the SIC (using its judicial functions) or the civil circuit judge, would consider if such a conduct is against the principle of good faith and honest commerce practices, and whether it can affect the decisions of consumers and the general operation of the market.

Finally, it must be said that there have not been many investigations related to predatory pricing during the previous years. The most important cases are Case 30835/2004: Mushrooms and Case 22624/2005: Adams Chewing Gum, explained below.

[2] Price Discrimination

The Constitution of Colombia sets the standard as to price discrimination and the constitutional court has considered Aristotle's concept of distributive justice to interpret the rule ("equality for the equals.")

Article 47 (2) of Decree 2153 prohibits any agreement setting sales or marketing conditions that discriminate third parties. In turn, Article 50 (2) prohibits vertical discrimination (exploitative abuses), which entails applying differential conditions to equivalent transactions putting suppliers or consumers in a position of disadvantage when compared with other suppliers or consumers in similar conditions. Article 50 (4) prohibits horizontal discrimination (anti-competitive abuses) which entails imposing different purchasing conditions on different consumers to eliminate or reduce competition.

Article 50 (5) of Decree 2153 prohibits regional predatory pricing which would enable a dominant firm to conduct a predatory campaign by financing it with the monopolistic prices that it charges in other areas of the country. When discrimination as abusive unilateral conduct is carried out, it can only be punished if the business has a dominant position. On the contrary, if objective factors such as volume discounts, transportation costs, or other circumstances explain the price differences, no violation takes place (e.g., Case 19444/2001 Celumovil-Comcel where mobile phone companies charged higher prices to customers for calls from landlines to mobiles than for calls

7. The investigated company was the biggest producer of mushrooms in Colombia, *Setas Colombianas S.A.*

from mobiles to landlines). The mobile phone carriers offered guarantees (settlement) to the SIC, and the investigation ended with no sanctions.

[3] Tying

In Colombia, tying (agreement or abusive conduct aimed at subordinating the supply of a product to accepting additional obligations or conditions that are not part of the business transaction) is prohibited as agreement and as a unilateral conduct. When the conduct is investigated as an abuse of dominance it is only considered unlawful when carried out by a company enjoying a dominant position.

Article 47 (7) of Decree 2153 deems per se illegal entering into agreements with the purpose or effect of subordinating the supply of a product to accepting additional obligations or conditions that are not a natural part of the business transaction. Article 50 (3) of Decree 2153 states that if a company enjoys a dominant position, tying is deemed abuse.

Loyalty discounts have also been examined in the past, and they are deemed illegal if they are found to be equivalent to tying.

[4] Horizontal Discrimination Anti-Competitive Abuses

Pursuant to Article 50 (4) of Decree 2153, it is considered that when a company enjoys a dominant position, it will incur in an abuse of dominance if it sells to a buyer in different conditions than the ones offered to another buyer, when this is done with the intention of diminishing or eliminating competition in the market.

In 1995 PROQUIMHUL filed an accusation against its competitor in the production of aluminium sulphide, PRODUCTOS QUÍMICOS PANAMERICANOS—PQP. PROQUIMHUL claimed that PQP caused the manufacturer of sulphuric acid, the main raw material to produce aluminium sulphide, to apply discriminatory conditions favouring PQP and putting PROQUIMHUL at a disadvantage in the market for aluminium sulphide in the southern part of Colombia.

The SIC did not find evidence of the alleged discrimination and PQP and FOSFADER were acquitted.

[5] Regional Predatory Pricing/Leveraging

There is a specific prohibition against *regional predatory pricing*, as a conduct of abuse of dominance, in Article 50 (5) of Decree 2153. A company will be accused of regional predatory pricing when it sells its products at different prices in different regions with the intention or the effect of diminishing or eliminating its competitors in that region. Here, the SIC is not concerned with pricing below costs, but with pricing differentials not based on the costs of the transactions in different regions. This conduct can therefore be seen as a form of price discrimination.

Whilst Article 50 (5) of Decree 2153 requires a demonstration of dominance before an infringement can be found, non-dominant companies may be caught by the general prohibition under Law 155. In this case, the authority will analyse the conduct using an approach like the *rule of reason*, considering all aspects of the conduct and weighing its pro-competitive and anti-competitive effects. The only case related to this infraction is Case 15653/2001: Ice cream cones—Induga.

[6] Obstruction or Blocking Access to Market or Distribution Channels

Under Colombian Law, the conduct of obstruction or blocking access to market or to distribution channels can evidently be investigated under the general prohibition contained in Article 1 of Law 155, considered together with Article 46 of Decree 2153. It can also be investigated as an agreement or abusive conduct aimed to impede the participation of a *Small or Middle Size Undertaking* (PYME by its initials in Spanish) in the market or distribution channels.

In Colombia, this obstructive conduct is prohibited both as an agreement and as a unilateral conduct, case in which it is considered as an abuse of dominance that is only illegal when committed by a company that enjoys a dominant position.

Pursuant to Article 47 (10) of Decree 2153, it is considered as per se illegal to enter into agreements with the purpose or effect of blocking access to the market or the distribution channels to PYMEs.

According to Article 50 (6) of Decree 2153, when a company enjoys a dominant position, it is considered as an abuse to enter a blocking conduct such as the one described immediately above against PYMEs.

Also, under Article 19 of Law 256 of 1996 (Law 256, Unfair Competition Law), manufacturers and distributors can be investigated because of exclusivity clauses agreed on between them which can be deemed in some cases as an unfair trade practice. In fact, entering exclusive dealing clauses in supply contracts to or with the effect of impeding access of competitors to the market or monopolizing distribution channels is considered an unfair competition conduct.

[D] Investigation (Authorities, Procedure, Powers, Burden of Proof, Appeal)

All anti-competitive conducts are subject to the same type of investigation, performed by the same authority, the SIC, under the same administrative procedure, and the same systems of analysis. In all cases the final decision of the SIC is subject only to a reconsideration plea before the superintendent. These decisions cannot be appealed to a higher authority. As said before, the final resolution issued by the SIC can be challenged before the administrative jurisdiction to obtain its annulment and the indemnification of the damages produced by the decision to the accused; meanwhile the decision is effective.

The competition authority has no judicial power to order the indemnification of the damages caused by the anti-competitive conducts. The persons affected by said conducts will have to seek indemnification before the civil judges using a civil action, a class action, or eventually an unfair competition action.

The conducts of abuse of a dominant position have a higher standard of proof because the authority will have to demonstrate that the investigated companies enjoy a dominant position, which requires a careful definition of the relevant market, and as said before, an exercise regarding market concentration and barriers to entry.

[E] Sanctions and Remedies

All anti-competitive conducts are subject to the same type of investigation, performed by the same authority, the SIC, under the same administrative procedure, the same systems of analysis.

[F] Precedent Cases

[1] Case 22624/2005: Adams Chewing Gum

Case 22624/2005: Adams chewing gum was decided by SIC against Cadbury Adams, a company with a dominant position in the market of mint flavoured gum. The product—Chiclet's Adams was presented to the public with a price of USD 200. Upon the entry of Confiteca to the market featuring "Tumix" (also, mint flavoured gum) at a price of USD 100, Cadbury Adams responded with "Chiclet's Clarks" at a price of USD 50. The SIC considered that this amounted to predatory pricing.

[2] Case 33361/2011: Beer-Bavaria

Case 33361/2011: Beer-Bavaria was decided by SIC in 2001. Heineken accused Bavaria of abuse of dominance with respect to the launch of Peroni beer and of tying that forced high-end bars and restaurants to exclusive advertise in favour of Bavaria as a condition to sell Bavaria products. Bavaria was able to demonstrate that the Sponsor Contracts to promote Peroni were temporary and that they did not include sales exclusivity, but rather advertisement exclusivity was what was required in few bars and restaurants. No sanctions were imposed on Bavaria.

[3] Case 15653/2001: Ice Cream Cones-Induga

Case 15653/2001: Ice cream cones-Induga was decided by SIC in 2001. Induga S.A., a powerful company with advanced technology and a dominant position, based in Medellin, introduced lower prices in the Atlantic Coast and in Medellin once a competitor accessed the market. The SIC determined that it was not reasonable that the price of the cones was higher in Medellin than in the coast. The decision was challenged and examined by the Council of State which issued its ruling in May 2013. The Council of State determined that Induga had no dominant position based on a relevant market analysis and that Induga did not sell its products below the prices at which it sold the same products in other regions of the country.

The decision was challenged before the administrative jurisdiction; the Council of State issued its judgment on May 23, 2013. This high court considered that *Induga* did not have a dominant position in the ice cream cones market. It established that, when defining the relevant market, the SIC did not consider other products with which consumers tend to replace ice cream cones, such as plastic recipients; the SIC did not consider that there was another competitor in the market with a share of 23% either. If these aspects had been included in this analysis, it would have been concluded that *Induga* did not have a dominant position.

The Council of State established that, even if *Induga* did have a dominant position, it was proven that this company did not sell its products in the Atlantic coast at a lower price than the one applied nation-wide; it was only proven that the prices at which *Induga* sold its products in Antioquia were lower than the prices at which it sold its products in Atlántico. Hence, there was no infraction of any Colombian competition law.

[4] Case 53403/2013: Mobile Calling Services-Comcel

Article 50 (6) of Decree 2153 expressly forbids firms with dominant positions from performing any unilateral conduct aimed to impede or deter entry of third parties to the markets and/or distribution channels. The SIC sanctioned *Comunicación Celular S.A. Comcel* for incurring in this anti-competitive conduct (Case 53403/2013: Mobile Calling Services-Comcel).

Allegedly, *Comcel* incurred a series of anti-competitive conducts in the process of Mobile Number Portability[8] (henceforward, MNP); this process allows users from different cellular companies to switch providers without changing their cell phone numbers. The MNP fosters free competition between the mobile calling services providers, since it encourages them to create strategies that encourage users to look for the best supplier.

Comcel was sanctioned for entering two main conducts:

- *Locking cell phones that the company operated:*[9] According to the SIC, *Comcel* prevented users from connecting their phones with other providers, since their phones could only be unlocked when they fulfilled certain requirements. Consequently, this company influenced its consumers' decisions, so that they would not switch providers. It was not proven that the conduct had a considerable effect, since only a few complaints about locked phones were brought forward in the process. The SIC, however, argued that the mere possibility of a harmful effect suffices for the conduct to be significant, and, hence, for this authority to penalize it. In this case, it was considered that

8. Proceso de Portabilidad Numérica.
9. Bloqueo de las bandas de los teléfonos operados por Comcel.

locking the cell phones that the company operated had a great potential for affecting the market.

- *Bulging MNP results:*[10] According to the SIC, *Comcel* gave its distributors great incentives to increase their portability outcomes. This led to the carrying of unreal procedures: Users that did not have the intention of performing a MNP process, had their cell phone lines transferred from other operators to *Comcel*. Although *Comcel* did not execute this deed directly, this company was accused of being aware of this conduct. The SIC considered that the company used a fraudulent strategy to alter MNP results, so that it appeared to be the operator with the greatest number of transfers. The latter falsely affected the position of the company in the market, regarding users' decisions, especially because the results were broadly exposed. In addition, *Comcel's* competitors lost some of the numbers they had been assigned. This conduct violated Article 1 of Law 155, which contains the general prohibition of anti-competitive practices.

The SIC imposed the company the highest fine so far imposed in Colombian Competition Law, approximately USD 40 million. *Comcel* has challenged the decision in the administrative jurisdiction.

[5] Case 3694/2013: Electric Meters-EBSA

The SIC decided an investigation against *Energía de Boyaca S.A.* EBSA, the only provider of the energy service for the department of Boyacá in Colombia (Case 3694/2013: Electric meters-EBSA) for abuse of dominance in the form of tying. The energy supply requires, among others, the usage of electric meters, which must be calibrated in different laboratories to properly perform it services.

The electric meter market, although complimentary to the energy market, is completely independent. There is a laboratory fully owned by *EBSA* where they perform electric meter calibration. Unlike the energy market, there are several laboratories not owned by *EBSA* that also provide calibration services.

On November 2010, *EBSA* issued an internal ordinance which required that electric meters calibrated on laboratories different from *EBSA's* had to pay a *homologating fee.* Such charge did not have to be assumed whenever they decided to calibrate the electric meter with *EBSA*.

The SIC determined that because the calibration of electric meters was a complimentary service associated to the energy supply, *EBSA* could determine market conditions in both markets and therefore could be liable of abuse of dominance in any of these markets. Such situation also showed the almost non-existent power of negotiation held by *EBSA's* competitors in that market. In addition, SIC found that there were other associated costs charged to third parties (such as a registration fee) that already covered any cost incurred by *EBSA* for the homologation process.

10. Abultamiento de las cifras sobre los resultados de los procesos de portabilidad numérica entre operadores.

In the instant case, SIC affirmed that charging that fee constituted an illegal competitive advantage that caused the effect of imposing an undue burden to competing laboratories. The authority ordered *EBSA* to refrain from charging the *homologating fee* and imposed a fine to the company.

§14.04 MERGER REVIEW

[A] Relevant Legislation

Merger control legislation in Colombia is set forth mainly in Law 155, Decree 2153, Law 1340, 2009, Circular No. 10,[11] and Resolution 2751, 2021 (Resolution 2751)[12] which contains the procedure and the guidelines related to merger control. Merger regulation for specific sectors is contained in other statutes.

The Organic Statute for the Financial System, Decree 663, 1993 (Decree 663) governs mergers in the financial and insurance sectors.[13] Legislation for mergers between airlines is basically contained in Article 1866 of the Commerce Code and Article 3.6.3.7.3 of the Colombian Aeronautic Regulation (RAC).[14]

In August 2009, a citizen filed a complaint requesting that the articles of law 1340, 2009 dealing with merger control be declared unconstitutional. According to the complaint, the mentioned articles of the law did not comply with the constitutional parameters for state intervention in the economy and violated the rights to free enterprise, private initiative, and free economic competition.

The constitutional court decided to uphold the law on the grounds that it is an obligation of the state to prevent anti-competitive conducts and for that reason it concluded that it is possible to establish a merger control system according to the Colombian Constitution.

The complaint also argued that the thresholds for merger review had to be established by law and could not be set by the SIC. The court ruled that as far as the law gave the authority to the SIC, to establish the thresholds, the intervention of the state in the economy was correctly exercised at the level of the law, and not at the level of the regulation.

Finally, the complaint argued that the fee imposed by the new law for the verification of conditioned mergers violated the constitutional principle of *"no taxation without representation"* and the Colombian tax law. The court considered that the mentioned fees are not taxes and therefore its imposition is constitutional.

11. External Bulletin No. 10 from the SIC.
12. Resolution 2751 of 2021 replaced the previous regulation contained in Resolution 10930 of 2015.
13. Decree 663 of 1993.
14. Commerce Code, Article 1866.

[B] Authorities

The SIC is the main authority for merger control in Colombia. As mentioned before, the SIC is an administrative entity controlled by the government. The president of Colombia is free to appoint and remove the superintendent from office at his or her discretion.

Pursuant to Article 2 of Law 1340, the SIC has the power to review mergers in all sectors of the economy, with two exceptions: (i) merger transactions in the financial sector are reviewed by the Superintendence of Finance (SF), which must hear the opinion of SIC and must apply the conditions that SIC recommends, if any; and (ii) operational agreements between airlines, which are reviewed by the Aeronautic Authority (Aerocivil).

As said before, the SIC is the National Competition Authority in charge of the application of the competition, unfair trade, consumer protection, data protection, intellectual property, and data protection legislations.

[C] Triggering Events and Thresholds

According to Article 9 of Law 1340, all transactions that consist of acquisitions, mergers, consolidations, or integrations (whatever the legal form of the transaction) between companies dedicated to the same activities or participating in the same vertical value chain, whose assets and sales individually or jointly meet the economic thresholds, are subject to merger control in Colombia.

The economic thresholds refer to combined local assets or local operational income equal to or more than 60,000 minimum monthly wages, approximately USD 13.7 million. However, if one or more undertakings have not established a local business in Colombia, the economic threshold calculation must consider the world-wide assets or worldwide operational income of the undertaking located abroad. If the economic threshold is not met, then the transaction is considered *de minimis* and the companies do not need to do anything.

If the economic thresholds are met, and the companies do not meet the market participation threshold (20%), they can file a *short form notification (no waiting period)* and proceed to the transaction immediately. The notification must be filed before the transaction enters effect in Colombia.

It is possible that the authority does not agree with the relevant market presented by the merging parties or with their market participation, which entails a risk of *gun jumping* if the parties file a *short form notification* and proceed immediately to make the transaction effective. However, nowadays this risk is mitigated by the new regulation, according to which, the parties can present the *short form notification* and wait for ten days. If the SIC does not challenge the market participations presented by the parties below 20%, then they may proceed with certainty, provided of course that the information they have used is real.

The market participation threshold is met when the companies, individually or jointly have a market participation equal or superior to 20% in any of the relevant markets affected by the transaction. If the transaction is vertical, the market participation is measured in each market.

If the companies meet all the above requisites including the economic plus the market participation thresholds, then they must file a *long form information (waiting period)* and must wait until the transaction is cleared by the competition authority to proceed with the transaction. There must be no commercial contact, share of information, or joint decision making between the companies until the transaction is cleared.

For the case of global transactions already cleared in other jurisdictions, Resolution 2751 expressly establishes the "carve out" option intended to keep the effects of the transaction without effects in Colombia.

Failure to comply with the merger control regulation is considered an antitrust infraction and the companies can be subject to a *gun jumping* investigation and fines that can go up to USD 24 million for the company and USD 470,000 for the natural persons involved.

Law 1340 has made it totally clear that SIC will review both horizontal and vertical transactions. Currently, there is a discussion as to whether merger control applies to conglomerate mergers in which there is no market overlap. It seems that this is not the case, however, since Law 1340 issued in 2009 did not refer to those cases.

SIC's position is that a merger transaction amounts to an entrepreneurial concentration requiring authorization from the competition authority when the companies involved cease to participate independently in the market and are, therefore, *permanently* controlled by the same management or decision centre, whatever the legal structure. SIC has not issued any doctrine on when joint ventures are caught. Given SIC's interpretation, however, it seems that only joint ventures that create a sort of permanent undertaking should be subject to merger control.

Colombian law offers two definitions of control: one is found in the Commerce Code and applies to corporations; the other is in the competition law and refers to undertakings in a broader way. According to the broader definition, control is the possibility of influencing, directly or indirectly, the business policy of a company or undertaking; the initiation, variation, or termination of the activities of the company; or the use of assets essential to the company's operations.

The definition of corporate control includes both internal and external control. Pursuant to Article 261 of the Commerce Code, internal control exists when a company, directly or through other subsidiaries, owns more than 50% of the capital stock of another company, or owns or commands enough voting stock to appoint the majority of its directors.[15] External control, on the other hand, exists when, by way of a contract or other relationship different from the ownership of stock, one person or company can exercise a dominant influence over a corporation.

The authority has also defined *"positive control"* as the possibility to take the decisions of the company and *"negative control"* as the possibility to veto the decisions of the company. It is important to report that the authority expects a company that has *"negative control"* to file for authorization if it attempts to acquire *"positive control"*.

15. Commerce Code, Article 261. Decree 410 de 1971. D. O. No. 33.339 del(June 16/1971).

Also, the authority distinguishes between *"sole control"* acquired or exercised by one company, and *"joint control"* when it is acquired or exercised by two or more companies.

As mentioned before, transactions that do not imply the acquisition of control are not caught by the merger antitrust legislation.

Colombia adheres to the effects theory, meaning that foreign transactions that produce effects in the Colombian market are subject to the review of the SIC. The same legislation governs both domestic and foreign mergers. SIC's doctrine requires authorization of foreign mergers where both parties to the merger market their products, directly or indirectly, in Colombia. Under the former doctrine of SIC, clearance was not necessary for foreign mergers when the products of one or both merging parties were sold in Colombia by independent companies that assumed the risk and made the decisions associated with the import and sale of the products. Nevertheless, one can consider this doctrine overruled after the *SABMiller – Bavaria* merger. In this case, SIC requested an antitrust filing, even though independent importers sold the products and brands of *SABMiller*.

[D] Exemptions

According to the current laws on merger review, the SIC only objects mergers generating an undue restriction on competition and most transactions should be approved. However, there are cases that although producing a big restriction on competition, can be authorized by the SIC based in an exception.

In Colombia, there are two types of exemptions to the merger control performed by the SIC. First, there is the so called *efficiency exception,* which refers to transactions that despite producing an undue restriction to competition generate efficiencies that exceed their negative impact on the market. Second, there is the so called *failing industry defence,* where one of the merging parties will imminently exit the market. There are also exceptions to the merger control conducted by the SIC that will be further explained below.

[1] Efficiencies

According to Article 12 of Law 1340, 2009, the SIC may[16] recognize the so called *efficiency exception and* decide not to object a merger transaction in cases where benefits for the consumers exceed the possible negative effects on competition and such benefits are unlikely to be achieved by other means.[17]

As seen above, reductions in price can be considered as efficiencies, but they are not the only ones. The law only requires that "benefits" exceed the negative impact of

16. The verb used in the rule is "may not" rather than "will not" object.
17. In this point, the rule resembles section 12 of the US Horizontal Guidelines imposing the "other means" requirement.

the merger. This can also be accomplished through innovation, better quality of the products, increased production, etc.

Due to the intrinsically speculative exercise that measuring the efficiency involves, the SIC only would analyse efficiency claims based on *"studies based on widely recognized methodologies"* and the merging parties must undertake to pass the benefits through to the final consumer. In that sense, vague and unfounded projections of efficiencies are not likely to be accepted by the SIC. In addition, the parties must show how the benefit will be transferred to the final consumers.

In addition, it is important to note that mergers approved under the *efficiency exception* are understood as "conditioned"[18] and therefore the SIC will review the actions undertaken by the merging parties and may request a collateral from the parties to assure their compliance with the conditions imposed.

A landmark case where the efficiency exemption was discussed was the ports merger (Case 255/2010: Tecsa, Maritrans, Granportuaria, Elequip —Nautiservicios). These companies provided logistic services at *SPRBUN*, a Port located in Buenaventura.[19] *SPRBUN* was a port with several logistic companies that usually ranked far below other ports in Colombia like Cartagena, in terms of efficiency. The port had problems like deficit of stevedores, lack of space, inefficiencies in handling reach-stackers, most of them due to the multiplicity of agents. To make the port efficient it was necessary that TECSA would take over most of the logistic operations, thereby reducing operation times, enhancing traceability of the containers, and increasing security and surveillance. Despite the high increase in market participation of *TECSA* (from 66% to more than 90%) in *SPRBUN*, the SIC concluded that the positive effects of the transaction would exceed the negative impact of the transaction, due to the creation of efficiencies and competitiveness in the national infrastructure. However, the SIC remembered that *TECSA* would have market power and compelled the company to comply with competition laws.

[2] Failing Industry Defence

The merging parties may argue this exemption when one of the companies is in an imminent state of failure. That means that although operating, the company is likely to disappear in the short term.

In Colombia, the failing industry defence is not expressly stated in the law, however the SIC has considered the experience of other jurisdictions to develop the exemption. It is important to note that the SIC will enhance scrutiny to determine whether this exemption applies to the case and therefore its usage is rather limited.

In that sense, the SIC has developed a test with three conditions that must be concurrently met by the companies arguing this defence:

18. In US antitrust argot, the efficiency claim will be deemed as a conduct remedy that will be closely reviewed by the SIC.
19. Resolution 255 of January 14, 2010.

- The failing company is likely to exit the market in the short term. Usually, the term must be inferior to one year and the reasons for exiting the market must be financially supported.
- The anti-competitive effects of saving the company from disappearing are not bigger than those created if the company exits the market. The SIC evaluates the existence of another buyer or other less critical solutions.
- Customers are not worse off after the merger than they would have been with the disappearance of the failing company. The SIC evaluates the market participation of companies after the company fails and will compare it with post-merger participation.

The landmark case regarding this defence is related to the cement and ready-mix industries (Case 13544/2006: Argos-Andino). *Argos* wanted to acquire an important share participation in *Andino*. Both *Argos* and *Andino* were competitors in the production and commercialization of Cement and ready mix in several regions of Colombia. In that case *Andino* could prove that absent the merger, the company would have been unable to meet its financial obligations due to the high level of indebtedness. Officers of *Andino* considered different investors before approaching *Argos* without success and due to the imminent exit of *Andino* the post-merger scenario was very similar to the market without ANDINO.

The *failing industry defence* has been successfully used a couple of times after the initial Case 13544/2006: *Argos-Andino,* in transactions related to the aeronautic industry: Case 30853/2015: Terpel-Quinter Rueda Family; Case 90622/2015: Terpel-Aviacom; and more recently case 9159: Aviatur-Chicó Tours.

[E] Pre-merger Control Regime or Post-merger Control Regime

In Colombia, merger control is performed *Ex Ante* both for the *long form information (waiting period)* or the *short form notification (no waiting period)*. Companies are strongly discouraged from performing merging activities (e.g., transfer of assets, employees, know how, closing of contracts, sensitive information, etc.) before obtaining authorization. Breach of merger control rules (i.e., merging before obtaining SIC's authorization) may lead to *a gun jumping* investigation. If the SIC finds that the companies merged before obtaining approval, then it may impose fines for breaching antitrust laws and can order the reversion of the merger transaction.[20] Failure to file is explained in further detail below.

[F] Closing the Transaction During the Waiting Period

Resolution 2751 brings the possibility of closing the transaction abroad during the waiting period. For instance, the SIC must be assured that such closing will not affect

20. As of July 2015, the SIC has not used the "reversion of the merger" prerogative stated in Article 13 of Law 1340, 2009.

the independence of the companies in Colombia. To accept a "*carve out*" for Colombia, intervening parties must present the following warranties:

- There will not be change of control in Colombia. Intervening parties' businesses must keep independence in Colombia.
- The acquiring company must refrain from influencing the competitive strategy, shareholders decisions, board of directors' decisions and/or other government bodies of the target company.
- Intervening parties must refrain from exchanging information deemed commercially sensitive and/or confidential for conducting their business.
- The provisions must be intended to be permanent. Temporary measures will be discarded by the SIC.

Resolution 2751 provides a short procedure to inform the SIC of the closing and the projected *carve out* provisions. Accordingly, intervening parties must present the SIC with the proposed structure of the projected *carve out* provisions and the mechanisms intended to keep the businesses permanently separated. The SIC will have five business days to analyse the provisions and decide whether they are proper to keep the businesses separated. If the SIC is not satisfied with the proposed provisions, then it will require the parties to modify and present the project again (the term will be defined by the authority). The SIC will have another five business days to issue a decision on the second proposal. Companies must refrain from closing everywhere, before the SIC issues a positive decision.

[G] Intra-group Transactions

Intra-group transactions are exempted from merger control in accordance with number 4 of Article 1 of Resolution 2751 issued by the SIC. There are two types of intra-group transactions that are explained below:

[1] Company Group

Companies that belong to the same group are exempted from merger review. Article 28 of Law 222, 1995 (Law 222) defines a *Group of Companies* as a set of companies under the same control and the same unity of purpose and direction. These conditions are explained in the following lines:

- Same Control: The same shareholder directly or indirectly controls two or more companies.
- Unity of purpose and direction: When the existence and the activities of all the controlled entities seek a common purpose defined by the parent company due to the direction it exercises over the controlled entities, notwithstanding the development of the individual object or activity of each of the companies in the group.

A relevant case to illustrate the legal institution of the *Group of Companies* is *GRUPO AVAL*, composed by four banks (*Banco de Bogota, AV Villas, Banco Popular* and *Banco de Occidente*) that share the same control and have a unity of purpose and direction.

[2] Shared Control

As said before, companies that respond to the same control, even if that control is shared, are exempted from merger review.

To define control, it is important to cite Article 260 of the Colombian Commerce Code defining a situation of control as the case where the decisional power of a company (controlled) is completely bestowed upon another (controlling), either directly or indirectly.

Colombian regulations presume a situation of control based in capital participation, vote power, and power to influence corporate decisions of the controlled company.[21] In that sense, even participation less than 50% of the shares may be deemed as control depending on the power to influence company's decisions (negative control).

[H] Substantive Test for Assessing Mergers

Pursuant to Article 11 of Law 1340, SIC must prohibit or object to mergers that will generate an undue restriction on competition. Of course, all mergers tend to restrict competition. As such, the SIC's objective is to determine whether those mergers will produce an *undue* restriction on competition.

Under Article 5 of Decree 1302, 1964 (Decree 1302), mergers exhibiting the following characteristics are presumed to produce an undue restriction on competition:

- where the merging parties engaged in anti-competitive activity prior to the transaction; and
- where the merged entity would acquire the capacity to impose unfair prices on consumers through the transaction.

Also, there are special sectors subject to regulation that impedes one company to acquire a certain percentage of the market, and there are other regulatory constraints that may force the SIC to block the transaction, not for competition reasons but due to regulatory constraints. In these cases, the authority does not advance a competition analysis.

One should consider that, according to Article 12 of Law 1340 and Decree 2153, SIC cannot object to mergers in which the parties can demonstrate, the *Efficiency Exception* as described above. Also, the SIC will apply the *Failing Industry Defence* if its thresholds are demonstrated as explained above.

21. *See* Article 27 Law 222, 1995.

If the merger transaction is not one of those that must be prohibited and if the exceptions just described do not apply, then the SIC will apply its substantive test. It is important to convey that the law does not explain the procedures or rationale that the SIC should use during its evaluation, and the guidelines issued by the SIC are not very specific in that respect. One can, however, identify some of the general elements in SIC's analytic process:

- SIC defines the general market based in the product market and the geographic market. The product market will be defined narrowly using the hypothetic monopolist test (*SSNIP Test*), to isolate the group of products (goods or services) that behave as perfect or imperfect substitutes of the product affected from the merger.
- In the supermarket cases: *Éxito – Carulla; Éxito – Cafam* and *Éxito/Cafam – Olímpica* the SIC used the *Isochronal Test* to define the relevant geographic market of the different supermarket chains within the large cities. The isochronal was rated at ten minutes time of transportation.
- SIC will consider and evaluate the competitive pressure that arises from perfect and imperfect substitutes, as well as from potential competition coming from national or international players. In 2011, the SIC authorized the *Caterpillar – Bucyrus* transaction, in which the authority considered competitive pressures from a relevant market larger than Colombia, which comprised a substantial part of Latin America.
- SIC will calculate the participation of the merging companies in the relevant market and apply concentration indexes such as HHI and CR4 to evaluate the effect of the merger. In markets that present a *leader—follower* structure, the SIC has also used the *Stackelberg Model* to assess market power before and after the merger takes place.
- SIC will then evaluate the different kinds of barriers for entering the market including import tariffs and duties, transportation costs, excess capacity, cost of building a plant in the country, etc., in an effort to evaluate the contestability of the market or the likelihood of entry of new competitors.
- If the parties have proposed conditions to the transaction, SIC will evaluate them and discuss them with the merging parties. In some cases, SIC will modify substantially the conditions offered by the parties and in general will prefer structural to behavioural remedies. Most likely, SIC will require divestment of part of the business.
- It is not very clear what set of circumstances will trigger an objection or a conditioned approval; but most likely it will be a negative mixture of the above elements.
- For instance, SIC would probably reject a merger that significantly increases market concentration, faces no perfect or even imperfect produce substitutes, does not have to cope with competition, enjoys high barriers to market entrance and limited contestability, and no possible structural remedies.
- Having said that, it is important to remember that in its whole history SIC has prohibited less than 1% of the informed mergers.

As said before, for some years now SIC has been applying reasoning and analysis like those developed both in the EU and the US. There is much debate as to the use of economic tools, such as the concentration indexes, which were prepared for developed economies, without adjustment to the size and specific characteristics of the Colombian economy. It must be considered that most markets in a developing economy are small and already concentrated, but this circumstance does not mean that there is no competition or that it will become impossible for new competitors to enter the market.

From the lines of merger cases that have been objected or conditioned, it is possible to deduct that SIC has moved from the *"Market Dominance Test"* it used initially, into a more comprehensive *"Substantially Lessening of Competition Test."* It is now clear that under Law 1340, issued in 2009, SIC has the capacity to review vertical mergers. There is much debate about the possibility of the authority to review conglomerate mergers.

Non-competition issues, such as convenience, political considerations, loss labour, etc., are not relevant in the merger review process and will not be considered or discussed by SIC.

[I] Notification Procedure and Timetable

It is important to convey that pursuant to Law 2010, 2019 (Law 2010), the parties that present a merger to the Colombian Competition Authority must pay a fee that is proportional to the size of the companies and the transaction. As mentioned before, Colombian merger control requires the previously described *short form notification (no waiting period)* when the economic thresholds are met but the market threshold is not; or *long form information (waiting period)* when both thresholds are met. Regarding merger whereby the assessment of the market threshold is complex, Resolution 2751 allows the intervening parties to file a *short form notification*. If the SIC is not satisfied with the market participation calculated by the parties, it has ten business days to request the parties to file the *long form information* instead. It is important to note that even though *short form notification* does not require a waiting period, in case of complex mergers it is advisable to refrain from closing for the next ten business days to mitigate any risk associated with the SIC not agreeing with the calculation of the combined market participation of the intervening parties.

In any case, the requisites either of these two systems must be complied with before the transaction takes effect in Colombia. Parties may execute agreements but must declare that performance is dependent on SIC clearance. Both parties are responsible for making the notification and presenting all relevant information to SIC.

[1] Mergers Carried Without Previous Clearance

Mergers executed without previous clearance from SIC are infractions of antitrust laws. The companies and their administrators are subject to *gun jumping* investigations and fines that are explained below.

It is, therefore, important that foreign mergers have no effect in Colombian territory until it has been approved by SIC. There is not yet a clear doctrine regarding the closing of foreign transactions before obtaining clearance with SIC, with a *carve out* or *hold separate* provisions for Colombia. However, it is advisable to include such a clause, as well as any other elements that help to assure SIC that the transaction will not have effects in Colombia before it has been cleared.

[2] Process and Timing

The chronology of the procedure works in two stages and goes like this:

Stage I:

- The petitioners file a pre-evaluation petition with a succinct description of the transaction and a demonstration of the payment of the fee.
- Within the following three days, SIC must determine whether it needs to review the transaction. SIC will end the proceedings if it decides the transaction does not require review.
- Within the three-day period, if SIC finds that review is necessary, it will order the parties to make a publication in a newspaper of sufficient circulation to enable interested parties to file any information pertinent to the analysis of the transaction, which should be done within ten working days of the publication.
- The petitioners can request that the SIC refrain from publication to preserve public order, in which case SIC can accept the petition while maintaining the confidentiality of the transaction and procedures.
- SIC has thirty working days (forty-five calendar days in most cases)[22] during which it studies the transaction to determine whether the merger poses a risk to competition, case in which the procedure should continue into Stage II; or if by the contrary, the merger does not affect competition, in which case SIC will approve it without conditions.

Stage II:

- If the procedure continues into Stage II, SIC must inform about it to the regulatory and control agencies in the sectors relevant to the transaction, so that they have the opportunity to present their technical advice regarding the transaction to the SIC, and to participate in the proceedings, which they can do at any point. While the agencies' views are not binding for the SIC, it must justify a decision to depart from those opinions.
- The interested parties must file the information requested for Stage II within fifteen days of the decision to continue the proceedings. They are free to

22. According to Article 62 of Law 4, 1913, when laws and official acts refer to terms of days, they are understood as working days, unless explicitly stated otherwise.

propose conditions and other measures that might reduce the anti-competitive effects associated with the transaction.

- SIC can request that the authorities and interested parties explain or supplement any information they have filed regarding the proceedings.
- Within this fifteen-day period, the petitioners can access the information filed by the authorities and third parties and attempt to rebut it.
- Within three months following the final filing date, SIC must make one of three possible decisions: simple authorization; conditioned authorization (i.e., clearance predicated on the application of suitable remedies); or objection.

The list of information that the interested parties must provide to the SIC is contained in Resolution 2751. The list is very detailed. It includes information concerning the terms of the transaction, the merging companies, competitors, consumers, market participation and conditions, barriers to entering the market, and any other information that may allow SIC assessing the effects of the transaction properly. One should note that SIC is free to delay its review until the information-gathering process is complete.

- Under Colombian law, if SIC exceeds the deadline, the transaction is automatically approved and SIC surrenders its authority over the case. This is known as positive administrative silence. However, one should note that this scenario is unlikely given that there have been only a couple of such instances in the past thirty years.
- If the parties to the merger remain inactive for two months at any point during the proceedings, SIC will consider the petition for authorization of the transaction abandoned.

[J] Consequences of a Failure to File

Mergers carried out without previous clearance from SIC are considered an infraction of antitrust laws and the companies and their administrators are subject to *gun jumping* investigations and fines. Fines are expressed in minimum monthly wages. The maximum fine that SIC may enforce amounts to 100,000 monthly wages, the equivalent to USD 23 million for the companies and 2,000 minimum monthly wages, the equivalent to USD 470,000 for the administrators or natural persons that carry out the transaction.[23]

In addition to that, in case SIC considers that the transaction produces an undue restriction on competition and must be prohibited, it could order to reverse the operation. Finally, it must be considered that an operation carried out in violation of competition laws can be declared by a judge absolutely null and void, which can have important economic repercussions. It must be pointed out that for merger purposes SIC

23. Law 1340, 2009, Article 25.

is not a judicial authority. Such a declaration must be obtained through an ordinary process before the general jurisdiction.

[K] Third-Party Involvement in Notification Process

SIC has not admitted third parties to fully participate in the merger review process. The authority will not grant them access to information submitted by the merging parties, notify third parties of its determinations, or permit them to file a reconsideration plea. Though third parties are free to present documents or express their opinions to SIC, the authority is not required to consider them. At its discretion, SIC may seek third-party testimony or information that might assist the authority in the review process.

Pursuant to paragraph 3 of Article 4, of Law 155, all the information the parties include in the antitrust filing is strictly confidential. Any public official who discloses any information regarding the procedure faces removal from office and criminal prosecution.

The Colombian economy is open to foreign investment. However, there are exchange, tax, labour, securities, and special-sector requirements that one must check about with local councils before entering a transaction.

[L] Remedies

Early in the review process, it is important for the merging companies to identify if the transaction should be subject to remedies, at least in a general way, so that the authority is aware of the intention or willingness of the parties to discuss them. In those cases, when SIC finds that the proposed transaction may pose undue restrictions to competition but believes there are options to correct such distortion, it will authorize the merger provided the parties undertake certain remedies.

Such conditions have ranged from elimination of exclusivity for distributors to the obligation of producing for a competitor at variable cost, allowing a competitor to use a percentage of installed capacity, and even the obligation to divest part of the business. SIC has shown a preference for structural remedies, such as divestments, over conduct or behavioural remedies.

SIC customarily requires that the parties comply with structural remedies within a certain time limit (generally, less than one year). Compliance with behavioural remedies is usually required for a limited period (generally, no more than three years), but there are cases in which an obligation has been imposed with no time limit. Pursuant to Article 11 of Law 1340, 2009, SIC must periodically review whether the parties have complied with the conditions and obligations imposed. Traditionally, SIC requires that an external auditor verifies the full compliance of the remedies and presents reports to the authority from time to time. Finally, SIC requests that the merging parties put in place a bank or insurance bond to guarantee full compliance with the remedies.

SIC has not made distinctions regarding the imposition of remedies in foreign-to-foreign mergers.

Even though SIC has not rendered an opinion on this issue, one could assume that the merger control authority would permit reasonable ancillary restrictions such as the non-competition clause for a limited period.

[M] Penalties

As described above, mergers carried out without previous clearance from SIC are considered an infraction of antitrust laws and the companies and their administrators are subject to *gun jumping* investigations and fines.

Fines are expressed in minimum monthly wages. The maximum fine that SIC may enforce amounts to 100,000 monthly wages, the equivalent to USD 23 million for the companies and 2,000 minimum monthly wages, the equivalent to USD 470,000 for the administrators or natural persons that carry out the transaction.[24]

[N] Appeal

Decisions issued by SIC are not subject to appeal. Rather, a disgruntled party or parties can seek a reconsideration plea before the same public official. The reconsideration plea must be filed within ten working days after notification of the decision. The superintendent must decide within the following two months, though the superintendent can extend this period if there is a need to gather additional evidence.

A party may challenge the final decision issued by SIC by means of a judicial action before the administrative jurisdiction. The party must file this action within the four months following the decision to object or prohibit the merger. However, this alternative is not very attractive to the parties because of the length of the procedure (five to twelve years).

[O] Specific Industries

There are industries exempted from merger control review undertaken by SIC, however, these industries must inform the relevant agency about the merger transaction. These industries are the financial and aeronautic industries and are explained in the following lines:

[1] Aeronautic Industry

According to the paragraph of Article 8 of Law 1340, the Civil Aeronautic Authority—*Aerocivil* is in charge of reviewing specific transactions between airplane operators. For instance, this agency deals among others, with share code agreements, joint commercial aviation operations, airfreight services, etc.

24. Law 1340, 2009, Article 25.

[2] Financial and Insurance Industries

The Superintendence of Finance—SF, is the governmental agency that controls and supervises financial institutions, banks, leasing companies, trading companies, etc. In that regard, Article 9 of Law 1340, 2009 states that merger transactions between companies under control of the SF are evaluated and authorized by such superintendence.

It is important to note that, Article 9 of Law 1340, 2009 provides that all the intervening companies must be under control of the SF for this entity to acquire jurisdiction over the merger. If one of the merging companies is not supervised by that superintendence, then the merger review is made by the SIC.

In these cases, the SF must request an opinion from the SIC, and if there are conditions to the transaction, those conditions must be defined by SIC.

CHAPTER 15

Competition Law in Ecuador

David A. Sperber Vilhelm[*]

§15.01 INTRODUCTION

Ecuador's first comprehensive and modern antitrust regulations were issued between 2009 and 2011. Executive Decree 1416[1] allowed for the direct application of Andean Community Decisions 608[2] and 616.[3] Decision 608 applies to abuse of dominant position and collusive practices or restrictive agreements, but it does not cover merger control.

Today, the Ecuadorian Competition Law (ECL, the "antitrust law"),[4] known officially as the Competition and Market Power Law (*Ley Orgánica de Regulación y Control del Poder de Mercado* – LORCPM), and its accompanying Rules ("RALORCPM")[5] constitute controlling law over competition issues.[6] Since their enactment, antitrust enforcement has been focused on anticompetitive conducts and unfair competition. More recently, since 2019, antitrust enforcement has also included gun

* The author thanks Charles Reeves and Cynthia Andino for their contributions.

1. Executive Decree 1614 of March 27, 2009.
2. Decision 608: Rules for the Protection and Promotion of Competition in the Andean Community, March 28, 2005. Decision 608 introduced a regional law regarding anticompetitive practices and abuse of dominant position. All sectors of economic activity are subject to it except when the Andean Community Commission decides to exclude a specific sector pursuant to a duly supported request from a Member State.
3. Decision 616 allows Decision 608 to be applied the Republic of Ecuador as of July 25, 2005. It enables Ecuador to apply Decision 608 when anticompetitive practices originate in Ecuadorian territory or in a third country which affects commerce in Ecuadorian territory. Bolivia and Ecuador may temporarily apply Decision 608 while they adopt a national competition law.
4. Ley Orgánica de Regulación y Control del Poder de Mercado – LORCPM. R.O. S. 555, October 13, 2011.
5. *Ibid.*
6. Reglamento a la Ley Orgánica de Regulación y Control del Poder de Mercado. R.O. 697, May 7, 2012.

jumping. The ECL governs all competition matters under national jurisdiction (i.e., cartels and restrictive agreements, unilateral conducts, merger control, unfair competition, and state aid). Its enforcement is vested in a single adjudicating body: The superintendency of competition ("superintendency", "SCPM" – *Superintendencia de Control del Poder de Mercado*).

§15.02 CARTELS

[A] Relevant Legislation

The ECL was enacted in 2011 and replaced Executive Decree 1614 of 2009. In turn it is regulated by its accompanying Rules.

Article 11 of the antitrust law establishes that:

> Prohibited Agreements and Practices: Any agreement, decision or recommendation, or concerted or consciously parallel practice, and in general all acts or conduct carried out by two or more independent persons are prohibited, and will be sanctioned in accordance with the rules of this law. This act applies [to acts or conduct] related to the production and exchange of goods or services, whose object or effect is to prevent, restrict, distort competition, or negatively affect economic efficiency or [the] general welfare.

The guiding principles for analyzing potential anticompetitive conduct is set forth in ECL Article 11, which provides a non-exhaustive list of anticompetitive conduct, including the following types of anticompetitive conduct between competitors:

(a) [Act in] concert to manipulate prices, interest rates, fees, discounts, or other commercial terms or transaction conditions, or to exchange information for these purposes or effect;
(b) [Act in] concert to distribute, restrict, limit, paralyze, establish obligations or control the production, distribution or commercialization of goods or services;
(c) [Act in] concert with clients, suppliers, or geographical areas to distribute or restrict supply sources;
(d) Restrict technological development or investment;
(e) Unjustifiably discriminate [in] prices, conditions, or negotiation modalities for goods or services;
(f) [Act in] concert [to create] unequal conditions for equivalent services, which unjustifiably places some competitors at a disadvantage compared to others;
(g) [Enter into] an agreement with the purpose of dissuading a person from a certain conduct, retaliating against it, or forcing it to act in a certain way;
(h) To agree on the quality of the products when it does not correspond to national or international technical standards;
(i) Bid-rigging, or in general all the conduct of suppliers or offerors, whatever the form they adopt, whose object or effect is to prevent, restrict, falsify or

distort competition, either in the presentation of offers and bids, or seeking to ensure the result for their own benefit, or that of another supplier or offeror, in a tender, auction, public auction, or other [process] established in the rules regulating government contracts, or private contracts open to the public;

(j) Boycott;
(k) To refuse unjustifiably purchase or acquisition demands, or offers of sales and provision of products or services, or to negotiate with current or potential suppliers, distributors, intermediaries, purchasers or users;
(l) To unjustifiably deny the admission of a person to an association, union or similar entity;
(m) To suspend, in a concerted and vertical line, the provision of a monopolist goods or services;
(n) To unjustifiably concert resale prices;
(o) To raise entry and/or exit barriers in a relevant market;
(p) To unjustifiably establish, impose, or suggest exclusive distribution or sales contracts, non-competition clauses, or similar;
(q) To do any act that prevents or hinders access or permanence of current or potential competitors in the market for reasons other than economic efficiency.

All agreements, practices, decisions, and/or recommendations that are declared anticompetitive are null and void, unless exempted in Article 12 of the ECL.

In order for the antitrust authority to be able to consider a conduct unlawful under the antitrust law it must:

(a) Prove the existence of an anticompetitive conduct such as those provided in Article 11 of the ECL, which lessens, distorts or restricts competition, and prove the participation of the investigated parties in such conduct;
(b) Prove the capacity of the investigated parties to be able to potentially cause harm to the general economic interest, general welfare, competitors or general consumers in a properly defined relevant product and geographic market; and
(c) Prove an actual or potential damage to the general economic interest, general welfare, competitors or consumers.

The modified Rules to the antitrust law establish five per se anticompetitive conducts:

(a) Price-fixing;
(b) Quantity fixing, limit(s) [on] production, distribution, and/or commercialization;
(c) Horizontal market allocation (by consumers, geographical, and/or product);

(d) Bid-rigging;
(e) Others to be determined in the future by the superintendency of competition.

The *de minimis* rule is not applicable to these conducts.

Other anticompetitive practices shall be treated under the rule of reason and be analyzed on a case-by-case basis, following the specific procedure established in the antitrust law. For instance, a given behavior could be seen as *prima facie* anticompetitive, but if such conduct lacks the capability of affecting the general economic interest, general welfare, competitors, or consumers protected by the ECL, then such conduct shall not be considered unlawful pursuant to the antitrust law.

On the other hand, the ECL does consider anticompetitive conduct legal if such conduct is proven to be pro-competitive, pro-efficient or if those accused of having engaged in such practices do not have enough market power to potentially cause damage to the general economic interest, general welfare, competitors, or consumers.

In addition, it is worth mentioning that the antitrust authority has held that agreements between competitors are not illegal when fostered by state action authorized by the Regulation Board of the ECL (*Junta de Regulación de la Ley Orgánica de Regulación y Control del Poder de Mercado*) or Congress.

Since the general economic interest, general welfare, competitors, or consumers concept is not defined in the antitrust law, its conceptual broadness has led to different interpretations in the case law since it was first introduced by the ECL in 2011. This broad concept grants the antitrust authority ample discretionary powers to determine its content; however, it also raises the burden of proof that the antitrust authority has to rule an anticompetitive conduct as unlawful.

Regarding the standard of proof for harm to the general economic interest, general welfare, competitors, or consumers, case law has held that the superintendency should prove the damage (e.g., Recapt[7]).

The National Supreme Court of Justice has not resolved a cartel case in application of the ECL.

[B] Extraterritoriality

The ECL is applicable to any conduct capable of producing effects in the Ecuadorian territory regardless of where it is practiced. Ecuadorian jurisdiction may be presumed if the economic conduct, whether conducted fully or partially outside of the country, if such conduct produces or is capable of producing effects in Ecuador. An anticompetitive conduct taking place outside of Ecuador is subject to the antitrust law if it targets, or has an effect on, the local market.

Article 5 of Decision 608 and Article 2 of the antitrust law adopt the so-called Effects Doctrine, which establishes the principle of extraterritorial application of the law.

7. SCPM. Resolution SCPM/CRPI/2015/019. October 8, 2019. Case Recapt.

The *Tissue* case[8] is the main precedent for the extraterritorial application of the antitrust law as it applies to the sanctioning of a cartel abroad. Under its rationale a collusive practice carried out exclusively abroad might fall under the jurisdiction of the national antitrust authorities if any Ecuadorian market is affected. At the same time, if two or more Andean Community country members are affected, then the general secretariat is competent to resolve the case.[9]

[C] Investigations

[1] Authorities

[a] Policy, Politics, and Institutions

The superintendency of competition, as noted above, is the enforcement body of the Ecuadorian antitrust law.

The antitrust law is enforced by the antitrust authority, which at present is vested in the superintendency of competition. The superintendent is appointed from a list of three qualified candidates that Ecuador's President remits to the Citizen's Participation and Social Control Council (*Consejo de Participación Ciudadana y Control Social*[10]). This council appoints the superintendent for a fixed term of five years, which is renewable for an additional term of five years. The SCPM is part of the "fifth power of the state" (Transparency and Social Control branch), and as such it is not subordinate to other branches of government.

The superintendency has a two-tier decision making. First, the National Intendancies (*Intendencias Nacionales*) investigates competition matters (investigatory body). The Intendant emits a non-binding final report to the Commission of First Instance ("commission", *Comisión de Resolución de Primera Instancia*), which issues resolutions and sanctions (resolution body).

Cartel investigations are carried out by the Intendancy of Collusive Agreements and Abuse of Market Power, which issues a non-binding report with recommendations to the commission, which takes the final decision on what measures are to be taken. The commission follows the recommendations issued by the Intendant and rarely takes a different position.

The three commissioners are appointed by the superintendent. They are usually lawyers and economists. They can be removed without cause by the superintendent. The superintendent, however, can only be removed with cause by Congress. The superintendent and the commissioners are appointed for five-year terms, which can be renewed once.

Pursuant to Articles 73 and 74 of the ECL, the commission's duties include, among others, the following:

8. CAN. SGCAN. Resolution N 2006. G.OA.C., Año XXXV, N. 3292, May 28, 2019.
9. *Ibid.*
10. CPCCS. www.cpccs.gob.ec.

(a) Decide on the existence of antitrust violations and apply the penalties set forth by the Ecuadorian antitrust law;
(b) Order the cessation of the anticompetitive practice, including under certain conditions or deadlines;
(c) Order precautionary measures;
(d) Carrying out activities, tending to reestablish the competitive process, even under certain conditions or deadlines, or declaring the unenforceability of contracts;
(e) Approve the terms of settlements in cartels, unfair competition, and unilateral conduct investigations;
(f) Resolve the immunity of leniency applicants, verifying if its conditions were fulfilled;
(g) Determine all remedies or measures to re-establish competition.

The resolution of the commission can be appealed to the superintendent or to the administrative court of appeals.

[b] Resources and Priorities

The enforcement of the antitrust law, despite its obvious technical content, sometimes has been politically driven, primarily for the following reasons: (i) the superintendent is indirectly appointed by the President of Ecuador; (ii) the superintendency's operations mainly depend on the National budget presented by the President of Ecuador to Congress; and, (iii) pursuant to the antitrust law, the antitrust authority has the absolute discretion to pursue the cases or claims it desires.

The superintendency's budget has decreased significantly in the last years. It continues to be seriously underfunded, especially taking into consideration the number of cases for which it is responsible.

Although the antitrust authority has expressly stated that cartels are hardcore offenses, its efforts to detect and sanction cartels have been low. The existence of a complex leniency program, as well as contradictory administrative precedents displayed by the antitrust authority, has contributed to a low-track record in punishing cartels.

[c] Inter-agency Cooperation

Ecuador has signed information cooperation agreements with fourteen competition authorities, as well as the International Competition Network (ICN), the Organization for Economic Cooperation and Development (OECD), and the United Nations Conference on Trade and Development (UNCTAD).

ECL's agreements with foreign competition authorities do not establish any obligation to provide confidential information, but they usually include provisions for coordinating parallel investigations, exchanging information, and consultations or staff exchanges between the authorities. Much of the actual coordination in merger and cartel investigations currently takes place outside of formal agreements, through direct and informal contacts or by way of waivers provided by relevant parties.

In practice, inter-agency cooperation with the antitrust authority has ranged from low to medium-low in merger and antitrust cases.

[2] Procedure

Pursuant to Article 53 of the Rules of the antitrust law, cartel investigations may be initiated by an individual or company, a government entity, as well as ex officio by the antitrust authority. Once a claim is filed, the SCPM reviews the claim, and if it complies with all the requirements the investigation starts.

Once an investigation is initiated pursuant to claim of a third-party, the antitrust law grants the investigated parties fifteen business days to submit their explanations regarding the alleged anticompetitive conduct. If the antitrust authority, after reviewing the explanations and evidence filed by the investigated parties, concludes that there are grounds to file formal charges against them, it issues a resolution opening a formal investigation within 10 business days and grants the Intendancy 180 business days for investigation. If necessary, an additional 180 business days may be granted. But, if on the contrary, the explanations filed by the investigated parties rules out the existence of anticompetitive conduct, the antitrust authority then issues a resolution closing the investigation.

Pursuant to Article 69 of the Rules of the ECL, after the intendancy closes its investigation, the parties' evidence production period shall last a maximum period of 60 business days, plus an additional 30 business days if necessary. The intendancy then emits a final report in 15 business days. If the final report determines recommendations for sanctions, then it is sent to the commission; otherwise, the case is closed. If the file is closed, either party can present an administrative motion for revision or an administrative appeal with the same antitrust authority. In some cases, the intendancy's final report with recommendations for sanctions can be appealed to the superintendent.

The commission has ninety calendar days to accept (totally or partially) or deny the intendancy's final report. The commission's resolution will determine the sanctions to be imposed, including monetary fines.

Notwithstanding the above-explained timeline set forth in the antitrust law, in practice investigations leading to the imposition of fines take between eighteen and twenty-five months.

Article 49 of the antitrust law grants other significant powers to the antitrust authority in exercising its duties, including those to:

(a) Hold hearings with the presumably responsible individuals, claimant, third-parties, witnesses and/or experts, take their declarations and order acts;
(b) Review books, accounting books, documents, information and other elements of the investigation;

(c) Dawn-raids;
(d) Resolve interim injunctions with or without notification to the parties;
(e) Fine with up to US 500,000 a person for not providing information, or it was incomplete or inaccurate;
(f) Fine the administrators and/or board directors with up to US 500,000 for participation in a cartel or other anticompetitive conduct.

Ecuador's Constitution, however, places limitations on the antitrust authority's investigatory powers in order to safeguard companies' and/or individuals' rights to defend themselves, such as due process of law, human rights, and the right to privacy.

Furthermore, during the procedure, pursuant to Articles 73 to 76 of the antitrust law, the commission can issue injunctions (i.e., cease and desist orders) ordering the accused parties to suspend the conduct under analysis until its final resolution is emanated (e.g., RTC versus BANRED).

In addition, Article 89 of the ECL provides the possibility for the investigated parties to present a pledge to cease the conduct in question. In that case, the commission can suspend the procedure term for 120 business days.

Once the commission or the superintendent issues a final resolution, the sanctioned party can appeal it to the administrative court of appeals within ninety business days. Since the ECL's decision involves the imposition of fines, the parties may give a bond to suspend the execution of the fine ordered by the administrative court of appeals until its decision, which can often take between two and three years. Generally, the administrative court of appeals does not suspend the execution of the commission or the superintendent orders and remedies.

[D] Sanctions and Remedies

[1] Administrative Sanctions

Article 79 of the antitrust law provides that the following sanctions may be imposed on the individual(s) or companies involved in a cartel:

(a) The cessation of the acts or conducts prohibited by the antitrust law and, if relevant, the removal of its effects;
(b) Fine of up to 12% of the national total gross income of the sanctioned party (not only the gross income of the relevant product). Exceptionally, if the benefit of the cartel is higher than 12%, then it can be sanctioned the total amount of the benefit;
(c) Order measures and remedies aiming at eliminating the distorting effects of competition;
(d) Publish the resolution in a major newspaper or other media;
(e) Request a judge to order the offending companies be dissolved, liquidated, spun-off, or split;
(f) Appoint an interim-controller until the remedies are executed.

Article 77 of the antitrust law makes companies liable for the conduct of individuals who acted on their behalf, with the help of, or for the benefit of the company—even if the act on which the company's representation is rendered ineffective.

Correspondingly, Article 77 also provides that those persons or corporations that violate the law's prohibitions, by act or omission, will be declared to be offenders. For the purposes of applying this law, the act of an economic operator is also attributable to the operators or persons who control it, except when their economic behavior is not determined by any of them.

When a fine is imposed on an association, union, or group of companies or economic operators that is insolvent, the association will be obliged to collect contributions from its members until the amount of the fine is covered.

The antitrust law does not contemplate the reduction of fines on the basis of "financial hardship" or "inability to pay". Moreover, the antitrust authority has not adopted this criterion in any known case.

Article 70 of the antitrust law stipulates a four-year statute of limitations period for initiating an investigation of an anticompetitive conduct. This period runs from the day the superintendency receives knowledge of the infringement or, in the case of continuous conduct, from the day they ceased. The statute of limitations can be stayed by the superintendency's issuance of a subpoena to the investigated party.

The statute of limitations on the sanctions imposed on an economic operator is eight years.

[2] Criminal Sanctions

The current antitrust law and the criminal code do not stipulate criminal sanctions for individuals or corporations involved in anticompetitive conduct.

[3] Private Actions and Follow-On Actions

Article 71 of the antitrust law allows any person damaged by an anticompetitive practice to civil law damages before a competent judge.

This section of the antitrust law, which recognizes the possibility of private antitrust litigation, has received virtually no enforcement. Since 2011 enactment of the ECL there have been no cases where a judge has granted compensation for damages caused by antitrust law violations.

It is important to note that Article 71 allows a person to seek civil damages (compensation for the loss of earnings and lost profits - there are no punitive damages) without a prior resolution from the superintendency.

[E] Cartel Leniency

Article 83 of the antitrust law gives the intendancy the power to negotiate and execute cartel leniency agreements. The commission subsequently approves or denies the leniency agreement. The leniency agreement may also be subject to review by the superintendent. Later, the commission determines if the beneficiary of the leniency application complied with its terms and conditions.

Leniency applicants normally receive full administrative benefits. These benefits are typically extended to the individuals involved in the infringement provided that they have also cooperated with the superintendency.

[1] Benefits and Types of Leniency

Under Ecuadorian antitrust law, the execution of the leniency agreement prevents administrative enforcement against the companies and individuals who have signed the agreement. In addition to extinction (in cases of full immunity) or reduction (in cases of partial immunity), there are other applicable administrative sanctions, as further detailed below.

It is important to note that the leniency program does not bar civil law claims for damages. The existence of a leniency agreement may technically allow, or even facilitate, such litigation. Generally, though, these agreements are confidential.

[2] Full Immunity

Provided that the superintendency is unaware of the existence of the violation up until the moment a leniency application is filed (i.e., before the launching of an administrative investigation into the matter), or even after the launching of an investigation, the first applicant for leniency will benefit from full immunity from the administrative fines.

Administrative immunity will only be extended to individuals involved in the anticompetitive practice, provided that they collaborate and confess to the practice and sign the agreement along with the company.

[3] Partial Immunity

Full leniency is only available to the first party to report a violation. The second party will benefit with fine reductions of 30%–50%; the third party will benefit with fine reductions of 20%–30%; and, additional parties will benefit with a fine reduction of up to 20%. The same percentages are extended to the individuals involved in the infringement provided that they also cooperate with the superintendency.

[4] Requirements

The basic principles of the Ecuadorian leniency program are: (a) full cooperation with the SCPM; (b) be the first one to confess to the violation; and (c) bring information to the authority about the anticompetitive practice. Moreover, the cooperating party shall stop its participation in the anticompetitive conduct and abide by confidentiality rules.

In short, basic requirements for a successful application are the following:

(a) The applicant must be the first to qualify with respect to the alleged or investigated infringement;
(b) The applicant must cease its involvement in the cartel as of the date of the leniency application, unless the superintendency decides it shall continue to benefit the investigation;
(c) The superintendency shall not have sufficient evidence to ensure the conviction of the applicant at the time the leniency is proposed or provides information to execute a dawn-raid;
(d) The applicant must confess its participation in the cartel and fully cooperate with the investigation;
(e) Must not eliminate evidence;
(f) Must not communicate to third-parties that a leniency application has been filed;
(g) Full cooperation with the SCPM; and
(h) Has not adopted acts to oblige other companies to participate in the cartel.

[5] Procedure

To benefit from the leniency program, the interested party must submit a proposal of a confidential meeting before the SCPM's general intendant. The proposal must contain the following information:

(a) The applicant's completed form;
(b) Brief description of the facts related to the violation, including explanation of the applicant's involvement;
(c) The evidence that demonstrates existence of a cartel;
(d) List of the names of the cartel's participants; and
(e) Signed collaboration agreement.

There is no guarantee of leniency until the execution of the leniency agreement (and ultimately its confirmation by the commission), but the applicant will not lose its position unless it is not able to provide a certain minimum threshold of evidence of the anticompetitive practice and its effects in Ecuador.

[F] Appeals

Once the commission issues a decision, the sanctioned company can file an appeal before the superintendent petitioning it to revert the decision. Appeals can also be filed directly to the administrative court of appeals. Administrative court of appeals decisions may in turn be appealed through the filing of a cassation petition at the National Court of Justice. Finally, as a last resort, a *writ of certiorari* to the constitutional court can be filed for alleged violations of fundamental constitutional rights.

Article 67 of the antitrust law allows that the following antitrust authority's decisions can be appealed:

(a) Imposition of Fines;
(b) Cease and Desist Orders;
(c) The dismissal or rejection of an economic concentration transaction or the imposition of remedies for its approval; and
(d) Dismissal of a claim filed with the antitrust authority.

In practice any administrative act (as defined in the administrative law) adopted by the antitrust authority that causes sufficient harm can be appealed by the parties affected by such decision.

Pursuant to Article 69 of the antitrust law, an appeal does not suspend the effects of the decision issued by the antitrust authority. Fines, however, can be suspended by the administrative court of appeals by substituting it with a bond or guarantee until its final decision has been issued.

Article 69 of the antitrust law requires that appeals to the administrative court of appeals should be filed within ninety business days of notice of the antitrust authority's decision. The antitrust authority then has ten business days to submit the file to the administrative court of appeals of the appellant's domicile. There is no fee to file this appeal.

[G] Precedent Cases

The National Supreme Court of Justice has not yet decided on any cartel cases. The complicated case currently being reviewed by the Andean Court of Justice is Kimberly-Clark del Ecuador S.A. ("KC") and Familia Sancela ("FG") annulment petition against the secretariat of the Andean Community. In June 2014, after a dawn-raid, KC and FG filed for leniency in the Tissue Case, which was approved by the superintendency. In the corresponding pleadings, KC provided incriminating information to the SCPM to obtain a full-exemption from the fines. The other cartel member was FG, which also filed for leniency. Zaimella was declared a non-member of the cartel.

Subsequently, ex officio, the superintendency denounced that a cartel between KC and FG existed at the Andean sub region of the tissue market under Decision 608 of the Andean Community. KC claims that the superintendency had used the confidential information it had provided in its leniency petition. For its part the SCPM affirmed that the evidence was obtained from the cartel investigation and not from KC's leniency petition. The secretariat of the Andean Community found that KC and FG had committed a hard cartel violation in Colombia and Ecuador for several years. It fined KC US$ 18 million and FG US$ 17 million. KC and FG then filed for annulment of the resolution with the secretariat of the Andean Community. That action is still pending at the Andean Community Court of Justice.

In 2017, the SCPM started a market investigation to determine whether the local cotton and textile companies were fixing prices. The holding in the case, where there had been a dawn-raid at the offices of the textile association, was that since the government set cotton prices and imports quotas there could have been no illegal collusion.

§15.03 UNILATERAL CONDUCT

[A] Relevant Legislation

Unilateral anticompetitive conduct is governed by Articles 7–10 of the antitrust law. Article 9 provides a long list of examples of conduct that can be undertaken by firms, either jointly or individually, which may be deemed antitrust violations. They include the more common unilateral practices of exclusive dealing, tie-ins, price discrimination, resale price maintenance, predatory pricing, and refusals to deal. They also include more arcane ones, such as excessive pricing, abuse of economic dependence, and significantly reducing production without cause.

Nevertheless, according to the statute, the practices stipulated in the list, and any others, will only be considered competition law violations if they also affect or restrict competition, the general welfare, or their competitors, or consumers, and constitute an abuse of a dominant position. Notwithstanding, the ECL's stipulated conduct are not per se illegal.

Since the list is not exhaustive, the SCPM may consider other practices to be unlawful depending on their potential to cause deleterious effects to competition. In all cases, the superintendency's assessment on the anticompetitive nature of a certain conduct will always contain an evaluation as to whether the practice is capable of causing a substantial and unjustified restraint on competition, affect the general welfare, or consumers.

In practical terms the focus is on the actual or potential harm of the conduct under investigation.

[B] Assessment of Dominance

Pursuant to Articles 7 and 8 of the antitrust law, a person or group of persons has a dominant position when, for a certain product or service, it is capable of acting independently regardless of their competitors, buyers, clients, suppliers, consumers, distributors, or other person in the relevant market in such a manner as that they have market power. Obtaining or strengthening market power in a way that does not threaten competition, economic efficiency, or the general welfare is not illegal.

In assessing whether a firm has market power in a relevant market, Article 8 requires that one or more of the following criteria must be considered:

(a) Their participation in that market, directly or indirectly, and their possibility of setting prices unilaterally or substantially restricting the supply in the relevant market, and other economic agents are not able to, in the present or in the future, counteract that power;
(b) The existence of barriers to entry and exit, of a legal, contractual, economic, or strategic nature; and, the elements that, foreseeably, can alter both these barriers and the offer of other competitors;
(c) The existence of competitors, customers, or suppliers and their respective ability to exercise market power;
(d) The possibilities of access of the economic operator and its competitors to sources, information, distribution networks, credit, or technology;
(e) Recent behavior;
(f) The disputability of the market;
(g) The characteristics of the supply and demand of the goods or services; and,
(h) The degree to which the good or service in question can be substituted for another of national or foreign origin.

Under the antitrust law, the unilateral conduct of a non-dominant firm cannot be sanctioned since only dominant firms are capable of affecting the general economic interest. Since no competition restraint is per se unlawful under the antitrust law, the antitrust authority's analysis predominantly focuses on the market share of the firms and its behavior.

The relevant market is established at the product and geographic levels. In order to determine the relevant product market, the antitrust authority analyzes the characteristics of the product, its price, its use, and its substitutes. As for the geographic market, the antitrust authority considers it to be the smallest region within which a sole competitor may impose a small but significant and non-transitory price increase (SSNIP test).

[C] Abuse of Dominant Position

An abuse of dominant position can be either exclusionary or exploitative. In cases of exclusionary abuses, the antitrust law punishes anticompetitive behavior that uses a dominant position to exclude competitors (either actual or potential) from the relevant market. In exploitative abuses cases, conversely, what is illegal is the imposition of abusive prices and commercial conditions that are different to the ones that would exist if there was effective competition in the market.

The concept of abuse of market power is defined in Article 9. First, it states that abuse of market power is prohibited. Second, it stipulates that abuse of market power occurs when one or more economic operators, on the basis of their market power, by any means, prevent, restrict or distort competition, or negatively affect economic efficiency or the general welfare.

Article 9 also provides a list of twenty-three examples of abusive conduct. The antitrust law requires the antitrust authority to prove a direct connection between the dominance and its abuse. Under this legislation, a unilateral conduct of a non-dominant firm cannot be considered abusive unless there exists a collective abuse of market power.

The list of non-exhaustive abuse of market power conducts are:

(a) One or more economic operators that affect, effectively or potentially, the participation of other competitors and the capacity of entry or expansion of the latter in a relevant market, through any means other than their own competitiveness or efficiency;
(b) One or more economic operators that increases their profit margins through the unjustified extraction of consumer surplus;
(c) One or more economic operators that due to the concentration of the means of production or commercialization, affect or may affect, limit or impede the participation of its competitors or harm direct producers or consumers;
(d) Predatory pricing or exploitative pricing;
(e) The unjustified alteration of the levels of production, of the market, or of the technical or technological development that negatively affect the economic operators or consumers;
(f) The unjustified discrimination of prices, conditions, or methods of setting prices;
(g) The application, in commercial or service relationships, of unequal conditions for equivalent services that unjustifiably place some competitors at a disadvantage compared to others;
(h) The unjustified conditional sale or tying;
(i) The unjustified purchase refusal, or the unjustified sale refusal;
(j) The incitement, persuasion, or coercion of third-parties not to accept, limit, or prevent the purchase, sale, or distribution of goods or services;
(k) The fixing, imposition, limitation, or unjustified establishment of conditions for the purchase, sale, or exclusive distribution of goods or services;
(l) The establishment of unjustified crossed subsidies, particularly aggravated when these are regressive subsidies;
(m) The subordination of acts, agreements, or contracts to the acceptance of obligations, supplementary or conditional benefits that, due to their nature or according to commercial use, are not related to their purpose;
(n) The unjustified denial of access for another economic operator to networks or other infrastructure in exchange for reasonable remuneration; as long as said networks or infrastructure constitute an essential facility;
(o) The implementation of exclusive or exploitative practices;

(p) Conditional discounts, such as those conferred through the sale of membership cards, loyalty cards, or other conditions, which imply any payment to access the aforementioned discounts;
(q) The abuse of an intellectual property right;
(r) The unjustified implementation of legal actions that have as a result the restriction of access or permanence in the market of current or potential competitors;
(s) To establish, impose, or suggest unjustified exclusive distribution or sale contracts, non-competition clauses or similar;
(t) The establishment of an unjustified resale price;
(u) Condition the purchase or sale of good or services to not using, acquiring, selling, or supplying goods or services produced, processed, distributed, or marketed by a third party;
(v) Behave in any manner to prevent or hinder the access or permanence of current or potential competitors in the market for reasons other than economic efficiency;
(w) The imposition of unjustified conditions on suppliers or buyers, such as the establishment of excessive and unjustified payment terms, return of products, especially when they are perishable.

The prohibitions provided in this article will also apply in cases where the market power of one or more economic operators has been established by a legal provision.

The assessment of the legal act that may contain them will not be admitted as a defense of conduct contrary to this law.

In order to sanction an abuse of market power conduct, the commission must find the following:

(a) Existence of a dominant position; and,
(b) Existence of an abusive conduct.

[D] Investigation (Authorities, Procedure, Powers, Burden of Proof, Appeal)

Please refer to the description provided in the cartel section regarding the applicable authority, its powers, the burden of proof, and the appeal process.

[E] Sanctions and Remedies

Please refer to the description provided in the cartel section regarding sanctions.

[F] Precedent Cases

The most important unilateral cases have been the following.

[1] Sinopharm and other v. Pfizer Ecuador

In 2011, the Ministry of Industry and Production decided this case by applying Decisions 608 and 616 of the Andean Community. The abuse of dominant position was for the unjustified and abusive implementation of legal actions that resulted in market restrictions to Viagra (Sildenafil) competitors based on a procedural patent. Pfizer Ecuador was fined $540,000.

[2] CNT E.P. v. Claro—CONECEL

In 2014, the commission applied the Ecuadorian Competition Act to sanction Claro for abuse of dominant position for blocking access to cellular towers that had been declared to be essential facilities. The commission ordered Claro to unilaterally revoke the exclusivity clause in the lease agreements with the towers' lessors. It fined Claro $138,500,000 (12% of its gross income) and subsequently increased the total fine to $220,000,000 in 2016 because the SCPM found that Claro had not complied with the ordered remedies. The antitrust authority's resolution was later overturned by a judge who ruled that Claro's constitutional rights had been violated.

§15.04 MERGER REVIEW

[A] Relevant Legislation

Since Decision 608 of the Andean Community does not have merger control regulation, Ecuador implemented a merger control regime in 2011 with the enactment of the antitrust law. Articles 14–24 govern merger investigations. This legislation establishes an ex ante merger control when one of two thresholds is met. Informative filings that do not meet the thresholds can also be filed. The superintendency, the national administrative competition authority, can approve, subordinate, or deny a filed transaction. The commission can intervene in cases where a merger has (or may have) anticompetitive effects in the relevant market. A new fast-track procedure has been in force since April 2020.

[B] Authority

As explained earlier, like in cartel and dominance cases, the authority that enforces merger control in Ecuador is the SCPM.

According to Article 21 of the antitrust law, the antitrust authority has the power to either approve, reject, or to condition the approval of certain economic concentration transactions (the "Concentration Transaction") to the fulfillment of certain undertakings (e.g., divestiture of certain assets or business lines, remedies).

[C] Triggering Events and Thresholds

[1] Qualitative Threshold: Acquisition of Control or Substantial Influence

The antitrust law requires the parties to notify and obtain the prior approval of the antitrust authority for certain Concentration Transactions, pursuant to the qualitative and quantitative thresholds provided in Article 16.

Concentration transactions affected by the antitrust law are those resulting in the direct or indirect acquisition of control or substantial/decisive influence of one or more companies, or those with shared management, lines of business, or assets. Article 14 provides a non-exhaustive list of concentration transactions of which the antitrust authority shall be notified. They include mergers, transfers of on-going business, stock acquisitions, shareholder agreements, joint-venture agreements, and any other agreement that grants de iure or de facto control of (or substantial influence over) management decisions or the company.

The antitrust authority established that a minority stake acquisition would amount to substantial influence provided that it grants the power to exercise a decisive influence in a company's daily business.

[2] Quantitative Thresholds

The Ecuadorian Competition Act has two criteria for mandatory filings, which are triggered by one of the following thresholds:

(a) Before or after the economic concentration, or in a transaction where the buyer will have or gain 30% or more of the relevant market(s); or,

(b) Separate or combined gross revenue of buyer and target in Ecuador exceeds 200,000 unified basic remunerations ($85,000,000 in 2022).[11] The Labour Ministry reviews this annually.

The filing has to be presented to the SCPM before the closing of a merger or acquisition that creates or effects a permanent change of control.

11. *Note*: banking and insurance markets have higher revenue thresholds, determined by the Market Power Control Board.

[D] Exemptions

Article 19 exempts the following concentration transactions from mandatory filings:

(a) Acquisition of shares without voting rights, or of bonds, debentures or any title convertible into shares without voting rights; or,
(b) Acquisition of liquidated companies or those that do not have registered activity in Ecuador during the previous three years.

The above exemptions to mandatory filing requirements shall be construed in a restrictive manner.

The material scope of notifiable transactions is wide-ranging since it includes all economic sectors. An exception to this is a transaction approved or created by a congressional act. Similarly, an exception can be obtained for a public-private partnership if it is approved by the competent administrative body. Another exception may be made for acquisitions that government entities or state-owned companies make.

Two filings have been presented to the SCPM by a "private" regulated bank that is wholly owned by the state. In these cases, the SCPM held that it had jurisdiction to review the transactions, which were approved by its commission.

[E] Pre-merger Control Regime or Post-merger Control Regime

If one of the thresholds is met, the general rule is that a mandatory filing shall be filed before a transaction is closed. Only informative filings can be filed after closing.

Since 2021 the rules of the antitrust law allow the notifying party to have meetings with the merger control intendancy to discuss market share and other matters.

[F] Intra-group Transactions

Based on the economic reality principle ("substance over legal form") set forth in Article 14, as well as the notification exemption for those concentration transactions in which the purchaser already owns more than 50% of the shares and votes of the target company, the antitrust authority has established case law where intra-group corporate reorganizations are not subject to merger control notification. It has also consistently ruled that internal group reorganizations (i.e., the acquisition or merger of entities within the same economic group) are exempt from mandatory notification requirements because they do not entail a change of control.

The parties can submit informative filings to the superintendency to avoid gun-jumping fines when the market share quota may be under discussion.

[G] Substantive Test for Assessing Mergers

Article 22 outlines a substantive test for analyzing concentration transactions to determine if there is an illegal concentration of economic power. The factors include:

(a) The competition status in the relevant markets;
(b) The market power of the acquirer and its main competitors;
(c) The need to develop and/or maintain competition of economic operators in the relevant market, taking into consideration its structure as well as current or potential competitors;
(d) Whether after the transaction market power has been generated or strengthened, or it has resulted in a foreseeable material decrease, distortion, or obstacle for the other economic operators and/or competitors;
(e) Whether the concentration:
  a. Improves production or commercialization systems;
  b. Promotes the country's technological or economic advancement;
  c. Improves the national industry's competitiveness in the international market as long as it does not significantly affect the economic well-being of national consumers;
  d. Harms the welfare of national consumers;
  e. Sufficiently offsets certain and specific restrictive effects on competition.

When reviewing a concentration transaction, the antitrust authority first defines the relevant product market (i.e., those products that are offered by both parties) and the geographic market (i.e., the territory where the merging entities offer the relevant products). It next considers the impact of the concentration transaction on the market structure by considering not only the merging parties' resulting combined market shares, but also barriers to entry, competition derived from imported products, efficiency gains, and potential competitors within a determined relevant market.

Most concentration transactions (approximately 80%) that the antitrust authority has reviewed since the merger control regime went into effect in 2011 have obtained the appropriate antitrust clearance. Roughly 18% of cases have resulted in fines and/or remedies while only one case has been denied.

Pursuant to the Merger Guidelines the existence of a high level of concentration in the relevant market (or a substantial increase in its level of concentration) as a consequence of a concentration transaction is a necessary, but not a sufficient condition, for the transaction to be denied. In Ambev InBev's acquisition of SABMiller, the local target had 92% of the relevant market and the buyer had 7%, but the transaction was approved with conditions and remedies.

The following were the conditions and remedies in this mega beer transaction:

(a) Total disinvestment of the AB InBev production plant in Guayaquil (Ecuador) and total disinvestment of other assets. This was the smaller production plant between AB InBev and SABMiller.
(b) The use of DINADEC S.A. (SABMiller's local distribution company acquired by the buyer) to allow access to AB InBev's nationwide distribution channel to local breweries.
(c) Implementation of separate contracts with clients and providers to include pro-competition conditions.
(d) Prohibition of exclusivity contract clauses.
(e) Creation and implementation of an e-commerce platform for the sale of independent craft beer producers.
(f) Open refrigerator space at the final sales points to craft beers and other drinks (up to 30% of refrigerator space for competitors).
(g) The sale of the *Biela*, *Dorada*, *Zenda*, and *Maltín* brands.
(h) Licensing the use of the *Brahma* brand, as well as production, distribution, and marketing of products of the brand.
(i) Limit the advertising budget of the *Pilsener*, *Club*, *Budweiser*, *BUD66*, and *Pony Malta* brands (main local brands).
(j) Maintain jobs and job stability for workers of both target and buyer companies in Ecuador; transfer 5% of the shares of the local company to workers through a trust (this option was removed from ECL Rules after this case).
(k) Provide access to the bottling process and bottle design of one bottle, its production system, training, and promotion to local craft breweries.

On November 15, 2017, after the remedies were approved by the commission, in an appeal the superintendent subsequently added a new condition within the divestment process. That condition was the sale of the *Club* beer brand (owned by SABMiller), which had a 10% national market share. This brand had been sold in Ecuador since 1966. Afterward, a court ruled that this disinvestment provision was not mandatory and thus *Club* currently remains part of AB InBev's local brands. Ultimately this acquisition was approved in Ecuador after AB InBev performed the required remedies. Heineken acquired the divested company the following year.

[H] Notification Procedure and Timetable

The antitrust law requires that only the buyer is obliged to notify the antitrust authority of a concentration transaction. The filing shall be made on or before eight calendars days after the closing. This is the shortest notification period in South America.

As per the timing of clearance, Article 21 provides that the antitrust authority has a maximum of sixty business days from the filing date to issue a decision. The intendancy can extend the analysis and approval for an additional sixty-business day period.

If no decision is issued within this period, the concentration transaction is considered to have been tacitly approved (administrative silence doctrine) with the same legal effects as an express approval.

In practice, however, the 120-business day period is repeatedly suspended by the antitrust authority through the issuance of several additional information requests that each add thirty business days to the process. Thus, the mandatory filing transaction can take between six and eleven months.

Since the antitrust law does not allow the parties to proceed with the closing of the concentration transaction prior to the antitrust authority's decision, it is important to note that there have been carve-outs to close the transaction in other jurisdictions. The antitrust authority has the power to undo the Ecuadorian portion of a concentration transaction deemed to be anticompetitive.

[I] Consequences of a Failure to File

Fines for "gun-jumping" can be issued for up to 12% of the local transaction's gross income. Gun jumping can also result from the transaction being voided. The commission has the power to undo the transaction and impose additional conditions and/or remedies.

Failure to provide requested information by the transaction parties and/or third parties can be sanctioned with fines of up to $500,000.

[J] Third Party Involvement in Notification Process

Only the parties that notified the antitrust authority of a concentration transaction can be a part of the notification process and access the confidential file. Third parties (such as competitors or clients of the parties) may be requested to file documents or testify as witnesses. But they are not allowed to access the confidential file.

[K] Remedies

The Ecuadorian Competition Act establishes structural and behavioral remedies. Since the antitrust law does not have a negotiation mechanism, the process may begin as soon as the parties or the intendancy determine that a remedy will be needed for the concentration transaction to be approved.

The parties shall not consummate the concentration transaction until the remedies ordered by the commission have been implemented, unless specified otherwise.

[L] Penalties

Fines for "gun-jumping" are up to 12% of the local transaction's gross income. The commission also has the power to void the transaction and impose additional conditions and/or remedies.

[M] Appeal

Please refer to the appeal heading in the Cartels Section, above.

[N] Specific Industries

The antitrust law does contain particular provisions regarding concentration transactions in the insurance, banking, and finance industries. In these cases, the separate or combined gross revenue of buyer and target in Ecuador shall not exceed 3,200,000 unified basic salaries for banks and financial institutions (2021: $1.36B) and 214,000 unified salaries (2021: $90.95M) for insurance companies. The Labour Ministry revises the unified basic salary annually.

Notwithstanding the above, it is important to note that certain regulatory frameworks have their own specific provisions regarding changes in control of regulated companies. For example, a change of control of a telecommunications company shall be subject to SCPM and ARCOTEL (Telecom Authority) approval if the change of control meets the thresholds set forth in the antitrust law.

CHAPTER 16

Competition Law in Mexico

Amílcar Peredo, Fernanda Garza Magdaleno & León Efrén Jiménez Domínguez

§16.01 INTRODUCTION

Competition enforcement in Mexico began in 1993 when the Federal Economic Competition Law (the "repealed law") came into force and the Federal Competition Commission ("FCC") was created. These events inaugurated a new age in economic regulation.

The repealed law was first amended in 2006 to grant the FCC new powers and to increase penalties. It was further amended in 2011 to strengthen the FCC's powers, criminalize collusive behavior, further increase penalties, and introduce the concept of "joint market power."[1] Until 2013, the FCC was an independent agency of the Ministry of Economy with technical and operational autonomy.

On May 2014, a new Federal Economic Competition Law (the "FECL") was published in the Federal Official Gazette ("FOG"). The FECL entered into force on July 7, 2014.

The FECL arose from the June 2013 amendments to Article 28 of the Mexican Constitution, through which two autonomous competition agencies, no longer part of the executive branch of government were created: (i) the Federal Economic Competition Commission, also known as COFECE (for its acronym in Spanish); and (ii) the Federal Telecommunications Institute, or IFT (for its acronym in Spanish). The IFT is the competition authority for the telecommunications and broadcasting sectors, while COFECE is the competition authority for all other industries. For purposes of this chapter, we refer to both authorities jointly as the "competition authorities".

The FECL essentially continues the framework of the repealed law concerning the analysis of monopolistic practices with few substantive and procedural modifications.

1. Although the law had several other amendments, these two had the greatest general impact for competition policy enforcement in Mexico.

Among the most significant changes that stem from the new regime are that new incremental powers were granted to the competition authorities, such as a new proceeding regarding barriers to competition and access to essential facilities. In addition, many of the changes to the FECL specifically deal with the organization, powers, and the composition of COFECE.[2]

§16.02 GENERAL ASPECTS OF THE MEXICAN COMPETITION REGIME

[A] Competition Authorities

As explained in the Introduction, in Mexico, the agencies in charge of enforcing the antitrust policy are COFECE and the IFT. As a result of the constitutional amendment, competition authorities are supposed to be entirely apolitical entities, as they are no longer part of the federal government but autonomous constitutional entities. As a result, decisions issued by these entities are independent, technically based, and objective.

Article 5 of the FECL stated that when one of such entities has information that the other is processing a matter under its jurisdiction, it shall require the submission of the corresponding file. In case the authorities do not agree on which is competent in a specific matter, the dispute shall be submitted to the judiciary who will reach a final decision. For many years, the subject matter jurisdiction of each agency remained undisputed. However, recently both authorities have claimed to have jurisdiction over the same markets related to the digital economy where the border of their jurisdiction is sometimes unclear.

The question of jurisdiction between both authorities arose recently in the following two cases:

(i) In 2019 in the context of a merger between Uber Technologies Inc. (Uber) and Cornershop, a Mexican grocery delivery start-up, notified to COFECE. This merger involved two economic agents that operated digital platforms. COFECE initiated the analysis, but the IFT requested COFECE to transfer authority over this matter because it considered itself as the competent authority to analyze the merger due to its subject matter. The judiciary finally decided that COFECE was the competent authority to analyze and decide the merger.

(ii) In 2021 in the context of an investigation initiated by the IFT regarding the existence of possible barriers to competition or essential facilities in the following investigated markets: (i) online search services, (ii) social networks, (iii) mobile operating systems, (iv) cloud computing services, and (v) related services. In this case, COFECE claimed jurisdiction on such markets. The judiciary finally determined that COFECE has jurisdiction to

2. IFT structure and characteristics were set forth in the Federal Telecommunications Law.

investigate the first three markets indicated above, and the IFT is competent to investigate the fourth market.

[B] Structure and Operation of the Competition Authorities

Through the 2013 constitutional reform, the membership of the governing board of the competition authorities was modified. The board of each authority is currently composed of seven commissioners who are nominated by the President of Mexico from a list of candidates proposed by an evaluation committee and ratified by the senate. Further, a series of principles are defined, such as autonomy, impartiality, transparency, and accountability which the competition authorities are required to observe in the performance of their duties.

The FECL also complies with the requirement in the constitutional amendment to separate COFECE's investigation powers from its authority to decide cases to ensure impartiality in decision making. This was achieved by transforming the Office of the Executive Secretary and dividing it into two different areas: (i) the "investigation authority", entrusted with carrying out investigations and issuing statements arising from their conclusions, recommending whether the COFECE's board ought to either close the case or open an administrative proceeding; and (ii) the "Technical Secretary" whose main duties are to review concentrations and to process trial-like proceedings which may conclude with the imposition of penalties for the investigated economic agents.[3]

As part of this separation of functions, the investigation authority does not require the board's consent to carry out an investigation (including issuance of inspection orders) or the imposition of coercive actions that, in addition to issuing warnings and fines in case of non-compliance and requesting the use of public enforcement agencies and imprisonment for up to thirty-six hours.

Further, the investigation authority may request the board to issue provisional remedies to ensure the effectiveness of all investigations and decisions, as well as to prevent damage that could be very difficult to compensate, including an order to cease and desist from engaging in the conduct under investigation (which was already contemplated in the repealed law), enforcement orders, and orders to prevent conducts related to the matter under investigation and to preserve information and documents required for the investigation.

3. IFT has a different organic structure. However, the Investigation Authority is also independent from the Executive Coordination, which supervises the Units in charge of processing concentrations and trial-like proceedings within the IFT.

[C] Scope of Application

The competition authorities have federal jurisdiction. The FECL provides that it is applicable to all areas of economic activity and is obligatory within the Mexican territory.[4]

The FECL applies to all economic agents, regardless of whether they are individuals, corporations, for-profit or non-profit organizations, federal, state, or municipal governments, associations, chambers of commerce, professional organizations, trusts, or any other form of participation in economic activities.

According to the FECL, the competition authorities may investigate any case in which a conduct has produced effects on the Mexican market, regardless of whether the illegal conduct was carried out within Mexico or abroad, by nationals or foreigners. Case-law has developed criteria establishing that the FECL may apply not only to conducts executed within Mexico but also to conducts that occur abroad when they produce effects in Mexico.[5]

§16.03 INVESTIGATIONS AND PROCEEDINGS REGARDING MONOPOLISTIC CONDUCTS

As previously mentioned, the FECL separates the authority that carries out investigations and the one that handles the administrative proceeding ("trial-like proceeding").

The investigation is carried out by the investigation division directors who are supervised by the head of the investigating authority. Both in practice and legally, this officer enjoys a significant degree of independence.

The FECL provides that the investigation of any type of monopolistic practices consists of two stages: (i) the investigation handled by the investigation authority that may conclude either with the closing of the file or with the issuance of a Statement of Probable Responsibility ("SPR"); and (ii) the trial-like proceeding handled by the technical secretary which begins with the notification of the SPR to the accused economic agents and follows the format of a judicial proceeding, providing the parties with due process rights.

[A] Investigation

To launch an investigation, the investigation authority needs an objective cause. An objective cause is any indication of the existence of monopolistic practices.

4. Article 1 of the law.
5. An example of a case in which COFECE penalized anticompetitive conducts carried out abroad, on the grounds of the harmful effect that they have caused within Mexico is case IO-005-2013, where seven global shipping companies were fined after COFECE found them responsible for the collusive conduct consisting in the allocation of the market of maritime transportation of vehicles and heavy machinery. In that case, there were several collusive agreements implemented globally on international routes, some of them involving several Mexican ports as points of origin or destination. The authority found that as a result, competition within Mexican territory was affected.

Investigations by COFECE of alleged anticompetitive conducts may be initiated by a third-party complaint, ex officio, as a consequence of a leniency application (only in case of collusive conducts) or as a consequence of a request filed by the president directly or through the executive branch.

The investigation period begins on the day in which a notice of the investigation's initiation is issued ("Notice of Initiation") and may last neither less than 30 business days nor exceed 120 business days thereafter. This period may be extended up to four times, for subsequent periods of 120 business days, whenever the investigation authority considers that there are justified reasons for doing so.

The scope of the investigation is restricted to the terms specified in the Notice of Initiation. However, if during an investigation, the authority considers that an additional product or geographic area shall be investigated it may open a new investigation. Nevertheless, in practice, the competition authorities usually set a wide definition of the investigated market which allows it to narrow down the investigation once it has enough evidence to do so.

In the repealed law, all investigations began with the publication of a summary of the Notice of Initiation issued by COFECE in the FOG. However, under the FECL, this was modified to allow the initiation of investigations without prior publication of the Notice of Imitation, as long as it was published during the first investigation period. The purpose of this amendment was to grant the investigation authority with the possibility of carrying out unannounced dawn raids.

Upon conclusion of the investigation, the investigation authority, within a sixty-day period, shall bring before the board an opinion that either proposes: (i) the initiation of the trial-like proceeding, if there exist objective elements that indicate a probable responsibility of the investigated economic agents, or (ii) the closing of the case when there are no elements to presume the responsibility of the investigated economic agents in an anticompetitive conduct.

The investigative opinion shall contain at least: (i) the identification of the investigated economic agent(s), and, if applicable, of the alleged offender(s); (ii) the investigated facts and their probable purpose or effect on the market; (iii) the evidentiary elements included in the investigation file and their analysis, (iv) the elements that support the proposal, (v) the legal provisions that may have been infringed (if applicable), and (vi) the consequences that may result from such violation.

The board of commissioners may order the closing of the case or the initiation of the trial-like proceeding within the next thirty days after having received the investigative opinion from the investigation authority.

During the investigation, none of the economic agents involved in the investigation may have access to the file.[6]

6. According to the Mexican Supreme Court, this is not a constitutional violation, since during the investigation phase does not grant the parties a due process right to be heard: "economic competition. ex officio investigation for the prevention and detection of monopolistic practices under federal law does not violate the guarantee to be heard."

The FECL establishes that all the information and documents gathered by the investigation authority during its investigations shall be classified as either reserved, or confidential, or public. Reserved information is that to which only those economic agents having a legal interest in the proceedings may have access, unless the owners of the information authorize disclosure. Confidential information is that considered sensitive and whose disclosure may potentially damage the competitive position of the economic agent providing the same, or which contains personal data that requires the owners' consent to be disclosed, or information whose disclosure may put at risk the safety of the economic agent, or that whose disclosure is legally prohibited. Due to its nature, confidential information is only available to those who provide it. Public information is information that has already been disclosed and is publicly available.

During the investigation, the competition authorities will not allow access to the file, even to economic agents involved, and during the rest of the proceedings, will only permit access to the file, excluding confidential information, to those agents with a legal interest.

Once the investigation proceeding is over, the head of the investigation authority must submit to the board a report either: (i) recommending closing the file if there are no grounds to presume responsibility of the investigated economic agents in the execution of a monopolistic practice,[7] or (ii) issuing a SPR to those economic agents that may be responsible for carrying out illegal conduct and therefore initiating an administrative trial-like proceeding.[8]

In case of leniency applications (only applicable in cartel investigations), there is an additional stage prior to the formal investigation where applicants provide to the competition authority evidence of the possible existence of cartel activity that may give the competition authority elements to initiate a formal investigation.

[1] Key Investigative Powers

The FECL gives the competition authority wide authority to gather the evidence it deems appropriate to carry out the investigations.

The FECL provides that any individual who has knowledge or is related to any fact investigated by COFECE, or with the subject matter of its ongoing procedures, has the obligation to provide, within a ten-day period, the information, objects, and documents under its possession by the means required; to appear for interviews in the place, hour, and date required, and to allow on-site inspections. Failure to cooperate in an investigation may result in a warning, and in case of non-compliance, in a fine of up to 3,000 times the current Measurement Unit ("MU"), which amounts to MXN 268,860 (approx. USD 12,908.40).[9]

7. In cases in which the investigation is initiated by a complaint, if the commission decides to close the investigation file, the plaintiff may appeal through an *amparo* action in a federal court.
8. Article 78 of the FECL.
9. The daily MU for 2021 is MXN 89.62. The exchange rate considered is USD 1 = MXN 20.8283 as of November 19, 2021.

The investigation authority has the following powers to gather information in its investigations:

[a] Requests for Information

The investigation authority is allowed to request any individual or company to submit the information or documents it deems necessary to carry out an investigation.

[b] Summon Individuals

The investigation authority is also allowed to summon individuals to appear before the competition authority to be interviewed in connection with the information they may have related to the investigated facts.

[c] Dawn Raids

The FECL repealed the obligation to publish the initiation of an investigation in the FOG, thus allowing COFECE to make unannounced dawn raids, in which the inspected parties are unaware of the commencement of the market investigation, and therefore, are unable to anticipate and prepare for the dawn raid.

COFECE may inspect any offices, premises, or any other location where it considers that it may find evidence connected with its investigation.

During a dawn raid the investigation authority may: (i) review, photocopy, or reproduce files; (ii) secure or seal offices or the areas where the information to be reviewed is kept, in order to ensure that it is not altered or withdrawn; (iii) ask general questions related to the information reviewed; and (v) take pictures or video, and reproduce any information related with the procedure. The inspected economic agent must refrain from obstructing the development of the inspection and is obligated to cooperate with the competition authority.

In case of dawn rides carried out by COFECE's investigation authority, there is a special procedure to separate documents qualified by the attorney-client legal privilege that shall be followed, pursuant to the recently issued COFECE's Regulatory Provisions for the assessment of information that stems from legal advice provided by economic agents ("Regulatory Provisions on Legal Privilege").

[2] Limitation Periods

The limitation period for COFECE to commence an investigation of unlawful concentrations or monopolistic practices was extended from five to ten years, calculated from the date in which the concentration took place or from the date in which the monopolistic practice ceased to exist.

[B] Trial-like Proceeding

If the investigation authority concludes that there is evidence that indicate probable responsibility of the investigated economic agents, it will issue a SPR that will be notified to the accused economic agents. The proceeding initiates with the notification of the SPR to the accused economic agents. The stages of the trial-like proceeding are the following:

a) After being served, the accused economic agents will have access to the file and a non-extendable forty-five-day period to reply to the SPR and submit documentary evidence, as well as to introduce other evidentiary elements that necessitate further processing.
b) After the constitutional reform, the investigation authority is considered a "party" to the trial-like proceeding. The FECL grants it with a non-extendable fifteen-day period to provide its views on the arguments and evidence put forward by the accused economic agents.
c) Thereafter, the procedural oversight authority shall order either the dismissal or admissibility of the evidentiary elements provided, and shall set the location, date, and time for evidentiary processing. The evidentiary elements shall be processed within a twenty-day period from the admission date.
d) Once the evidence is processed and within the following ten-day period, the authority may order further evidence gathering or summon the parties (including the investigation authority) for closing arguments.
e) Within ten days following the deadline to submit closing arguments, the accused economic agent has the right to request an oral hearing before the board of commissioners to render any statements they deem appropriate.
f) The competition authority shall issue the resolution within a non-extendable forty-day period.

The final decision and sanctions imposed must be based in arguments and evidence, so that it can be deemed as duly grounded in fact and law.[10]

[C] Information Protected by Legal Privilege

On September 30, 2019 the Regulatory Provisions on Legal Privilege were published in the FOG and entered into force. These provisions set out a proceeding for processing communications between individuals and companies involved in proceedings carried out by COFECE and their lawyers when such communications are intended to provide legal advice.

10. Under Mexican legislation this means that evidence and arguments should be enough to prove that the facts of the case are consistent with how the law was applied to decide and sanction, to the specialized court satisfaction.

According to the provisions, COFECE will neither take into consideration protected communications nor regard them as evidence.

The procedure contemplated in the provisions applies during the investigation and the trial-like proceeding.

[D] Appeal

As a consequence of the June 2013 amendments to Article 28 of the Mexican Constitution, on August 2014 the judiciary created specialized courts in competition and telecommunications matters (the "specialized courts"). The main activity of these specialized courts is to rule on "*amparo*" actions[11] filed against the decisions issued by the competition authorities. The FECL granted additional powers to the specialized courts to resolve jurisdictional conflicts that may arise between COFECE and IFT. In addition, the FECL also clarifies that civil actions filed to recover compensatory damages arising from anticompetitive behavior will be solved by the specialized courts.[12]

Pursuant to the constitutional amendment, currently the competition authorities' final decisions may only be challenged through an indirect *amparo* action before the specialized courts. Formerly, there were two types of defenses that could be used to challenge the orders or decisions issued by the CFC: (i) an administrative appeal or (ii) an *amparo* action. However, as a result of the 2013 constitutional amendment, the administrative appeal was repealed, leaving the *amparo* action as the only appeal available to challenge final orders and decisions.

The rules applicable to an *amparo* action are set forth in Articles 103 and 107 of the Federal Constitution and more specifically in the Amparo Law; these rules are quite complex and beyond the scope of this chapter, but in general terms, allow the parties subject to enforcement by the competition authorities to challenge the decisions, or even the FECL or its regulations, in case there are grounds to consider these contravene human rights acknowledged in the constitution or international treaties.

If the plaintiff is successful, then the order or decision violating the specific right will be annulled by the specialized court, usually the competition authority shall issue a new act, without repeating the infringement, although the precise effect of this depends on the circumstances of each case.

11. An *amparo* action is a trial in which either a specific provision of a Law or an administrative decision (or both) can be challenged in a Federal Court, on the basis that it violates constitutional and/or conventional human rights.
12. As of today, however, the specialized courts hold jurisdiction only over administrative matters.

§16.04 CARTELS

[A] Relevant Legislation

The FECL identifies collusive conducts as absolute monopolistic practices. In accordance with Article 53 of the FECL, absolute monopolistic practices include contracts, agreements, arrangements, or combinations thereof among economic agents with the aim or effect of an absolute monopolistic practice. The FECL does not require the existence of a written agreement to penalize a cartel. In order to penalize such an agreement, the competition authority must prove through different means of evidence that the arrangement was entered into by competitors.

These conducts are illegal per se and are the following:

- Price fixing;
- Restricting the supply or demand of goods and/or services;
- Territory and client allocation among competitors.
- Bid rigging; or
- Exchanging of market information with any purpose or effects referred in the previous sections.

Absolute monopolistic practices are considered per se illegal. Conducts identified as such are automatically illegal without further investigation and without considering market share or possible efficiencies. In Mexico, only horizontal and not vertical restraints are illegal per se.

In case of collusive practices, the competition authorities will only need to prove that the agreement among competitors took place, without the need to assess if it had an adverse impact to competition or consumers. In this regard, the Mexican Supreme Court has acknowledged that indirect evidence may suffice to support liability derived from cartel activity.[13]

In addition, and only for absolute monopolistic practices, the Federal Criminal Code ("FCrC") is applicable, as this type of practice is also considered criminal conduct in Mexico.

[B] Immunity/Leniency

The FECL establishes an immunity and leniency program to reduce or eliminate potential criminal and administrative liability for engaging in absolute monopolistic practices.

Any economic agent or individual who has participated directly, or on behalf of companies in an absolute monopolistic practice, may acknowledge its participation before the investigation authority and apply for leniency, either prior to the initiation of an investigation or during an ongoing investigation (prior to the issuance of the SPR).

13. *See* "Amparo en Revisión 453/2012 of the Second Chamber of the Mexican Supreme Court of Justice.

Both economic agents and their employees may be included within the same application and may receive the same benefits.

The immunity and leniency program reduces the maximum applicable fine according to the applicant's position within the program (immunity or reductions of 100% only for the first applicant, and leniency or reductions up to 50%, 30%, or 20% to subsequent applicants), assuming that the applicant has submitted sufficient evidence regarding the alleged practices in order to be granted immunity or leniency. Also, there would not be any criminal liability for the applicants and their employees or managers.

The conditions for being granted full immunity are: (i) being the first economic agent and/or individual involved in the conduct, providing sufficient supporting evidence to allow the investigation to be initiated or allow the presumption of the existence of an absolute monopolistic practice; (ii) cooperate fully and continuously throughout the investigation, and trial-like proceeding; and (iii) take all the necessary actions to cease the anticompetitive practice.

The identity of the applicant (whistle-blower) is maintained under strict confidentiality during the leniency proceeding, the investigation, and the trial-like proceeding. Therefore, its identity is not disclosed to any third parties, the media, or even other authorities (international cartels).

Nevertheless, economic agents that have been granted immunity or leniency may still be subject to a civil claim by parties who suffered damages or losses as a result of the illegal conduct.

It is worth mentioning that, in addition to the FECL, on March 4, 2020, the Regulatory Provisions on Immunity and Reduction of Penalties Program issued by COFECE, were published in the FOG. This binding instrument seeks to further regulate the leniency program set forth in the FECL. It contains: (i) a procedure to request coverage under the immunity program, (ii) the definition and scope of the obligation of the economic agent to cooperate with COFECE fully and continuously, and (iii) the procedure to be followed by COFECE to remove immunity to any economic agent who fails to comply with its obligations.

[C] International Inter-agency Cooperation

Regarding international cartel investigations, inter-agency cooperation is not only expected but also necessary for the effective conclusion of this type of investigation. This practice is common within antitrust agencies around the globe, and the Mexican competition authorities (specially COFECE) are not an exception.

It is normal practice, that after receiving an immunity or leniency application in which a previous application has been submitted with another antitrust enforcement agency in another jurisdiction, COFECE requests inter-agency cooperation to the extent available.

Pursuant to the FECL, however, any information contained in a file (whether immunity/leniency or an investigation or administrative proceeding file) may not be disclosed to any other party, including any foreign antitrust agency. Thus, to be able to disclose or receive any such information, the competition authority may request the parties involved in an investigation to issue either a procedural or full waiver, waiving its right to keep confidential the information provided.[14]

[D] Sanctions and Remedies

[1] Administrative Sanctions

The FECL contemplates sanctions for individuals and economic agents engaging in absolute monopolistic practices, as follows:

- For the economic agent that directly participated in the absolute monopolistic practice: a maximum fine of 10% of the economic agent's annual income.
- For the economic agent that contributed, facilitated, or instigated the execution of monopolistic practices: a maximum fine equivalent to 180,000 times the MU, which amounts to MXN 16,131,600.00 (approx. USD 774,503.92).
- For having participated in an absolute monopolistic practice on behalf of an economic agent: (i) the ineligibility to act as a company's board member, manager, director, executive, agent, representative, or legal representative for a maximum five-year period, and (ii) a maximum fine equivalent to 200,000 times the MU, which amounts to MXN 17,924,000.00 (approx. USD 860,559.91).

Criminal sanctions that may be imposed to individuals that participated in an absolute monopolistic are: (i) prison ranging from 5 to 10 years and (ii) a fine ranging from 1,000 to 10,000 times the MU, which amounts to MXN 89,620.00 to MXN 896,200.00 (approx. USD 4,302.80 to USD 43,028.00).

Penalties may be doubled in case of a second violation.[15] The competition authority shall consider, when imposing a penalty, the severity of the violation, the damage caused, the degree of intent, market share held, the size of the market in question, the duration of the practice, previous history, and the financial capacity of the agent, among other factors.

[2] Criminal Sanctions

Since 2011, the competition authorities have been able to request the beginning of a criminal investigation against those who engage in absolute monopolistic practices

14. A procedural waiver only allows the commission to disclose (only to other antitrust authorities) the procedural status of a specific on-going investigation. A full waiver allows the commission to disclose any information, documents, and even the identity of the parties involved in an investigation.
15. The FECL states that for purposes of this law, a second offense will be considered as having occurred when an agent who has been penalized for a violation, commits another violation of the same type or nature, within a lapse of no more than ten years between the first and the second violation.

(cartel activity), but it is not responsible for prosecuting criminal charges against economic agents involved in antitrust violations. The FECL provides that the head of the investigation authority is the authority that may request the Federal Attorney General's Office (public prosecutor) to begin a criminal investigation. In criminal proceedings, the competition authority acts only as a complainant, but the proceedings are carried out by a federal prosecutor (*Ministerio Público*) and the criminal courts. Once the prosecutor has received the complaint, it is obligated to begin an investigation.[16]

The main legislation applicable to criminal proceedings in the antitrust field are the FCrC and the National Code of Criminal Procedure ("NCCP").

Article 254 *bis* of the FCrC considers all absolute monopolistic practices (price fixing, supply restriction, territory and client allocation, bid rigging, and exchange of information with the intention or effect of the previous conduct) as criminal offenses.

Since antitrust criminal offenses are federal in nature and governed by the FCrC and the NCCP, the federal public prosecutor has jurisdiction and can act throughout Mexico. In addition to the foregoing, the FCrC applies, among others, to acts carried out abroad but which have an effect in Mexico.[17]

In Mexico, individuals may only be held criminally liable (not corporations) if they were directly involved in carrying out the illicit conduct, either to benefit themselves or to their principals.

Economic agents who successfully applied for leniency in an antitrust investigation are not subject to criminal liability.

As previously mentioned, only individuals may be charged and convicted of a criminal offense. The FCrC provides that individuals who participated in absolute monopolistic practices would be penalized with: (i) prison ranging from five to ten years and (ii) a fine ranging from 1,000 to 10,000 times the MU, which amounts to MXN 89,620.00 to MXN 896,200.00 (approx. USD 4,302.80 to USD 43,028.00).

It should be noted that this criminal fine is different from the administrative fine that can be imposed by COFECE pursuant to the FECL, following an administrative proceeding.

For many years, COFECE was not active in requesting the beginning of criminal investigations arising from absolute monopolistic practices. However, during 2020, COFECE made public that its investigation authority filed complaints with the Attorney General's Office against several individuals who, presumably coordinated to manipulate the results of public tenders on the health sector. COFECE has been increasingly vocal in the relevance of penalizing collusive practices under the criminal law.

[E] Relevant Cases

After its creation, COFECE has been very active investigating and sanctioning cartel activity, including international cartels and conducts carried out in many relevant

16. Article 254*bis* of the FCC.
17. Articles 2 and 3 of the FCrC.

economic sectors such as healthcare (mainly consisting in collusive conducts through bid riggings),[18] the financial sector,[19] basic consumer goods (such as tortillas, sugar, eggs, poultry, etc.),[20] among others.

Three of the most notable recent cartel decisions issued by COFECE are the following:

(a) Investigation IO-001-2016 into collusive practices in the drug distribution market. In this case COFECE decided to impose penalties on five companies and twenty-one individuals for their participation in five anticompetitive conducts related to price fixing, market allocation, and supply limitations. The total fine amounts to MXN 903,479,260.71 (approx. USD 43,377,484.51). In addition, this resolution imposed for the first time in the history of COFECE, the sanction consisting of disqualification of certain individuals. This implies the prohibition to act as directors in any company of the economic group of the economic agent they currently represented for periods ranging from six months to four years.

(b) Investigation DE-011-2016 into collusive practices in the market for full-service laboratory and blood bank studies, and related goods and services, contracted by the National Health System. In this case COFECE decided to impose penalties on eleven companies and fourteen individuals for bid rigging in public tenders organized by the Mexican public health system and for exchanging information with such purpose. The total fine imposed amounted to approximately MXN 626,457,527.54 (approx. USD 30,077,227.98).

(c) Investigation number IO-006-2016 into collusive practices in the trade of government debt securities in the secondary market. In this case, COFECE found evidence that 7 banks and 11 traders entered into 142 illegal agreements to sell or buy at a certain price, or not to trade or acquire certain government securities. This conduct affected some operations in the secondary market for government securities between 2010 and 2013. The total fine imposed amounted to approximately MXN 35,075,883.36 (approx. USD 1,684,049.27).

18. For instance, investigations: (i) DE-011-2016 of cartel conduct regarding laboratory and blood bank services, as well as related goods and services, contracted by the National Health System in Mexico; and (ii) DE-020-2014: Investigation of cartel conduct in the market for polyethylene gloves.

19. For instance, investigations: (i) IO-003-2015 of cartel conduct in the pension fund market, and (ii) IO-006-2016 of cartel conduct in the trade in debt securities issued by the Mexican government.

20. For instance, investigations: (i) IO-006-2013 of a cartel conduct in the market for manufacturing, distribution, and marketing of sugar in Mexico; and (ii) IO-005-2009 of a cartel in the manufacturing and distribution of poultry in Mexico City.

§16.05 ABUSE OF DOMINANCE

[A] Relevant Legislation

Abuse of dominance conducts identified in the FECL as relative monopolistic practices are analyzed under the "rule of reason", which means that it is necessary to assess the impact of the conduct in the market to determine whether it is illegal and can be sanctioned.

Article 56 of the FECL identifies certain conducts that qualify as relative monopolistic practices and are thus subject to competition enforcement. According to Article 54 of the FECL, these conducts are illegal if:

(i) The economic agent carrying out the practice has substantial market power;
(ii) They have an exclusionary object or effect; and
(iii) They do not generate market efficiencies that would outweigh the damages caused.

[1] Assessment of Market Power

In Mexico, there are two broad approaches to assessing market power. First, a firm's share within a relevant market (if a firm has a small share of the market, it is highly unlikely to have substantial market power). Second, quantitative measures of a firm's pricing power are often used, such as its price-cost margins or its profitability over time (if a firm is unable to maintain prices significantly above competitive levels, it is unlikely to have substantial market power). In addition, other evidence of the potential actions of the firm under investigation and of its competitors and consumers are also considered (in particular, if entry of other competitors is sufficiently easy then it is unlikely that a firm will have significant market power).

In practice, a combination of all these approaches is commonly employed by COFECE in order to determine the presence or absence of substantial market power.

[a] Market Definition/Market Shares

Although there are no explicit market share thresholds, shares in excess of 40%–50% may suggest substantial market power. COFECE traditionally follows the approach of relying primarily on market share estimates to decide when an economic agent has substantial market power. Nevertheless, market share by itself is not enough to conclude that an entity has substantial market power, since COFECE must consider other market conditions related to the actual competitive restraints faced by the allegedly dominant party.

[b] Quantitative and Other Measures

Before concluding whether a firm has substantial market power (only taking into account, market shares), it is also necessary to establish if the firm is protected by substantial barriers to entry and other considerations.

In addition, in some industries in Mexico, relatively large customers act as a significant constraint on market power. These large customers can have sufficient buying power so as to limit the ability of the firm under investigation to increase prices.

[c] Joint Market Power

With respect to the analysis of relative monopolistic practices, the FECL maintains the possibility of analyzing the joint market power of two or more companies.

[2] Conducts That may be Penalized

Article 56 of the FECL identifies a set of thirteen conducts that qualify as relative monopolistic practices and are thus subject to competition enforcement, namely: (i) vertical market segmentation, (ii) imposition of resale prices, (iii) bundling, (iv) exclusivities, (v) refusal to deal, (vi) boycott, (vii) predatory pricing, (viii) loyalty discounts or conditioned sales, (ix) cross-subsidies, (x) establishing discriminatory conditions, (xi) increase the cost of rivals, (xii) denial of treatment related to essential facilities, and (xiii) margin squeeze.

[3] Object and Effect

Relative monopolistic practices may only be sanctioned when they have an anticompetitive (exclusionary) purpose or effect, consisting in any of the following:

- to unduly displace other firms
- prevent other firms from having access to the market, or
- establish advantages in favor of one or more people.

The FECL explains that the displacement required for a relative monopolistic practice to be illegal may occur not only in the market where the practice is taking place, but also in related markets.

[4] Efficiencies

Relative monopolistic practices are illegal and shall be punished if the abovementioned requirements are met, unless the economic agent proves that the efficiencies that they produce positively affect economic competition and market access, and thus outweigh the possible anticompetitive effects and result in an improvement of consumer welfare.

Some of the efficiencies that may be considered are:

- The introduction of new goods or services.
- The use of residual lots, defective or perishable products.
- Cost reductions resulting from creating new techniques and production processes.
- Technological advancement.

[5] Sanctions and Remedies

The administrative sanctions for carrying out a relative monopolistic practice are:

- For the economic agent that participated in the relative monopolistic practice: a maximum fine of 8% of the economic agent's annual income,
- For the economic agent that contributed, facilitated, or instigated the execution of monopolistic practices: a maximum fine equivalent to 180,000 times the MU, which amounts to MXN 16,131,600.00 (approx. USD 774,503.92).
- For having participated in a relative monopolistic practice on behalf of an economic agent: (i) the ineligibility to act as a company's board member, manager, director, executive, agent, representative, or legal representative for a maximum five-year period and (ii) a maximum fine equivalent to 200,000 times the MU, which amounts to MXN 17,924,000.00 (approx. USD 860,559.91).

It is important to note that that there is no criminal liability arising from the execution of relative monopolistic practices.

[6] Settlement

There are no immunity and leniency program or criminal sanctions for relative monopolistic practices. Notwithstanding, a special settlement proceeding is available in investigations concerning relative monopolistic practices and illegal concentrations.

The economic agent interested in concluding the investigation before its completion, shall express in writing its willingness to settle before the investigation authority issues an SPR. The applicant should state: (i) the commitment to suspend, eliminate, or correct the illegal practice or concentration; and (ii) the proposed legally and economically feasible means to avoid or eliminate the relative monopolistic practice or illegal concentration under investigation.

[7] Relevant Cases

One of the recent relevant abuse of dominance cases is case IO-001-2015 concerning refusal to deal and discriminatory discounts. In this case, COFECE penalized the credit information company *Dunn and Bradstreet, SA, Sociedad de Información Crediticia*

("DUN") for denying treatment to *Círculo de Crédito, SA de CV, Sociedad de Información Crediticia* ("CC") in the market of gathering and processing credit information of companies in Mexico. DUN refused to sell or provide CC its primary database of companies and a segment of the database owned by DUN that contained credit reports of companies, even though according to the Mexican financial regulation, credit information societies must exchange their primary databases among themselves. A fine of MXN 27,455,091.12 (approx. USD 1,318,162.84) was imposed to DUN. The conduct consisting of discriminatory discounts was finally not sanctioned since the accused economic agents were able to prove that it was not carried out.

There is another relevant ongoing investigation handled by COFECE regarding abuse of dominance in the market of digital advertising and related services in Mexico.

§16.06 BARRIERS TO COMPETITION AND ESSENTIAL FACILITIES

[A] Definition

One of the most significant aspects of the constitutional reform is that the competition authority was granted with the following new incremental powers to effectively carry out its purpose: (i) order measures to eliminate barriers to competition; (ii) regulate access to essential facilities; and (iii) order the divestiture of assets, rights, social parts, or shares of the economic agent, in the proportions necessary to eliminate anticompetitive effects.

Article 3 of the FECL defines barriers to competition as any structural market characteristic, act, or deed performed by economic agents or any legal provision issued by any level of government with the purpose or effect of impeding access to competitors or limiting their ability to compete, which impedes or distorts competition and market access.

Article 60 of the FECL sets forth that in determining the existence of essential facilities it shall determine:

- If the facility is controlled by one or several economic agents with substantial market power or that have been declared preponderant by the IFT;
- If the facility cannot be feasibly replicated by another economic agent due to technical, legal, or economic conditions;
- If the facility is indispensable for supplying goods or services in one or more markets, and has no close substitutes;
- The circumstances under which the economic agent came to control the facility; and
- Other criteria provided in the Regulatory Provisions.

[B] Special Proceeding

Article 94 of the FECL sets forth a new, different, and independent, proceeding for determining essential facilities or barriers to competition and an enforcement against unlawful concentrations, and absolute and relative monopolistic practices.

The special proceeding to decide on essential facilities and barriers to competition is very similar to the one applicable to monopolistic practices, with a few variations.

First, it consists of two stages, a preliminary stage to process the investigation carried out by the investigation authority and a subsequent administrative proceeding handled by the office of the technical secretary.

Second, the terms and stages of both the investigation and the proceeding are shorter. For instance, this investigation may only last up to three investigation periods (each of 30–120 days) and the administrative proceeding is also reduced since it does not allow for intervention of the investigation authority as a party submitting arguments during this phase. Other aspects of the proceeding differ from the proceeding regarding monopolistic practices, like the opportunity granted to the economic agents at any moment of the special proceeding and until the file is deemed completed, to submit a proposal of suitable and economic feasible measures to eliminate the competition problems identified.

Third, this type of investigation may only be initiated ex officio or at the request of the executive branch, and its initiation must be published in the FOG.

Fourth, the final decision issued by the competition authority may include:

- Recommendations to Public Authorities.
- An order to an economic agent to eliminate a barrier that unduly affects free market access and the competition process.
- The determination on the existence of essential facilities and guidelines to regulate.
- The divestiture of the involved economic agent's assets, rights, partnership interest or stock, in the necessary proportions to eliminate the anticompetitive effects.

[C] Penalties

A maximum fine equivalent to 10% of the economic agent's income that controls an essential facility, for failing to comply with the regulation related thereto and for failing to comply with an order to eliminate a barrier to competition may be imposed.

[D] Relevant cases

The following are two landmark cases regarding essential facilities and barriers to competition:

a) Case IEBC-001-2015: This is COFECE's first investigation related to the determination of essential facilities and was related to the market for the supply of air transportation services used by the Mexico City International Airport ("AICM"). The investigation authority found that the market lacked: (i) clear rules in the allocation and supervision of take-off and landing schedules (slots) and related infrastructure, (ii) a procedure for new airlines or those already established to obtain additional slots, and (iii) an effective application of the relevant regulations in force. According to the investigation authority, this resulted in several inefficiencies in the air passenger transportation services market.

   In its preliminary ruling, the investigation authority pointed out the existence of an essential input in the market for landing and take-off services at the AICM that generated anticompetitive effects in the market of passenger air transportation to and from Mexico City. Thereafter, the second stage of the procedure began. Economic agents, authorities, and regulators with a legal interest were able to and offered the evidence they considered pertinent.

   COFECE's board determined the existence of, among other issues, a lack of clear rules, and effective application of the regulations in force, related to the mechanism for assigning and supervising the use and supervision of slots at the AICM. Therefore, COFECE imposed guidelines and measures to be adopted by the AICM to correct the deficiencies found in these procedures.

b) Case IEBC-002-2015: This is COFECE's first case on barriers to competition and is related with ground transportation in the State of Sinaloa, Mexico. This investigation was initiated at the request of the Ministry of Economy.

   After its investigation, the investigation authority found that the ground transportation market in the State of Sinaloa had regulatory obstacles that hindered competition. According to Sinaloa's Transit Law, any individual or legal entity interested in providing local cargo transportation needed a concession and a zone permit, without which, it was unable to carry goods within the State. However, to obtain concessions and permits, an interested party was required to undergo a complex process whose operating rules made it difficult for new operators to enter the market.

   In February 2017, COFECE's board issued a resolution stating that Sinaloa's ground transportation market had barriers to effective competition that generated anticompetitive effects. As a result of this, in its resolution, COFECE required the executive and legislators of Sinaloa to carry out legal and administrative reforms. Following the board's decision, the state government and its local Congress enacted, in June 2017, changes to its transit law. With these changes, most of the regulatory barriers found in this procedure were eliminated.

§16.07 OPINIONS AND OTHER PROCEEDINGS

[A] Opinions

The competition authorities have the authority to issue opinions on general matters (laws, regulations, executive orders, rulings, and circulars), programs, or policies that may have anticompetitive effects. These opinions on legislative proposals and public policy are not binding or mandatory. The competition authorities may issue these opinions ex officio, at the request of an interested party, or at the request of the President of Mexico and/or the chambers of the Federal Congress, according to the nature of each opinion.

In addition, the FECL grants the competition authorities with the authority to issue formal opinions, i.e., binding opinions on economic competition matters not sufficiently clear in the law or in previous administrative or judicial interpretations. An opinion is issued at the request of an interested party only when COFECE is provided or has in its possession sufficient elements to take a decision without having to commence an investigation and considers that the opinion is necessary or useful due to, for instance, the significance of the goods or the extent of the conduct in the markets. Thus, the competition authorities have broad discretionary powers to agree to this type of request, provided that no request will be agreed to if its subject matter is under review by the competition authorities or any court of law or if it is hypothetical.

[B] Proceedings on Market Conditions

The FECL also provides that the competition authorities may rule on market conditions, i.e., effective competition issues, existence of market power in the relevant market, or other similar terms. The competition authorities may issue such resolutions or opinions, provided that the legal or regulatory provisions, agreements, or decrees issued by the executive branch expressly establishes such need.

The resolutions in this proceeding may be issued ex officio, at the request of the executive branch, at the request of the agency that coordinates the corresponding industry or at the request of the affected party. These resolutions are relevant because they allow other authorities to trigger regulatory mechanisms, for instance, regarding tariff control.

§16.08 MERGER REVIEW

[A] Relevant Legislation

Article 61 of the FECL defines a "concentration" as: "the merger, acquisition of control, or any act through which companies, associations, shares, partnership interests, trusts or assets in general are joined together, and carried out among competitors, suppliers, clients or any other economic agent". The FECL requires economic agents to notify concentrations with the competition authority (COFECE or IFT, depending on the sector) when they exceed certain thresholds.

When a concentration exceeds a relevant threshold, the economic agents involved shall obtain merger clearance before the transaction is executed. However, the FECL also allows for economic agents to submit concentrations voluntarily. While the filing is mandatory when any of the thresholds is exceeded, if a concentration does not exceed any of the thresholds, the parties may submit a voluntary filing, in which case the antitrust authority shall review and decide whether the transaction should be authorized or not.

Specific binding rules that govern the merger review process are detailed by the antitrust authorities through secondary regulatory provisions. Criteria on efficiency gains, threshold calculation, characteristics of the documents required for a pre-merger notice are some of the matters covered in those regulations.[21]

Although they are not compulsory rules, the Merger Guidelines issued by the antitrust authorities in Mexico provide general orientation based on experience of the competition authority to provide economic agents guidelines to understand the applicable criteria in the pre-merger review process. COFECE and IFT guidelines cover many of the same concepts.

Competition authorities update their guidelines at least every five years. In April 2021, for instance, COFECE updated its Merger Guidelines with the purpose of covering relevant matters that were not previously included, namely:[22] (i) treatment of collaboration agreements (types of JVs are described and discussed, among other topics); (ii) possible solutions when a multiplicity of sellers or acquirers are obligated to notify a concentration; (iii) binding filing criteria and;[23] (iv) clarification regarding the amount of the transactions; among other criteria.

The IFT has also issued its own guide entitled: "Guidelines for the control of concentrations in the telecommunications and broadcasting sectors",[24] which has been updated on March 4, 2022.

New regulation on electronic systems has become essential for the antitrust practice. COFECE has successfully established a system known as the "SINEC" (Electronic System of Concentrations, for its acronym in Spanish) through which the merger review process is handled. Currently, all merger review cases are processed through SINEC, which has eliminated the need for paper filings before COFECE.

This has led to the issuance of rules applicable to COFECE's electronic platforms, such as the Regulatory Provisions on the Use of Electronic Media before the

21. IFT regulatory provisions:http://www.ift.org.mx/industria/autoridad-investigadora/documentos-materia-economica; COFECE regulatory provisions:https://www.cofece.mx/wp-content/uploads/2019/08/19.08.01-Disposiciones-Regulatorias-de-la-LFCE-ultima-reforma.pdf
22. Published in the FOG on April 8, 2021.
23. Due to the COVID-19 pandemic, binding filing criteria became relevant and were included in this update. Among other criteria, they explain the type of documents an entity should submit to demonstrate the potential risk of its exit from the market.
24. (*Guía para el control de concentraciones en los sectores de telecomunicaciones y radiodifusión*)

COFECE[25]and the Guidelines for Filing Concentration Notices by Electronic Means before COFECE.[26]

[B] Economic Thresholds

Article 86 of the FECL provides three scenarios under which a concentration must be notified and approved by COFECE prior to its closing. If any of such thresholds are met, the mandatory pre-merger notice requirement will be triggered. Those scenarios are described below:

(i) If the transaction, or series of transactions, irrespective of the place of execution, results in a direct or indirect amount in Mexico greater than the equivalent of 18 million MU in force, MXN 1,613,160,000.00 (approx. USD 77,450,392.01).

The transaction will meet this threshold if the value or purchase price assigned to the Mexican part of the transaction, if any, exceeds the amount of USD 77,450,392.01. If no purchase price is being assigned to the Mexican part of the transaction, this threshold does not apply and tests 2 and 3 below should be considered.

(ii) If the transaction or series of transactions cause an aggregation of 35% or more of the assets or share capital of an economic agent, whose assets in Mexico or annual sales originated in Mexico, are greater than the equivalent to 18 million MU in force, MXN 1,613,160,000.00 (approx. USD 77,450,392.01).

The transaction will meet the first threshold of this test if the acquirer is expected to accumulate the 35% or more of the share capital or assets of the target. However, to meet this limit, target must have assets in Mexico or annual sales originated in Mexico in excess of MXN 1,613,160,000.00 (approx. USD 77,450,392.01).

(iii) If the transaction or a series of transactions cause an aggregation in Mexico of assets or share capital which amounting to more than the equivalent of 8.4 million MU in force, approximately MXN 752,808,000.00 (approx. USD 36,143,516.27) and two or more economic agents participate, whose assets or annual sales volume in Mexico on an individual or aggregate basis are greater than 48 million MU in force, MXN 4,301,760,000.00 (approx. USD 206,534,378.71)

The first threshold of this limit is met if the proposed transaction results in the accumulation in Mexico by the acquirer of share capital or assets of more than MXN 752,808,000.00 (approx. USD 36,143,516.27). If this test is exceeded, it should be reviewed whether, the acquirer and seller jointly or

25. Refer to: https://www.cofece.mx/wp-content/uploads/2021/02/ComDisRegUsoMedEle-18-07-2019.pdf
26. Refer to: https://www.cofece.mx/wp-content/uploads/2019/07/Lineamientos-concentraciones-reforma-18-jul-2019.pdf

separately have assets or annual sales volume in Mexico greater than MXN 4,301,760,000.00 (approx. USD 206,534,516.27).

[C] Exemptions

According to Article 93 of the FECL the following exemptions apply:

(i) Corporate restructures where the economic agents[27] involved belong to the same economic interest group. No third entities involved.

(ii) When an economic agent increases its participation in a company's capital stock which it has controlled (i) since its incorporation or commencement of operations or, (ii) as result of a previous authorization from COFECE.

(iii) When the transaction causes the incorporation of any sort of trust, where the economic agent transfers its assets, stock, partnership interest or participation units without the purpose or necessary consequence of transferring them to a company other than the trustor and the fiduciary institution.

However, if the guaranty trust is executed, this shall be notified before COFECE in case the thresholds referred to in number 1.1 above are met.

(iv) When the transaction includes legal acts of foreign companies, regarding stock, partnership interest or participation units, or under trust agreements entered into abroad and related to companies not residing in Mexico for tax purposes, provided that companies involved (i) do not acquire control over Mexican companies, (ii) do not accumulate stock, partnership interests, participation units, or participation in trust or assets in general in Mexico in addition to those which they directly or indirectly owned prior the transaction.

(v) When the acquiring party is a variable income investment company and the object of the transaction is acquisition of stock, obligations, assets, securities, or documents with funds resulting from the placement of the investment company's shares in a public offering, except if as a result or because of the transactions, the investment company may have significant influence over the decisions of the economic agents involved in the concentration.

(vi) In case of the acquisition of stock, assets, titles, or the representative documents of the capital stock of companies or whose underlying assets represents equity of legal entities, and which are traded on stock exchanges, when such acquisition does not entitle the purchaser to own 10% or more of such capital sock, obligations convertible into stock, assets, securities or documents, and the acquirer does not have the ability to:

27. Any individual or company, either for profit or non-profit, federal, state or municipal public administration agencies and entities, associations, business chambers, and professional associations, trust or any other form of participation in economic activity.

a. Appoint or remove members of the board, directors, or managers of the issuer;
b. Imposing, directly or indirectly, decisions on the general meetings of stockholders, partners or equivalent bodies;
c. Holding ownership rights that allow, directly or indirectly, to exercise voting rights of 10% or more of a legal entity's capital stock; or
d. Directing or influencing, directly or indirectly, the management, operation, strategy or the main policies of a legal entity, by means of equity holdings, contractually or otherwise.

(vii) In case of acquisition of stock, partnership interest, participation units, or trusts is performed by one or more investment funds (i) merely for speculation, and ii) which do not have investments in companies or assets that participate or are employed in the same relevant market as the economic agents involved in a concentration.

If a transaction meets any of the abovementioned exemptions, it does not need to be cleared or notified.

[D] Pre-merger Control Regime or Post-merger Control Regime

As previously established, the Mexican legal system follows a pre-merger control regime. *Ex-ante* powers of the Mexican antitrust authorities are exercised through the pre-merger review process provided in the FECL and its regulatory provisions. As explained above, if a transaction triggers any of the thresholds, notice of the transaction must be filed with the competent competition authority at any time prior to closing. Voluntary filings are reviewed under the same rules as mandatory ones.

The competition authority's resolution may authorize, block, or subject the authorization to conditions intended to prevent negative effects to free market access and economic competition that may result from the transaction.

A draft of the agreement to be executed by the parties (or an executed agreement in which a standstill obligation subject to antitrust approval is included) shall be enclosed in the filing, as well as general corporate and financial information, and general market information.

According to the FECL, the parties are not allowed to close a notifiable transaction without clearance from the corresponding competition authority. Otherwise, the transaction will be considered null and void, and administrative, criminal, and civil liability may arise. As a consequence, the legal acts concerning the transaction may not be registered in the corporate ledgers, and public notaries are neither authorized to formalize any corporate act within a public deed nor record it in the Public Commercial or Property Registry.

In addition, the FECL provides specific penalties for unlawful concentrations (defined as those which damage or restrict competition).

While the Mexican system is based on a pre-merger review basis, the competition authorities carry out activities to verify that completed transactions comply with the

FECL and with their resolutions. In this respect, antitrust authorities may investigate concentrations that did not trigger a mandatory filing within a year after closing. Approved concentrations may also be investigated by the Mexican antitrust authorities when the resolution is based on false information.

Once the competition authority has issued a favorable resolution, it will grant the notifying parties a term to close the transaction and to subsequently give notice to the competition authority. Failure to give notice of the closing will result in fines depending on the length of time the notifying parties have failed to give notice of the closing.

In a transaction that, in the competition authority's view, could have significant effects on the relevant markets, the resolutions may be subject to certain conditions or remedies established and agreed upon by both the notifying parties and the competent competition authority. In this regard, the competition authority will determine the deadlines to comply and may verify that they are being carried out.

Some of the most relevant transactions in which COFECE has imposed conditions have been: (i) the purchase of Aeromexico shares by Delta, two airlines with significant presence in the AICM; (ii) the concentration between two supermarkets *Organización Soriana* and *Controladora Comercial Mexicana*, which at the time were among the economic agents with greatest market power in their respective markets; in which COFECE authorized the transaction subject to the divestiture of a number of stores where the concentration would have had anticompetitive negative effects; (iii) the concentration between Monsanto Company and Bayer Aktiengesellschaft, two relevant pesticide and drug companies, with certain manufacturing lines overlaps in which COFECE authorized the transaction subject to the divestiture of the genetically modified cotton seed business; among others.

[E] Intra-group Transactions

As provided in Article 93 of the FECL corporate restructure is not subject to filing requirements.

[F] Consequences of a Failure to File

Under Article 88 of the FECL, a mandatory filing is a joint obligation for the parties directly participating in the transaction. In case a factual or legal impossibility takes place, provided said impossibility is proved to the antitrust authorities, the buyer may file the notice on its own.

As stated before, if a mandatory filing is not submitted before COFECE or the IFT, (i) the transaction will be considered null and void (it will not produce legal effects in Mexico) and (ii) the legal acts concerning the transaction may not be registered in the corporate ledgers, and public notaries are neither authorized to formalize it, nor record it in the Public Commercial or Property Registry.

A verification process may be carried out by COFECE or the IFT in order to determine whether the parties failed to file the notice, where applicable.

[G] Third-Party Involvement in Notification Process

The economic agents directly taking part in the concentration must notify the same.

When those directly involved cannot give notice, whether because it is legally or practically impossible and this is proved to the competition authority, or in the case provided for in Article 88 of the FECL, either the surviving company, the one acquiring control of the companies or associations, or the one intending to carry out the transaction or accumulate shares, equity interests, beneficial interests in a trust, or assets that are the object of the transaction, may do so.

In the notification, the parties must designate a common representative unless, for duly justified reasons, this cannot be done. If no justified reason is given for not naming a common representative, COFECE must name one, ex officio.

Those involved in the transaction may not exchange information that may create a situation that may give rise to the imposition of a penalty under the FECL.

[H] Penalties

Regarding sanctions, according to Article 127-VIII of the Law, the parties participating in a concentration that was not submitted before the antitrust authorities, either companies or/and individuals, may be sanctioned with fines of up to 5% of their annual income for failing to notify a concentration when legally required to do so. However, for foreign companies that does not report financial information to pay income taxes in Mexico, a maximum fine of up to MXN 35,848,000 (approx. USD 1,721,119.82) may be imposed per individual or company participating in the transaction.

[I] Appeal

As stated previously in this chapter, in accordance with the constitutional amendment, the *amparo* action is the only recourse available to challenge a concentration decision. As stated above, this action must be filed before the specialized courts.

[J] Specific Industries

There are no special regulations in Mexico regarding concentrations in specific industries. However, sector regulation (for instance, Port Act or Hydrocarbons Act) imposes the obligation to obtain COFECE's positive opinion to carry out certain transactions or acts, for instance, assignment of rights or possibility of control within regulated agents. This positive opinion mechanism is similar to the pre-merger concentration review.

§16.09 CONCLUSIONS/FINAL COMMENTS

After approximately seven years from the constitutional reform that created two autonomous competition agencies, these authorities have been active in exercising their powers to investigate and sanction anticompetitive practices as well as reviewing and deciding on concentrations.

COFECE has already developed substantial enforcement experience and has effectively penalized many cartels and abuse of dominance practices. The range of cases that have been decided is broad and involves important sectors of the Mexican economy and includes enforcement against international cartels. COFECE has also been developing relevant experience exercising its newly acquired incremental powers and has issued several resolutions on proceedings related to barriers to competition and essential facilities.

Regarding mergers, COFECE has also developed important experience and is very active in developing consistent merger review methodologies and criteria. Most mergers notified with COFECE are authorized without conditions.

There is a current trend to address the competition challenges of the digital economy. Both competition authorities are increasingly involved in building capacity and tackling these new challenges from the enforcement perspective and from the preventive perspective in merger analysis.

Finally, COFECE has begun to request criminal prosecution of cases. Although there have not been any criminal proceedings decided yet, we may expect that activity in this respect will also increase in the following years. Effective enforcement of cartels from a criminal perspective will be key to strengthen the enforcement of collusive conducts in the following years.

CHAPTER 17

Competition Law in Paraguay

Felix Santiago Bofferón

§17.01 INTRODUCTION

[A] Background: Legal Framework

Law No. 4956/2013 on "Defense of Competition" (the "Law") and its pertinent regulation under Decree No. 1490/2014 (the "Decree"), rule an area of substantial importance for the efficient performance of any market, i.e., the competition. This is especially important for a market such as the Paraguayan one, which is undergoing a stage of full development and expansion, which is why it demands an adequate normative framework for the performance of its business agents within the competition system, aimed towards an efficient allocation of the economic resources.

The market structure in Paraguay also highlights the importance of having such regulatory framework, since most of these markets continue to be characterized by a strong tendency towards concentration, i.e., with economic agents having a high degree of participation and de facto control over certain products and services. This situation arises, in most cases, in a marked asymmetry between the parties involved in commercial relations, which in turn constitutes an essential prerequisite for the existence of restrictions and limitations to competition freedom, market distortions and, of course, abuses against the weaker party in the relationship; all to the detriment of the general interest and the progress of the country. Since the entry into force of the Law, the enforcement has moved to predominantly focus on merger control.

Although Paraguay had certain rules on the subject, including some with constitutional rank,[1] there was a notable absence of a specific body of law grouping

1. National Constitution. CN. "Article 107. Freedom of competition. Every person has the right to engage in the lawful economic activity of his preference, within a system of equal opportunity. Competition in the market is guaranteed. The creation of monopolies and the artificial raising or

together a complex of rules that would give shape to a regulatory system aimed at establishing the conditions under which the relationship between the variables of supply and demand should develop, without losing sight at the same time of the custody, at least indirectly, of the consumer.

The Law came into force in 2013[2] and was regulated in 2014.[3] However, only as of 2016, with the appointment of the head of the Research Directorate (technical research body), the competition authority (CONACOM) gave practical start to its technical functions. Although it is true that CONACOM has become increasingly effective, it still has limited application against anticompetitive practices in the Paraguayan market due to deficiencies in the legal and structural framework (material resources).[4]

[B] Core Principles and Scope of Application

In general terms, the Law is circumscribed to a model of competition regulation with origins in the European Union (EU), and approaches the three thematic axes normally legislated by this kind of framework, namely: prohibited agreements, abuse of dominant position, and merger control. Although each of these thematic axes has one specific chapter within the text of the Law, they are all subject to the application of the core principles explicitly or implicitly established in the framework, such as: the application of the *rule of reason* (in principle, there are no conducts or agreements subject to sanctions per se) and, linked to this, the adoption of the doctrine of economic efficiency gains as endpoint of the relevant acts and conducts.

Similarly, the Law establishes the principle of economic reality for the analysis and judgment of the relevant acts and conducts, as well as for extending the accusation and responsibility of the legal persons for infringing the Law to: (i) their representatives, when involved in the execution of the concerned acts or conducts, and (ii) their controllers, when determining the economic behavior of the infringing legal person.[5]

As for the scope of application, both subjective and objective, the principle of extraterritoriality is embodied in its text, establishing as condition for the application of the framework: (i) that the concerned acts have the character of *Economic Activities*

---

lowering of prices that hinder free competition shall not be allowed...." Law No. 1034/83, "TITLE IV COMMERCIAL COMPETITION CHAPTER I GENERAL PROVISIONS. Article 105. - Commercial competition may be freely exercised if it does not harm the interests of the national economy and within the limits established by the provisions of this Code, special laws or what the parties may contractually agree upon. Article 106. The agreement limiting competition shall be valid if it is limited to a specific area and activity and for no more than five years, if its purpose is not to harm third parties. If no term has been stipulated or a term longer than that established in this Article has been agreed upon, its duration shall be five years. Article 107. Whoever is the sole supplier of a service or product shall be obliged to supply it to all interested parties under equal conditions and price".

2. Law No. 4956/2013 Competition Defense.
3. Decree No 1490/2014.
4. The CONACOM's budget for 2021 was USD 780.000. In contrast, the average budget for Latin American agencies in 2018 was USD 10.7 million (OECD, 2020. "Competition Trends 2020," p.19). Available at: http://www.oecd.org/competition/oecd-competition-trends.htm.
5. Article 3°, subsection 3, and Article 5°, of the Law; and Article 91° of Decree).

(for profit or nonprofit), and (ii) that the same produce and effect on the competition, whether in all or in part of the national territory, even in the event of acts executed outside the national territory or by persons addressed abroad (Doctrinal Effects). The Law provides no sector exemptions, and CONACOM exercises its jurisdiction across all industries.

In this chapter, we attempt to analyze the substantive aspects related to the various topics addressed by the Law, both in its static and in its dynamic aspect, as well as an exposition of the aspects that, in our opinion, hinder the effective application of the regulations in Paraguay.

§17.02 PROHIBITED AGREEMENTS: CARTELS

[A] Relevant Legislation

Undoubtedly, one of the guiding principles on which a regulatory system for the promotion and protection of the competitive process should place greater emphasis, both in its static aspect (the determination of the factual assumptions and the effects resulting from the adequacy of a specific conduct to such assumptions, or in the criminal nature of the typicality) and in its dynamic aspect (detection, prosecution, and sanction) is what is generally known as prohibited agreements, which subsumes the most reprehensible institute in the competitive field, the cartel.[6]

The Law is no exception to the regulations of its kind, and as already mentioned in the introduction, it addresses the topic of Prohibited Agreements in its Chapter II, Article 8,[7] which establishes, under the title "*Agreements restricting competition*", as follows:

> Any agreement, decision, concerted or consciously parallel practice, regardless of whether they are written or verbal, formal or informal, which has the purpose, produces or may produce the effect of preventing, restricting or distorting competition in all or part of the national market, consisting of the following conducts, among others, is prohibited, provided that they constitute some of the aforementioned hypotheses:
>
> (a) Fixing or imposing, directly or indirectly, or collectively recommending, purchase or sale prices or other transaction conditions in an abusive manner;
> (b) Unjustifiably limit, restrict or control the market, production, distribution, technical development or investments to the detriment of competitors or consumers;
> (c) To allocate markets, customers or sources of supply;
> (d) Unjustifiably applying unequal conditions to third contracting parties for equivalent services that cause them a competitive disadvantage;
> (e) Subordinating the conclusion of contracts to the acceptance, by the other contracting parties, of supplementary services which, by their nature or in

6. It is empirically proven that the cartels and horizontal agreements result in a welfare loss for the economy as a whole.
7. Following the line of Article 101 of the Lisbon Treaty (2007), formerly Article 85 of the TCE or Treaty of Rome (1957).

accordance with trade usage, have no relation whatsoever with the object of such contracts;

(f) Collusive bidding;

(g) Restrictions on production or sales, in particular by means of market quotas;

(h) Concerted refusal to purchase; and;

(i) Unjustified collective refusal to participate in an agreement, or admission to an association, which is decisive for competition.

In order to determine whether or not the practices referred to in this Article should be sanctioned under the terms of this Law, the Enforcement Authority shall analyze the efficiency gains derived from the conduct accredited by the economic agents that favorably affect the process of competition and free concurrence.

Following the legislative technique of Article 101 of the Lisbon Treaty, the Law addresses the issue through a wording that contains a generic prohibition of the prohibited conduct "...agreement, decision, concerted or consciously parallel practice... which has the purpose, produces or may produce the effect of preventing, restricting or distorting competition in all or part of the national market...", to then state a non-exhaustive list of anticompetitive behaviors which would seem to be considered per se to fall within the prohibited generic framework and, being so, should be sanctioned for their mere commission.

This would seem to follow the usual practice in the matter of sanctioning this type of conduct, or at least the most "serious"[8] ones under the per se rule. The intent-based rules that forbid an agreement or practice by its nature or form are based upon the assumption that certain practices intrinsically constitute "unreasonable" restrictions of competition, to exempts authorities from further investigation into their specific effects for their punishment.[9]

However, there are provisions within the Law itself that, in our opinion, seem to exclude the application of a per se sanctioning criterion for prohibited agreements:

- The first part of the Article 1 of the Law aimed at enshrining its purpose would seem to lean towards the competitive process as a protected legal good, and not towards the welfare of consumers or competitors, at least not in a direct and preferential manner. Such Article expresses "The purpose of this Law is to defend and promote free competition in the markets".
- Article 3 of the Law, located within the title reserved to general provisions, states in its numeral 3 that in order to assess the practices, conducts, or recommendations that have the effect or purpose of restricting, limiting, hindering, distorting, or preventing the existing or future competition in the

8. See the OECD 1998 Recommendations at p. 2. These so-called hard-core cartels constitute "the most egregious violations of competition law as they injure consumers in many countries by raising prices and restricting supply, thus making goods and services completely unavailable to some purchasers and unnecessarily expensive for others."

9. Case Continental T.V., Inc. v. GTE Sylvania Inc., 433 U.S. 36, 58 (1977) at p. 50: "There are certain agreements or practices which because of their pernicious effect on competition and lack of any redeeming virtue are conclusively presumed to be unreasonable and therefore illegal without elaborate inquiry as to the precise harm they have caused or the business excuse for their use." See also Case Broadcast Music, Inc. v. CBS, 441 U.S. 1, 19–20 (1979).

relevant market, the authority will take into account whether these practices, conducts, or recommendations "...generate economic efficiency gains of the subjects involved".

- The same conditioning referred to in the previous paragraph is expressly included in Article 8 of the Law, which regulates this institute of prohibited agreements, expressly adding that the sanctioning of such practices is conditioned to a prior analysis by the authority on potential "efficiency gains" derived from such conducts.
- And, specifically, the Article 8 of the Law requires price/quantity fixing agreements to be "abusive" in order to be prohibited, and establishes that limitations to production, distribution, and technical development shall be prohibited only if "they negatively affect consumers"

In the absence of a clear and precise definition of the treatment that our system provides for this type of conduct, a comprehensive interpretation of the rule would seem to indicate that it does not fall within the line of regulations that provide for a sanction per se of this type of agreements, because that in all cases, for the purpose of their sanction, they should be analyzed by the authority under the sieve of the principle of *reason rule*.

On the other hand, it is very important to consider that the authority has had limitations to access direct evidence of cartels and therefore build solid cases. The absence of a leniency program constitutes a critical weakness of the Law, and the deficient legal basis to conduct dawn raids further weakens the ability of the authority to uncover anticompetitive behavior.[10] These tools could help the CONACOM to obtain relevant evidence of illegal conducts since cartel detection is highly complex, even for sophisticated and experienced authorities.

May be this is the reason why since 2016 the CONACOM has initiated only one formal investigation about cartel cases. Since 2020, CONACOM has initiated only one investigation for a possible cartel in a public tenders (bid rigging).[11]

This case was recently resolved by the authorities and constitutes the first precedent for the application of the law regarding cartel cases.[12]

10. Article 29 of the Law set forth CONACOM's powers and attributions. Said powers do not include the power to carry dawn raids or inspections. Nevertheless, Article 75 of the Decree (which regulates the Law) sets forth the authority's right to carry out *"inspections"* with or without prior notice, and among other measures, to examine books, records, documents etc., "...*with judicial authorization*". This legal framework has two essential problems: i) the power to carry dawn raids or inspections is not foreseen by law but rather in a regulatory decree giving rise to an uncertainty over the constitutionality of the tool; and, ii) the competent judge (civil or criminal) in charge of granting the authorization is not specified. These weaknesses cause the authority to be reluctant to use it to gather evidence through inspections.
11. Insumos Médicos S.A., Eurotec S.A. and Medical Pharma S.A. regarding alleged violation of Article 8 of Law No. 4956 - File No. 1/2020.
12. Resolution D/AL N°82/212 dated November 9, 2021.

[B] Extraterritoriality

As mentioned in the general introduction, the Law adopts the "Doctrinal Effects" and therefore introduces the principle of extraterritorial application of the law. This principle is embodied in Article 3, and it is applicable for all the law's thematic axes, establishing as general condition for the application of the framework, without prejudice to the other specific requirements demanded for each topic (prohibited agreements, abuse of dominant position, or mergers): (i) that the concerned acts have the characters of economic activities (for profit or nonprofit); and (ii) that the same produced and affected the competition, whether in all or in part of the national territory, even in the event of acts executed outside the national territory or by persons addressed abroad. However, to this day there are no cases about cartels in which this extraterritoriality principle was applied.

[C] Investigations

[1] Authorities

[a] Policy, Politics, and Institutions

The Law created a public, autonomous, and autarkic entity called the National Competition Commission (CONACOM for its initials in Spanish) as the Competent Authority.

The two main bodies of CONACOM are: (i) the Board of Directors, which is the highest authority of the institution and is composed by three members; and (ii) the Research Directorate (which has two departments, one for conducts and one for mergers), which is constituted as the entity's technical and executive body and is headed by a research director. Both the members of the board of directors and the director of research are appointed by the executive power from shortlists presented by a body called the Board of Qualifications, whose composition involves representatives of the state and the private sector.

[b] Resources and Priorities

Despite the fact that this is a new field of application in Paraguay, it is worth to highlight that CONACOM has managed to maintain a technical profile and, as far as it is possible to know from its actions, it has not been affected by political interferences that tend to undetermine the foundations of institutions, especially those with an incipient development such as CONACOM. It is reasonable to deduce that these virtues of institutional "genesis" are based on an institutional design that, although it cannot be as infallible, at least provides the entity with the necessary institutional independence required by its sensitive function. The fact of being an autonomous and autarkic entity, in whose composition the state and the private sectors share roles, seems to have contributed, at least in its beginnings, to the preservation of the technical and aseptic profile that the authority radiates at a local level, at least among the other operators of the system.

However, this respectable technical reputation acquired by the institution has not gone in hand with a dynamic intervention in the field of prosecution of conducts, especially cartels, despite the fact that international experience has shown these tasks, especially the latter, should be a primary purpose for a competition agency, even more so in small markets such as the Paraguayan one, which usually present themselves as favorable scenarios due to their concentrated structure for collusive practices.

It is likely that this shortcoming is based on deficiencies in the regulatory framework, as mentioned in section 17.02[A] (inexistence of a leniency program, deficient legal basis to conduct dawn raid) and, the lower inter-agency cooperation displayed by the other Paraguayan state agencies with the CONACOM, as well as the budgetary limitations faced by the authority. Similarly, with respect to the agency's priorities, it is important to mention that CONACOM's Board of Directors issued in July (2021) a resolution determining the economic sectors that will be considered priorities for the agent's mission during the period 2021–2022,[13] considering them as those in which the competition policy may have the greatest effect in terms of economic growth and welfare for people, but clarifying that this determination will not imply a limitation to CONACOM's scope of action in other economic sectors. The process for the determination of these priority sectors included field work through surveys to associations and companies, in order to know the perception of the main market players in this regard.

Finally, this process identified eight priority economic sectors for competition policy in Paraguay, which are construction—cement, public procurement, electricity sector, financial sector (means of payment system—credit cards), telecommunications sector, pharmaceutical industry sector, health insurance sector, and supermarket sector.

Consequentially, a greater presence of the agency in this sectors is to be expected, both in the exercise of its functions of promoting or advocating competition, and in the exercise of its "enforcement" powers, the latter being certainly the one that will present the greatest challenges, especially in the behavioral area, due to the limited experience acquired so far in this area for the reasons of substance and form already explained above.

[c] Inter-agency Cooperation

The Law establishes in its Article 7 that "All conducts restraining competition that are incompatible with the obligations derived from International Treaties and Conventions approved or ratified by the Republic of Paraguay are prohibited."

In line with this provision, Paraguay has signed multilateral and bilateral agreements on the matter:

13. Resolutión D/AD N° 52/2021.

- Paraguay has signed the Fortaleza Protocol of Defense of Competition in December 1996.
- In 2002, Paraguay signed the Agreement on the Implementation of the Fortaleza Protocol.
- In 2004, through Common Market Council ("CMC") Decision No. 4/2004, Mercosur approved the consensus on the cooperation among competition agencies. In 2006, it also approved CMC Decision 15/2006 establishing a system of exchange of information and consultation in the field of merger control.
- In 2010, Mercosur approved the CMC Decision No. 43/2010, containing an Agreement for the Defense of Competition in Mercosur, which replaced the Fortaleza Protocol. This agreement was ratified by Paraguay in January 5, 2018.[14]

Moreover, CONACOM has initiated a process aimed at establishing formal bases for bilateral collaboration with competition agencies of other jurisdictions, in order to make possible consultations on relevant aspects for the application of competition laws and to facilitate the exchange of information. Within the framework of this process, it has signed a series of agreements such as:

_ the inter-institutional cooperation agreements signed with the National Commission for the Defense of Competition (CNDC) of Argentina and the Tribunal for the Defense of Free Competition (TDLC) of Chile, on March 15 and 22, 2024, respectively;

- the inter-institutional cooperation agreement signed with the National Institute for Competition Defense and Protection of Intellectual Property (INDECOPI) of Peru on October 29, 2021;[15]
- the technical cooperation agreement signed with the Federal Economic Competition Commission (COFECE) of Mexico on July 2021;[16]
- the technical cooperation agreement signed with the National Economic Prosecutor's Office of Chile on May 18, 2021;[17]
- the renewal of the technical cooperation agreement with the Commission for the Defense and Promotion of Competition (CDOC) of Honduras signed on May 18, 2021;[18]

14. Law 6020/2018 which incorporates Mercosur's Antitrust Agreement.
15. https://www.conacom.gov.py/noticias/la-conacom-y-el-indecopi-de-peru-suscriben-un-convenio-de-cooperacion-interinstitucional
16. https://www.conacom.gov.py/noticias/la-conacom-y-la-cofece-de-mexico-renuevan-su-convenio-de-cooperacion-tecnica
17. https://www.conacom.gov.py/noticias/la-conacom-y-la-fiscalia-nacional-economica-de-chile-suscriben-un-convenio-de-cooperacion-tecnica
18. https://www.conacom.gov.py/noticias/la-conacom-y-la-cdpc-de-honduras-renuevan-su-convenio-de-cooperacion-tecnica

- the technical cooperation agreement signed with the Commission for the Promotion of Competition (COPROCOM) of Costa Rica on April 2021;[19]
- the inter-institutional cooperation agreement signed with the Administrative Council for Economic Defense (CADE) of Brazil on October 24, 2018;[20] and
- The inter-institutional cooperation agreement signed with the Authority for Consumer Protection and Defense of Competition (ACODECO) of Panama on June 8, 2018.[21]

[D] Sanctions and Remedies

[1] Administrative Sanctions

Any breach of the provisions of the Law are punishable by CONACOM with: (i) Warning and intimation of cessation of the infringing acts; (ii) declaration of nullity, and (iii) fines of up to 150% of the profits obtained with the offending practice, or up to 20% of gross revenues from the sale of the products subject of infringing practice in the relevant market in the last twelve months.[22]

The Law provides for the extension of the responsibility and for the performance of acts sanctioned by it to the "... natural persons who, acting as the legal persons included in the scope of its application, have intervened in the execution of the sanctioned acts by this Law", as well as the controllers of the people involved in the eventual transgression.[23] Under the Paraguayan process of law, CONACOM bears the burden of proof in case of infraction to the Law. Once the infringement has been proven, the investigated parties must prove the existence of efficiency gains that offset its negative effects.[24]

[2] Criminal Sanctions

The Law does not provide criminal sanctions for individuals found responsible for behaviors contrary to the regulations.

However, in 2019 a set of laws was sanctioned and enacted to comply with the evaluation requirements of GAFILAT (Financial Action Task Force of Latin America) for the fight against money laundering and corruption, among which it is important to highlight, due to its content, Law 6.452/19 "Which amends several provisions of the

19. https://www.conacom.gov.py/noticias/la-conacom-y-la-coprocom-de-costa-rica-suscriben-un-convenio-de-cooperacion-tecnica
20. https://www.conacom.gov.py/noticias/convenio-de-cooperacion-tecnica-entre-la-conacom-y-el-cade
21. https://www.conacom.gov.py/noticias/acuerdo-CONACOM-ACODECO
22. Article 63 of the Law.
23. The principle of economic reality (Article 3°, subsection 3, and Article 5°, of the Law; and Article 91° of Decree).
24. Article 3° of the Decree.

Criminal Code",[25] introducing among other criminal offenses, Private Bribery, within a new chapter added to the Criminal Code under the title "Punishable Acts Against Competition." These criminal offenses describe conducts that could be configured in cases of bid rigging and provide for prison sentences of up to three years.[26] Thus, although the Law does not provide for criminal penalties, as from the entry into force of the above mentioned regulations, the configuration of an infringement provided for in the Law (Bid Rigging[27]) could give rise to the application of criminal penalties to those who were actors in such infringement, in case of configuring the conduct typified by the new criminal regulations

[3] *Private Actions and Follow-On Actions*

The Private damages actions are allowed by the Law,[28] and they can be presented to the civil courts follow-on to a CONACOM's decision, based on the Article 1833 of the Paraguayan Civil Code.

[E] Leniency

Without a doubt, the absence of a leniency program that allows companies to come forward to the CONACOM to report the existence of a cartel constitutes a critical weakness of the Paraguayan antitrust system.

[F] Appeal

At the administrative level, CONACOM's decision is final and binding. From CONACOM's final decision, it is possible to file a reconsideration motion (before the same authority) or a motion for clarification, which aims to clarify omissions, contradictions, or obscurities in such decision. Also, a dissatisfied party can always take CONACOM's decision to court. The definitive CONACOM's decisions can be appealable in before the Court of Accounts. The Court of Accounts is a national court that deals with administrative matters.

25. Its source is the United Nations Convention against Corruption, approved in Paraguay by Law N° 2535/05.
26. Article 268b. Private bribery...Whoever, as the person in charge or representative of a company, association, entity or organization of any kind, requests, allows himself to be promised or accepts in commercial traffic a benefit for himself or for a third party in exchange for accepting the offer of products, goods or services of another, in disadvantageous conditions for other competitors in the market, shall be punished with imprisonment of up to two years or with a fine...". (and in certain cases up to 3 years). "Art. 268c. Private bribery...Whoever, with the purpose of obtaining a competitive advantage over other competitors in the market, offers, promises or guarantees to a manager or representative of a company, association or organization, a benefit in exchange for favoring him in the acquisition of his products, goods or services, under disadvantageous conditions for other competitors in the market, shall be punished with imprisonment for up to two years or with a fine..." (and in certain cases up to 3 years).
27. Article 8° of the Law, and Article 6 of Decree.
28. Article 64° of the Law.

[G] Precedent Cases

Recently, CONACOM resolved its first case of law enforcement regarding cartels. Given the importance of this precedent, we believe it is appropriate to briefly summarize the background of this case, in order to expose the line of argument followed by the authority to resolve it.

It is the first case in which the Paraguayan authority investigated an alleged cartel case, which, according to the Investigation Directorate (DI) of CONACOM, operated in the bidding market for the provision of medical supplies, and involved two national companies (EUROTEC S.A. and IMEDIC S.A.) and two natural persons to whom the representation of these companies was attributed.[29] Bid Rigging is a form of horizontal restriction to competition. As such, it is included in the prohibition of the Law.

In this specific case, and based on journalistic publications, the Directorate of Investigation of CONACOM (DI) initiated an investigation on eight of these processes (substantiated between January 2018 and April 2020). To this end, it requested information and documentation from the companies under investigation, public agencies, and from the National Public Procurement Directorate.

Based on the information collected, the DI determined that each bidding process analyzed constituted a market in itself as it contained a unique set of products independent from the other bids, and that the geographic market was national. In addition, based on the application of the checklist to detect collusion in public procurement tenders of the OECD Guidelines for Combating Bid Rigging in Public Procurement (2009), and the OECD Corruption and Collusion in Public Procurement (2010), the DI considered to have detected clear indications of collusion in the analyzed processes:

- Type 1 Evidence: Competitors socialize regularly.
  - Two brothers were the legal representatives of two of the companies under investigation.
  - At the same time, they had shareholdings and board memberships in companies competing in the same bids.
- Type 2 Evidence: Competitors have the same address or telephone number.
  - Two of the investigated companies reported the same physical and electronic address to receive tax notifications and even those related to the processes in which they participated.
- Type 3 Evidence: Competitors submit similar applications or materials.
  - The bid maintenance guarantee policies of two of the investigated companies were contracted with the same insurance company, with correlative numbering and managed by the same individual.
- Type 4 and 5 Evidence: The companies submit their documentation at the same time and entrust the same persons to carry out tasks inherent to the bids.

29. The Paraguayan Law provides for the application of sanctions to those individuals who, acting as legal representatives, managers, or directors of legal entities involved in practices in violation of said law, determine their behavior (Article 3 of the Law).

    - The DI detected that passwords used to submit the bids were correlated and that, in some cases, the bids were submitted by the same person.
- Type 6 Evidence: companies take turns to be the winning bidder.
    - The DI detected patterns of bid suppression among the investigated companies[30] as the same companies did not tend to bid in the same tenders, indicating that they might divide lots or items.

As is usually the case in this type of cases, the DI based its accusation on indirect evidence. In general, it is difficult for the investigating bodies to have access to direct evidence. In these cases, indirect or circumstantial evidence, such as that alleged by the DI, becomes relevant and is generally the only means of proof, especially in jurisdictions such as Paraguay, which do not yet have more adequate tools, such as dawn raids powers or a leniency regime.

The DI considered proven the existence of collusive behavior of these companies under the modality of bid rigging through the "suppression of offers", formulating its accusation[31] and requiring the application of an exemplary and dissuasive fine, close to the maximum applicable,[32] both for the investigated companies and for their legal representatives involved, including the disqualification to participate, directly or indirectly, in public procurement processes with the Paraguayan State for a period of five years.

Finally, and after the administrative summary was substantiated, the CONACOM's Board of Directors issued a resolution on November 9, 2021 (Resolution D / AL No. 82/2021) and resolved to: ABSOLVE the accused companies and representatives, based on the following arguments (essentially, all defendants based their defenses on the following arguments, each of which was addressed by the board of directors in the resolution):

- The defendants argued that the DI's accusation was based essentially on circumstantial, indirect evidence, which, in the defendants' view, violated the constitutional principle of presumption of innocence. With respect to this argument, the board validated the actions of the DI on the basis of indicia, based on a series of national and comparative legal, jurisprudential, and doctrinal sources, which validate indicia as a source of conviction about the occurrence of an investigated fact,[33] and even more so in the field of competition law enforcement, and especially in the prosecution of cartels, given the

30. An agreement between competitors whereby one or more companies agree to abstain or withdraw a previously submitted bid, so that the bid is awarded to the agreed winner.
31. Technical Report of Accusation of the DI dated February 24, 2021.
32. Up to 150% of the profits obtained with the infringing practice or up to 20% of the gross turnover from the sale of the products subject to the infringing practice in the relevant market affected in the last 12 months.
33. The mentioned precedents include, among others, a resolution of the Peruvian competition authority, INDECOPI (Res. 051/210 of August 13, 2010 in the "*Oxígenos Medicinales*" case); a Judgment of the Spanish Supreme Court in the "*Aceites Toledo*" case (Appeal 6171/19-96, of July 15, 2002); a Judgment of the Supreme Court of the Eastern Republic of Uruguay of September 3, 2020, in the case "*Fabrica Nacionales de Cervezas c/ Ministerio de Economía y Finanzas s/ Acción*

unlikelihood that those responsible for this type of conduct will leave direct material traces of it.

- The accused companies also alleged that they could not engage in the conduct attributed to them, since they would have to have a dominant position in the market, which was not proven by the DI. In this regard, the board dismissed this argument with a simple reference to the non-existence of such requirement for the configuration of the prohibited conduct, stating that "...this is irrelevant for the case at hand", and that market power is not a requirement "...sine qua non for the configuration of the offense consisting of an agreement restricting competition". This position is closely linked to the development that the board makes later in this resolution on what it understands to be the standard by object and effect established in our system for the analysis and eventual sanction of this type of conduct. In this regard, the board states that, according to this standard, an agreement prohibited by its object does not merit that the authority undertakes the task of proving its effects, without prejudice to assessing the efficiency gains that could have been generated by it, but that in all cases must be alleged and proven by the parties that invoke them.[34]
- Likewise, the defendants alleged the non-existence of a patrimonial damage to the state, since the investigated bids concluded in awards that were in line with the reference prices, and in some cases below them, reason for which they argued that ultimately, any eventual "agreement" derived in efficiency gains by making it possible to award the cheapest bids, even below the reference price. This argument was rejected by the board of directors when it was stated, clearly and correctly in our opinion, that the non-existence of an artificial price increase as a result of the agreement does not release the agreement from its infringement nature, because even if such efficiency gains could exist, the Law is clear in its Article 3 when it conditions the valuation of such gains to be obtained by alternative ways to conducts or agreements prohibited by the law.[35] The board of directors also states its opinion that the efficiencies alleged by the defendants do not fit the efficiency typology foreseen in our legislation (productive or dynamic).[36]
- Finally, the argument put forward by the defendants and which was the most sensitive for the resolution adopted by the board of directors, was based on the fact that the companies EUROTEC S.A. and IMEDIC S.A. could not incur in bid

de Nulidad - Excepción de Inconstitucionalidad". And reference is also made to the existing legal basis in the Decree, which establishes in its Article 6° that the authority must take into account in order to determine the existence of a collusive bidding "... d) the indications of coordination in the documentation submitted in the bids or tenders."

34. Resolution D/AL N°82/212, from November 9, 2021, p. 92.
35. Article 2°, sub-section 3 of the Law.
36. In this regard, and without prejudice to agreeing with the position of the Board of Directors, it is necessary to clarify that the reference to efficiencies provided for in Article 25 of the Decree is clearly enunciative and not exhaustive as the Board of Directors would seem to consider in this opinion.

> rigging through the "suppression of offers"; since their joint non-participation in the bids investigated in bids of identical items or parties was due to the fact that they could not do so without violating the Public Contracting Law, which prohibits companies linked to each other by a partner or associate (as is the case of these companies), to submit offers for the same item of goods or services, in the same contracting procedure.[37] In this regard, the board states in its resolution that "...the accumulation of indirect evidence or indications in the file, pointed out by the DI in the first place, and subsequently confirmed by the representatives of the defendants at the time of justifying their actions in compliance with the provisions of Art. 40, inc. g) of the Public Procurement Law, generate the presumption of the existence of the conduct imputed to EUORTEC and IMEDIC, and make us reach a sufficient conviction that they carried out a concerted practice, and, certainly, with the potential to produce such effect, provided that we assume that the accused companies are independent companies among themselves, as stated by the DI."[38] However, the board of directors based its decision of absolution on the principle of legal exemption provided for in Article 2, paragraph 4 of the Law,[39] concluding that, having proven and recognized the existence of common partners among the accused companies "...the only way of not incurring in the prohibition established..." in the Public Contracting Law for such companies ".... is through the coordination between the companies that share partners or associates, regardless of the social quotas held by the common partner or associate and the power he/she could exercise in the strategic decision making of the companies in question", adding that the corporate structure of the accused companies could even lead to the conclusion that they are part of the same business group, and as such they would not enjoy the independence required to be considered competitors, lacking in such case the aptitude to collude horizontally.[40]

Beyond the decision of the authority in this process, it is important to highlight the importance of the fact that the local authority addressed and resolved a case in this area of investigation, even without the recommended tools by the experience of comparative jurisdictions, since there is no doubt that the coordination of offers among competitors destroys the essential objective of the competitive process, which is none other than obtaining better quality goods at a better price, as a result of the expected struggle or dispute among competitors. At the same time, it highlights the importance of the advocacy role that the authority must assume in order to promote the development of substantive regulations that contribute to strengthen the competitive process or the modification of those that hinder it, as is the case, in our understanding, of the aforementioned provision of the Public Contracting Law. On this point, it is worth

37. Law 2051/03, Article 40°, section g).
38. Resolution D/AL N°82/212, from November 9, 2021, p. 82.
39. "The exercise of a right, power or exceptional prerogative, granted or recognized by law, shall not be considered an anti-competitive practice or abuse of a dominant position..."
40. Resolution D/AL N°82/212, from November 9, 2021, pp. 102 and 103.

mentioning that after the resolution of this precedent, the Board of Directors of CONACOM issued a formal opinion with respect to the wording of Article 40, paragraph g) of Law 2051/03 and the wording of Article 21, paragraph m) of the draft law of the "Public Procurement and Supply"([41]) bill, which is intended to replace the current Public Procurement Law, concluding that such wording "*...restricts competition*" and due to its broadness has the effect of "*...to forcing the communication and coordination of independent companies by the mere fact of having shareholders in common*", recommending its modification to comply with its purpose "*...to prevent the simulation of competition in public procurement processes...by persons who are not independent among themselves*".[42]

§17.03 UNILATERAL CONDUCTS

[A] Relevant Legislation

As mentioned before, the Law addresses the behavioral and structural phenomena usually regulated by antitrust regulations, and among the firsts it addresses those of a plural nature (involving the participation of two or more agents, as is the case with Prohibited Agreements) and those of a unilateral nature, as is typically the abuse of dominant position, reserving for this institute the Third Chapter under the title of Abusive Conduct.

Within this chapter, Article 9 of the Law expressly prohibits the abuse of dominant position in the following terms: ""The abusive exploitation by one or more of the natural or legal persons referred to in Article 3 of this Law, of their dominant position in all or part of the relevant market is prohibited", and then, within the same article, it goes on to list certain conducts as species of the prohibited generic conduct, namely:

1. The imposition, directly or indirectly, of unfair prices or other commercial conditions, or of unfair services;
2. The limitation of production, distribution or technical development to the unjustified detriment of competitors or consumers;
3. The unjustified refusal to satisfy demands for the purchase of products or the rendering of services;
4. The unjustified application, in commercial or service relations, of unequal conditions for equivalent services, which place some competitors in a disadvantageous situation with respect to others;
5. The subordination of the conclusion of contracts to the acceptance of supplementary benefits that, by their nature or according to the uses of commerce, are not related to the object of such contracts; and,
6. Obtaining or attempting to obtain, under threat of rupture of commercial relations, prices, payment conditions, sales modalities, payment of additional charges and other conditions of commercial cooperation not included in the general conditions of sale that have been agreed upon."

41. That replicates the actual wording of paragraph g) Art. 40 of Law 2051/03.
42. Formal opinion of the Board of Directors. D/13/21, December 1, 2021.

The concept of abuse of dominant position is not defined by the Law as an integral concept, since it requires the concurrence of two copulative requirements for the punishable conduct to be configured.

The Law, following the line of influence of the European competition law, conditions the configuration of this unilateral conduct to the concurrence of two copulative requirements: dominant position and abuse, expressly excluding the possibility of sanctioning or reproaching the first of such requirements when configured individually, providing in the last paragraph of Article 9 of the Law, that "Those who hold a dominant market position shall not be liable, for that circumstance alone, to sanctions established in this Law", unless, enjoying such position, it is proven that they have adapted their conduct to some of the factual assumptions referred to in the article as specific typologies of abuse, even adding a subjective requirement which is controversial and to which we will refer below "...with the purpose of obtaining undue advantages and causing harm to others, which would not have been possible in the absence of such position of dominance."

[B] Assessment of Dominance

With respect to the abuse requirement, the Law establishes (at least enunciatively) those conducts that could potentially constitute it. But with regards to the dominance requirement, the Law builds this idea without providing a specific concept, but granting the criteria that must be considered to determine its configuration.

Article 9 establishes that "... a natural or legal person enjoys a dominant position when for a given product or service it is not exposed to effective and substantial competition". It then establishes the parameters that must be taken into account to determine whether or not such exposure exists with respect to one or more market agents, namely:

1. The degree to which the good or service in question is substitutable by others, whether of domestic or foreign origin; the conditions for such substitution and the time required for the same;
2. The extent to which regulatory restrictions limit the access of products or suppliers or demanders to the market in question; and,
3. The degree to which the allegedly responsible party can unilaterally influence price formation or restrict supply or demand in the market and the degree to which its competitors can counteract such power.

According to the International Competition Network (ICN), the domain can be established in terms of behavior, structure and/or durability. Numeral 3 of the above-transcribed paragraph of the Paraguayan regulation, considers the behavioral dimensions for the definition of dominance (commonly used in the EU, Canada, the United States, Australia, and most Latin American countries, among others), since it takes into account the ability of companies to act independently of competitive market constraints.[43]

As for the structural dimension, it is covered by numerals 1 and 2 of Article 9 of the Law, but it is very important to note that within this structural dimension, the standard does not contemplate, at least directly, as a criterion or parameter the market share of the agent(s) involved.

The Law does not specify a certain market share threshold needed for a company to be considered to have enough market power to be able to act unilaterally or independently in a relevant market ignoring both its competitors and its customers. However, the Law indirectly establishes a threshold of 45% as a reference of dominant position. This is so given that in the chapter of the law intended to regulate the merger control regime, the Law establishes that the purpose of such regime is to establish whether the operations evaluated "...are compatible with this Law...", determining that such compatibility is met by "...those concentrations that do not pose a significant obstacle to effective competition, as they do not create or strengthen any dominant position in the national market or in a substantial part of it..."[44] Moreover, the Law establishes that one of the alternative thresholds that generate the obligation to notify a concentration operation is that "As a consequence of the operation, a share equal to or greater than 45% (forty-five percent) of the national market of a given product or service, or of a defined geographic market within the same, is acquired or increased."[45]

In other words, if the Law determines that concentration operations that do not create or reinforce a dominant position are compatible with the Law, and determines the obligation to notify those that may generate the acquisition or increase of a market share equal to or greater than 45%, it is clear then that the legislator wanted to draw attention to a market share that reaches or exceeds that threshold, indirectly making the market share an additional evaluation criterion that the authority should not ignore through a comprehensive interpretation of the Law.

With respect to the temporal dimension, it should be noted that the Law does not require as a condition that companies to hold their dominant position for a specified period of time.

Finally, it is necessary to return to an important aspect related to the legal framework of abuse of dominant position in Paraguay, and that is that it incorporates a subjective requirement as a condition to determine whether a conduct that is framed within the figure of abuse of dominant position is subject to sanction. The last paragraph of Article 9 of the Law establishes that "Those who hold a dominant market position shall not be liable, by that circumstance alone, for sanctions established in the present Law, unless it is proven through administrative proceedings that the same have carried out any of the activities prohibited by the present Law, with the purpose of

43. Article 9°, subsection b), number 3 of the Law: "The degree to which the allegedly responsible party can unilaterally influence price formation or restrict supply or demand in the market and the degree to which its competitors can counteract such power."
44. Article 13 of Law.
45. Article 14, numeral 1 subsection a) of Law.

obtaining undue advantages and causing harm to others, which would not have been possible in the absence of such dominant position."

For this condition, it is possible that the regulatory framework about the abuse of dominant position in the Law presents problems of application, since it includes intention as an element to punish the existence of an abuse (intention to obtain advantages unduly and harm another competitor). Usually, the concept of abuse is an objective notion related to the market effects stemming from the behavior of an undertaking in a dominant position and not to the intention behind that conduct.[46]

The experience in this type of case is very limited in Paraguay. It was not until 2021 that CONACOM began the first formal investigation into a possible case of abuse of a dominant position due to an unjustified refusal to sell.[47]

[C] Investigation (Authorities, Procedure, Powers, Burden of Proof, Appeal)

Please refer to the description provided in the cartel section.

[D] Sanctions and Remedies

Please refer to the description provided in the cartel section.

[E] Precedent Cases

Case "Teledeportes Paraguay S.A. s/ alleged infringement of Law No. 4956/2013".

As highlighted in the cartel case analyzed in the respective section, this case constitutes the first precedent in the matter since the entry into force of the Law and the constitution of the enforcement authority. As stated by the board of directors itself in its resolution "... it is the first case submitted to the consideration of CONACOM's Board of Directors in which an alleged abuse of a dominant position is analyzed in the light of our Antitrust Law. Therefore, the results of this analysis will constitute the basis on which the concrete content of the prohibition contained in Article 9 of our Law could be outlined or rather unveiled or unraveled."[48]

---

46. This is for instance the approach adopted by the European Commission in Case 85/76 *Hoffmann-La Roche v Commission* [1979] ECR 461: "the concept of abuse is an objective concept relating to the behavior of an undertaking in a dominant position which is such as to influence the structure of a market where, as a result of the very presence of the undertaking in question, the degree of competition is weakened and which, through recourse to methods different from those which condition normal competition in products or services on the basis of the transactions of commercial operators, has the effect of hindering the maintenance of the degree of competition still existing in the market or the growth of that competition."
47. Teledeportes Paraguay S.A. regarding alleged violation of Law No. 4956/2013 – File No. 3/2020. Resolution A/D No. 29/2021 https://www.conacom.gov.py/institucion/unidades/directorio.
48. Resolution D/AL N° 87 (23.11.2021), p. 104.

It is therefore clear that it is important to analyze the particularities of this case and the positions taken by the CONACOM bodies, which, as in the first cartel investigation case, differ in substantial aspects.

Background of the case:

- Teledeportes Paraguay S.A. (the defendant) is a company belonging to the economic group Millicom, which in Paraguay is vertically integrated in the value chain of the television industry, including, as regards this specific case, the official first division soccer championships (professional and/or honor division) in the Republic of Paraguay in all its stages (Paraguayan Soccer). In such chain, the defendant is the programmer that produces and provides the TV content related to Paraguayan Soccer, and integrates such content through a cable channel "Tigo Sport", and markets the same to cable operators in the country. It should be noted that the Millicom group, through its subsidiaries Telecel S.A. and Servicios y Productos Multimedios S.A., is also the largest cable operator in the country.
- The defendant, since approximately 2007, is the holder of the exclusive rights granted by the Paraguayan Soccer Association (APF), for the transmission, broadcasting, and/or commercial exploitation of the images and sound of Paraguayan Soccer, in all its stages, in the Republic of Paraguay and in the rest of the world, at least until the end of the year 2023. This exclusive right granted to the defendant consists in consequence in an intellectual property right once the Paraguayan Soccer content is produced and transmitted through Tigo Sport's cable signals.
- This case arises from a complaint filed by the companies AMX Paraguay S.A. and TUVES Paraguay S.A. (the complainants) against the defendant at the beginning of 2020, for an alleged violation of the Law, consisting of an Abuse of Dominant Position, due to the unjustified refusal to supply signals for the transmission of Paraguayan Soccer to the Complainants.
- The complainants alleged to have requested on numerous occasions to the defendant the conditions of onerous access to the possibility of retransmitting the signals of *TIGO SPORT* and *TIGO SPORT* +, and more specifically those related to the Paraguayan Soccer content, as other Pay TV operators in Paraguay do.

On April 15, 2021, based on the complaint filed and based on the information obtained in the development of the investigation of the case, the Investigation Directorate of CONACOM (DI), filed an accusation against the defendant for an alleged infringement of Article 9 of Law No. 4956/2013 "Defense of Competition", consisting of abuse of dominant position for an unjustified refusal to supply signals for the transmission of Paraguayan Soccer.[49]

49. Article 9°, inc. a) 3. "...Abuse may consist on: ... the unjustified refusal to satisfy demands for the purchase of goods or the rendering of services."

Relevant Market

When defining this essential element in any antitrust matter, considering the arguments put forward by the DI, as well as the criticisms made by the defendant with respect to the definitions proposed,[50] the board of directors finally resolved to define the Relevant Market (RM) by product and geography as follows:[51]

- Upstream Market: the wholesale distribution market of signals that include the live broadcasting of soccer matches of the first division championships organized by the APF, with national scope, in which the alleged infringement of refusal to supply an essential input to compete in the downstream market would occur.
- Downstream Market: affected (and in which the economic group of which the defendant is part also operates), is the pay TV market, including cable operators of Distribution, UHF, DATDH, IPTV, and Personal Flow (OTT), with national scope.

Regarding this definition, it is important to highlight the position taken by the board of directors with respect to the analysis made by the DI to define the RM, especially considering: the existing lack of market information in our country, and the budgetary deficiencies that afflict the authority and limit its ability to conduct studies of high technical content to support its allegations. Thus, the board considered that the analysis of substitutability carried out by the DI as support for the definition of the RM, is in line with the standards set by the doctrine and comparative jurisprudence in that, given the difficulty of collecting data and information to assess substitutability by performing the hypothetical monopolist test, the determination of the RM may have to be made in view of the characteristics and utilities of the product, or by resorting to other indications that generate a conclusion on the matter.[52]

Dominant Position:

With respect to this other essential element for the configuration of the conduct under investigation, the DI considered proven the dominant position of the defendant in the Upstream Market since it holds 100% of such market, considering it holds the exclusive broadcasting rights of the Paraguayan Soccer matches. On the other hand, with respect

50. The Defendant objected to the mechanics used by the DI for the definition of the RM (retail and wholesale), pointing out that such construction was made only under the protection of the DI's manifestations in previous merger transactions, information submitted by the parties, opinions of the sector regulator and foreign precedents, but in the total absence of technical empirical evidence resulting from economic analysis (substitutability tests, price analysis, price elasticity and cross-price of demand, etc.), resulting in an unfounded conclusion by the DI that the Respondent holds a "monopoly" in the wholesale pay TV market (upstream), and an unfounded limitation of the retail RM (downstream).
51. Resolution D/AL N° 87 (November 23, 2021), p. 97.
52. The board of directors thus endorses the DI's argumentation for the definition of the RM based on the information provided by the parties, by the regulator, and even the precedents gathered from the European jurisdiction and the regional competition agencies (Argentina, Chile, and Brazil).

to the downstream market, the DI also considered that the dominant position of the defendant was proven based on a structural analysis of the market on the basis of market shares,[53] of the HHI index (Herfindahl-Hirschamann)[54] and the dominance threshold.[55] Likewise, in the latter market, the DI pointed out that the information emerging from the aforementioned analyses showed that the high atomization of demand threatened the countervailing power of the same, i.e., that operators wishing to have the content of Paraguayan Soccer had little, if any, bargaining power vis-à-vis the defendant. To all this, to reinforce the argument of dominant position of the DI, it was added, in its opinion, the high barriers to entry, especially due to the vertical integration of the economic group of the defendant, which conspired to discourage any attempt to challenge such market.

Analyzing the arguments and evidence presented by the DI and the defendant[56] regarding the configuration of this requirement, the board of directors contrasted them with the conditions set forth in the Law to conclude that an economic agent enjoys a dominant position.[57] And in this task it concluded that:

- The defendant enjoys a dominant position in the upstream market because it is not exposed to substantial and effective competition,[58] not only because it has the exclusive rights to exploit the Paraguayan Soccer,[59] but also because:
  a) The Paraguayan Soccer product is a market in itself, or a product that cannot be substituted by other national or foreign content, according to the conclusions reached by the authority when analyzing the Relevant Market in these proceedings, as well as in merger transactions involving

53. The economic group to which the defendant belongs (Millicom Group), reached a market share of 61.8% in this market in 2020, according to the analysis of the DI based on the data provided by the parties and by the regulator (National Telecommunications Commission—CONATEL).
54. This exceeded 4,200 points in 2020, suggesting competitive concerns derived from this concentration threshold.
55. Located between 43% and 32%, and which was, according to the DI, highly surpassed by the defendant.
56. With respect to that particular requirement, it rejected the DI's conclusions on the grounds that they were not supported by objective empirical bases emerging from technical market studies. In this regard, for example, it rejected the DI's reasoning that the exclusive rights granted to the Defendant give rise, by themselves, to the configuration of a monopoly in the upstream market.
57. Article 9, inc. "...(b) In order to establish the existence of a dominant position in a market, the following circumstances shall be considered: (1) The extent to which the good or service in question is substitutable for others, whether of domestic or foreign origin; the conditions for such substitution and the time required for substitution; (2) The extent to which regulatory restrictions limit access by products or suppliers or demanders to the market in question; and (3) The extent to which the allegedly responsible party may unilaterally influence price formation or restrict supply or demand in the market and the degree to which its competitors may counteract such power."
58. Resolution D/AL N° 87 (23.11.2021), p. 103.
59. Circumstance that by itself, according to the Board of Directors, is usually considered sufficient to determine the existence of a dominant position in the local soccer market, citing comparative jurisprudence of the Spanish (MEDIAPRO case) and Uruguayan (*Asociación Uruguaya de Futbol* case) competition authorities.

companies of the Millicom group, and the allegations made by representatives of said group on such occasions;[60]

b) Although there are no regulatory barriers limiting the access of products, suppliers, and demanders to the market in question, there are legal barriers (such as the exclusive rights conventionally granted to the defendant) and structural barriers (the huge investments that potential competitors of the defendant would have to make to access the market under competitive conditions) that prevent the respondent from being exposed to effective and substantial competition; and
c) Being the only company that has exclusive rights over the input product of Paraguayan Soccer, it would also have such a bargaining power vis-à-vis the complainants of the same, which would allow it to have a decisive influence over the conditions of supply of the product, and on the other hand, from its own refusal to supply the licenses to the Complainants, it is clear that the defendant has the ability to reduce or restrict the supply or the demand in the market.

Abuse:

With respect to this element, the DI based the existence of this element on the understanding that, since the complainant was the exclusive owner of the rights in question, which in its opinion constituted a monopoly, and having proven the omission in the response to the complainants' request for the supply of the input in question, and moreover, there was an express acknowledgment of the refusal to respond to such requests, and that such refusal lacked any justification whatsoever, the DI considered that the complainant had failed to provide the input in question to the complainants, and that it had not provided any justification whatsoever,[61] and that therefore, the abusive conduct prohibited by the Law should be considered configured and accredited.

Finally, and in order to prove the subjective and voluntary element to which our legislation conditions the sanction of the Abuse of Dominant Position,[62] the DI understands that, since the purpose of the complainant is the development of TV and soccer content, there would be no logical argument for it to renounce the possibility of obtaining a greater maximization of benefits by selling or licensing the rights in favor

60. Resolution D/AL N° 87 (23.11.2021), p. 101.
61. In this regard, the DI argued that the only justification alleged by the defendant was that such refusal was based on the legitimate exercise of copyrights over the required input, but that such argument was inadmissible because the legitimate exercise of such categories of rights cannot be invoked to "...unjustifiably or abusively restrict the free market or competition" and that "...one of the limits of copyrights are the regulations that govern the free market and competition". Another circumstance alleged by the DI with the same purpose was the history of provision of this input to almost a hundred competing operators of the Millicom group downstream (Resolution D/AL N°87, p. 19 and 37).
62. Article 8° establishes as one of the conditions for sanctioning the conduct, that the same be carried *out* "...with the purpose of obtaining undue advantages and causing harm to others, which would not have been possible in the absence of such position of dominance".

of the complainants, except for the undue purpose of eliminating or diminishing downstream competition in favor of the subsidiaries of the economic group of which it is a part.[63] The DI also considered that the intent to injure is clear, with respect to the complainants because they are the two competitors with the greatest chances of exerting competitive pressure; and with respect to consumers, because they see their options for accessing the denied input reduced.

For its part, with respect to the configuration of this element, the defendant presented an argument that would be essential in the resolution of the case and which is linked to the principle of legal exemption enshrined in Article 2 clause 4 of the Law. In this sense, the defendant argued that the Law is clear as regards the cases of exclusion of sanctions, one of them being the principle of legal exemption, by virtue of which, the exercise of a right cannot constitute an abuse of dominant position, and being, according to the defendant, its refusal to assign retransmission rights protected by the intellectual property right that it holds over the content, such refusal cannot be considered an infringement, being that on the basis of such right, the defendant ".... has the freedom of choice of its commercial contractors and the free availability of its property."[64]

Finally, with respect to this critical element for the definition of the case, the board concluded that:

- It was proven that the complainants repeatedly requested the defendant to have the product in question.[65]
- It was proven that the defendant did not respond to such requests and that it even expressly acknowledged the refusal in a note sent to the authority within the framework of the processing of the case.
- That, in view of the aforementioned certainties, the final decision depended on proving that such refusal was unjustified.
- With respect to this issue, the DI attempted to prove the lack of justification by limiting itself to a literal analysis of the regulations, without considering elements that typify the specific type of abuse, which, although not expressly enshrined in the Law, are the products of case law and doctrine linked to the application of regulations that constitute the sources of Paraguayan law, at least with respect to this type of conduct,[66] and, as such, must be considered at the time of an adequate legal hermeneutic of the Law.
- That in this sense, the fact alleged by the DI that the defendant provides the required input to other market operators in Paraguay is insufficient to support the qualification of the refusal as unjustified, since if such argument is accepted to resolve this case against the defendant, it would collide with the

63. As mentioned earlier, Millicom group owns the largest subscription television operator in the country.
64. Resolution D/AL N° 87 (November 23, 2021), p. 29.
65. The rights to access the broadcast of Paraguayan Soccer matches.
66. Considering the substantial similarity between the provisions of Article 9 of the Law, and Article 2 of Spanish Law 15/2007 and 102 of the TFUER.

right of each company to choose with whom to contract, which is an essential pillar of market economies, since it is a derivation of the Right of Property.

The resolution shows the board's interest in stating its position that competition law must be applied under strict compliance with the principle of priority of norms, emphasizing that, as in many other constitutions, the Paraguayan Constitution recognizes the right of companies to freely dispose of their property, including intellectual property, and the right to choose their contractual partners, and that therefore, the holder of a property right, especially intellectual property, enjoys exclusive rights that include the possibility of denying third parties licenses with respect to such property.

In support of this position, it refers to the "Communication from the Commission - Guidelines on the Commission's monitoring priorities in its application of Article 82 of the CE Treaty,"[67] to emphasize that any company, whether dominant or not, must have the right to choose who to trade with and freely dispose of its property, and that exceptions restricting or limiting such rights must be carefully justified, especially in the case of intellectual property rights, which are usually the result of large-scale investments, which motivate the restriction arising from exclusivity, at least for a certain period of time, as a mechanism to stimulate investment and development.

In line with the aforementioned, the board of directors holds that nevertheless, there are certain exceptional circumstances in which the exercise of the exclusionary right of ownership may involve abusive behavior in the terms of the prohibition contained in Article 9 of Law No. 4956/2013, but for this to occur —and it is here that the board takes a position that in our opinion is of great value in the task of unraveling the scope of our regulations, at least as regards the type of conduct involved in this case—there must be certain concurrent requirements, enshrined by jurisprudence and comparative doctrine,[68] as follows:

(i) The refusal relates to a product or service that is objectively essential to be able to compete effectively in a downstream market, i.e., that has no actual or potential substitute on which competitors in the downstream market can rely to counteract the negative consequences of the refusal.
(ii) The refusal is likely to result in the elimination of effective competition in the downstream market.
(iii) Finally, that such refusal is likely to be detrimental to consumers.

Based on these assumptions enshrined in its resolution, the board finally concluded that in this particular case, the DI could not prove with concrete, solid and convincing evidence, the lack of rationality or economic logic of the defendant's conduct, since it did not prove that the sole purpose of such conduct was to harm a competitor or restrict competition, and this given that the DI could prove neither the

67. The Board of Directors resorts to the same source to establish its position on the evidentiary standard that should govern the analysis of this type of conduct, and in this regard determines that such standard is that of "*...solid and convincing evidence*" (Resolution D/AL No. 87 (November 23, 2021), p. 112).
68. Resolution D/AL N° 87 (November 23, 2021), p. 116.

essentiality of the product,[69] nor the exclusion of effective competition,[70] and therefore considered as not accredited the existence of a prohibited practice in the investigated modality, and resolved to acquit the defendant through Resolution D/AL No. 87, dated November 23, 2021.

By way of conclusion, it should be noted that through this resolution, the board of directors establishes an interesting referential framework of analysis for this type of conduct. It analyzes and resolves the denounced infringement as an alleged case of abuse of dominant position in related markets, a typology characterized by the existence of an agent that holds a dominant position in a certain relevant market, and intends to project or extend its market power to another relevant market different but close or neighboring to the dominant one. Similarly, regarding the typicity of the abusive conduct under investigation, it clearly establishes that the refusal of treatment, supply, license, or denial of an input requires, in addition to the concurrence of the express requirements contemplated in the Law, other elements developed by doctrine and jurisprudence, providing a more precise and predictable framework of analysis for market operators, at least with respect to this type of conduct in particular.

§17.04 MERGER CONTROL

[A] Relevant Legislation

The system of merger control governed by the Law is intended for evaluating the compatibility business combinations with the regime established by said framework and with the national market, or a substantial part of the same, as set forth in Article 13 of the Law. In this regard, said article provides an evaluation criterion stating that compatible with the Law are the operations of concentration not entailing a significant obstacle against an effective competition, as they neither create nor reinforce any dominant position whatsoever in the national market or in a substantial part thereof.

On this issue, it is worth noting that the regulation system within which the Law is circumscribed, is that of the *rule of reason*, which is why the mere existence of a dominant position, or its creation or reinforcement as a result of a concentration operation, is not enough per se for deeming such operation as unauthorized; provided that the enforcing authority must prospectively analyze if the creation or reinforcement of such possible dominant position entails a significant obstacle against an effective

69. In this regard, the board of directors stated that the input object of the denial is difficult to conceive as essential to compete downstream, when the complainants entered the subscription television market and remained in the same attracting a large number of clients, without counting on this input, at least since 2007 when the first contract was signed between the APF and the Respondent.
70. In this regard, the board of directors stated that it is difficult to reasonably conceive that the refusal (the only case credited to their understanding) generates the exclusion of competition in downstream marking, since the complainants have entered and remained in it and have captured a significant mass of clients, even in spite of the refusal.

competition, based on the criteria set forth by the very law and its decree.[71] That is to say, the mere increase of market share, even when the same implied the creation or reinforcement of a dominant position, does not constitute, singlehandedly, a conclusive evidence of incompatibility of the operation with the market and with the Law.

[B] Authorities

Please refer to the description provided in the cartel section.

[C] Triggering Events and Thresholds

[1] Qualitative Threshold: Acquisition of Control or Substantial Influence

The definition of the operations that are subject to merger control is a key element for an efficient merger control framework, since too broad a definition could lead to the reporting of transactions that are unlikely to have a real effect on the market structure, but whose analysis would generate unnecessary "costs" for the authority and the parties involved. On the other hand, too narrow a definition could lead to leaking troublesome operations.

The Law defines in its Article 12[72] three cases that, for the purposes foreseen in the same are deemed as operations of concentration:

(a) When two or more individuals within the scope of application of the Law, previously independent from one another, *merger*;
(b) When one or more natural or legal persons, whether national or foreign, control at least one or more legal persons, by acquiring shares of the capital, or purchasing assets, or contract, or by any other means acquired, directly or indirectly, control over the totality or a part of one or more legal persons; and

71. To this effect, the authority must know and analyze in depth the structure of the markets involved, the actual and potential competition (inside and outside the republic), the market position of the participants, alternatives of substitutability of the products or services affected, barriers to market entry and exit, efficiency gains alleged by the participants, etc., that is, a complex accumulation of elements and data that allow the authority to reasonably assume how the market will be in the future in case the analyzed concentration operation is carried out. All these elements of analysis are foreseen as such in the Law (Article 13) and the Decree (Article 24 and other concordant provisions).

72. The Law: "Article 12.- Definition of concentration. 1. For the purposes provided for in this Law, a concentration operation shall be deemed to take place: a) when two or more of the previously independent entities within the scope of application of this Law merge; b) when one or more domestic or foreign individuals or legal entities control at least one or more legal entities, through the acquisition of shares in the capital, or the purchase of assets, or by contract or by any other means, acquire, directly or indirectly, control over the entirety of one or more other legal entities, 2. The creation of a common legal entity that performs on a permanent basis the functions of an independent economic entity shall constitute a concentration operation as provided for in paragraph 1 (b) of Article 12..."

(c) When two or more natural and/or legal persons within the scope of application of the Law create one common legal person, which carries out, on a permanent basis, the functions of an independent business entity.

From the foregoing it is clear that the regulation takes as criteria for the definition of concentration operations: (a) the existence of a merger per se, (b) the existence of a takeover, and (c) the creation of a common legal entity (Corporate Joint Venture).

Mergers and Joint Ventures

Regarding the merger alternative, and considering the principle of extraterritoriality enshrined in the Law for its scope of application, there are not many aspects on which to delve, given that, to a greater or lesser extent, there is a uniform conception of the essence of the legal institute of merger, beyond the conceptual variations that may arise among the different legal systems.[73]

On the other hand, the alternative of the corporate Joint Venture, foreseen as a special one within the type of concentrations foreseen by the Law, does not seem to present important challenges regarding the determination of the scope and content of such legal institute (beyond the fact that it is not regulated as such in the Paraguayan legal system) due to the wide diffusion and use of this associative modality in international commerce.

Regarding the regulation of the "taking of control" as a criterion for determining the existence of a concentration operation, it is appropriate to deepen the analysis of the content and scope that the Law reserves for this economic and legal phenomenon.

What is understood as control takeover by the Law?

For the determination of the existence or not of a control takeover, in the terms foreseen in the Law, the same follows the criterion of *"decisive influence"*. For the Law, when one or more legal persons, by taking shares in the capital, by acquiring assets items, by contract, or by any other means, have the possibility of exerting a decisive influence on the activities of an entity within the scope of application of this Law, a control takeover takes place, and therefore one of the cases defined as concentration is materialized.

Considering the requirements contemplated in the Law for the configuration of an assumption of control, it is worthwhile to focus on the entity that the law requires to be affected by the decisive influence of the Controlling Entity. Such role is reserved by the Law to "...one or more legal persons".[74] Therefore, this legal framework would

73. The Paraguayan Civil Code includes institute's essential notes in its Article 1192, which establishes that "By means of a merger, two or more companies are dissolved without liquidation, in order to constitute a new one, or one of them absorbs another or others that are dissolved without liquidation. The new company, or the absorbing one, becomes the holder of the rights and obligations of the dissolved ones, as soon as the merger agreement is formalized..."

74. Article 12 numeral 3 of the Law: "For the purposes of this Article, control results from rights, contracts or other means which, by themselves or together, and taking into account the factual and legal circumstances, confer the possibility of exercising decisive influence over the activities

seem to leave out of the objective scope of application of the merger control regime of the Law, certain operations that although they could affect the structure of a market[75] do not necessarily imply the taking of control of a legal person, at least in the sense that the Law grants to such situation.

A clear example of the aforementioned is found when contrasting the acts that the Law considers as typologies of a concentration operation subject to its scope of application, with the nature and characteristics of the regime of transfer of commercial establishments (or *transfer of goodwill*) regulated by Law 1.034/83. Such contrast, added to what has been stated by the national and comparative doctrine on the subject, clearly reveals that the aforementioned regime of *transfer of goodwill* does not constitute a mechanism to acquire control or "decisive influence" over all or part of one or more legal entities, at least not always. And although this regulatory deficiency has not been exploited to date to evade the application of the Law with respect to this type of operations, a legislative revision of the definition provided by Article 12 of the Law would be appropriate in order to shield the system from this type of regulatory leaks.

[2] Quantitative Thresholds

In a merger control framework, the thresholds play a substantial role, because it determine what type transactions are there must be mandatory notified. Usually, the objective thresholds (based on turnover of merging parties, assets of merging parties, or amount of transaction) are the most commonly used and are recommended internationally, for instance by the ICN and the Organization for Economic Cooperation and Development (OECD).[76]

As per the terms of the Law, the concentration operations shall be subject to notice, assessment and authorization, conditioned or not, or to rejection by CONACOM, with the occurrence of at least one of the following circumstances;[77]

(a) as a result of the merger, the acquirer achieves share equal to or more than 45% in the national market of a determined product or service, or in a geographic market defined within the same; or
(b) the global gross turnover in the Republic of Paraguay of the group of participants of one concentration, exceeds in the last fiscal year the amount of

of a subject included in the scope of application of this Law, in particular: (a) rights of ownership or use of all or part of the assets of a legal person; (b) rights or contracts that make it possible to decisively influence the composition, deliberations or decisions of the organs of a legal person."

75. It is very important to remember that the merger control, in essential, is a competition policy tool that seeks to complement the enforcement of behavior regulations and identify situations in which a change in market structure will likely affect market outcomes, and harm consumers and/or, the competitive process.
76. ICN, Recommended Practices for Merger Notification Procedures; OECD, Recommendation of the Council on Merger Review, March 23, 2005 – C (2005)34.
77. Article 14 of the Law.

one hundred thousand monthly minimum salaries.[78] The global gross turnover includes the amounts resulting from the sale of products and performance of services carried out by the same during the last financial year corresponding to their ordinary activities, upon reductions of sales or discounts on sales, as well as of the Value Added Tax (VAT), the excise, and other taxes directly related with the volume of the business.

The Law uses the combined thresholds system. Although the combination of alternative thresholds (in this case, market share and gross billing) is useful, the use of combined threshold can also generate undesirable effects for the system to requiring large firms to notify even very small acquisitions that are not expected to lead to any significant anticompetitive effects in the market.

In this line, the OECD recommend of "...the best practice is to define the size thresholds separately for each merging party, in order to avoid a reporting merger situation where a relatively large company exceeding a threshold makes a de minimis acquisition of a much smaller company, which is unlikely to have a significant effect on competition."[79]

[D] Exemptions

Regarding the exceptions to the merger control framework, Article 12 of the Law follows the line of the EU merger regulation[80] and specifically excludes from the merger control system the activities of banks, credit institutions, or other financial institutions or insurance companies, whose normal activities include transactions and dealing in securities for their own account or for the account of others, holding on a temporary basis securities which they have acquired in an undertaking with a view to reselling them, provided that they do not exercise voting rights in respect of those securities, in order to determine the competitive behavior of that undertaking or provided that they exercise such voting rights only with a view to preparing the disposal of all or part of that undertaking or of its assets or the disposal of those securities and that any such disposal takes place within one year of the date of acquisition.[81] The same exception applies to cases of acquisition of control by virtue of legal provisions related to insolvency, bankruptcies, or other similar processes.

[E] Pre-merger Control Regime or Post-merger Control Regime

It is one of the most controversial axes of the Law. Article 14 of the Law establishes as a general rule that merger notifications must be submitted within ten business days

78. Approximately US$ 33.000.000 in our day.
79. OECD, Peer Review of Competition Law and Policy in Honduras. DAF/COMP/LACF (2011) 3, 2011, p. 30.
80. Council Regulation (EC) No 139/2004 (the EC Merger Regulation).
81. Article 12, Inc. 5, a) of the Law.

after their conclusion, but at the same time, there is a prior authorization process regulated in the Regulatory Decree.

On the other hand, the Law does not contain an explicit prohibition to carry out a merger or acquisition before obtaining the authorization of CONACOM (that is, to sanction the cases of Gun Jumping).

The concurrence of these circumstances generates a deep uncertainty about the true nature (ex ante or ex post) of the notification regime established in the Law, with the legal and practical problems that this implies, and about which we will not refer with more precision in the chapter of Penalties.

To date, this legal void has not generated any substantial controversy regarding a concentration operation. However, the certainty and security that a regime as sensitive as this one must present for those affected should motivate the correction of this deficiency in the regulatory framework.

[F] Intra-group Transactions

The comprehensive and systematic interpretation of the Law, especially of the provisions of Article 12 that characterizes the assumptions of concentration, and the application of the principle of economic reality established by the regulations, allow to conclude, and so has also been interpreted by CONACOM,[82] that intragroup corporate reorganizations are not subject to merger control notification, because:

(a) The Article 12 requires as a condition for a merger to be subject to the control regime of the law, that it involves "... two or more subjects ... previously independent ..."; and
(b) The transactions between companies under the control of the same economic group (including joint ventures) do not imply a change of control, and therefore cannot affect the market structure since control of the acquired entity remains within the same group economic.

[G] Substantive Test for Assessing Mergers

Evaluation criteria

According to the Law, an operation shall be compatible with the market whenever it does not create or reinforce a dominant position that constitutes a significant obstacle for effective competition. For this to be determined, the authority must analyze:

(i) the degree of increase in concentration that the operation might generate;
(ii) the possibility that the operations facilitates individual or arranged actions against the competition; and

82. Resolution D / AL N ° 5, February 2020, file *"Consultation on the scope of Art. 12 of Law 4956/13 on the Competition Defense"*.

(iii) the efficiency gains emerging from the operation (the burden of proof lying on the involved parties)[83]

Economic efficiencies

Achievement of economic efficiencies is an important argument when analyzing an operation, and even more so if they can have the effect of creating a substantial market power. The decree makes express reference to two modalities of economic efficiencies: productive (reduction of costs) and dynamic (innovation and development). But, it is necessary to clarify that the reference to efficiencies provided for in Article 25 of the Decree is clearly enunciative and not exhaustive. The parties should be claiming the economic efficiencies and to prove them or explain how they benefit consumers.

[H] Notification Procedure and Timetable

[1] Process of Analysis by the Authority

Filing rules

There are constant debates on this point with regards to the regime adopted by the Law for the notification of operations (*ex post* control or *ex ante* control?). This occurs due to deficiencies in the regulatory framework, since it does not clearly determine the nature of the system.[84] However, from a comprehensive analysis of the regulatory framework (Law and Decree), it can be concluded that it states two options for notifying concentration operations:

(a) Ex post: within ten business days counted from the date of written completion of the agreement or publication of the acquisition offer, of exchange, or of the acquisition a control share.[85] It is important to mention that the Law does not establish a suspensory effect, and therefore there is no express legal impediment for the parties to finalize the transaction before the authority pronounces itself, always at the risk of a possible conditioning or a rejection.
(b) Ex ante or previous authorization: other than timing of the notice, the rules on evaluation, terms, and decision are the same for both modalities.[86] This alternative is regulated only in the decree and not in the Law, which generates

83. Article 26 of the Decree.
84. The wording of the law generates confusion as to the ex ante or ex post condition of the notifications. And the lack of an express prohibition to carry out the operation before obtaining CONACOM's authorization is another element of confusion, and it excludes the possibility to sanction Gun Jumping eventual cases.
85. Article 14, subsection 1) of the Law: *"Merger transactions must be notified and registered in the Antitrust Merger Registry to the Enforcement Authority, within 10 (ten) days of their execution counted from the day following the date of the written conclusion of the agreement or the publication of the offer to purchase, exchange or acquisition of a controlling interest."*
86. Article 14 of the Decree.

legal uncertainty for its application and proof of this is that to date no operation has been notified under this mechanism.

Parties compelled to filing

In the event of a concentration by control takeover, the obligation falls on the party acquiring the control. In the case of a merger, the obligation rests on both parties jointly. It is not clear who is responsible for notifying in a joint venture, since the Law considers this case as included within the regime of taking control, but not necessarily in this type of associative phenomena one of the parties has control over the other.

Filing information required

In the Paraguay merger control regime, the parties involved are obliged to submit extensive information regarding the notified transaction. The information required in a notification is provided by the decree.[87] Similarly, the Law states that CONACOM shall prepare guidelines. In 2021, CONACOM issued the first guide for the notification of concentration transactions, seeking to harmonize the process and clarify the requirements imposed on notifiers.[88] The filing must include, among others, the following information:

(a) Identification of the individual or legal entity filing the notice and other individuals or legal entities involved in the merger.
(b) Description of the structure of ownership and control of each of the parties involved in the Merger Operation.
(c) Financial Statements of the individuals or legal entities involved pertaining to the precedent fiscal year.
(d) Description of the Merger Operation and the type of transaction and the pertaining act in question, as well as the clauses under which the parties are bound to non-compete.
(e) Statement mentioning the individuals and legal entities involved in the transaction with direct or indirect shareholding, who take part in the administration or in any activity of other individuals or legal entities producing or commercializing goods and services equal, similar or substantially related to goods or services of the individuals or legal entities involved in the merger.
(f) Value of the transaction.
(g) List and description of the goods and services produced or offered by the individual or legal entities involved in the merger.
(h) Market shares of the companies involved and their competitors, if such information is available.
(i) Information on merger authorizations in other jurisdictions.

87. Articles 16 and 21 of the Decree.
88. Resolution A/D No. 29/2021 (https://www.conacom.gov.py/institucion/unidades/directorio).

(j) Location of the plants or establishments of the individuals or legal entities involved the location of their main distribution centers and the relationship they keep with such individuals or legal entities.
(k) If so decided by those filing the notice, analysis, reports. or documents seeking to prove that the merger is compatible with the market.

In addition, in case that an operation be considered as a complex operation and therefore exceeds the fast track analysis stage, the CONACOM may request for additional information, as among others:

(a) Information on the economic and/or financial objectives and/or basis of the Merger Operation.
(b) Detailed information on the products and services involved in the Merger Operation.
(c) Detailed information on the relevant markets affected by the Merger Operation.
(d) Information on the competitors and the degree of competition relevant markets affected by the Merger Operation
(e) Information on customers or consumers, the production process, and the installed capacity of individuals or legal entities.
(f) Costs of production, distribution, sales, and supplies of individuals or legal entities;
(g) Information on distribution and commercialization, distribution channels, prices, transportation costs of the individuals or legal entities.
(h) Information on foreign trade and consumption, tariffs, countervailing duties and other import restrictions in the markets of products and services involved in the Merger Operation.
(i) Information on the factors which determine the ease or difficulty of access to the market in which the Merger Operation must exist.
(j) A detailed description of the effects of the transaction on the markets for the products and services involved, as well as economic efficiencies generated by it.

Evaluation

The analysis regime foreseen in the Paraguayan system is developed in two stages. The second is intended for operations which, in the judgment of the authority, are more complex.

(a) First stage (fast track): Sets forth a maximum term of thirty business days. Within this stage, CONACOM may authorize those operations that are evidently not a significant obstacle for the competition, or dispose the opening of the second stage, given the complexity of the operation. Adding the additional terms foreseen for remedying the lack of documents as required by the Law, this stage could come to an effective maximum duration of fifty business days approximately.

(b) Second stage: This stage cannot exceed 60 business days. Said term may be suspended for the requirement of additional information. For this reason, this stage may reach an effective maximum duration of 110 business days approximately, which, added to the maximum 50 business days of the first stage, may take the procedure to an effective maximum term of 160 business days approximately.

Hearings

Before making a decision, CONACOM must call the involved parties in the transaction for a hearing (only those who have passed to the second stage of the analysis). In said hearing, the parties have the possibility to orally express their points of view, submit amendment proposals for the concerned operation or conditions for their viability, all of which may be considered by the enforcement authority. It is common for the parties to expect the arrival of this hearing in order to discuss alternatives or propose conditions for the approval of the transactions being questioned by CONACOM. But it is advisable (and this has been suggested informally by the authority on several occasions) that the parties, when notifying the operations and providing the required information, also present their proposed behavioral or structural conditions (if any) and require that CONACOM call for hearings as necessary to discuss them, without having to wait until the final preliminary hearing to do so.

Decision

Upon completion of the evaluation procedure, CONACOM has the authority to:

(a) Upon conclusion of the first stage (fast-track): (i) authorize the operation; or (ii) defer the same to the second stage.

(b) Upon conclusion of the second stage: (i) authorize the operation; (ii) reject the same; or (iii) authorize the operation with structural or behavioral conditions (disinvestment, changes in conditions of the operation, rules of conduct, etc.).

Tacit authorization

The Law allows the tacit authorization of a Merger Operation in the event that the authority does not resolve on its rejection, authorization, or conditional authorization, after ninety business days, but this term is suspended for the collection of additional information. To date there are no cases of tacit authorization.

[I] Consequences of a Failure to File

Failure to notify a concentration transaction that falls within the scope of application of the Law is considered a misdemeanor, and it may give rise to the penalties provided therein (Article 62 of the Law, and Article 34 of Decree). In this regard please refer to the description provided in the cartel section.

In addition to the aforementioned sanctions, for the specific case of concentration transactions, the decree establishes CONACOM's power to, after declaring the operation null and void, order the "deconcentration" of non-notified operations, or to annul those notified and unauthorized operations that also materialize according to Articles 35° and 37° of Decree.

[J] Third Party Involvement in Notification Process

According to the regime foreseen in the Law, only the parties that notified the transaction to the CONACOM are part of the process. Third parties, such as competitors or clients of the parties, may be requested to file documents or may be invited to testify as witnesses, but are not allowed to access the file. There has not been any merger cases interrupted by third parties.

[K] Remedies

From 2016 to March 2022, the National Competition Commission ("CONACOM") has resolved thirty seven merger operation,[89] of which thirty three were authorized (89%), one resulted declared improcedent, two resulted declared desisted, and one was denied by the authority.. [90] Of the operations authorized, twenty seven were not subject to any conditions, while the remaining six were authorized with conditions, mostly of behavioral nature, although some of a structural nature were also imposed.[91] The

89. https://www.conacom.gov.py/ambitos-de-actuacion/concentraciones/listado-de-operaciones-de-concentracion
90. *"Frigomer S.A. and Frigorífico Norte S.A. regarding Notification of Concentration Operation. File No. 190/2020."* Resolution D/AL N° 18/2020 dated September 21, 2020.
91. The structural remedies imposed were the following: i) obligation to deploy a higher capacity network with coaxial cables *("Servicios y Productos Multimedios S.A., Get Line Internet S.A., TV Cable Paraná S.A. and Cable 3 Fronteras S.A regarding Notification of Concentration Operation" - File No. 015/2017");* ii) refraining from carrying out works aimed at expanding vault capacity in the interior of the country *("Prosegur S.A., Wackenhut S.A. and G4S US Holdings Limited regarding Notification of Concentration Operation - File. No. 105/2017")*; iii) obligation to deploy a higher capacity network with coaxial cables ("*Servicios y Productos Multimedios S.A. and Cable Visión del Sur S.A. regarding Notification of Concentration Operation – File No. 033/2018*"); iv) limit the number of service stations operated by the acquirer to a maximum of 50% in certain districts of the country ("*Copetrol S. A. and Petrobras Paraguay Distribution Limited / Petrobras Paraguay Operaciones y Logísticas S.R.L. / Petrobras Paraguay Gas S.R.L. s/ regarding Notification of Concentration Operation – File No. 072/2018");* and v) limit the number of service stations operated by the acquirer to a maximum of 50% in the city of Asunción *("Copetrol S.A. and Axion Energy Paraguay S.R.L. s regarding Notification of Concentration Operation - File No. 060/2019")*.

preference for behavioral conditions creates difficulties for the authority to effectively implement such prescribed conditions. Although these operations affected various sectors (food industry, agribusiness, security, transportation and logistics, machinery supply, gas distribution, pharmaceutical, purchase and slaughter of livestock, among others), the technology telecommunications, and fuel and lubricants sectors were the most active.

[L] Penalties (Gun Jumping)

Regardless of the deficiency highlighted in the normative framework that regulates the modality of notification (prior or ex post), an essential concern emerges as a result of such deficiency. Such concern is linked to the effect that the notification (and the process initiated therefrom) generate on the consummation or concretion of the notified transaction, while the same is subject to analysis by the authority.

Our legislation does not expressly prohibit the parties from consummating the notified transaction before the authority issues its decision. That is to say, it does not expressly typify Gun Jumping as a fault, reason for which, its concretion does not constitute a cause of nullity of the transaction.[92] This could cause an extremely complex situation in the event that the parties involved in a transaction, in the absence of an express legal limitation, and protected by the constitutional principle of legality, decide to consummate the transaction and subsequently a decision of the authority decides to condition it, or even more serious, not to authorize it.

In the absence of an express prohibition for gun jumping, and not constituting a ground for declaring the transaction null and void, it is reasonable to assume that if this situation (even today hypothetical) were to materialize, it would place the authority and the other affected parties before a highly complex scenario of legal and economic uncertainty, whose derivations and implications are difficult to imagine and project, but which undoubtedly would not collaborate with the development and consolidation of the still incipient Paraguayan antitrust regime.

[M] Appeal

Please refer to the description provided in the cartel section.

[N] Specific Industries

The scope of application of Article 3 of the Law is absolute, since it includes natural and legal persons, private or public, without any exception, and this is also applicable to the merger regime.

---

92. Article 35 of the Decree provides as grounds for nullity of the transaction: i) failure to notify; ii) provision of fraudulent information; and iii) failure to comply with compliance schedules.

The law does not exclude any specific sector of the economy from the scope of the Law, nor does it with respect to regulated sectors.

In this regard, the Article 61 of the Law expressly establishes that "...All public institutions and regulatory entities are obliged to supply information or issue the reports that are requested. In case of non-compliance with this obligation, they will be sanctioned with fines applied to the responsible officials and the head of the public institution or regulatory entity, in accordance with the Laws and regulations...The National Competition Commission (CONACOM) is the only competent public institution to evaluate the restrictions to free competition and to instruct and resolve the procedures that it regulates."

CHAPTER 18

Competition Law in Peru

Alfredo Bullard González, Alejandro Falla Jara & Andrea Cadenas

§18.01 INTRODUCTION

Peru is located in the South American Pacific zone and is the third largest country in the region. It is an emerging, market-oriented economy characterized by a high level of foreign trade and foreign investment.

Before 1990, the Peruvian economy was characterized by intense protectionism, price controls, and government direct intervention in different sectors. Until 1990, the state also owned all the public service companies such as telecommunication and rail operators. In 1990, the economic model changed. The market was liberalized to attract foreign investment and promote competition, publicly owned natural resources and public service industries were reorganized and privatized, and the state's intervention in the economy was restricted. All these reforms were consolidated in the new Peruvian Constitution enacted in 1993.

According to the new constitution, the economic model is now market oriented. The economy's engine is the private initiative, free prices are set by supply and demand, and competition between private firms is sought to be promoted. The state, from then on has been relegated to the role of supervising the proper functioning of the market, rather than being an agent that intervenes directly in the economy. In that sense, the role of the state in the economy is defined by the principle of subsidiarity, according to which the state shall not develop business activities unless privates cannot and will not be able to satisfy a social demand.

Competition law and policy was formally introduced in Peru in 1991 with the enactment of Legislative Decree N° 701. It was consolidated with the establishment of a duty to protect competition at the constitutional level in the Peruvian Constitution of 1993 and with the opening, in the same year, of an autonomous governmental agency, the National Institute for the Defense of Competition and Protection of Intellectual Property (hereinafter, INDECOPI). Such legislative decree sanctioned anticompetitive conducts such as abuse of dominance, concerted practices or any other that could limit, restrict, or distort competition in a way that would affect the general economic interest within the Peruvian territory.

Legislative Decree N° 701 was in force for more than fifteen years before it was replaced in June 2008 by Legislative Decree N° 1034—Law for the Repression of Anticompetitive Conducts. This new competition law was enacted with the purpose of making the legislation compatible with the Free Trade Agreement signed by Peru and the United States of America. Even though Legislative Decree N° 1034 sets its goal as the achievement of "consumer welfare," it clarifies that the means to that goal should follow economic efficiency. To date, the Peruvian competition policy prohibits horizontal and vertical cartels, collusions, and the abuse of dominant position.

Under Legislative Decree N° 1034 and its amendments, the competition policy in Peru has achieved important milestones. Apart from investigations, enforcement, and advocacy actions, the Leniency Program for cartels' detection has been successfully applied by INDECOPI in the last years, and in 2019 the Antitrust Rewards Program Guidelines were approved. On 2019 a consolidated version of Legislative Decree N° 1034 and its amendments was published through Supreme Decree 030-2019-PCM (hereinafter, the Peruvian Competition Law).

Since 2021, Peru has a new regulatory framework for merger control applicable to all sectors. Specifically, on June 14, 2021, Law N° 31112—Merger Control Act and its regulations, approved by Supreme Decree No. 039-2021-PCM, came into force. This new regime has replaced the previous merger control regime established by Law N°26876—"Law against Monopoly and Oligopoly in the Electricity Sector", which was only applicable to the electricity sector.

§18.02 CARTELS

[A] Relevant Legislation

"Horizontal collusive practices" are prohibited by Article 11 of the Peruvian Competition Law. This category of "horizontal collusive practices" considers concerted agreements, decisions, recommendations, or in general concerted practices between competitors that have the object or effect of restricting, preventing, or distorting competition.

Specifically, cartels are prohibited by Article 11.2 of the law, when it states that horizontal concerted practices that are not supplementary or ancillary to other legal agreements shall be per se punishable if they aim to:

(i) Fix prices or other trade or service conditions;
(ii) Limiting production or sales, especially by shares;
(iii) Allocating customers, suppliers, or geographical areas; or,
(iv) Establish positions or abstentions in bids, tenders or other contractual form or public acquisition under the current legislation.

Cartels are subject to a "per se" rule (absolute prohibitions) which determines that a practice will be considered unlawful by itself without the need of evaluating whether it affects competition or not. Under this rule, to punish a conduct it is not necessary to demonstrate the actual or potential anticompetitive damage.

[B] Extraterritoriality

According to Article 4 of the Peruvian Competition Law, its provisions only apply to conducts that have an effect over all or part of the Peruvian Territory, even if those conducts are originated abroad.

[C] Investigations

The main cause of action against the breach of antitrust rules is administrative proceedings handled by the Competition Commission. The goal of the proceedings is to determine administrative liability by declaring the existence of a breach (or not) to the competition law and to impose administrative sanctions, when applicable.

[1] Authorities

INDECOPI is the authority in charge of the prosecution, investigation, and sanction of anticompetitive practices. It has exclusive jurisdiction in the enforcement and promotion of the competition legislation. INDECOPI's bodies in charge of the application of the Peruvian Competition Law are the following:

- The National Direction of Competition Investigation and Promotion (previously named the Competition Commission's Technical Secretariat) (hereinafter, the Competition Direction) is the technical autonomous agency that acts as prosecutor and is in charge of investigations, initiated ex officio or after claims. The Competition Direction is also in charge of handling the administrative procedures before the Competition Commission and to issue technical opinions regarding the existence of alleged anticompetitive conducts.
- The Competition Commission is the agency with technical and operational autonomy responsible for the enforcement of the Peruvian Competition Law for all economic activities except for the telecommunications market. The competition agency in charge of the enforcement of the Peruvian Competition Law in the telecommunications market is the Organism for the Supervision of Private Investment in Telecommunications (OSIPTEL).
- INDECOPI's Tribunal is the body responsible for reviewing Antitrust Commission's decisions as a second and final instance.

[2] *Inter-agency Cooperation (International)*

INDECOPI has entered into a series of agreements with other Latin-American competition agencies, such as the National Economic Prosecutor's Office of Chile (FNE) and the Superintendence of Industry and Commerce of Colombia (SIC), and more recently with the United States' Federal Trade Commission. These agreements seek to allow information exchange between competition agencies regarding the application and enforcement of competition law.

[3] *Procedure*

Any individual or company can request the opening of formal proceedings by filing a complaint with reasonable preliminary grounds on the existence of an infringement to the law and paying a fee, without the need to provide evidence of the alleged damage suffered by the anticompetitive conduct. After a claim, the Competition Direction shall start a preliminary investigation with a term of forty-five working days, which can be extended for a similar term.

The Competition Direction can also start ex officio investigations if it suspects the existence of anticompetitive practices. The basis for such investigations can be obtained from informal complaints, market analysis, sudden price changes, information from the media, or other market indicia.

Investigations are usually initiated with dawn raids. According to the Peruvian Competition Law, the Competition Direction has the power to conduct dawn raids, with or without prior notification, at the premises of the natural or legal person, business associations and autonomous properties, and examine books, records, documents, and goods, being entitled to check on the development of the production processes and take the statement of the persons found at the premise. During the dawn raid, the authority can take copies of physical files, magnetic or electronic, as well as any document that is deemed relevant or taking photographs or filming as may be necessary.

Moreover, the Competition Direction has the power to summon and question any officer or official representative of any legal person or entity, without any previous judicial authorization.

After the preliminary investigation, the Competition Direction can decide to start an administrative sanctioning procedure with an indictment or close the investigation without charges. Claimants can appeal such decision to the tribunal within fifteen business days.

The Competition Direction will issue a decision starting the administrative procedure if it considers there are sufficient grounds to believe an anticompetitive practice has been carried out. In its indictment, the Competition Direction shall identify the alleged individuals or companies who incurred in the anticompetitive conduct, including an explanation of the facts that sustain the indictment, and the characterization of the alleged infringement to the Peruvian Competition Law.

The indictment shall be notified to the Commission, claimants, and defendants within a period of no more than five business days. Defendants will be given a period of thirty business days to present their defense. The Competition Direction's decision to initiate an administrative sanctioning procedure with its indictment can be appealed.

Once the procedure has been initiated, the trial period cannot exceed seven months from the deadline to answer the charges. The Competition Direction may act or the parties may offer the following forms of evidence: (a) documents, (b) party's statements, (c) testimonies, (d) dawn raids, (e) experts reports, or, (f) other evidence deemed to be necessary to clarify the facts alleged or charged.

The Competition Direction has thirty business days after the trial period to issue the technical report that contains its analysis and conclusions about the alleged infringement. The technical report should analyse the evidence presented by all parties involved, determine the existence or absence of an administrative infringement, the identification of those responsible, and propose fines and remedies.

If no evidence of the existence of anticompetitive practices is found by the Competition Direction, then the technical report shall conclude the nonexistence of the administrative infringement. Parties will have fifteen business days to make allegations and request a hearing with the Commission.

The Commission may grant the hearing requested if considered necessary to gather further evidence or proof needed to reach its final decision. The parties may present final allegations within the next ten business days after the hearing has been carried out. No additional evidence can be filled after the final allegations.

The Commission's final decision must be issued within thirty business days from the deadline that the parties have to present their final allegations. Such decision will be notified to the parties within ten business days.

[D] Sanctions and Remedies

[1] Administrative Sanctions

Anticompetitive conducts are subject to a monetary fine, which will be defined according to the severity of the infringement, with the following fines:

- In case of a minor violation, the fine shall be up to five hundred (500) UIT[1] (approximately USD 544,200) provided that such fine does not exceed 8% of the sales or gross income earned by the offender, or its economic group, with regard to all its economic activities during the fiscal year immediately preceding the issuance of the decision of the Commission;
- In case of a major violation, the fine shall be up to 1,000 UIT (approximately USD 1.08 million) provided that such fine does not exceed 10% of the sales or gross income earned by the offender, or its economic group, with regard to all

1. Taxing Reference Unit, established for 2021 at S/ 4,400.00 or USD 1,075.92, approximately.

its economic activities during the fiscal year immediately preceding the issuance of the decision of the Commission; or,

- In case of a serious violation, the fine shall be higher than 1,000 UIT, provided that such fine does not exceed 12% of the sales or gross income earned by the offender, or its economic group, with regard to all its economic activities during the fiscal year immediately preceding the issuance of the decision of the Commission.

In case of professional or business associations, or economic agents who have started their operations after January 1 of the preceding fiscal year, the fine shall not exceed, in any case, 1,000 UIT (approx. USD 1.08 million). Also, a fine of up to 100 UIT (approx. USD 108,000) could be applied to the legal representatives or individuals of the corporate bodies of the responsible corporations, irregular companies, business associations, autonomous equities, or trusts involved in the infringement.

In addition to the fine, the Peruvian Competition Law establishes that the Commission has the power to impose remedies to restore competition or prevent anticompetitive conducts, such as orders to cease a conduct, the obligation to contract under specific conditions, the unenforceability of anticompetitive clauses or provisions, among others.

[2] Criminal Sanctions

After the Peruvian Competition Law eliminated the criminal liability for antitrust infringements in 2008, amidst the COVID-19 pandemic in August 2020, Law N° 31040 reintroduced the crime of "abuse of economic power" in the Criminal Code. Such crime provides a term of imprisonment of no less than two and no more than six years for those who abuse their dominant position in the market, or participate in restrictive practices or agreements in product, commercial, or services activities, in order to block, restrict, or distort competition. Law N° 31040 does not differentiate between conducts subject to a per se rule and those subject to the rule of reason (abuse of dominance, non-cartel agreements, and vertical restraints). Furthermore, it does not consider the provisions of the Peruvian Competition Law regarding the Leniency Programme and does not provide for a sanction exemption for collaboration with the authorities.

[3] Private Actions and Follow-on Action

Article 49 of the Peruvian Competition Law provides statutory basis for antitrust damages actions by recognizing the right to sue economic damages arising from anticompetitive behavior. Once the administrative proceeding before INDECOPI (or OSIPTEL) is concluded, any person who has suffered damages as a result of an anticompetitive conduct, can sue before the Judicial Power a civil claim for damages, even if they have not been part of the administrative procedure followed by INDECOPI. In this case, the person must be able to show a causal link between the damages suffered and the conduct declared anticompetitive. Under the Peruvian legal framework, damages seek to compensate the consequences of an anticompetitive conduct and not to deter unlawful actions.

In addition, the Peruvian Competition Law has granted the Commission the legal standing to sue for damages derived from anticompetitive conducts in defense of the diffuse and collective interests of the affected consumers, provided there is a previous and favourable report from the Technical Secretariat and after the administrative decision about the anticompetitive conduct has become final. In this context, in 2021, INDECOPI issued the Guidelines on Actions for Damages on behalf of consumers as a consequence of anticompetitive conducts (hereinafter, the Damages Guidelines),[2] which contain the rules, conditions, and restrictions INDECOPI must follow to sue damages on behalf of consumers.

For instance, the Damages Guidelines establish that INDECOPI will only bring actions for damages in order to compensate direct purchasers of the goods or services involved in an anticompetitive conduct. The guidelines also recognize that although INDECOPI is entitled to bring actions for any anticompetitive conduct prohibited by the Peruvian Competition Law, the Commission shall prioritize actions to recover damages derived from cartels. In addition, the Damages Guidelines limit the Commission's power by stating that it shall not promote damages actions for cartels detected after a Type A leniency applicant who was the first to provide information to the authority when it did not have any indicia of the conduct. However, the same limitation has not been established for other type of leniency applicants.

[E] Leniency

Article 26 of the Peruvian Competition Law sets the basis for the Leniency Program when it provides that any person may request the Competition Direction to be exempted from sanctions in return for evidence that helps identify and establish the existence of an illegal practice.

After Legislative Decree No. 1205 enacted in 2016 amended the law to clarify the rules for granting leniency benefits for the second and subsequent applicants, in August 2017, INDECOPI's Competition Commission approved the Leniency Program Guidelines.[3] These guidelines establish the requirements for the application and granting of benefits to cartel participants that report the conduct and collaborate with the authority.

These guidelines state that the program is aimed at offenders, natural or legal persons, who can provide evidence that helps to prove the existence of a cartel, as well as to sanction it; and that it does not apply to those who have coerced other agents to comply with the cartel. Following the law, these guidelines differentiate the type of benefit according to the opportunity in which the application is presented:

2. Available at: https://bit.ly/3BmzGqE.
3. Available in Spanish at: https://bit.ly/35P8cvz.

- Type A Leniency, which includes 100% exemption of the fine granted to the first applicant if the information is provided before the cartel is detected by the authority;
- Type B Leniency can provide 50%–100% fine reduction if the application is presented after the Competition Direction already has some indicia of the conduct; and,
- Type C Leniency applies when the first application has already been filed by another collaborator and/or when the sanctioning procedure has already begun. Depending on each case and the value of the information provided, the fine reduction can be of 20%–50%.

The benefits of fine exoneration or fine reduction do neither limit the imposition of corrective remedies, nor limit the civil liability for the damages caused by the cartel. Only in the case of Leniency Type A, the benefit also includes the non-imposition of corrective measures of restitution.

In addition, in December 2019, the Competition Commission approved the Antitrust Rewards Program Guidelines, pursuant to Article 28 of the Peruvian Competition Law.[4] This program is complementary to the Leniency Program and applies only to individuals who while not having participated in the cartel can provide relevant information to detect it. The program is therefore designed to incentivize family members, former employees of the defendants, or any person who may provide relevant information about a cartel to collaborate with the agency in exchange of monetary rewards.

For such purpose, the Antitrust Rewards Program Guidelines establish that whistle-blowers may receive a reward determined by two amounts: (i) a base amount of USD 51,000 approximately, and (ii) a variable amount determined according to the success of the procedure and the fines imposed to the offenders, with a limit of USD 102,000 approximately.

[F] Appeal

The Commission's final decision can be appealed within fifteen business days of being notified, by defendants and third parties with a legitimate interest. The Competition Direction may appeal the decision that declares the investigated parties as not responsible, as well as the imposed fine.

The appeal shall be granted by the Commission without suspensory effects unless the Commission states otherwise. No reconsideration is allowed against the acts and decisions issued by the Competition Direction or the Commission.

The motion to appeal shall be decided with a term of 120 business days. The tribunal decision shall be notified to the parties involved in the procedure and to third parties incorporated as parties in the procedure. The tribunal is not allowed to increase sanctions imposed by the Commission.

4. Available in English at: https://bit.ly/3dsup6u.

[G] Precedent Cases

INDECOPI's Organization and Functions Act grants the Tribunal with the power to set binding precedents, which are to be mandatory followed by the Commission. They are not binding though to OSIPTEL or the judiciary. It is important to consider that even without an express precedent; the Competition Commission tends to follow INDECOPI Tribunal's criteria.

Since the enactment of the Peruvian Competition Law, the tribunal has set two precedents in competition law matters, one related to vertical agreements and the other regarding the scope of application of the law. The tribunal also set a precedent on the revision of conditions imposed under the previous merger control law applicable only to the electricity sector, Law N° 26876, Electricity Sector Antimonopoly and Oligopoly Law. As this regime is no longer active since the entry into force of Law N° 31112, the new merger control law applicable to all the sectors, this precedent case is ineffective.

– Group Multipurpose S.R.L. and DISPRA E.I.R.L. against QUIMPAC S.A. and CLOROX DEL PERU S.A.

Resolution N° 0068-2009/SC1-INDECOPI[5] of February 24, 2009 of INDECOPI's Tribunal approved the following binding precedent (*"Precedente de Observancia Obligatoria"*) regarding vertical collusive practices.

Article 12 of the Peruvian Competition Law states that vertical collusive practices have "the object or effect of restricting, preventing or distorting competition." The tribunal interpreted that when such article refers to vertical collusive practices that "have the object or effect" to restrict competition two situations must be differentiated:

(i) Vertical collusive practices that have an identified anti-competitive purpose, directly derived from the terms and conditions of the vertical agreement involved, and that have the potential to cause a particular harmful result on competition and consumer welfare, which are referred to in the law when it states that vertical collusive practices that "have the object" to restrict competition are prohibited. The tribunal clarified that the "object" element should not be considered as the intention or subjective purpose of the parties.

(ii) Vertical collusive practices that, without having an identified anticompetitive purpose derived from an agreement, can generate negative effects on competition and consumer welfare, which are referred to in the law when it states that vertical collusive practices that "have the effect" to restrict competition are prohibited.

Given that according to the Peruvian Competition Law vertical collusive practices with the object or effect to restrain competition are subject to the rule of reason, the tribunal established that the analysis of the conduct in both previously mentioned situations should consider the following methodology:

5. Resolution N° 0068-2009/SC1-INDECOPI available in Spanish at: https://bit.ly/3iKQnFe.

- Establish if any of the parties involved holds a dominant position in the relevant market.
- Establish the existence of a vertical collusive practice.
- Balance the anticompetitive objectives of the practice versus the related efficiencies.
- If the anticompetitive objectives of the practice are greater than the related efficiencies, it shall be determined if the vertical collusive practice had a negative result or the potentiality to cause a particular harmful result on competition and consumer welfare. If such real or potential effects do not exist, the vertical collusive practice shall not be considered as an infringement, even if it was designed with the object to restrict competition.

– Ex officio case against Salaverry Port Dockers trade union, and others

Resolution N° 0479-2014/SCD-INDECOPI[6] of November 1, 2014, of INDECOPI's Tribunal approved the following binding precedent regarding the scope of application of the Peruvian Competition Law.

Article 3 of the Peruvian Competition Law provides that "conducts that are consequence of a law" are out of its scope. In this precedent, the tribunal interpreted that this provision requires the existence of a law authorizing a conduct or a legal obligation to execute the conduct.

The tribunal determined that the interpretation of such legal provision must be conducted on a literal or restrictive basis, so that the authority may consider a conduct exempted from the antitrust regime only when such exclusion is expressly derived from a law. For these purposes, the tribunal established a three-step analysis to assess potential exemptions to the application of the Peruvian Competition Law:

(i) Analyze, under a restrictive interpretation, whether a certain legal norm authorizes a certain conduct or not.

(ii) If the conduct is authorized, the competition authority shall not sanction it, regardless of its anticompetitive effects. If, however, a law authorizes a certain conduct but there are reasonable grounds to believe such authorization is being exercised in an unreasonable manner, the competition authority shall inform of such behavior to the competent authority in charge of enforcing such law.

(iii) If a conduct is not expressly authorized by a law, then the competition authority shall analyze it considering the criteria and applicable precedents under Peruvian Competition Law.

6. Resolution N° 0479-2014/SDC-INDECOPI available in Spanish at: https://bit.ly/3m5eJLI.

§18.03 UNILATERAL CONDUCT

[A] Relevant Legislation

Conducts classified by Article 10 of the Peruvian Competition Law as an "abuse of dominance" are the following:

- Refusal to deal.
- Discrimination.
- Tying.
- Predation.
- Abuse of legal procedures or *sham litigation*.
- Other conducts with an equivalent effect.

According to the Peruvian Competition Law, these practices shall be assessed under the "rule of reason" standard (relative prohibition in the terms of the law). Under this standard, the competition agency needs to prove that the practice has a restrictive effect on competition and negative effects on consumer welfare.

[B] Assessment of Dominance

[1] Relevant Market

The definition of relevant market is a key element to determine a firm has a dominant position in a given market. According to Article 6 of the Peruvian Competition Law, the relevant market must be defined comprising the relevant product or services market, as well as the relevant geographical market.

The identification of the relevant product market aims to establish which set of products are suitable substitutes to each other. The relevant geographical market can be defined as the area that includes all the commercial suppliers or commercial locals that consumers consider substitutes of the commercial supplier or commercial local analysed.

Therefore, the key in determining the relevant market is substitution. Such substitution can be derived from two dimensions: (i) the substitution on the demand side, and (ii) the substitution on the supply side. Particularly, to determine the relevant market, the competition agency shall look for the evidence and data that demonstrate how consumers react to a change in the price of products (substitution by the demand's side).

[2] Market Power/Dominant Position

Once the relevant competitors are recognized in a previously defined relevant market, it is possible to determine the market share of an agent. Usually in Peru, sales are the main variable used to estimate market shares, even if sometimes companies with a large presence on the market do not have market power, or vice versa. Factors such as a high elasticity of demand or low barriers to entry to the market hinder the market power of any company. Also, a market with few substitutes, legal barriers, or high capital requirements will boost and reinforce the dominant position of a company with high market share.

INDECOPI often uses the Herfindahl-Hirschman index (HHI). This indicator shows the market concentration, which helps determine whether a company has the capacity to alter prices or not.

[C] Abuse of Dominant Position

Peruvian Constitution states in Article 61 that: "The State facilitates and oversees competition. It fights any practice that would limit it and the abuse of dominant or monopolistic positions. No law or arrangement may authorize or establish monopolies". Therefore, holding a dominant position is not prohibited in Peru.

The use of market power can be understood in two ways, depending on the circumstances. The first is the use of the efficiencies derived from economies of scale. The second is that size gives the possibility of obtaining illicit benefits that could not have been obtained other way.

An *"illegal abuse of dominance"* must be understood as the use of dominant power to cause exclusionary effects. Damages derived from a free and fair competition through price, quality, and condition commercialization cannot be sanctioned.

Therefore, under Peruvian Competition Law, a conduct will be sanctioned ex post only if it has exclusionary effects. The abuse of dominance with exploitative effects is not considered illegal in Peru, because it does not affect the structure of the market, is not meant to reinforce the market power of the dominant, and does not set in disadvantage to other competitors since this behaviour usually causes the entry of new competitors attracted by the profits of the dominant.

[D] Exclusionary Practices Typified in the Peruvian Competition Law

[1] Predation

When price predation occurs, the predator first sells its products or services at a loss to exclude its competitors from the market, and then raises its prices above competitive levels to recoup in excess the initial loss. Three conditions make predatory pricing viable: (i) the undertaking should have a dominant position, (ii) entry costs to the market should be high, and (iii) the predator must be able to recoup losses and generate effective profits in a short term. However, an undertaking's dominant position could also exist in a different market. For example, if a company with dominant position in Arequipa's market uses its monopolistic profits in that market to subsidize its entry to Lima's market.

Predatory practices are considered to be typified in the open clause regulated in subparagraph h) of Article 10.2 of the Peruvian Competition Law.

[2] *Discrimination*

Price discrimination[7] can be defined, as a situation in which units of a same good or service are commercialized by a company with dominant position at different prices,[8] which means: a same good is sold at different prices. That difference can be determined comparing the price of the good or service regarding different consumers or in operations made by the same supplier.[9]

In general, it is considered that price discrimination can generate a negative effect to competition when it is used as a mechanism to exclude from the market other competitors or to prevent the access of new competitors to the market. That could occur, for example, in some cases, if a company with a dominant position grants "special prices" only to its clients who also buy to its competitor. Furthermore, the Peruvian Competition Law determines that discrimination should place certain competitors in disadvantage towards others.

Discrimination is regulated by the Peruvian Competition Law on Article 10.2.b):

> 10.2. The abuse of dominant position in the market may consist of conducts with exclusionary effects such as:
>
> b) To apply, in business relations or services, different conditions for equivalent services positioning, without justification, certain competitors in an unfavorable condition with respect to others. There is no abuse of dominant position in case of granting discounts or bonuses usually used and accepted in business practices, which may be given or granted due to compensatory and specific circumstances, such as pre-paid, volume or others usually given, under equal terms.[10]

7. The price discrimination is one of many practices of establishment of non-uniformed prices, as well as the tariff in two parts, the establishment of discounts per quantities, tied sakes and the discrimination per quality.
8. Units that are physically equal can be considered as different goods according to their different costs of production, when commercialized in different markets. This way, the sale of equal goods at different prices is not a case of price discrimination unless those goods are produces at identical costs.
9. There are three types of price discrimination. In first place, the first-degree or perfect discrimination takes place when the company can charge a different price to each consumer according to what he is willing to pay for the good. It has by purpose the extraction of all the surplus of the consumer. On the other hand, the second-degree discrimination is characterized by the non-intention of adjusting the prices to the elasticity of the consumers' demands, as the prices structure is the same for all of them. Last, the third-degree decimation differs from the case before as the company cannot identify the will of pay of each consumer, and due to that, it discriminate prices between consumers of totally independent groups or markets. The company can identify the elasticity of the demands on the different groups or markets and adjust the price according to that, charging a lower price to consumers whose demand is most sensible.
10. The existence of differences in the level of the demand has been considered in previous INDECOPI resolutions as sufficient justification for the establishment of a differentiated commercial treatment. For example, Resolution No. 001-98-INDECOPI-CLC from the January 9, 1998, the proceeding followed between the National Industry Society against the Company "Minera del Centro del Perú S.A.", established the following: "*3.5. The Commission considers that from a legal point of view, the geographical price differentiation does not result to be punishable by it, as the price differentiation existent could be justified by the existence of differentiated costs – transaction or transportation costs for example-, or for being about*

[3] Tying

In a tied sale, a seller of various products who has a dominant position in the market in the supply of any of them, establishes that the clients will only be able to buy that particular product (the one that enjoys of the dominant position) if they accept to buy a product of a different type (over this second product, the supplier does not have a dominant position). An essential element in the definition of this conduct is the pressure applied over the buyer so that he or she acquires all the products supplied by the seller.

The sanction imposed to this type of behaviours has its origin in the possibility that companies have to appeal to this type of activities with the only intention of extending their market power over a particular market (of the dominant product) to another one (of the tied product) and eventually exclude of that market the existing competitors.

Usually, tying is a normal and legitimate practice that generates benefits to the market and consumers. Therefore, there are circumstances in which tied sales may have positive effects on competition, generating positive consequences such as: (a) Efficiency increase: Tied sales can generate efficiency, as they reduce transaction costs for consumers. (b) Assure quality: Tied sales assure quality and the optimum functioning of the sold product.

Tied sales are regulated in Article 10.2.c) of the Peruvian Competition Law which establishes that:

---

operations made in different markets, in which the consumers count with a different elasticity in the demand, that would reflect a different degree of substitution of the good or the access to supplying sources."

Similarly, in Resolution No. 007-1999/TDC-INDECOPI emitted by the Courtroom in the proceeding followed by the Newspaper *El Comercio* against Aero Continente for abuse of dominant position in the way of price discrimination, the following was said: *"When a situation of restriction in the offer of the service takes place, the conditions of the market described before determine that those companies that require to hire air freight and cargo service of immediate nature, must be able to pay a high price for this kind of service. This higher price reflects the cost of excluding every other types of cargo that compete to access the air transportation service. This occurs in the case of the service of diaries and magazine distributions. The companies that distribute this type of products are willing to pay more for the transport in the morning flights that the price that those companies that send other type of cargo are willing to pay (including the case of perishing goods such as shellfishes). This explains why the raise of prices affects more the cargo transport of diaries and magazines. In consequence, the Tribunal considers that the differentiation of tariffs questioned by El Comercio is explained because Aero Continente has identified a special nature services demand, constituted by the air freight and cargo of diaries and magazines. That demand requires handling merchandises daily and immediately, in the first morning flights. This way, given the particular conditions of the service required, the accused has established a special tariff for the transportation of diaries and magazines that the Courtroom considers justified. This way, according to the criteria exposed in point III.2 of the present resolution, if reasonable explanations for the differentiated prices policy established by a company exist and if, on the other hand, from the analysis of the facts, the aim of restricting competition is not appreciated, the practice should be considered licit. It must be taken in count that, if not, the application of the regulations contained in Legislative Decree No. 701 would conduct to a system veiled of price control that finally, would produce a bigger distortion in the resources assignment in the market."*

> 10.2 The abuse of dominant position in the market may consist of conducts with exclusionary effects such as:
>
> (...)
>
> c) Subordinating the celebration of contracts to the acceptance of additional provisions that, by their nature or commercial use, are not related to the aim of such contracts.

[4] *Refusal to Deal*

Refusal to deal is, in principle, a legal conduct. It is an inherent part of every person's free will and freedom to contract. However, a company with dominant position is subject to certain specific obligations, as is the case of not refusing, without objective reason, to deal with a provider (in case of monopsony) or with a client (in case of a monopoly). The refusal does not necessarily have to be explicit and clear. Any behavior that has the effect of not satisfying the request or the systematic delay of its attention could be categorized under this heading.

The Peruvian Competition Law recognizes this practice as an abuse of dominance under the relative prohibition standard in letter a) of Article 10.2: "To deny to supply or accept offers, of products or services, without justification."

According to the Peruvian Competition Law and INDECOPI's caselaw, a refusal to deal will be considered as an anticompetitive practice and therefore unlawful, when these four elements are proven:

- The undertaking that refuses to deal has a dominant position on the relevant market.
- A refusal to deal has taken place, through the undertakings actions (communications) or elusive responses.
- The refusal to deal is not justified by an objective and reasonable justification.
- The refusal to deal has an exclusionary effect on competition.

[5] *Abuse of Legal Procedures or Sham Litigation*

As it is known, incumbents can find it attractive or convenient to avoid or delay the entrance of new competitors to the market, opposing to the granting of permits or certifications required to initiate operations in the market. In addition, they can also find it useful to legally question the validity of the permits or authorizations granted to competitors.

The elements that characterize *Sham Litigation* as an abuse of dominant position are: (i) the repeated use of legal actions against competitors, and (ii) the abusive use of such actions. Being this the last and most difficult element to identify, it has been considered that it is configured if two conditions are met. First, the absence of an objective basis for a reasonable triumph of the legal actions initiated; and, second, it must be identified if the procedural activity tries to affect the correct functioning of the market, through multiple legal actions.

Sham Litigation is described as an infringement in Article 10.2.f) of the Peruvian Competition Law under the following terms:

> 10.2 The abuse of dominant position in the market may consist of conducts with exclusionary effects such as:
>
> (...)
>
> f) To abuse and reiterate legal or administrative procedures, whose effect is to restrict the competition.
>
> (...)

[E] Investigation

[1] Initiative

According to the Peruvian Competition Law, the Competition Direction is the technical autonomous body that acts as prosecutor and is in charge of investigations, initiated ex officio or after claims. The Competition Direction is also in charge of handling the administrative procedures before the Competition Commission, and to issue technical opinions regarding the existence of alleged anticompetitive conducts.

Investigations can be initiated ex officio or on the basis of complaints from competitors. The Competition Direction decides as to whether or not to initiate an investigation or admit the complaint.

The infringement procedure may be initiated when the reported conduct is being performed, when there is a threat of it and even when its effects have already stopped. Any decision to not initiate an investigation cannot be appealed administratively by the complainant.

[2] Powers

According to the Peruvian Competition Law, the Competition Direction has the power to conduct dawn raids, with or without prior notification, at the premises of the natural or legal person, business associations and autonomous properties, and examine books, records, documents and goods, being entitled to check on the development of the production processes and take the statement of the persons found at the premise. During the dawn raid, the authority can take copies of physical files, magnetic or electronic, as well as any document that is deemed relevant or taking photographs or filming as may be necessary.

Moreover, the Competition Direction has the power to summon and question any officer or official representative of any legal person or entity, without any previous judicial authorization.

[3] The Procedure

After the preliminary investigation, the Competition Direction can decide to start an administrative sanctioning procedure with an indictment or close the investigation without charges. Claimants can appeal such decision to the tribunal within fifteen business days.

The Competition Direction will issue a decision starting the administrative procedure if it considers there are sufficient grounds to believe an anticompetitive practice has been carried out. In its indictment, the Competition Direction shall identify the alleged individuals or companies who incurred in the anticompetitive conduct, including an explanation of the facts that sustain the indictment, and the characterization of the alleged infringement to the Peruvian Competition Law.

The indictment shall be notified to the Commission, claimants, and defendants within a period of no more than five business days. Defendants will be given a period of thirty business days to present their defense. The Competition Direction's decision to initiate an administrative sanctioning procedure with its indictment can be appealed.

Once the procedure has been initiated, the trial period cannot exceed seven months from the deadline to answer the charges. The Competition Direction may act or the parties may offer the following forms of evidence: (a) documents, (b) party's statements, (c) testimonies, (d) dawn raids, (e) experts reports, or (f) other evidence deemed to be necessary to clarify the facts alleged or charged.

The Competition Direction has thirty business days after the trial period to issue the technical report that contains its analysis and conclusions about the alleged infringement. The technical report should analyse the evidence presented by all parties involved, determine the existence or absence of an administrative infringement, the identification of those responsible and propose fines and remedies.

If no evidence of the existence of anticompetitive practices is found by the Competition Direction, the technical report shall conclude the nonexistence of the administrative infringement. Parties will have fifteen business days to make allegations and request a hearing with the Commission.

The Commission may grant the hearing requested if considered necessary to gather further evidence or proof needed to reach its final decision. The parties may present final allegations within the next ten business days after the hearing has been carried out. No additional evidence can be filled after the final allegations.

The Commission's final decision must be issued within thirty business days from the deadline that the parties have to present their final allegations. Such decision will be notified to the parties within ten business days.

[4] Sanctions and Remedies

Anticompetitive conducts are subject to a monetary fine, which will be defined according to the severity of the infringement, with the following fines:

- In case of a minor violation, the fine shall be up to 500 UIT[11] (approx. USD 544,200) provided that such fine does not exceed 8% of the sales or gross income earned by the offender, or its economic group, with regard to all its economic activities during the fiscal year immediately preceding the issuance of the decision of the Commission;
- In case of a major violation, the fine shall be up to 1,000 UIT (approx. USD 1.08 million) provided that such fine does not exceed 10% of the sales or gross income earned by the offender, or its economic group, with regard to all its economic activities during the fiscal year immediately preceding the issuance of the decision of the Commission; or,
- In case of a serious violation, the fine shall be higher than 1,000 UIT, provided that such fine does not exceed 12% of the sales or gross income earned by the offender, or its economic group, with regard to all its economic activities during the fiscal year immediately preceding the issuance of the decision of the Commission.

In case of professional or business associations, or economic agents who have started their operations after January 1st of the preceding fiscal year, the fine shall not exceed, in any case, 1,000 UIT (approx. USD 1.08 million). Also, a fine of up to 100 UIT (approx. USD 108,000) could be applied to the legal representatives or individuals of the corporate bodies of the responsible corporations, irregular companies, business associations, autonomous equities, or trusts involved in the infringement.

In addition to the fine, the Peruvian Competition Law establishes that the Commission has the power to impose remedies to restore competition or prevent anticompetitive conducts, such as orders to cease a conduct, the obligation to contract under specific conditions, the unenforceability of anticompetitive clauses or provisions, among others.

[5] Appeal to the Competition Tribunal

The Commission's final decision can be appealed within fifteen business days of being notified, by defendants and third parties with a legitimate interest. The Competition Direction may appeal the decision that declares the investigated parties as not responsible, as well as the imposed fine.

The appeal shall be granted by the Commission without suspensory effects, unless the Commission states otherwise. No reconsideration is allowed against the acts and decisions issued by the Competition Direction or the Commission.

The motion to appeal shall be decided with a term of 120 business days. The tribunal decision shall be notified to the parties involved in the procedure and to third parties incorporated as parties in the procedure. The tribunal is not allowed to increase sanctions imposed by the Commission.

11. Taxing Reference Unit, established for 2021 at S/ 4,400.00 or USD 1,088.51 as of November 2021, approximately.

[F] Precedent Cases

There are no binding precedent cases under the Peruvian Competition Law in the matter of abuse of dominance.

§18.04 MERGER REVIEW

[A] Relevant Legislation and Authorities

From 1997 to 2021, Peru had a merger control regime applicable only to the electricity sector, which was governed by Law N° 26876—Electricity Sector Antimonopoly and Oligopoly Law and its Regulations approved by Supreme Decree N° 017-98-ITINCI. These regulations established that any merger or concentration procedure conducted in the electricity market (power transmission, generation, and distribution) required the prior approval from INDECOPI as the competition authority. Roughly twenty transactions were notified and assessed during the effectiveness of this law, with only three of them being approved with conditions and none denied.

On January 7, 2021, Law N° 31112, a new merger control applicable to all the sectors of the economy was enacted. This law, along with its Regulations, approved by Supreme Decree 039-2021-PCM, its Threshold Calculation Guidelines, and Notification Forms, entered into force on June 14, 2021, thus repealing Law N° 26876, and subjecting all the concentration operations meeting the jurisdictional thresholds and having effects in Peru to the prior authorization of INDECOPI.

[B] Triggering Events and Thresholds

According to Article 6 of Law N° 31112, transactions that involve a transfer or change in the control of an economic agent must obtain a prior merger authorization by INDECOPI if they meet or exceed the following jurisdictional thresholds:

(i) The total sum of the value of annual sales or gross income or the value of the assets in the country of the companies involved in the concentration during the fiscal year prior to notification should be equal to or greater than 118,000 UIT, approximately USD 133 million.
(ii) The value of the annual sales or gross income or the value of the assets in the country of at least two of the companies involved in the concentration during the fiscal year prior to notification should be each equal to or greater than 18,000 UIT, approximately USD 20 million.

For these purposes, the Law and its Regulations establish the four kinds of transactions that typically fall within the concept of "concentrations". These are:

(i) Mergers.
(ii) Acquisition of control through purchase of shares or other contractual forms.

(iii) Constitution of joint ventures permanent and full function or associative contracts that give two or more economic agents control over one or more economic agents.
(iv) Acquisition of control over productive assets (operative in the past twelve months) (i) to whom a defined income volume is attributable, (ii) that can reinforce or increase the market share of the acquirer, and (iii) that have generated income during the year prior to notification.

INDECOPI has the power to initiate ex officio investigations and review closed operations falling below the thresholds when they may potentially restrict competition as a result of:

(i) Transactions in concentrated markets.
(ii) Acquisition of competitors with small market participation and growth potential.
(iii) Acquisition of competitors that have recently entered the market.
(iv) Successive acquisition of competitors in the market.
(v) Other operations with similar effects.

Concentrations involving first landing economic agents that had no income in the country during the previous year cannot be reviewed. INDECOPI's power is subject to a time limit of one year from the closing of the operation. INDECOPI may force the sale of the acquired shares/assets, among other remedies as a result of the exercise of its ex officio power to review closed transactions. However, agents are allowed to present a voluntary notification when the thresholds are not met.

[C] Exemptions

Law N° 31112 excludes from its scope of application transactions which do not involve a change of control over an economic agent, such as internal corporate growth, temporary control assumed by an agent as a result of a legal mandate (e.g., in bankruptcy procedures), and the regular activity of financial entities.

[D] Substantive Test for Assessing Mergers

The merger test established in the Law and its Regulations to review mergers intends to determine if the transaction under analysis creates a significant restriction to competition on the involved markets. According to Article 7 of Law N° 31112, the Competition Commission will evaluate the following aspects of the market:

- Market structure;
- Current or potential competition;
- The evolution of supply and demand;
- Distribution or commercialization sources;

- Legal barriers and other kinds of barriers (technological, horizontal, or vertical restrictions) for market entrance;
- The economic and financial power of the involved agents;
- The creation or strengthening of a dominant position;
- The production of economic efficiencies.

For economic efficiencies to be taken into consideration, they must be productive, allocative or innovative efficiencies that meet the following requirements:

- they must be proven by the applicant;
- they must be inherent to the concentration;
- they must be aimed to outweighing identified restrictive effects on competition stemming from the concentration and improving consumer welfare;
- they must be transferable to the consumer; and
- they must be verifiable by the authority.

[E] Notification Procedure and Timetable

Before the beginning of the procedure, the economic agents participating in the concentration can make individual or joint consultations to the Competition Direction. These consultations might be related to the notifiable nature of a given concentration, the concepts to be considered for threshold calculation and other procedural questions.

There are two notification forms which contain the necessary information to be presented for the assessment of the concentration and its possible effects on competition: The Ordinary Notification Form and the Simplified Notification Form.

The Simplified Notification Form contains less burdensome information requirements. Transactions eligible for presenting a simplified notification form comprise (i) non-overlap concentrations, horizontal or vertical, where the economic agents involved in the concentration or their respective economic groups do not carry out economic activities in the same product market and in the same geographic market, or, they do not participate in the same production or value chain; and (ii) operations that involve a change from joint to single control over an economic agent.

Law N°31112 establishes a two-phase review procedure, after which INDECOPI can decide to:

(i) clear the notified transaction;
(ii) clear the concentration subject to remedies proposed by the notifying parties or those imposed to compensate the restrictive effects of the concentration in the market; or
(iii) prohibit the concentration

The first stage is the notification phase: after the submission of the notifying form, the Competition Direction assesses the information filed by the parties to determine whether all the requirements have been met in a period of ten business days. If any of them is missing, a ten-business-day period is granted to the parties for rectification, after which the Competition Direction declares the application admissible or inadmissible within a period of five business days.

Once the notification is admitted, Phase I involves the Competition Commission's evaluation as to whether the concentration falls within the scope of the Law, as well as whether it raises serious competition concerns. This stage lasts a maximum period of thirty business days. At the end of this term, the Competition Commission may alternatively decide to:

(i) Dismiss the authorization request notified because it does not fall within the scope of the Law,
(ii) Clear the concentration, after concluding the notified transaction falls within the scope of the Law and that there is not enough evidence to presume it will have anticompetitive effects on the market, or
(iii) Decide to pursue a Phase II evaluation if serious competition concerns were identified in the Phase I evaluation of the Competition Commission.

If the Commission does not issue a decision within the provided period, the concentration is automatically authorised in application of positive administrative silence.

Phase II lasts a maximum of ninety business days, after the Commission has notified the parties that the transaction has moved on to the next stage of evaluation and the publication of a brief summary of the concentration and its potential risks in order to allow third parties to present relevant information. This period may be extended for an additional period of thirty business days, with due justification by the authority for such extension. This period could also be extended for fifteen additional business days if the parties involved require hearings.

Both in Phase I and Phase II, the Commission is allowed to suspend the course of the period if the parties have proposed commitments in order to analyse them.

After the final decision is issued imposing conditions or prohibiting the concentration, the notifying parties may appeal such decision within fifteen business days of its notification, after which the tribunal has maximum ninety business days to issue a final decision.

[F] Consequences of a Failure to File

According to Article 23 of Law N° 31112, an act of concentration under the scope of the Law for which the participant has not requested and obtained prior authorization from INDECOPI, will have no legal effect whatsoever, and all of the acts derived from the execution of the concentration will be considered void.

The Competition Commission is also allowed to order corrective measures in order to undo the transaction, such as issuing mandates for the sale of the acquired rights or assets.

[G] Third Party Involvement in Notification Process

Under Law N° 31112, third parties with legitimate interest can participate in the procedure, having the right to access to the file of the case, and obtain copies of non-confidential information. Furthermore, they can submit relevant information concerning the concentration without being considered parties to the procedure.

Third parties can request to intervene in the procedure within a term of ten business days after the Commission publishes a summary of the reasons justifying the transition to a Phase II procedure. In the case of the ex officio review, the limit is ten business days from the publication of the Admission Resolution.

The Competition Commission also has the power to request technical information from other public entities, such as regulators, which are obliged to abide.

[H] Remedies and Penalties

Law N° 31112 allows the parties to propose conditions to the authority at any time during the procedure before the final decision is issued. In that sense, the parties can propose commitments to mitigate or reduce potential negative impacts on competition, and the authority can accept them and clear the transaction under those conditions.

Notwithstanding this, INDECOPI maintains the power to subject the concentrations to conditions that it has designed separately if it considers them necessary to mitigate the potential anticompetitive effects of the concentration, without there being any restriction on whether these conditions shall be structural or behavioural.

Failure to notify a concentration operation is sanctionable with a fine of up to 500 UIT (approx. USD 544,200), provided it does not exceed 8% of the sales of the offender or its economic group. The execution of a transaction before obtaining clearance is sanctionable with a fine of up to 1,000 UIT (approx. USD 1.08 million), provided it does not exceed 10% of the sales of the offender or its economic group. Likewise, the execution of a transaction that has been prohibited by INDECOPI is sanctionable with a fine of up to 12% of the sales of the offender or its economic group.

[I] Appeal

The Competition Commission's decision regarding a notified transaction may be appealed to INDECOPI's tribunal. The tribunal will issue its decision within a period of ninety business days.

CHAPTER 19

Competition Law in Uruguay

*Juan Manuel Mercant & Jonathan Clovin**

§19.01 INTRODUCTION

The Uruguayan Constitution contains various scattered articles that in one way or another are related to competition law. Indeed, Articles 7, 10, 32, 36, 50, 53, and 85 n. 17 all somehow relate to competition.

Article 7 of the Constitution establishes that: "[t]he inhabitants of the Republic have the right to be protected in the enjoyment of their life, honor, **liberty**, security, **work** and **property**. No one can be deprived of these rights except in accordance with the laws that are *established for reasons of general interest*" (our emphasis). This constitutional provision establishes, among others, three fundamental rights of the rule of law that are also key for competition: the right to freedom, the right to work, and the right to property.

Right to freedom. In addition to being enshrined in Article 7 of the Constitution, it is reiterated in Article 10, which reads: "[t]he private actions of people who in no way attack public order or harm a third party, are exempt from the authority of the magistrates. No inhabitant of the Republic will be forced to do what the law does not mandate, or impeded to do what it does not prohibit." That is, the principle of freedom governs, and is limited only by public order, the rights of other third parties and the laws. As far as competition law is concerned, it is important to zoom in one of the many manifestations of the right to freedom, which is "freedom of business". According to Carlos López Rodríguez, following Font Galan, freedom of business is made up of three

* The authors would like to acknowledge the work of Javier Napoleone who co-authored the previous edition of this chapter with Juan Manuel Mercant and whose excellent work served as a basis for this updated edition.

basic dimensions: (i) freedom of access to the market, (ii) freedom of business decision, and (iii) freedom of cessation of business in the market.[1]

Freedom of access to the market implies the inexistence of legal or commercial barriers to enter or access a market in such a way that anyone can begin to carry out (legal) business activity in the economic sector of their choice.

Freedom of business decision is essentially linked to the previous one, since it implies the free choice of the sector and type of activity to be carried out. It implies autonomy in the management of the company and its activity.

The freedom of cessation would be the opposite of the freedom of access to the market and implies that people are free to cease their activity without external restrictions.

Right to property. The right to property is enshrined in the aforementioned Article 7 and also especially in Article 32 of the Constitution, which states: "Property is an inviolable right, but subject to the provisions of the laws that are established for reasons of general interest. No one may be deprived of their right to property except in cases of public necessity or utility established by law and always after receiving fair and prior compensation from the National Treasury. When the expropriation is declared due to public necessity or utility, the owners will be compensated for the damages they suffer due to the duration of the expropriation procedure, whether or not the expropriation is consumed; even those that derive from variations in the value of the currency."

Right to work. In addition to being enshrined in Article 7 of the Constitution, it is reiterated especially in Articles 36, 50, and 53. Article 36 provides: "Any person can engage in work, cultivation, industry, commerce, profession or any other lawful activity, except for the general interest limitations established by law." As anticipated, this article not only reiterates the right to work, but is closely related to the freedom of business decision, which only yields to limitations imposed by the general interest and included in a law.

Article 50 establishes: "The State will guide the Republic's foreign trade, protecting productive activities whose destination is export or that replace imported goods. The law will promote investments for this purpose, and will preferably channel public savings for this purpose. Every trustified commercial or industrial organization will be under the control of the State. Likewise, the State will promote decentralization policies, in order to promote regional development and general well-being."

Finally, in relation to labor law and the constitution, Article 53 provides: "Work is under the special protection of the law. Every inhabitant of the Republic, without prejudice to their freedom, has the duty to apply their intellectual or physical energies in a way that benefits the community, which will strive to offer, in preference to citizens, the possibility of earning their livelihood through the development of an economic activity."

As should be clear from reading the aforementioned articles, the constitutional rights to freedom, property, and work are not absolute, but rather they yield to those

1. LÓPEZ RODRÍGUEZ, Carlos E. Defensa de la Competencia, La Ley Uruguay.

laws that are established for reasons of general interest and public order. These concepts are flexible or indeterminate in content, and they are defined from time to time according to the evolution of society over time. In this sense, the Supreme Court of Justice, in its Judgment No. 525/2000 established: "It is important to indicate that the guidelines that define the general interest are not rigid or unalterable, but that they vary with the evolution of each environment and each era. Hence, the legislative solutions do not coincide, and what matters, ultimately, is that the new provisions consult the general interest at the time they are being issued, adjusting to the existing political, economic and social conditions..."[2]

Broadly speaking, and following Carlos E. López Rodríguez, the general interest is the opposite concept to that of individual interest and requires, as its name indicates, the character of generality: interest that responds to that of all or the generality of the inhabitants of the Republic.[3] On the other hand, the concept of "public order" refers to the normal functioning of society and its institutions. In this sense, the Supreme Court of Justice has affirmed in relation to the concept of public order, that "public order means the consecration of norms in favor of the indispensable preservation of the organization of social life."[4]

Likewise, Couture in his *Vocabulary* defines public order as the "set of assessments of a political, social, economic or moral nature, typical of a given community, at a given historical moment, which form the basis of its positive laws and which it tends to protect."[5]

Another provision of the constitution that should be mentioned is Article 85 n. 17, which gives the legislature the ability to "grant monopolies, requiring two-thirds of the votes of the total members of each Chamber. To institute them in favor of the State or the Local Governments, an absolute majority of votes of the total number of members of each Chamber will be required." Such is the power granted to the legislature to approve the granting of monopolies, eliminating competition in a given market. In line with the provisions of the articles referred to earlier, and the constitutional principles of freedom, property, and work, these monopolies could only be considered valid to the extent that they are granted for reasons of general interest or public order. That is, they are meant to be the exception, not the rule.

As of today there are various state monopolies, such as that of water supply in favor of *Obras Sanitarias del Estado* ("OSE"), that of land-based telecommunications in favor of *Administración Nacional de Telecomunicaciones* ("ANTEL"), and that of electric transmission and distribution of energy in favor of the *Administración Nacional de Usinas y Transmisiones Eléctricas* ("UTE"), among others.

The constitution points to a general principle that all markets will be governed by free competition, except in exceptional cases, when the conditions of Article 85 n. 17

2. Supreme Court of Justice, Judgment No. 525/2000 dated 12/20/2000. Available at: http://bjn.poderjudicial.gub.uy/BJNPUBLICA/hojaInsumo2.seam?cid=12705
3. López Rodríguez, Carlos E. Defensa de la Competencia, La Ley Uruguay.
4. Supreme Court of Justice, Judgment No. 148/2007.
5. Couture, Eduardo. Ed. Depalma, Buenos Aires, 1976, p. 437.

are met, and that by express will of the legislative power the monopolistic economic organization is chosen for a particular market.

However, such theoretical freedom of trade lacked an important practical element in order to achieve it, until relatively recently.

Competition law constitutes a novelty in Uruguayan legislative history. It is an area of the law that two decades ago (considering that the first competition law was enacted back in 2000) was not considered by Uruguayan practitioners, most of whom were not even aware of its existence. This was even truer for the real subjects of competition law: Uruguayan companies.

Before the entry into force of the Law on the Promotion and Defence of Competition No. 18,159 in 2007, there were already different isolated regulations on the matter of competition.

Budget Law No. 16,736 of January 5, 2000 for the period 1995–1999. The first legal provision that specifically dealt with antitrust issues was Article 699 of the Budget Law for the period 1996–2000, which established that: "[t]he Office of Planning and Budget is committed to reviewing all regulations and legal and administrative restrictions to competition between individuals that limit the supply of goods and services. The Executive Power will establish by decree the opportunity in which the cessation of each administrative restriction will begin to take effect, reporting to the Legislative Power. The Executive Power will propose, within the year of validity of this law, the pertinent modifications to each legal restriction." This was a rule that imposed tasks, but it was not directly applicable, that is, the prior activity of the Office of Planning and Budget was necessary, as well as a reaction from the executive power.

Urgency Law No. 17.243 of July 14, 2000. In the middle of the following year, the Urgency Law was approved which expressly alluded to "competition rules" and prohibited collusive agreements and practices. Unlike the timid progress of the Budget Law mentioned above, this regulation established operative norms that included specific prohibitions:

Article 13: "*Companies that carry out economic activities*, whatever their legal nature, *are subject to the rules of competition*, without prejudice to the limitations established by law and for reasons of general interest (Articles 7 and 36 of the Constitution of the Republic) or that result from the public service nature of the activity in question". While making reference to the "*rules of competition*", it does not clarify what these would be. Likewise, it is interesting to note the subjective scope of this rule, which referred exclusively to "*companies*" that "*carry out economic activities.*" The concept of "*company*" is not entirely clear in Uruguayan law, although in general it can be identified as the conjunction of capital and organized labor. The rule was careful not to identify this concept with no reference to any of the other existing legal concepts (e.g., commercial or civil, among others, companies), but it was doubtful whether the rule was applicable to individual natural persons. The precedent for this rule can be found in Decision No. 21/94 of the Council of the Southern Common Market or MERCOSUR. On the other hand, once again the limit already anticipated in the constitution with respect to laws that would be passed in the "general interest" was reiterated.

Article 14: "Agreements and concerted practices between economic agents, decisions of business associations and the abuse of the dominant position of one or more economic agents that have the effect of preventing, restricting or distorting competition and free access to the market for the production, processing, distribution and marketing of goods and services are prohibited, such as:

A) Impose permanently, directly or indirectly, purchase or sale prices or other transaction conditions in an abusive way for consumers;
B) Restrict, unjustifiably, the production, distribution and technological development, to the detriment of companies or consumers;
C) Unjustifiably apply unequal conditions to third parties in the case of equivalent benefits, thus placing them at a significant disadvantage against the competition;
D) Subordinate the conclusion of contracts to the acceptance of complementary or supplementary obligations that, by their very nature or due to commercial customs, are not related to the object of those contracts, to the detriment of consumers;
E) In a systematic way, sell goods or provide services at a price lower than cost, without reasons based on commercial uses, in breach of tax or commercial obligations;

The application of these rules proceeds when the distortion in the market generates significant damage to the general interest".

The above article is the immediate precedent for Articles 2 and 4 of our current competition law, Law No. 18,159, which is discussed in depth further in this chapter. Our legislator had thus initially spoken in favor of a generally applicable "*rule of reason*", over its alternative known as " *per se* rule" (that is at least until the 2019 reform, when the "per se" rule for certain hard-core cartel practices was finally introduced). In other words, for a conduct to be prohibited under this rule, it must have the *effect* of preventing, restricting, or distorting competition. This meant that any of the behaviors enumerated in the article could be prohibited, but only in so far as it had the aforementioned effect on competition. This principle is maintained in the current wording, and it is contemplated in Article 2 of Law No. 18,159 as a general rule.

In addition to the above, the article under analysis introduced strict conditions of applicability of the rule: that the effect (in addition to preventing, restricting, or distorting competition) had to distort the market in such a way as to generate a relevant damage to the general interest. It seemed that the legislative intent was to protect the aggregate welfare of society as a whole (as opposed to protecting consumer welfare as is the objective of most antitrust systems worldwide, and as it would come to be in Uruguay too a few years later). This had very significant implications when it came to test whether a practice was prohibited or not since it had to overcome several tests: (i) verify the existence of (a) a concerted practice, (b) decisions by associations of undertakings, or (c) abuse of dominant position; and (ii) verify that it had the *effect* of preventing, restricting, or distorting competition; and (iii) show that the distorting effect in the market was of such magnitude that it generated a significant detriment to the interest general. The required standard, in particular to meet the third prong of the test, was extremely high.

Article 15: "The Executive Power shall regulate the provisions of this Chapter and shall provide the pertinent measures for the application of said provisions. Any dispute that arises that refers to the matter regulated in this Chapter may be submitted by the parties to arbitration, in accordance with the provisions of Title VIII of Book II of the General Code of Procedure (Law No. 15,982, of October 18, 1988). The regulations will promote the qualification of specialized centers for this purpose." Arbitration was thus imposed as a dispute resolution method, without clarifying whether it was applicable in the private sphere or between private agents and the enforcement body (which was yet to be created). The executive power finally regulated these provisions by issuing Decree No. 86/001, to which we refer below.

Budget Law No. 17.296 of February 23, 2001. Articles 157 and 158 of Law No. 17,296 established sanctions for non-compliance with the provisions of Law No. 17,243 and created powers of the enforcement body. The sanctions included, in ascending order: a warning, a warning with publication, and a fine from 500 UR to 20,000 UR, which could be applied jointly or independently, depending on the circumstances of the case and in view of the seriousness of the offense. A cessation of prohibited practices could also be ordered. Likewise, it was established that the criteria to be considered for the purpose of determining the seriousness of the infringement were the damage caused, the modality and scope of the restriction of competition, the participation of the infringer in the market, the duration of the prohibited practice, and any recidivism or antecedents of the offender.

Decree No. 86/001. Decree No. 86/001 dated March 20, 2001 regulated the provisions of Law Nos. 17,243 and 17,296. It appointed the general directorate of commerce as the enforcement body and established the procedure for action in complaints made ex officio or at the request of a party.

Law No. 17,566 of September 19, 2003. Article 89 of this law entrusted the telecommunications regulator (URSEC) with the task of preventing anticompetitive behavior and abuse of dominant position in its regulated markets, without prejudice to the provisions in force in the matter of public services and legally established monopolies.

General considerations on the regulations prior to Law No. 18,159. Although the aforementioned norms meant progress in national legislation in relation to competition, they did not cover all the aspects that needed to be addressed in order for a competition law system to function. For example, they lacked a fundamental pillar of competition law such as the control of economic concentrations. Furthermore, the regulations, in addition to being scarce, contained aspects that fundamentally undermined its prospects of ever be implemented. In this sense, for example, the condition established in the final paragraph of the prohibition provided for in Article 14 of Law No. 17,243 made its application practically impossible, since in addition to imposing a double condition (rule of reason and relevant damage to the general interest), it did not provide any definition of "relevant damage" to the "general interest". The foregoing can probably be justified in the fact that the rules were included in emergency and budget laws, when in reality, a systematic rule is required that contains a precise, specific, and all-encompassing norm on the matter (later enshrined in Law No. 18,159). Finally, the previous regulations entrusted the tasks of control and application of the antitrust provisions to the general directorate of commerce, when it is convenient to have an enforcement body specialized in the matter.

Law No. 18.159. The main pillar upon which competition law in Uruguay has been built is Law No. 18,159 for the Promotion and Defence of Competition (the "*Law*"). Taking into account the shortcomings identified in the previous legislation, and recognizing the need for a systematic policy to collect all relevant aspects of the Law of Competition, after two years of study within the Legislature, Law was enacted on July 20, 2007 and its regulatory Decree No. 404/007, was passed on October 29, 2007 (the "*Decree*"). It set the cornerstones under which the actual competition system has further developed in Uruguay.

The new Law dealt exclusively with competition law, establishing a general system that covers the entire subject. In its first article entitled "Object" it states: "This law is of public order and aims to promote the welfare of current and future consumers and users, through the promotion and defense of competition, the stimulus to efficiency economic and the freedom and equality of conditions of access of companies and products to the markets". The first article of the law contains the fundamental concepts that color Uruguayan competition law indelibly. In this sense, it is established that the law is of public order and aims to "promote the welfare of current and future consumers and users" (thereby definitely curing the previous norms' aggregate welfare standard issue).

From the parliamentary process of the law, it clearly transpires that the most debated issue was that of the control of concentrations. Two opposing positions arise from these debates regarding the need and convenience or not of a prior control system of economic concentrations that would require the prior authorization of the enforcement body. As a result of these debates, the Law ended up opting for a system of ***prior notification*** to the applicator, and only required *prior authorization* when a de facto monopoly was created as result of the concentration. Indeed, under Articles 7 and 9 of the Law in its original version, to the extent that certain acts of economic concentration exceeded the established thresholds, it was sufficient to merely notify the regulator, without the possibility for the enforcement body to oppose or even condition the concentration. Only in cases where the act of economic concentration created a de facto monopoly was it necessary to request prior authorization from the enforcement body. This was partially modified by the reform introduced in 2019, as we see below, and Uruguay now has a pre-merger control fully in force, casting a much wider net.

The international systems regarding the form of structural supervision of the market and the control of economic concentrations are varied, and in our country this issue was much debated prior to the enactment of the Law. There were several legislators who at the time and prior to the enactment of the Law expressed their preference for a prior authorization system (and not just mere communication or notification). For example, in the stenographic version of July 13, 2005, Professor Siegbert Rippe stated: "Regarding the first question, I must say that if I, the Executive

Branch—public authority—**have prior control, I can determine if it is convenient, or not, if it merits, or not, that such a process of business concentration occur**. (...) In this case, I can say that I do not authorize this type of business. Then, the business is not done, the monopoly does not take place and neither does the merger or acquisition of the company take place. Thus, companies will continue to act within a framework of free competition. If I have no prior control, I have a fait accompli. That's the point: the deed is done. My legal system enabled the formation of de facto monopolies because it did not repress them and I cannot sanction a posteriori what I did not prevent, having the opportunity to do so." In the same sense, in the stenographic version of August 10, 2005, Mr. Iván Posada stated: "the issue of prior control is the substantial basis of the project. I believe that if there is no prior control, we are establishing a legislation for the defense of competition and freedom of trade that will not have consequences, if there are companies that have a monopoly or almost monopoly control, and the only thing they need to do under this new proposal is a mere communication, the law will end up being an innocuous and inoperative thing because it will not be able to prevent these situations from occurring."

For his part, and expressing an opinion contrary to those we have just mentioned, the then Secretary of the Ministry of Economy and Finance, in the stenographic version of the same August 10, 2005, said "It is clear that, consistently with what we said before, the project **does not include the prior control of concentrations**. We understand that from the conceptual point of view, economic theory is clear in that the structure of markets does not determine behaviors and does not determine results. The characteristics of the Uruguayan economy and international experience **suggest that prior control can have many costs in terms of efficiency without the benefits of avoiding potentially harmful concentrations**. In any case, if they were harmful, they would be punished by way of conduct. Therefore, we think that the considerations of efficiency, competitiveness and employment should prevail, and then the resources—which are surely going to be scarce—should be concentrated in preventing and punishing the conducts in the incipient stage of this legislation and not in controls of concentrations, with all the problems we've seen. (...) **We consider it inconvenient to have tough legislation with regard to prior control of concentrations.**"

Likewise, José Manuel Quijano, in the session of October 2–5, 2006, established in this regard that "Article 7 has to do with the notification of concentrations and it is discussed whether it should be ex post or ex ante. There are several arguments in favor of both positions. With regard to the notification of concentrations **being ex post**, I am going to mention five arguments that seem central to me: 1°) ex post control facilitates investments instead of discouraging them; 2nd) global legislation goes in that direction; 3°) in Uruguay the markets frequently present high degrees of concentration; 4th) if concentration is reduced by administrative decision, the economic units will deviate from the minimum efficiency scale, and 5th) there is no causal relationship—at least mathematically—in economic theory between market structure and anti-competitive behavior. On the other hand, I believe that some reasons can be put forward in **favor of ex ante control**: 1) ex ante control is used in various legislations without discouraging investment; 2nd) it can be agile and efficient and in all cases it is a control; 3°)

there is no change in global legislation tending to eliminate ex ante control; 4th) ex post control is difficult to carry out because, for example, once the merger has been completed, it is very difficult to disarm it, and 5th) the markets are very different from each other, even in small economies such as Uruguay, both in number of companies, as in degrees of concentration and on an efficient scale."

Another issue addressed in the parliament sessions in relation to the then bill was that of the enforcement body. As the Undersecretary of Economy and Finance indicated in the session of December 21, 2006, the authority systems that exist at the level of Comparative Law are varied: "It is thus that in the different countries we have, from the most extreme case, which is New Zealand—where there are practically no sectorial regulation bodies and everything is subject to a kind of general competition regulator—up to situations in which the sectorial regulation bodies have power even above the enforcement bodies. In other cases various hybrid mechanisms grant cross functions or force coordination as occurs, for example, in England and Germany. In other words, the institutional arrangements in this regard are various. Obviously, to define this, it is necessary to take into account the specificities of the country, what regulated sectors exist, what characteristics, trajectory and experience the regulatory bodies have and how many resources society can allocate to it. Keep in mind that if you have abundant resources it is one thing, but if you have to limit them, you should look for other alternatives. **The option that we propose is that there is an authority of general application of this law in the Commission for the Promotion and Defence of Competition, but in the cases of sectorial regulation bodies that already have among their functions that of promoting competition—the URSEA, URSEC and the Central Bank have the specific rule—today it is interpreted that there is a concurrence of competences.** This means that if someone has a case in the communications sector, they can go to claim both the URSEC and the General Directorate of Commerce. **That creates problems, therefore, we prefer to have a clear definition of who is used in each case.** One of the options would be to remove the logic of promotion from the regulatory bodies and for everything to remain in the orbit of the ministerial body. That is not the option we prefer, but the one that is proposed in the project. **For this option, the protection and promotion of competition, which is already a legal mandate for the sectorial regulation bodies—URSEA, URSEC and Central Bank, for the moment and, in the event that there may be others in the future, it will be made explicit—It also makes the enforcement authorities act in cases where there are problems in the markets they regulate.**"

As a final comment regarding the parliamentary process, in the session of October 25, 2006, Professor Camilo Martínez Blanco listed the strengths of the then bill, today Law No. 18,159:

> In the first place, that it is of *public order* and, as they are mandatory norms, they remove the private negotiation possibilities that may circumvent the law.
>
> Secondly, we talk about *competition as a value*, a subject that will have to be worked more deeply, since building all this is not an easy task ...
>
> Another strong point, *is its universal* scope that is enshrined in Article 3, which are made by both the state and the liberal professions or other agents, including non-profit.

Structure of Law No. 18,159. Here is a brief outline of the structure of the Law:

Chapter I: General provisions

Deals with the fundamental aspects of our law, such as its object (Art. 1), general principles (Art. 2), subjective scope (Art. 3), prohibited practices (Art. 4), relevant market (Art. 5), abuse of dominant position (Art. 6), and notification of concentrations (Arts. 7–9).

Chapter II: Procedure for the Investigation and Punishment of Prohibited Practices

Establishes the competence of the enforcement body (Art. 10), includes procedural provisions on preparatory measures (Art. 11), complaints (Art. 12), preventive termination (Art. 13), evidence (Art. 14), precautionary measures (Art. 15), cessation and conciliation commitments (Art. 16), and sanctions (Arts. 17–20).

Chapter III: Enforcement Body

Establishes the competence of the Commission for the Promotion and Defense of Competition in relation to the application of the provisions of the law in question, functioning as a decentralized body of the Ministry of Economy and Finance. It regulates all aspects of the operation of the enforcement body (integration, term of office, renewals, representation, presidency, dismissal, functions, powers, area of shared competence, among others).

Chapter IV: Final Provisions

The provisions relating to the prescription of actions (Art. 28), reference to the rules of Decree 500/991 (Art. 29), derogations (Art. 30), and regulations (Art. 32) are included.

The structure of the law itself is based on two fundamental pillars, namely: (A) Prohibition of anticompetitive conduct; and (B) Control of economic concentrations. Likewise, the Commission for the Promotion and Defense of Competition is created as the main specialized enforcement body on the matter.

Objectives of Law No. 18.159. The parliamentary process prior to the approval of Law No. 18,159 recognized the existence of the historical debate on the objective and the legal good protected by competition law:

> Historically, there has been a lot of discussion in different places about what the ultimate goal of competition policies is. We said that competition is an instrument—not an end in itself-, which should ultimately aim to improve the well-being of consumers, both current and future. In other words, it is necessary to ensure that there are markets that contribute to the well-being of current consumers, and that also promote healthy investment processes (efficient) from which future consumers will be favored.
>
> There is a lot of confusion about the objective of competition policies because, historically, they may have been used to grant sectorial or regional benefits, or the central objective of consumer welfare may have been confused with having interference in competitive processes between companies (which is more commonly known as 'unfair competition'), with trying to improve positions of some companies compared to others. There may also have been small business promotion aspects. In short, there will be other policies that will surely aim to

> grant benefits, in accordance with the policies followed at the sectorial, regional and small and medium-sized enterprises level, but competition policies are not the ideal ones to have good results in this regard. This is a critical element.
>
> Therefore, *competition policy has a central objective, which is the welfare of* current and future *consumers* and is, ultimately, in addition to complementing openness policies, a form of indirect regulation that the State exercises to control the exercise of power, in particular, of what economists call 'market power'. Basically, this indirect regulation to control the exercise of power occurs in global terms through two groups of policies.[6]

According to the authors, Law No. 18,159 has adopted the correct interpretation of the true protected legal interest, which is stated unambiguously from Article 1 of said law: "(Purpose) This law is of public order and is intended to **promote the well-being of current and future consumers and users**, through the promotion and defense of competition, the stimulation of economic efficiency and the freedom and equality of access conditions for companies and products to the markets."

Confirming this, the Commission for the Promotion and Defense of Competition has taken a clear position on the matter and said that "the objective of the law on the promotion and defense of competition is not to protect the particular interests of competitors, but the rights of consumers through the protection of free competition."[7]

In another resolution, advisers to the Commission for the Promotion and Defense of Competition stated that "the law that regulates the matter that summons us is a law of public order, and it is said law that establishes that all markets will be governed by the principles and rules of free competition (except the limitations established by law for reasons of general interest), and aims to promote the welfare of current and future consumers and users, through the defense of competition, the purpose of this institution not being that of matters related to unfair competition."

In this sense, Representative Alfredo Asti expressed during the parliamentary debates: "... The reason is that they are, obviously, the weakest link in what is a commercial deal. They are the ones who are absolutely dispersed; those with little information; those who have little chance to act when they are harmed." And he continues: "In our understanding it is clear that in this article, the law reaffirms the protection of a primary legal objective: ' the well-being of current and future consumers." And it does so through three tools, placed on the same level of importance: the defense of competition, economic efficiency and equal access to markets."

In Judgment No. 575/2010, the Highest Administrative Court (Tribunal de lo Contencioso Administrativo) clarified the relationship between the objective of the law (the welfare of consumers) and the broader concept of general interest: "That regarding the notion of general interest, the proposal made by the defendant regarding the fact that the central objective of the defense of competition is the welfare of consumers and that the criterion for evaluating the existence of a general interest is that of reasonableness, it is considered to be correct. The Court understands applicable, for these purposes, the concept of general interest developed in a work published by Juan

6. Parliamentary debates held on August 10, 2005. House of Representatives, Undersecretary of Economy and Finance.
7. Resolution 64/013 of the Commission.

Manuel MERCANT in which it is stated that: 'Basically, it intends to indicate that the effects of anti-competitive conduct should be evaluated not in relation to an isolated aspect of the productive system but considering as a whole the consequences of these behaviors on the economic values recognized by the community. Such is the approach of Jorge Otamendi. More specifically, the general economic interest is not the interest of a particular competitor or a group of competitors but of society in general, with particular attention to consumers. According to Guillermo Cabanellas in his work already mentioned. The appropriate method for evaluating the extent to which the general economic interest is harmed or benefited is to compute, on the one hand, the benefits that may derive for the community, or a sector of it, and on the other the damages that result, considered in a similar, taking into account in both cases considerations of an economic nature'. (Juan Manuel Mercant 'Key concepts to analyze the norm as defense of competencia' LJU Section Doctrine T. 132)."

Scope of Law No. 18.159. With regard to the subjective scope of applicability of the Law, in its section 3 states that the principles and rules of free competition are applicable to all individuals or legal entities who carry out economic activities, either on a profit or non-profit basis, within the Uruguayan territory or that take place abroad but with effects in the Uruguayan territory.

Although the principle is the application of equal treatment to all economic agents, section 2 of the Law includes an odd provision, rarely seen among free competition regulation. This provision sets forth that the exercise of a right, power, or exceptional benefit granted or recognized by law shall not be deemed as an anticompetitive practice or an abuse of dominant position. In consideration that the Uruguayan economy has several highly regulated markets, including the existence of numerous de jure monopolies, the goal of this inclusion was to safeguard such monopolies and avoid any interpretation that through the Law, *de jure* monopolies would have been tacitly repealed. Among the monopolized sectors of the economy, there is the transformation, transmission, and distribution of electricity, landline communications, and distribution and refinery of oil. Nevertheless, the exclusion to the scope of applicability of the Law is solely limited to the activity in which the governmental agency has the monopoly. For all other activities that the governmental agency may carry out, outside the scope of privilege, such excess would fall under the scope of applicability of the Law and be subject to its full application.

The applicability, control, and enforcement of the Law, and overall oversight of the market is entrusted to the Commission for the Promotion and Defense of Competition (the "*commission*"). The commission is an administrative body hierarchically dependent on the Ministry of Economy, but with technical autonomy[8] in the matters it deals with. It is composed of three commissioners, which are designated by the executive power, for a term of six years, with the ability of being re-elected.

8. Although subject to hierarchy of the Executive Branch, which impacts on the appeal system herein below described, the fact that the Commission is vested with technical autonomy means that it may freely decide its cases and would not be subject to any disciplinary measure on account of its decisions.

On October 26, 2021, the parliament approved the *Rendición de Cuentas y Balance de Ejecución Presupuestal* corresponding to fiscal year 2020 which, together with other issues, introduced relevant amendments to Articles 10 and 27 of Law No 18,159.

Until then, Article 27 of the LPDC provided that, in those sectors that were subject to the control or superintendence of specialized regulatory bodies "such as" the Central Bank of Uruguay (hereinafter, the "BCU"), the Regulatory Unit of Energy and Water Services (hereinafter, the "URSEA"), and the Regulatory Unit of Communications Services (hereinafter, the "URSEC"), the protection and promotion of competition would be the responsibility of such bodies.

Therefore, in all other sectors not subject to the control of specialized regulatory bodies, the protection and promotion of competition—by default—would be the responsibility of the commission.

However, the wording of this article gave rise to certain interpretative doubts, particularly due to the expression "such as", since it was unclear whether the commission was only inhibited from acting in such sectors or whether there were possibly other regulated sectors in which it could not intervene, since the expression "such as" potentially indicated a non-exhaustive list.

Through this amendment, the wording of Article 27 is modified by eliminating the expression "such as" and establishing expressly that the BCU, the URSEA, and the URSEC will only retain:

1. Their "regulatory powers in matters of promotion and defence of competition", and;
2. The powers to grant authorizations—with or without prior non-binding consultation to the Commission—for those acts of concentration referred to in Articles 7 to 9 of the Law (merger control provisions) and which have as a target (a) entities regulated and supervised by it; or, (b) shares, quotas, or other equity participation securities in an entity regulated by it. In such cases, no term shall apply, nor shall any tacit authorization be granted pursuant to Article 9.

Regarding the investigation, analysis, and sanctioning of prohibited practices, Article 10 of the Law is also amended, and grants the commission, without exceptions, the power to act ex officio or upon complaint.

In these cases, the commission must merely notify the BCU, the URSEA, or the URSEC when the practices refer to the market whose regulation and control is expressly assigned to them. This second change will come into effect six months after the approval of this law, i.e., in April 2022.

These legislative changes eliminated one of the main uncertainties regarding the jurisdiction of the commission in this matter: since the wording of Article 27 referred to specialized regulators "such as" the BCU, the URSEC, and the URSEA, until now there was a question mark as to whether such list was exhaustive, opening the possibility that other specialized regulators from other sectors could dispute the competence of the commission.

Therefore, it can be said that the commission now has jurisdiction over all matters in this area, with the exception of the authorization of economic concentrations in sectors regulated by the BCU, the URSEA, and the URSEC and their capacities as regulators of these markets.

Notwithstanding the foregoing, the new wording is not free from possible difficulties. The first is that it will be necessary to determine the exact scope of the expression "regulatory competences in matters of promotion and defense of competition" retained by the BCU, the URSEA, and the URSEC. Second, although there will be very obvious cases, it will not always be easy to determine whether the subject of a given concentration transaction is a regulated or unregulated subject, which may generate competition conflicts between the commission and the regulators. Finally, the elimination of the deadlines foreseen to authorize economic concentrations may not be positive, since these processes usually require clear timelines.

Reform of Law No. 18,159. On August 13, 2018, the executive branch signed a bill (the "Bill") to modify Law No. 18,159, and immediately forwarded it to the legislative branch for consideration and parliamentary processing.

The project, with minor modifications to its original wording introduced during the parliamentary process, was approved in the Senate on September 11, 2019, and then promulgated by the executive branch dated September 20, 2019 (the "*Reform*").

The Reform proposed important changes and further aligned Uruguayan competition law with international standards in many ways.

Even though it is not mentioned in the explanatory memorandum of the project, the initiative was a result of a set of recommendations issued by the United Nations in the report on Uruguay published on October 12, 2016 (the "Report").[9] The Report was the result of Uruguay undergoing a "*Voluntary Peer Review of Competition Law and Policy*", within the framework of the United Nations Conference on Trade and Development (**UNCTAD**). The Reform implemented some (although clearly not all) of the recommendations made by UNCTAD.

The Reform's main changes were the introduction of a general prior authorization regime for the control of economic concentrations, as well as the introduction of the "per se" rule for hardcore cartels.

§19.02 GENERAL OVERVIEW OF THE LAW

[A] Main Principles

The Law in its section 2 lists the general principles applicable to the markets—from whose application the practices or behaviors declared as prohibited derive—and states

9. Report issued by UNCTAD and written by Pamela Sittenfeld, lawyer and member of the Expert Advisory Group of the Competition and Consumer Protection program in Latin America (COMPAL). It can be found at the following address: http://unctad.org/es/PublicationsLibrary/ditcclp 2016d1_es.pdf.

that "All markets are governed by the principles and rules of free competition, except for the limitations established by law, due to reasons of general interest." Thus, a series of substantive principles on which all the system is based and that enable the assessment of the behaviors of the companies and determine the behaviors that shall be prohibited.

Although the Law does not list such principles, they derive from the analysis of the different sections, specially sections 1, 2, 3, and 4, and that might be summarized in a general principle or rule: the free operation of the market in all its aspects is the final objective intended to be achieved and protected, since the main principle is that a competitive system enables the better allocation of resources and efficiencies among all participants in the market (consumers and producers).

[B] Applicability of the Rule of Reason

The main characteristic of the Law is that, despite confusing references to the "by object/by effect" dichotomy (which betray the European inspiration for the text) it is based on the applicability of the US-style "*rule of reason*". This principle had been ratified by the commission and also the courts. Section 2 of the Law sets forth the applicability of the rule of reason and prohibits the abusive use of a dominant position, and any individual or concerted practices, conducts, or recommendations thereof, if they result in or purport to restrict, limit, hinder, distort, or impede the actual or future competition within a relevant market and there are no justifications, as explained below.

Even though the Law provides a list of conducts or practices which may be considered as anticompetitive in the first place, they have to be analyzed under the rule of reason to effectively determine if they result or not in an anticompetitive practice prohibited by the Law.

A source of debate among Uruguayan practitioners is that the Law sets forth that not only conducts that have an anticompetitive effect are the ones punishable, but also the behaviors that have as "*object*" such goal. Through such inclusion, some understand that the mere potentiality or intention of an anticompetitive effect is being punished.

Furthermore, paragraph 3 of section 2 of the Law establishes that in order to assess the legitimacy or illegitimacy of the behaviors, the commission may take into account whether such practices, behaviors, or recommendations generate gains of economic efficiency to the subjects, economic units, and companies involved, the possibility of obtaining the same through alternative mechanisms and the benefit transferred to consumers.

Finally, the Law deems that the conquest of the market by an economic agent resulting from the natural process based on "higher efficiency" of such agent is not anticompetitive.

[C] Determination of the Relevant Market

For the purposes of analyzing any anticompetitive conduct, it is quintessential to undergo an analysis of the relevant market, where such conduct bears its effects. To determine which is the relevant market that might be affected in each case, the Law establishes certain guidelines and the commission through one of the first resolutions issued by it[10] and establishes the general criteria for such purposes.

Section 5 of the Act *in fine* establishes that "to analyze, among other factors, the existence of substitutive products or services, as well as the geographical area comprising the market, and to define the area of effective competition concerned." The notion of "substitutability" is thus introduced. The capacity of companies of imposing their conditions in the market will depend on substitutability, that is to say, the real or potential alternatives existing for the products or services being offered. Although this is essentially an economic issue, we may comment that the above-mentioned notion of substitutability may be focused either from the point of view of the demand (substitutability of the demand) or from the point of view of the supply (substitutability of the supply). Thus, the substitutability of the demand means that, under certain conditions (e.g., an increase in price or a decrease in the quality of a product or service), the consumers will be willing to redirect their consumption to other products or services. In turn, substitutability of the supply aims at determining which products belong to the same market, considering the possibility that other companies that are not for the time being offering the respective products may in a short term and with low costs, participate in such market, becoming then potential competitors to be included in the definition of the relevant market.

Although there is a healthy amount of debate on this point in the Antirust world, determining the relevant market should be the first step in any Uruguayan antitrust investigation. This is what clearly transpires from the applicable regulations, specifically Article 5 Law No. 18,159 on the Defense of Free Competition in Commerce; Article 6 of its Regulatory Decree No. 404/2007 and Resolution No. 2/09 of the Commission for the Promotion and Defense of Competition.

The value of this prior step is universally recognized in the jurisprudence and practice of competition authorities around the world, and Uruguay is no exception. See, for example, the jurisprudence of our highest administrative court on this point: "In competition cases, firstly, the determination of the relevant market and its geographical scope is imposed, being key to the correct elucidation of this type of matter. This methodology has been included as a solution of principle by article 5 of the Law."[11]

In Uruguay, most of the cases handled by the Commission for the Promotion and Defense of Competition uses and depart from the definition of the relevant market, as we consider to be the correct form. Notwithstanding this, Resolution No. 2/009 that establishes the general criteria for determining the relevant market admits that said definition is not an absolutely necessary element in all cases: "However, despite the

10. Criteria for the definition of the relevant market. Resolution No. 2/2009, dated May 25, 2009.
11. Judgment of the Highest Administrative Court No. 972/2017.

importance that this analysis will have in most cases, it should be noted that: Determination of the relevant market will not always be necessary to make decisions in the cases analyzed. Even when it is a necessary study, it will not always be the first step of the investigation, which must be determined by criteria of procedural efficiency." This limitation was also emphasized by the commission in its recent guidelines for the analysis of economic concentrations.

§19.03 ANTICOMPETITIVE PRACTICES[12]

As anticipated, Article 2 of the Law generically prohibits: "...the abuse of dominant position, as well as all practices, conducts or recommendations, whether individual or concerted...", classifying as potential anticompetitive practices unilateral conducts—including the abuse of dominant position, but not limited, at least theoretically, to that hypothesis—and concerted ones—both horizontal and vertical agreements—as potential anticompetitive practices.

With regard to the enumeration and classification of prohibited practices, our legislation departs both from the fundamentally generic enunciation of US law and from the clear separation between abusive unilateral conduct and concerted practices typical of European Community law. Instead, the Law proposes a broad but merely enunciative list of practices that may be considered anticompetitive, emulating the solution of other Latin American legal systems such as Argentina (Law No. 27,442) or Chile (Decree Law No. 211), a solution also tested in Article 6 of the MERCOSUR Protocol.

Thus, Article 4 of the Law in its current wording—after the amendment adopted by the Reform—expressly declares the following practices, among others, to be expressly prohibited, and: "insofar as they configure any of the situations set forth in Article 2 of the Law," among others[13] to the following practices:

"(A) Directly or indirectly agreeing or imposing purchase or sale prices or other transaction conditions";
"(B) Limiting or restricting the production, distribution and technological development of goods, services or productive factors, to the detriment of competitors or consumers";
"(C) Applying unequal conditions to third parties in the case of equivalent benefits, thus placing them at a significant disadvantage vis-à-vis competition";
"(D) Subjecting the conclusion of contracts to the acceptance of complementary or supplementary obligations which, by their very nature or by commercial usage, have no connection with the subject matter of such contracts"; "(E) Preventing access to the market by third parties to the same or similar services, thus placing them at a significant disadvantage vis-à-vis competitors or consumers";

12. For an in-depth analysis of Anticompetitive practices under Uruguayan competition law, we recommend the excellent and recently published work of our esteemed colleague Renato Guerrieri, in *Derecho de la Competencia*, Thomasset et al., 1ª edición, junio 2020, FCU, ISBN 978-9974-2-1123-0.
13. Article 4 of the Law states, "The enumeration is for illustrative purposes only".

"(E) Preventing the access of competitors to infrastructures that are essential for the production, distribution or commercialization of goods, services or productive factors";

"(F) Obstruct access to the market by potential market entrants";

"(G) Establish zones or activities where some or some of the economic agents operate exclusively, the remaining ones refraining from operating in the same";

"(H) Unjustifiably refusing the sale of goods or the rendering of services"; and

"(I) The same enunciated practices, when they are resolved through associations or guilds of economic agents."

As already mentioned, the Reform was prompted by the conclusions of UNCTAD's voluntary peer review of Uruguay where—following international best practices—it was recommended to introduce a series of amendments to the Law. Among them, with respect to anticompetitive practices, the most salient aspects of the Reform were the following: (i) eliminating a series of qualifiers of some of the conducts set forth in Article 4 of the Law ("abusively", "in an unjustified manner" and "unjustifiably") essentially because they were redundant by virtue of the application of the rule of reason; (ii) to eliminate the former subparagraph E) of Article 4 of the Law relating to collusive practices in the context of public or private bids or tenders for prices, and to include such conduct in the list of "per se" practices under Article 4 bis of the Law; and (iii) to introduce the "per se" rule of analysis with respect to certain concerted practices under the list of the current Article 4 bis of the Law, being an exhaustive enumeration, in order to *"enhance the value of legal certainty since the transformation of the rule of analysis is sought"*.

In addition, as of the wording introduced by the Reform, the aforementioned Article 4° bis is incorporated to the Law, which expressly declares the following concerted practices, conducts or recommendations among competitors prohibited, under the "per se" rule:

"(1) *To establish, directly or indirectly, prices or other commercial or service conditions";*

"(2) Establish the obligation to produce, process, distribute or commercialize only a restricted or limited quantity of goods or the provision of a restricted or limited number, volume or frequency of services"; "(3) Divide, distribute, distribute, distribute or commercialize only a restricted or limited quantity of goods or the provision of a restricted or limited number, volume or frequency of services";

"(3) To divide, distribute, apportion, allocate or impose portions, zones or market segments of goods or services, customers or sources of supply";

"(4) Establishing, arranging or coordinating bids or forbearance in bids, tenders or auctions";

"(5) *The same enunciated practices, when they are resolved through associations or guilds of economic agents."*

Finally, Article 6 of the Law defines abuse of dominant position as an anticompetitive practice in terms of: "...when the agent or agents who are in such a situation [of dominance] act in an undue manner, with the purpose of obtaining advantages or causing damages to others, which would not have been possible in the absence of such dominant position."

As a corollary of the aforementioned list of anticompetitive practices, several analytical and interpretative difficulties appear in the facts:

First, Article 4 of the Law intermingles, within a common category, practices as dissimilar as horizontal agreements, vertical agreements, and manifestations of abuse of dominant position, and lists in a generic way as potentially anticompetitive, multiple conducts that in other jurisdictions only constitute manifestations of abuse of dominant position. Such is the case of certain unilateral practices such as the refusal to sell, the creation of entry barriers, and tied sales.

At present, following the literal wording of the Law, unilateral conducts of economic agents that do not hold a dominant position could eventually be considered anticompetitive, which we understand would not be appropriate and would represent a departure from the main models in comparative law and an infringement of the principle of legal certainty. In any case, the standard to determine the anticompetitive nature of these conducts—the anticompetitive effect or object—should coincide with having sufficient market power to effectively engage in such conducts and cause a significant adverse effect. Therefore, on the facts, everything leads us again to manifestations of abuse of dominant position.

Second, we find several references that in our opinion are misleading or at least inaccurate. In particular:

(i) Article 4° literal A) of the Law unduly encompasses a series of totally dissimilar anticompetitive practices, some unilateral—including manifestations of abuse of dominant position—and others concerted, subject to different rules, such as predatory pricing, resale price fixing, and collusive price fixing agreements;

(ii) Article 4 letter D) of the Law prohibits tied sales in terms of the imposition: "of complementary or supplementary obligations", instead of alluding to the acquisition of another product or service, as is proper of this prohibited practice;

(iii) Article 4, paragraph E) of the Law in its previous wording and Article 4 bis, paragraph 4) refer to prohibited practices in the framework of bids or price contests exclusively in terms of collusive agreements (known as "bid rigging", in which respect we refer to what is developed in Chapter IX of this work), and do not explicitly include other conducts characteristic of such procedures, such as, for example, in the drafting of bidding documents; and

(iv) In general terms, Article 4 of the Law in its original wording required for the configuration of certain practices a special degree of illegitimacy—"abusively", "in an unjustified manner", "unjustifiably", concepts that should have been expressly defined, and also be extensible to all anticompetitive practices, even though there is no express text in the regulations, by virtue of the application of the rule of reason, since in many cases there are superabundant references. Therefore, through the Reform these qualifiers were eliminated, except in the case of refusal to market.

Third, we note the lack of some provisions whose inclusion would simplify the analysis of potentially anticompetitive conducts and would allow for greater certainty and predictability in the enforcement work, namely:

(i) Unlike other laws, the Law does not propose the categorization or hierarchy of conducts according to their level of seriousness. Indeed, neither in the Law nor in the Decree is there any mention of the so-called hard core anticompetitive conducts ("hardcore restrictions" or the "object box") as it is usually called in comparative law with respect to restrictions that are difficult to justify even by applying the rule of reason, such as collusive price-fixing or market-sharing agreements. A first advance in this sense is noted with the Reform, which among other things introduces the rule of "per se" analysis with respect to certain concerted practices as we have seen.

(ii) In the Law and the Decree we do not find institutes comparable to the "de minimis" doctrine of European Community law, nor the so-called safe haven and safe harbor, that is, the exemption from sanctions and/or presumption of legality in situations where the allegedly infringing economic agent holds a low market share, and/or where it is evident that the possible anticompetitive damage will be remote.

(iii) Some key concepts are also not specified, among them: (i) the minimum market share that an economic agent should possess as a rule in order to determine and/or presume that it holds a dominant position; and (ii) the precise definition of the anticompetitive object—the meaning and scope of which has generated endless debates in comparative law as we shall see—, and of the anticompetitive effect.

None of this can be seen in the national regulatory instruments, and so far there has been no significant development in the casuistry of the commission or other sectorial enforcement bodies in this regard.

And fourth, with respect to the list of prohibited practices, which is merely enunciative and not exhaustive, although we understand that this solution is necessary insofar as the legislator cannot anticipate every potentially anticompetitive commercial strategy, it is not free from criticism. In particular, the potential infringement of legal principles such as typicity and legal certainty, and the constitutional principle of freedom contained in Article 10, paragraph 2 of our constitution, which provides that everything that is not prohibited by law is permitted, must be taken into account. The Reform's explanatory memorandum recognizes this tension, and states: "—in the face of the conflict between the legal certainty of an exhaustive list and the effectiveness of the rule—it is decided to protect the latter", emphasizing: "... the impossibility of foreseeing in advance all the practices or conducts in which companies could engage."

By object/by effect. As anticipated, Article 2 of the Law prohibits: "...all practices, conducts or recommendations, individual or concerted, that have **as their effect or object**, to restrict, limit, hinder, hinder, distort or prevent current or future competition in the relevant market."

The central elements to be analyzed are then the anticompetitive "effect or object", which are of alternative and non-cumulative verification—that is, a practice may be considered anticompetitive if it has a restrictive effect or object—, thus requiring a separate consideration in each case. This solution, although it may be questionable since the verification of prohibited practices without an anticompetitive effect is legislatively recognized, arises from the literal wording of the rule itself, and also from jurisdictional pronouncements both in Uruguay and in other jurisdictions.

Meanwhile, the concept of "anticompetitive object" is one of the most controversial and complex in competition law. The notion is inspired by European Community law—in our opinion, unwisely, by virtue of the practical and interpretative difficulties that this notion has entailed there—and neither the Law, the Reform, the Decree nor any other regulatory provision provides any clarification or explanation of the scope of the concept. Therefore, in any legal system, unraveling its meaning becomes a complex doctrinal and jurisprudential interpretative task.

The consequence of typifying an anticompetitive practice by virtue of its object is that it would not be necessary to evidence the verification of concrete restrictive effects, since they are alternative and non-cumulative requirements according to Article 2 of the Law. This is not the same as presuming or assuming that such effects have occurred or could occur, which beyond being usually raised in the facts, should be inappropriate.

In our opinion, the prohibition of practices exclusively on the basis of their anticompetitive purpose is objectionable, since according to Article 1 of the Law, the objectives of the defense of competition consist, among other things, of "promoting the welfare of current and future consumers and users". Therefore, it would be natural to require necessarily the accreditation of anticompetitive effects in all cases in order to prohibit a conduct. This has been expressed in the national doctrine and the Highest Administrative Court: "If the conduct has no impact on competition, it is irrelevant for the purposes of the Law. It may be an illegal practice for constituting, for example, an act of unfair competition, but without distortion of competition, it will not violate the Law..."[14]

All that being said, the anticompetitive conducts regulated by the Law can be fundamentally subdivided into two, cartels and unilateral conducts. And in consideration that the law treats the proceedings and sanctions thereto in a uniform matter, such issue is thereafter considered.

§19.04 CARTELS

Originally, one of the peculiarities of Uruguayan antitrust was that, under section 4 of Law No. 18.159, agreements among competitors internationally known as "cartels" were not prohibited "per se". Article 4 in its original wording provided a list of conducts that were prohibited, but only provided that such conduct proves to be anticompetitive under the analysis of the rule of reason. Among such list, were a series of conducts

14. Judgment of the Highest Administrative Court No. 400/2014.

expressly targeted to prevent the cartelization of the different economic agents, through the coordination of conducts with the goal of hindering competition. Such conducts expressly mentioned price-fixing or imposition of other conditions; the coordination of presentations to public or private public bids for the provision of goods and services; or the unjustified distribution of areas or activities among competitors, refraining from acting in the others' area or activity. Therefore, at least in theory, one could try to justify a cartel among competitors with efficiencies, or proving that the conduct had had no anticompetitive effects.

The Reform of Law No. 18.159 put an end to that Uruguayan peculiarity. The Reform includes a new Article 4BIS which introduces an exhaustive list of practices prohibited per se (i.e., in and of themselves), referring to practices, conduct, recommendations, or concerted practices among competitors. This absolute prohibition therefore no longer admits justifications under the rule of reason. The concept of agreement between competitors is the critical element in the legal definition, as well as the object of such agreements; Agreements among competitors that will be considered *per* se illegal are: agreements on prices or other commercial conditions; agreements to limit the production of goods or services; agreements to share markets; coordination in bids, price contests or auctions; as well as the same practices carried out through a trade union or business association.

In this way, our legislation began to have two types of anticompetitive practices: those practices subject to the rule of reason (justifiable), and others prohibited per se (not justifiable).

The introduction of anticompetitive practices per se (i.e., where it is sufficient to prove that the practice was verified for it to be considered prohibited and, therefore, punishable) can be classified as a positive change for the system as a whole.

On the one hand, it will surely imply an economy resources, since if the existence of the practices listed in the new Article 4 BIS is verified, it is no longer necessary to analyze whether there are justifications and, therefore, the waste of resources is avoided, both for the enforcement bodies and from the parties involved.

However, the introduction of anticompetitive practices per se is not without risks and/or impacts that should be mentioned. The main known risk presented by the system of anticompetitive practices per se is known as "false positive", for identifying situations where a per se prohibition, established for the purpose of achieving maximum efficiency to avoid useless waste of resources, qualifies practices as anticompetitive that in fact generate efficiency gains (research and/or development or other forms of virtuous cooperation agreements among competitors is the typical example). As the Reform was drafted, the application will be without exceptions.

A second aspect is that the legal battles that in these cases will be based mainly on the facts and not on economic theory. As a consequence of the latter, an intensification of requests for information from the enforcement bodies can be expected and also a significant increase in "leniency applications" by a cartel participant to obtain total or partial exemption from sanctions.

Another questionable aspect in our view is that the text was adopted without a *"de minimis "* exception. This is known at the international law level as an exception for those agreements among competitors that are so insignificant that no anticompetitive effects can be anticipated. Such a proposal was made on two occasions during the parliamentary process, and yet not incorporated.

As there are no specific requirements or special formalities established, the express or tacit, written or oral agreements may be included in this prohibition. A concerted practice of several companies (without the existence of a written agreement) may lead the commission to the conclusion that a collusive agreement exists, provided that there is no alternative reasonable explanation for such coordination. All the foregoing gives rise to the very developed theories of "conscious parallelisms," "coordinated practices," or "parallel practices" whose considerations are very useful in these cases.

In connection with the procedure and sanctions that may occur in a cartel investigation, please refer to the *Procedure and Sanctions* section, under Unilateral Conducts.

With regard to the extraterritoriality of the actions of the commission, specifically of cartels that act outside of Uruguay and also have an effect within Uruguayan territory (or vice versa), our local legislation does not have any specific provision that gives powers to the commission (or other regulators, as applicable). Even though the scope of applicability of the Law provides that foreign entities that have an economic impact in Uruguay must abide such Law, no precedent of the commission endeavors in such investigations.

Although there is an increasing control over all types of anticompetitive conducts, especially on cartels, there are no specific policies, politics, or institutions being passed or imposed in order to attack these form of conducts. Consequently, the commission neither has specific resources to tackle this form of anticompetitive practice, nor is there any directive to prioritize the seizure of cartels.

Uruguay forms part of certain international agencies in matters of competition, such as within the MERCOSUR (formed by Uruguay, Argentina, Brazil, Paraguay, and Venezuela). On December 16, 2010, the members of MERCOSUR entered into an agreement for the Defense of Competition in MERCOSUR, with the purposes of exchanging information between the agencies of countries that form part of it.

The commission has the power to act under its own initiative ("*ex officio*") or upon a claim filed by an interested party.

The Law establishes a wide range of denouncing parties, who may be any person, either an individual or a legal entity, public or private, national or foreign. However, the Law enables the commission not to commence any investigation procedure, when the claim submitted is considered by the commission as "evidently improper," so as to avoid ungrounded claims with the mere purpose of slandering individuals or companies.

When the enforcement agency considers that there may be prohibited practices being developed, it will carry out an investigation aiming at the clarification of the events and the identification of those responsible. Customarily, the commission acts ex officio when certain matters become of public knowledge or concern. Otherwise, the majority of the conducts that are investigated on account of a claim are filed by a person (whether individual or legal entity).

According to the commission's latest published annual report (2019), 70% to 80% of the cases originate in complaints and the remaining matters are initiated ex officio.[15]

[A] Relevant Cases

The most well-remembered national precedent so far is the *Pulpa del Tomate* case, where the commission detected and sanctioned a cartel whose object consisted of fixing prices in the purchase of tinted tomato pulp containers. This case is particularly interesting because it combines the characteristic features of collusive practices, such as the leniency of the repentant for the purpose of detecting the agreement, the exchange of information, and the use of a third party—a common printing house—, constituting a "hub and spoke" type of agreement.

In the case *Timopel S.A. v. Pancini Industrial del Sauce S.A., Barraca Deambrosi S.A., Gibur S.A., Vulcania S.A. and Domingo Ghelfa – Claim*,[16] the commission concluded that the cited parties were part of a cartel. This cartel had as a purpose the fixation of prices in the purchase of cardboard containers for the products produced by them.

After four years of investigation, the commission proved the existence of a collusive agreement, through the following elements: (i) that the parties involved had access to the information about sales of each other, (ii) the possibility of corroborating that the parties to the agreement met the agreed standards and, (iii) in case any of them did not abide by it, the possibility of sanctioning such party in breach. Even though no written agreement existed between the involved parties, it was clear to the commission the existence of this cartel and the concerted practices carried out by it. As a result of such conducts, the commission applied different fines to the parties involved that ranged from 100,000 Indexed Units to 4,000,000 Indexed Units.

The commission objected and sanctioned the practice, concluding: "The defendants acknowledge the existence of an agreement to which they were part of together with the plaintiff, coinciding also in the determination of the time frame and the fact that Timopel S.A. would have withdrawn from it in mid-2010... the agreement would be based on the logic that a higher production—volume of boxes—, achieved by working together, would allow them to obtain better prices for the 'sieved tomato pulp' containers. To that end, they would have hired the services of Impresora Visión, who would have quoted them a lower price due to the volume contracted and the subsequent delivery to be made in one or two places, in order to reduce the freight cost of the containers produced...", adding that the following would be proven: "(a) access to information on the conditions of sale applied by the members of the agreement,

15. Commission for the Promotion and Defense of Competition 2014 Report. Available in Spanish at https://www.mef.gub.uy/innovaportal/file/15663/4/memoria-2014.pdf.
16. *Timopel S.A. v. Pancini Industrial del Sauce S.A., Barraca Deambrosi S.A., Gibur S.A., Vulcania S.A. and Domingo Ghelfa – Claim*, Resolution No. 24/014, dated April 1, 2014.

alleged rivals of competition, using as a propitious means the participation of Impresora Visión SA... (b) power of corroboration of compliance with the conditions imposed by the participants of the agreement, which is found in the traffic of information indicated in subparagraph (a). The participation of the printing company is key in this control, as well as the procedure applied by Deambrosi SA to grant bonuses in supermarkets... c) the application of 'sanctions' to those who deviate from the agreed or expected behaviour. In this case, the sanction would have operated in the lowering of prices of sieved and crushed pulp, precisely the same type of product produced by the complainant"; and synthesizing: "The horizontal agreement verified between the parties, deserves to be qualified as collusive, since no elements emerge from this investigation that manage to explain it in reasons of economic efficiency, having as effect or object to control competition and even to restrict it ... by departing from the rules of free competition, inevitably causing a damage to the general interest".

However, the principal novelty presented by this case was the fact that the commission applied the institute of leniency for the first time since the enactment of the Law.[17] Its applicability was brought into practice due to the fact that the collusive agreement was exposed by a former member of the cartel. For the purposes of applying the institute of leniency, the commission entered into a clemency agreement under which Timopel S.A. had to fulfill certain conditions for leniency to enter into effect, in connection with the provision of evidence as to effectively expose the cartel. As a result thereof and by the conclusion achieved by the commission, Timopel S.A., was exonerated from any fines, which arises from the commission's final resolution.

Another domestic precedent is the *Maritime Agents* case,[18] where the commission detected the existence of a rate-fixing agreement in the market for services provided by maritime agencies that lasted at least a decade, with the participation of the sector's trade union, which even consulted the commission on the legality of suggesting rates—an extreme taken as a mitigating factor of its responsibility. It was a price suggested by the union that operated as a minimum tariff.

Also noteworthy is the *Meat Market* case, where the commission promoted a preparatory measure consisting of a study of the meat market, and in particular of price formation and the possible existence of price-fixing agreements between competitors and with the intervention of trade associations. Although it was determined that the prices were fixed in general terms in the same sense as those announced in the press, the commission concluded that there were no elements that would allow linking the price movements with anticompetitive conducts. However, the commission made a recommendation to market players regarding the risk of making price announcements.[19]

17. The legal grounds set forth in the Law with regard to leniency are further described under the Sanctions section, within Proceedings and Sanctions.
18. Comisión, Resolución No. 72/2012, caso Cristalpet c/ Agentes Marítimos.
19. Comisión, caso *Medida preparatoria sobre mercado de la carne.*

§19.05 UNILATERAL CONDUCTS

Unilateral practices—as the term itself indicates—consist of anticompetitive conducts committed by a single economic agent, generally involving the imposition of commercial conditions that constitute manifestations of abuse of a dominant position. In comparative law, the classification of unilateral prohibited practices is reserved in principle exclusively to the actions of economic agents holding a dominant position—although this solution does not expressly arise from Uruguayan law.

In Uruguay, following the literal wording of the Law, unilateral conducts of economic agents that do not hold a dominant position could eventually be considered anticompetitive, which, in our opinion, would not be appropriate. There could even be absurd scenarios such as sanctioning refusals of commercialization by an economic agent with marginal market share. Faced with an analogous situation under Brazilian law, the OECD pointed out that in the face of an unorthodox and ambiguous formulation, the provisions would have the potential to be misapplied, a conclusion that we understand is transferable to Uruguay.

The Law also provides definitions as to what is considered market dominance and when an abuse of such position exists.

Section 6 of the Law defines market dominance as when one or more agents, in a relevant market, may substantially affect the relevant variables thereof, regardless of the behaviors of their competitors, purchasers, or providers. In the same section, it is defined the abuse of dominant position when the agent or agents who have market dominance, act in an improper manner, with the aim of obtaining advantages or causing damages to others, that might not have been possible in case such dominant positions did not exist.

It is clear that the Law allows the existence of economic agents who may have a dominant position and the exercise thereof, but it is strictly forbidden for such agents to adopt any form of conduct that may qualify as abusive.

Even though the Law, nor the Decree provide with guidelines as to determine when an economic agent has a dominant position, in practice, the commission has incorporated the standard criteria (not always) of the "*Hypothetical Monopolist Test,*" through the assessment of an increase in prices (even those not very significant as to amounts and terms), is conducted without a detriment of the sales. In case of verifying such circumstance, the agent concerned shall have a dominant position that enables it to behave as such. In case of not having such position, when increasing the prices, it would suffer a loss on the side of sales.

Thus, in order to determine whether a company has a dominant position or not, a structural analysis of the market concerned and of the relevant players should be performed and also about the existence of barriers to enter such market, the effective and potential competition, together with other issues related to the substitutability of products, etc.

The dominant position or dominant position supposes the possibility that a company has to substantially affect the relevant variables of a market regardless of the behaviors of its competitors, suppliers, customers, etc. The dominant position is characterized by the disregard of those who have such a position with respect to their competitors, buyers, and consumers and/or the power to oppose the maintenance of effective competition.

The dominant position cannot be assimilated to a monopoly, since what characterizes the dominant position is not the exclusivity of a market but the lack of effectiveness of the existing competition in that market to significantly alter the behavior of the dominant company. According to Cabanellas,[20] jurisprudence and doctrine have developed several of the elements necessary to determine the existence of a dominant position. Such elements include the following: (i) number of companies operating in the relevant market, (ii) market share of the company in the relevant market, (iii) absolute size of the company, (iv) price-cost ratio of the company,[21] (v) relationships with suppliers and distribution channels, (vi) elasticity of demand, (vii) pricing power, and (viii) analysis of conjunctural situations.

At the level of the European Commission, various approaches have been made to identify the existence of a dominant position. In general, they start from a structural approach to the market (analyzing, among other things, market participation and entry barriers) and the position of the company in question in said market, and then move on to a behavioral approach (where checks the independent and autonomous action of the company in question) and finally the victim's position can be analyzed to see if there is a dependency or not.

In Uruguay, the criterion of dominance or dominant market power is legally defined in Article 6 paragraph 1 of the Competition Law, which states: "For the purposes of the provisions of Article 2 of this law it is understood that one or more agents enjoy a dominant position in the market when they can substantially affect the relevant variables of the market, regardless of the conduct of their competitors, buyers, or suppliers." In this way, and according to the definition given by our legislator, in order to determine the existence of a dominant position, it must be analyzed whether the agent is in a position to act independently in the relevant market, without having to consider the reactions of its agents, competitors, and buyers, and without them being able to avoid or compensate for it.

Camilo Martínez Blanco understands that "to attend to whether the company in question acts relatively independently of the market because it does not feel challenged."[22] In a similar way, Marcelo Amorín maintains that there is a dominant position when "the company that is capable of exercising this influence is left out of effective competition, since it can act without taking into account the possible reactions of its competitors."[23] It should be noted that this is the criterion followed by most countries when evaluating whether or not an agent has a dominant position.

20. Cabanellas De Las Cuevas, Guillermo. Antitrust Law and Defense of Competition. Editorial Heliasta. pp. 655 ff.
21. See Lerner's index (L = (price-cost) / price. The further L is away from 0 (positive), the more market power a competitor has.
22. Martínez Blanco, Camilo. *supra*, p. 195.
23. Amorín, Marcelo. Abuse of dominant position and imposition of prices in Studies on the Defense of Competition and Consumer Relations, p. 93.

An important clarification regarding the analysis of the dominant position in a market is that a significant market share does not in itself constitute sufficient evidence of the existence or not of market power.

Regarding market share, Law No. 18,159 does not establish minimum percentages from which it must be considered that there is a dominant position. The only indirect reference is found in the original wording of Article 7 of the Law (now modified), which established the need to notify any act of economic concentration to the commission when, as a consequence of the concentration operation, a participation equal to or greater than 50% of the relevant market. By virtue of this reference, it was possible to infer the legal parameter from which a stake greater than 50% may be indicating a dominant position.

For its part, the commission has stated: "The dominant position is also defined as the possibility of an agent to adopt behaviors in relation to prices, quality of goods and / or services independently or the possibility of reducing the level of innovation that would be required in a market in which it does not enjoy such a position (...) It is important then, based on the legal definition, to bear in mind that the agent must have the power to act independently of its competitors in order to evaluate the existence of a dominant position"(Resolution No. 57/2013).

On another occasion, the commission stated: "In order to assess the market power of the investigated companies, in addition to market share, the following factors should be considered basically: competitors: number of competitors and their respective market share; entry conditions: absence or existence of entry barriers; compensatory purchasing power" (Resolution No 37/2011).

There could also be a "collective dominant position," which occurs for example when: (i) companies that participate in the same market enter into collusive agreements or practices and act in concert or (ii) companies that are subject to control unified; and provided that it becomes clear that there is no competitive behavior between said companies.[24]

On one occasion, the controversial and innovative—and in our judgment misguided—theory of "atypical dominant position" was attempted by the commission. In a case of predatory pricing, the commission stated: "That the existence of an atypical dominance position in this case by Abal Hnos. SA, derives from its strength at the international level, as it is a subsidiary of the multinational company Philip Morris International, and not from its specific market share in the local market, given that it has the financial capacity to sustain for a prolonged period the strategy of setting prices below the variable average cost ..." This theory was luckily dismissed by the Highest Administrative Court, arguing among other issues: (i) "that in the relevant Uruguayan market, Abal Hnos did not hold a dominant position vis-à-vis the complaining competitor"; (ii) that its condition of a subsidiary of an multinational company: "... does not per se imply anti-competitive conduct"; and (iii) that "Therefore, for predatory pricing to be classified as an anticompetitive practice in a legal system such as ours, based on the 'rule of reason', it must be inextricably associated with the

24. Judgment of the Highest Administrative Court No. 972/2017.

subjective aspect given by the exercise of a dominant position by an agent in such a position in a relevant market that, as stated, Abal did not have."[25] In this case, the Highest Administrative Court also ruled on the market share threshold under which, in Uruguayan Law, there would be a presumption of non-dominance: "The Court does not share the view upheld by the Commission for the Promotion and Defense of Competition position in regard to the existence of an 'atypical' dominant position by the plaintiff, as a subsidiary of the Company PHILIP MORRIS INTERNATIONAL, as this would imply a undue extension of the relevant market under investigation on a practically global scale. (...) Thus, according to the doctrinal references mentioned above, for an economic agent to be considered to have a 'dominant position', it must own at least 40% or more of the relevant market (...)."

The Highest Administrative Court also ruled on the notion of dominant position on other occasions: "There are two notions of dominant position; one dating from the neoclassical followed by the Chicago school, for this the relevant thing is that the company is in a position to manifest unilateral behavior in terms of prices and quantity of products offered. In another line, what is transcendent is the position with respect to suppliers and competitors, with the possibility of deteriorating their market shares, to the point that they may disappear, which would make the market less efficient."[26]

The illegal anticompetitive practice is not that of having a dominant position, but that of abusing it. This requires considering whether the company in question acted in the same way as it would have acted in a normal competitive situation or if, on the contrary, it used clearly disproportionate or abusive means ("*unduly*" according to our law) to defend itself against competition, taking advantage of the fact that competition was limited by its presence in the market. On this issue, the Highest Administrative Court frequently quotes the work of Martinez Blanco on the matter: "an agent occupies a dominant position if his economic power allows him to act in the market without taking into account the reaction of his competitors. or intermediate or final consumers. And, in our legal system it is not illegal to occupy a dominant position. The fact of occupying a dominant position is not negative in itself, if it is the result of the agent's own efficiency; but if that power is used to inhibit competition, it is undoubtedly an anti-competitive practice that constitutes an abuse. (Cf. Camilo Martinez Blanco: 'Basic Manual of the Law of Competition' p. 69)."[27]

In turn, various behaviors can be considered normal for any company in the market and could be adopted without any problem by non-dominant companies, while the same behaviors can be prohibited for a dominant company. From this objective conception, the idea is derived that the dominant company has, because it is, a special responsibility in its behavior to continue maintaining a competitive attitude, a responsibility that non-dominant companies do not have.

In addition to the prohibition of abuse of dominant position stated in Articles 2 and 6 of the Law, Article 4 the Law provides a list of conducts, which may be

25. Judgment of the Highest Administrative Court No. 972/2017.
26. Opinion of Judge Dr. Lombardi, Judgment of the Highest Administrative Court No. 575/2010, *see also* Judgment No. 372/2011 and Judgment No. 187/2013.
27. Judgment No. 42/009 and Judgment No. 357/2009.

considered as anticompetitive conducts, provided they are considered as such under the rule of reason analysis above-mentioned.

[A] List of Anticompetitive Conducts

Originally article 4 of the Law provided the following list of practices, which would presumably result in an anticompetitive conduct, subject to a rule of reason analysis:

- "To concert or to impose directly or indirectly purchase or sale prices or other conditions for transactions on an abusive basis."
- "To limit, restrict or concert on an unjustified basis the production, distribution and technological development of goods, services or factors of production, to the detriment of competitors or consumers."
- "To apply without justification to third parties unequal conditions in the case of equivalent benefits, thus placing them in an important disadvantage before competitors."
- "To subordinate the execution of agreements to the acceptance of additional or supplementary obligations that, due to their own nature or for the commercial uses, are not related to the object of such agreements."
- "To impede the access of competitors to infrastructures which are essential for the production, distribution or trade of goods, services or factors of production."
- "To hinder without justification the access to the market of potential participants therein."
- *"To establish without justification areas or activities where one or more of the economic agents operate on an exclusive basis, and refraining the remaining ones from operating in the same"*
- *"To reject without justification the sale of goods or the provision of services."*

The Reform introduced certain changes to Article 4. In addition to moving all the cartel behavior to the newly created Article 4BIS (see above), it made certain adjustments in the wording of Article 4, eliminating certain qualifications previously included in some of the prohibited practices (e.g., "abusively"— literal a—, "unjustifiably"— literal b—, "unjustifiably"— literal c).

The authors of this chapter understand that these adjustments were technically appropriate, since this class of practices will always require an analysis regarding whether or not they are justified under the rule of reason enshrined in Article 2, it also makes no sense to require a justification or additional requirement in Article 4.

All in all, it must be noted that if a conduct above-mentioned does not meet the substantial requirements to be considered as an anticompetitive conduct, i.e., that it passes muster under the rule of reason, it will not be prohibited. Likewise, any other behavior that even when it is not contemplated in such listing is framed within any of the cases analyzed above of Article 2 of the Law, will be contrary to the rule therein contained, and therefore, prohibited.

[B] Relevant Cases

One of the landmark cases decided by the commission in its history was in connection with the establishment of guidelines on how to bill for the services rendered by the members of the corresponding associations or group of professionals. As a result of the study conducted by the commission, it resolved that the issuance of guidelines by each professional association resulted in all collusive agreements and even though they were not mandatory to the members that formed part of each of the associations, they were highly persuasive and applied uniformly by such members. Consequently, the commission in its resolution ordered the different professional associations (Uruguayan Bar Association, Association of Notary Publics of Uruguay and CPAs and Economists Association) to repeal the guidelines originally passed by each of them, so that the professional fees would be left to free competition.

However, such decision of the commission was found null and void by the Highest Administrative Court (*Tribunal de lo Contencioso Administrativo*), through decision 400/2014, dated September 30, 2014. The Highest Administrative Court found that the publication of guidelines by different professional associations was not an anticompetitive practice, given that the professional associations proved that they do not conduct any sort of control of the applicability of such guidelines as had determined the commission. Moreover, the tribunal argued that given that in Uruguay it is not mandatory for professionals to enroll in professional associations, they cannot be considered as having market dominance. Lastly, the administrative tribunal found that the commission had not provided sufficient proof of the "*abuse*" committed by the professional associations, especially considering that under the Uruguayan regime, the applicability of the rule of reason prevails upon such conducts. Consequently, the court declared the commission's decision null and void, thus, allowing the professional associations to reinstate their billing guidelines.

The commission has been particularly active and has used Article 4 to attack minimum resale price maintenance practices (*Baranur* case— Resolución No. 158/2016, caso Baranur c/ Samsung y otros, and the *Alimentos Congelados* case). The *Alimentos Congelados* case[28] is particularly illustrative, in which behind a mechanism of "suggested prices" that distributors informed to retailers, there were hidden pressures from a third agent, who exerted pressure so that distributors demanded in a concerted manner from retailers the setting of minimum retail prices for their products, under the threat of this third agent to suspend purchases from distributors in case of non-compliance. It was even evidenced the existence of a punishment to a distributor for not having achieved the task of aligning prices in the retail market. In the case at hand, both the instigating agent and the material executors of the prohibited practice were held responsible for it.

In the *Alimentos Congelados* case, although the commission did not find efficiency gains that justify the practice of "RPM" given the characteristics and homogeneity of the goods marketed, it did recognize that: "In general, the establishment of

28. Highest Administrative Court, Judgment No. 208/2018.

minimum sales prices is usually considered efficient as a way of counteracting the effect known as "free rider". That is, there are selling firms that make investments in the sale itself, such as customer service, demonstrations, information on operation, use of the good itself, etc., and other selling firms that provide customer service without any added service and at lower prices, it is possible for consumers to obtain information on the product in question in the selling premises of the first type, but make the purchase in the firms of the second type. The problem here is that if the manufacturing companies—or wholesale distributors—sell to the firms of the second type, there is a risk that the former will not capture all the investment made and will therefore be discouraged from continuing to invest in sales and at some point from continuing to trade; while if the products are sold only to the firms of the first type, there is a risk of not having adequate distribution to consumers. Another argument in favor of the establishment of sales prices by distributors has to do with possible initial investment costs necessary to establish themselves, in the sense that the minimum prices would act as a protection for the initial investment necessary to be made. Other arguments in favor are that they allow for intra-brand competition not at the price level, but in terms of quality, after-sales service, commitment to the brand itself, etc."[29]

The other paradigmatic case in terms of resale price maintenance in Uruguay is *Baranur* where, based on a complaint alleging an unjustified exclusion from the electronics market, the commission controversially changed the object of the investigation and sanctioned multiple companies—in some cases, based on essentially circumstantial evidence—, for an alleged concerted practice of minimum "RPM" of televisions. In this case, the commission ignored several arguments put forward by the agents, such as that: (i) the exchange of information regarding retail prices ("PVP") would not necessarily imply the imposition of "RPMs"; (ii) there would have been televisions offered simultaneously in different sales channels in the local market at prices different from the alleged negotiated "RPM"; (iii) the non-conclusion of sales to Baranur would not be linked to the adequacy of the "RPM" but to other commercial arguments; and (iv) the consumption through non-traditional sales channels-where Baranur operated—would be extremely low compared to the consumption through traditional sales channels.

To support the sanction in *Baranur*, the commission highlighted the harm to consumers and the limitation to competition that the resale price fixing practice would generate, since the agents would have to respect a minimum resale price, without being able to compete below it, generating an artificial overprice. This is without prejudice to disregarding the market share held by the infringing agents.

29. Comisión, Report No. 73/2011, caso *Mercado de alimentos congelados*.

§19.06 PROCEEDINGS AND SANCTIONS

[A] Procedure

[1] Preparatory Measures

Upon coming across an anticompetitive conduct, before commencing a formal investigation the commission may request certain preparatory measures as to ascertain the admissibility of certain claim or to gather information. This provides the commission the ability to get acquainted beforehand with the specifics of a certain relevant market where the alleged anti-competitive conduct is being carried out, as well with its composition and standard practices carried out therein.

As preparatory measures, the commission may require information from any person, individual or legal entity, either public or private. Moreover, the commission has the power of requesting ordinary courts the application of evidentiary measures, on a confidential basis and without prior notice to the investigated parties, such as exhibitions and obtainment of copies of civil and commercial documents, books of trade, books of minutes of corporate bodies, accounting data bases, and correspondence.

Furthermore, the Law establishes that in case the commission requires information of those involved in the behavior under investigation, and they fail to provide the requested information, such failure may shift the burden of proof against the party in breach, in connection with the information that they failed to produce.

Also, the Law guarantees to those involved—to whom the commission had requested information—that in no case are they obliged to provide information that implies the obligation to disclose business secrets, plans, "know-how," inventions, formulas and patents, provided that they evidence that such provision would imply the breach of professional secrecy or breach intellectual property rights.

In addition, the commission is empowered to order the precautionary suspension of the investigated behaviors or practices at any stage of the proceedings, when it determines in its discretion that such practice or behavior is capable of causing serious damages.

Moreover, the Law empowers the commission to request ordinary courts for interim measures if it deems convenient, on a confidential basis and without notice, before starting the administrative proceedings or during the continuance thereof. For such purposes, the ordinary courts shall be competent, and the rules included in the General Code of Procedure regarding interim measures are deemed applicable, except for the obligation to provide an injunction bond, from which the commission is exempted.

[2] The Investigation

Once the investigation has commenced, either when a claim has been filed or an ex officio investigation has been initiated by the commission, the alleged offenders are notified of such investigation and have the right to present their defense, within a term of ten business days. Within such term, the alleged offenders are mandated to present all of the evidence they may have in their power to be acquitted from the charges.

After the alleged offenders have presented their initial defense, the commission has a ten-business-day period to ascertain whether to carry on with its investigation or to close the case at this early stage of the proceedings, in case no sufficient grounds arise about the existence of an anticompetitive practice.

If the determination of the commission is to carry on with its investigation, it shall order the production of the evidence provided or requested by the parties in their respective presentations (i.e., claimant in its initial claim and the alleged offender in its initial defense), where all of the legally admitted means of evidence can be presented and requested to be produced. In addition, the commission has the ability to refuse the production of certain evidence on grounds such as inadmissibility, illegality, or unnecessary.

Once the investigation has been finalized, of which the commission does not have a legal or regulatory term to meet, the parties involved in the proceedings are given fifteen business days to duly analyze the file to present their corresponding defenses and may even present complementary evidence to that already provided in the file, but may not incorporate new evidence than that which could have been already provided. Such complementary evidence, if admissible, shall be produced within sixty business days. After such term has elapsed, the parties shall have a new opportunity to examine the file and present their final defenses. Thereafter, the commission has sixty business days to finally resolve on the case.

Notwithstanding the above, the Law incorporates the possibility that the commission may, at any stage of the proceedings, suspend them for a term not exceeding ten calendar days in order to enter into an agreement with the presumptive offender, to suspend or modify the conduct that initiated the investigation. The only limitation to this suspension and the possibility to enter into such agreement is set forth in cases where anticompetitive nature of the conduct is manifest and the identity of the offender is evident. The possibility of suspending for ten days the proceeding so that the denouncing party and the denounced party consider possible settlements, provided that the investigated behavior consists in a case of "abuse of dominant position" (section 6) and only the denouncing party is damaged by the same, is also provided for.

[B] Sanctions

The Law imposes a series of sanctions to the anticompetitive conducts incurred by the participants of the market.

The penalties that the commission may impose would be the following: (a) an admonition, (b) an admonition with the publication of the resolution, at the expense of the offender, in two newspapers sold at the national level, (c) a fine to be determined by the commission between a minimum amount of 100,000 Indexed Units[30] and a

30. As of July 18, 2021, approximately USD 11,350.

maximum amount equivalent to the higher of the following amounts: (i) 20,000,000 indexed units, (ii) the equivalent to 10% of the annual turnover of the offender; and (iii) the equivalent to three times the damage caused by the anticompetitive practice, if assessable.

Consequently, the fines that the commission can impose are of substantive nature, especially in consideration with the size of the market economy of Uruguay. It is important to point out that in the last cases, the commission has imposed severe sanctions. In other words, there is a tendency to apply stricter sanctions upon the finding of an anticompetitive practice.

For the purposes of the determination of the penalty, the Law sets forth the following criteria for the commission to evaluate: the economic importance of the damage caused; the degree of participation of the responsible persons; the intent; the repetition; and the attitude assumed during the development of the administrative proceedings.

In addition, the Law establishes the possibility of applying fines not only to the legal entity who carried out the anticompetitive practice, but also to those members of the management bodies who had "*actively contributed*" in the development of such practice, and also to the controlling companies and its management bodies.

This notwithstanding, to date, the highest sanction ever applied by the commission was in an abuse of dominant position (a beer company that was being sanctioned for the third consecutive time) for a little less than USD 2,000,000. Other sanctions were generally considerably lower.

Another particularity of the Uruguayan competition regime, contrary to other regimes, is that it does not provide for the imposition of criminal sanctions to the offenders of the Law.

[C] Ancillary Consequences

Moreover, the operations or agreements (or any of their clauses) carried out in breach of the provisions of the Law may be declared null and void. Such consequence, although it is not expressly mentioned in the Law, derives from our general civil law principles (section 8, paragraph 2 of the Uruguayan Civil Code).

Furthermore, the breach of prohibitive rules might eventually constitute an illicit event that may generate a civil tortious liability in case of causing damages to third parties. Such responsibility that would be governed by sections 1319 and 1321 of the Uruguayan Civil Code implies that any illicit event (including the abuse of a right established in section 1321) generates civil liability and the corresponding damages and losses must be paid. In case there is already an administrative decision establishing that a certain conduct violated the rules of defense of competition set forth in the Law, it is probable that such precedent would have an important incidence in the civil claim. However, the judge will not be bound by such administrative decision, since the same is not binding upon the tribunal.

[D] Leniency

As a form of promoting the filing of claims the Law incorporates the institute of "Leniency" or also called the "Statute of Clemency for the Repentant" as a mitigating circumstance in the application of penalties.

Section 17 of the Act provides that:

> In the case of concerted practices among competitors, the report filed by one of the members of the agreement or the contribution of the same to obtain sufficient evidence to sanction the remaining offenders shall be considered as a special mitigating circumstance.

The Law through the introduction of this institute aims to promote that members of cartels or parties of collusive agreements denounce the existence of such anti-competitive agreements and if sufficient evidence is produced, it might be taken into account by the Commission to mitigate the penalties imposed on the denouncer, or even exempting it from any penalty whatsoever.

The act does not provide a list of eligibility for leniency and only refers to a member of the concerted practice agreement. This member may be an individual or a legal entity, particularly in consideration that fines may be imposed as well on the members of the legal entity who have actively contributed in the consecution of such practice.

However, it is relevant to point out that in no case the mere denouncing of a cartel or an anticompetitive agreement constitutes an automatic immunity to the penalties the commission may impose. Upon said filing the commission has the discretion of deciding whether the claim and the provision of the relevant information will act as a mitigating circumstance or not.

Despite the above-mentioned, as arises from the Decree, leniency is not to be applied to entities that have created or initiated the cartel or anticompetitive conduct. Moreover, the leniency in the application of conducts can be applied only to the first entity who denounces such activity, although they may benefit from a reduction in the penalty to be imposed if they present sufficient proof of other cartels or anti-competitive agreements, entered into with other competitors.

It must be noted that the incorporation of a leniency program in the Law did not constitute an innovation in the Uruguayan law regime as such institute is set forth in both tax and criminal matters.

[E] Appeal

Once the final resolution by the commission has been rendered, and as a consequence of an anticompetitive conduct, a sanction has been imposed to an offender, such offender may intend to challenge the resolution passed by the commission.

The resolutions passed by the commission are subject to the ordinary regime of administrative appeals, which means that a resolution by the commission may be challenged, either on the merits of the decision or on its legality, before the commission, seeking for the revocation of the resolution ("*recurso de revocación*") and, jointly, an administrative appeal before the ultimate hierarchical organ, this is, before the Executive Power ("*recurso jerárquico*"). It is important to note that through the means of the administrative appeals, any of the organs in charge of its resolution in addition to being able to enter into the merits of the decision, may modify the content of the decision rendered by the commission.

The term to file said administrative actions is of ten calendar days as from the date in which the sanctioned party is notified of the resolution by the commission.

Once the administrative action has been filed, the administration has a term of 200 days as from the filing to issue a resolution. In case, the term expires without any resolution from the administration, the action shall be deemed rejected, and the sanctioned party would have the ability to file for the annulment of the resolution before the Highest Administrative Court ("*Tribunal de lo Contencioso Administrativo*"). Such filing only proceeds in case the appellant filed both administrative appeals simultaneously, before the organ that issued the resolution and its maximum hierarchical organ.

The term to file an annulment action before the Highest Administrative Court is of sixty days as from the notification of the rejection of the administrative action or as from the expiration of the 200 day term for the resolution of the administrative action (this is, after the administrative action has been tacitly rejected).

The Supreme Administrative Court may confirm or annul the resolution, as applicable, solely on the basis of illegality, but in no case may it modify its content.

§19.07 PRE-MERGER ANALYSIS

Under the original drafting of the Law, Uruguay had set forth a peculiar kind of pre-merger review system under the form of a mere prior notification of ten days prior to closing, and in certain exceptional circumstances (the creation of a de facto monopoly, a scenario which never occurred in practice), of prior authorization by the commission before its conclusion. This previous regime imposed a light burden on companies (since in most cases the only obligation was to provide information to the regulator about the transaction that had no possibility to challenge the transaction itself). This has however been changed in the Reform which introduced a unified pre-merger control system.

The Reform introduced pre-merger control (prior authorization) for certain economic concentrations. Prior authorization shall be required with respect to any act of "economic concentration" when the gross annual turnover in the Uruguayan territory of all the participants in the operation, in any of the last three financial years, is equal to or greater than UI 600,000,000 (six hundred million indexed units). As of April 2022, this amount is approximately equivalent to USD 78.000.000.

In their appearance as invited to comment on the Reform before Parliament, one of the proposals of the authors of this chapter was: (i) to incorporate a dual threshold, that is, that the turnover of each of at least two of the participants meets a certain threshold, and (ii) to have an exception when the value of the transaction or the assets does not exceed a certain figure of the total. Unfortunately this suggestion was not taken up ((ii) was only later incorporated as a presumption that a transaction should be treated under the fast track procedure, a consolation).

Upon request for prior authorization with respect to a concentration, the enforcement body may: (i) expressly or tacitly authorize it; (ii) subject the concentration to certain conditions; or (iii) deny authorization. The concentration may not be implemented until express or tacit authorization has been obtained; the latter shall occur when sixty calendar days have elapsed since the notification and the enforcement body has not issued its decision.

On July 15, 2020, the executive branch issued and then published on its website the updated version of regulatory decree No—404/007 (hereinafter, the "Decree") that was pending by virtue of the amendments introduced by the Reform.

The following is a summary of the issues or aspects that we consider most relevant of the Decree on the central issue:

Regarding the turnover threshold in the national territory for the purposes of the request for prior authorization (600,000,000 Indexed Units, approximately USD 78.000.000 in July 2020), it is provided that for its calculation:

(a) the turnover values, including taxes, of all the participants of the act of concentration, as well as of the entities controlled by them, of those who control them, and of the entities under the control of those who also control the participants shall be aggregated; and
(b) the value of the UI to be taken into account should correspond to the business day prior to the date of the request for authorization and, if applicable, the interbank exchange rate of the business day prior to the date of the request for authorization shall be considered.

Regarding the analysis of the concentration by the application body, the following factors are included as factors to be included: consideration of the relevant market, the degree of concentration, external competition, entry barriers, the effect on upstream and downstream competition, and efficiency gains.

Regarding the moment of filing, it is clarified that the request for authorization must be made prior to the perfecting of the concentration act (depending on the type of concentration in question) and if it is subject to the fulfillment of suspensive conditions or acts of fact that imply the taking of control or substantial influence, it must be made prior to the occurrence of such situations.

Regarding the deadlines and phases for analysis, it is indicated that:

(a) the legal analysis period of sixty calendar days available to the enforcement body to decide on the request for authorization shall begin to run from the date on which the request for authorization was correctly and completely made and shall be interrupted when there are requests for information:

(b) the enforcement body shall inform the parties whether the request for authorization was made correctly and completely within ten business days, and the parties shall in turn have ten business days to remedy these observations—upon expiration of this period without raising observations, the request for authorization shall be deemed not to have been filed and the parties may not resubmit a new request for authorization before ten more business days have elapsed; and
(c) two phases for the evaluation of concentrations were introduced in the process, namely: (i) a first phase that may not extend beyond the first twenty calendar days, reserved for those concentrations that due to their impact, in the opinion of the enforcement body, do not constitute a substantial lessening of competition, there being in turn a presumption that the concentrations do not constitute a substantial lessening of competition when the amount of the concentration or the value of the assets located in Uruguay that are absorbed, acquired, transferred or controlled does not exceed the amount equivalent to 5% of the threshold of 600.000,000 Indexed Units); and (ii) a second phase (within the remaining forty calendar days) for those concentrations that, in the opinion of the enforcement body, could negatively affect the conditions of competition in the relevant market(s) under consideration. In this second stage, the enforcement body may request additional information from the parties or third parties and will even give notice of the concentration so that third parties may make allegations on possible changes or impacts on the conditions of competition in the affected markets.

Since the enforcement body may accept, reject or condition economic concentration operations, the following is regulated regarding possible conditions:

(a) the conditions must proportionally counteract the immediate or potential effects, which may harm competition and arise as a result of the concentration operations under consideration;
(b) both the parties and the enforcement body may unilaterally suggest such conditions;
(c) a specific process is established in which the enforcement body may request the parties to submit proposals for mitigation measures. The parties will have fifteen working days to respond and the enforcement body 15 working days to evaluate them;
(d) the conditions may be structural (e.g., sale of assets or business) or behavioral (e.g., commitment not to develop a certain practice); and
(e) the non-acceptance by the companies of the conditions or of the compliance program and its deadlines, established by the enforcement body, will imply the denial of the authorization.

Regarding the efficiency gains that may be argued by the parties, they may only be computed if they arise directly from the concentration and cannot be achieved without it, and they must be transferable to the consumer. The Decree lists possible efficiency gains, as well as those that will not be acceptable and are all aligned with international parameters.

Regarding the suspensive effect of the new prior authorization regime, the Decree clarifies that concentrations may not be perfected until the authorization resolution is issued or has been tacitly authorized due to the expiration of the term.

Mergers derived from legal acts carried out abroad must be notified before they produce legal or material effects in the national territory. In case of rejection, the Decree clarifies that the merger may not proceed, under penalty of judicial and administrative actions aimed at declaring the lack of legal effects of the act.

Eight months after the entry into force of the Reform, the commission presented and published in December 2020 its Guide for the Economic Analysis of Economic Concentrations (the "Guide"), prepared jointly with the Argentine economist Diego Petrecolla.

In general terms, in the Guide the commission recognizes that: (i) most economic concentrations do not have negative effects on competition but are rather pro-competitive, (ii) vertical and conglomerate concentrations are less likely to lead to anticompetitive outcomes than horizontal concentrations, and (iii) its intervention consists in considering how the operations affect competition over time, and in detecting and not allowing operations that create, enhance, or consolidate market power or facilitate its exercise, an analysis that is highly dependent on the specificities of each case.

In specific terms, the Guide analyzes in detail key aspects in the field of merger control such as (i) the distinction between types of economic concentrations, (ii) the definition of the relevant markets, (iii) the participants, market shares, and concentration level of the relevant market, (iv) the potential anticompetitive effects both unilateral and coordinated in each type of economic concentration, (v) the weighting of other aspects such as the counterveiling power of vigorous buyers, competition from imported products and barriers to entry, (vi) the potential efficiency gains in economic concentrations, and (vii) the possible remedies or conditions to restore competition, among others.

Below are selected highlights of the Guide:

> The definition of the relevant market is only a methodology and not an end in itself, and the calculation of market shares and supply-side concentration is relevant but should be assessed in conjunction with other factors such as barriers to entry and market contestability.
>
> The adoption of internationally recognized methodological criteria, such as the Hypothetical Monopolist Test or the Herfindahl-Hirschman Index (but sadly not the usual accompanying safe harbors).
>
> With respect to horizontal mergers, the consideration of their potential unilateral and coordinated anticompetitive effects.
>
> With respect to vertical mergers, the consideration of their potential anticompetitive effects—input foreclosure, customer foreclosure, and coordinated effects—, this point also being analyzed with respect to conglomerate mergers.

With respect to barriers to entry, which are specific to each market, the most frequent ones are described, analyzing the elements to determine whether the entry or expansion of competitors after the operation would be viable, timely and sufficient.

With respect to efficiency gains, some are listed that may meet the commission's criteria (cost reductions, elimination of double marginalization, alignment of investment objectives, and price and cost reductions) and others are listed with possible ambiguous effects (research and development, improvements in procurement, management and cost of capital, network effects, and product repositioning).

The commission may decide not to object to a concentration with anticompetitive effects, if it involves a "firm in crisis", subject to certain conditions that competition will deteriorate to a lesser or similar degree than without the operation.

With respect to remedies or conditions to restore competition, they must be limited to addressing only competition issues and not other interests or objectives, not being a mechanism to regulate markets or solve existing, non-merger specific problems. The remedies are also classified into structural and behavioral, and the implementation of each of them is analyzed, and it is clarified that they are not necessarily mutually exclusive.

The commission acknowledges the existence of ancillary restrictions in the context of a merger—for example, non-competition or non-solicitation clauses—and recognizes that these are generally harmless.

As for issues still unresolved or introduced, the Guide: (i) does not clarify the commission's interpretation of concepts such as "concentration" and "change in the structure of control", (ii) does not define "safe harbours" or "safe havens"-that is, thresholds below which it could be presumed or concluded that concentrations do not have anticompetitive effects, apart from a reference to operations in which the upstream market share is greater than 30% that will be looked at more intensively in the framework of customer foreclosure effects in vertical mergers, (iii) does not include levels or delta of HHI that would be considered less concentrated, and (iv) does not define a dominance threshold in terms of market share.

In summary, the Guide includes guidelines and criteria necessary for analyzing economic concentrations and determining whether or not to grant authorization which are, generally speaking, positive and clear guidelines in line with the Reform and the best practices internationally, notwithstanding some issues that still need to be resolved or were introduced.

[A] Economic Concentrations

Section 7 of the Law sets forth that any economic concentration that results in a modification in the controlling structure of the participating companies, and that meets the threshold, has to be subjected to the commission's prior authorization. However, the term "economic concentration" is very broadly and loosely defined, and unfortunately so far Uruguay lacks more official guidance from the commission on exactly what is understood under this concept. In particular, the referred section of the Law provides with a non-limitative list of events that shall result in an economic concentration.

In the first place, the Law provides that the merger of two or more companies (through absorption or creation), in the terms of our Companies Law No. 16,060, as amended, would give rise to an economic concentration. Also, the Law lists as a transaction that would give rise to an economic concentration to the acquisition of shares, quotas or corporate interests.

In addition to the acquisition of shares, the Law provides for the acquisition of business, industrial or civil enterprises. In this last case, it refers to a typical operation under Uruguayan law which is the transfer of an "*ongoing business concern*", meaning the acquisition of the whole set of tangible and intangible assets for the development of an activity (industrial or commercial) organized for the production or marketing of goods or provision of services.

Moreover, the definition of "economic concentration" also lists the total or partial acquisition of corporate assets implying a transfer in the control of the productive units, whether of tangible or intangible assets.

Lastly, as is customary in legislative practice in our country, the Law provides a catch-all category by stating that any other kind of legal operation that implies the transfer of control of all or a portion of an economic unit or company may result in an economic concentration. This is a residual category in which any other form of legal business whereby a transfer of control is carried out will be deemed included.

Consequently, in cases where no economic concentration takes place, such as in cases of intra-group mergers or any other form of intra-group transactions, it is not necessary to notify the commission of such transactions.

[B] Exemptions to the Pre-merger Prior Authorization Obligation

Furthermore, section 8 of the Law establishes that the parties are exempted from notifying the commission of an economic concentration in any of the following cases:

- First, the purchase of companies in which the purchaser had already at least 50% of the shares thereof. The idea behind this exception is that there is no actual transfer of control.
- Second, the acquisitions of bonds, debentures, obligations, and any other debt instrument of the company or shares without voting rights. This exemption goes in the same line, since the purchase of such instruments does not imply a transfer of control.
- Third, the acquisition of a sole company by a sole foreign company that does not already possess assets or shares of other companies in the country. This exception has been incorporated from the analysis undertaken of comparative law at the moment of passing the bill, so that in the cases of a first landing in the country, the notification requirement is not an element that may discourage the company, and is commonly referred to as the "first landing" exception.

- And lastly, the acquisitions of companies declared in bankruptcy, but only in cases where only one possible buyer is bidding for the company. This is normally included with the aim of making the purchase of companies without activity easier, so as to avoid the liquidation and closing of the same.

[C] Consequences for Failing to Obtain Prior Authorization from the Commission

It is worth detailing the sanctions foreseen in the Law and the Decree in case of not complying with the duty to request prior authorization for economic concentrations, since they can be very serious.

The sanctions foreseen by the Law and the Decree are serious and abundant:

> Article 34 of the Decree:
>
> *The sanctions shall consist of:*
>
> A) Warning.
>
> B) Warning with publication of the resolution, at the expense of the offender, in 2 (two) newspapers of national circulation.
>
> C) Fine to be determined between a minimum amount of 100,000 U.I. (One Hundred Thousand Indexed Units) and a maximum amount of whichever is higher of the following values:
>
> 1) 20:000,000 U.I. (Indexed Units twenty million).
> 2) The equivalent to 10% (ten percent) of the offender's annual turnover.
> 3) The equivalent of three times the damage caused by the anticompetitive practice, if determinable.
>
> [...]
>
> These penalties may also be applied to those who fail to comply with the obligations set forth in Article 14 of the Law being regulated. Likewise, they may also be applied in those cases in which the provisions set forth in articles 7° and 9° of the Law being regulated are not complied with.

Article 37 of the Decree:

> In addition to the sanctions that the Enforcement Body imposes on the legal entities that carry out conducts prohibited by the law being regulated, it may also impose fines on the members of its administrative and representative bodies that have actively and intentionally contributed to the development of the practice.
>
> It will be understood that the members of the administrative and representative bodies have actively contributed in the development of a practice prohibited by article 2 of the law being regulated, as long as the same is resolved through the corresponding decision making bodies and there is no record in the minutes that the participant abstained or voted against the measure.
>
> The conducts developed by a legal entity controlled by another, will also be imputable to the controlling entity. In the same way, the responsibilities that may correspond to the members of the administrative and representative bodies of the controlled company may also be imputed to those who perform the same functions in the controlling company."

Article 39 of the Decree:

> The administrators, directors and de facto or de jure representatives of the participants, whether or not they are registered with the General Directorate of Registries in
>
> compliance with Article 86 of Law No. 16,060 of September 4, 1989, as amended by Article 13 of Law No. 17,904 of October 7, 2005, under the terms set forth in Article 19 of the Law being regulated.
>
> The registrable acts relating to an economic concentration may not obtain the definitive qualification of the General Registry Directorate until the authorization of the Enforcement Body is verified. In the case of non-registrable acts, such authorization shall be recorded in the document and shall be controlled by the intervening notary public or the parties as the case may be.

Article 44 of the Decree:

> In case of authorization, the participants may proceed with the concentration without further proceedings under the terms of the authorization. In case of rejection of the merger, the merger may not be carried out under any form pursuant to the provisions of Article 9 of the Law being regulated. Nor may it be carried out without compliance with the conditions to which the act of concentration is subject if the authorization is granted under such terms. If the act of concentration is carried out without the due authorization, the Enforcement Body shall promote the judicial and administrative actions aimed at declaring the lack of legal effects of the act.
>
> The Enforcement Body will communicate to the General Directorate of Registries the acceptance or rejection of the corresponding request of the economic concentration operation.
>
> Acts carried out in contravention of the provisions of Article 9 of the Law being regulated shall not produce legal effects, without prejudice to the sanctions that the Enforcement Body is empowered to impose in accordance with the provisions of Articles 17 and 19 of the Law being regulated.
>
> The Enforcement Body may impose sanctions in the following cases:
>
> (a) If the act of economic concentration is not communicated in time
>   a) If the act of economic concentration is not communicated in due time and form.
>   b) Failure to comply with the conditions set forth in the merger resolution of concentration.
>   c) If the concentration is not authorized and the business is carried out.

So far no sanctions have ever been applied under the new prior authorization regime (since its entry into force in April 2020). Under the old notification regime, the commission imposed sanctions for failing to notify in cases it had detected itself in the press, and applied the lowest possible form of sanctions provided by the Law (warnings or very low fines under USD 500).

Note however that the commission has already opened several investigations in possible cases of failure to obtain prior authorization. Those investigations are pending at the time we write these lines.

Index

T

U

V

W

www.ingramcontent.com/pod-product-compliance
Lightning Source LLC
LaVergne TN
LVHW020003031026
849161LV00023B/852

* 9 7 8 9 4 0 3 5 3 6 9 5 8 *